AF674186

MED Essence
YOUR PERSONALISED STUDY GUIDE

NEET (UG)

Handwritten Notes

Physics

ENRICHED WITH
PYQ Punch • NEET Accelerate

FREE
ONLINE SUPPORT
See Inside Cover

MED Essence
YOUR PERSONALISED STUDY GUIDE

NEET (UG)

Handwritten Notes

Physics

ENRICHED WITH
PYQ Punch • NEET Accelerate

Ankit Goyal
B.Tech., IIT Delhi

arihant
SUCCESS AND NOTHING LESS

arihant
SUCCESS AND NOTHING LESS

ARIHANT PRAKASHAN (Series), MEERUT

All Rights Reserved

© Publisher

No part of this publication may be re-produced, stored in a retrieval system or by any means, electronic, mechanical, photocopying, recording, scanning, web or otherwise without the written permission of the publisher. Arihant has obtained all the information in this book from the sources believed to be reliable and true. However, Arihant or its editors or authors or illustrators don't take any responsibility for the absolute accuracy of any information published and the damage or loss suffered thereupon.

All disputes subject to Meerut (UP) jurisdiction only.

卐 Administrative & Production Offices

Regd. Office

'Ramchhaya' 4577/15, Agarwal Road, Darya Ganj, New Delhi -110002
Tele: 011- 47630600, 43518550

卐 Head Office

Kalindi, TP Nagar, Meerut (UP) - 250002
Tel: 0121-7156203, 7156204

卐 Sales & Support Offices

Agra, Ahmedabad, Bengaluru, Bareilly, Chennai, Delhi, Guwahati, Hyderabad, Jaipur, Jhansi, Kolkata, Lucknow, Nagpur & Pune.

卐 **PRICE** ₹445.00

卐 **PO No. :** TXT-29-T069522-2-26

Published by Arihant Publications (India) Ltd.

For further information about the books published by Arihant, log on to www.arihantbooks.com or e-mail at info@arihantbooks.com

Follow us on

Preface...

A Word for Aspiring NEET Scholars

First of all, congratulations on starting one of the most challenging and rewarding journeys of your life—the preparation for **NEET (National Eligibility cum Entrance Test)**. *The path ahead may seem difficult, but remember, it is also full of chances for learning and personal growth..*

These **handwritten notes** *have been crafted with the aim to guide you through the vast and intricate landscape of Physics, one of the most fundamental yet challenging subjects in the NEET syllabus. As someone who has been through the rigorous grind of IIT preparation, I understand the importance of clarity, simplicity, and conceptual depth when it comes to mastering Physics. This is exactly what I've tried to bring into these notes.*

The notes are designed to help you develop a deep understanding of core concepts, which is crucial for tackling the application-based questions often found in NEET. I have tried a different approach with diving each topic into digestible segments that you can easily comprehend and retain.

The Features like **NEET Accelerator**, *will help you build a strong foundation while keeping the subject engaging.*

The NEET exam demands not only knowledge but also the ability to apply that knowledge efficiently under time constraints. With Features like **MCQ Punch** *and* **PYQ Punch** *will help you strike the right balance between theory and questions. They will not only clarify your concepts but also give you the confidence to approach any problem, no matter how tricky it seems at first.*

Remember, success in NEET is not about rote learning or memorizing facts. It's about developing a clear understanding and applying it in innovative ways. These notes are not just a tool to help you study; they are meant to be a companion in your journey, designed to build your problem-solving skills and foster a deeper connection with the subject.

I encourage you to go through these notes with patience, consistency, and an open mind. Don't hesitate to revisit any topic as many times as necessary. Believe in yourself, stay focused, and keep pushing forward. With the right approach, hard work, and these notes in hand, you are well on your way to achieving your NEET goals.

Best wishes for your preparation. May you achieve all the success you aim for!

Ankit Goyal
B. Tech., IIT Delhi

Key Features

MCQ Punch

Conceptual/Numerical solved MCQs helpful for better conceptual understanding

MCQ PUNCH

Q2. If a vector $2\hat{i} + 3\hat{j} + 8\hat{k}$ is perpendicular to the vector $4\hat{j} - 4\hat{i} + \alpha\hat{k}$, then the value of α is :

Sol. As 2 vectors are perpendicular, their dot product is 0.

$$2\hat{i} + 3\hat{j} + 8\hat{k}$$
$$-4\hat{i} + 4\hat{j} + \alpha\hat{k}$$
$$-8 + 12 + 8\alpha = 0 \quad \Rightarrow \quad \alpha = -\frac{1}{2}$$

PYQ PUNCH

Q4. The area of a rectangular field (in m^2) of length 55.3m and breadth 25m after rounding off the value for correct significant digits is : (NEET 2022)

Sol. $L = 55.3 \rightarrow 3\ SD$; $B = 25 \rightarrow 2\ SD$

$A = L \times B$

$= 55.3 \times 25\ m^2$

$= \underset{S.D}{13}\underset{NSD}{82.5}\ m^2 = 1400\ m^2$

PYQ Punch

Selective PYQs helpful in Theory-PyQ syncing along with learning enhancement.

NEET Accelerate

- $\cos^2\alpha + \cos^2\beta + \cos^2\gamma = 1$
- $\sin^2\alpha + \sin^2\beta + \sin^2\gamma = 2$
- Angle of $\vec{AB}$ is θ not ϕ.

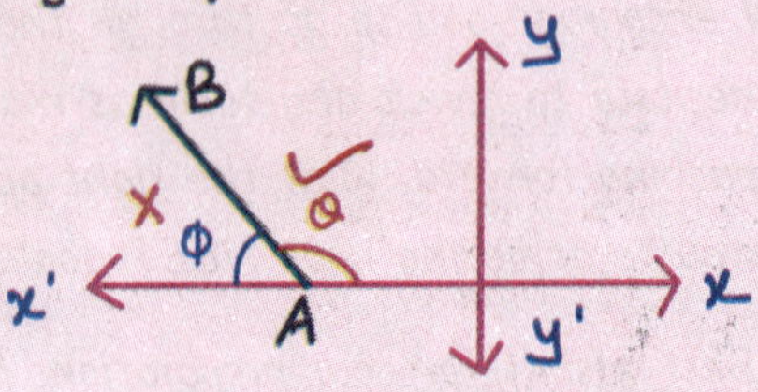

NEET Accelerator

Specialised Tips. Tricks & conceptual Info, most Important from NEET preparation prospective

Contents

Contents

1. Vector

Vector Quantity

- Having magnitude and direction both.
- Follow triangle law of vector addition.
- Example: Velocity, Acceleration, Force etc.
- Symbol of vector: $\vec{AB}$ or $\vec{r}$.
- Symbol of magnitude of vector: $|\vec{AB}|$ or $|\vec{r}|$.

Graphical Representation of Vector

- **Length**
- Represents magnitude of the vector.
- **Ends**
- One is tail and other is head.
- Together represents the direction of the vector.
- Direction is from tail to head. or A to B

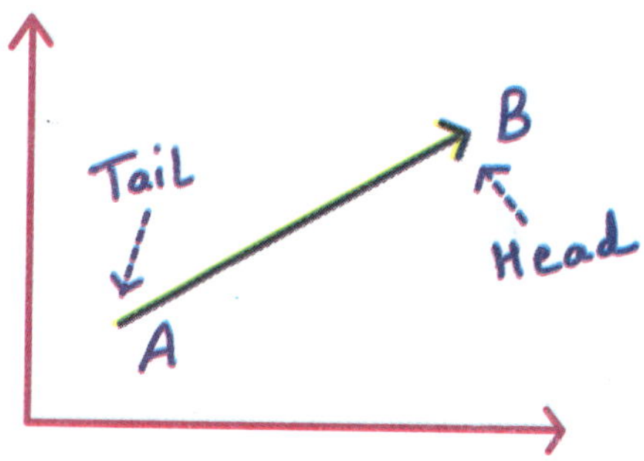

Properties of Vector

1. **Shifting of Vector**
- A vector can be moved over the graph freely provided its length and direction are kept same.

2. **Interchanging head & tail**
- Interchanging the positions of head and tail changes the direction of vector by 180°.

3. **Angle of the vector**
- It is the angle made by the vector with the +ve axes.
- α : Angle with +ve x-axis
- β : Angle with +ve y-axis
- γ : Angle with +ve z-axis

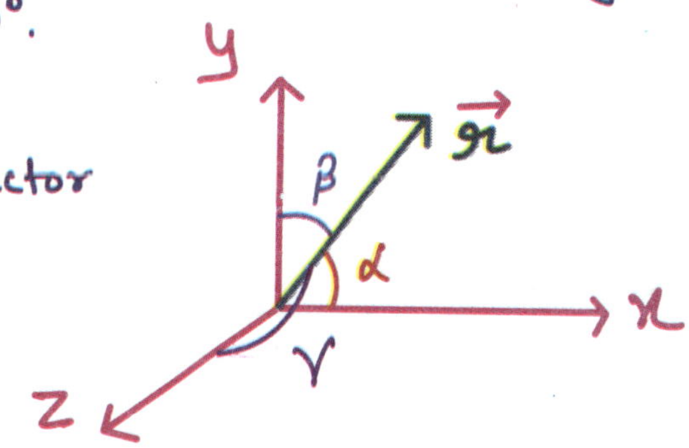

NEET Accelerate

- $\cos^2\alpha + \cos^2\beta + \cos^2\gamma = 1$
- $\sin^2\alpha + \sin^2\beta + \sin^2\gamma = 2$
- Angle of $\vec{AB}$ is θ not ϕ.

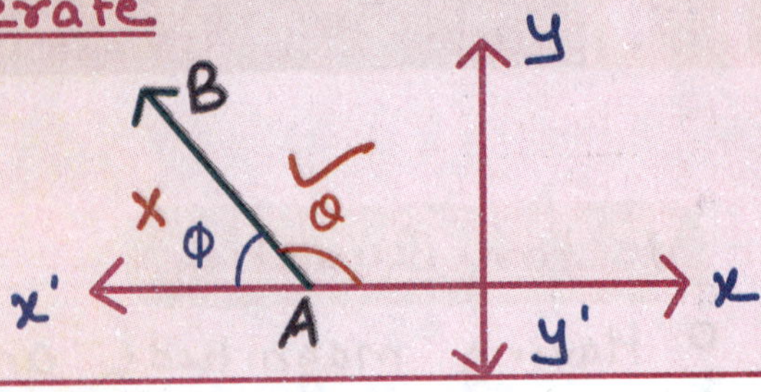

4. Angle between two vectors

- It is the angle formed between two vectors when they are connected by their tails.

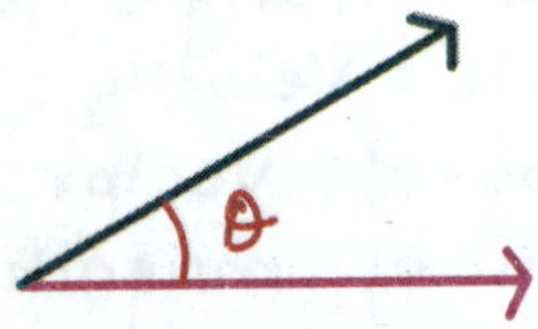

5. Multiplication of a vector by a constant k

	+ve k	−ve k
▸ Magnitude	Becomes k times	Becomes k times
▸ Direction	Same	Reverses

General Form of a vector

Representation

$\vec{r} = a\hat{i} + b\hat{j} + c\hat{k}$

where $\hat{i} \rightarrow$ +ve x-direction

$\hat{j} \rightarrow$ +ve y-direction

$\hat{k} \rightarrow$ +ve z-direction

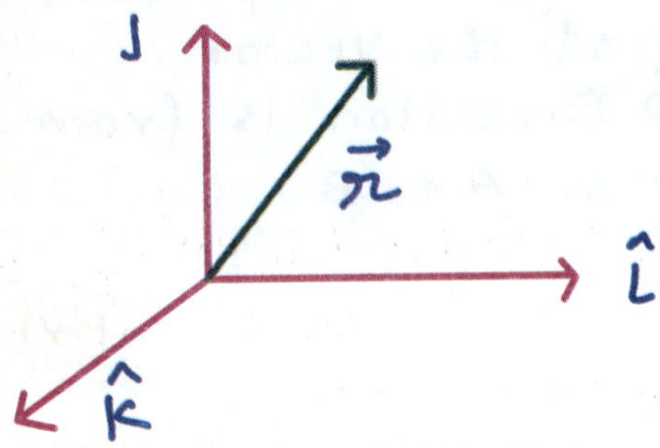

Magnitude

$|\vec{r}| = \sqrt{a^2+b^2+c^2}$

Angle

- $\cos\alpha = \dfrac{a}{\sqrt{a^2+b^2+c^2}}$
- $\cos\beta = \dfrac{b}{\sqrt{a^2+b^2+c^2}}$
- $\cos\gamma = \dfrac{c}{\sqrt{a^2+b^2+c^2}}$

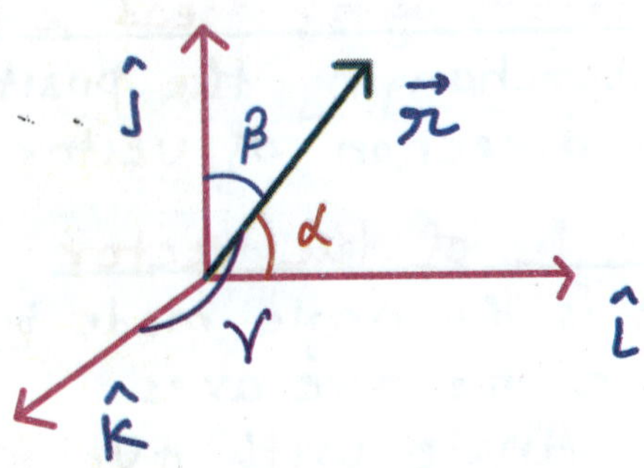

Triangle Law of Vector Addition

◎ Given

- $|\vec{a}| = a$
- $|\vec{b}| = b$
- $\theta \rightarrow$ Angle between $\vec{a}$ & $\vec{b}$.

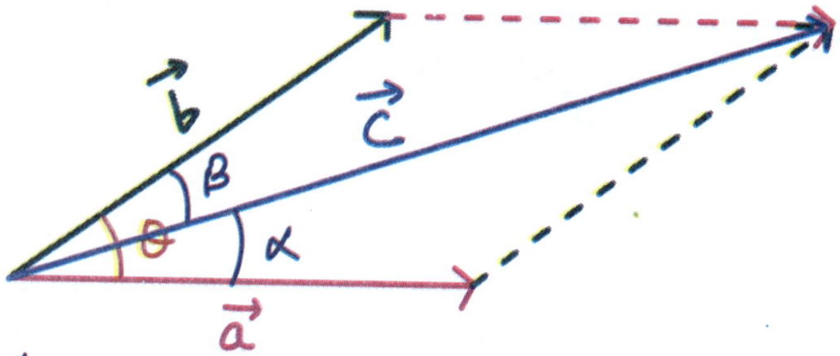

◎ Results

- $\vec{c}$ is the resultant vector.

  $\vec{c} = \vec{a} + \vec{b}$

- $|\vec{c}| = \sqrt{a^2 + b^2 + 2ab\cos\theta}$

- $\tan\alpha = \dfrac{b\sin\theta}{a + b\cos\theta}$

  $\alpha \rightarrow$ Angle between resultant vector and $\vec{a}$ vector.

- $\tan\beta = \dfrac{a\sin\theta}{b + a\cos\theta}$

  $\beta \rightarrow$ Angle between resultant vector and $\vec{b}$ vector.

NEET Accelerate

- Resultant vector's tail is connected with the tail of first vector and head is connected with the head of last vector.
- If magnitudes of two vectors are equal and equal to magnitude of their resultant vector, then angle between the two vectors is 120°.

Position Vector

- It represents the position of the particle in vector form.

  $\vec{r} = x\hat{i} + y\hat{j} + z\hat{k}$

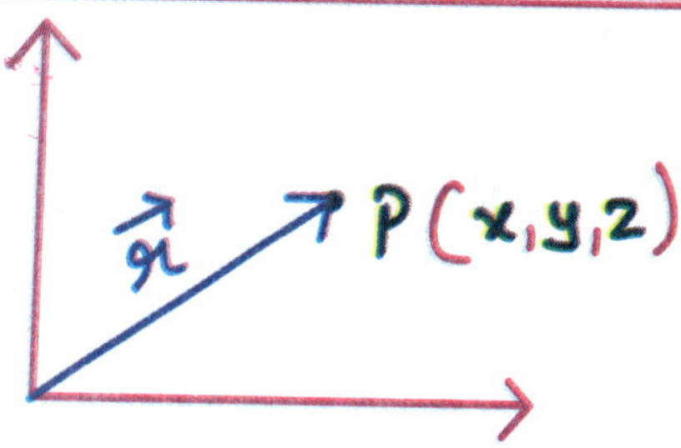

Displacement Vector

- $\vec{r} = \vec{r}_2 - \vec{r}_1$

  $= (x_2 - x_1)\hat{i} + (y_2 - y_1)\hat{j} + (z_2 - z_1)\hat{k}$

- $|\vec{r}| = \sqrt{(x_2-x_1)^2 + (y_2-y_1)^2 + (z_2-z_1)^2}$

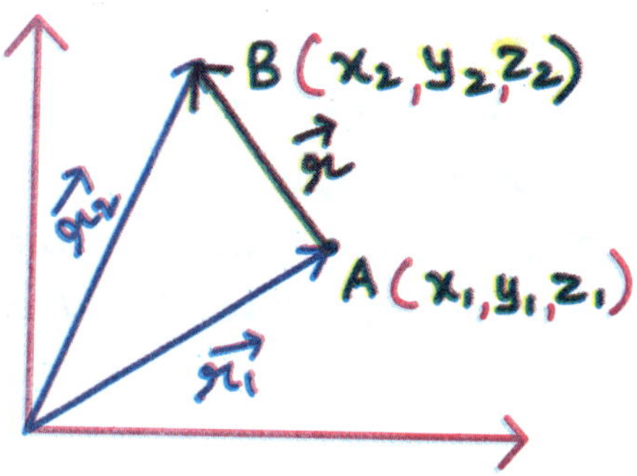

Difference of two vectors

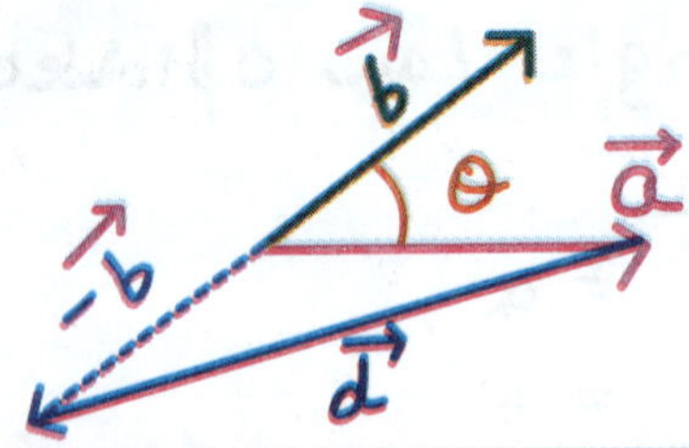

- $\vec{d} = \vec{a} - \vec{b}$
- $|\vec{d}| = \sqrt{a^2 + b^2 - 2ab\cos\theta}$

NEET Accelerate

- In vector addition or subtraction, it is not necessary that magnitude of resultant vector is greater than the magnitude of the vectors.
- For 90° angle between 2 vectors, the magnitude of sum of two vectors is equal to the magnitude of difference of the two vectors.
- For 2 vectors having same magnitude and angle between them is 120°,

$$|\vec{d}| = \sqrt{3}\,|\vec{c}|$$

Maximum and Minimum Value of Resultant

- **Maximum**
- $|\vec{c}_{max}| = |\vec{a}| + |\vec{b}|$ when $\theta = 0°$
- **Minimum**
- $|\vec{c}_{min}| = ||\vec{a}| - |\vec{b}||$ when $\theta = 180°$

Resolution of Vector

- A vector can be resolved into 3 rectangular components in a 3-D space while can be resolved into 2 rectangular components in a 2-D plane.
- It is resolved to make the calculation easy.
- For example, a particle moves in the horizontal direction due to horizontal force and in vertical direction due to vertical force only.

How to resolve a vector

- θ ke saath wala component $\cos\theta$ hota hai
- Dusra component $\sin\theta$ hota hai.

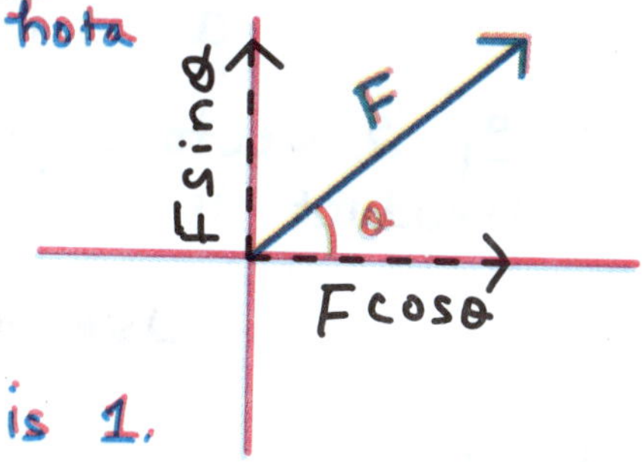

Unit Vector ($\hat{r}$)

- It is a vector whose magnitude is 1.
  - $\hat{r} = x\hat{i} + y\hat{j} + z\hat{k}$
  - $|\hat{r}| = \sqrt{x^2 + y^2 + z^2} = 1$
- It is used to represent the direction of the vector.

MCQ PUNCH

Q1. If a unit vector is represented as $0.5\hat{i} + 0.8\hat{j} + c\hat{k}$, then the value of c is:

Sol. Mag $= \sqrt{0.5^2 + 0.8^2 + c^2} = 1$

$\rightarrow c = \sqrt{0.11}$

Products of Vectors

Scalar or Dot Product

- Gives scalar quantity.
- $\vec{a}.\vec{b} = |\vec{a}||\vec{b}|\cos\theta$
  $= ab\cos\theta$

Vector or Cross Product

- Gives Vector quantity.
- $\vec{a} \times \vec{b} = |\vec{a}||\vec{b}|\sin\theta\ \hat{n}$
  $= ab\sin\theta\ \hat{n}$

Scalar Product in Component Form

$\vec{a} = a_x\hat{i} + a_y\hat{j} + a_z\hat{k}$

$\vec{b} = b_x\hat{i} + b_y\hat{j} + b_z\hat{k}$

$$\vec{a} \cdot \vec{b} = a_x b_x + a_y b_y + a_z b_z$$

Properties of Scalar Product

- It is commutative in nature.
  $\vec{a} \cdot \vec{b} = \vec{b} \cdot \vec{a}$

- It is distributive in nature.

$$\vec{a}\cdot(\vec{b}+\vec{c}) = \vec{a}\cdot\vec{b}+\vec{a}\cdot\vec{c}$$

- If 2 vectors are perpendicular, then their dot product is 0.

Use of Scalar Product

- It is used to find the angle between 2 vectors.

$$\cos\theta = \frac{\vec{a}\cdot\vec{b}}{|\vec{a}|\times|\vec{b}|}$$

- It is used to find unknown coefficient if 2 vectors are perpendicular.

MCQ PUNCH

Q2. If a vector $2\hat{i}+3\hat{j}+8\hat{k}$ is perpendicular to the vector $4\hat{j}-4\hat{i}+\alpha\hat{k}$, then the value of α is :

Sol. As 2 vectors are perpendicular, their dot product is 0.

$$2\hat{i}+3\hat{j}+8\hat{k}$$
$$-4\hat{i}+4\hat{j}+\alpha\hat{k}$$
$$-8+12+8\alpha = 0 \Rightarrow \alpha = -\frac{1}{2}$$

Vector Product in Component Form

$$\vec{a} = a_x\hat{i}+a_y\hat{j}+a_z\hat{k} \quad ; \quad \vec{b} = b_x\hat{i}+b_y\hat{j}+b_z\hat{k}$$

$$\vec{a}\times\vec{b} = \begin{vmatrix} \hat{i} & \hat{j} & \hat{k} \\ a_x & a_y & a_z \\ b_x & b_y & b_z \end{vmatrix} = (a_y b_z - b_y a_z)\hat{i} - (a_x b_z - b_x a_z)\hat{j} + (a_x b_y - b_x a_y)\hat{k}$$

$$\vec{b}\times\vec{a} = \begin{vmatrix} \hat{i} & \hat{j} & \hat{k} \\ b_x & b_y & b_z \\ a_x & a_y & a_z \end{vmatrix} = (b_y a_z - a_y b_z)\hat{i} - (b_x a_z - a_x b_z)\hat{j} + (b_x a_y - a_x b_y)\hat{k}$$

Direction of Vector Product

Clock-Method

- Clockwise

$\hat{i} \times \hat{j} = \hat{k}$
$\hat{j} \times \hat{k} = \hat{i}$
$\hat{k} \times \hat{i} = \hat{j}$

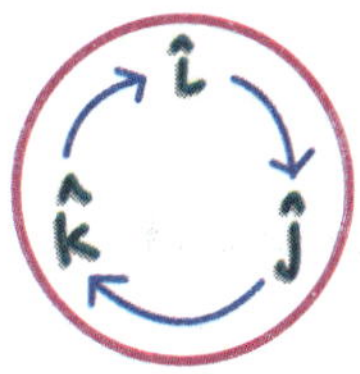

- Anti-clockwise

$\hat{i} \times \hat{k} = -\hat{j}$
$\hat{k} \times \hat{j} = -\hat{i}$
$\hat{j} \times \hat{i} = -\hat{k}$

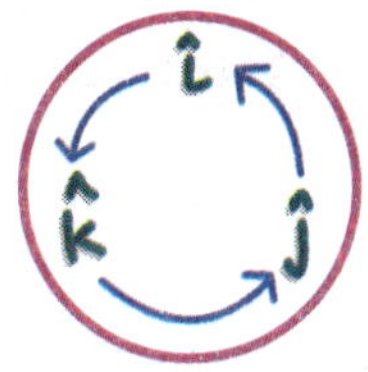

Right hand thumb rule

- Put the fingers of right hand in the direction of first vector.
- Curl the fingers in the direction of 2nd vector.
- Thumb gives the direction of resultant vector.

Properties of Vector Product

- It is not commutative in nature.

$$\vec{a} \times \vec{b} \neq \vec{b} \times \vec{a}$$

- It is distributive in nature.

$$\vec{a} \times (\vec{b} + \vec{c}) = \vec{a} \times \vec{b} + \vec{a} \times \vec{c}$$

- If two vectors are parallel, then their vector product is 0.
- Direction of resultant vector is perpendicular to both the vectors.

Use of Vector Product

- It is used to find the angle between 2 vectors.

$$\sin\theta = \frac{|\vec{a} \times \vec{b}|}{|\vec{a}| \times |\vec{b}|}$$

- It is used to find unknown coefficient if 2 vectors are parallel.

- For 2 parallel vectors

$\vec{A} = a_1\hat{i} + b_1\hat{j} + c_1\hat{k}$

$\vec{B} = a_2\hat{i} + b_2\hat{j} + c_2\hat{k}$

the ratio of their coefficients are same i.e.

$$\frac{a_1}{a_2} = \frac{b_1}{b_2} = \frac{c_1}{c_2}$$

MCQ PUNCH

Q3. $\vec{A}$ and $\vec{B}$ are two vectors and θ is the angle between them. If $|\vec{A} \times \vec{B}| = \sqrt{3}\,\vec{A}.\vec{B}$, then the value of θ is :

Sol. $|\vec{A} \times \vec{B}| = \sqrt{3}\,\vec{A}.\vec{B}$

$\Rightarrow AB\sin\theta = \sqrt{3}\,AB\cos\theta$

$\Rightarrow \tan\theta = \sqrt{3}$

$\Rightarrow \theta = 60°$

Projection of Vector

- Projection/ component of $\vec{b}$ on $\vec{a}$ is given as

Projection Length = $\vec{b}.\hat{a}$

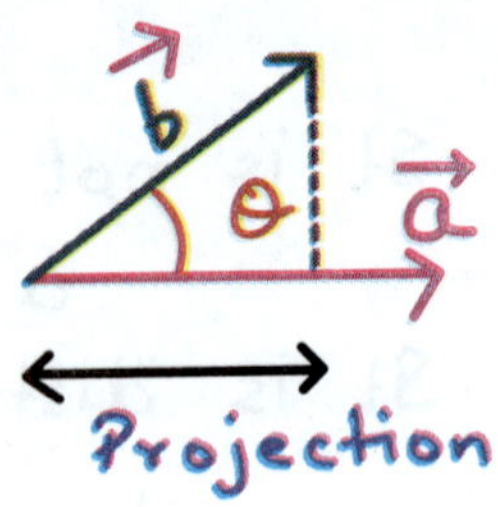

Triple Product

- $(\vec{a} \times \vec{b}).\vec{a} = 0$
- $(\hat{i} \times \hat{j}) \times \hat{k} = 1$

2. Units & Dimensions

Systeme Internationale (SI Unit)

- Given by CGPM (General Conference on Weights & Measures)
- Divides the units into 3 parts.

Fundamental Units

- These units are independent of each other.
- These are 7 in numbers

Derived Units

- These units are derived from fundamental units.

Supplementary Units

- These units have no dimensions.
  - Plane Angle (rad)
  - Solid Angle (sr)

Quantity	Units	Symbol
Mass	kilogram	kg
Length	metre	m
Time	second	s
Temperature	kelvin	K
Current	Ampere	A
Amount of Substance	mole	mol
Intensity of Light	Candela	Cd

Note: It is not necessary to have only these 7 as fundamental units.

Prefix of Units

Power	Number	Prefix	Symbol
18	10^{18}	Exa	E
15	10^{15}	Peta	P
12	10^{12}	Tera	T
9	10^{9}	Giga	G
6	10^{6}	Mega	M
3	10^{3}	kilo	k
2	10^{2}	hecta	ha
1	10^{1}	deka	da
-1	10^{-1}	deci	d
-2	10^{-2}	centi	c
-3	10^{-3}	milli	m
-6	10^{-6}	micro	μ
-9	10^{-9}	nano	n
-10	10^{-10}	Angstrom	Å
-12	10^{-12}	pico	p
-15	10^{-15}	fermi / femto	f
-18	10^{-18}	atto	a

Phone ki Memory Se yaad Rakhe

Tb → Terabyte
Gb → Gigabyte
Mb → Megabyte
kb → kilobyte

Conversion of Unit

Conversion of Prefix

- Conversion of picokelvin into Megakelvin.
  Steps to follow

⇒ 1 picokelvin = 10^{-12} k & 1 Megakelvin = 10^{6} k

⇒ $\frac{1 \text{ picokelvin}}{1 \text{ Megakelvin}} = \frac{10^{-12} \text{ k}}{10^{6} \text{ k}}$

⇒ 1 picokelvin = 10^{-18} Megakelvin

Conversion of Unit with Numerical Value

- In this conversion, numerical values are attached with unit.
- $n_1 \alpha^a \beta^b \gamma^c = \frac{n_1}{x^a y^b z^c}(x\alpha)^a (y\beta)^b (z\gamma)^c = n_2 (x\alpha)^a (y\beta)^b (z\gamma)^c$

▷ $n_2 = \frac{n_1}{x^a y^b z^c}$

MCQ PUNCH

Q1. The density of a material in CGS system of units is 4 g/cm³. In a system of units in which unit of length is 10 cm and unit of mass is 100g, the value of density of material will be

Sol. $n_1 \alpha^a \beta^b = \frac{n_1}{x^a y^b}(x\alpha)^a (y\beta)^b = n_2 (x\alpha)^a (y\beta)^b$

$\alpha = g$; $a = 1$; $x = 100$; $n_1 = 4$

$\beta = cm$; $b = -3$; $y = 10$; $n_2 = ?$

$$n_2 = \frac{n_1}{x^a y^b} = \frac{4}{100^1 \times 10^{-3}} = 40$$

Dimensions

- It is the power of fundamental unit in a derived unit.
- For example, dimension of length and time in speed (ms^{-1}) is 1 and -1.

Dimensional Formula

- It is the representation of fundamental units by a capital character.
- Length → [L] Mass → [M]
  Time → [T] Current → [A]

Operations on Dimensional Formula

Addition / Subtraction

- M + L = Not possible
- M − L = Not possible
- M + M = M not 2M
- M − M = M not 0

Multiplication / Division

- No boundation
- M × L = ML
- $M \div L = \frac{M}{L}$

Applications of Dimensional Formula

Homogeneity

- An equation ~~is~~ may be correct if dimensional formula of all the terms in an equation is same.
- It is used to find the dimensions of unknown quantities.

PYQ PUNCH

Q2. A force defined by $F = \alpha t^2 + \beta t$ acts on a particle at a given time t. The factor which is dimensionless, if α & β are constants, is **(NEET 2024)**

a. $\frac{\beta t}{\alpha}$ b. $\frac{\alpha t}{\beta}$ c. $\alpha \beta t$ d. $\frac{\alpha \beta}{t}$

Sol. $F = \alpha t^2 + \beta t$

Dimension of each term should be same.

$[F] = [\alpha t^2]$ $[F] = [\beta t]$

$[MLT^{-2}] = [\alpha T^2]$ $[MLT^{-2}] = [\beta T]$

$\alpha = [MLT^{-4}]$ $\beta = [MLT^{-3}]$

Option a. $\frac{\beta t}{\alpha} = \frac{[MLT^{-3}T]}{[MLT^{-4}]} \neq 1$ ✗

Option b. $\frac{\alpha t}{\beta} = \frac{[MLT^{-4}T]}{[MLT^{-3}]} = 1$ ✓

Conversion

- $n_1 U_1 = n_2 U_2$
  - For example

    $n_1 [M_1^a L_1^b T_1^c] = n_2 [M_2^a L_2^b T_2^c]$
- System of Unit
  - MKS: m, kg, sec
  - CGS: cm, g, sec
  - FPS: Foot, pound, sec

Conversion from MKS to CGS

- $n_1 U_1 = n_2 U_2$
- $[kg^a m^b s^c] = x[g^a cm^b s^c]$
- $x = \left[\frac{kg}{g}\right]^a \left[\frac{m}{cm}\right]^b \left[\frac{s}{s}\right]^c$

- 1 N = 10^5 Dyne
- 1 J = 10^7 Erg
- 1 $kg/m^3 = 10^{-3} g/cm^3$

Derivation

- In a limited sense, dimensional formula can be used to derive formulaes.
- If a physical quantity P depends upon other physical quantities Q, R & T, then

$$P = k\, Q^a R^b T^c$$

PYQ PUNCH

Q3. If force F, acceleration A and time T are chosen as the fundamental physical quantities. Find the dimensions of energy. **(NEET 2021)**

Sol. $E = k\, F^a A^b T^c$

$[ML^2T^{-2}] = [MLT^{-2}]^a [LT^{-2}]^b [T]^c$

$[M^1 L^2 T^{-2}] = [M^a L^{a+b} T^{-2a-2b+c}]$

Comparing Dimensions

$a = 1 \quad a+b = 2 \quad -2a-2b+c = -2$

$a = 1 \;;\; b = 1 \;;\; c = 2$

Dimension of E is $[FAT^2]$

Least Count

- It is the minimum measurement by an instrument.
- For example, least count of wall watch is 1sec.

Significant Digits

- Measured Value
  - Significant Digits (SD)
    - Certain Digits
    - 1st Doubtful Digit
  - Insignificant Digits (ISD)
    - All digits after 1st doubtful digit

- Depends upon the least count of the instrument.
- Doesn't depend upon the unit of the quantity.
- Countable numbers have infinite significant digits.

Rules to Identify Number of Significant Digits

Number < 1

- All the starting zeroes are insignificant.
- Ex 0.00201000 has 6 significant digits.

Natural Number

- All the trailing zeroes are insignificant.
- Ex 20103400 has 6 significant digits.

Number greater than or equal to 1 and in decimal form

- All the digits are significant.
- Ex 201.00 has 5 significant digits.

Rules of Round-off

- If the insignificant digits lie after the decimal, then they are simply removed.
  - 225.3 (S.D) 124 (ISD) ⇒ 225.3
- If the insignificant digits lie before the decimal, then they are replaced by the zero.
  - 22 (S.D) 5.3124 (ISD) ⇒ 220

- If Ist I.S.D is less than 5, keep the doubtful digit same.
  - 225.3424 (S.D: 225.3, ISD: 424) ⇒ 225.3
- If Ist I.S.D is greater than 5, raised the doubtful digit by 1.
  - 225.3624 (S.D: 225.3, ISD: 624) ⇒ 225.4
- If Ist I.S.D is equal to 5 and D.D is even, then keep the D.D same.
  - 225.4524 (S.D: 225.4, ISD: 524) ⇒ 225.4
- If Ist I.S.D is equal to 5 and D.D is odd, then raise the D.D by 1.
  - 225.3524 (S.D: 225.3, ISD: 524) ⇒ 225.4

Significant Digits in Operation

Multiplication / Division

- Number of Significant digits in a result is equal to the minimum of Significant digits in the questions.
- Insignificant digits are rounded off.
- Multiply / Divide and Round off.

PYQ PUNCH

Q4. The area of a rectangular field (in m^2) of length 55.3m and breadth 25m after rounding off the value for correct significant digits is : (NEET 2022)

Sol. $L = 55.3 \rightarrow 3$ SD ; $B = 25 \rightarrow 2$ SD

$A = L \times B$

$= 55.3 \times 25 \ m^2$

$= 1382.5 \ m^2 = 1400 \ m^2$ (S.D: 13, NSD: 82.5)

Addition / Subtraction

- Number of digits after the decimal in the final answer is same as the minimum digits after the decimal in the question.
- Add / Subtract and round off.

PYQ PUNCH

Q5. Taking into account of the significant figures, what is the value of 9.99m − 0.0099 m? (NEET 2020)

Sol. 9.99 → 2 digits after decimal
0.0099 → 4 digits after decimal

$$\begin{array}{r} 9.99 \\ -0.0099 \\ \hline 9.9801 \end{array} \Rightarrow 9.98 \rightarrow \text{2 digits after decimal}$$

Significant Digits in Scientific Notation

- Conversion of units should always take place in scientific notation.
- Example : 234.00 m has 5 S.D.
  23400 cm has 3 S.D ✗
  234.00×10^2 cm has 5 S.D ✓
- Rounding off 99.9 to 2 S.D. is 1.0×10^2

Errors

- Occurs while taking readings.
- Types of Error

Systematic Error
- Reason can be detected and rectified.
- Use when single reading is given in the question.

Random Error
- Reason is difficult to detect and rectify.
- It can be reduced by ↑ the no. of observations.
- Example - change of Temp. and humidity.
- Use when more than 1 reading is given in the question.

Systematic Error:

Equipment
- Faulty instrument
- Tear and wear of the instrument.
- Least count limitation.

Procedure
- Measuring technique limitation.

Personal
- Carelessness of the operator.
- Lack of knowledge.

PYQ PUNCH

Q6. The errors in the measurement which arise due to unpredictable fluctuations in temperature and voltage supply are: (NEET 2023)

a. Personal Error
b. Least Count Error
c. Random Error
d. Instrumental Error

Sol. Random Error

Arithmetic For Random Error

- Rule says that if the observations are increased by x times, then error get reduced by x times.
- Method

▷ $x_m = \frac{x_1 + x_2 + x_3 + \dots}{5}$

↑ True Value

▷ $\Delta x_1 = x_m - x_1$

$\Delta x_2 = x_m - x_2$

⋮

$\Delta x_n = x_m - x_n$

▷ $\Delta x_m = \frac{|\Delta x_1| + |\Delta x_2| + \dots + |\Delta x_n|}{n}$

↑ Absolute Error

▷ $x = x_m \pm \Delta x_m$

↑ Measured Value

- **Relative Error or Fractional Error**

$$= \pm \frac{\Delta x_m}{x_m}$$

- **Percentage Error**

% Error = Relative Error × 100

$$= \pm \frac{\Delta x_m}{x_m} \times 100$$

PYQ PUNCH

Q7. Time intervals measured by a clock give the following readings 1.25s, 1.24s, 1.27s, 1.21 s and 1.28 s. What is the percentage relative error of the observations? (NEET 2020)

Sol. $x_m = \frac{1.25 + 1.24 + 1.27 + 1.21 + 1.28}{5} = 1.25$

$\Delta x_1 = x_m - x_1 = 1.25 - 1.25 = 0$

$\Delta x_2 = x_m - x_2 = 1.25 - 1.24 = 0.01$

$\Delta x_3 = x_m - x_3 = 1.25 - 1.27 = -0.02$

$\Delta x_4 = x_m - x_4 = 1.25 - 1.21 = 0.04$

$\Delta x_5 = x_m - x_5 = 1.25 - 1.28 = -0.03$

$$\Delta x_m = \frac{|0| + |0.01| + |-0.02| + |0.04| + |-0.03|}{5} = 0.02$$

$$\%\ \text{Error} = \frac{\Delta x_m}{x_m} \times 100 = \frac{0.02}{1.25} \times 100 = 1.6\%$$

Arithmetic For Systematic Error

Addition

- $a = \bar{a} \pm \Delta a$; $b = \bar{b} \pm \Delta b$

  $c = a + b = \bar{a} + \bar{b} \pm (\Delta a + \Delta b)$
- Absolute error is added.

Subtraction

- $a = \bar{a} \pm \Delta a$; $b = \bar{b} \pm \Delta b$

  $c = a - b = \bar{a} - \bar{b} \pm (\Delta a + \Delta b)$
- Absolute error is added.

Multiplication

- $a = \bar{a} \pm \Delta a$; $b = \bar{b} \pm \Delta b$

  $\bar{c} = \bar{a}\bar{b}$

  $\frac{\Delta c}{\bar{c}} = +\frac{\Delta a}{\bar{a}} + \frac{\Delta b}{\bar{b}}$
- Relative Error is added.

Division

- $a = \bar{a} \pm \Delta a$; $b = \bar{b} \pm \Delta b$

  $\bar{c} = \bar{a}/\bar{b}$

  $\frac{\Delta c}{\bar{c}} = +\frac{\Delta a}{\bar{a}} + \frac{\Delta b}{\bar{b}}$
- Relative Error is added.

Trick to solve Error Questions

- Given $P = \frac{Q^a R^b}{S^c T^d}$

$$\%\ \text{error in } P = \left(+a \times \frac{\Delta Q}{\bar{Q}} + b\frac{\Delta R}{\bar{R}} + c\frac{\Delta S}{\bar{S}} + d\frac{\Delta T}{\bar{T}}\right) \times 100$$

PYQ PUNCH

Q8. In an experiment, the percentage of error occurred in the measurement of physical quantities A, B, C and D are 1%, 2%, 3% and 4% respectively. Then the maximum percentage of error in the measurement of X, where $X = \frac{A^2 B^{1/2}}{C^{1/3} D^3}$, will be

(NEET 2019)

Sol. $\% \frac{\Delta X}{X} = + 2\frac{\Delta A}{A} \times 100 + \frac{1}{2}\frac{\Delta B}{B} \times 100 + \frac{1}{3}\frac{\Delta C}{C} \times 100 + 3\frac{\Delta D}{D} \times 100$

$= + 2 \times 1\% + \frac{1}{2} \times 2\% + \frac{1}{3} \times 3\% + 3 \times 4\%$

$= 16\%$

Error in Time Period of Simple Pendulum

- Time Period $T = 2\pi\sqrt{\frac{l}{g}}$
- Error in Time Period

$$\frac{\Delta T}{T} = + \frac{1}{2}\frac{\Delta l}{l} + \frac{1}{2}\frac{\Delta g}{g}$$

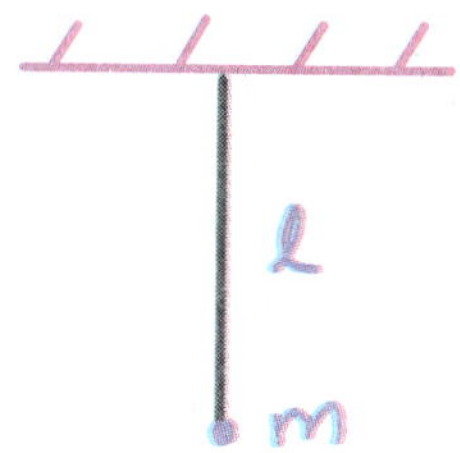

Dimensional Formula for Various Physical Quantities

Class 11th	Class 12th
Pressure – $ML^{-1}T$	Electric Potential – $ML^2T^3A^{-1}$
Work – ML^2T^{-2}	Resistance – $ML^2T^{-3}A^{-2}$
Power – ML^2T^{-3}	$R = \sqrt{\frac{\mu_0}{\varepsilon_0}} = \omega L = \frac{1}{\omega C}$
Gravitational Constant – $M^{-1}L^3T^{-2}$	Capacitance – $M^{-1}L^{-2}T^4A^2$
Spring Constant – MT^{-2}	Permittivity – $M^{-1}L^{-3}T^4A^2$
Coefficient of Viscosity – $ML^{-1}T^{-1}$	Planck's Constant – ML^2T^{-1}
Angular Momentum – $M^1L^2T^{-1}$	$\frac{L}{R} = RC = \sqrt{LC}$ – T

3. Motion in a Straight Line

Some Basic Terms

Rest	No change of position with respect to surrounding.
Motion	Change of position with respect to surrounding.
Initial Time	It is referred to a time when an observer starts taking the observation. It is generally taken as $t = 0$.
Initial Position	It is the position of the particle at initial time.
Initial Speed	It is the speed of the particle at initial time.

Distance vs Displacement

Distance	Displacement
○ Total path length. ○ Scalar ○ Always positive ○ Can't decrease with time.	○ Shortest path length. ○ Vector ○ Can be positive or negative. ○ Can decrease with time.

◉ For uniform motion

Displacement = Distance

◉ For non-uniform motion

Displacement ≤ Distance

Distance and Displacement for Circular Path

○ Particle is moving from A to B.

▹ Displacement $x = 2R\sin\left(\frac{\theta}{2}\right)$

▹ Distance $\overset{\frown}{AB} = R\theta$

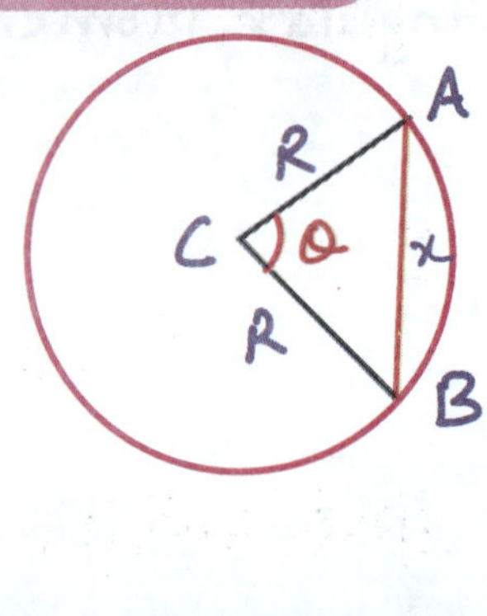

Average Speed

- It is the total change of distance in given time.

$$S_{avg} = \frac{\text{Total Distance}}{\text{Total Time}}$$

Different cases of Average Speed

- **Case I : Distances and speeds are given**

$$S_{avg} = \frac{x_1 + x_2}{\frac{x_1}{v_1} + \frac{x_2}{v_2}}$$

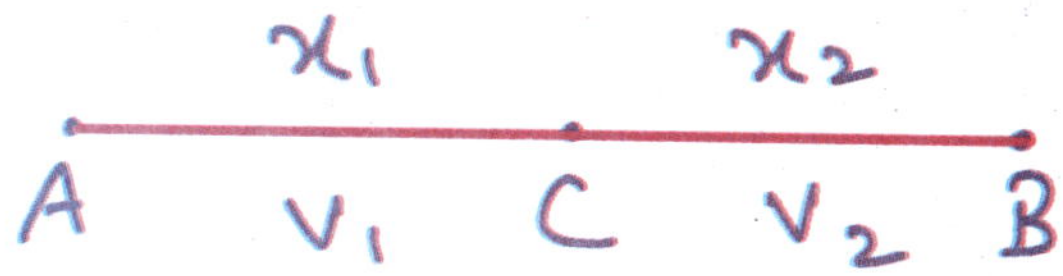

PYQ PUNCH

Q1. A vehicle travels half the distance with speed v and the remaining distance with 2v. Its average speed is (NEET 2023)

Sol. $x_1 = x_2 = x$; $v_1 = v$; $v_2 = 2v$

$$S_{avg} = \frac{x_1 + x_2}{\frac{x_1}{v_1} + \frac{x_2}{v_2}} = \frac{x + x}{\frac{x}{v} + \frac{x}{2v}} = \frac{4v}{3}$$

- **Case II : Distances and Time are given**

$$S_{avg} = \frac{x_1 + x_2}{t_1 + t_2}$$

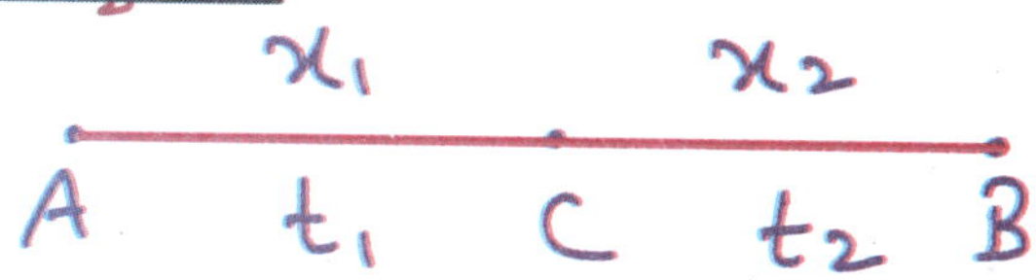

- **Case III : Speeds and Time are given**

$$S_{avg} = \frac{v_1 t_1 + v_2 t_2}{t_1 + t_2}$$

- **Case IV : Different Speed equal Time**

$$S_{avg} = \frac{v_1 + v_2}{2}$$

◎ Case V : Same Distances different Speeds

$$S_{avg} = \frac{2V_1V_2}{V_1+V_2}$$

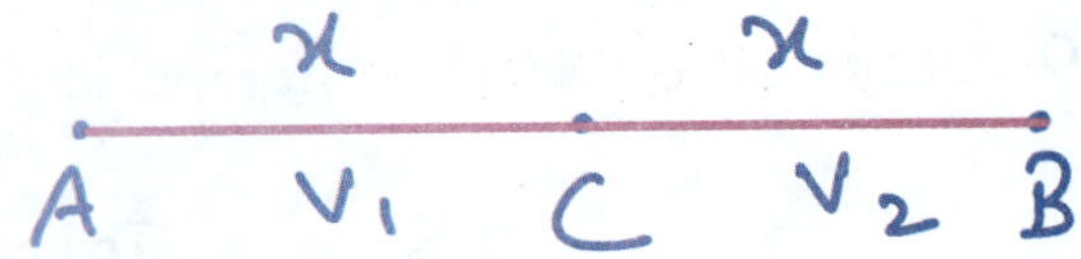

MCQ PUNCH

Q2. A car moves from X to Y with a uniform speed V_u and returns from Y with a uniform speed V_d. The average speed for this round trip is

Sol. $x_1 = x_2 = x$; $V_1 = V_u$; $V_2 = V_d$

$$S_{avg} = \frac{2V_1V_2}{V_1+V_2} = \frac{2V_uV_d}{V_u+V_d}$$

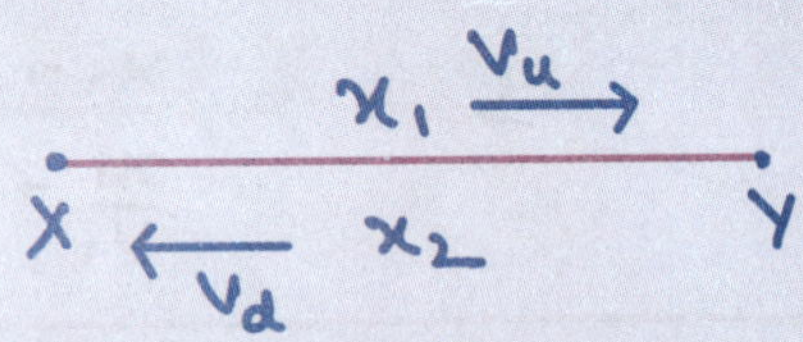

Instantaneous Speed

- Small distance (dx) covered in small time (dt).

$$S_{ins} = \frac{dx}{dt}$$

Instantaneous Speed Comes from differentiation of position w.r.t. time

Average Velocity

$$\vec{V}_{avg} = \frac{\text{Displacement}}{\text{Total Time}} = \frac{\vec{x}_2 - \vec{x}_1}{t_2 - t_1}$$

Instantaneous Velocity

$$\vec{V}_{ins} = \frac{d\vec{x}}{dt}$$

$$= \frac{dx}{dt}\hat{i} = V_x\hat{i}$$

V_x : Speed in x-direction

NEET Accelerate

- On a circular path with uniform speed v

$$V_{avg} = \frac{V\sin(\theta/2)}{(\theta/2)}$$

- For uniform motion

$$V_{avg} = S_{avg} \quad \text{and} \quad V_{ins} = S_{ins}$$

- In non-uniform motion, speed may constant.

Average Acceleration

- It is the change of velocity every second.

$$\vec{a}_{avg} = \frac{\text{Change of Velocity}}{\text{Total Time}} = \frac{\vec{V}_f - \vec{V}_i}{t_f - t_i}$$

- Acceleration opposite to motion is retardation.

$$\text{Retardation} = -\text{Acceleration}$$
$$r = -a$$

Instantaneous Acceleration

- $$\vec{a}_{ins} = \frac{d\vec{v}}{dt}$$
$$= \frac{dv}{dt}\hat{i} = a_x\hat{i}$$

a_x : Acceleration in x-direction

- Isne dharti pe janam liya hai keval velocity ko badalne ke liye. Velocity can be changed either by changing the magnitude or the direction.
- Two types of acceleration are:

Tangential	Centripetal
▹ It only changes the magnitude of the velocity.	▹ It only changes the direction of the velocity.
▹ It acts along the velocity.	▹ It acts perpendicular to velocity.
▹ $a_t = \frac{dv}{dt} = \frac{d^2x}{dt^2}$	▹ $a_c = \frac{v^2}{r}$

PYQ PUNCH

Q3. A particle of unit mass undergoes 1-D motion such that its velocity varies according to $v(x) = bx^{-2n}$, where b and n are constants and x is the position of the particle. The acceleration of the particle as a function of x is given by: **(NEET 2015)**

Sol. $a = \frac{dv}{dt}$

$\Rightarrow \frac{d}{dt}(bx^{-2n})$

$\Rightarrow b(-2n)x^{-2n-1}\frac{dx}{dt}$

$\Rightarrow -2bnx^{-2n-1}v$

$\Rightarrow -2bnx^{-2n-1}(bx^{-2n})$

$= -2b^2nx^{-4n-1}$

Equations of Motion

1. $\vec{v} = \vec{u} + \vec{a}t$

2. $\vec{s} = \vec{u}t + \frac{1}{2}\vec{a}t^2$

3. $v^2 = u^2 + 2\vec{a}.\vec{s}$

4. $\vec{S}_{n^{th}} = \vec{u} + \frac{\vec{a}}{2}(2n-1)$

5. $\vec{V}_{avg} = \frac{\vec{v} + \vec{u}}{2}$

Special Points to Remember

- Valid for Constant Acceleration
- u: Initial ~~Speed~~ Velocity
- v: Final ~~Speed~~ Velocity
- a: Constant acceleration
- s: ~~Distance~~ Displacement
- S_n: Displacement in n^{th} second

MCQ PUNCH

Q4. The distance travelled by a particle starting from rest and moving with an acceleration $4/3\ ms^{-2}$ in the third-second is :

Sol. $\vec{S}_{nth} = \vec{u} + \frac{\vec{a}}{2}(2n-1)$

$$= 0 + \frac{4}{3\times 2}(2\times 3-1) = \frac{10}{3}\ m$$

Q5. A particle has initial velocity $(2\hat{i})$ and acceleration $(0.3\hat{i})$. The magnitude of velocity after 10 sec will be

Sol. $\vec{v} = \vec{u} + \vec{a}t$

$$= 2\hat{i} + 0.3\hat{i} \times 10$$
$$= 2\hat{i} + 3\hat{i}$$
$$= 5\hat{i}$$

$|\vec{v}| = 5$ units

Tricks to use motion's equations in non-uniform motion

Given : 2 different accelerations over the path AC.

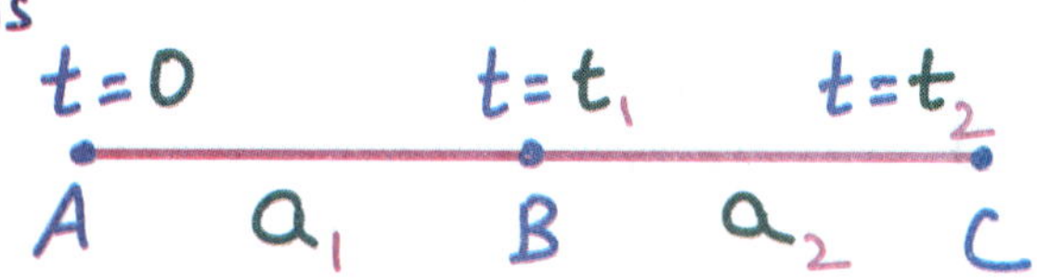

Method :

- For each path (AB & BC), we apply equations of motion separately.
- The final velocity of 1st case becomes initial velocity of 2nd case.

Rest to Rest Motion

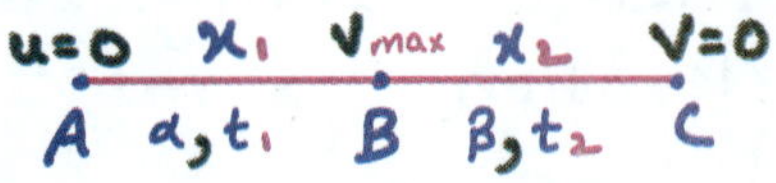

α : Acc of AB
β : Retard of BC
S : Total Distance
T : Total Time

- $\alpha t_1 = \beta t_2$
- $\alpha x_1 = \beta x_2$
- $V_{max} = \alpha t_1 = \beta t_2 = \left(\frac{\alpha\beta}{\alpha+\beta}\right)T$
- $S = \frac{\alpha t_1^2 + \beta t_2^2}{2} = \frac{\alpha\beta T^2}{2(\alpha+\beta)}$

NEET Accelerate

- If a car moving with speed u stops after covering the distance S, then on doubling the speed, it stops after covering the distance 4S.

$$S \propto u^2$$

- Body moving with constant acceleration from A to C.

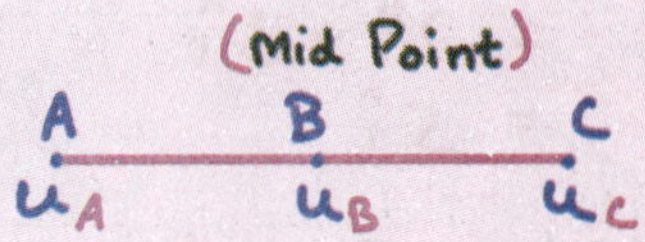

$$u_B = \sqrt{\frac{u_A^2 + u_B^2}{2}}$$

Free Fall or Motion Under Gravity

- A body is said to be under free fall when only gravity acts on the body.
- Acceleration during free fall is always g and downwards, no matter whether body is going up or down.
- Motion doesn't depend upon the mass of object.

Sign Convention

- Upward direction is taken as positive.
- Downward direction is taken as negative.
- Acceleration a is always $-g$.

$$a = -g$$

Cases of Free Fall

◎ Case I : Ball is dropped from height h

- Given : $u = 0$; $s = -h$; $a = -g$

$$v = -\sqrt{2gh} \quad ; \quad t = \sqrt{\frac{2h}{g}}$$

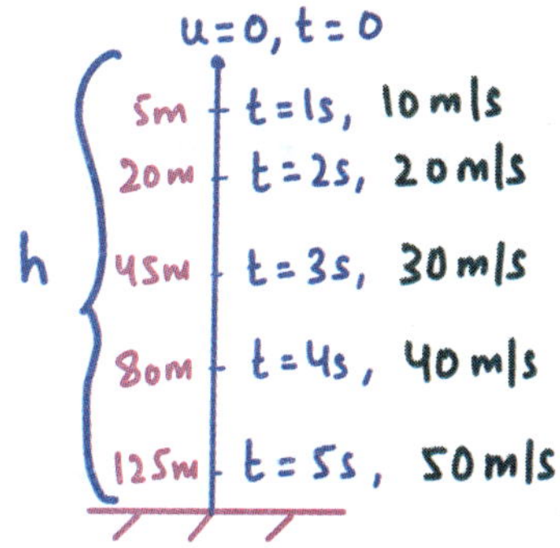

Time	Distance covered	Speed
1st sec	5m	10 m/s
2nd sec	15m	20 m/s
3rd sec	25m	30 m/s
4th sec	35 m	40 m/s
5th sec	45 m	50 m/s

- Ratio of distances covered every sec is 1:3:5:7...

PYQ PUNCH

Q6. The ratio of the distances travelled by a freely falling body in the 1st, 2nd, 3rd and 4th second : (NEET 2022)

Sol. 1:3:5:7

◎ Case II : Ball is thrown downward

- Given : $u = -u$; $s = -h$; $a = -g$

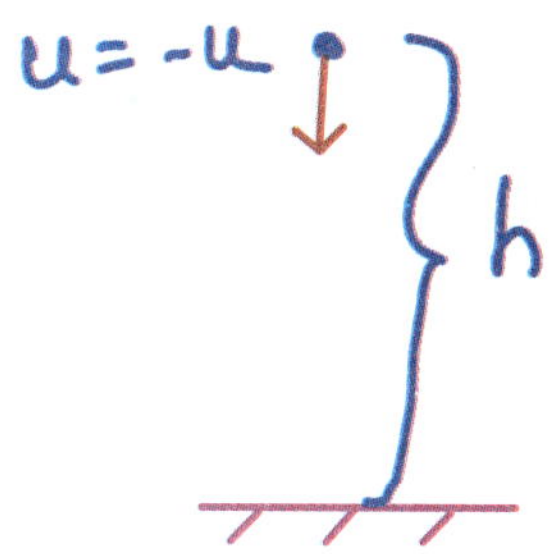

$$v = -\sqrt{u^2 + 2gh}$$

$$t = \frac{\sqrt{u^2 + 2gh} - u}{g}$$

◎ Case III : Ball is thrown upward

- Given : $u = u$; $a = -g$

At max height h

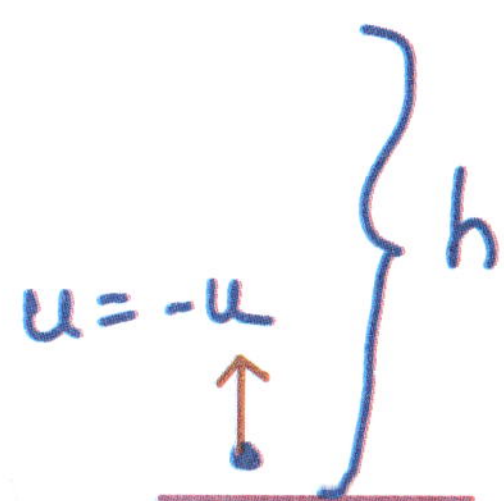

$$v = 0 \quad ; \quad h = u^2/2g$$

- Time of ascent t_a = Time of descent $t_d = u/g$
- Time of flight $t = t_a + t_d = 2u/g$

◎ Case IV : Ball is thrown upward from height h

- Given : $u = u$; $a = -g$; $S = -h$

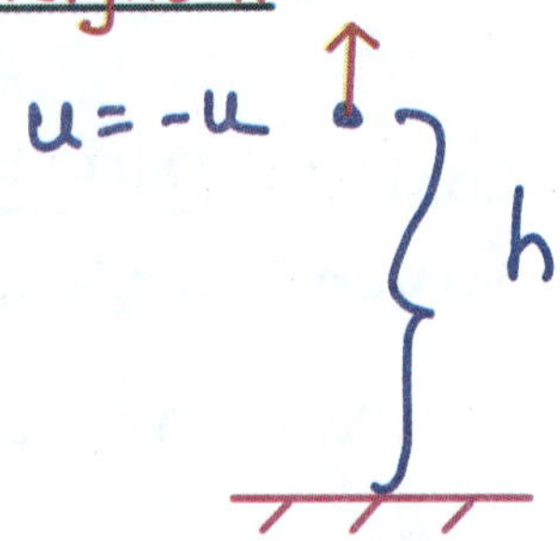

Velocity at Ground $v = -\sqrt{u^2 + 2gh}$

Time of flight $t = \dfrac{\sqrt{u^2 + 2gh} + u}{g}$

◎ Case V : Dropped from hot air balloon moving upward with constant speed u

- Though the object is dropped, its initial speed is same as the speed of balloon and acceleration is g downward.
- All the formulae of case IV are applicable here.

NEET Accelerate

- A ball is thrown upward with a speed u, then it will be at the same height h for 2 different times t_1 and t_2 such that

$t_1 + t_2 = \dfrac{2u}{g}$; $t_1 t_2 = \dfrac{2h}{g}$

Graphs

- Area and slope of every graph represents some physical quantity.
- $\text{Slope} = \dfrac{\text{Y-axis}}{\text{X-axis}}$; Area = Y-axis X X-axis

Position - Time Graph

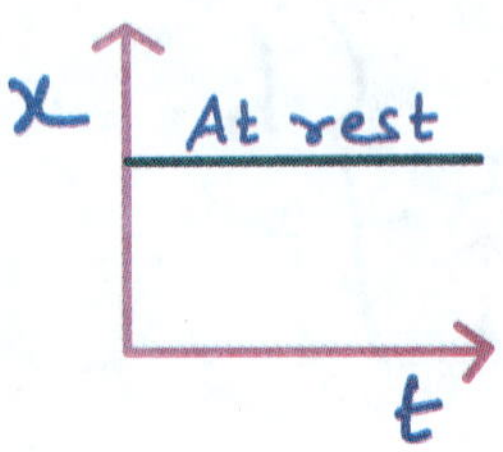

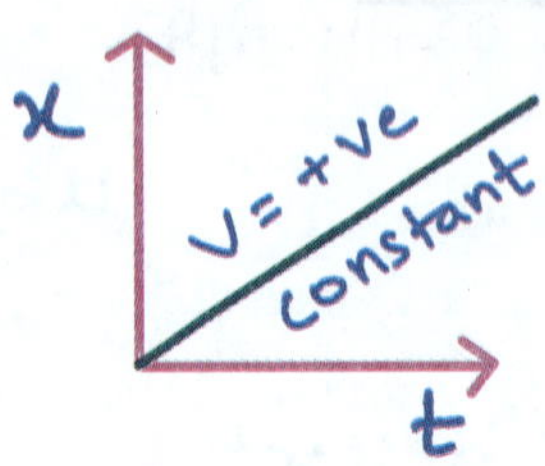

$\text{Slope} = \dfrac{\text{Displacement}}{\text{Time}}$ = Velocity

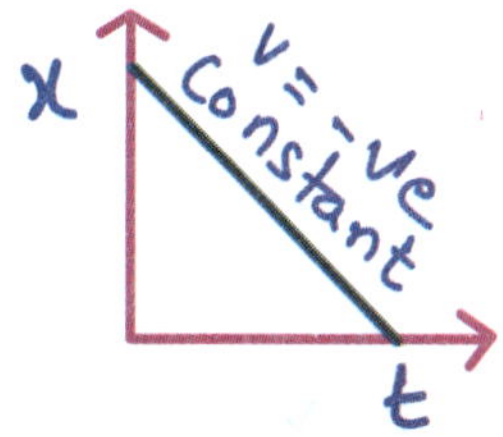

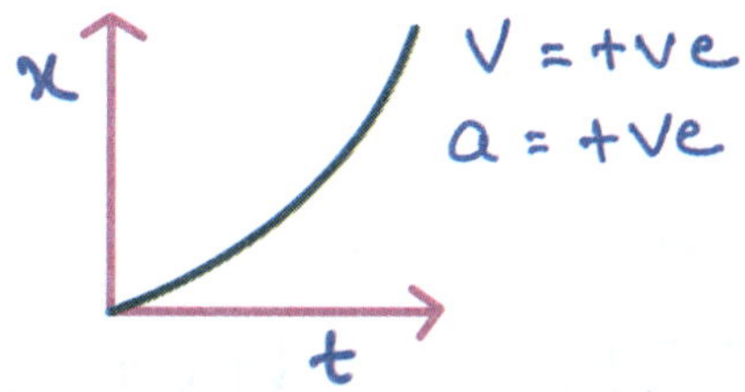

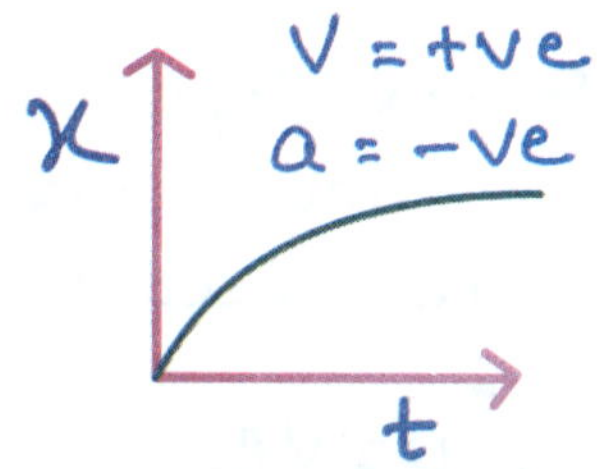

Velocity - Time Graph

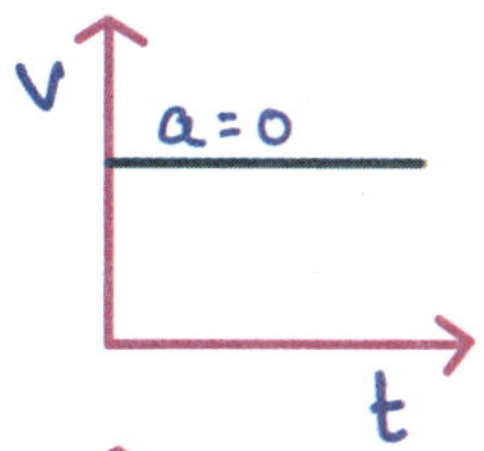

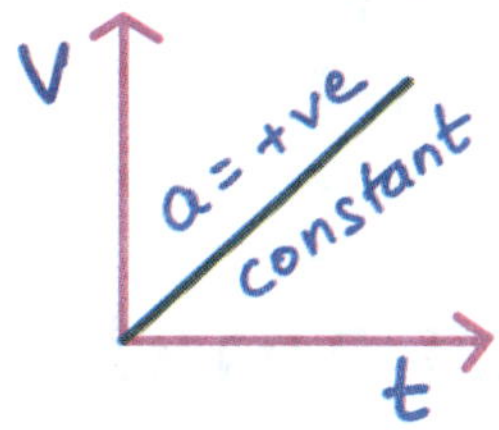

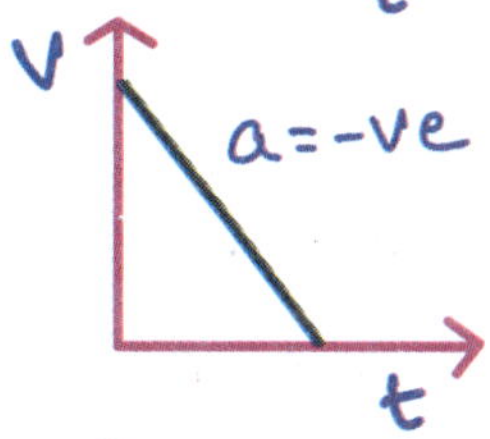

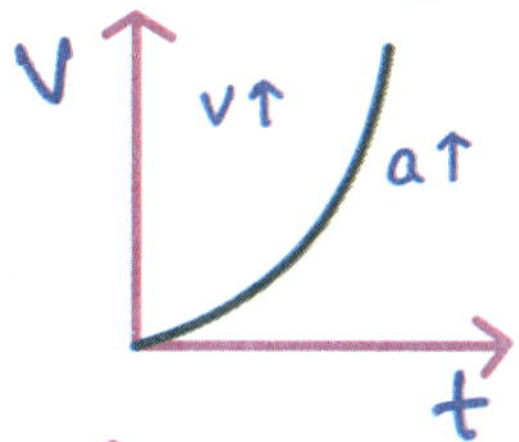

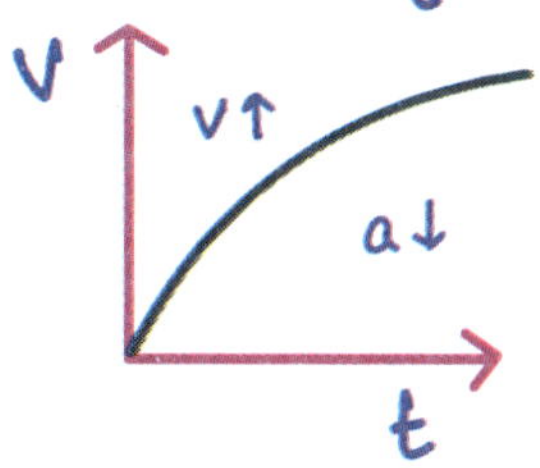

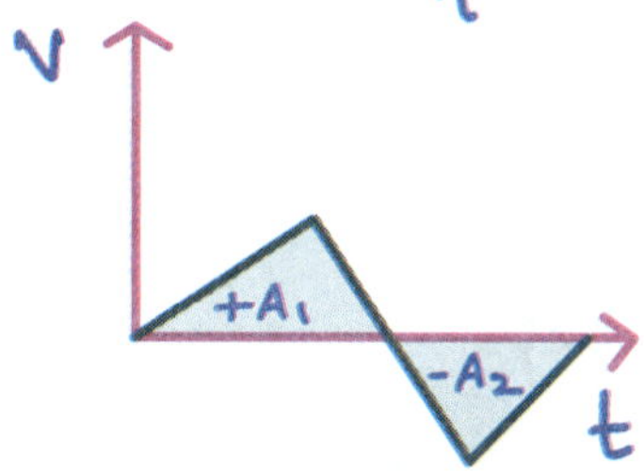

- Slope $= \dfrac{\text{Velocity}}{\text{Time}}$ = Acceleration
- Area = Velocity × Time = Displacement
- $x = \int_{t_1}^{t_2} v\,dt$
- Disp. $= A_1 + A_2$
- Distance $= |A_1| + |A_2|$

Acceleration - Time Graph

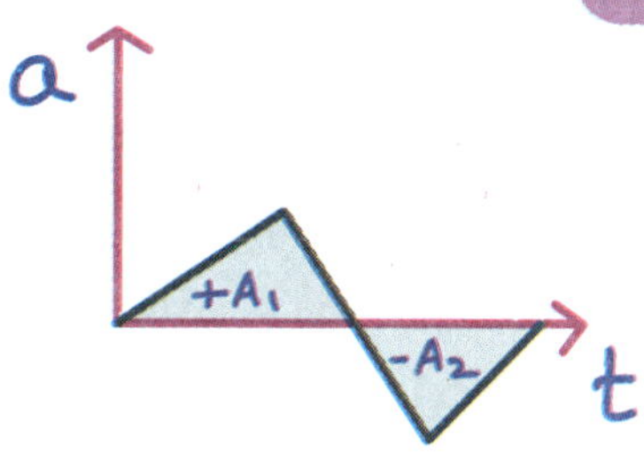

Area = Acc × Time
= Change of Velocity
$= A_1 + A_2$

Conversion of Graph

- Moving Down : x-t to v-t to a-t
- Curved line becomes inclined straight line (ISL).
- +ve slope ISL becomes Horizontal Straight Line (HSL) above X-axis.

- –ve slope ISL becomes Horizontal Straight Line (HSL) below X-axis.
- HSL becomes straight line over x-axis.

Curve ⟶ ISL ⟶ HSL ⟶ X-axis

PYQ PUNCH

Q7. The velocity (v) - time (t) plot of the motion of a body is shown. The acceleration (a) - time (t) is represented as: (NEET 2024)

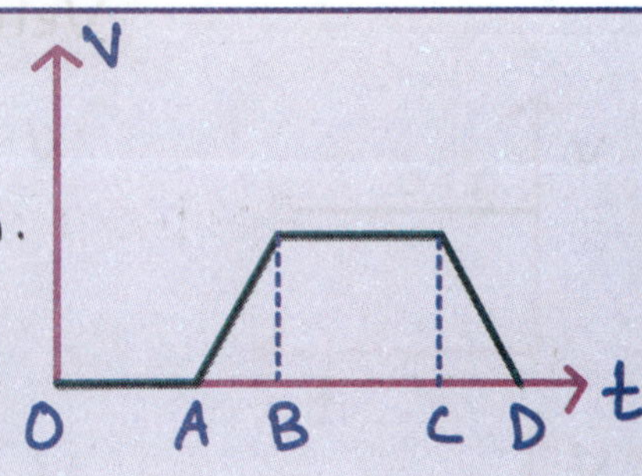

Sol.

OA : X-axis to X-axis
AB : +ve ISL to above HSL
BC : HSL to X-axis
CD : –ve ISL to below HSL

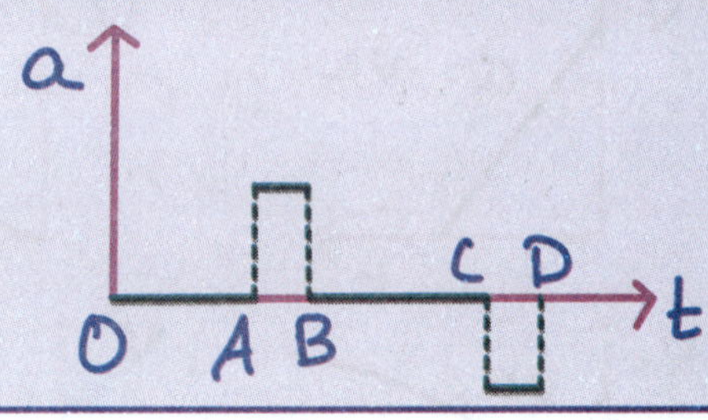

- **Moving Up** : a-t to v-t to x-t
- Reverse the previous steps

X-axis ⟶ HSL ⟶ ISL ⟶ Curve

Relative Motion

- It is the motion of one body with respect to another body.
- Jis body ke respect mein calculation hoti hai wo apne aap ko bhagwan maanti hai. Sari calculation uske around hoti hai. Wahi origin hai, wahi stationary hai.

- **Relative Position**
- Position of 1 w.r.t. 2 $\vec{r}_{12} = \vec{r}_{1G} - \vec{r}_{2G}$
- Position of 2 w.r.t. 1 $\vec{r}_{21} = \vec{r}_{2G} - \vec{r}_{1G}$

Relative Velocity

- Velocity of 1 w.r.t 2 $\quad \vec{v}_{12} = \vec{v}_{1G} - \vec{v}_{2G}$
- Velocity of 2 w.r.t 1 $\quad \vec{v}_{21} = \vec{v}_{2G} - \vec{v}_{1G}$

Relative Acceleration

- Acceleration of 1 w.r.t 2 $\quad \vec{a}_{12} = \vec{a}_{1G} - \vec{a}_{2G}$
- Acceleration of 2 w.r.t 1 $\quad \vec{a}_{21} = \vec{a}_{2G} - \vec{a}_{1G}$

Applications of Relative Velocity

Time taken to Cross (T)

- **Moving in Same Direction**

Given : $V_A > V_B$

$$T = \frac{L_A + x + L_B}{V_A - V_B}$$

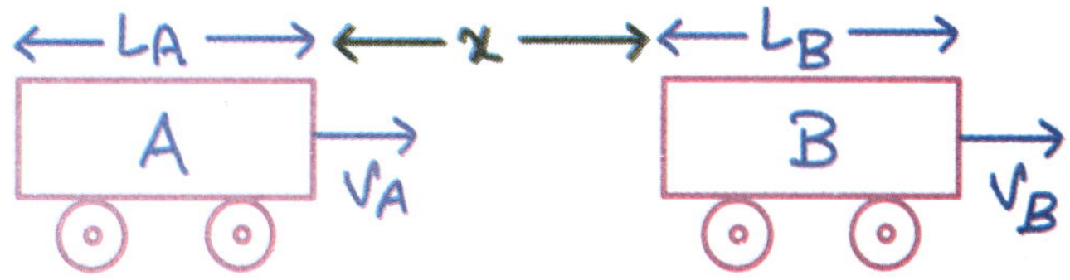

- **Moving in Opposite Direction**

$$T = \frac{L_A + x + L_B}{V_A + V_B}$$

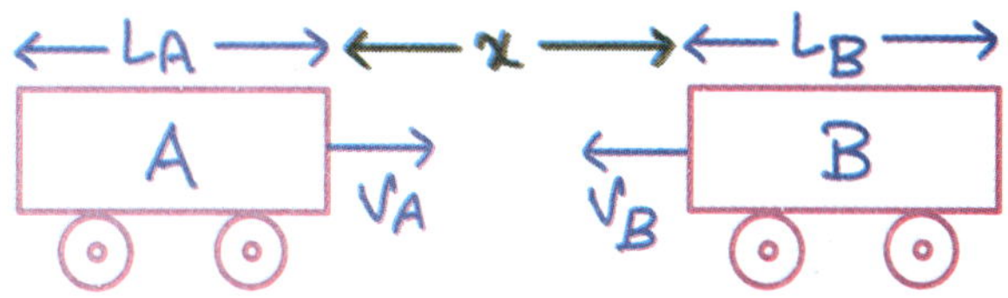

MCQ PUNCH

Q8. A bus is moving with a speed of 10 m/s on a straight road. A scooterist wishes to overtake the bus in 100 sec. If the bus is at a distance of 1 km from the scooterist, with what speed should the scooterist chase the bus ?

Sol. Moving in Same Direction

$$T = \frac{L_A + x + L_B}{V_A - V_B}$$

Taking $L_A = L_B = 0$; $x = 1000\text{ m}$

$V_B = 10\text{ m/s}$; $T = 100\text{ sec}$

$V_A = 20\text{ m/s}$

Time on Escalator

Given: Escalator Length x

Escalator Speed u ; Person Speed v

- Time to cross the stationary escalator $t_1 = x/v$
- Time to cross a moving escalator $t_2 = x/u$
- Time to cross a moving escalator while walking in the same direction

$$t = \frac{t_1 t_2}{t_1 + t_2}$$

- Time to cross a moving escalator while walking in the opposite direction

$$t = \frac{t_1 t_2}{t_1 - t_2}$$

Swimmer in the river

- Same formulae as escalator.

Collision of Balls

- Relative Acceleration $= 0$
- Relative Speed $= u_1 + u_2$
- Time of Collision $t = \frac{h}{u_1 + u_2}$
- Position of Collision from Ground $= u_1 t - \frac{1}{2} g t^2$

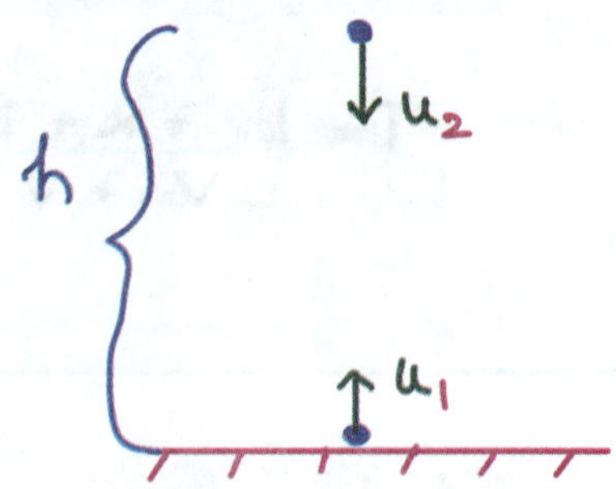

NEET Accelerate

- All the equations of motion are completely applicable in relative motion provided relative acceleration is constant.
- Relative speed increases while moving in opposite direction.

$$V_r = V_1 + V_2$$

- Relative speed decreases while moving in same direction.

$$V_r = V_1 - V_2$$

4. Motion in a Plane

Application of Vector

- Motion of each direction is independent of other direction.
  2-D Motion $\Rightarrow [1\text{-D}]_{x\text{-axis}} + [1\text{-D}]_{y\text{-axis}}$
- Displacement, velocity, acceleration and force along x-axis is independent of displacement, velocity, acceleration and force along y-axis.
- Just resolve the vector quantities into x-axis and Y-axis and follow all the rules of motion in a straight line.
- Time being a scalar quantity links both the axes i.e. time is same in both co-ordinates.

Equations of Motion in a Plane

- All the equations of motion studied in the motion in a straight line are valid here for constant acceleration.
-

X-axis	Y-axis
$V_x = u_x + a_x t$	$V_y = u_y + a_y t$
$S_x = u_x t + \frac{1}{2} a_x t^2$	$S_y = u_y t + \frac{1}{2} a_y t^2$
$V_x^2 = u_x^2 + 2a_x S_x$	$V_y^2 = u_y^2 + 2a_y S_y$
$(S_n)_x = u_x + \frac{a_x}{2}(2n-1)$	$(S_n)_y = u_y + \frac{a_y}{2}(2n-1)$
$(V_{avg})_x = \frac{V_x + u_x}{2}$	$(V_{avg})_y = \frac{V_y + u_y}{2}$
$V_x = \frac{dx}{dt}$	$V_y = \frac{dy}{dt}$
$a_x = \frac{dV_x}{dt}$	$a_y = \frac{dV_y}{dt}$

Instantaneous Velocity

- Change of distance in one direction is independent of the change of distance in any perpendicular direction.
- $\vec{V}_{ins} = \frac{d\vec{r}}{dt}$ where $\vec{r} = x\hat{i} + y\hat{j}$

$$= \frac{dx}{dt}\hat{i} + \frac{dy}{dt}\hat{j}$$

$$= V_x\hat{i} + V_y\hat{j}$$

V_x : x-dir speed
V_y : y-dir speed

- $|\vec{V}_{ins}| = \sqrt{V_x^2 + V_y^2}$

Instantaneous Acceleration

- $\vec{a}_{ins} = \frac{d\vec{v}}{dt}$ where $\vec{V} = V_x\hat{i} + V_y\hat{j}$

$$= \frac{dV_x\hat{i}}{dt} + \frac{dV_y\hat{j}}{dt}$$

$$= a_x\hat{i} + a_y\hat{j}$$

a_x : x-dir acc
a_y : y-dir acc

- $|\vec{a}_{ins}| = \sqrt{a_x^2 + a_y^2}$

PYQ PUNCH

Q1. The x and y coordinates of the particle at any time are $x = 5t - 2t^2$ and $y = 10t$ respectively, where x and y are in meters and t in seconds. The acceleration of the particle at $t = 2s$ is : (NEET 2017)

Sol. $V_x = \frac{dx}{dt} = 5 - 4t$; $V_y = \frac{dy}{dt} = 10$

$a_x = \frac{dV_x}{dt} = -4$; $a_y = \frac{dV_y}{dt} = 0$

$$|\vec{a}_{ins}| = \sqrt{a_x^2 + a_y^2}$$

$$= \sqrt{(-4)^2 + 0^2} = 4 m/s^2$$

Projectile Motion (PM)

- Projectile is an object which is thrown in air.
- In PM, we study the trajectory of an object which is thrown at an angle θ to horizontal with speed u.
- The acceleration of the object is always g (downward) while the horizontal acceleration is always zero.

$$a_x = 0 \quad ; \quad a_y = -g$$

- Direction of motion is always in the direction of velocity. In PM, it is tangential to the curve.

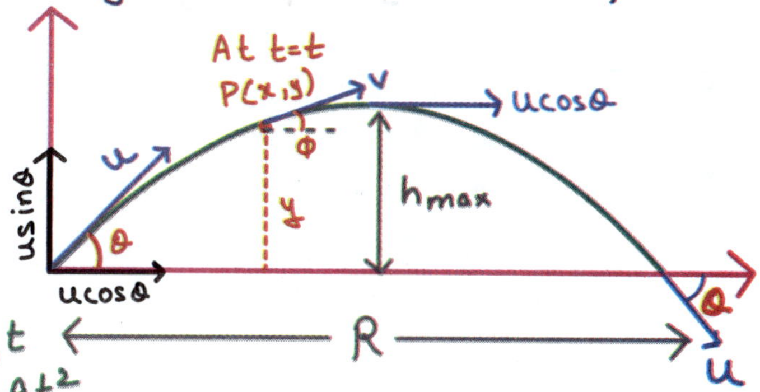

- X-axis
  - $u_x = u\cos\theta$
  - $a_x = 0$
  - $t = t$
  - $V_x = u\cos\theta$
  - $x = u\cos\theta t$
- Y-axis
  - $u_y = u\sin\theta$
  - $a_y = -g$
  - $t = t$
  - $V_y = u\sin\theta - gt$
  - $y = u\sin\theta t - \frac{1}{2}gt^2$

Formulae

Time

- Time of ascent t_a = Time of descent $t_d = \frac{u\sin\theta}{g}$
- Time of flight $t = t_a + t_b = \frac{2u\sin\theta}{g}$

Range

- $R = \frac{u^2\sin 2\theta}{g}$

Maximum Range

- $R_{max} = \frac{u^2}{2g}$ at $\theta = 45°$

Maximum Height

- $h_{max} = \frac{u^2\sin^2\theta}{2g}$

Angle with Horizontal

- $\tan\phi = \frac{V_y}{V_x}$

Complementary Angles

- Same range for two different angles θ_1 and θ_2.
- $\theta_1 + \theta_2 = 90°$
- $H_1 + H_2 = \frac{R^2}{16}$, where H_1 and H_2 are max height for θ_1 and θ_2.

Equation of Trajectory

$$y = x\tan\theta - \frac{1}{2}\frac{gx^2}{u^2\cos^2\theta}$$

Equation of Parabola

$$y = x\tan\theta\left[1 - \frac{x}{R}\right]$$

Angle of Projection with Vertical

- The particle is projected at an angle α with the vertical direction.
- Speed of projection is u.
- Angle of projection with horizontal direction becomes
  $\theta = 90° - \alpha$
- Everything else remains the same.

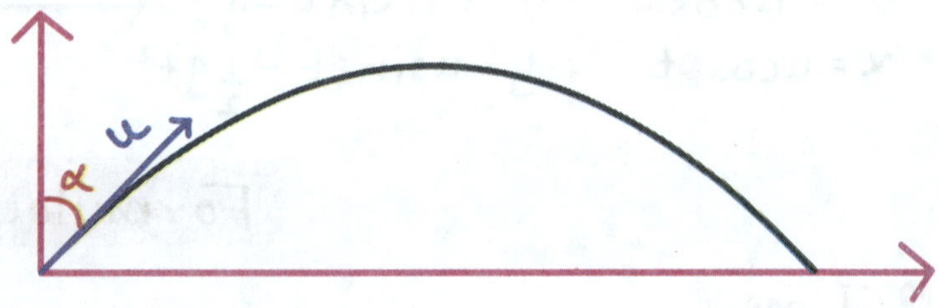

PYQ PUNCH

Q2. A bullet is fired from a gun at the speed of 280 m/s in the direction 30° above the horizontal. The maximum height attained by the bullet is: (NEET 2023)

Sol.
$$h_{max} = \frac{u^2 \sin^2\theta}{2g}$$
$$= \frac{(280)^2 \times \sin^2 30°}{2 \times 9.8}$$
$$= 1000 \text{ m}$$

Q3. A ball is projected with a velocity of 10 m/s, at an angle of 60° with the vertical direction. Its speed at the highest point of its trajectory will be: (NEET 2022)

Sol. Angle with horizontal
$$\theta = 90° - \alpha$$
$$= 90° - 60°$$
$$= 30°$$

Speed at highest point $= u\cos\theta$
$$= 10\cos 30°$$
$$= 5 \text{ m/s}$$

NEET Accelerate

- Angle of return = Angle of projection = θ
- Velocity at top point is only horizontal = $u\cos\theta$
- Speed of return = Speed of throw = u
- h_{max} and R are related by $h_{max} = \frac{R\tan\theta}{4}$
- A ball is thrown upward with a speed u, then it will be at the same height h for 2 different time t_1 and t_2 such that
  - $t_1 + t_2 = \frac{2u\sin\theta}{g}$
  - $t_1 t_2 = \frac{2h}{g}$

Horizontal PM from some height

X-axis	Y-axis
$u_x = u$	$u_y = 0$
$a_x = 0$	$a_y = -g$
$t = t$	$t = t$
$V_x = u$	$V_y = -gt$
$x = ut$	$y = -\frac{1}{2}gt^2$

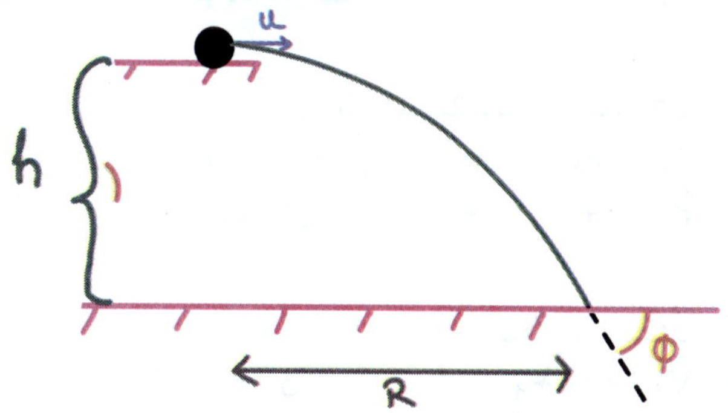

Formulae

- Time $t = \sqrt{\frac{2h}{g}}$ → Same time as free fall because initial vertical velocity is 0.
- Range $R = u\sqrt{\frac{2h}{g}}$
- Speed at any time $= \sqrt{u^2 + (gt)^2}$
- $\tan\phi = \frac{V_y}{V_x}$

PM from some height at angle θ

X-axis	Y-axis
$u_x = u\cos\theta$	$u_y = u\sin\theta$
$a_x = 0$	$a_y = -g$

- Time $t = \frac{u\sin\theta}{g} + \sqrt{\left(\frac{u\sin\theta}{g}\right)^2 + \frac{2h}{g}}$
- Range $R = u\cos\theta\, t$

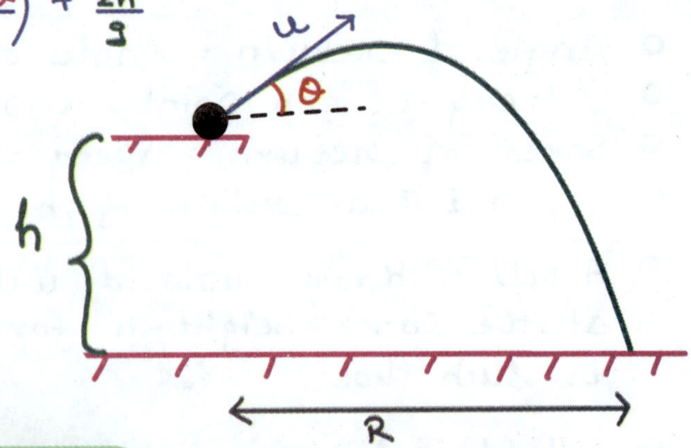

Relative Motion in a Plane

- The concept of relative motion in a straight line is completely valid here.

Relative Position

- Position of 1 w.r.t. 2 $\vec{r}_{12} = \vec{r}_{1G} - \vec{r}_{2G}$
- Position of 2 w.r.t. 1 $\vec{r}_{21} = \vec{r}_{2G} - \vec{r}_{1G}$

Relative Velocity

- Velocity of 1 w.r.t. 2 $\vec{v}_{12} = \vec{v}_{1G} - \vec{v}_{2G}$
- Velocity of 2 w.r.t. 1 $\vec{v}_{21} = \vec{v}_{2G} - \vec{v}_{1G}$

Relative Acceleration

- Acceleration of 1 w.r.t. 2 $\vec{a}_{12} = \vec{a}_{1G} - \vec{a}_{2G}$
- Acceleration of 2 w.r.t. 1 $\vec{a}_{21} = \vec{a}_{2G} - \vec{a}_{1G}$

River Man Problem

- Speed of river flow = u
- Speed of swimmer in still water = v_{MR}

Shortest time to cross the river

- Must swim perpendicular to the flow of river i.e. AB.
- Path seen from the ground is AC.

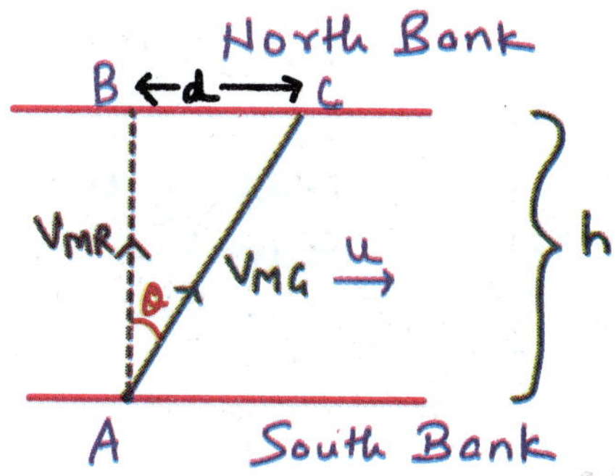

- Time to cross $t = \frac{h}{V_{MR}}$
- Drift $d = u \times \frac{h}{V_{MR}}$
- Velocity of Man w.r.t. ground

$$V_{MG} = \sqrt{u^2 + V_{MR}^2}$$

- Angle of swim w.r.t. ground

$$\tan\theta = \frac{u}{V_{MR}} = \frac{d}{h}$$

◎ <u>Shortest path to cross the river</u>

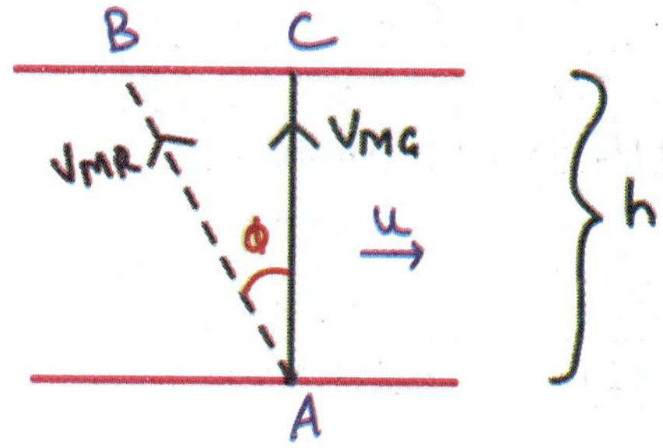

- Shortest path is exactly opposite end i.e. AC.
- Must swim at an angle ϕ with perpendicular to the flow of river.
- Drift must be 0.
- Time to cross $t = \frac{h}{V_{MR}\cos\phi}$
- Angle of swim w.r.t. river $\sin\phi = \frac{u}{V_{MR}}$

PYQ PUNCH

Q4. The speed of the swimmer in still water is 20 m/s. The speed of the river water is 10 m/s and is flowing due east. If he is standing on the south bank and wishes to cross the river along the shortest path, the angle at which he should make his strokes w.r.t. north is. (NEET 2019)

Sol. $\sin\phi = \frac{u}{V_{MR}} = \frac{10}{20} = 0.5$

$\phi = 30°$

Rain Man Problem

- Rain is falling with speed V_R.
- Man is running horizontal with speed V_M.

Rain falling Vertically

- Rain falling downward.
- Man running eastward.
- Velocity of rain w.r.t. man

$$\vec{V}_{RM} = \vec{V}_R - \vec{V}_M$$

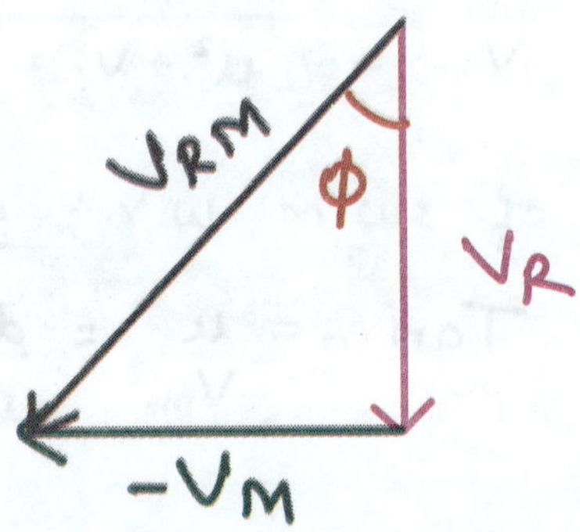

- $\tan\phi = \dfrac{V_M}{V_R}$

Rain appears to fall vertically

- Rain is falling at an angle θ with vertical.
- Man running eastward.
- Rain appears to fall downward.
- $\sin\theta = \dfrac{V_M}{V_R}$

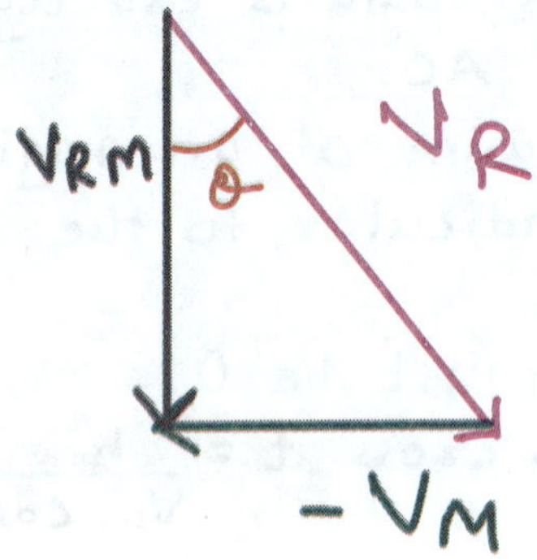

5. Newton's Laws Of Motion

Force

- It is a push or pull on an object that results from the interaction of two bodies.

Type of forces

Contact force
- Objects interact by touching.
- Friction
  Tension
  Normal
  Spring force

Non-Contact force
- Objects interact without touching.
- Gravitational force
  Magnetic force
  Electrostatic force
  Nuclear force

Normal Force

- Whenever two bodies are in contact, they exert a force on each other called as Normal force.
- It acts perpendicular to the surfaces in contact. It is a push force.
- Number of normals on a body is equal to the number of surfaces in contact.
- It is a self adjusting force.

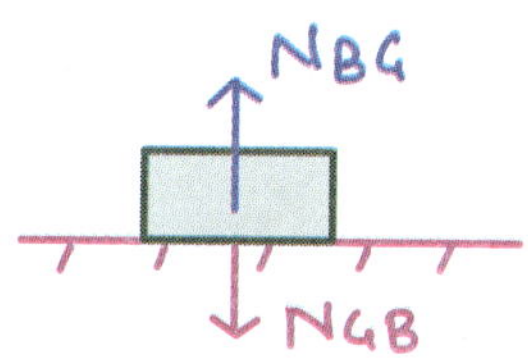

Useful Cases of Normal

Inclined Plane	Ball	Ladder 1	Ladder 2
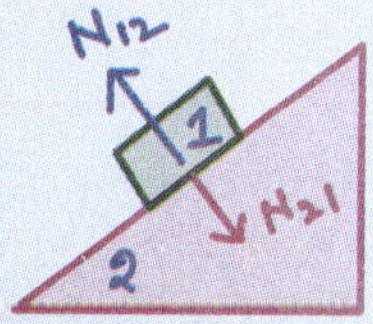	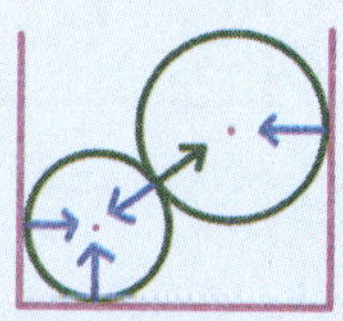	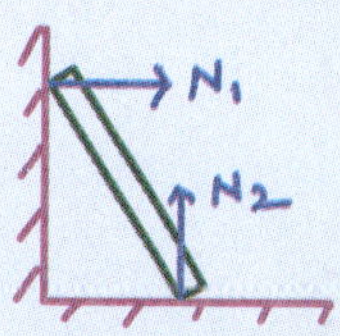	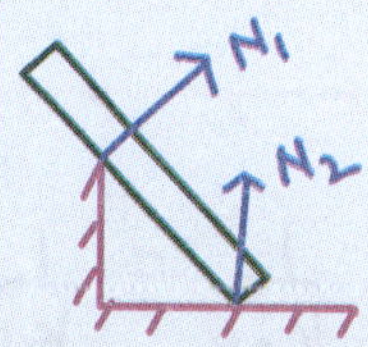
Perpendicular to the inclined plane.	Passes through centre of the ball.	Perpendicular to the surface of wall.	N_1: perpendicular to the surface of ladder.

Tension

- When a string or a wire is held tightly, a force gets generated in it called as Tension.
- Tension acts along a string.
- For a massless string, tension is constant throughout the string.
- It is a pull force.

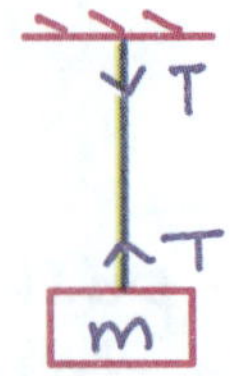

Spring Force

- When a spring is extended or compressed from its natural length, then a force gets generated in it called as Spring force.

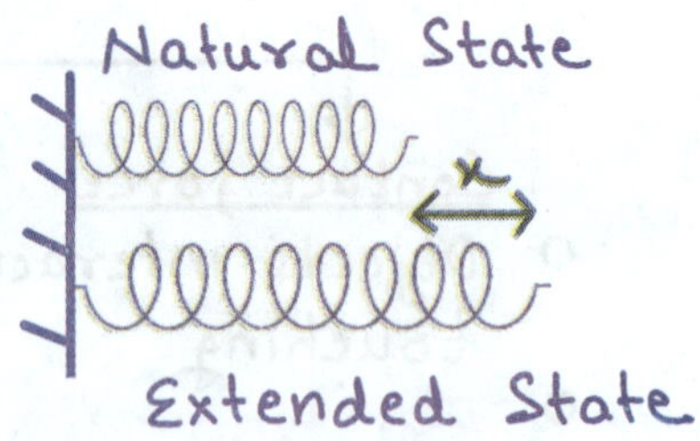

- $F \propto x$ or $F = kx$
  where K is called as Spring Constant
- K depends upon the length of the spring (l) and the material of the spring. $K \propto \frac{1}{l}$

Spring in Combination

Series

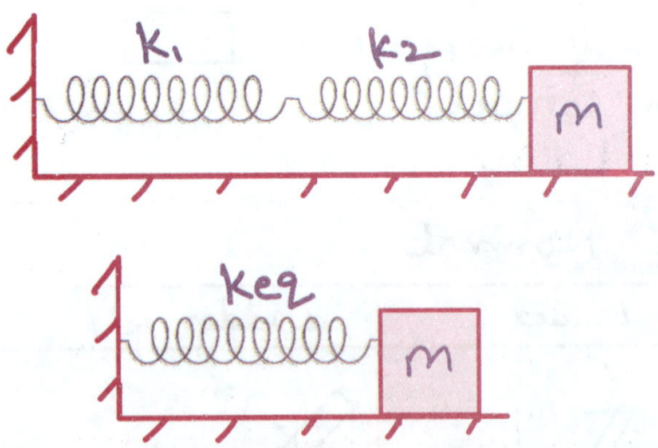

$$\frac{1}{K_{eq}} = \frac{1}{K_1} + \frac{1}{K_2}$$

Parallel

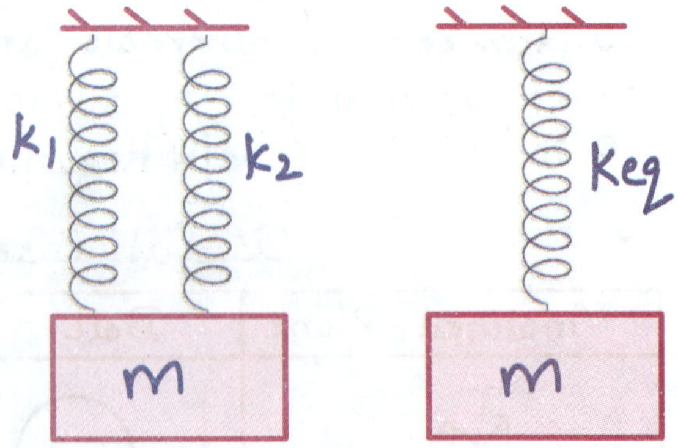

$$K_{eq} = K_1 + K_2$$

Cutting of Spring

- If a spring is cut into 2 parts of length ratio $l_1 : l_2$ then new spring constants are

$$k_1 = \frac{(l_1 + l_2)k}{l_1} \quad , \quad k_2 = \frac{(l_1 + l_2)k}{l_2}$$

- If a spring is cut into 3 parts of length ratio $l_1 : l_2 : l_3$ then new spring constants are

$$k_1 = \frac{(l_1 + l_2 + l_3)k}{l_1} \quad , \quad k_2 = \frac{(l_1 + l_2 + l_3)k}{l_2} \quad , \quad k_3 = \frac{(l_1 + l_2 + l_3)k}{l_3}$$

Free Body Diagram (FBD)

- It is the pictorial representation of all the forces acting on a particle.
- Steps to draw FBD ÷
  - Identify the body / system whose FBD has to be drawn. Let it be m_1.
  - Make a list of all the forces acting on it.
    $m_1 g$: Gravity due to Earth (downward)
    N_1 : Normal due to ground (upward)
    N_2 : Normal due to m_2 (downward)

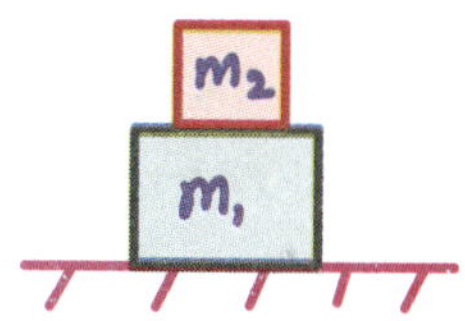

  - Considering body as a point mass, draw all the forces acting on it with their tails on this point.

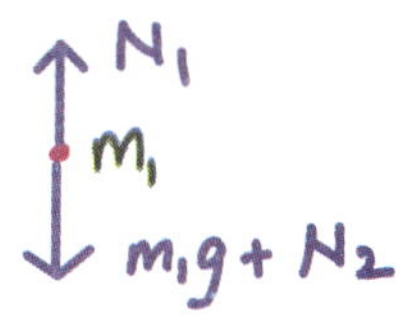

Frequently Used FBD

Inclined Plane

FBD of m

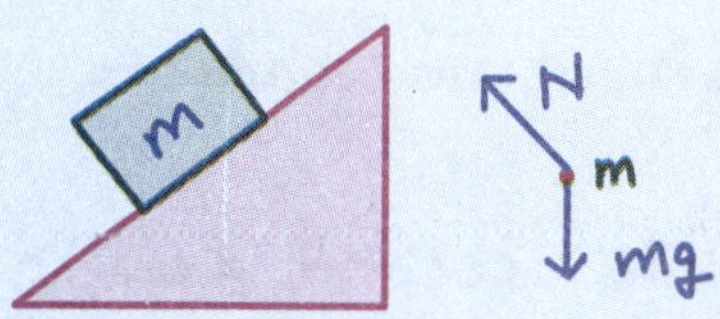

Pulley

FBD of m_1 & m_2

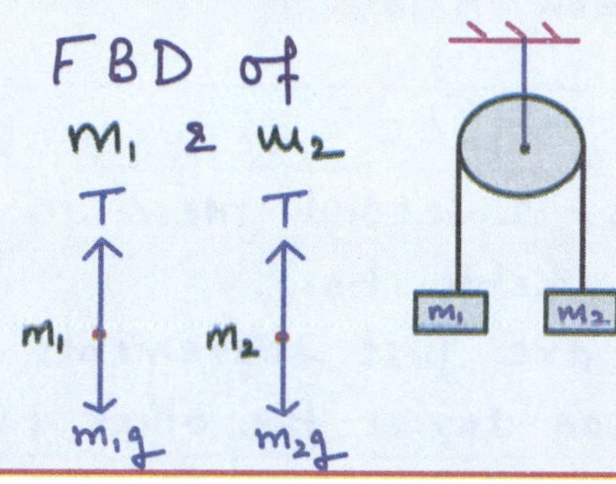

Blocks on Ground

FBD of m_1 & m_2

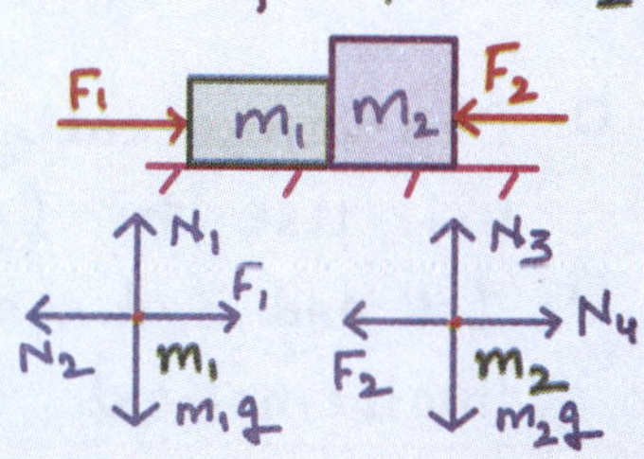

Newton's Laws of Motion

1. First law of motion or Law of Inertia

- Inertia is a property of a material, which resists the change of state of motion of the body.

  Inertia ∝ mass

- First law states that a body continues in the state of rest or a state of uniform motion until and unless an external force is applied on it.

2. Second Law of Motion or Law of momentum

- Momentum is the measure of motion contained in a body.

  $\vec{p} = m \times \vec{v}$

- Second law states that the rate of change of momentum is directly proportional to the net external force.

$$p = \text{constant} \xleftarrow[\text{External Force}]{\text{For Zero}} \vec{F}_{ext} = \frac{d\vec{p}}{dt} \xrightarrow[\text{mass}]{\text{For Constant}} \vec{F}_{ext} = m\vec{a}$$

- If no external force acts on a body then there is no change in the momentum of the body. This is called as Conservation of momentum.

3. Third Law of Motion or Action-Reaction Law

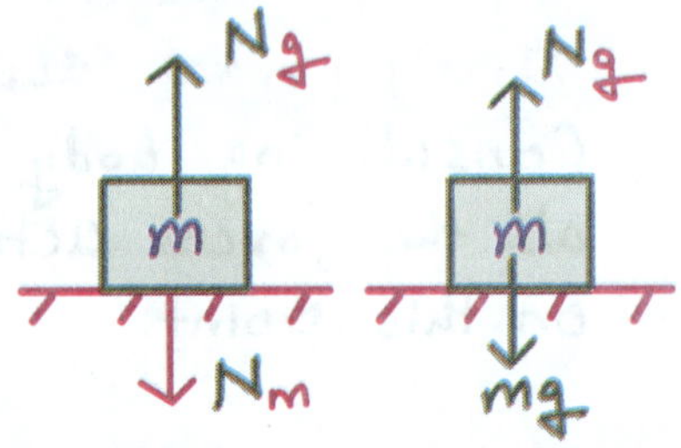

- Every action has equal and opposite reaction. $N_g = N_m$
- Action-reaction forces never act on a same body.
- Since N_g and mg are acting on a same body, hence they don't form action-reaction pair.

NEET Accelerate

- Mathematically har 1 second mein jo momentum badalta hai use hi force kehte hai.
- 1st and 3rd laws are just statements while second law is mathematical. We can derive the other two laws from 2nd law.

Change of Momentum and Force due to it

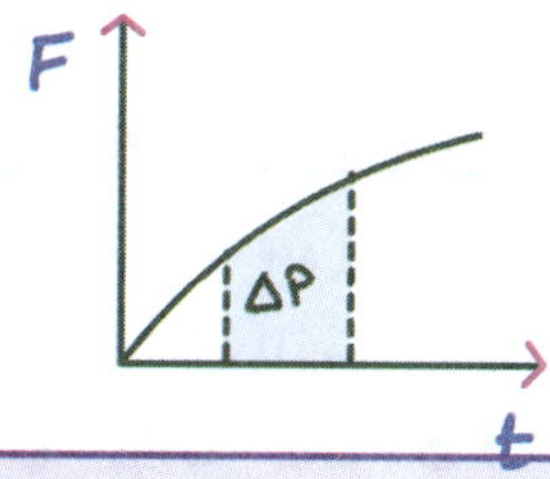

- $\Delta\vec{P} = \int \vec{F} dt$ Area of Force-Time Graph
- $\vec{F} = \frac{d\vec{P}}{dt}$ Slope of Momentum-Time Graph

PYQ PUNCH

Q1. The force 'F' acting on a particle of mass 'm' is indicated by a force-time graph shown below. The change in momentum of the particle over the time interval from zero to 8 sec is (NEET 2014)

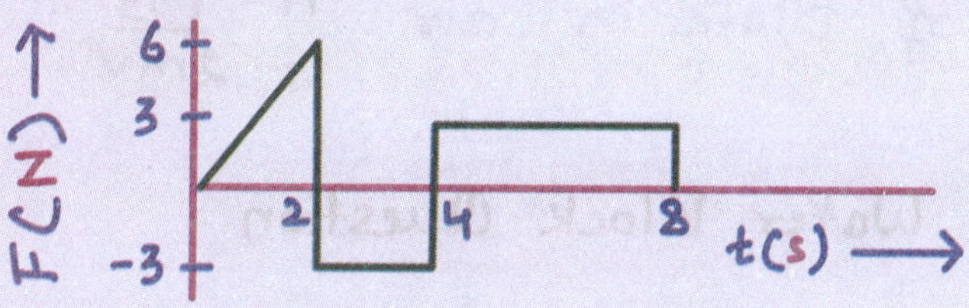

Sol. Change in momentum = Area of Force-Time Graph

$$= \frac{1}{2}\times 2\times 6 - 3\times 2 + 3\times 4 = 12 \text{ Ns}$$

Rebounding Ball

Ball strikes a surface perpendicularly

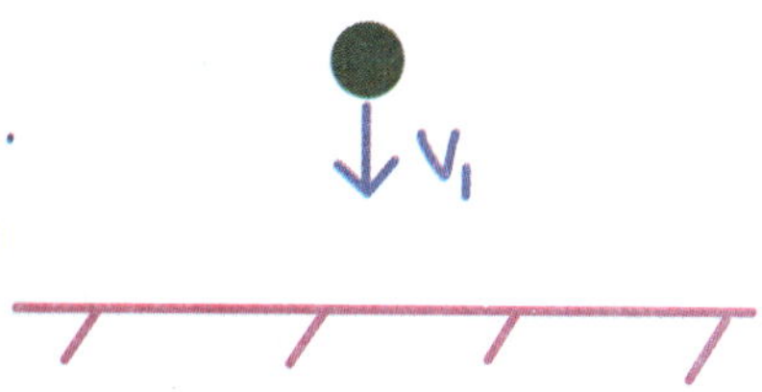

- Ball strikes with v_1 & returns back with v_2.
- Momentum Change of ball $\Delta P = m[v_2 + v_1]$
- Force on Surface $F = \frac{m[v_2+v_1]}{\Delta t}$
- If $v_1 = v_2 = v$, then $\Delta P = 2mv$, $F = 2mv/\Delta t$

Ball strikes a surface at an angle

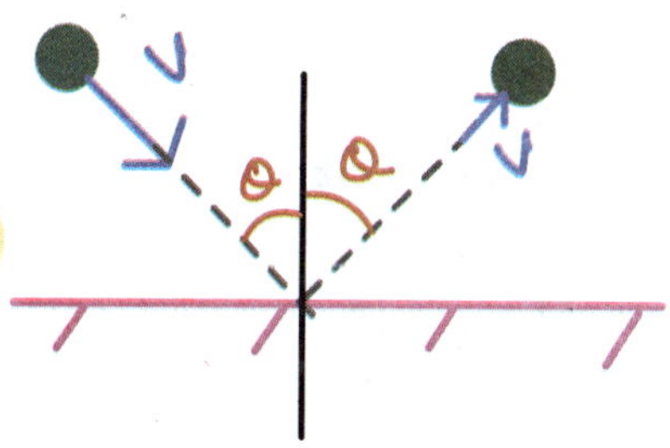

- Ball strikes & returns back with v.
- Momentum Change of ball $\Delta P = 2mv\cos\theta$
- Force on Surface $F = \frac{2mv\cos\theta}{\Delta t}$

Bullet Plate Question

Bullet striking a plate & gets embedded

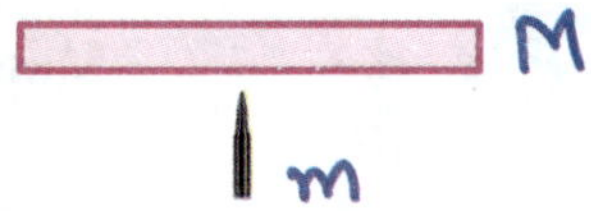

- Bullet strikes with speed v.
- n bullet strike per second.
- Force on plate $F = nmv$
- For floating of plate in air $n = \frac{Mg}{mv}$

Bullet striking a plate & returns with same speed

- Force on plate $F = 2nmv$
- For floating of plate in air $n = \frac{Mg}{2mv}$

Water Block Question

Water striking a block & falls down

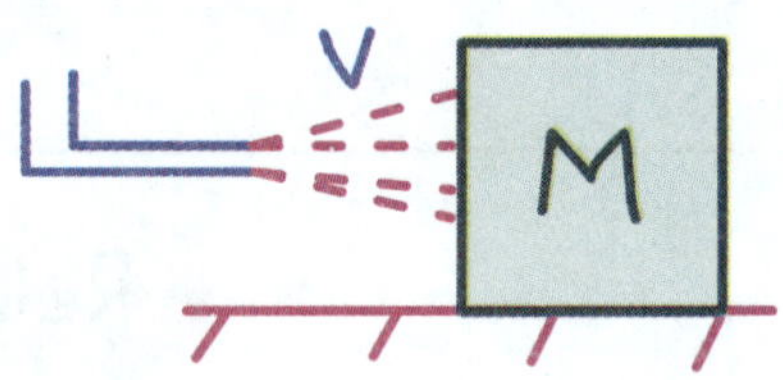

- Jet of water with speed v strikes the block.
- Water flow rate is $\dot{m} = \rho A v$
- Force on block $F = \dot{m}v = \rho A v^2$

  where ρ is density and A is jet's area of cross-section.

Water striking a block & returns with same speed

- Force on block $F = 2\dot{m}v = 2\rho A v^2$

NEET Accelerate

- If the change of momentum and force are Δp & F during striking & stopping, then change of momentum & force becomes $2\Delta p$ & 2F on striking & rebounding at same speed.
- If sand drops on a conveyor belt at a rate of M kg/s, then the required force to keep it moving with constant speed is Mv.

Impulse

- It is a measure of impact during collision.
- I = Change of Momentum

$$\vec{I} = \vec{p_f} - \vec{p_i} = \int \vec{F}dt$$ → Area of Force-Time Graph

- $\vec{I}_{avg} = \vec{F}_{avg} \Delta t$

MCQ PUNCH

Q2. If a cricketer catches a ball of mass 150 gm moving with a velocity of 20 m/s, then he experiences a force of (Time taken to complete the catch is 0.1 sec)

Sol. $\vec{F}_{avg} = \dfrac{\vec{I}_{avg}}{\Delta t} = \dfrac{\vec{p_f} - \vec{p_i}}{\Delta t}$

$= \dfrac{0 - .15 \times 20}{0.1} = -30\text{ N}$

$|\vec{F}_{avg}| = 30\text{ N}$

Equilibrium

- At equilibrium, net external force on the body is zero.
- Body may be at rest or moving with uniform velocity.
- Conditions :
  - $F_{ext} = 0$
  - $a = 0$
  - $\vec{v}$ = constant

Types of Equilibrium

Stable

- Body returns to the original position after slight displacement.

Unstable

- Body doesn't return to the original position after slight displacement.

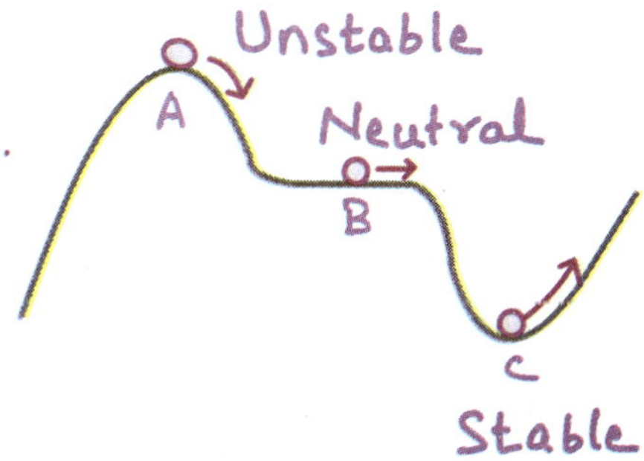

- **Neutral**
- Body remains at the same place after slight displacement.

PYQ PUNCH

Q3. A particle moving with velocity is acted by three forces shown by the vector traingle PQR. The velocity of the particle will increase, decrease or remains constant.

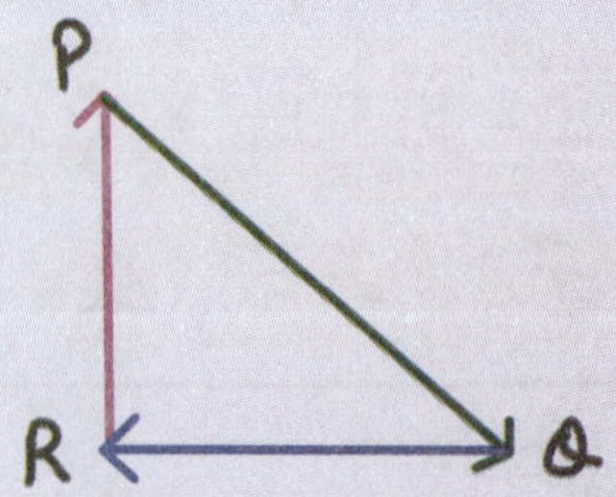

(NEET 2019)

Sol. Three forces $\vec{RP}$, $\vec{PQ}$ and $\vec{QR}$ are forming a triangle, hence $F_{net} = 0$

Thus $\vec{v}$ is constant.

Conservation of Momentum

- In the absence of any external force, linear momentum remains conserved.

$$\vec{p} = \text{Constant} \quad \text{for } F_{ext} = 0$$

- Momentum can be conserved in a particular direction also.

$$\vec{p_x} = \text{Constant for } F_x = 0 \quad , \quad \vec{p_y} = \text{Constant for } F_y = 0$$

Special Cases of Conservation of Momentum

- **A stationary object explodes in many parts**

- No external force, hence momentum remains conserved in all directions.

$$(p_i)_x = (p_f)_x \quad , \quad (p_i)_y = (p_f)_y$$

- Internal force of explosion changes the Kinetic Energy of the system.

PYQ PUNCH

Q4. A shell of mass m is at rest. It explodes into three fragments having mass in the ratio 2:2:1. If the fragments having equal mass fly off along mutually perpendicular direction with speed v, the speed of the third fragment is? **(NEET 2022)**

Sol. Let the masses be 2m, 2m and m.

In explosion, momentum is conserved in all directions.

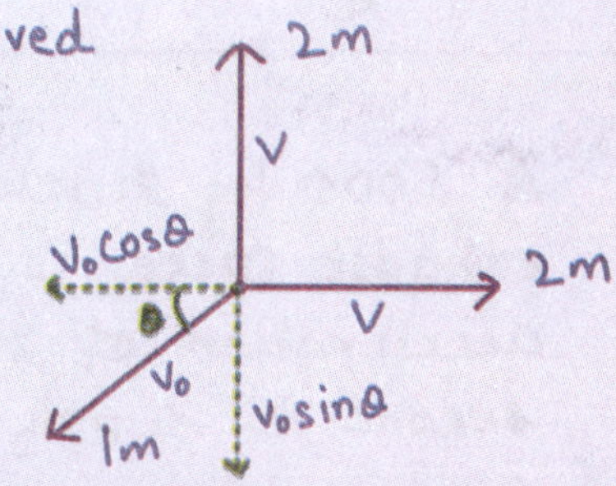

In X-axis

$$V_0\cos\theta = \frac{2mv}{m} = 2v \quad \text{—}(1)$$

In Y-axis

$$V_0\sin\theta = \frac{2mv}{m} = 2v \quad \text{—}(2)$$

Square and add equations (1) and (2)

$$V_0 = 2\sqrt{2}\,V$$

Gun Bullet System

- Recoil Speed of Gun

$$V_G = \frac{m_b v_b}{M_G}$$

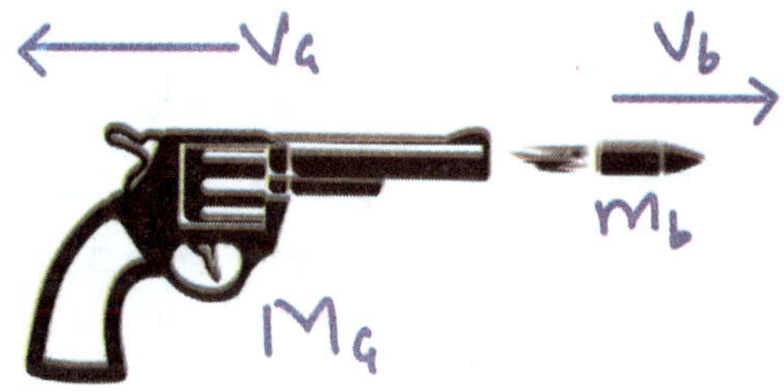

- If n bullets are fired from the gun every second, then force on the gun $\vec{F_G} = -n\,m_b\,\vec{V_G}$
- $\frac{K.E_G}{K.E_b} = \frac{m_b}{M_G}$

Rocket Propulsion

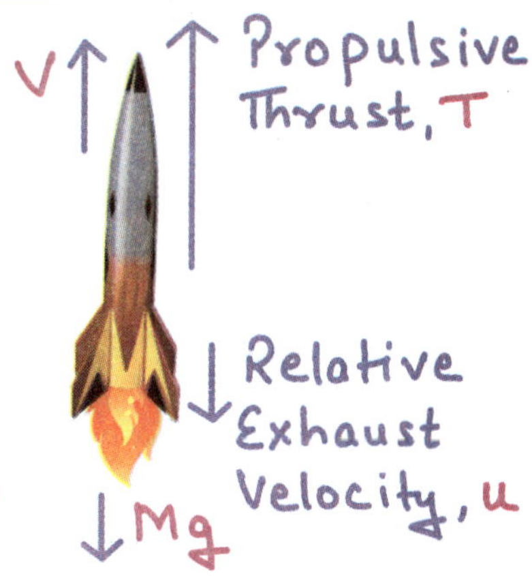

- Rocket works on the principle of Conservation of Momentum.
- Rocket Dynamics :
  - Exhaust is coming out at a constant rate r
  - Speed of rocket at any instant be v

- Gases are ejected at a constant relative speed u w.r.t. rocket.
- Acceleration of rocket $a = \frac{ur}{M} - g$
- Thrust to move with constant acceleration $T = (u-v)r$
- Thrust to move with constant Speed $T = Mg = ur$
- Remaining mass at time t $M_t = M - rt$

MCQ PUNCH

Q5. A 5000 kg rocket is set for vertical firing. The exhaust speed is 800 m/s. To give an initial upward acceleration of 20 m/s², the amount of gas ejected per second to supply the needed thrust will be $(g = 10\ m/s^2)$

Sol. $a = \frac{ur}{M} - g$

$20 = \frac{800 \times r}{5000} - 10 \Rightarrow r = 187.5\ kg/s$

Q6. A 600 kg rocket is set for a vertical firing. If the exhaust speed is 1000 m/s, the mass of the gas ejected per second to supply the thrust needed to overcome the weight of rocket is

Sol. $Mg = ur$

$600 \times 10 = 1000 \times r$

$r = 6\ kg/s$

Constraint Motion

- Motion of one object is restricted by the motion of other object.
- For example, a person sitting in the car has a same velocity and acceleration as of car. Hence, the motion of a person is constrained to the motion of the car.

Application of Newton's Laws of Motion

- Among the various things, the laws are mainly used to find the acceleration of the bodies.
- Steps to apply ÷
  - First identify any constraint relation among the bodies in the system.
  - Draw FBD of the body / system.
  - Apply Newton's 2nd law of motion in each direction separately.

Special Cases To Remember

Single Block

- $a_x = \frac{F}{m}$
- $a_y = 0$
- $N = mg$

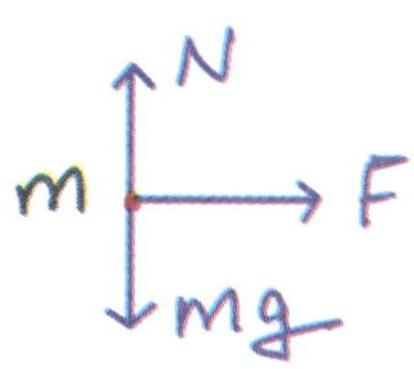

Two Block System

- Same Acceleration a.
- $a = \frac{F}{m_1 + m_2}$

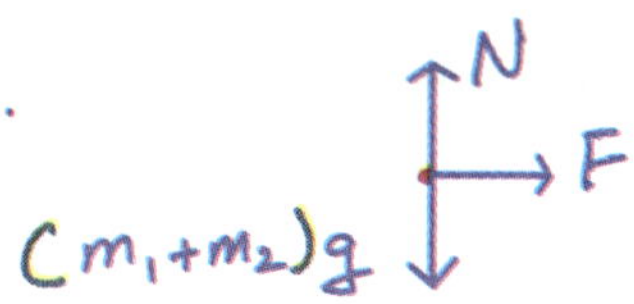

- Normal Reaction

N = Total Front Mass x Common Acc

$= m_2 \times a$

More than Two Block system

- Same Acceleration a.
- $a = \frac{F}{m_1 + m_2 + m_3}$

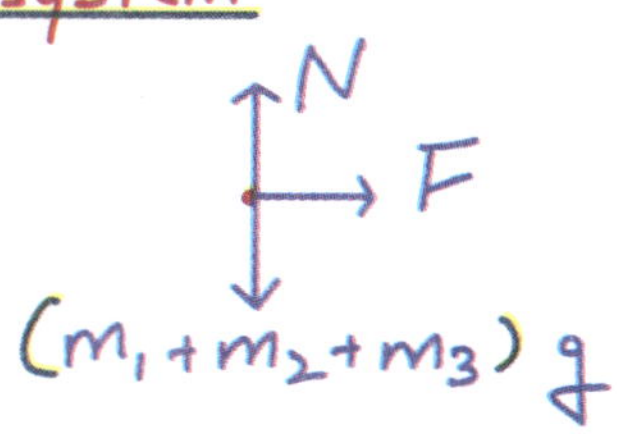

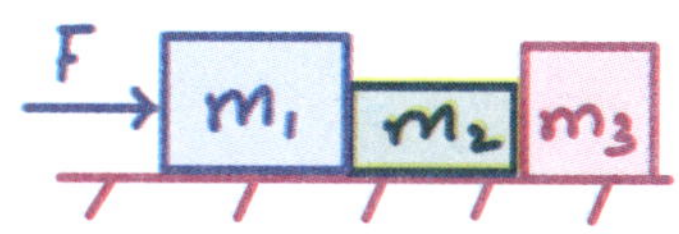

- Normal Reaction

N = Total Front Mass x Common Acc

Normal between m_1 & m_2, $N_1 = (m_2 + m_3)a$

Normal between m_2 & m_3, $N_2 = m_3 a$

PYQ PUNCH

Q7. Three blocks A, B and C of masses 4 kg, 2 kg and 1 kg respectively are in contact on a frictionless surface, as shown. If a force of 14 N is applied on the 4 kg block then the contact force between A and B is (NEET 2015)

Sol. $a = \dfrac{F}{m_1+m_2+m_3} = \dfrac{14}{4+2+1} = 2\,m/s^2$

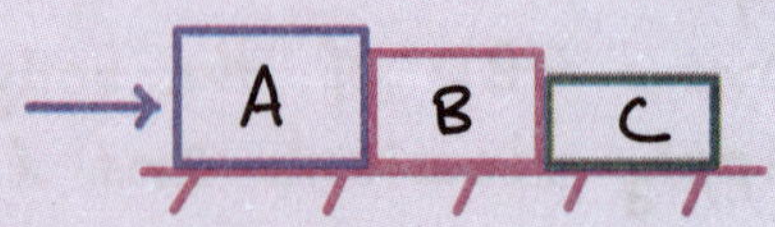

N = Total Front mass × Acc

$= 3 \times 2 = 6N$

Block System attached to String Horizontally

- Same Acceleration a.
- $a = \dfrac{F}{m_1+m_2+m_3}$

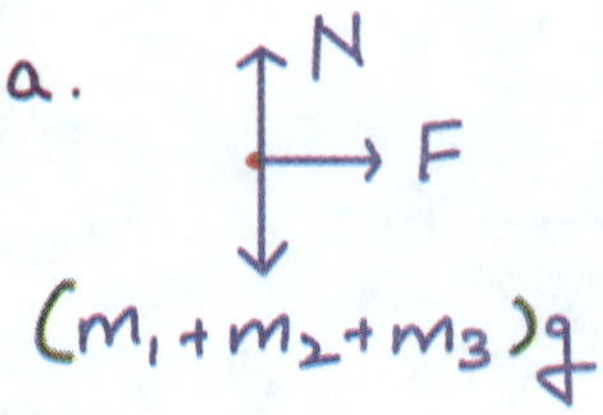

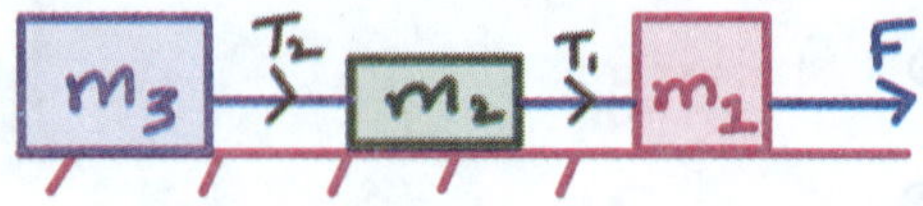

- Tension

T = Total Back Mass × Common Acc

Tension in string between m_1 & m_2, $T_1 = (m_2+m_3)a$

Tension in string between m_2 & m_3, $T_2 = m_3 a$

Block System attached to String Vertically

- Same Acceleration a.
- $a = \dfrac{F-(m_1+m_2+m_3)g}{m_1+m_2+m_3}$

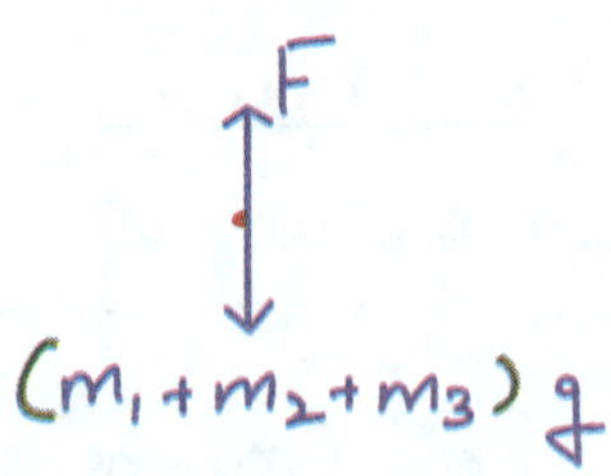

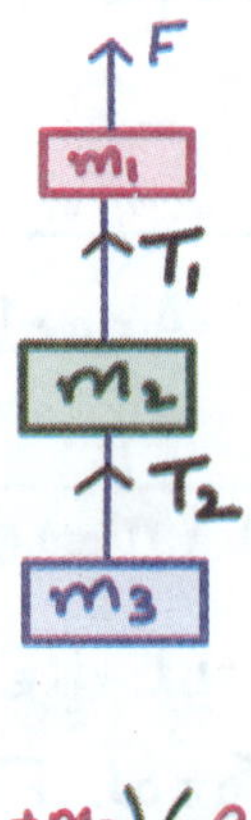

- Tension

T = Total Back Mass × (Common Acc + g)

Tension in string between m_1 & m_2, $T_1 = (m_2+m_3)(a+g)$

Tension in string between m_2 & m_3, $T_2 = m_3(a+g)$

Block on Inclined Plane

- Block slides down with an acceleration

  $a = g\sin\theta$

- $N = mg\cos\theta$

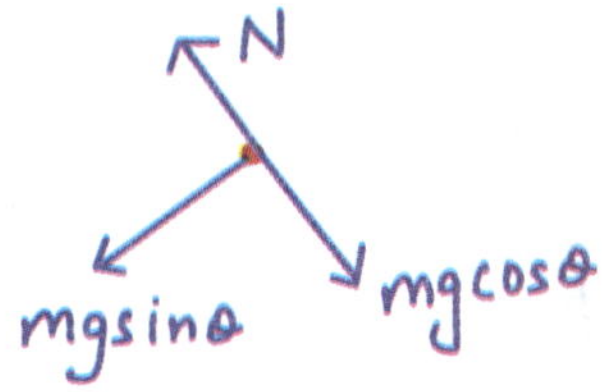

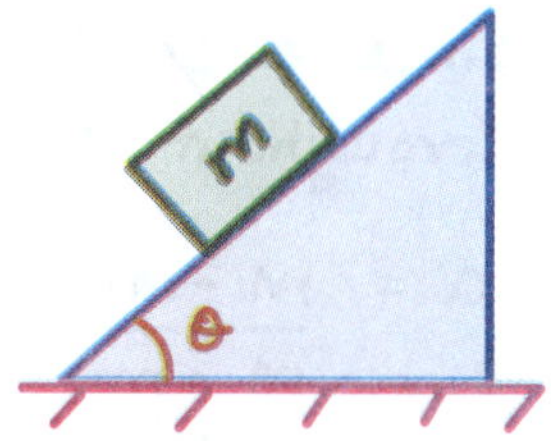

PYQ PUNCH

Q8. A small block slides down on a smooth inclined plane, starting from rest at time $t = 0$. Let S_n be the distance travelled by the block in the interval $t = n-1$ to $t = n$. Then the ratio $\frac{S_n}{S_{n+1}}$ is : (NEET 2021)

Sol. Given $u = 0$

For an inclined plane, $a = g\sin\theta$

Distance covered in n^{th} sec

$$S_{n^{th}} = u + \frac{a}{2}(2n-1)$$

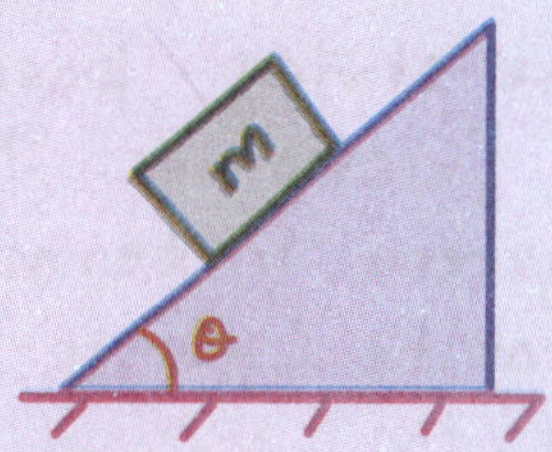

$$S_n = 0 + \frac{g\sin\theta}{2}(2n-1) = \frac{g}{2}\sin\theta(2n-1)$$

$$S_{n+1} = 0 + \frac{g\sin\theta}{2}(2(n+1)-1) = \frac{g}{2}\sin\theta(2n+1)$$

$$\frac{S_n}{S_{n+1}} = \frac{2n-1}{2n+1}$$

Monkey on a string

- Climbing Upward

  $T = Mg + Ma$

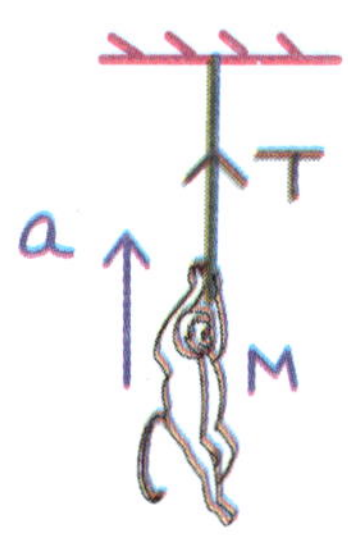

- Falling Down

  $T = Mg - Ma$

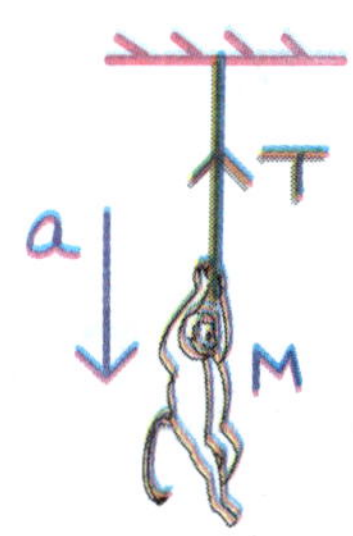

Pulley Block System I

- Constraint motion : Acc of all the blocks are same. Let it be a.
- Since a single string, hence tension is same throughout the string.
- $a = \left(\dfrac{m_1 - m_2}{m_1 + m_2}\right) g$
- $T = \dfrac{2 m_1 m_2 g}{m_1 + m_2}$

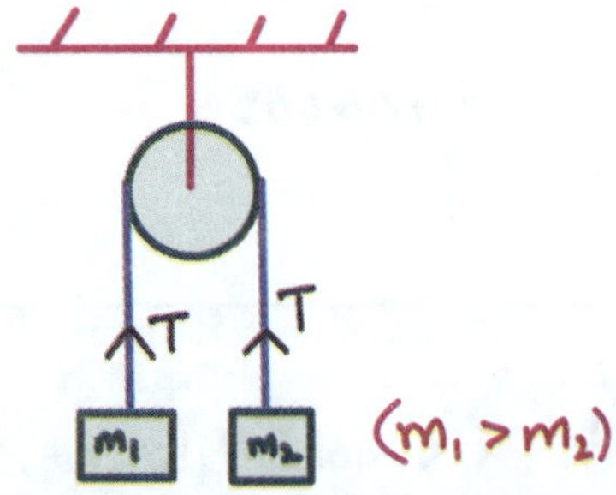

PYQ PUNCH

Q9. Two bodies of mass 4 kg and 6 kg are tied to the ends of a massless string. The string passes over a pulley which is frictionless. The acceleration of the system in terms of acceleration due to gravity (g) is (NEET 2020)

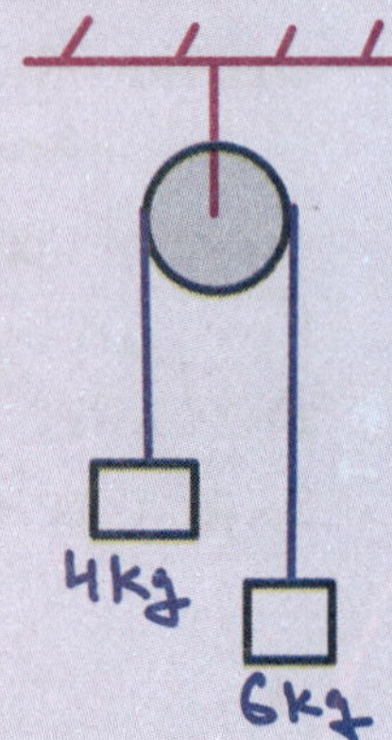

Sol. $a = \left(\dfrac{m_2 - m_2}{m_1 + m_2}\right) g$

$= \left(\dfrac{6 - 4}{6 + 4}\right) g = g/5$

Pulley Block System II

- $a = \dfrac{m_2 g}{m_1 + m_2}$
- $T = \dfrac{m_1 m_2 g}{m_1 + m_2}$

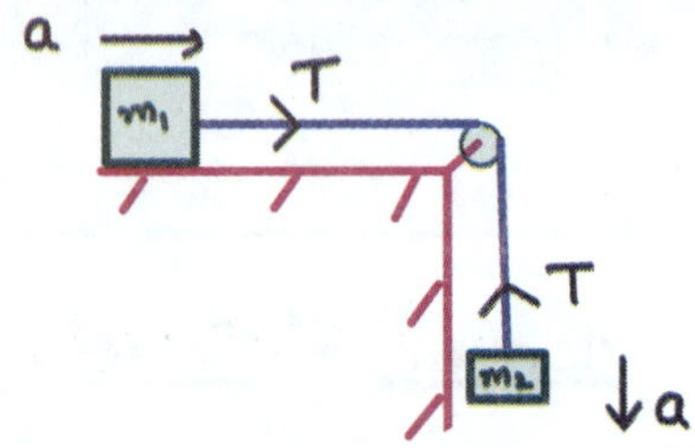

Pulley Block System III

- $a = \dfrac{(m_1 \sin\theta - m_2) g}{m_1 + m_2}$
- $T = \dfrac{m_1 m_2 (\sin\theta + 1) g}{m_1 + m_2}$

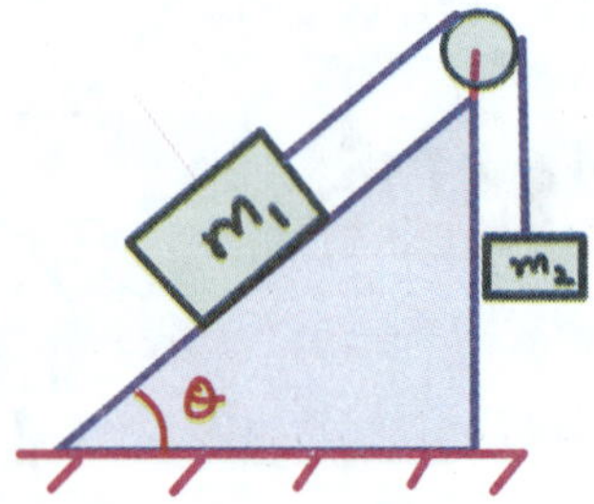

Cutting of String in a Spring - String mass System

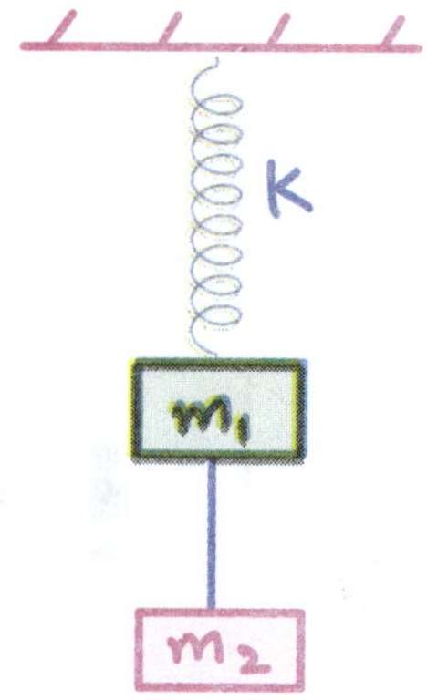

- Initially system is in equilibrium.
- String between the blocks is cut
- Tension becomes Zero in the String while spring keeps exerting the same force at that instant.
- Acceleration of m_1 and m_2 immediately after the string is cut

$a_1 = \frac{m_2}{m_1} g$

$a_2 = -g$

PYQ PUNCH

Q10. Two blocks A and B of masses 3m and m respectively are connected by a massless & inextensible string. The whole system is suspended by a massless spring as shown in figure. The magnitudes of accelerations of A and B immediately after the string is cut are respectively. **(NEET 2017)**

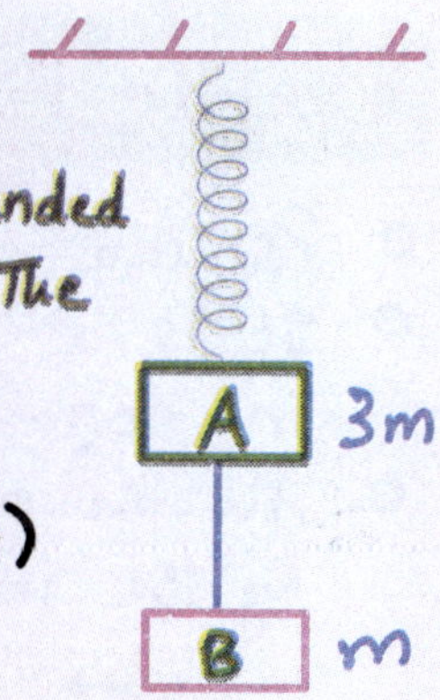

Sol. $m_1 = 3m$, $m_2 = m$

$a_1 = \frac{m}{3m} g = \frac{g}{3}$; $a_2 = -g$, $|\vec{a}_2| = g$

Weight of an Object

True Weight

- It is the gravitational pull of the Earth.

$W_T = mg$

Apparent Weight

- It is the Normal reaction on the body.

$W_a = N$

Weight in Lift

Accelerating Upward	Accelerating Downward	Zero Acceleration or Constant Speed
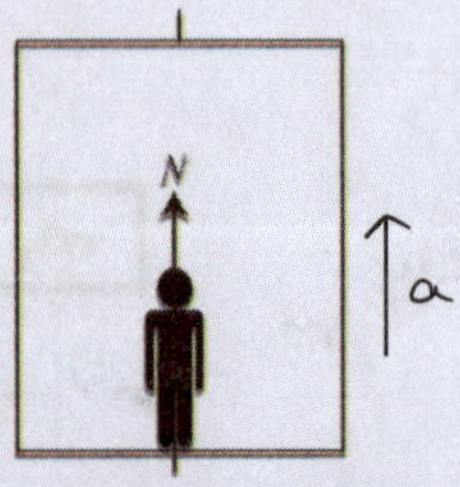	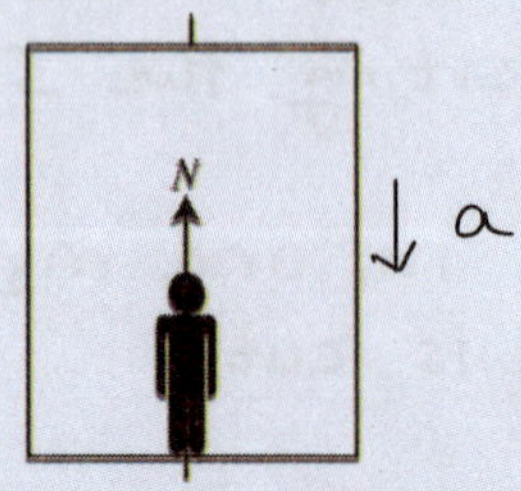	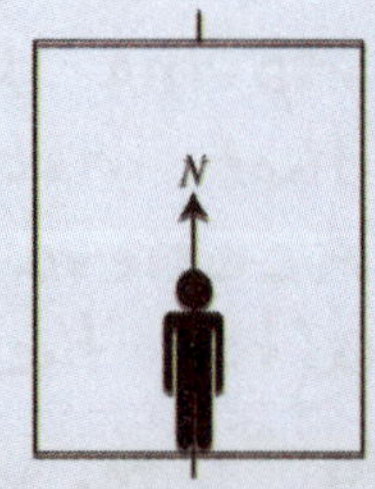
○ $N = m(g+a)$ ○ Weight increases	○ $N = m(g-a)$ ○ Weight decreases	○ $N = mg$ ○ Weight remains same

Pseudo Force

- Pseudo means false.
- It is a false force used to validate the Laws of Motion in non-inertial frame (accelerating frame)
- All the other forces acting on an object are not affected by the introduction of Pseudo force.

$$\vec{F}_{pseudo} = -m\vec{a}_{frame}$$

Most General Cases of Pseudo Force

◉ Acceleration of Inclined Plane so that block does not slip

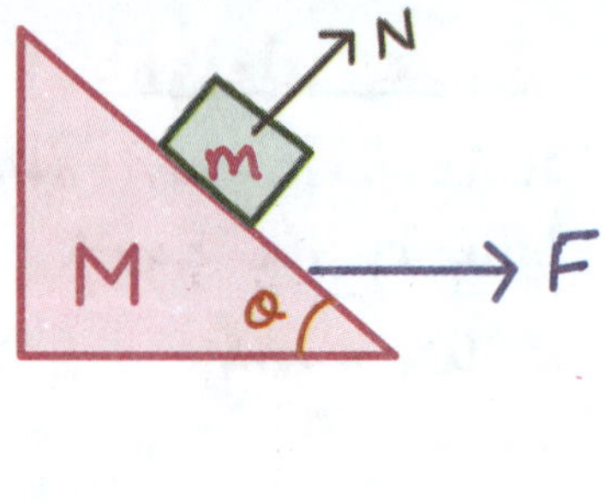

- $F = (M+m)\, g \tan\theta$
- $a = g\tan\theta$
- $N = Mg/\cos\theta$

Acceleration of Inclined Plane so that block free fall

- $F = Mg\cot\theta$
- $a = g\cot\theta$
- $N = m(g\cos\theta - a\sin\theta)$

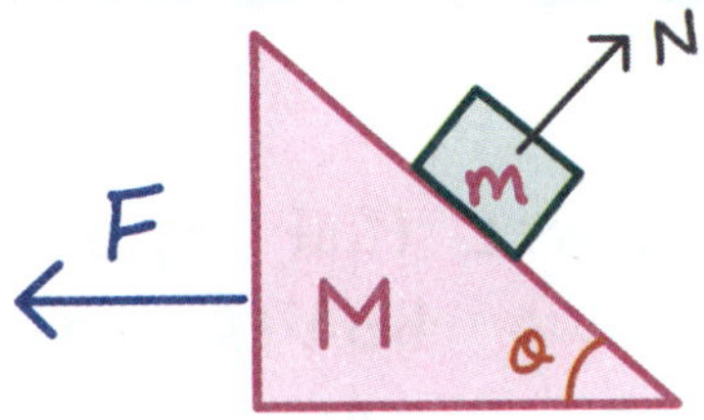

Pendulum in Accelerating Car

- $\sin\theta = \frac{a}{\sqrt{a^2+g^2}}$
- $T = m\sqrt{a^2+g^2}$

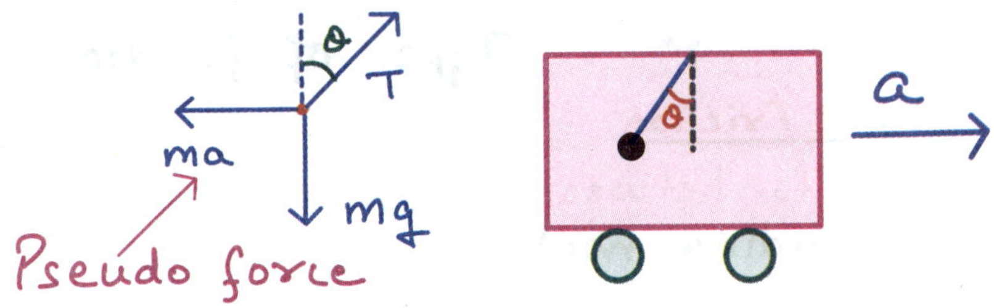

Pendulum in a car on a circular track

- Taking turn with speed V
- $\tan\theta = \frac{v^2}{rg}$
- $T = m\sqrt{\left(\frac{v^2}{r}\right)^2 + g^2}$

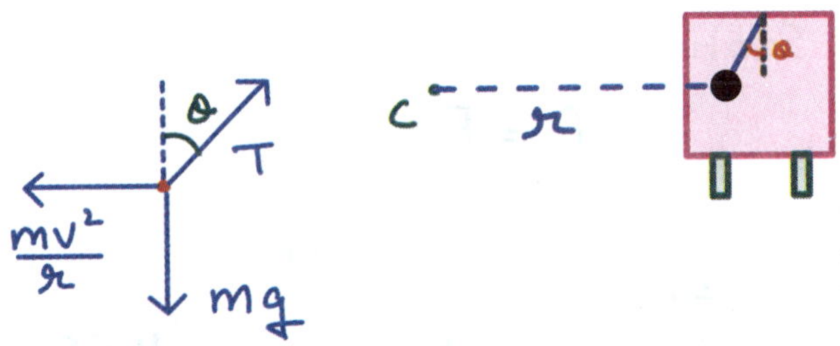

PYQ PUNCH

Q 11. A car is moving in a circular horizontal track of radius 10 m with a constant speed of 10 m/s. A bob is suspended from the roof of the car by a light wire of length 1.0 m. The angle made by the wire with the vertical is : (NEET 2013)

Sol. $\tan\theta = \frac{v^2}{rg} = \frac{10^2}{10\times10} = 1$

$\theta = 45^\circ$

6. Friction

- It is a force that opposses the ~~motion~~ relative motion between two bodies in contact.
- It can stop a moving body or move a body at rest.
- It always act parallel to the Surfaces in contact.

Types of friction

Static Friction

- It acts between the surfaces when there is a impending motion.
- The aim of static friction is to resist the impending motion by acting in opposite direction.
- It is a self adjusting force.
- Static friction

$$f_s = F_{ext}$$

Block at rest

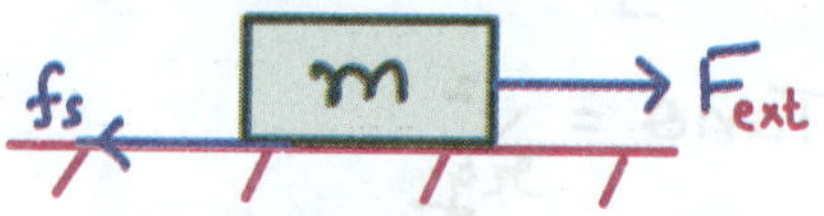

- Maximum value of Static friction is called as limiting Friction.

$$f_L = (f_s)_{max} = \mu_s N$$ → where N is the Normal Reaction between the surfaces in which friction is acting.

where μ_s is the coefficient of static friction.

μ depends upon the
- nature of surfaces in contact. → Smooth or Rough, Polished or Unpolished, Wet or Dry
- material of surfaces in contact.

NEET Accelerate

- Though the value of static friction varies from

$$0 \leq f_s \leq (f_s)_{max}$$

However, $f_s = F_{ext}$ if $F_{ext} < (f_s)_{max}$

$f_s = \mu_s N$ if $F_{ext} \geq (f_s)_{max}$

- More the value of μ, more is the friction. However, it doesn't depend upon the surface area in contact.

Kinetic Friction

- It acts between the surfaces when there is a relative motion.
- Unlike static friction, its value is fixed.
- Kinetic friction

$$f_k = \mu_k N$$

Block is moving

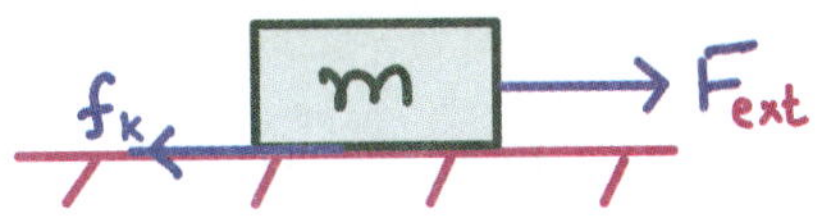

where μ_k is the co-efficient of kinetic friction.

- It always act in opposite direction of motion.

Graph of friction vs force applied

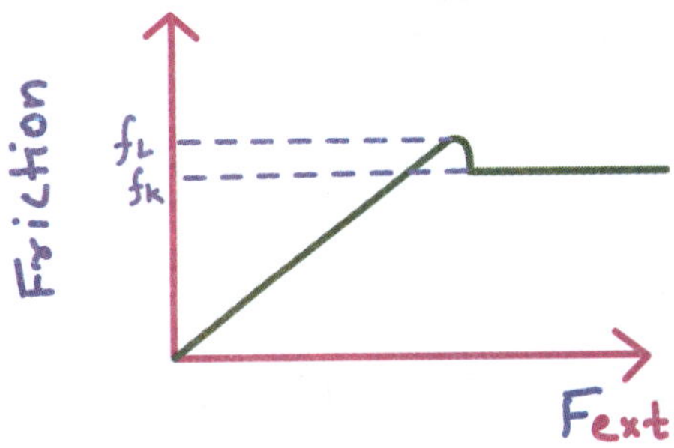

$\mu_s > \mu_k$

NEET Accelerate

- On a same body, both static and kinetic frictions can act together but on a same surface either of them can act at a time.

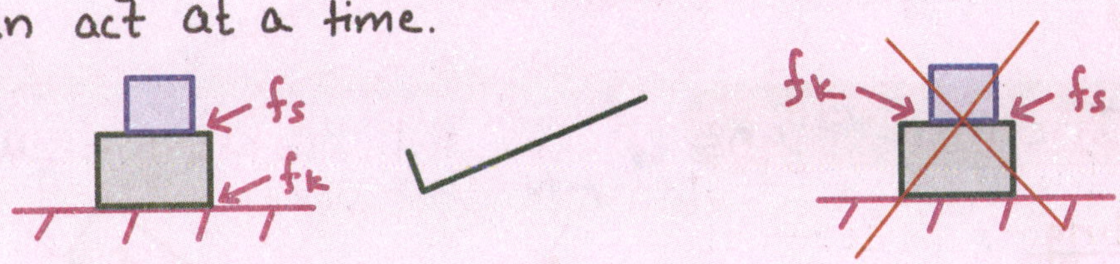

- Though practically $\mu_s > \mu_k$ but generally in numericals $\mu_s = \mu_k = \mu$.
- It is easy to pull than push because friction force reduces due to decrease in Normal reaction.

- Rolling friction $f_r < f_k < f_s$ or $\mu_r < \mu_k < \mu_s$

Contact force between Ground and Block

- **For no sliding**
- $f_s = F_{ext}$
  - $|\vec{F_c}| = \sqrt{N^2 + f_s^2}$
- $(f_s)_{max} = \mu N = \mu mg$
  - $|\vec{F_c}|_{max} = \sqrt{N^2 + (\mu mg)^2}$

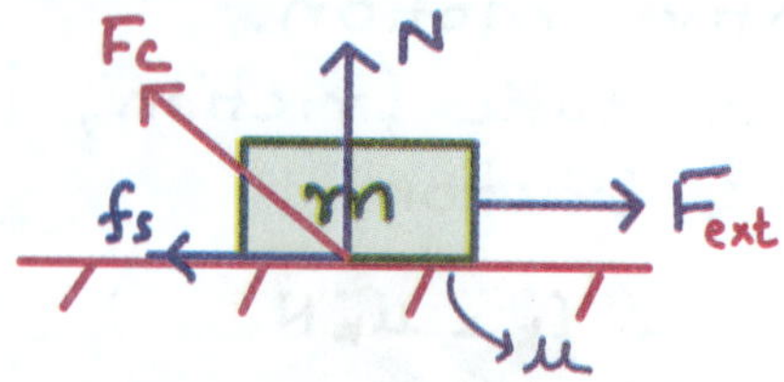

Block at rest

- **Block is moving**
- $f_k = \mu mg$
  - $|\vec{F_c}| = \sqrt{N^2 + (\mu mg)^2}$

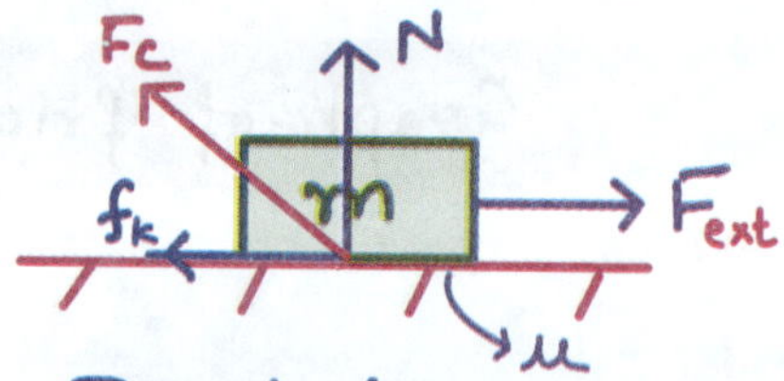

Block is moving

Angle of friction

- It is the angle formed between the Contact force and the Normal Reaction.
  $\tan\theta = \frac{f}{N}$
- Maximum angle of friction
  $\tan\theta = \mu$

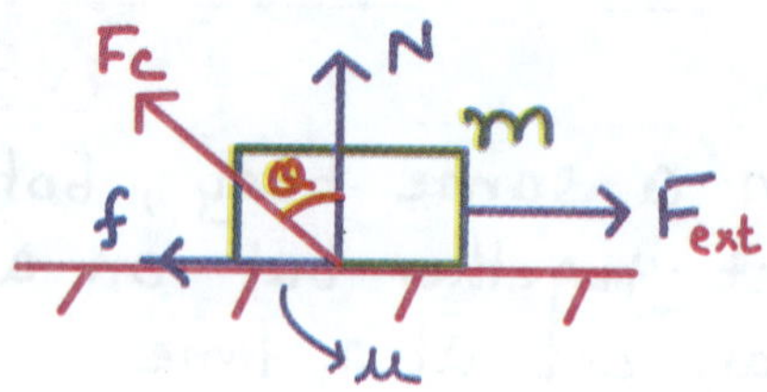

Block on Inclined Plane

- **For no sliding**
- $f = mg\sin\theta$
- $N = mg\cos\theta$

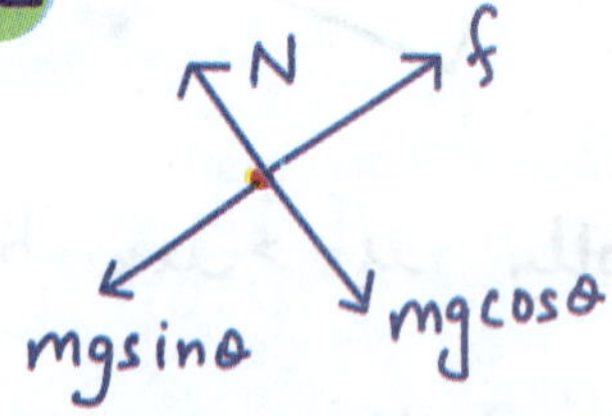

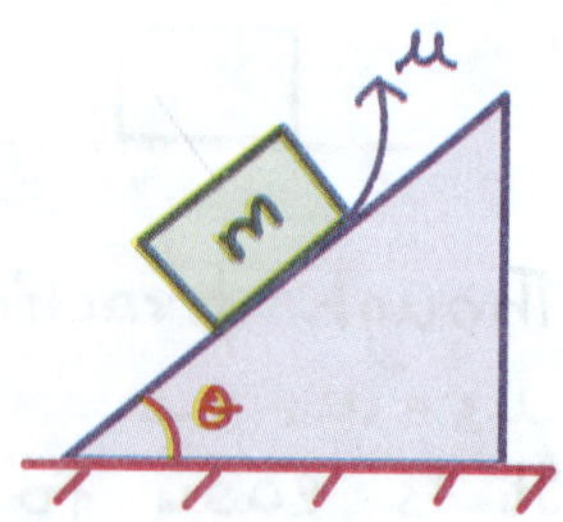

- **Angle of Repose**
- It is the maximum angle (θ) of a rough inclined plane with horizontal such that the block kept on it remains at rest.

$$\mu = \tan\theta$$

- Every rough curved surface is considered as rough inclined plane.

- **For sliding** ($\theta > \tan^{-1}\mu$)
- $N = mg\cos\theta$
- $f = \mu mg\cos\theta$
- $a = g(\sin\theta - \mu\cos\theta)$

Min and Max force to move an object on incline plane

Minimum	Maximum
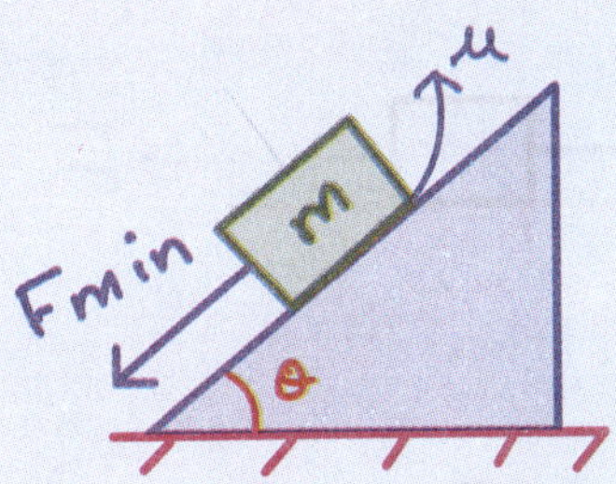	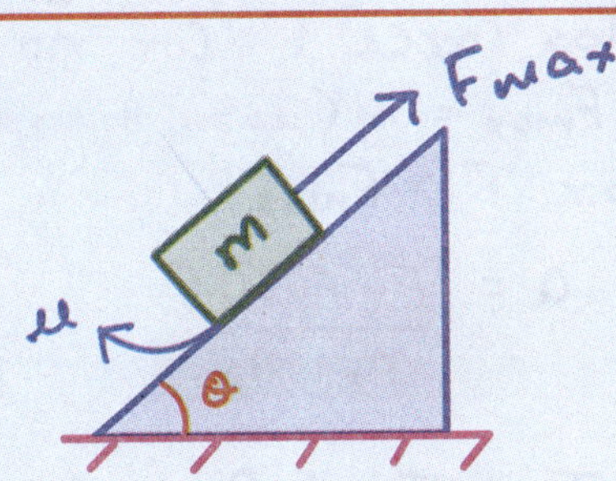
• Force must act down $F_{min} = mg(\mu\cos\theta - \sin\theta)$ • If $F_{ext} > F_{min}$, body has downward acceleration $a = \frac{F_{ext}}{m} + g[\sin\theta - \mu\cos\theta]$	• Force must act up $F_{max} = mg(\mu\cos\theta + \sin\theta)$ • If $F_{ext} > F_{max}$, body has upward acceleration $a = \frac{F_{ext}}{m} - g[\sin\theta + \mu\cos\theta]$

Insect on a Curved Surface

- Maximum angle upto which the insect can climb is

$\tan\theta = \mu$

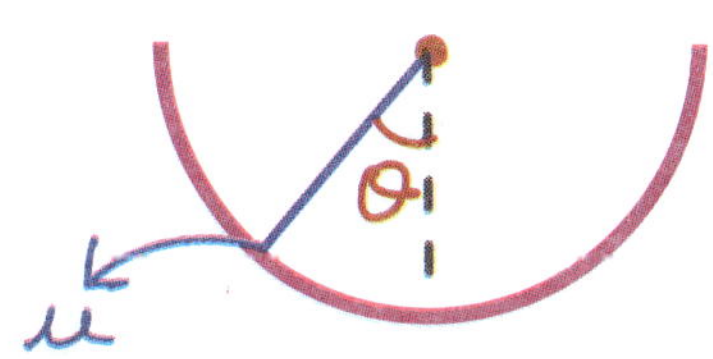

Tricks for solving friction questions

Horizontal force on a block for no sliding for given Force

- $F_{min} = F_{given} - \mu N$
- $F_{max} = F_{given} + \mu N$

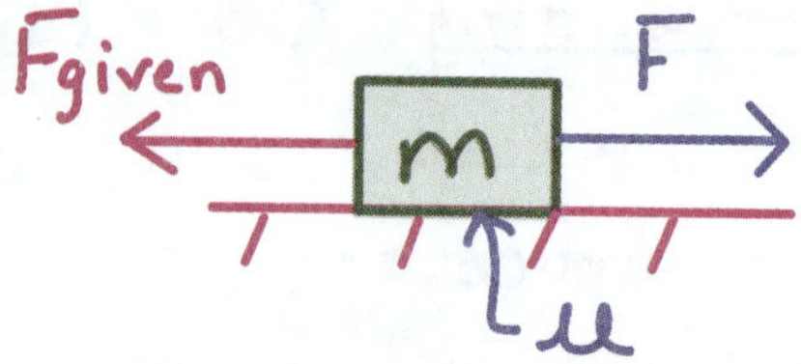

Min value of F for no sliding

- $F_{min} = \dfrac{\mu mg}{\sqrt{1+\mu^2}}$
- $\tan\theta = \mu$

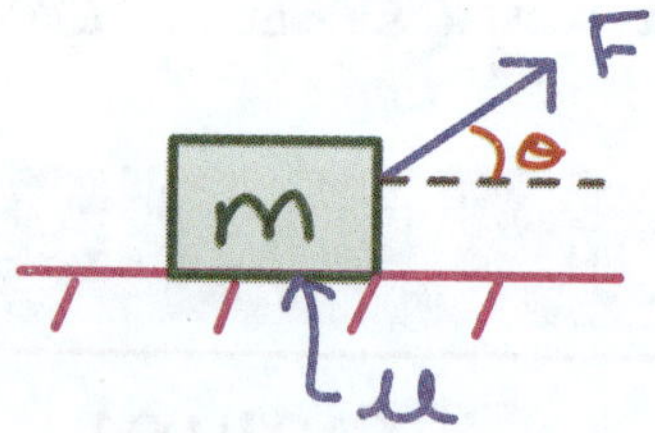

Two blocks string-mass system

- Max force F for no sliding
  - $F_{max} = g(\mu_1 m_1 + \mu_2 m_2)$
- For $F > F_{max}$
  - $a = \dfrac{F - F_{max}}{m_1 + m_2}$

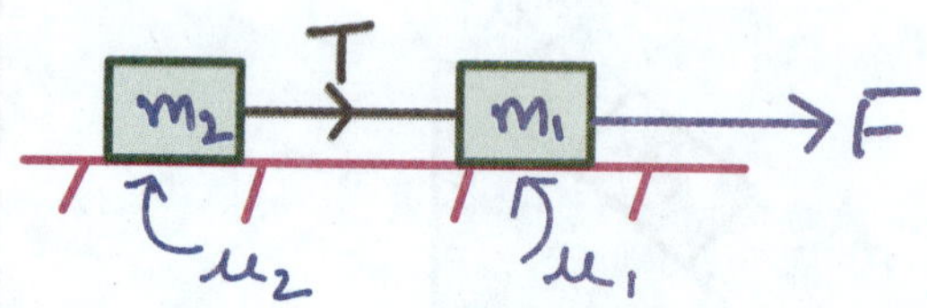

  - T = Total Back Mass × Acceleration + Total back friction
    $= m_2 \times a + \mu_2 m_2 g$

Three blocks string-mass system

- $F_{max} = g(\mu_1 m_1 + \mu_2 m_2 + \mu_3 m_3)$
- For $F > F_{max}$
  - $a = \dfrac{F - F_{max}}{m_1 + m_2 + m_3}$

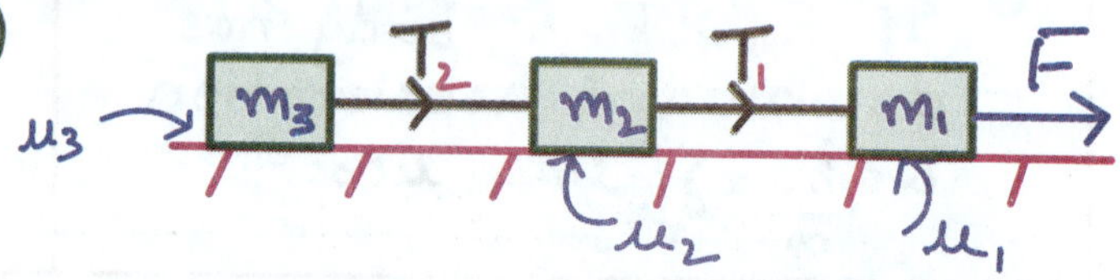

  - T = Total Back Mass × Acceleration + Total back friction
    $T_1 = (m_2 + m_3) \times a + \mu_2 m_2 g + \mu_3 m_3 g$
    $T_2 = m_3 \times a + \mu_3 m_3 g$

Chain hanging on table

- Part of the chain is hanging.
- Maximum value of x for no sliding

$$x_{max} = \frac{\mu L}{1+\mu}$$

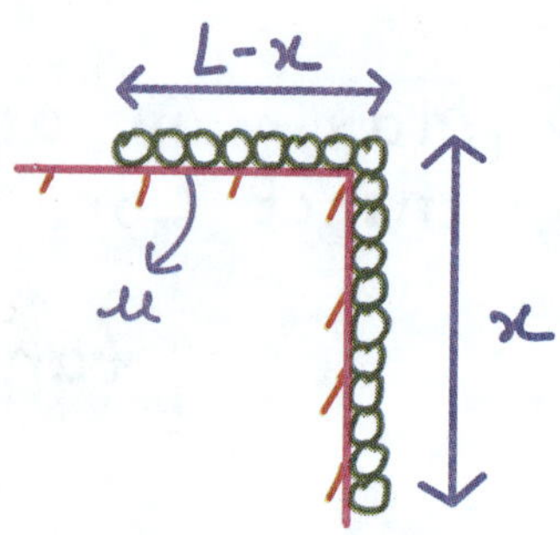

Hanging Block over the pulley

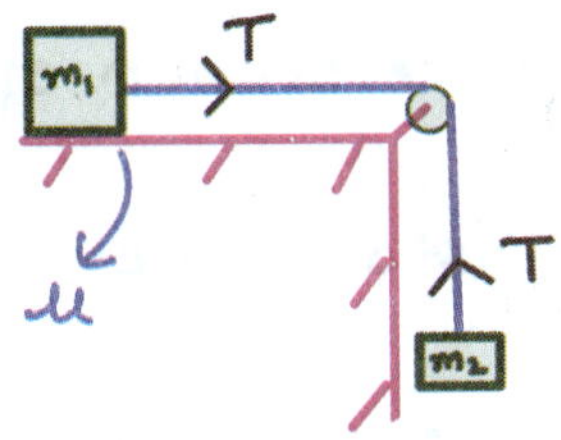

- For no sliding
  - $(m_2)_{max} = \mu m_1$
  - $T = m_2 g$
- For sliding $(m_2 > \mu m_1)$
  - $a = \frac{g[m_2 - \mu m_1]}{m_1 + m_2}$
  - $T = \frac{m_1 m_2 g (1+\mu)}{m_1 + m_2}$

PYQ PUNCH

Q1. Calculate the acceleration of the block and trolley system shown in the figure. The coefficient of kinetic friction between the trolly and the surface is 0.05. ($g = 10\, m/s^2$, mass of the string is negligible and no other friction exists).

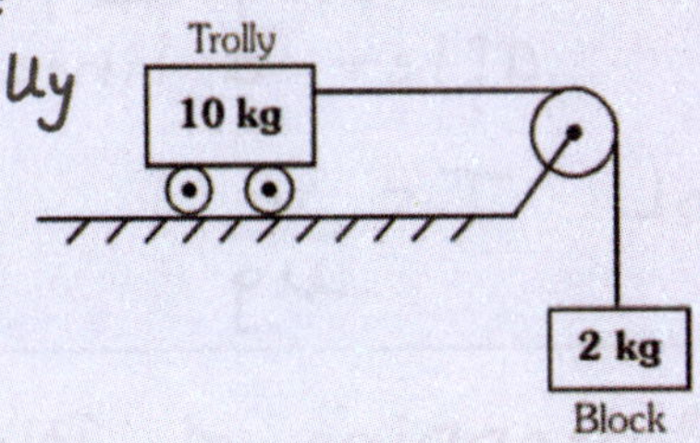

(NEET 2020)

Sol. $a = \frac{g[m_2 - \mu m_1]}{m_1 + m_2}$

$= \frac{10(2 - 0.05 \times 10)}{10 + 2}$

$= 1.25\, m/s^2$

Block on Conveyor Belt

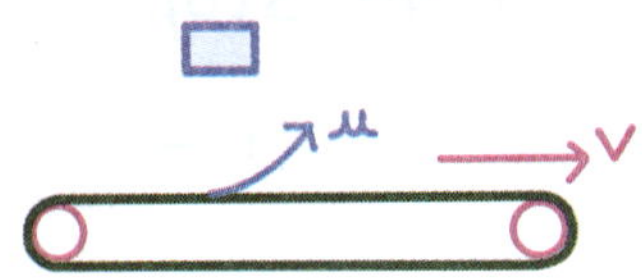

- Conveyor belt speed v.
- Block dropped on belt.
- Acceleration of the block

  $a = \mu g$
- Distance moved by the block before coming to rest

  $S = \frac{v^2}{2\mu g}$
- Time to stop $t = \frac{v}{\mu g}$

Stopping of block on ground

- Block is pushed on a horizontal rough ground with an initial speed V_0.
- Acceleration of the block $a = \mu g$
- Distance covered $S = \frac{V_0^2}{2\mu g}$
- Time to stop $t = \frac{V_0}{\mu g}$

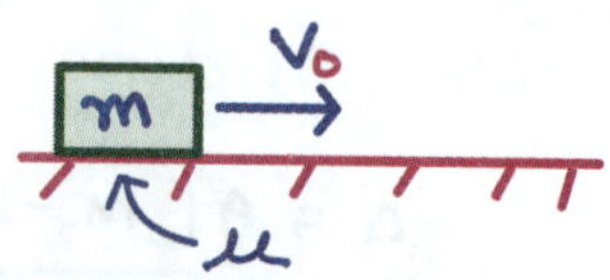

MCQ PUNCH

Q2. A block B is pushed momentarily along a horizontal surface with an initial velocity V. If μ is the coefficient of sliding friction between B and the surface, the block B will come to rest after a time

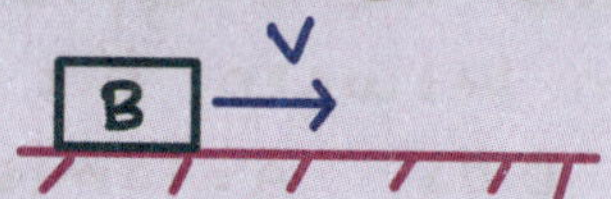

Sol. $T = \frac{V}{\mu g}$

Stopping of Block on Incline

- Block pushed upward with initial speed u.
- Block stops after covering the distance

$$S = \frac{u^2}{2g(\mu\cos\theta + \sin\theta)}$$

- Time to stop

$$t = \frac{u}{g(\mu\cos\theta + \sin\theta)}$$

Reaching of block at bottom of Incline

- For $\theta < \tan^{-1}(\mu)$, block slides down
- Let S be the sliding distance
- Speed at bottom

$$v = \sqrt{2gS(\sin\theta - \mu\cos\theta)}$$

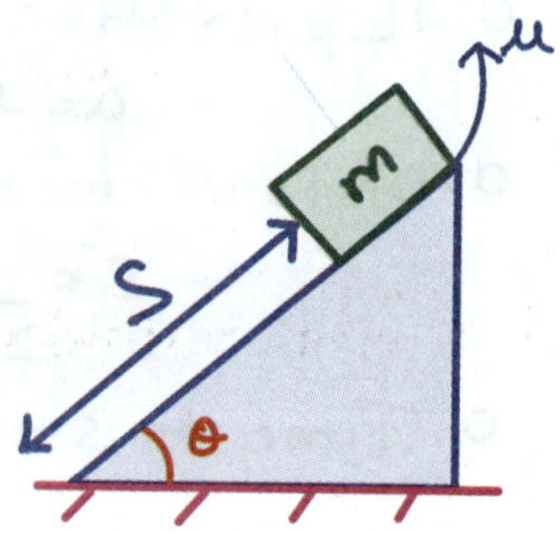

- Time to reach at bottom

$$t = \sqrt{\frac{2s}{g(\sin\theta - \mu\cos\theta)}}$$

Block pushed against vertical wall

- Minimum force on the block for it not to fall down

$$F_{min} = \frac{mg}{\mu}$$

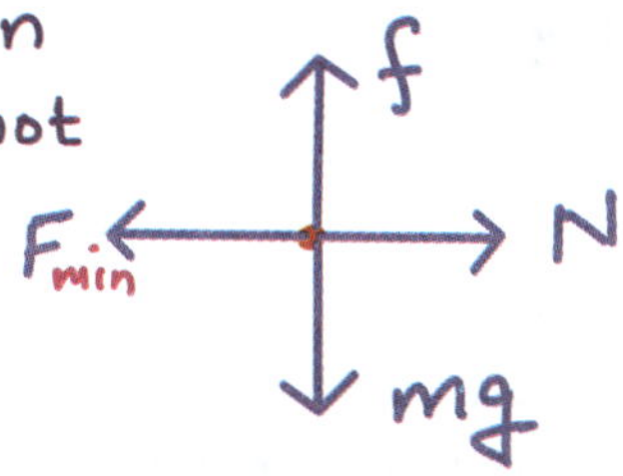

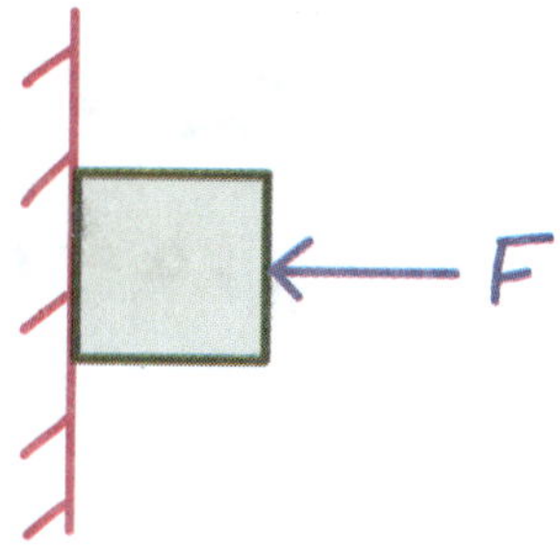

Inclined plane half smooth half rough

- Block is placed at the top of the wedge. It slides down and stops at the bottom.

$$\mu = 2\tan\theta$$

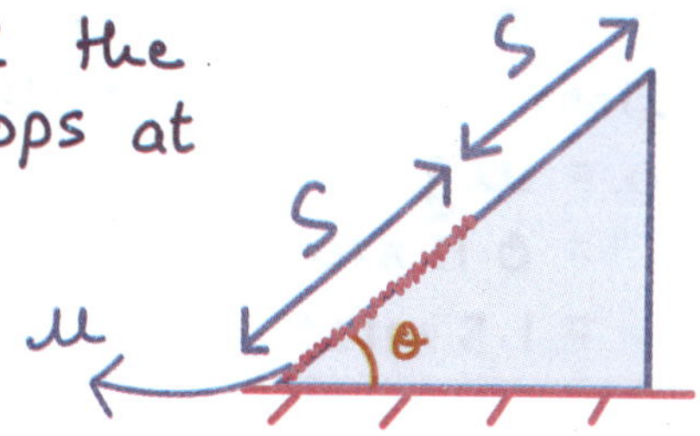

Inclined plane partially smooth partially rough

- Smooth Surface Length = n × Rough Surface Length
- Block is placed at the top of the wedge. It slides down and stops at the bottom.

$$\mu = (n+1)\tan\theta$$

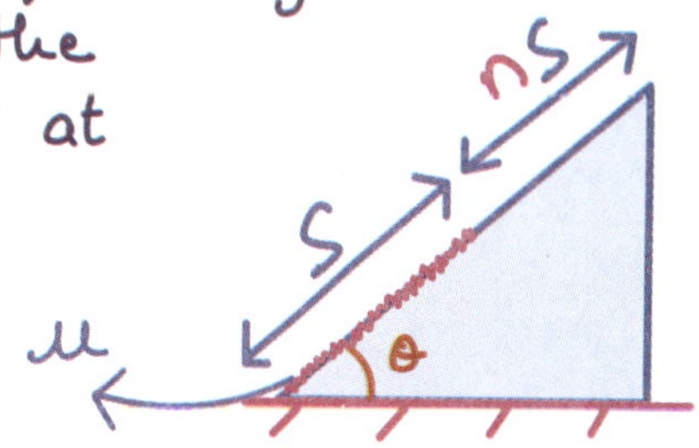

Block at the front of the truck

- Use Pseudo force
- Min acceleration of the truck for the block to not fall down

$$a_{min} = \frac{g}{\mu}$$

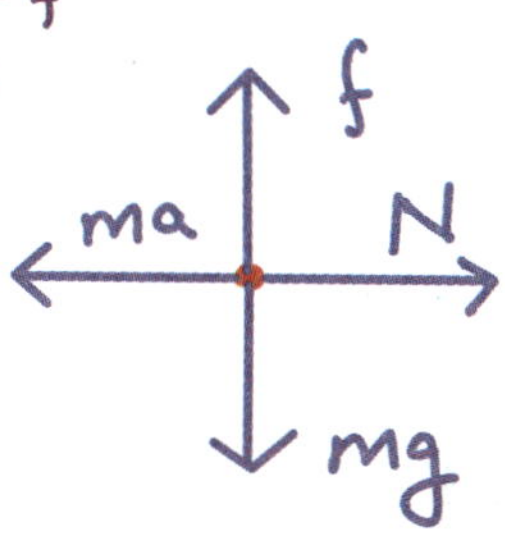

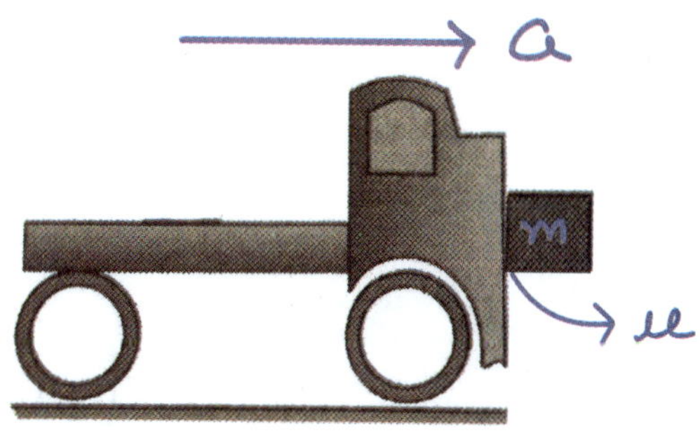

Block over Block

- **Force applied on lower block and ground is smooth**
- Maximum value of F for which two blocks keep on moving together

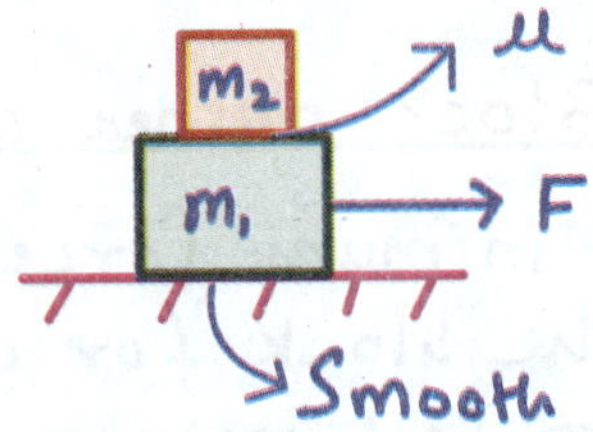

$$F_{max} = (m_1 + m_2)\mu g$$

$$a = \mu g$$

PYQ PUNCH

Q3. Calculate the maximum acceleration of a moving car so that a body lying on the floor of the car remains stationary. The coefficient of static friction between the body and the floor is 0.15 ($g = 10 m/s^2$). (NEET 2023)

Sol. $a = \mu g$

$= 0.15 \times 10$

$= 1.5 m/s^2$

7. Circular Motion

Basic Terms

Angular Displacement

- It is the angle covered by the particle during circular motion.

$$\theta = \frac{\text{Arc Length}}{r}$$

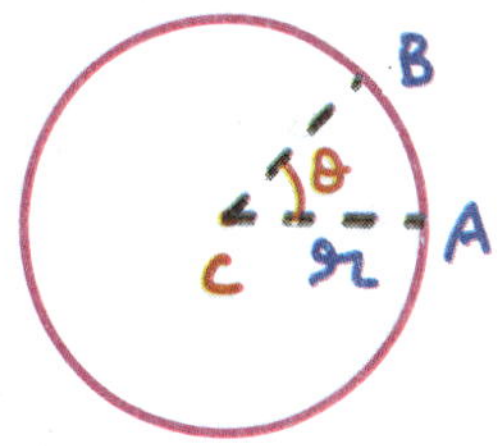

- Unit always in radian.
- 2π rad = 360° = 1 turn
- RPM is rounds per minute
- $x \text{ RPM} = \frac{x}{60} \times 2\pi \text{ rad}$

Angular Velocity

- It is the rate of change of angular displacement.

$$\omega_{avg} = \frac{\theta_2 - \theta_1}{t} \qquad \omega_{ins} = \frac{d\theta}{dt}$$

- Unit is rad/sec
- It is an axial vector.
- Direction is found out using Right Hand Thumb Rule. It is along axis of rotation.

Angular acceleration

- It is the rate of change of angular velocity.

$$\alpha = \frac{d\omega}{dt}$$

- Unit is rad/sec^2
- Direction is along the axis of rotation.
- Positive α increases the ω.
- Negative α decreases the ω.

Kinematical Equation

Linear Motion	Circular Motion
For constant acceleration only	For constant angular acceleration only
$v = u + at$	$\omega = \omega_0 + \alpha t$
$S = ut + \frac{1}{2}at^2$	$\theta = \omega_0 t + \frac{1}{2}\alpha t^2$
$v^2 = u^2 + 2aS$	$\omega^2 = \omega_0^2 + 2\alpha\theta$
$S_{nth} = u + \frac{a}{2}(2n-1)$	$\theta_{nth} = \omega_0 + \frac{\alpha}{2}(2n-1)$

PYQ PUNCH

Q1. The angular speed on a fly wheel moving with angular acceleration changes from 1200 rpm to 3120 rpm in 16 seconds. The angular acceleration in rad/s^2 is (NEET 2022)

Sol. $\omega_0 = 1200 \text{ rpm} = \frac{1200}{60} \times 2\pi \text{ rad} = 40\pi \text{ rad}$

$\omega = 3120 \text{ rpm} = \frac{3120}{60} \times 2\pi \text{ rad} = 104\pi \text{ rad}$

$\alpha = \frac{\omega - \omega_0}{t} = \frac{104\pi - 40\pi}{16} = 4\pi \text{ rad/s}^2$

Uniform Circular Motion

- **Speed**
- Remains constant
- $v = r\omega$

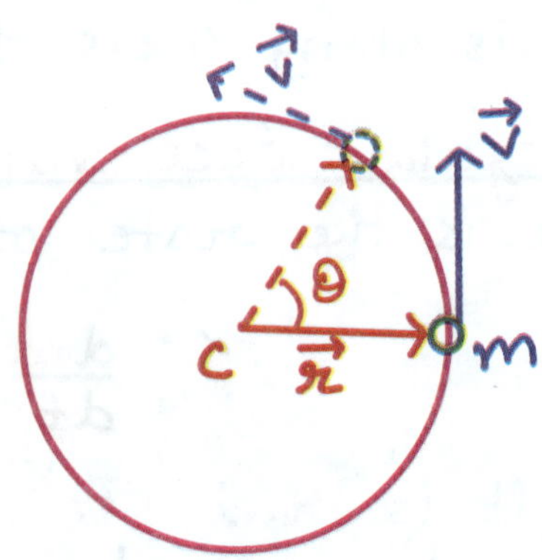

- **Velocity**
- Continuously changes
- At any instant

$\vec{v} = r\omega(-\sin\theta\,\hat{i} + \cos\theta\,\hat{j})$

- Always tangential to the curve.
- Always perpendicular to both position and acceleration vectors.

Acceleration

- It is always directed towards the centre, hence called as Centripetal Acceleration.
- $a_c = \omega^2 r = \frac{v^2}{r}$
- This acceleration only changes the direction of velocity.
- Direction changes as particle rotates.
- Tangential acceleration $a_t = 0$

Time Period

Time Period of rotation $T = \frac{2\pi r}{v} = \frac{2\pi}{\omega}$

PYQ PUNCH

Q2. A particle moving in a circle of radius R with a uniform speed takes a time T to complete one revolution. If this particle were projected with the same speed at an angle 'θ' to the horizontal, the maximum height attained by it equals 4R. The angle θ is given by : (NEET 2021)

Sol. For circular motion, $u = \frac{2\pi R}{T}$

For projectile motion

$$\Rightarrow h_{max} = \frac{u^2 \sin^2\theta}{2g} = \left(\frac{2\pi R}{T}\right)^2 \frac{\sin^2\theta}{2g}$$

$$\Rightarrow 4R = \frac{4\pi^2 R^2 \sin^2\theta}{2T^2 g}$$

$$\Rightarrow \theta = \sin^{-1}\left(\frac{2T^2 g}{\pi^2 R}\right)^{1/2}$$

Centripetal Force

- It is the force which provides required centripetal force for circular motion.
- It is always directed towards the centre.
- $F_c = \frac{mv^2}{r} = m\omega^2 r$
- It is not a force in itself. It is just the resultant of all the forces acting towards the centre.
  - In planetary motion, gravitational force works as a centripetal force.
  - In atom, electrostatic force works as centripetal force.
  - Particle tied to a string & rotating in a circular motion, tension provides required Centripetal Force.
- Never represent centripetal force in FBD.

PYQ PUNCH

Q3. A bob is whirled in a horizontal plane by means of a string with an initial speed of ω rpm. The tension in the string is T. If speed becomes 2ω while keeping the radius same, the tension in the string becomes : (NEET 2024)

Sol. Tension provides the required Centripetal Force

$F_c = m\omega^2 r$

for $\omega = \omega$

$T = m\omega^2 r$ -------- (1)

for $\omega = 2\omega$

$T' = m(2\omega)^2 r$

$= 4m\omega^2 r$

$T' = 4T$

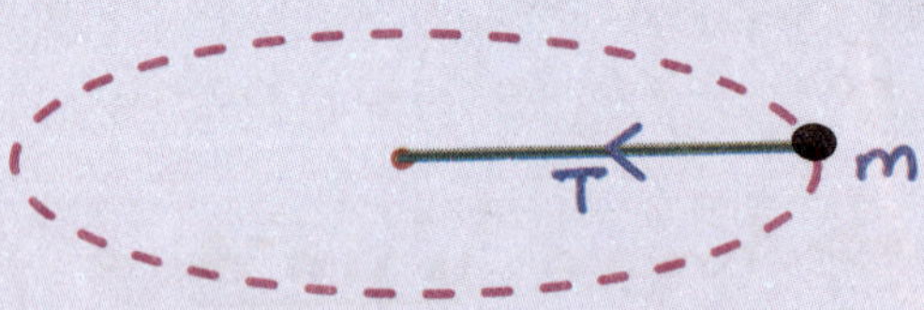

Non-Uniform Circular Motion

- Both magnitude (speed) and direction of velocity change.

- $a_c = \frac{v^2}{r} = \omega^2 r$
- $a_t = \frac{dv}{dt} = r\alpha$
- $a_{net} = \sqrt{a_c^2 + a_t^2}$

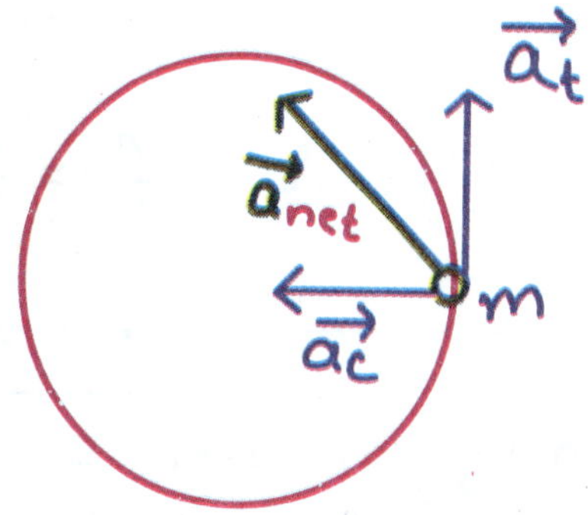

PYQ PUNCH

Q4. A uniform circular disc of radius 50cm at rest is free to turn about an axis which is perpendicular to its plane and passes through its centre. It is subjected to a torque which produces a constant angular acceleration of 2 rad/s². Its net acceleration at the end of 2.0 is approximately: (NEET 2016)

Sol. $\alpha = 2\ rad/s^2$ $\quad r = 50cm = 0.5m$

$a_t = r\alpha = 2 \times 0.5 = 1\ m/s^2$

$\omega = \omega_0 + \alpha t = 0 + 2\times 2 = 4\ rad/s$

$a_c = \omega^2 r = 4\times 4\times 0.5 = 8\ m/s^2$

$a_{net} = \sqrt{a_c^2 + a_t^2} = \sqrt{8^2+1^2} = \sqrt{65}\ m/s^2$

Banking of Road

- Road is banked
- To increase the maximum permissible speed of turn.
- To decrease the tear and wear of the tyre.

- **Without Banking**
- Friction provides the required centripetal force.
- Maximum permissible speed of turn is

$v_{max} = \sqrt{\mu r g}$

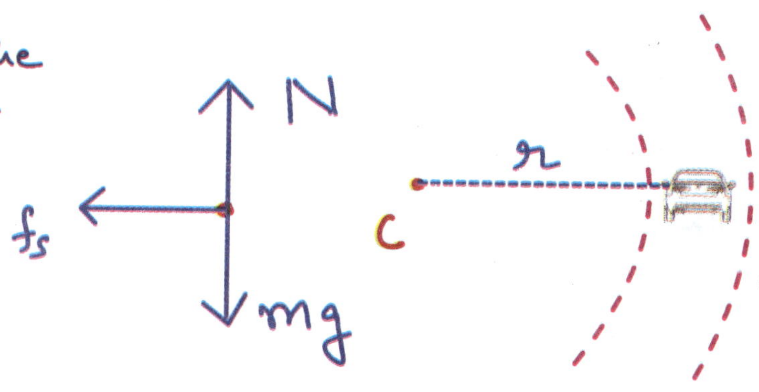

- It is independent of mass of the car
- Centripetal force, $f_c = f_s = \frac{mv^2}{r}$

MCQ PUNCH

Q5. A 500 kg car takes a round turn of radius 50m with a velocity of 36 km/hr. The centripetal force is

Sol. $36\ km/hr = \frac{36 \times 5}{18} = 10\ m/s$

$F_c = \frac{mv^2}{r}$

$= \frac{500 \times 10^2}{50}$

$= 1000\ N$

With Banking

- Normal and friction together provide the required centripetal force.
- Maximum permissible speed of turn is

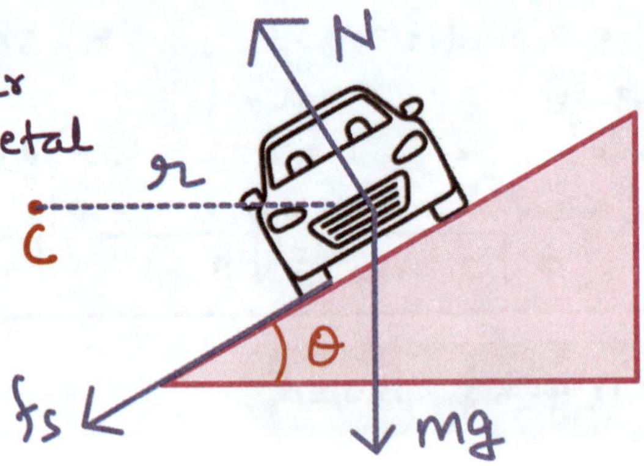

$$V_{max} = \sqrt{\frac{rg(\mu + \tan\theta)}{1 - \mu\tan\theta}}$$

- Both normal and friction contributes in Centripetal Force.

With Banking but no friction

- Normal provides the required centripetal force.
- Maximum permissible speed of turn is

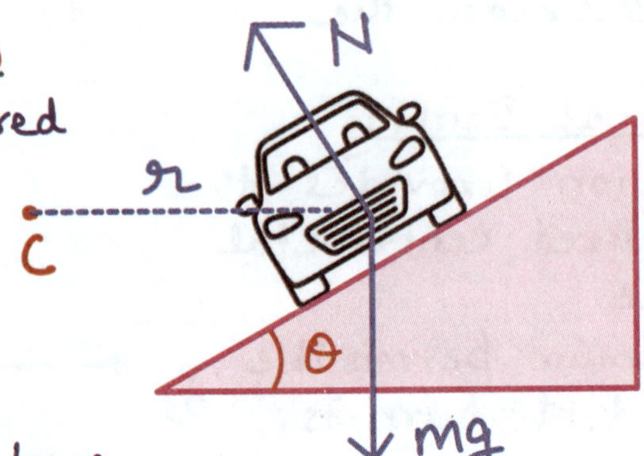

$$V_{max} = \sqrt{rg\tan\theta}$$

- Component of normal causes the turn.

MCQ PUNCH

Q6. A car of mass 1000 kg negotiates a banked curve of radius 90 m on a frictionless road. If the banking angle is 45°, the speed of the car is

Sol. $v = \sqrt{rg\tan\theta} = \sqrt{90 \times 10 \times \tan 45^\circ} = 30\text{ m/s}$

Vertical Circular Motion

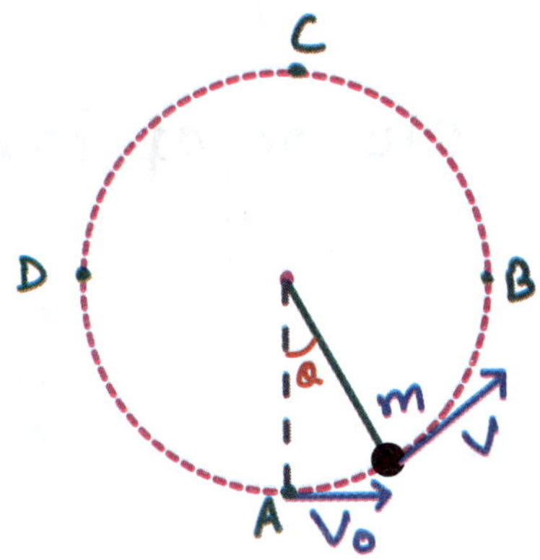

- **Speed**
  - It varies with angle
  - Decreases from A to C and increases from C to A.

$$V = \sqrt{V_0^2 - 2gr(1-\cos\theta)}$$

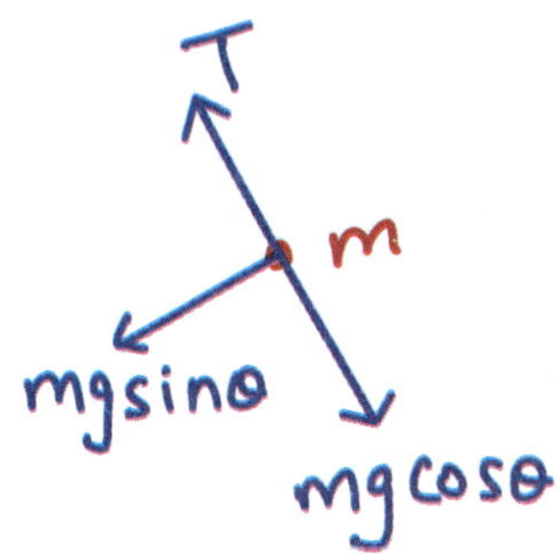

- **Tension**
  - Tension at any angle

$$T = \frac{mv^2}{r} + mg\cos\theta$$

  - $T_A\ (\theta = 0^\circ) = \frac{mv_0^2}{r} + mg$
  - $T_B\ (\theta = 90^\circ) = \frac{mv_0^2}{r} - 2mg$
  - $T_C\ (\theta = 180^\circ) = \frac{mv_0^2}{r} - 5mg$

	$\theta = 0^\circ$	$\theta = 180^\circ$
Speed	Max	Min
Tension	Max	Min

- **Tangential Acceleration**
  - $a_t = g\sin\theta$
  - For $0^\circ < \theta < 180^\circ$, ↓ Speed
  - For $180^\circ < \theta < 360^\circ$, ↑ Speed
- **Critical Speed** (V_{cr})
  - It is the minimum speed at the lower-most point for it to complete the vertical circle.

$$V_{cr} = \sqrt{5gr} = V_0$$

- $V_B = \sqrt{3gr}$
- $V_C = \sqrt{gr}$

PYQ PUNCH

Q7. What is the minimum velocity with which a body of mass m must enter a vertical loop of radius R so that it can complete the loop? (NEET 2016)

Sol. $V_{min} = \sqrt{5gR}$

Motion of Particle for Varying Initial Speed

$V_0 \leq \sqrt{2gr}$	$\sqrt{2gr} < V_0 < \sqrt{5gr}$	$V_0 \geq \sqrt{5gr}$
• Oscillate • 0 to 90° • Path is Circular	• Slacking • 90° to 180° • Parabolic after slacking	• Complete Circle • 0 to 360° • Circular

Slacking

- ~~Speed~~ Tension becomes zero.
- Particle becomes independent after point E and follows parabolic path.
- Angle of slacking

$$\cos\theta = \frac{2gr - V_0^2}{3gr}$$

- Speed at slacking

$$V_E = \sqrt{\frac{V_0^2 - 2gr}{3}}$$

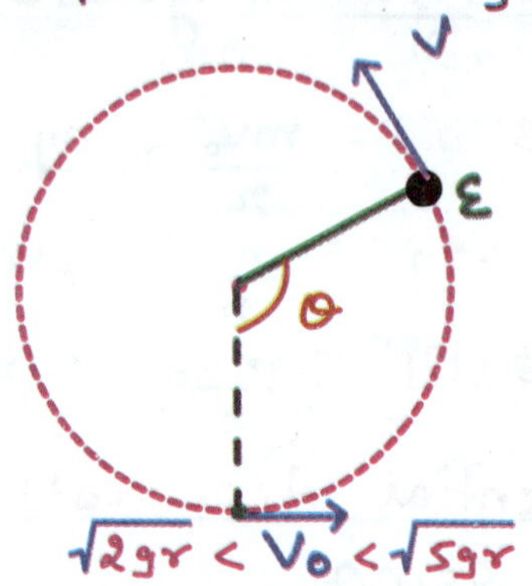

Object connected to massless rod

- Motion is always circular as rod never gets slacked.

Critical Speed

- $V_0 = \sqrt{4gr}$
- $V_B = \sqrt{2gr}$
- $V_C = 0$

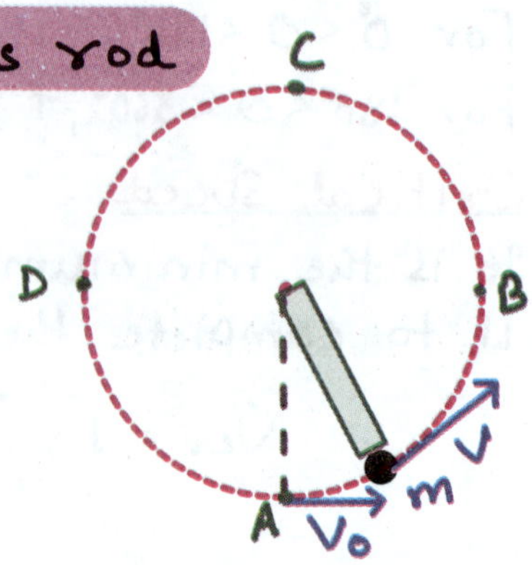

NEET Accelerate

- Speed reduces by a value of 2 for every 90° of rotation.
- If speed at bottom is
  $V_A = \sqrt{10gr}$
  then it becomes
  $V_B = \sqrt{8gr}$
  $V_C = \sqrt{6gr}$

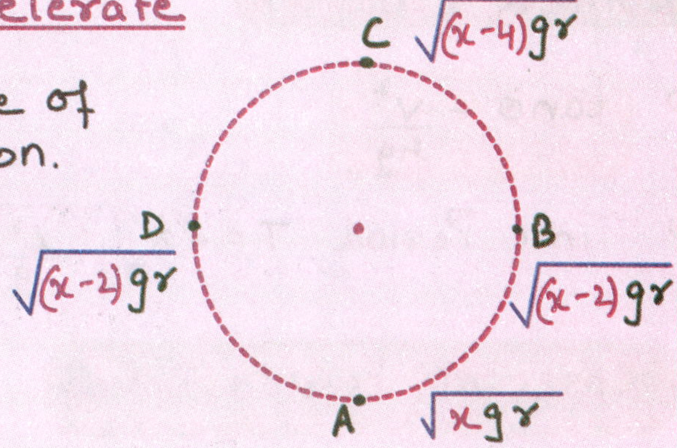

- The maximum chance of string to get break is lower-most point because at this position, the tension is maximum.

Special Cases of Vertical Circular Motion

Water Slide

- Min h for which person complete the slide

$$h = \frac{5r}{2}$$

- $V_A = \sqrt{5gr}$ (Critical Speed)

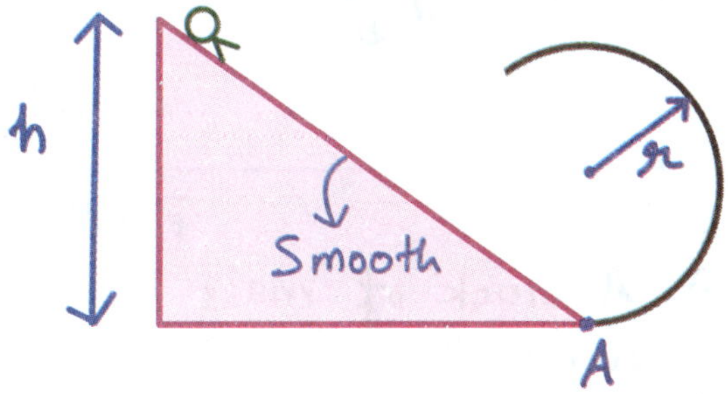

Sliding over Hemispherical Bowl

- Particle leaves the contact from the bowl for

$$\theta = \cos^{-1}\left(\frac{2}{3}\right)$$

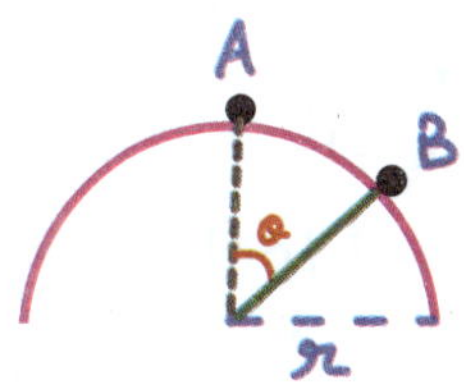

- Speed at Separation

$$V = \sqrt{2gr(1-\cos\theta)}$$

Motion in a Slot

- Critical speed is

$$V_0 = \sqrt{4gR}$$

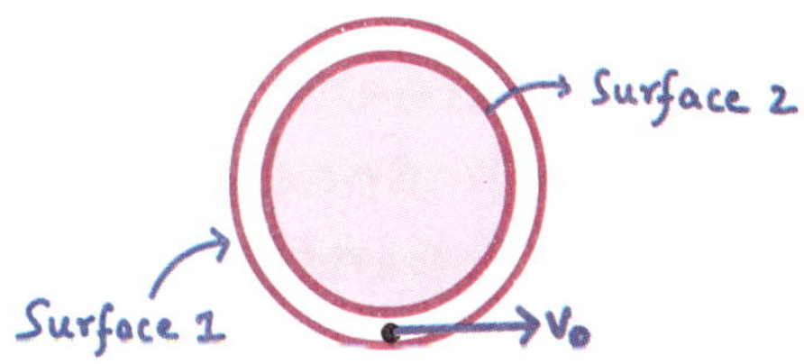

- Initially in contact with Surface 1. As moves up, contact becomes with Surface 2

Conical Pendulum

- $\tan\theta = \frac{v^2}{rg}$
- Time Period $T = 2\pi\sqrt{\frac{(l^2 - r^2)^{1/2}}{g}}$

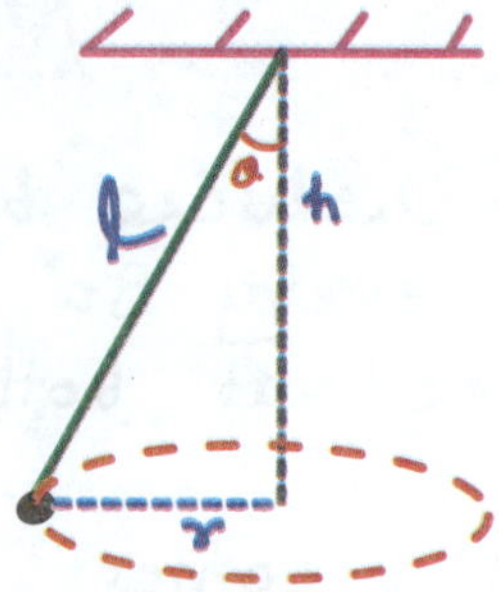

Cases of Pseudo Force

◎ Block attached to a rotating Tumbler

- Minimum angular velocity of tumbler for the block not to fall down

$$\omega_{min} = \sqrt{\frac{g}{\mu r}}$$

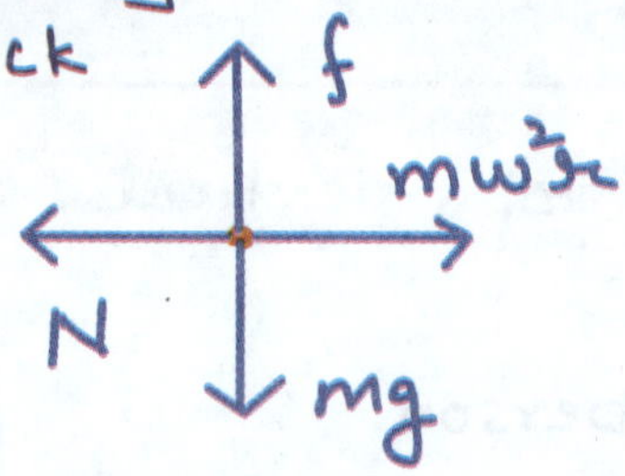

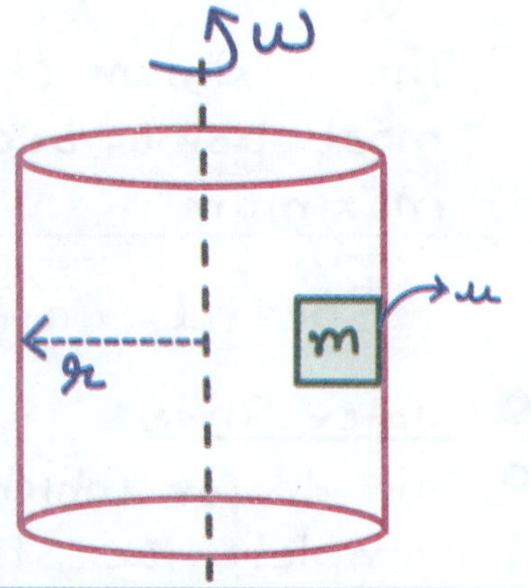

PYQ PUNCH

Q8. A block of mass 10 kg is in contact against the inner wall of a hollow cylindrical drum of radius 1 m. The coefficient of friction between the block and the inner wall of the cylinder is 0.1. The minimum angular velocity needed for the cylinder to keep the block stationary when the cylinder is vertical and rotating about its axis, will be ($g = 10\,m/s^2$)

(NEET 2019)

Sol. $\omega_{min} = \sqrt{\frac{g}{\mu r}} = \sqrt{\frac{10}{0.1 \times 1}} = 10$ rad/s

◎ Pendulum inside a car taking Circular turn

- Car taking a turn at a constant speed v.
- Angle of pendulum

$$\tan\theta = \frac{v^2}{rg}$$

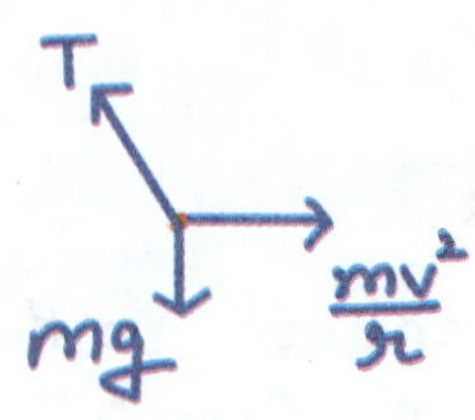

8. Work, Energy & Power

Work

- Said to be done by a force when there is a displacement.

Constant Force	Variable Force
▹ $W = \vec{F}.\vec{s} = Fs\cos\theta$ ▹ F = Force ▹ S = Disp. 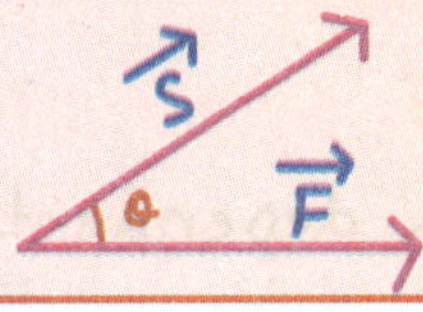	▹ $\int dW = \int \vec{F}.d\vec{s}$ ▹ $W = \int_{x_1}^{x_2} F_x d_x + \int_{y_1}^{y_2} F_y d_y + \int_{z_1}^{z_2} F_z d_z$

- Scalar quantity
- Dimensional Formula $[ML^2T^{-2}]$
- Unit Joule
- Unit in CGS is Erg
- $1\ J = 10^7$ Erg

Work Dependency on Angle

$0° \leq \theta < 90°$	$\theta = 90°$	$90° < \theta \leq 180°$
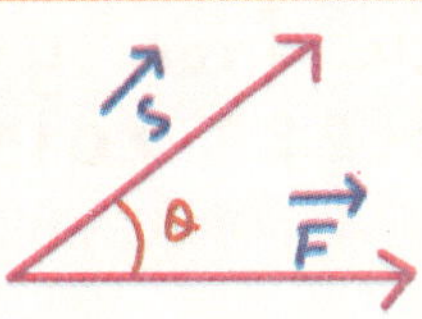	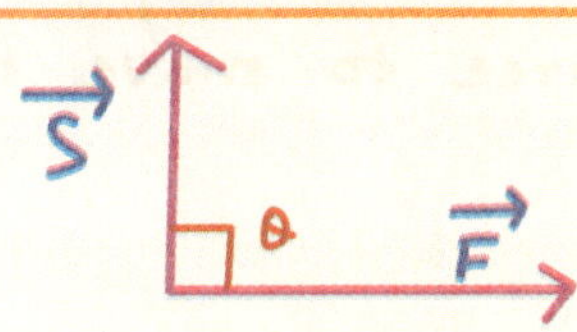	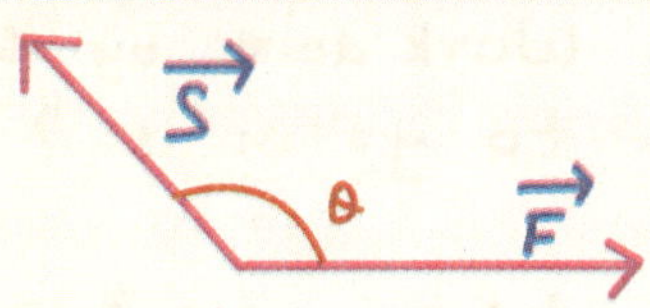
▹ $W > 0$	▹ $W = 0$	▹ $W < 0$
▹ Work is done in favor of the force	▹ Force is not doing any work.	▹ Work is done against the force.

Types of Forces

- **Conservative Forces** (CF)
- Work done by this force is path independent.
- $\vec{F}_{CF} = -\left(\frac{dU}{dr}\right)$
- Work done over a closed loop is zero.

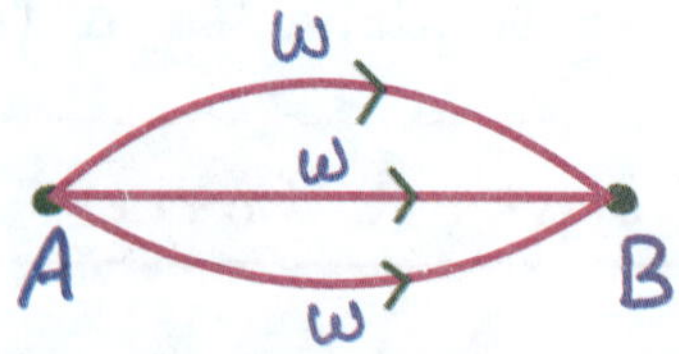

- **Non-Conservative Forces** (NCF)
- Work done by this force is path dependent.
- Work done over a closed loop is non-zero.

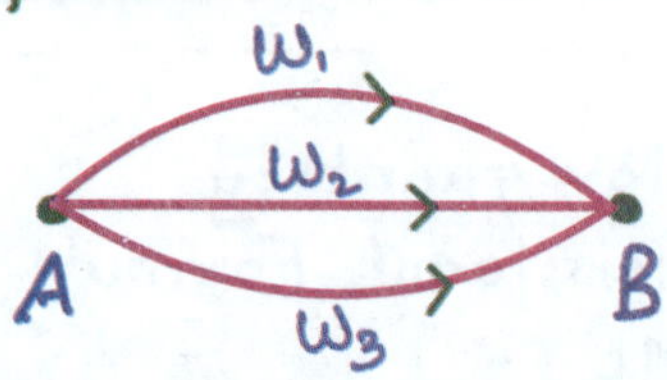

Tricks for finding WD by Variable Force

- **Position Dependent Force**
- Given : $F = Ax^2 + Bx + C$
- Use : $W = \int_{x_1}^{x_2} \vec{F}\cdot d\vec{x} = \int_{x_1}^{x_2} (Ax^2 + Bx + C)\, dx$

PYQ PUNCH

Q1. A force $F = 20 + 10y$ acts on a particle in y-direction. Work done by this force to move the particle from $y = 0$ to $y = 1\text{m}$ is ? (NEET 2019)

Sol.

$$W = \int_{y_1}^{y_2} (Ay^2 + By + C)\, dy$$

$$= \int_0^1 (10y + 20)\, dy$$

$$= 25\text{ J}$$

Time Dependent Force

- Given : $F = At^2 + Bt + C$
- Step 1: Find Velocity using integeration

$$V = \int_{t_1}^{t_2} \frac{F}{m} dt$$

- Step 2: $W = \int_{x_1}^{x_2} \vec{F}.\vec{dx} = \int_{t_1}^{t_2} Fv dt$

Symbols

x = Position
x_1 = Initial Position
x_2 = Final Position
t = time
t_1 = Initial time
t_2 = Final time
V = velocity
a = acceleration
F = Force

Time Dependent Position

- Given : $x = At^2 + Bt + C$
- Step 1: Find Velocity using differentiation

$$V = \frac{dx}{dt}$$

- Step 2 : Find Acceleration using differentiation

$$a = \frac{dv}{dt}$$

- Step 3: $W = \int_{x_1}^{x_2} \vec{F}.\vec{dx} = \int_{t_1}^{t_2} Fv dt = m\int_{t_1}^{t_2} av dt$

MCQ PUNCH

Q2. A body of mass 3 kg is under a constant force which causes a displacement s in meters in it, given by the relation $s = \frac{1}{3}t^2$, where t is in seconds. Work done by the force in 2 seconds is

Sol. $v = \frac{ds}{dt} = \frac{2t}{3}$; $a = \frac{dv}{dt} = \frac{2}{3}$

$$W = m\int_{t_1}^{t_2} av dt = 3\int_0^2 \frac{2}{3} \times \frac{2t}{3} dt = \frac{8}{3} J$$

Time Dependent Velocity

- Given : $V = At^2 + Bt + C$
- Step 1 : Find Acceleration using differentiation

$$a = \frac{dv}{dt}$$

- Step 2: $W = \int_{x_1}^{x_2} \vec{F}.\vec{dx} = \int_{t_1}^{t_2} F v dt = m\int_{t_1}^{t_2} a v dt$

Graphical Characteristics of Graph

Slope

- Differentiation of work w.r.t. position gives Force.

$$\frac{dW}{dx} = F$$

Area

- Area of force - displacement graph gives Work.

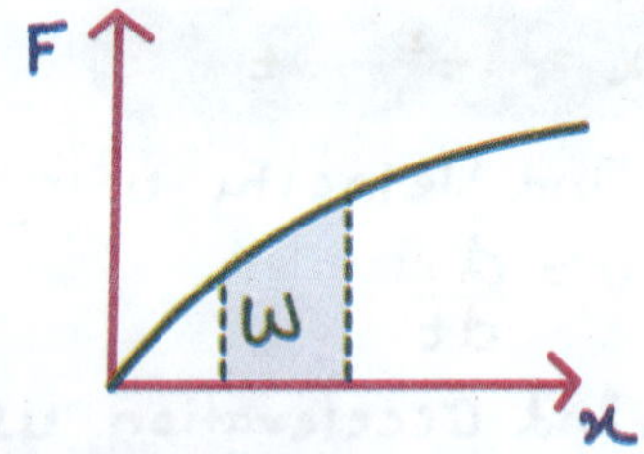

Work Done by different Forces

Normal Force

Lift accelerating upward	Lift accelerating downward
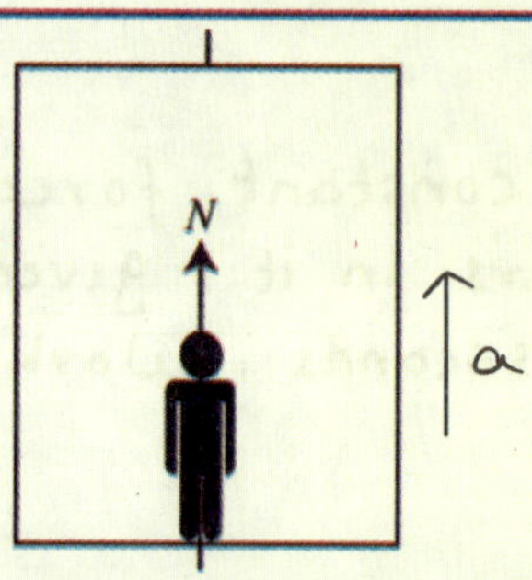 - Normal acts upward and greater than mg - Apparent weight (N) increases. - If moving upwards $W_N > 0$ - If moving downward $W_N < 0$	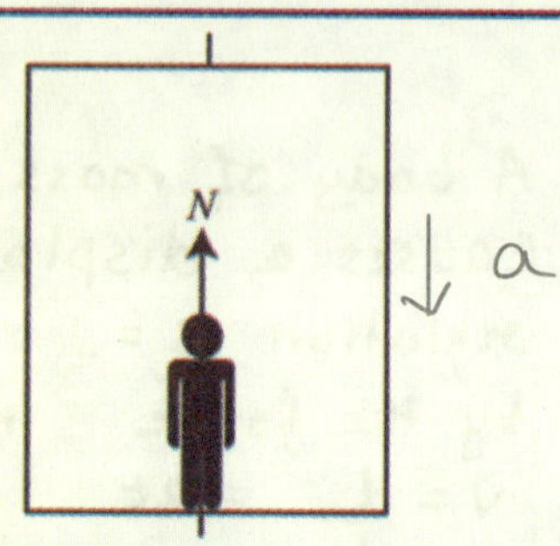 - Normal acts upward and less than mg. - Apparent weight (N) decreases. - If moving upwards $W_N > 0$ - If moving downward $W_N < 0$

◎ Tension

Vertical Circular Motion	Horizontal Circular Motion	Pulley
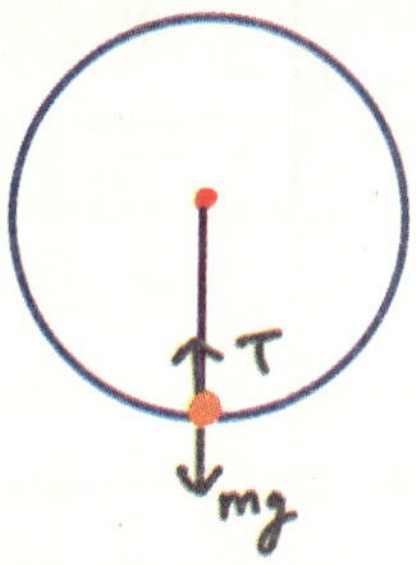 $W_T = 0$	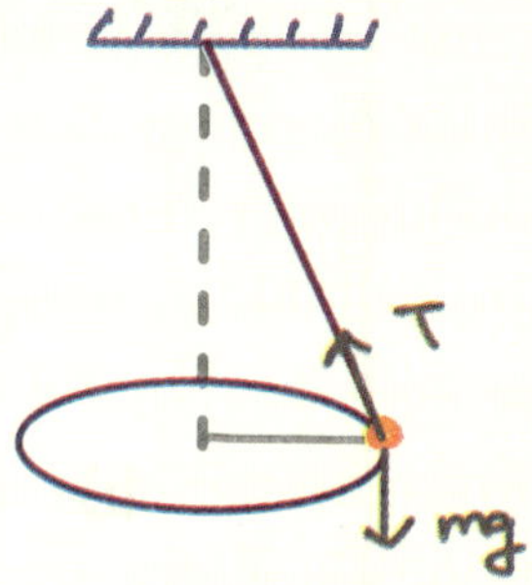 $W_T = 0$	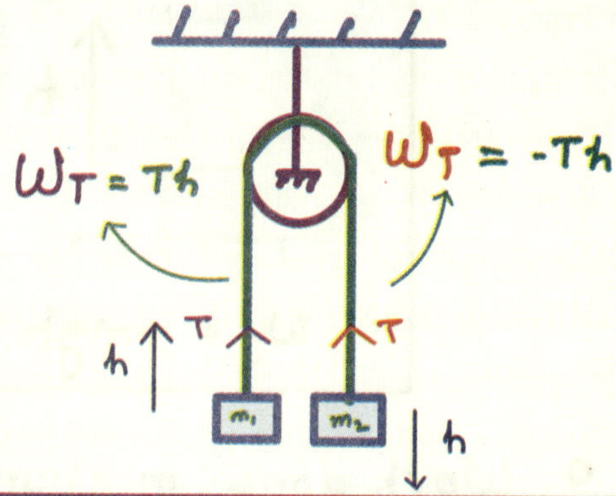

NEET Accelerate

- In circular motion, the work done by tension is always zero.
- In linear motion, the work done by tension is non-zero.

◎ Friction : Work done is path dependent.

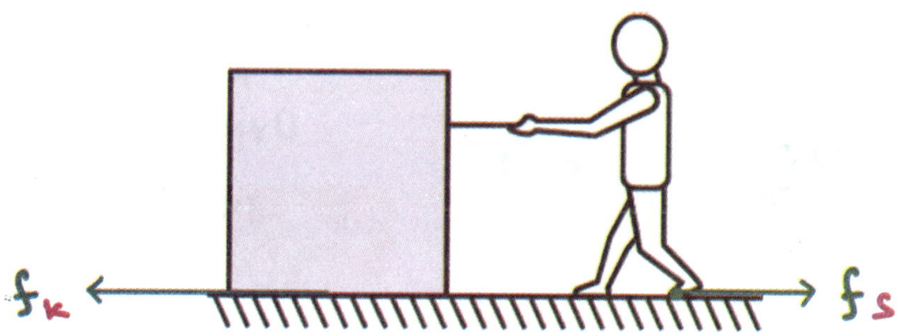

Static Friction	Kinetic Friction
◦ $W_s = f_s x$	◦ $W_k = -\mu N x$
◦ Work done is either 0 or positive.	◦ Work done is always negative.

- **Gravity** : Work done is path Independent.

Body going Up	Body going down
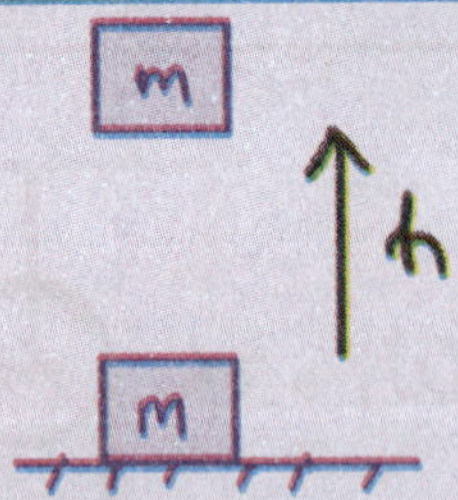	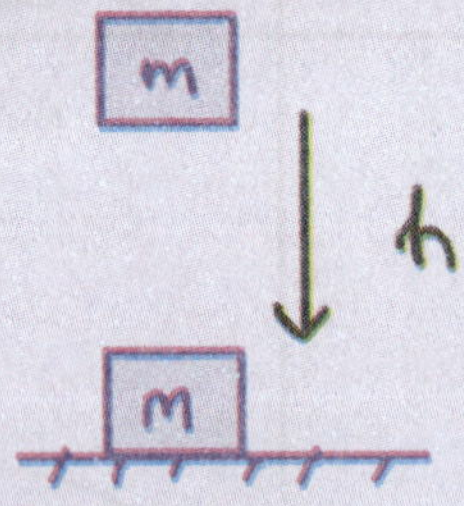
$W_g = -mgh$	$W_g = mgh$

- **Work done in changing the orientation**

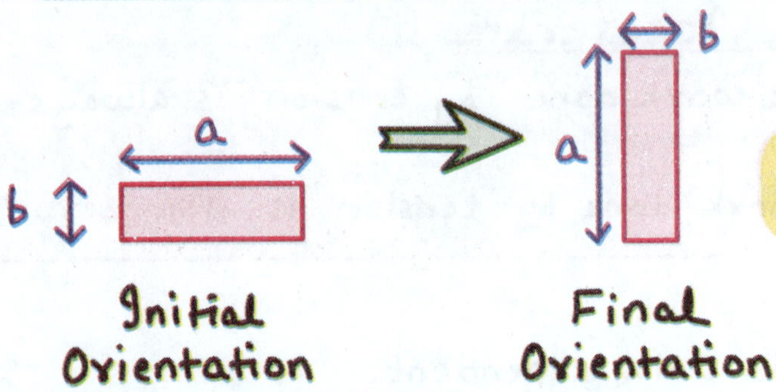

$$W_g = -mg\left(\frac{a}{2} - \frac{b}{2}\right)$$

- **Work Done in pulling a chain**

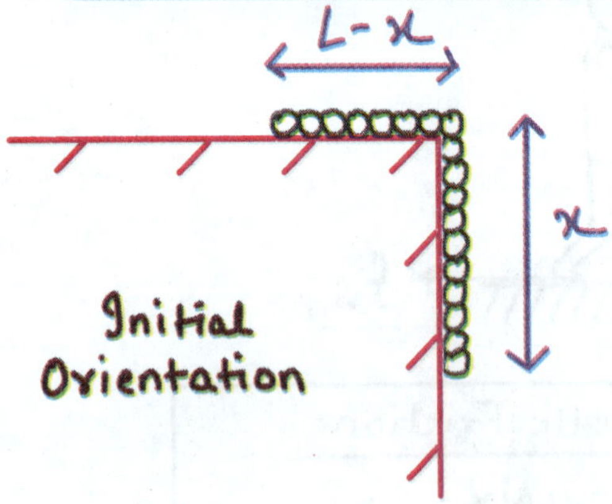

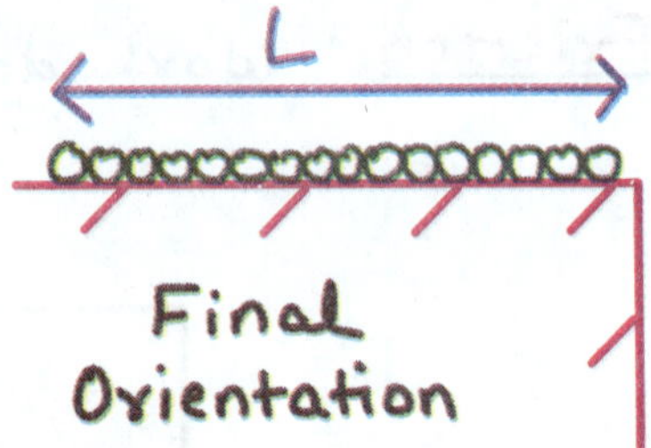

$$W_g = -\frac{Mgx}{L}\left(\frac{x}{2}\right)$$

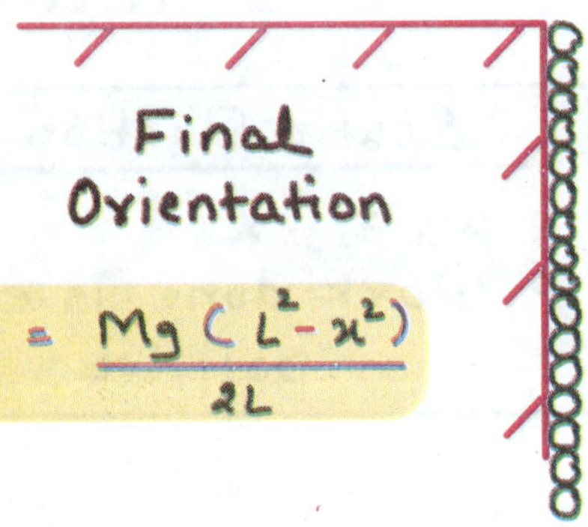

$$W_g = \frac{Mg\,(L^2 - x^2)}{2L}$$

Spring Force : Work done is path Independent.

Compressed / Stretched	Free State
○ $W_s = -\frac{k}{2}[x_2^2 - x_1^2]$ ○ Work done is always negative.	○ $W_s = -\frac{k}{2}[x_2^2 - x_1^2]$ ○ Work done is always positive.

NEET Accelerate

- When a compressed / elongated spring is left free, its temperature increases.
- For a constant force F, work done is inversely proportional to spring constant.

$$W = \frac{F^2}{2k}$$

- If W is the work done in increasing the length x of a spring, then to further increase its length by x, work required is $3W$.

Energy

- It is the ability to do work.
- Unit same as work.

Mechanical Energy

Kinetic Energy (KE)

- Energy possessed by virtue of motion.
- $KE = \frac{mv^2}{2} = \frac{p^2}{2m}$, where p is momentum
- For same p, lighter object has more KE.

- **Graphs**

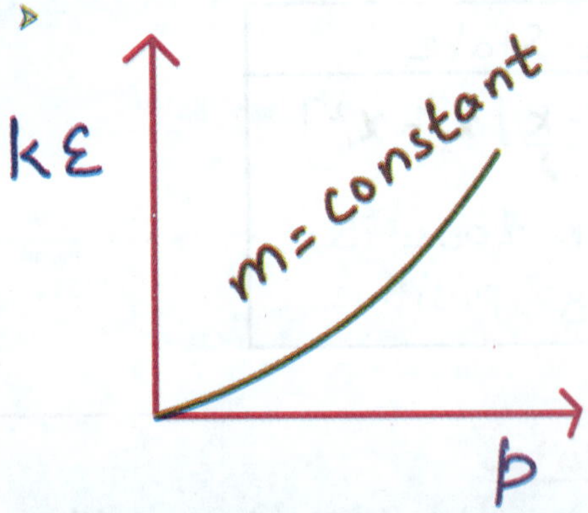

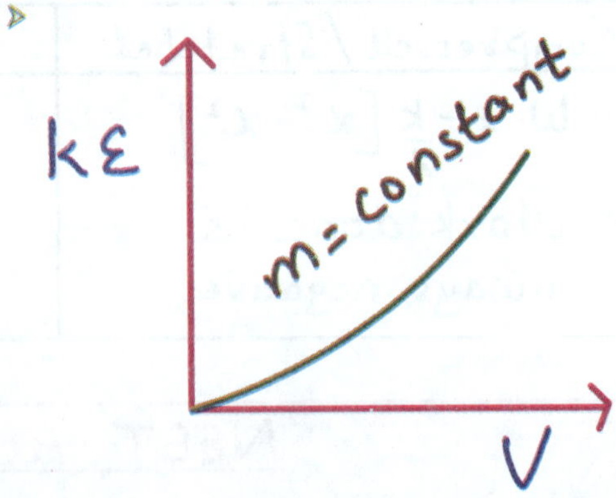

- **KE during Projectile Motion**

  - Initial KE = $\frac{mu^2}{2}$ = Final KE
  - KE at top point = $\frac{m(u\cos\theta)^2}{2}$

- **Potential Energy (PE)**
- Energy due to interactions of two bodies.
- Changes due to work by conservative forces only.
- In a self occuring process, it always decreases.
- Gravitational PE = mgh
- Elastic PE of a spring = $\frac{k(x_2^2 - x_1^2)}{2}$
  - If initial length is 0 i.e. $x_1 = 0$, then $PE \propto x^2$.
  - If a spring is left free after elongation or compression, its temperature increases.
  - In a catapult, PE get converted into KE.

PYQ PUNCH

Q3. The Potential Energy of a long spring when stretched by 2 cm is U. If the spring is stretched by 8 cm, the potential energy stored is : (NEET 2023)

Sol. $PE \propto x^2 \Rightarrow \frac{PE_1}{PE_2} = \left(\frac{x_1}{x_2}\right)^2 \Rightarrow PE_2 = 16U$

Theorems

1. Change of Potential Energy is equal to negative of Work done by conservative forces only.

$$U_f - U_i = -W_c$$

2. <u>Work Energy Theorem</u> (WET)
- Change of Kinetic Energy is equal to work done by all forces.

$$KE_f - KE_i = W_{CF} + W_{NC} + W_{other}$$

3. <u>Conservation of Mechanical Energy</u> (COME)
- If work is done by conservative forces only, then mechanical energy remains conserved.

$$K.E_i + P.E_i = K.E_f + P.E_f$$

NEET Accelerate

- From 1st theorem, only CF can change the PE.
- From 2nd theorem, every force desires to change KE.
- In 3rd theorem, NCF lag toh sakti hai par kaam nhi karni chaiye.
- Escape velocity, launching of satellite, motion of a satellite ke saare questions 3rd theorem se hi honge.
- During work done by NCF, only WET is applicable.

Special Applications of 3 Theorems

◎ <u>Maximum extension of a vertical spring</u>

- Suddenly released

$$K.E_i + P.E_i = K.E_f + P.E_f$$

$$0 + 0 = 0 + \frac{1}{2}kx^2 - mgx$$

$$\Rightarrow x = \frac{2mg}{k}$$

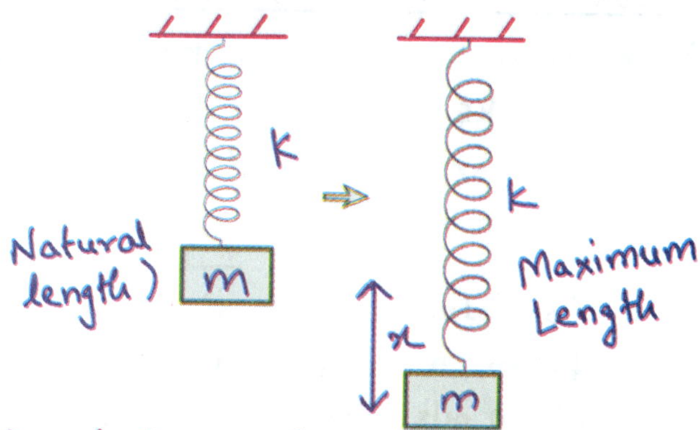

▹ Loss of Gravitational PE = Gain of Spring PE

- Slowly released

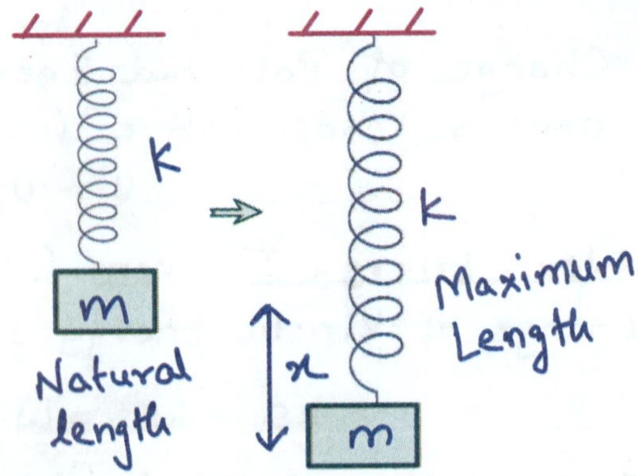

- We do work to make it fall slowly, hence COME is not applicable here

$$F = mg = kx$$

$$x = \frac{mg}{k}$$

Maximum Compression of a spring on a smooth surface

$$K.E_i + P.E_i = K.E_f + P.E_f$$

$$\frac{1}{2}mv_0^2 + 0 = 0 + \frac{1}{2}kx^2$$

$$\Rightarrow x = \sqrt{\frac{m}{k}}\,v_0$$

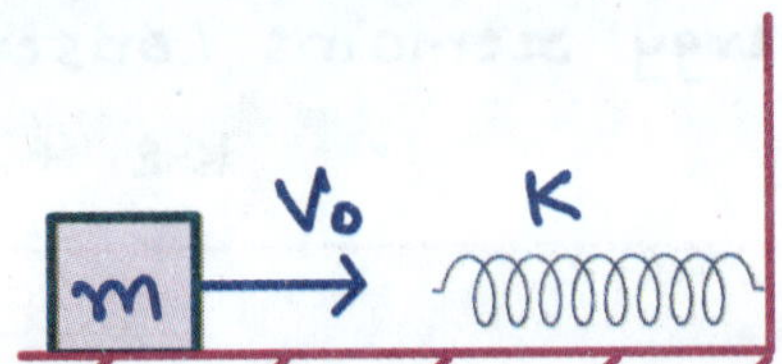

Speed of chain when it becomes vertical

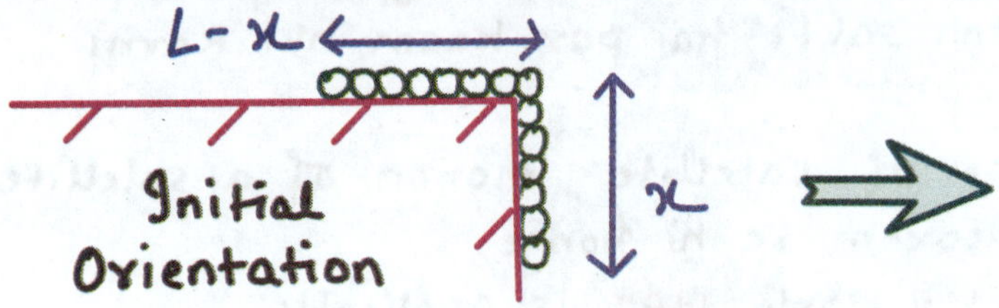

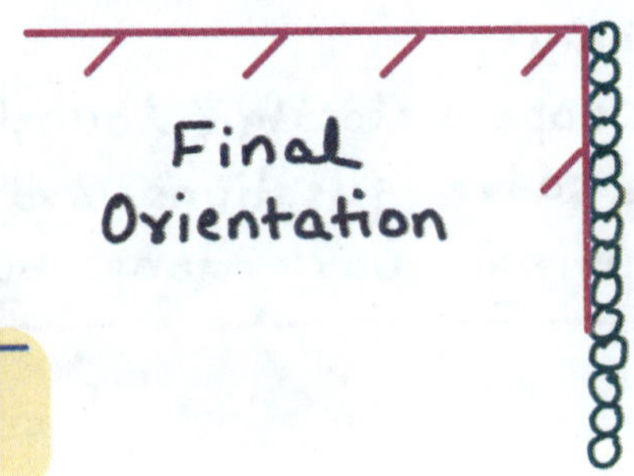

$$V = \sqrt{gL\left[1 - \frac{x^2}{L^2}\right]}$$

Work done by Air Friction

- Friction is a NCF, hence we apply WET

$$kE_f - kE_i = W_g + W_f$$

$$W_f = -mgh + \frac{1}{2}mv_0^2$$

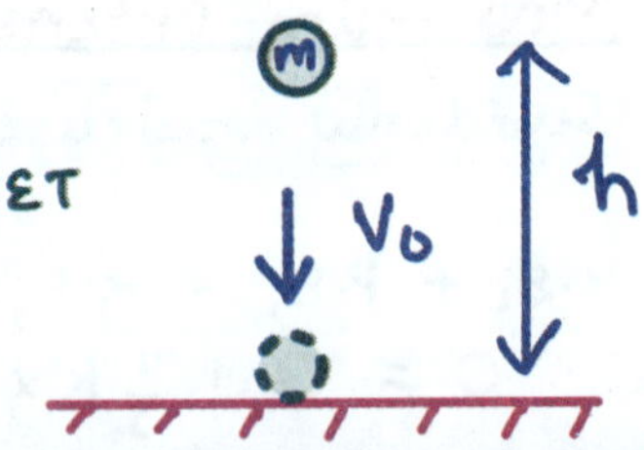

PYQ PUNCH

Q4. Consider a drop of rain water having mass 1gm falling from a height of 1km. It hits the ground with a speed of 50 m/s. The work done by the resistive force of air is: (NEET 2017)

Sol.
$$W_f = -mgh + \frac{1}{2}mv_0^2$$
$$= -10^{-3}\times 10\times 1000 + \frac{1}{2}\times 10^{-3}\times 50^2$$
$$= -8.75\,J$$

Bullet through a block

- Let v_1 be the initial speed of the bullet and v_2 be the speed of the bullet when it pierces x distance in the block.

$KE_f - KE_i = W_f$, where f is the frictional force on the block.

$\frac{1}{2}m(v_2^2 - v_2^{1}) = -fx$

Equilibrium

At A	At B	At C
F = 0	F = 0	F = 0
Unstable	Neutral	Stable
$\frac{d^2U}{dx^2} = -ve$	$\frac{d^2U}{dx^2} = 0$	$\frac{d^2U}{dx^2} = +ve$

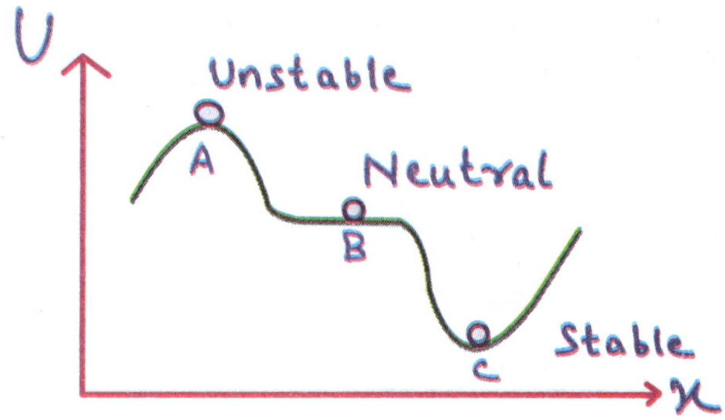

Power

- Rate of doing work
- Unit is Watt (W)
- 1 Hp = 746 W
- $P_{avg} = \frac{\text{Total Work}}{\text{Total Time}}$
- $P_{ins} = \frac{dW}{dt} = \vec{F}.\vec{V}$
- Slope of Work-Time graph gives Power.

PYQ PUNCH

Q5. At any instant of time t, the displacement of any particle is given by $2t - 1$ (SI Unit) under the influence of 5N. The value of instantaneous power is : (NEET 2024)

Sol. $P_{ins} = \vec{F}.\vec{V}$ ⟶ From Variable Force Concept

$= 5 \times 2$

$= 10W$

$V = \frac{dx}{dt} = 2$

Important relations for Constant Power (P)

- **Speed and Time**

$$V = \sqrt{\frac{2P}{m}}\, t^{1/2} \Rightarrow V \propto t^{1/2}$$

- **Position and Time**

$$x = \sqrt{\frac{8P}{9m}}\, t^{3/2} \Rightarrow x \propto t^{3/2}$$

- **Position and Speed**

$$x = \frac{m}{3P} v^3 \Rightarrow x \propto v^3$$

- **Acceleration and Time**

$$a = \sqrt{\frac{P}{2m}}\, t^{-1/2} \Rightarrow F \propto t^{-1/2}$$

MCQ PUNCH

Q6. A particle of mass m is driven by a machine that delivers a constant power of k watts. If the particle starts from rest, the force on the particle at time t is :

Sol. For constant power,

$$a = \sqrt{\frac{k}{2m}}\, t^{-1/2}$$

$$\Rightarrow F = ma = \sqrt{\frac{mk}{2}}\, t^{-1/2}$$

Special Cases of Power

- **Power of a Pump**
- Given : Fluid Density ρ
  Speed of flow v
  Area A
  Mass per unit length fluid μ

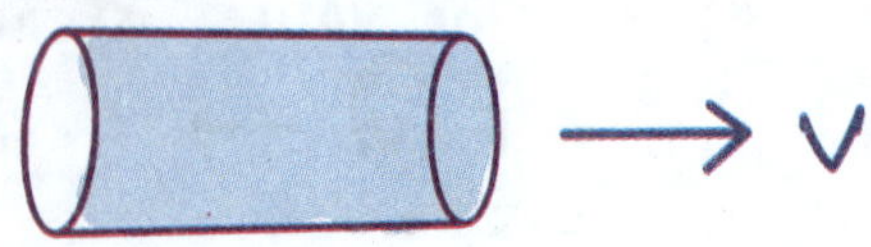

- Use :
  - $\rho A = \mu$
  - $P = \rho A v^3$
  - $P = \mu v^3$

MCQ PUNCH

Q7. An engine pumps water through a hose pipe. Water passes through the pipe and leaves it with a velocity of 2m/s. The mass per unit length of water in the pipe is 100 kg/m. What is the power of the engine ?

Sol. Power of the engine,

$P = \mu v^3$

$= 100 \times 2^3 = 800\ W$

- Rate at which KE is provided to liquid
- $P = \dot{KE} = \frac{1}{2}\rho A v^3$

9. Center of Mass

Center of Mass (COM)

- It is a point where whole mass of the system is assumed to be concentrated.
- An external force on COM only causes translatory motion of the body.
- It can lie inside or outside the body.
- Position of COM depends upon the frame of reference.

COM of Discrete Particles

- With respect to origin
- Position of COM

$$\vec{r}_{cm} = \frac{m_1\vec{r}_1 + m_2\vec{r}_2}{m_1 + m_2}$$

- X-Coordinates of COM

$$\vec{x}_{cm} = \frac{m_1\vec{x}_1 + m_2\vec{x}_2}{m_1 + m_2}$$

- Y-Coordinates of COM

$$\vec{y}_{cm} = \frac{m_1\vec{y}_1 + m_2\vec{y}_2}{m_1 + m_2}$$

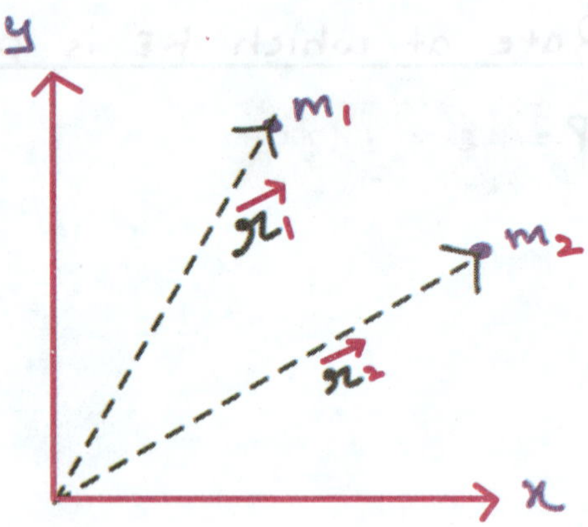

MCQ PUNCH

Q1. Three masses are placed on the x-axis; 300g at origin, 500g at x=40 and 400g at x=70cm. The distance of the COM from the origin is :

Sol. $$\vec{x}_{cm} = \frac{m_1\vec{x}_1 + m_2\vec{x}_2 + m_3\vec{x}_3}{m_1 + m_2 + m_3}$$

$$= \frac{300\times 0 + 500\times 40 + 400\times 70}{300+500+400}$$

$$= 40 \text{ cm}$$

◎ **With respect to a particle**

- COM from m_1

$$r_1 = \frac{m_2 d}{m_1 + m_2}$$

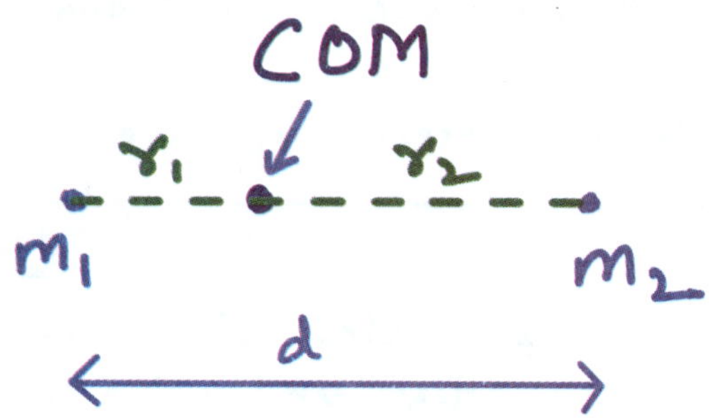

- COM from m_2

$$r_2 = \frac{m_1 d}{m_1 + m_2}$$

Points to remember for 2 mass system

- COM always lie on the line joining 2 masses.
- COM is near to the heavier mass.
- $m_1 r_1 = m_2 r_2$
- $r \propto \frac{1}{m}$

PYQ PUNCH

Q2. Two particles of mass 5 kg and 10 kg respectively are attached to the two ends of a rigid rod of length 1m of negligible mass. The centre of mass of the system from 5 kg particle is nearly at a distance of ? (NEET 2020)

Sol. $r_1 = \frac{m_2 d}{m_1 + m_2}$

$= \frac{10 \times 1}{10 + 5}$

$= 66.67$ cm

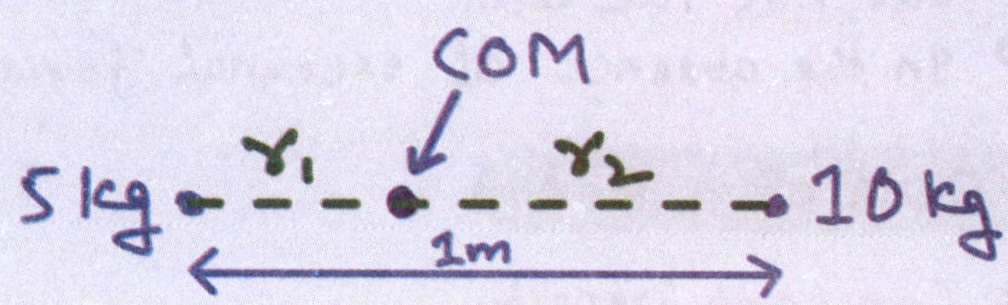

Motion of COM

◎ **Velocity of COM**

- $$\vec{v}_{cm} = \frac{m_1 \vec{v}_1 + m_2 \vec{v}_2}{m_1 + m_2}$$

$\vec{v}_1$: Velocity of mass m_1

$\vec{v}_2$: Velocity of mass m_2

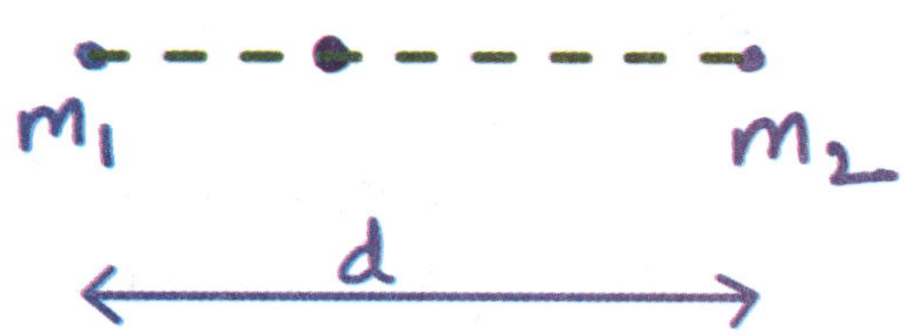

- V_{cm} can only be changed by External Force.
- Internal forces can change the speed of the bodies but not the V_{cm}.
- In the absence of external force, V_{cm} is constant.

MCQ PUNCH

Q3. Two particles which are initially at rest, move towards each other under the action of their internal attraction. If the speeds are v and 2v at any instant, then the speed of center of mass of the system will be:

Sol. Initial speed of the bodies is zero.

$\Rightarrow (V_{cm})_{initial} = 0$

In the absence of external force, V_{cm} remains constant, hence

$(V_{cm})_{final} = 0$

Acceleration of COM

- $$\vec{a}_{cm} = \frac{m_1\vec{a}_1 + m_2\vec{a}_2}{m_1 + m_2}$$

$\vec{a}_1$: acceleration of mass m_1

$\vec{a}_2$: acceleration of mass m_2

- Internal forces can change the acceleration of the bodies but not the a_{cm}.
- In the absence of external force, a_{cm} is zero.

COM of a Rod

Constant Density

$\lambda = \lambda_0$

$x_{cm} = \frac{L}{2}$

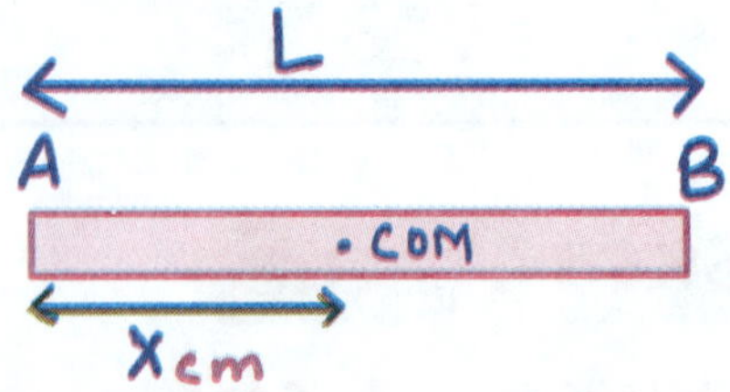

Variable Density

$\lambda = \lambda_0 x^1$	$\lambda = \lambda_0 x^2$	$\lambda = \lambda_0 x^n$
$X_{cm} = \frac{2L}{3}$	$X_{cm} = \frac{3L}{4}$	$X_{cm} = \left(\frac{n+1}{n+2}\right)L$

PYQ PUNCH

Q4. If the linear density of a rod of length 3 cm is proportional to x, where x is the distance from one end of the rod, the distance of the center of gravity of the rod from this end? (NEET 2002)

Sol. $\lambda \propto x$

$X_{cm} = \frac{2L}{3} = \frac{2}{3} \times 3 = 2\text{ cm}$

COM of Continuous Bodies

Shape	Diagram	COM
Semi-Circular Ring	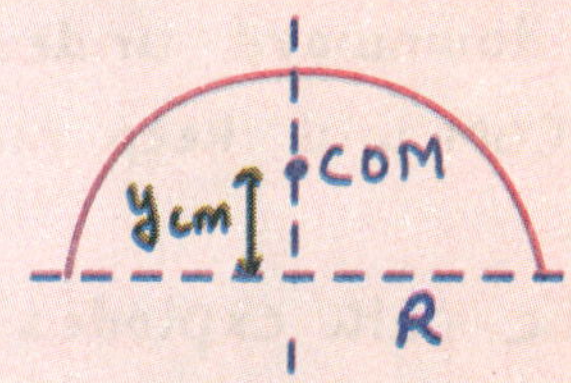	$\frac{2R}{\pi}$
Semi-Circular Disc	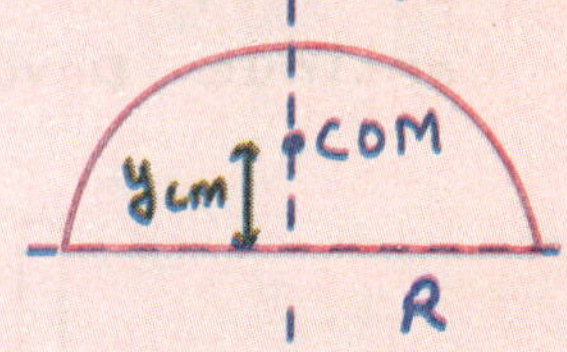	$\frac{4R}{3\pi}$
Hollow Hemisphere	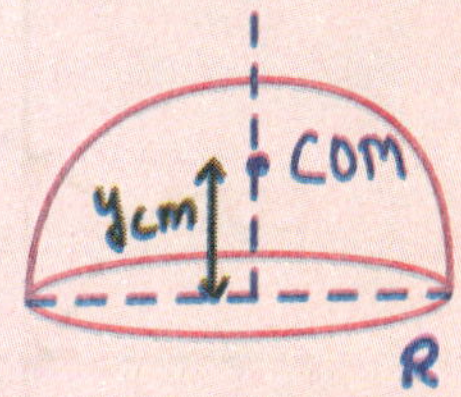	$\frac{R}{2}$
Solid Hemisphere	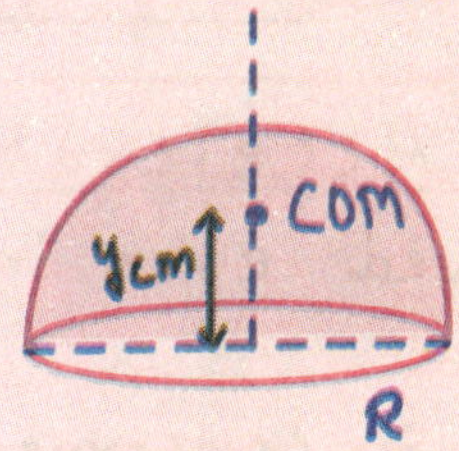	$\frac{3R}{8}$
Hollow Cone	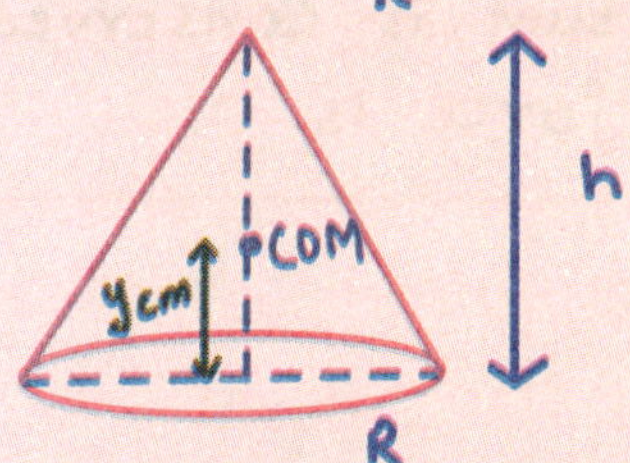	$\frac{h}{3}$
Solid Cone	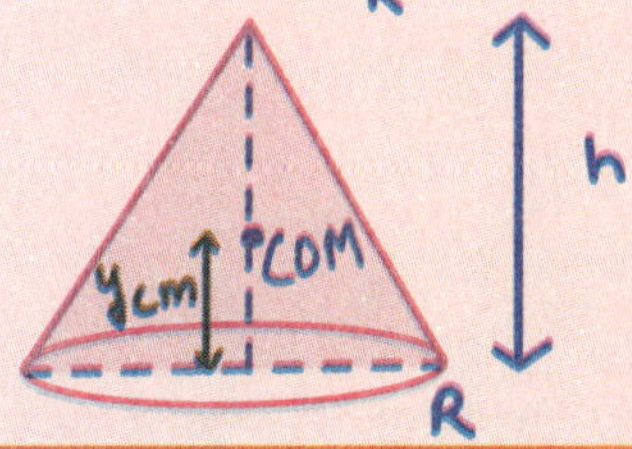	$\frac{h}{4}$

Conservation of Linear Momentum

Conditions

- $F_{ext} = 0$
- $a = 0$
- v = Constant

Special Cases of Conservation of Momentum

A moving object explodes in many parts

- A body falling vertically downward under gravity breaks in various parts. In this case, COM will keep moving continuously in vertical direction.
- A shell following parabolic path explodes somewhere in two or more parts but COM will continue parabolic path.

Falling of vertical rod on smooth surface

- Center of mass falls down vertically.

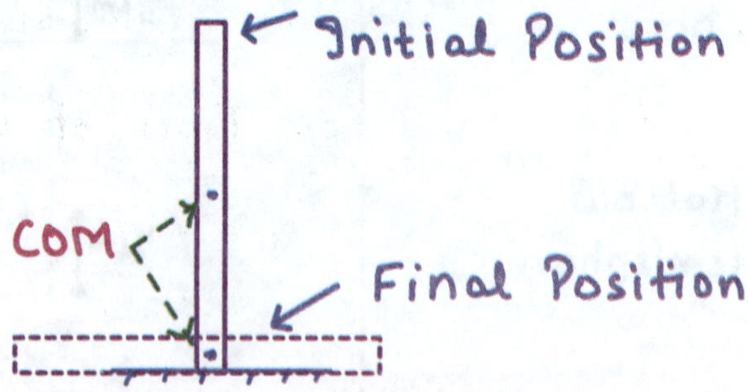

NEET Accelerate

- Momentum can be conserved even in the presence of external force.
- In such cases, momentum is conserved in that direction only where net external force is 0.

10. Collision

Collision

- It is the phenomenon of interaction of two bodies for a short interval of time.

Impulse

- It is the measure of impact during the collision.
- I = Change of Momentum

$$\vec{I} = \vec{p_f} - \vec{p_i} = \int \vec{F} dt$$ → Area of Force-Time Graph

- $$\vec{I}_{avg} = \vec{F}_{avg} \Delta t$$

where $\vec{F}$ is the Impulsive Force and
Δt is the time of interaction.

Types of Collision

	Perfectly Elastic	Plastic	Perfectly Inelastic
Momentum	Conserved	Conserved	Conserved
Kinetic Energy	Conserved	not-Conserved	not-Conserved
Deformation	×	✓	✓
Coefficient of Restitution (e)	1	$0 < e < 1$	0

Collision in 1-D

- Head-on-Collision is always 1-D.
- Perfectly Elastic Collision
- Apply
  - Conservation of momentum.

$$m_1\vec{v_1} + m_2\vec{v_2} = m_1\vec{v_1}' + m_2\vec{v_2}'$$

Before Collision After Collision

- Conservation of kinetic Energy.

$$\frac{1}{2}m_1v_1^2 + \frac{1}{2}m_2v_2^2 = \frac{1}{2}m_1v_1'^2 + \frac{1}{2}m_2v_2'^2$$

- To make calculation easy, coefficient of restitution can also be applied

$$e = \frac{\vec{V}_{separation}}{\vec{V}_{approach}} = \frac{\vec{V_2'} - \vec{V_1'}}{\vec{V_1} - \vec{V_2}} = 1$$

o Fractional loss of Energy

$$\text{Body A} = \frac{V_1^2 - V_1'^2}{V_1^2} \quad ; \quad \text{Body B} = \frac{V_2^2 - V_2'^2}{V_2^2}$$

PYQ PUNCH

Q1. Body A of mass 4m moving with speed u collides with another body B of mass 2m, at rest. The collision is head on and elastic in nature. After the collision, the fraction of energy lost by the colliding body A is : (NEET 2019)

Sol.

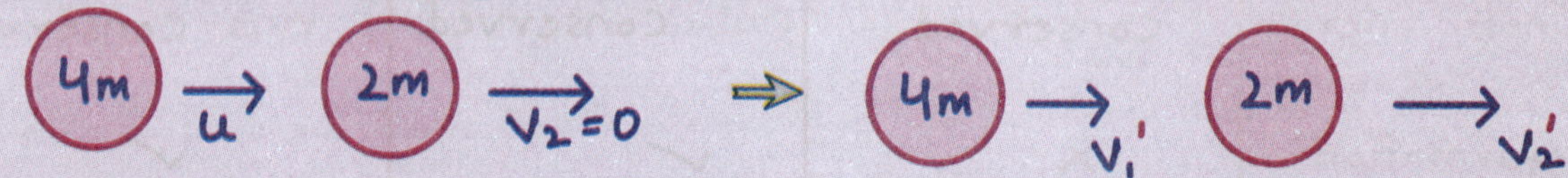

Conservation of momentum

$$m_1\vec{V_1} + m_2\vec{V_2} = m_1\vec{V_1'} + m_2\vec{V_2'}$$

$$\Rightarrow 4mu + 0 = 4mV_1' + 2mV_2'$$

$$\Rightarrow 2u = 2V_1' + V_2' \text{ ---- eq. 1}$$

Coefficient of restitution

$$1 = \frac{\vec{V_2'} - \vec{V_1'}}{\vec{V_1} - \vec{V_2}} = \frac{V_2' - V_1'}{u}$$

$$\Rightarrow u = V_2' - V_1' \text{ ---- eq. 2}$$

From equations 1 and 2

$V_2' = \frac{4u}{3}$ and $V_1' = \frac{u}{3}$

Fractional loss of Energy of A

$$= \frac{V_1^2 - V_1'^2}{V_1^2} = \frac{(u)^2 - \left(\frac{u}{3}\right)^2}{(u)^2} = \frac{8}{9}$$

- If mass of 2 bodies is same
  - Velocities get exchanged.
  - $\vec{v}_1' = \vec{v}_2$
  - $\vec{v}_2' = \vec{v}_1$
- 

PYQ PUNCH

Q2. Two identical balls A and B having velocities of 0.5 m/s and −0.3 m/s respectively collide elastically in one-dimension. The velocities of B and A after the collision respectively will be: (NEET 2016)

Sol. Since masses are same

$V_B' = V_A = 0.5$ m/s

$V_A' = V_B = -0.3$ m/s

Plastic Collision

- Apply
  - Conservation of momentum.

$$m_1\vec{v}_1 + m_2\vec{v}_2 = m_1\vec{v}_1' + m_2\vec{v}_2'$$

Before Collision — After Collision

- Coefficient of restitution

$$e = \frac{\vec{V}_{separation}}{\vec{V}_{approach}} = \frac{\vec{v}_2' - \vec{v}_1'}{\vec{v}_1 - \vec{v}_2}$$

- Fractional loss of Energy

$$\text{Body A} = \frac{v_1^2 - v_1'^2}{v_1^2} \quad ; \quad \text{Body B} = \frac{v_2^2 - v_2'^2}{v_2^2}$$

- Net loss of Energy

$$\Delta KE = \frac{1}{2}\left(m_1\left(v_1^2 - v_1'^2\right) + m_2\left(v_2^2 - v_2'^2\right)\right)$$

- A part of lost kinetic Energy deforms the body or lost in the form of heat.

PYQ PUNCH

Q3. A moving block having mass m, collides with another stationary block having mass 4m. The lighter block comes to rest after collision. When the initial velocity of the lighter block is v, then the value of coefficient of restitution e will be : (NEET 2018)

Sol.

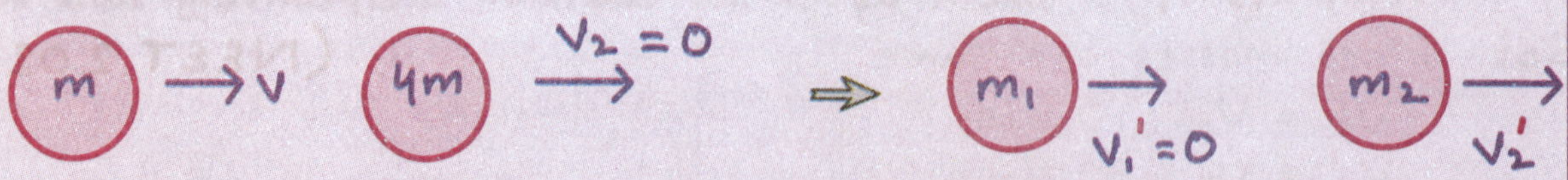

Conservation of momentum

$$m_1\vec{V_1} + m_2\vec{V_2} = m_1\vec{V_1'} + m_2\vec{V_2'}$$

$\Rightarrow$ $mv + 0 = 0 + 4mV_2'$

$\Rightarrow$ $v = 4V_2'$ --- eq.1

Coefficient of restitution

$$e = \frac{\vec{V_2'} - \vec{V_1'}}{\vec{V_1} - \vec{V_2}} = \frac{V_2'}{v} \text{ --- eq. 2}$$

From equations 1 and 2

$e = 0.25$

Perfectly Inelastic Collision

- Two bodies stick to each other.
- Apply
  - Conservation of momentum.

$$m_1\vec{V_1} + m_2\vec{V_2} = (m_1 + m_2)\vec{V'}$$

Before Collision — After Collision

- Fractional loss of Energy

$$\text{Body A} = \frac{V_1^2 - V'^2}{V_1^2} \quad ; \quad \text{Body B} = \frac{V_2^2 - V'^2}{V_2^2}$$

- Net loss of Energy

$$\Delta KE = \frac{1}{2}\left(m_1\left(v_1^2 - v_1'^2\right) + m_2\left(v_2^2 - v_2'^2\right)\right)$$

- A part of lost kinetic Energy deforms the body or lost in the form of heat.

PYQ PUNCH

Q4. Two bodies A and B of same mass undergo completely inelastic one dimensional collision. The body A moves with velocity v_1 while body B is at rest before collision. The velocity of the system after collision is v_2. The ratio is: (NEET 2024)

Sol.

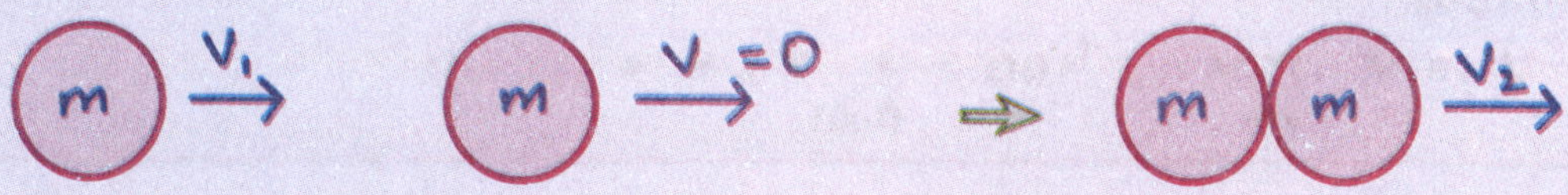

Conservation of momentum

$$m_1\vec{v_1} + m_2\vec{v_2} = (m_1 + m_2)\vec{v}'$$

$$\Rightarrow m v_1 + 0 = 2m v_2$$

$$\Rightarrow \frac{v_1}{v_2} = \frac{2}{1}$$

Collision of Bullet with Pendulum

- **Plastic Collision**

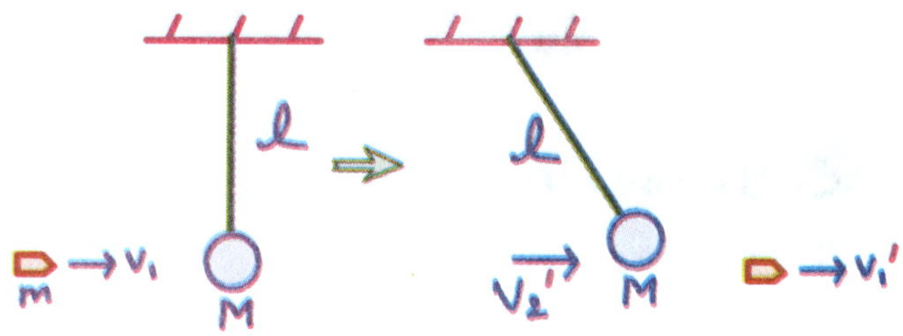

- $$V_1' = \left(\frac{m + Me}{m + M}\right)V_1$$

- $$V_2' = \left(\frac{m(1+e) + 2Me}{m + M}\right)V_1$$

- Height upto which bob rises

$$h = \frac{V_2'^2}{2g}$$

- $$V_1' = V - \frac{M}{m}V_2'$$

MCQ PUNCH

Q5. A bullet of mass 10 g moving horizontal with a velocity of 400 m/s strikes a wooden block of mass 2 kg which is suspended by light inextensible string of length 5 m. As a result, the centre of gravity of the block is found to rise a vertical distance of 10 cm. The speed of the bullet after it emerges out horizontally from the block will be :

Sol. $m = 10\,gm = 0.01\,kg$; $M = 2\,kg$

$h = 10\,cm = 0.1\,m$; $V_1 = 400\,m/s$

Using

$$V_2' = \sqrt{2gh} = \sqrt{2 \times 9.8 \times 0.1} = 1.4\,m/s$$

Now

$$V_1' = V - \frac{M}{m}V_2' = 400 - \frac{2}{0.01} \times 1.4 = 120\,m/s$$

Inelastic Collision

- Bullet gets embedded in the bob.
- $V' = \left(\frac{m}{m+M}\right)V_1$
- Height upto which bob rises

$$h = \frac{V'^2}{2g}$$

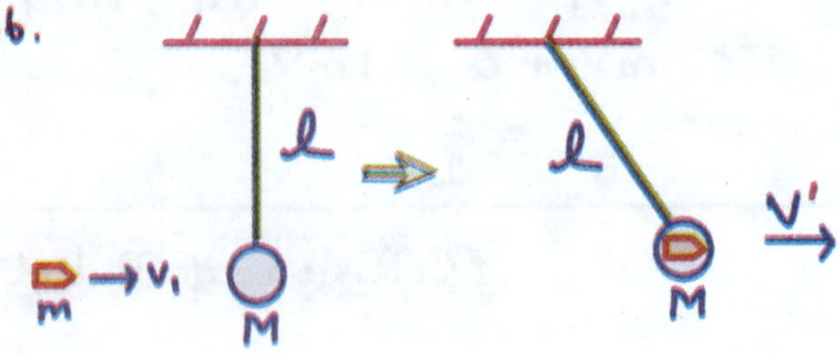

Collision in 2-D

- No head-on-collision.
- Two bodies move in different directions.

Elastic Collision

- Apply
  - Conservation of kinetic Energy.

$$\frac{1}{2}m_1v_1^2 + \frac{1}{2}m_2v_2^2 = \frac{1}{2}m_1v_1'^2 + \frac{1}{2}m_2v_2'^2$$

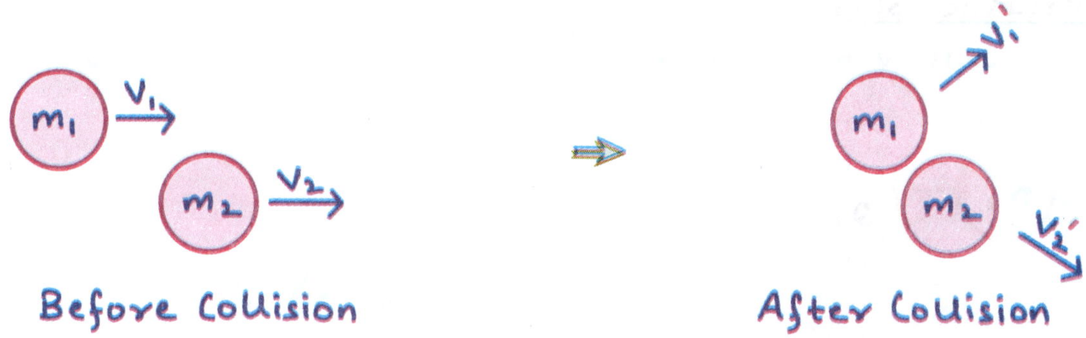

MCQ PUNCH

Q 6. On a frictionless surface, a block of mass M moving at speed v collides elastically with another block of same mass M which is initially at rest. After collision, the first block moves at an angle θ to its initial direction and has a speed of v/3. The second's block speed after the collision is :

Sol. By conservation of kinetic Energy

$$\frac{1}{2}m_1v_1^2 + \frac{1}{2}m_2v_2^2 = \frac{1}{2}m_1v_1'^2 + \frac{1}{2}m_2v_2'^2$$

$$\Rightarrow Mv^2 + 0 = M\left(\frac{v}{3}\right)^2 + Mv_2'^2$$

$$\Rightarrow v_2' = \frac{2\sqrt{2}\,v}{3}$$

- If two bodies have same mass and one of them is at rest initially then
  - $\theta_1 + \theta_2 = 90°$

    i.e. 2 masses move perpendicular to each other.

Inelastic Collision

- Apply conservation of momentum separately in x-axis and y-axis.

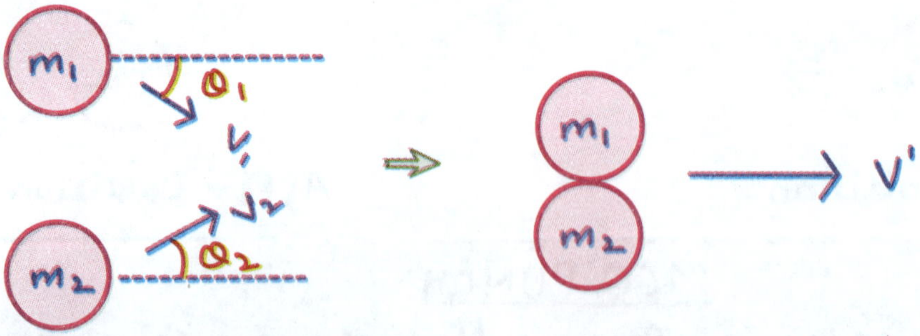

Before Collision After Collision

- In x-axis

$$m_1 v_1 \cos\theta_1 + m_2 v_2 \cos\theta_2 = (m_1 + m_2) V'$$

- In y-axis

$$m_1 v_1 \sin\theta_1 = m_2 v_2 \sin\theta_2$$

MCQ PUNCH

Q7. A mass m moving horizontally (along the x-axis) with velocity v collides and sticks to a mass of 3m moving vertically upward (along the Y-axis) with velocity 2v. The final velocity of the combination is :

Sol. In x-axis

$$mv = (m + 3m) v'_x$$

$$\Rightarrow v'_x = \frac{v}{4}$$

In y-axis

$$3m \times 2v = (m + 3m) v'_y$$

$$\Rightarrow v'_y = \frac{3v}{2}$$

Now

$$V' = v'_x + v'_y$$

$$= \frac{v}{4}\hat{i} + \frac{3v}{2}\hat{j}$$

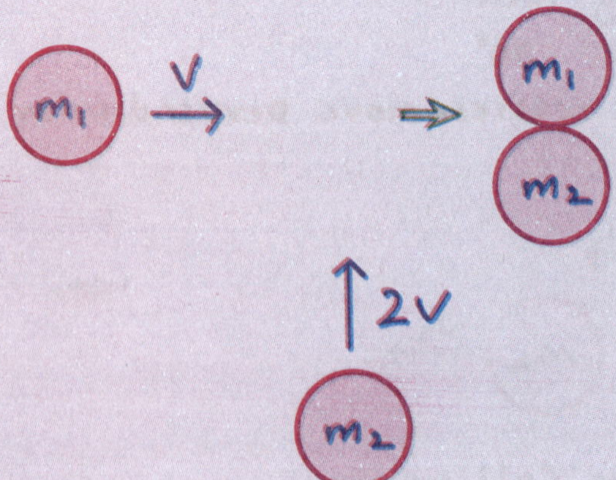

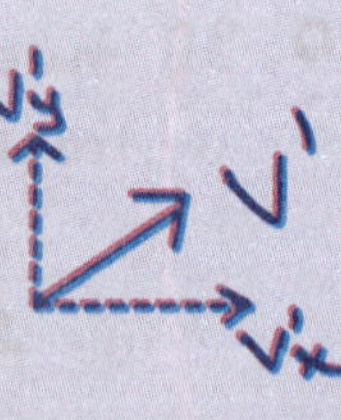

11. Rotational Motion

Axis of Rotation

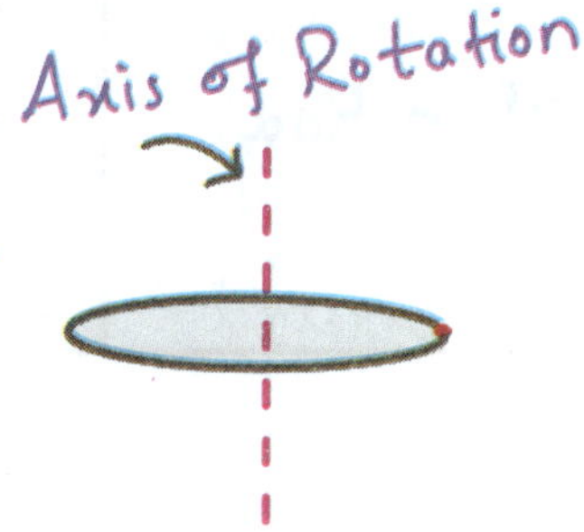

- An axis around which an object rotates.
- It can lie inside or outside the object.

Moment of Inertia (MOI)

- It is the resistance to the change of state of rotational motion.
- Depends upon the
  - Mass of the object.
  - Distance of mass from the axis of rotation.

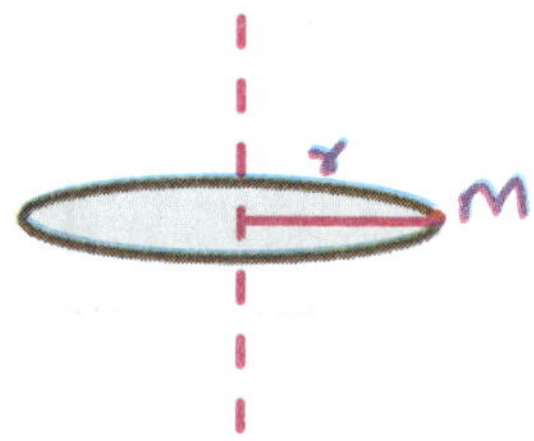

$$I = mr^2$$

- For a same object, MOI can change as it depends upon the axis of rotation also.

MOI of Discrete System

- MOI of individual mass gets added up.

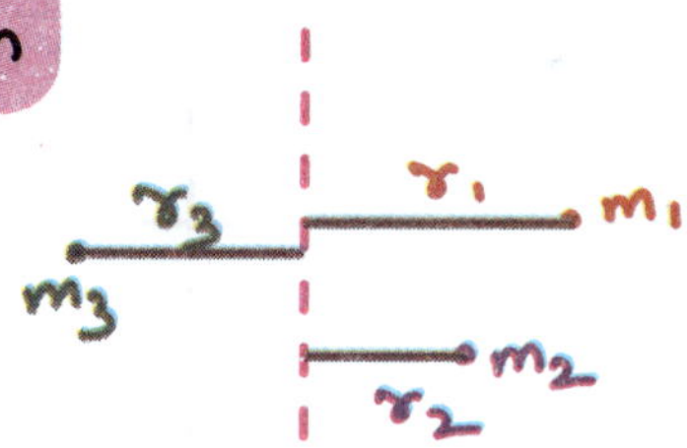

$$I = m_1 r_1^2 + m_2 r_2^2 + m_3 r_3^2 + \ldots$$

PYQ PUNCH

Q1. A light rod of length l has two masses m_1 and m_2 attached to its two ends. The moment of inertia of the system about an axis perpendicular to the rod and passing through the center of mass is **(NEET 2016)**

Sol. $r_1 = \frac{m_2 l}{m_1 + m_2}$; $r_2 = \frac{m_1 l}{m_1 + m_2}$

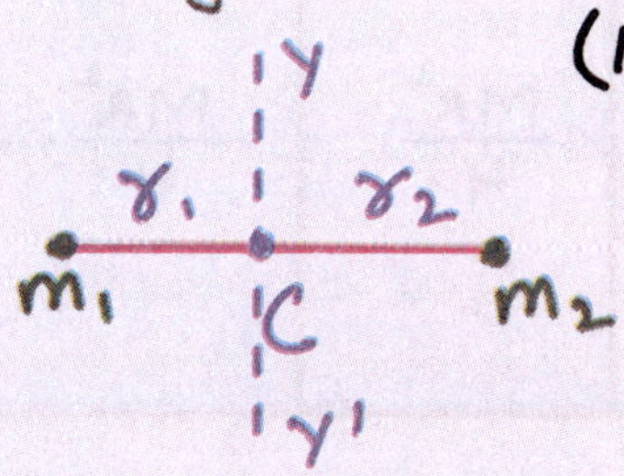

$$I = m_1 r_1^2 + m_2 r_2^2$$

$$= \frac{m_1 m_2 l^2}{m_1 + m_2}$$

Shape	$I_{xx'}$	$I_{yy'}$	$I_{zz'}$	Diagram
Thin Rod	0	$\frac{ML^2}{12}$	$\frac{ML^2}{12}$	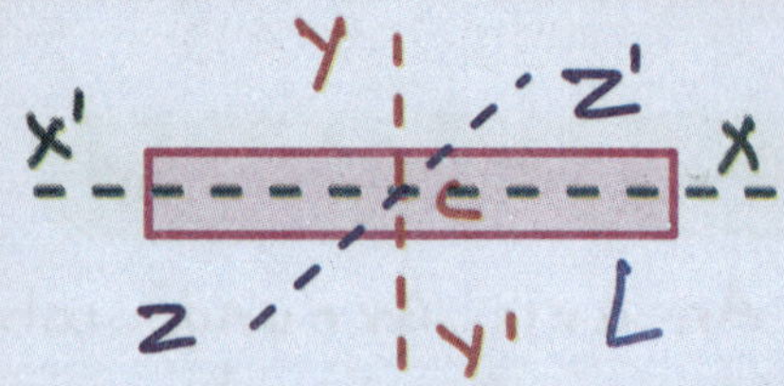
Rectangular Lamina	$\frac{Ma^2}{12}$	$\frac{Mb^2}{12}$	$\frac{M(a^2+b^2)}{12}$	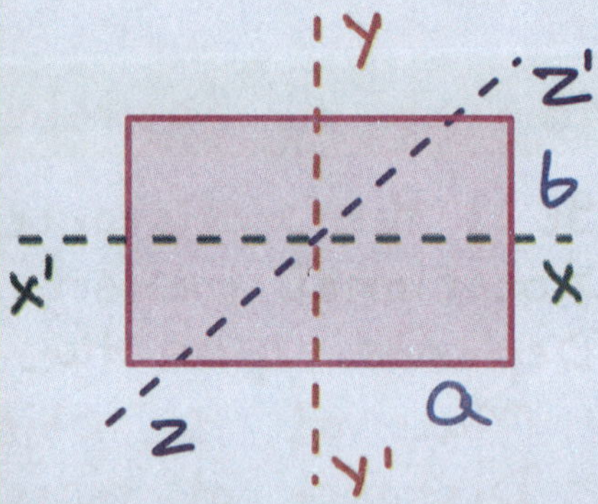
Square Lamina	$\frac{Ma^2}{12}$	$\frac{Ma^2}{12}$	$\frac{Ma^2}{6}$	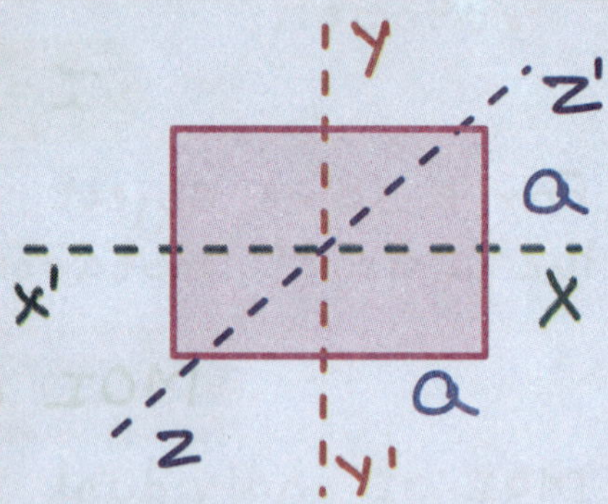
Ring	$\frac{MR^2}{2}$	$\frac{MR^2}{2}$	MR^2	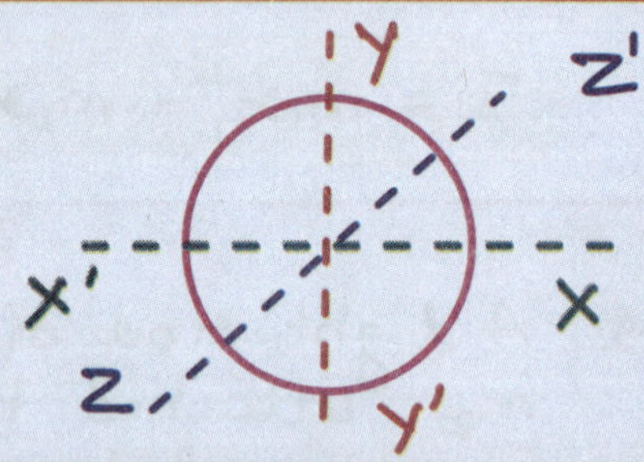
Disc	$\frac{MR^2}{4}$	$\frac{MR^2}{4}$	$\frac{MR^2}{2}$	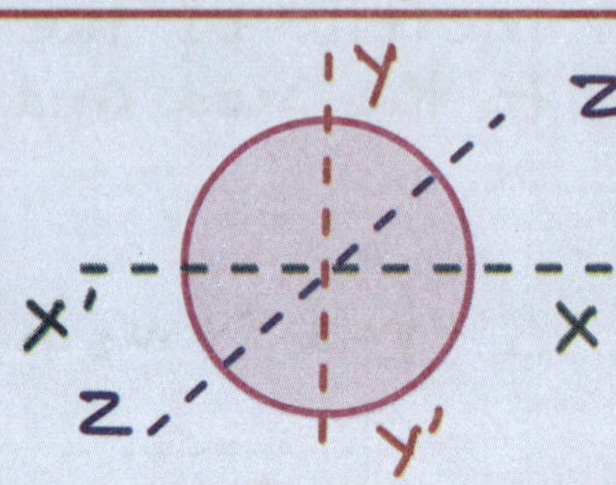

Shape	$I_{xx'}$	$I_{yy'}$	$I_{zz'}$	Diagram
Hollow Cylinder		MR^2		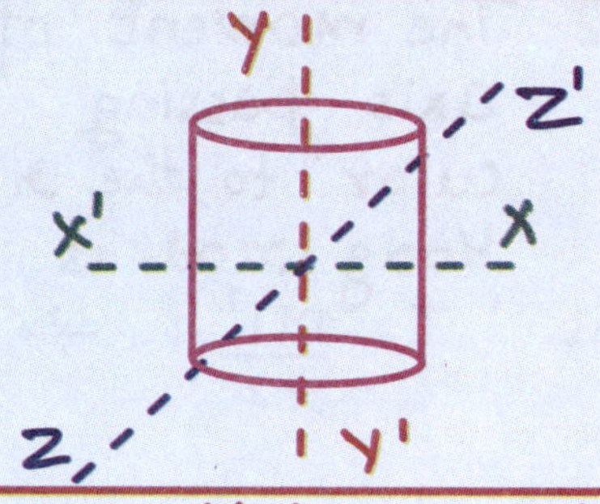
Solid Cylinder		$\frac{MR^2}{2}$		
Hollow Sphere	$\frac{2}{3}MR^2$			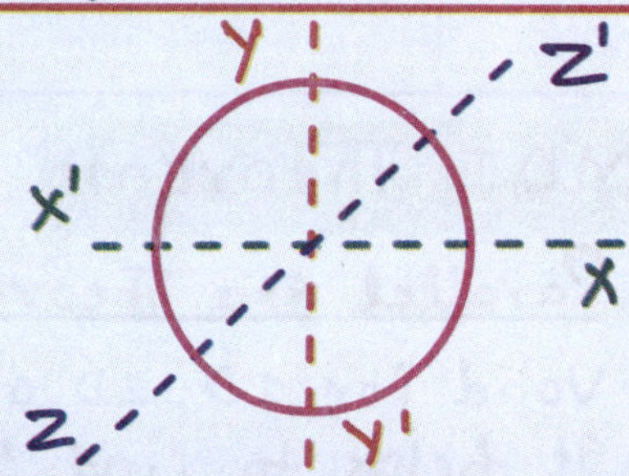
Solid Sphere	$\frac{2}{5}MR^2$			
Thick Ring	$\frac{M}{2}\left(\frac{r_2^4 - r_1^4}{r_2^2 - r_1^2}\right)$ where $M = \sigma\pi(r_2^2 - r_1^2)$			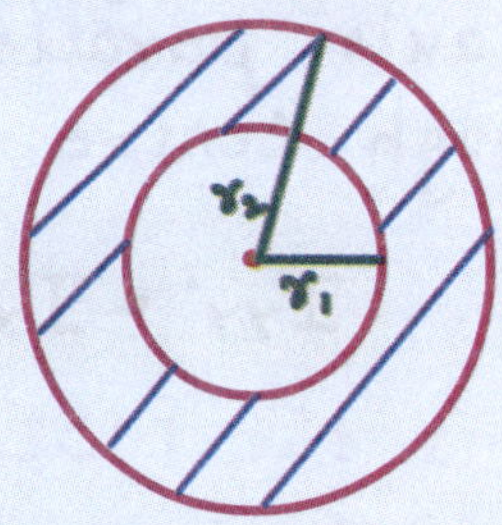
Thick Hollow Sphere	$\frac{2M}{5}\left(\frac{r_2^5 - r_1^5}{r_2^3 - r_1^3}\right)$ where $M = \rho \times \frac{4}{3}\pi(r_2^3 - r_1^3)$			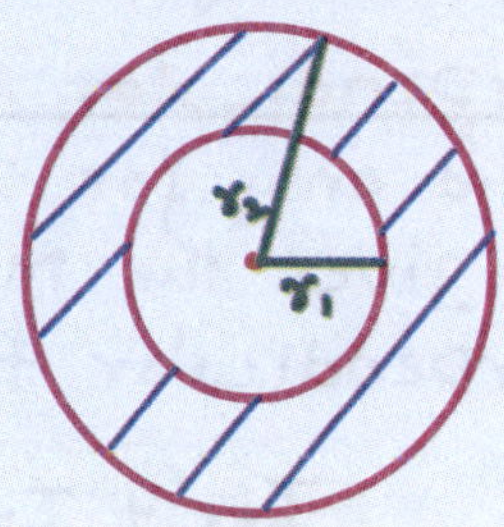

Points

- Rectangular lamina can be considered as thin rod to find $I_{xx'}$ and $I_{yy'}$.
- Cylinder means solid cylinder.
- Sphere means solid sphere.
- Hollow cylinder is made up of rings, hence same MOI.
- Solid cylinder is made up of disc, hence same MOI.

PYQ PUNCH

Q2. The moment of inertia of a thin rod about an axis passing through its mid-point and perpendicular to the rod is 2400 g cm². The length of the 400g rod is : (NEET 2024)

Sol. $I = \frac{ML^2}{12} \Rightarrow L = \sqrt{\frac{12I}{M}}$

$= \sqrt{\frac{12 \times 2400}{400}} = 8.5\text{cm}$

MOI Theorems

Parallel Axis Theorem

- Valid for 1D, 2D and 3D bodies.
- It helps to find the MOI around an axis parallel to the axis passing through centre of mass.

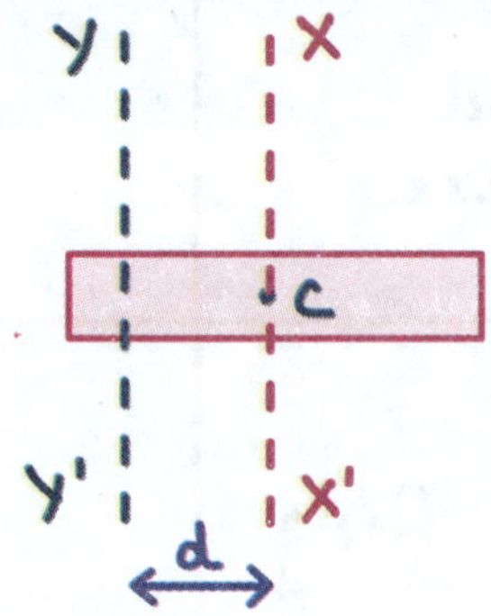

$$I_{yy'} = I_{xx'} + Md^2$$

$I_{xx'}$ is the MOI around an axis passing thr. COM.

- MOI along $I_{xx'}$ is the minimum.

Perpendicular Axis Theorem

- Valid only for 2D bodies.
- It gives the MOI around an axis perpendicular to a known axis.

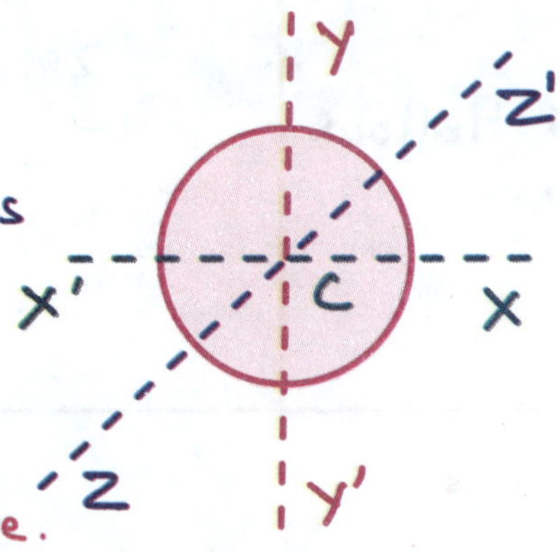

$$I_{xx'} + I_{yy'} = I_{zz'}$$

$I_{xx'}$ & $I_{yy'}$ are the axes in the plane of 2D body & passing through its centre.
$I_{zz'}$ is the axis ⊥ to the 2D body

Important MOI using the theorems

Along the ends of Thin Rod

$$I_{yy'} = I_{xx'} + M\left(\frac{L}{2}\right)^2 = \frac{ML^2}{3}$$

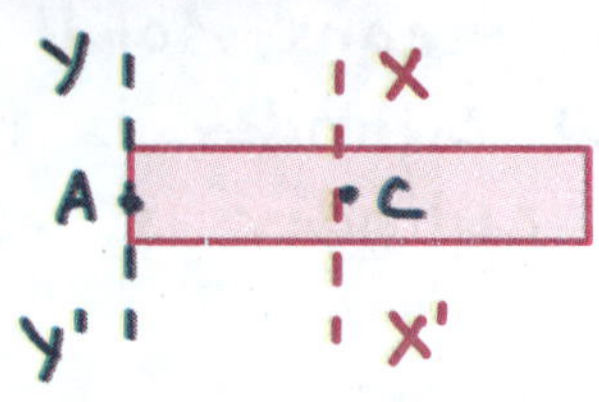

MCQ PUNCH

Q3. The moment of inertia of a thin uniform rod of mass M and length L about an axis passing through its mid-point and perpendicular to its length is I_0. Its MOI about an axis passing through one of its ends and ⊥ to its length is :

Sol. $I_{yy'} = I_{xx'} + M\left(\frac{L}{2}\right)^2$

$$= I_0 + \frac{ML^2}{4}$$

◎ **Along any axis of Square in its plane passing thr. Centre**

$$I_{11'} = I_{22'} = \frac{Ma^2}{12}$$

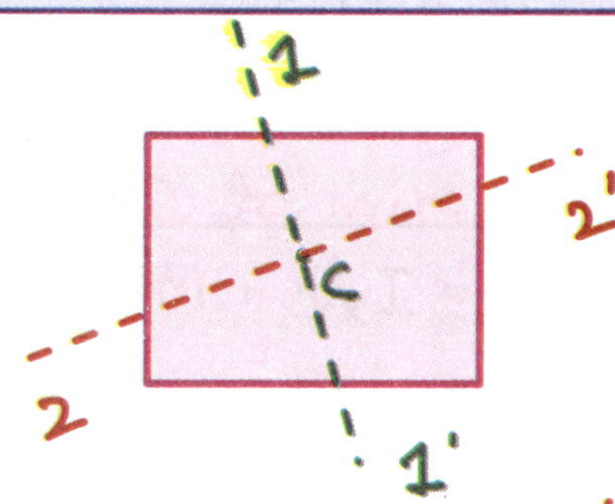

◎ **Along the rim of Ring and ⊥ to it**

$$I_{11'} = I_{22'} + MR^2$$
$$= MR^2 + MR^2$$
$$= 2MR^2$$

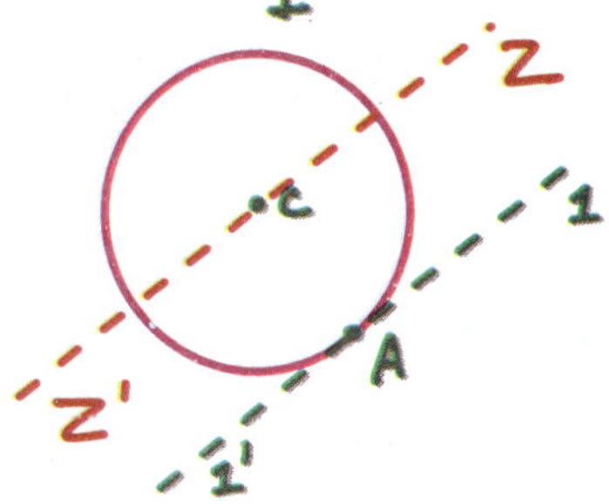

◎ **Along the rim of Disc and ⊥ to it**

$$I_{11'} = I_{22'} + MR^2$$
$$= \frac{MR^2}{2} + MR^2$$
$$= \frac{3}{2}MR^2$$

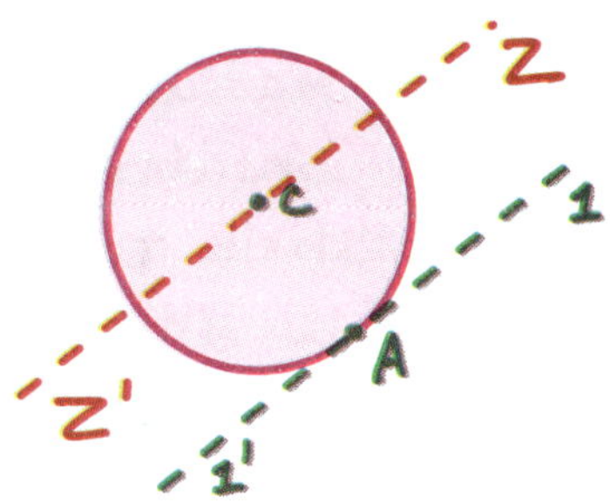

◎ **Along the rim of Ring and in its plane**

$$I_{yy'} = I_{xx'} + MR^2$$
$$= \frac{MR^2}{2} + MR^2$$
$$= \frac{3}{2}MR^2$$

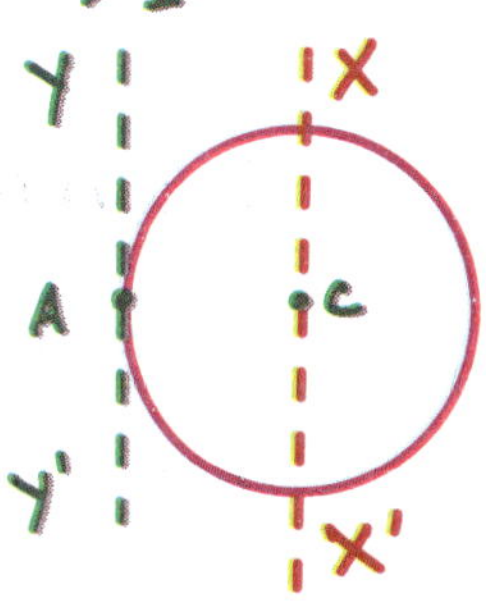

◎ **Along the rim of Disc and in its plane**

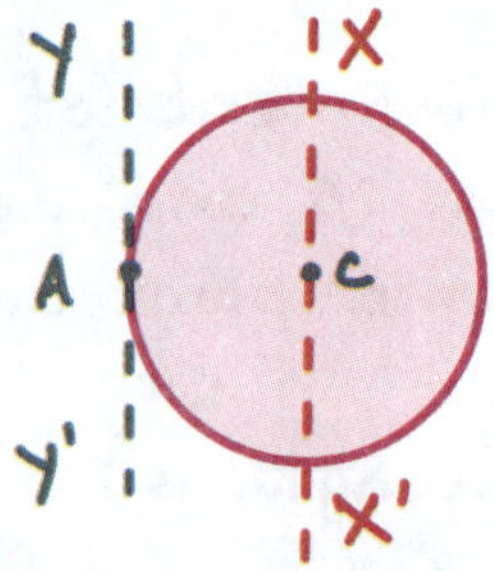

$$I_{yy'} = I_{xx'} + MR^2$$
$$= \frac{MR^2}{4} + MR^2$$
$$= \frac{5}{4}MR^2$$

◎ **Along the rim of Hollow Sphere**

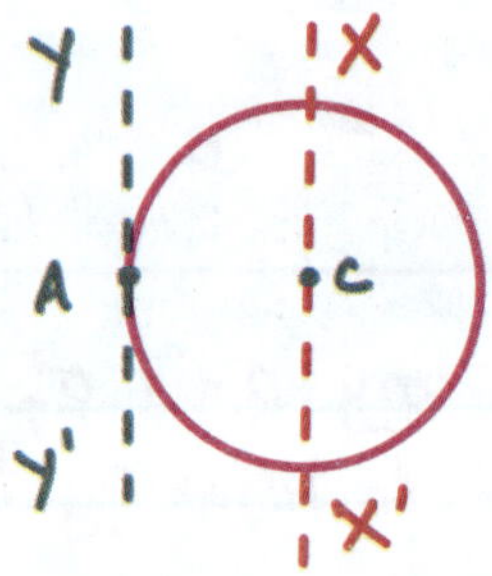

$$I_{yy'} = I_{xx'} + MR^2$$
$$= \frac{2}{3}MR^2 + MR^2 = \frac{5}{3}MR^2$$

◎ **Along the rim of Solid Sphere**

$$I_{yy'} = I_{xx'} + MR^2$$
$$= \frac{2}{5}MR^2 + MR^2 = \frac{7}{5}MR^2$$

Addition of MOI

- Just like discrete mass system, MOI of continuous mass system can be added along a common axis.

MCQ PUNCH

Q4. Three identical spherical shells, each of mass m and radius r are placed as shown in figure. Consider an axis XX', which is touching to two shells and passing through diameter of third shell. MOI of the system consisting of these three spherical shells about XX' axis is

Sol. MOI along XX' of

Sphere 1, $I_1 = \frac{5}{3}MR^2$

Sphere 2, $I_2 = \frac{5}{3}MR^2$

Sphere 3, $I_3 = \frac{2}{3}MR^2$

Total $I = I_1 + I_2 + I_3 = 4MR^2$

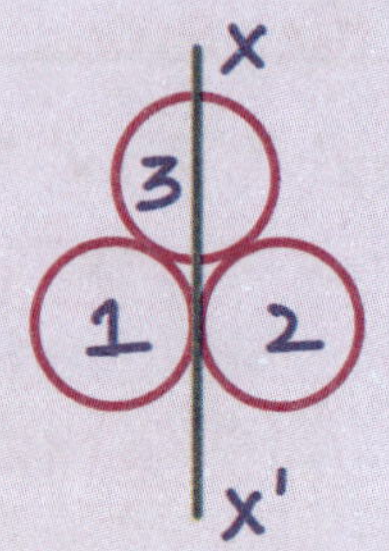

Subtraction of MOI

- MOI can be subtracted along the common axis.
- For area, $m = M/n^2$
- For volume, $m = M/n^3$

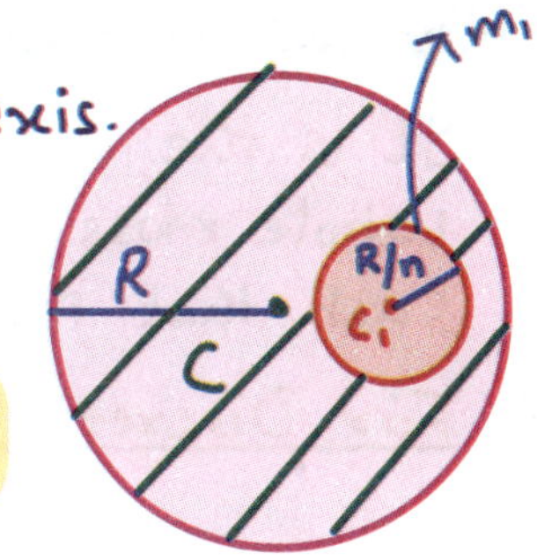

$$I_{remain} = I_{complete} - I_{removed}$$

PYQ PUNCH

Q5. From a circular ring of mass M and radius R, an arc corresponding to a 90° sector is removed. The MOI of the remaining part of the ring about an axis passing through the centre of the ring and perpendicular to the plane of the ring is k times MR^2. Then, the value of k is (NEET 2021)

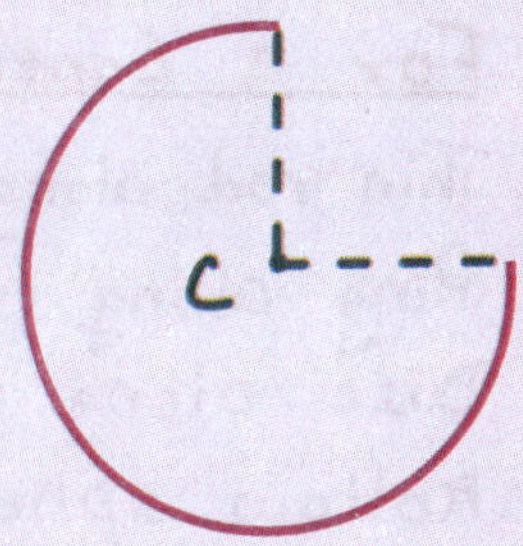

Sol. Mass of Complete ring $= M$

MOI of Complete ring about C, $I_1 = MR^2$

Mass of removed part $= M/4$

MOI of removed part about C, $I_2 = \frac{M}{4}R^2$

MOI of remaining part about C

$$I = I_1 - I_2 = \frac{3}{4}MR^2 = kMR^2$$

$\Rightarrow k = 3/4$

Q6. From a disc of radius R and mass M, a circular hole of diameter R, whose rim passes through the center is cut. What is the MOI of the remaining part of the disc about a perpendicular axis, passing through the center? (NEET 2016)

Sol. MOI of Complete disc about C, $I_1 = MR^2/2$

Mass of cut disc, $m_1 = M/4$

MOI of cut part along C,

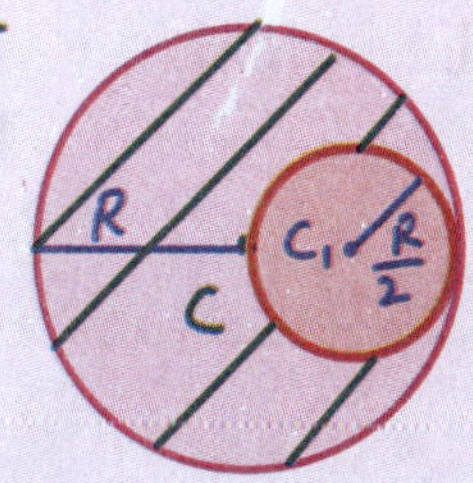

$$I_2 = \frac{3}{2} \times \frac{M}{4}\left(\frac{R}{2}\right)^2 = \frac{3}{32}MR^2$$

MOI of remaining part $= I_1 - I_2 = \frac{13}{32}MR^2$

Radius of Gyration (k)

- It is the distance from the axis of rotation where whole mass of the system is assumed to be concentrated such that MOI remains the same.
- For Discrete Mass System

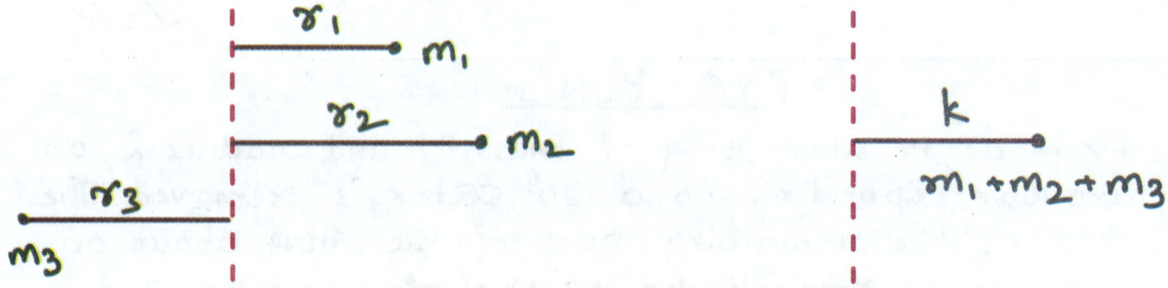

$$k = \sqrt{\frac{m_1 r_1^2 + m_2 r_2^2 + m_3 r_3^2 + \ldots}{m_1 + m_2 + m_3 + \ldots}}$$

- For a Continuous Mass System
  - Thin rod along center axis, $k = L/\sqrt{12}$
  - Ring along Center axis, $k = R$
  - Disc along Center axis, $k = R/\sqrt{2}$
  - Hollow sphere along central axis, $k = \sqrt{\frac{2}{3}}R$
  - Solid sphere along central axis, $k = \sqrt{\frac{2}{5}}R$

PYQ PUNCH

Q7. The ratio of the radius of gyration of a thin uniform disc about an axis passing through its centre and normal to its plane to the radius of gyration of the disc about its diameter is : (NEET 2022)

Sol. Radius of Gyration of disc about normal axis,

$$k_1 = R/\sqrt{2}$$

MOI of disc about diameter, $I = MR^2/4$

Radius of Gyration of disc about diameter,

$$k_2 = R/2$$

$$k_1 : k_2 = \sqrt{2} : 1$$

Kinetic Energy

Translation Motion	Rotational Motion	Rolling Motion
$T.K.E = \frac{1}{2}mv^2$	$R.K.E = \frac{1}{2}I\omega^2$	Total K.E = $\frac{1}{2}mv^2 + \frac{1}{2}I\omega^2$

- Total K.E $= \frac{1}{2}mv^2 + \frac{1}{2}I\omega^2$; $I = mk^2$; $\omega = v/r$

$$= \frac{1}{2}mv^2 + \frac{1}{2}mk^2 \times \frac{v^2}{r^2}$$

$$= \frac{1}{2}mv^2\left(1 + \frac{k^2}{r^2}\right)$$

where, k is the radius of gyration.

Total Kinetic Energy of Regular Bodies

Ring / Hollow Cylinder

- $k = R$
- Total K.E $= mv^2$

Disc / Solid Cylinder

- $k = R/\sqrt{2}$
- Total K.E $= \frac{3}{4}mv^2$

Hollow Sphere

- $k = R\sqrt{\frac{2}{3}}$
- Total K.E $= \frac{5}{6}mv^2$

Solid Sphere

- $k = R\sqrt{\frac{2}{5}}$
- Total K.E $= \frac{7}{10}mv^2$

PYQ PUNCH

Q8. A solid sphere is in rolling motion. In rolling motion, a body possesses translational kinetic energy K_t, as well as rotational kinetic energy K_r, simultaneously. The ratio $K_t : K_t + K_r$ for the sphere is : **(NEET 2018)**

Sol. For Sphere, $K_t = \frac{1}{2}mv^2$; $K_{total} = \frac{7}{10}mv^2$

$$\frac{K_t}{K_t + K_r} = \frac{5}{7}$$

Torque

- It is the measure of turning effect of force.
- Depends on the direction of action of force and the axis of rotation.

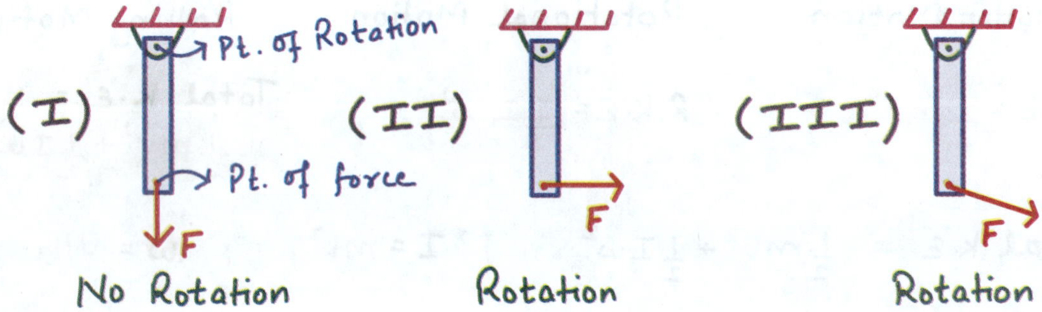

- $\vec{\tau} = \vec{r} \times \vec{F} = rF\sin\theta\,\hat{n}$

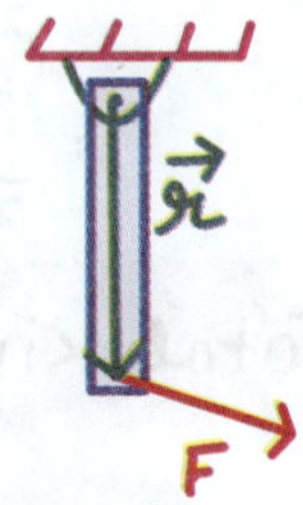

$\vec{r}$ is the position vector joining pt. of rotation and the pt. of force.

Tricks to solve Torque Questions

1. $\vec{r}$ and $\vec{F}$ both are given

- P: Point of force
- O: Point of Rotation
- Torque of Force F at pt. P around O is given by

$$\vec{\tau} = \vec{r} \times \vec{F}$$

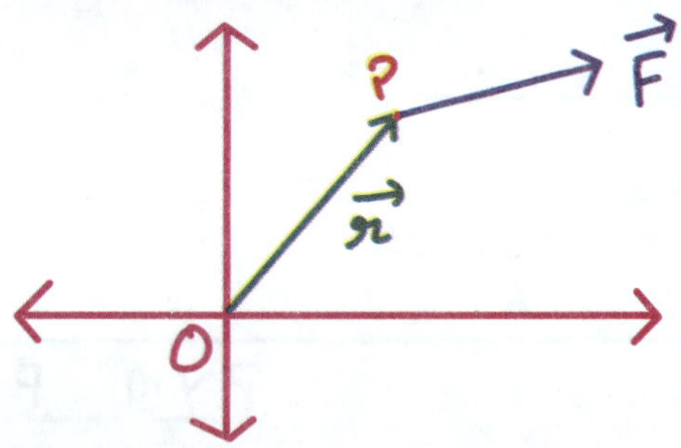

PYQ PUNCH

Q9. Find the torque about the origin when a force of $3\hat{j}$ N acts on the particle whose position vector is $2\hat{k}$ m. (NEET 2020)

Sol. $\vec{r} = 2\hat{k}$, $\vec{F} = 3\hat{j}$

$$\vec{\tau} = \vec{r} \times \vec{F}$$
$$= 2\hat{k} \times 3\hat{j} = -6\hat{i}\ \text{N-m}$$

2. Coordinates of pt. of force and rotation are given

- Step 1

  $\vec{r} = (x_2 - x_1)\hat{i} + (y_2 - y_1)\hat{j} + (z_2 - z_1)\hat{k}$
- Step 2

  $\vec{\tau} = \vec{r} \times \vec{F}$

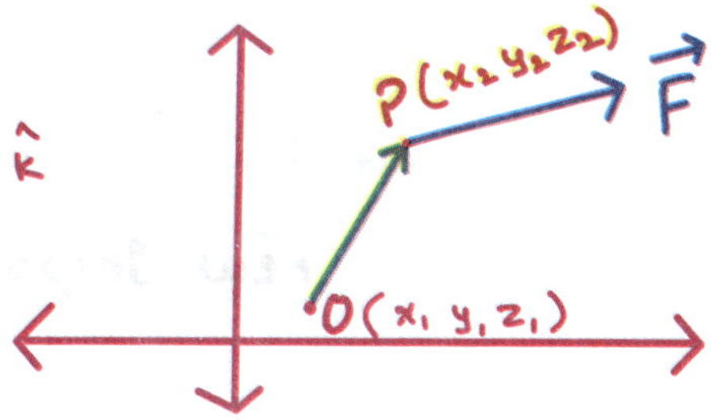

PYQ PUNCH

Q10. The moment of the force, $\vec{F} = 4\hat{i} + 5\hat{j} - 6\hat{k}$ N at (2, 0, −3), about the point (2, −2, −2), is given by (NEET 2018)

Sol.

$$\vec{r} = (x_2 - x_1)\hat{i} + (y_2 - y_1)\hat{j} + (z_2 - z_1)\hat{k}$$
$$= (2-2)\hat{i} + (0+2)\hat{j} + (-3+2)\hat{k}$$
$$= 2\hat{j} - \hat{k}$$

$$\vec{\tau} = \vec{r} \times \vec{F} \qquad \begin{array}{c} \\ \vec{r} \\ \vec{F} \end{array}\begin{vmatrix} \hat{i} & \hat{j} & \hat{k} \\ 0 & 2 & -1 \\ 4 & 5 & -6 \end{vmatrix}$$

$$\vec{\tau} = -7\hat{i} - 4\hat{j} - 8\hat{k}$$

3. Mag of r & F, and angle between them are given

- Torque of Force F at pt. P around O is given by

  $\tau = rF\sin\theta$

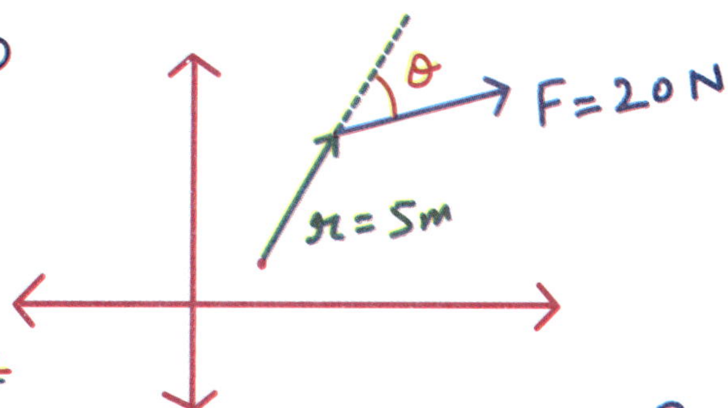

4. Force acting along a line

- Force acting at pt P along the line.
- Torque about pt O is given by

  $\tau = r_\perp F$

where $r_\perp = \left| \dfrac{ax_1 + by_1 + c}{\sqrt{a^2 + b^2}} \right|$

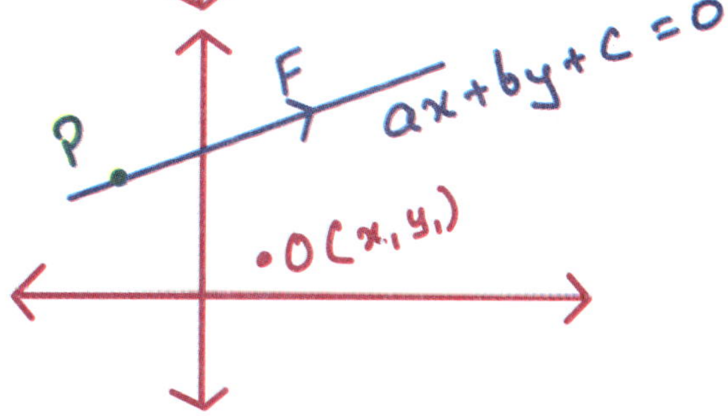

Relationship between torque and Angular Acceleration

- $\vec{\tau} = I\vec{\alpha}$
- I is calculated along the same axis where τ is calculated.

Few Important Relations

- $\vec{v} = \vec{\omega} \times \vec{r}$
- $v = \omega r$
- $\vec{a_t} = \vec{\alpha} \times \vec{r}$
- $a_t = \alpha r$
- $a_c = \omega^2 r$
- $a_{net} = \sqrt{a_t^2 + a_c^2}$

- For constant α
  - $\omega = \omega_0 + \alpha t$
  - $\theta = \omega_0 t + \frac{1}{2}\alpha t^2$
  - $\omega^2 = \omega_0^2 + 2\alpha\theta$

PYQ PUNCH

Q11. A rope is wound around a hollow cylinder of mass 3 kg and radius 40 cm. What is the angular acceleration of the cylinder, if the rope is pulled with a force of 30 N? **(NEET 2017)**

Sol. $\tau = rF$

$= .4 \times 30 = 12\text{ N}$

$I_{cyl} = MR^2 = 3 \times .4^2 = .48$

$\alpha = \tau / I$

$= 12/.48 = 25\text{ rad/s}^2$

Couple

- Even though the net force on a body is Zero, these forces may form a couple to rotate the body.
- Torque

  τ = Force × Distance btw them

  $= Fl$

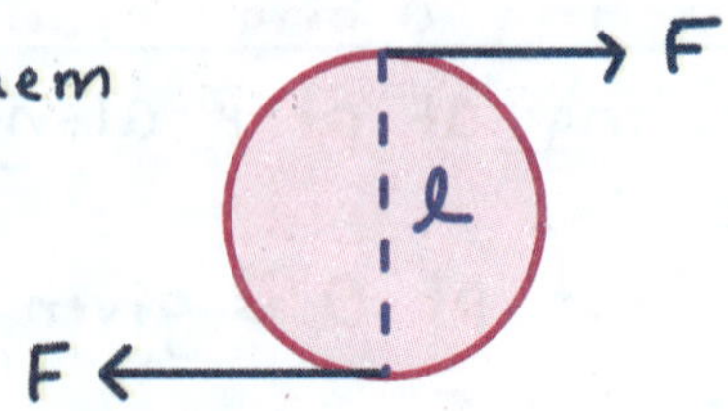

- This torque is independent of axis of rotation.

Equilibrium

- For a body to be in equilibrium
  - $F = 0$
  - $\tau = 0$

How to find Tension / Normal in Equilibrium

Rod attached to the strings

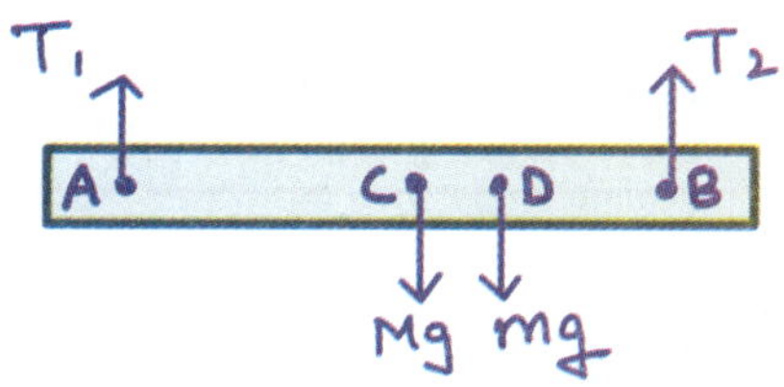

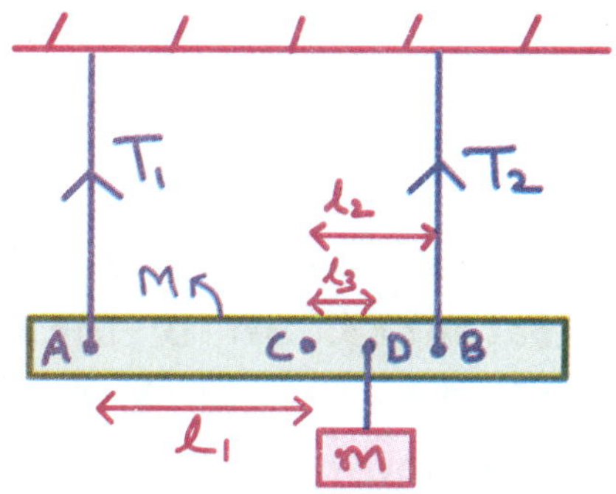

- $F = 0$

$\Rightarrow T_1 + T_2 = Mg + mg$

- $\tau_C = 0$

$\Rightarrow T_1 l_1 + mg l_3 = T_2 l_2$

$T_1 l_1 + mg l_3$ → Torque of forces acting upwards in left or acting downwards in right.

$T_2 l_2$ → Torque of forces acting upward in right or downward in left.

Rod placed on Wedges

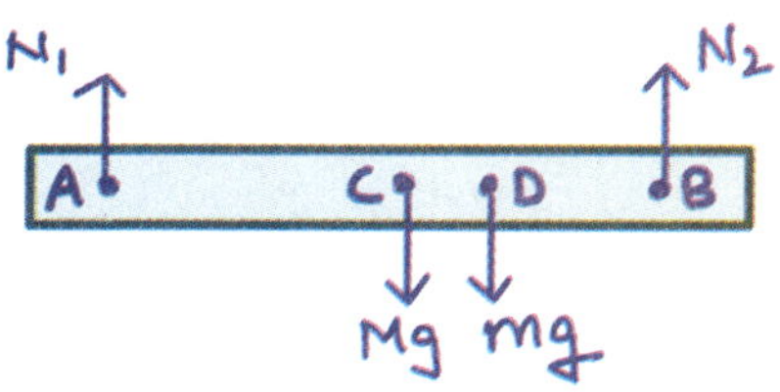

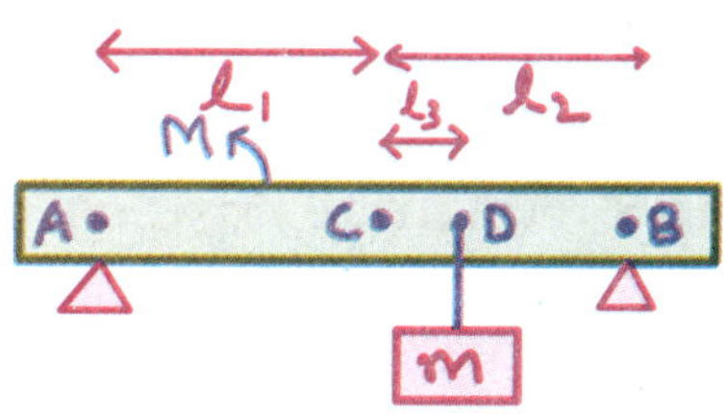

- $F = 0$

$N_1 + N_2 = Mg + mg$

- $\tau = 0$

$N_1 l_1 + mg l_3 = N_2 l_2$

Balancing on Single Wedge

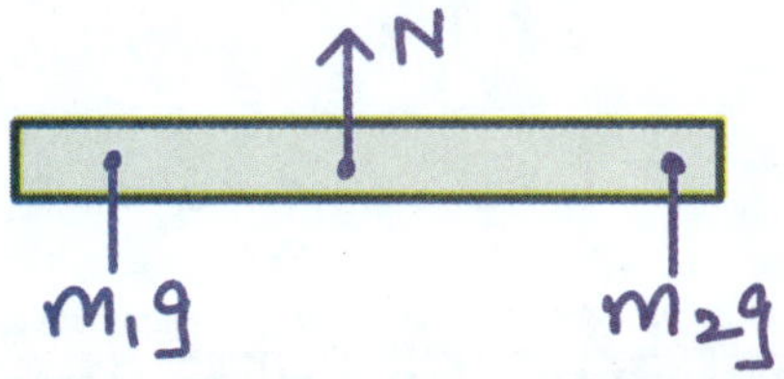

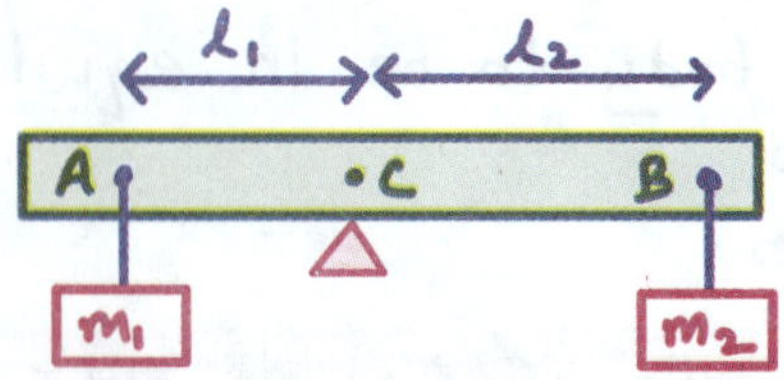

- $F = 0$
  $N = m_1g + m_2g$
- $\tau = 0$
  $m_1gl_1 = m_2gl_2$

$$m_1l_1 = m_2l_2$$

PYQ PUNCH

Q12. A uniform rod of length 200 cm and mass 500 g is balanced on a wedge placed at 40 cm mark. A mass of 2 kg is suspended from the rod at 20 cm and another unknown mass is suspended from the rod at 160 cm mark as shown in the figure. Find the value of m such that the rod is in equilibrium. (NEET 2021)

Sol.

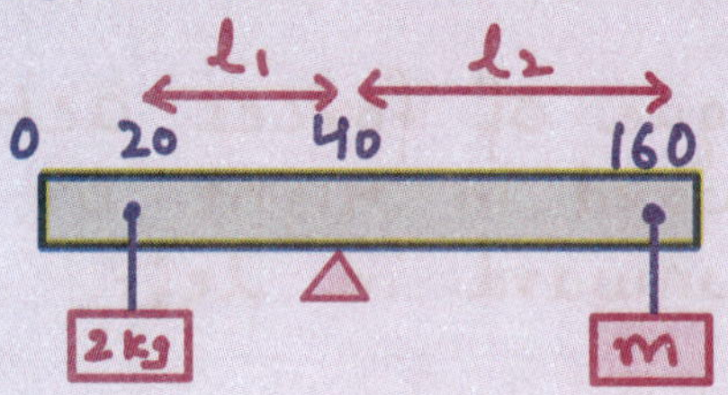

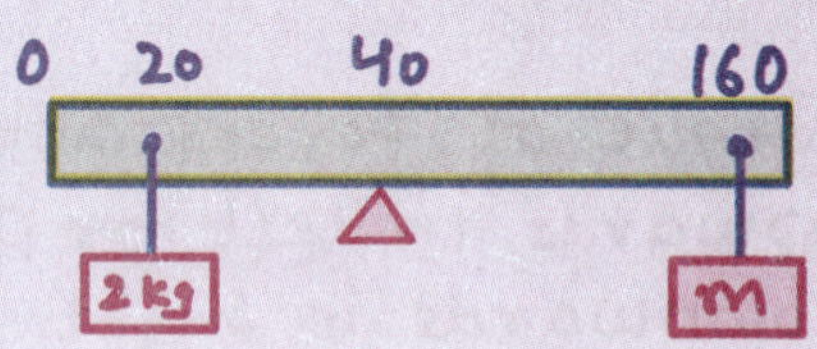

$m_1l_1 = m_2l_2$

$2 \times 20 = m \times 120$

$m = \frac{1}{3}$ kg

Angular Momentum ($\vec{L}$)

- It is the measure of motion contained in a rotating body about the point of rotation.

$$\vec{L} = \vec{r} \times \vec{p}$$

- A point mass or a particle can also has angular momentum.

Angular Momentum of a particle

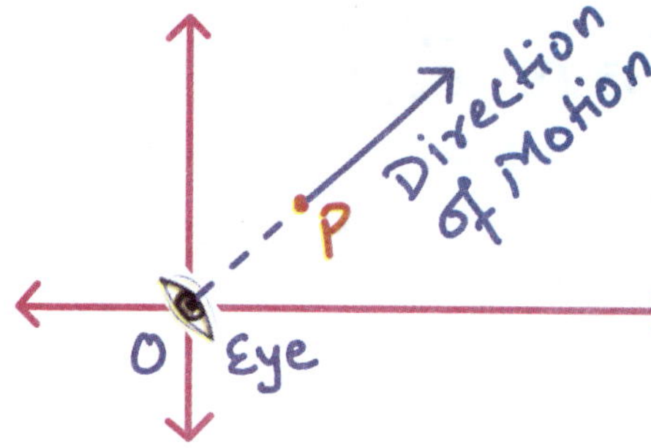

Linear Motion

- Eye ball remains in the same position while particle moving.
- $\vec{L}_0 = 0$

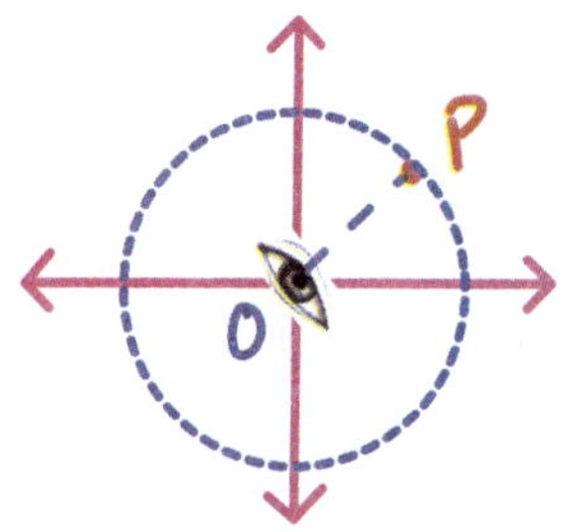

Pure Rotational Motion

- Eye ball keeps on rotating as the particle moves.
- Distance remains the same.
- $\vec{L}_0 = mr^2\vec{\omega}$

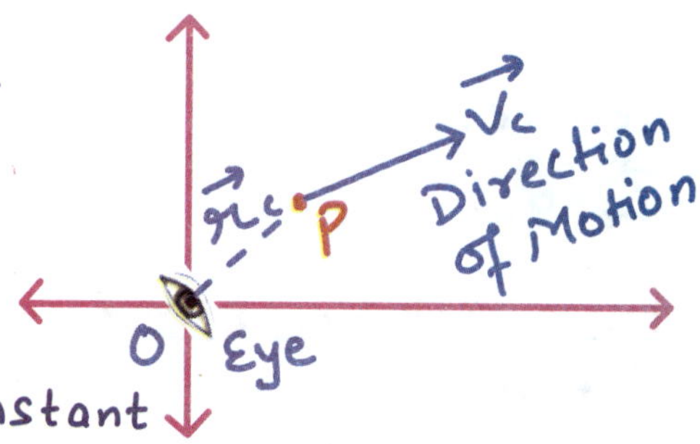

Rotational + Linear Motion

- Eye ball keeps on rotating as the particle moves.
- Distance keeps on changing.
- $\vec{L}_0 = \vec{r_c} \times \vec{p_c}$
- Angular momentum remains constant even the particle position changes.

MCQ PUNCH

Q13. A particle of mass m in the X-Y plane with a velocity v along the straight line AB. If the angular momentum of the particle with respect to origin O is L_A when it is at A and L_B when it is at B, then compare L_A and L_B.

Sol. Since particle moving in a straight line, hence

$L_A = L_B$

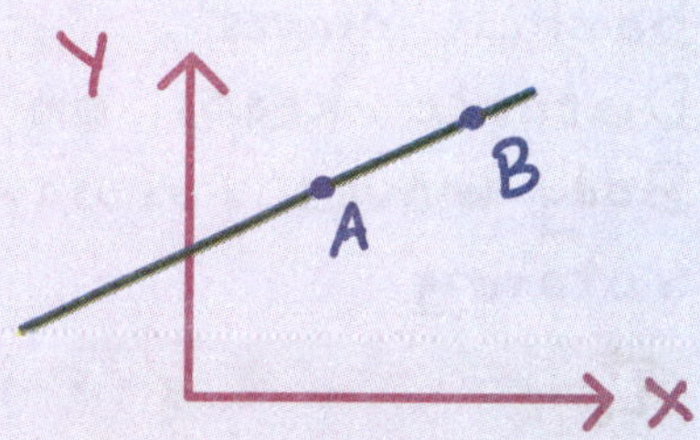

Angular Momentum of a Projectile

- $\vec{L}_o = m(\vec{r}_c \times \vec{v}_c)$

where

$\vec{r}_c = u\cos\theta t\,\hat{i} + (u\sin\theta t - \frac{1}{2}gt^2)\hat{j}$

$\vec{v}_c = u\cos\theta\,\hat{i} + (u\sin\theta - gt)\hat{j}$

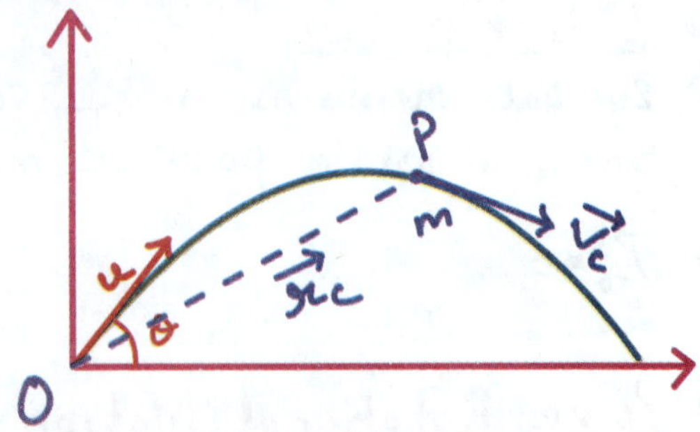

Angular Momentum of Continuous Body

Linear Motion

- Eye ball remains in the same position while body moving.
- Body not rotating around its centre.
- $\vec{L}_o = 0$

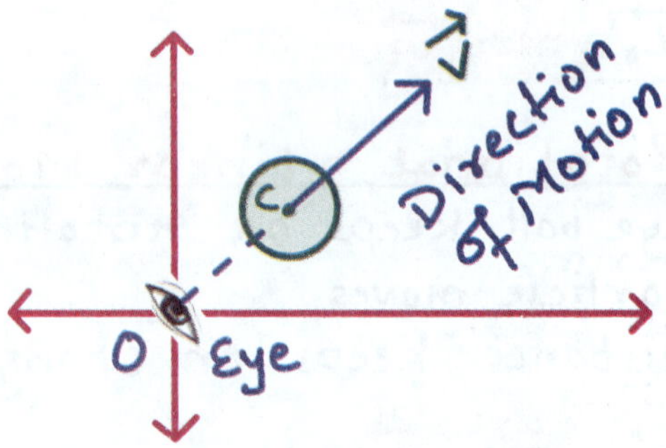

Pure Rotational Motion

- Eye ball keeps at the same place.
- Body rotating around its Centre of Mass.
- Centre of mass is stationary.
- $\vec{L}_o = I_c\vec{\omega}$

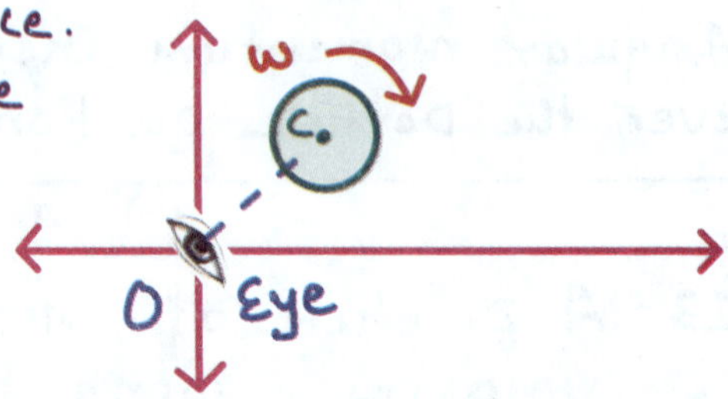

Rolling Motion

- Eye ball keeps on rotating as the particle moves.
- Distance keeps on changing.
- Body moves forward while rotating.
- $\vec{L}_o = I_c\vec{\omega} + \vec{r}_c \times \vec{p}_c$

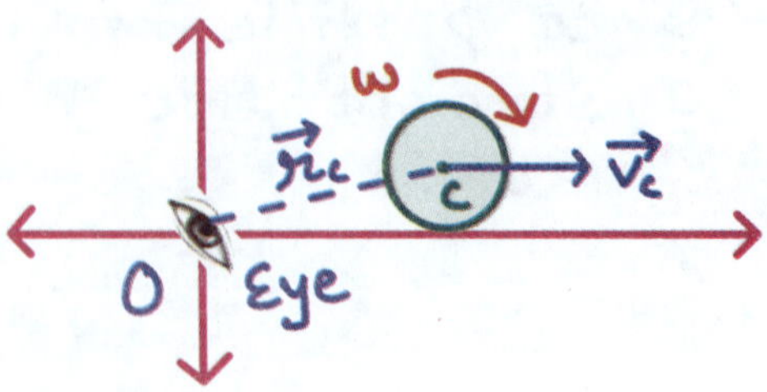

Conservation of Angular Momentum (CAM)

- Angular momentum is related to torque by

$$\vec{\tau}_{ext} = \frac{d\vec{L}}{dt}$$

- In the absence of external torque, angular momentum is conserved.

$$\vec{L_i} = \vec{L_f}$$

$$I_1\omega_1 = I_2\omega_2$$

$$m_1v_1r_1 = m_2v_2r_2$$

Few Important cases of CAM

Stone tied to a String passing through a table

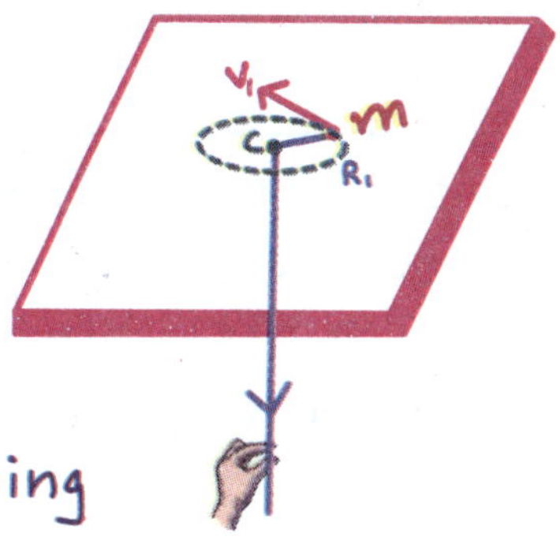

- Initially rotating with speed v_1 in a circle of radius R_1.
- String is pulled down so that radius of circle becomes R_2.
- Speed v_2 becomes $v_2 = \frac{v_1R_1}{R_2}$
- Initial and final tension in the string

$$T_1 = \frac{mv_1^2}{R_1} \quad \text{and} \quad T_2 = \frac{mv_2^2}{R_2}$$

- Ratio of $\frac{T_1}{T_2} = \left(\frac{R_2}{R_1}\right)^3$

Disc over disc

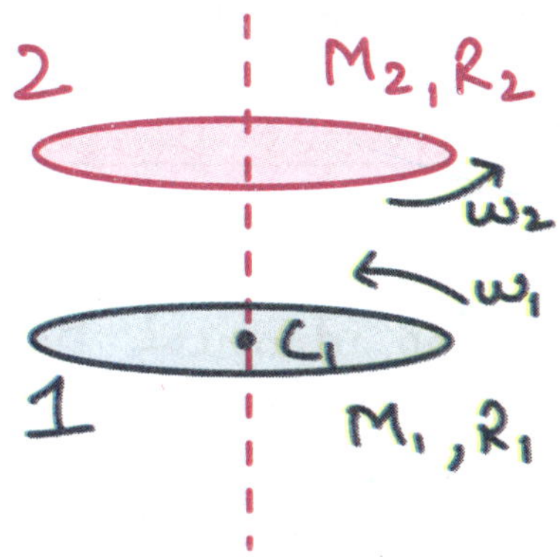

- Disc 1 is rotating with angular Speed ω_1 & Disc 2 with ω_2.
- When brought in contact, common angular speed becomes

$$\omega = \frac{I_1\omega_1 + I_2\omega_2}{I_1 + I_2} \rightarrow \omega_1 \text{ \& } \omega_2 \text{ in Same direction}$$

$$\omega = \frac{I_1\omega_1 - I_2\omega_2}{I_1 + I_2} \rightarrow \omega_1 \text{ \& } \omega_2 \text{ in opposite direction}$$

PYQ PUNCH

Q14. Two discs are rotating about their axes, normal to the disc and passing through the centres of the discs. Disc D_1 has 2 kg mass and 0.2m radius and initial angular velocity of 50 rad/s. Disc D_2 has 4 kg mass, 0.1 m radius and initial angular velocity of 200 rad/s. The two discs are brought in contact face to face, with their axes of rotation coincident. The final angular velocity of the System is (NEET 2013)

Sol. $I_1 = \frac{1}{2}M_1R_1^2 = \frac{1}{2}\times 2\times 0.2^2 = 0.04\ kgm^{-2}$

$I_2 = \frac{1}{2}M_2R_2^2 = \frac{1}{2}\times 4\times 0.1^2 = 0.02\ kgm^{-2}$

$$\omega = \frac{I_1\omega_1 + I_2\omega_2}{I_1+I_2} = \frac{0.04\times 50 + 0.02\times 200}{0.04+0.02} = 100\ rad/s$$

Disc placed gently over another rotating disc

- Disc 1 is rotating with angular Speed ω_0
- Disc 2 is placed gently over it.
- Common angular speed

$\omega_1 = \omega_0$ & $\omega_2 = 0$ $\quad \omega = \frac{I_1\omega_1}{I_1+I_2}$

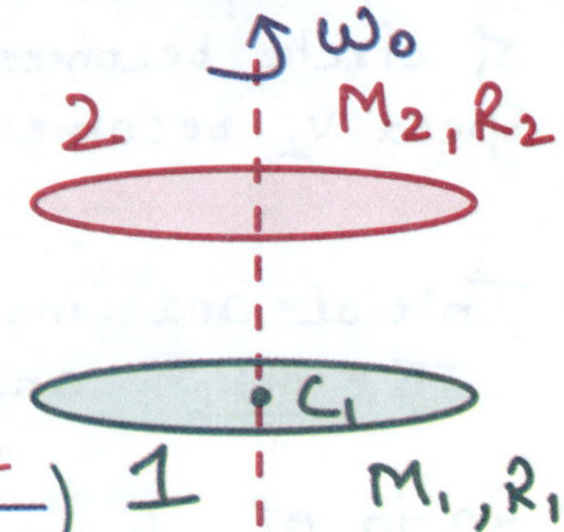

- $K.E_i = \frac{1}{2}I_1\omega_0^2$ $\quad$ o $K.E_f = \frac{1}{2}\left(\frac{I_1^2\omega_0^2}{I_1+I_2}\right)$
- Loss of Kinetic Energy $\Delta K.E. = \frac{1}{2}\left(\frac{I_1 I_2\omega_0^2}{I_1+I_2}\right)$

Particles placed at the end of rotating body

- Rod is rotating around its central axis with ω_0.
- Two identical particles are placed at its ends.
- Common angular speed

$$\omega = \frac{I_0\omega_0}{I_0+2I_m}$$

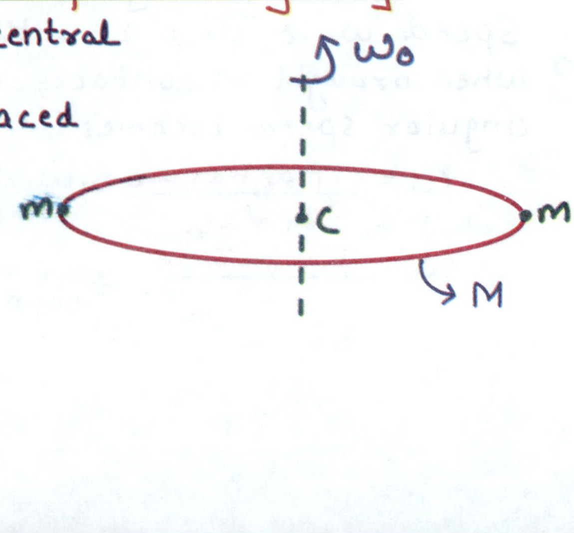

MCQ PUNCH

Q15. A thin circular ring of mass M and radius r is rotating about its axis with constant angular velocity ω. Two objects each of mass m are attached gently to the opposite ends of a diameter of the ring. The ring now rotates with angular velocity given by:

Sol. $I_0 = Mr^2$ $\quad I_m = mr^2$

$$\omega = \frac{Mr^2\omega}{Mr^2 + 2mr^2} = \frac{M\omega}{M+2m}$$

- **Relation with Rotational Kinetic Energy**
- $R.k.E = \dfrac{L^2}{2I}$

Work Done by Torque

- It is the work done in rotating a body.

Constant Torque	Variable Torque
◦ $W = \vec{\tau}.\vec{\theta}$ ◦ τ = Torque ◦ θ = Angular Displacement	◦ $\int dW = \int_{\theta_1}^{\theta_2} \vec{\tau}.d\vec{\theta}$

Rolling Motion

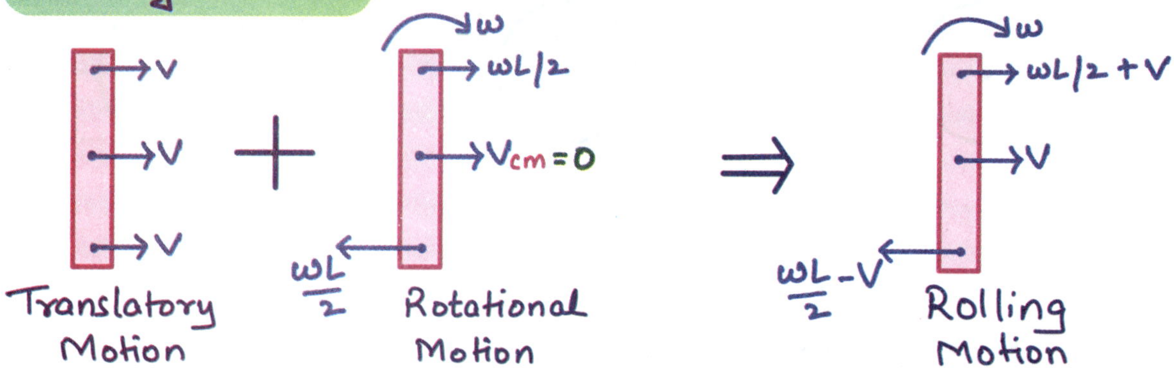

- Super-imposition of translatory motion and rotational motion gives Rolling Motion.

Pure Rolling Motion

- For pure rolling, speed of points of contact must be same.

$$V_P = V_{P'}$$

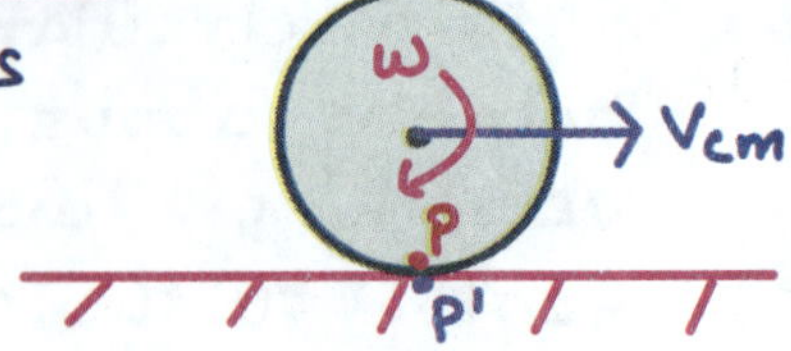

- If body is rolling on ground, then

$$V_P = V_{P'} = 0$$

$$V_{cm} = r\omega$$

- Speed at any point P on the rim is given by

$$V_P = 2\omega r \sin\frac{\theta}{2} = 2v\sin\frac{\theta}{2}$$

- And direction is perpendicular to line joining pt P with O.
- Speed of top point

$$V_T = 2v\sin\frac{180^\circ}{2} = 2v$$

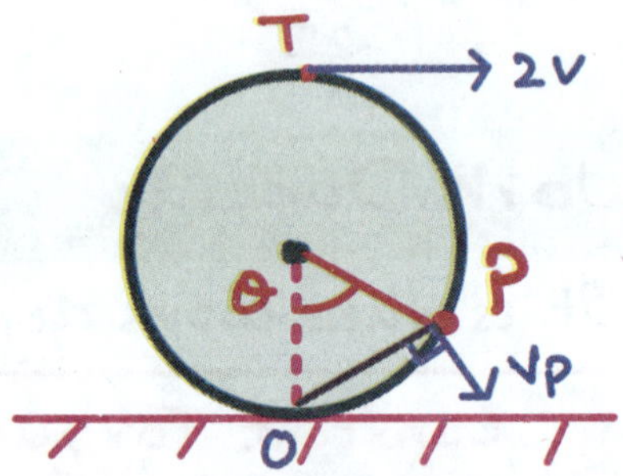

NEET Accelerate

- If $v = \omega r$, frictional force is 0 and pure rolling.
- If $v > \omega r$, frictional force is backward & kinetic.
- If $v < \omega r$, frictional force is forward & kinetic.

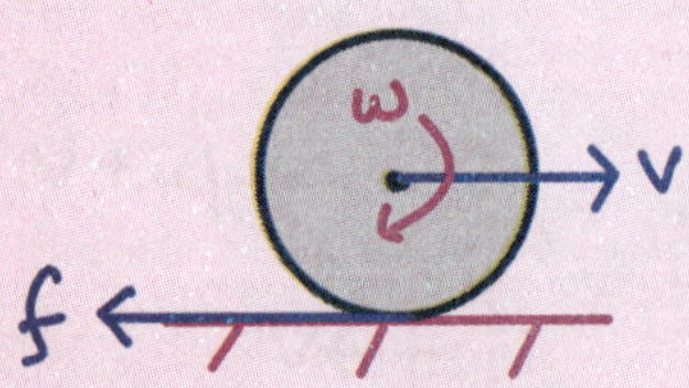

$V > \omega r$

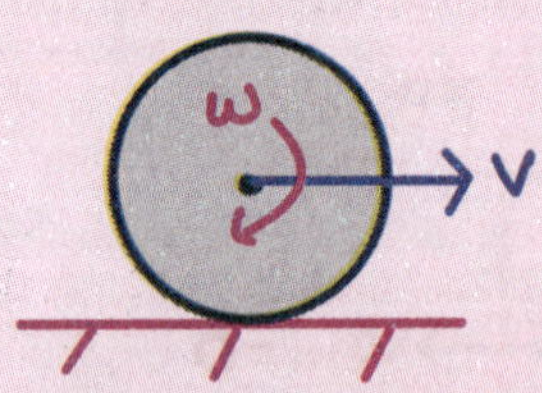

$V = \omega r$

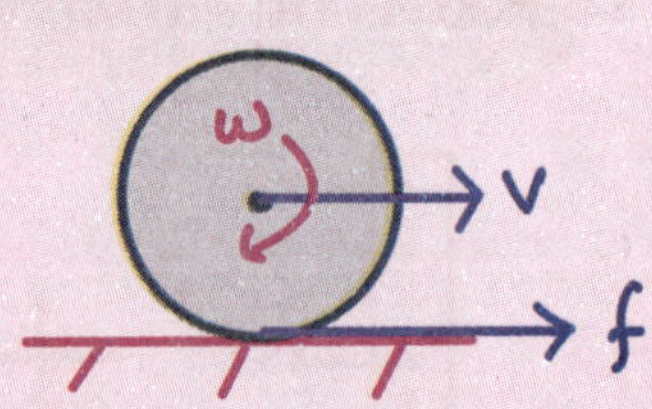

$V < \omega r$

- In a bicycle, friction acts forward on rear wheel while it is backward on front wheel.

Rolling Motion due to Ext Force on Rough Horizontal Surface

- $a_{cm} = \dfrac{FR(R+h)}{m(k^2+R^2)}$
- $f = -F\left(\dfrac{k^2-Rh}{k^2+R^2}\right)$

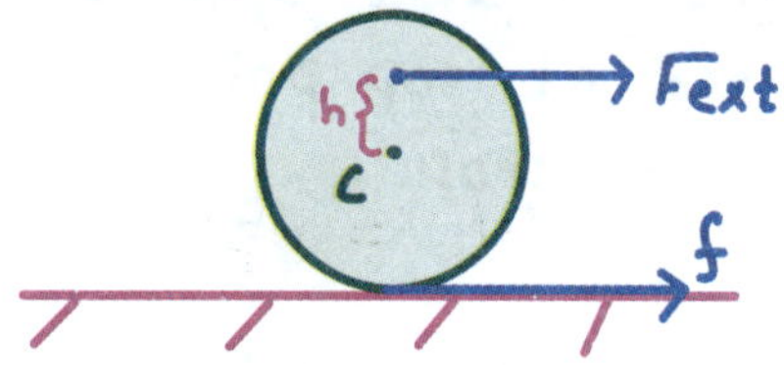

- $k^2 = Rh$
  - $f = 0$
  - No friction
  - Pure rolling
- $k^2 > Rh$
  - $f < 0$
  - Friction backward
  - Pure rolling
- $k^2 < Rh$
  - $f > 0$
  - Friction forward
  - Pure rolling

Rolling Motion on rough inclined plane

- Work done by friction is Zero.
- Acceleration, $a = \dfrac{g\sin\theta}{\left(1+\frac{k^2}{R^2}\right)}$ (Always Downward)
- Friction, $f_s = \dfrac{mg\sin\theta}{\left(1+\frac{R^2}{k^2}\right)}$ (Always Upward)

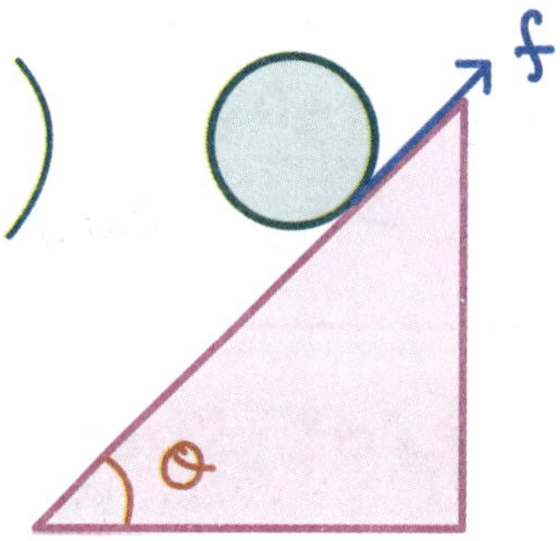

- Rolling Down
  - Friction acts upward.
  - Time to reach bottom. $t = \sqrt{\dfrac{2L}{g\sin\theta}\left(1+\dfrac{k^2}{R^2}\right)}$
  - Speed at bottom, $v = \sqrt{\dfrac{2gL\sin\theta}{\left(1+\frac{k^2}{R^2}\right)}}$

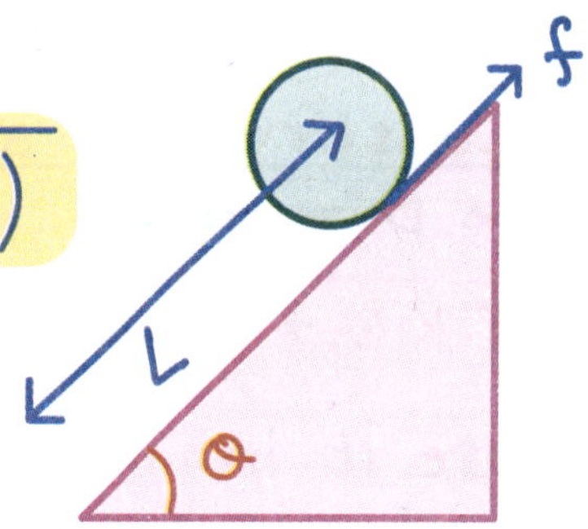

NEET Accelerate

- One who has larger k, has lesser acceleration and take more time to reach bottom.

$$t_{\text{ring or hollow cylinder}} > t_{\text{hollow sphere}} > t_{\text{disc or cylinder}} > t_{\text{sphere}}$$

Going up with Speed u

- Friction acts upward.
- Speed at top point = 0
- Time to stop $t = \frac{u}{g\sin\theta}\left(1+\frac{k^2}{r^2}\right)$
- Distance travelled on inclined plane

$$S = \frac{u^2}{2g\sin\theta}\left(1+\frac{k^2}{r^2}\right)$$

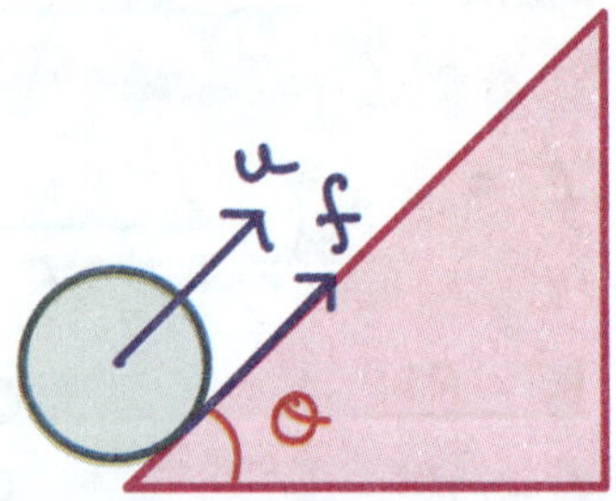

PYQ PUNCH

Q16. A solid cylinder of mass 2 kg and radius 50 cm rolls up an inclined plane of angle inclination 30°. The centre of mass of cylinder has speed of 4 m/s. The distance travelled by the cylinder on the inclined surface will be (Take g = 10 m/s²). (NEET 2019)

Sol. $r = 0.5m$; $\theta = 30°$; $m = 2kg$; $u = 4m/s$; $k = R/\sqrt{2}$

$$S = \frac{u^2}{2g\sin\theta}\left(1+\frac{k^2}{r^2}\right) = \frac{4^2}{2\times10\times\sin30°}\left(1+\frac{1}{2}\right) = 2.4m$$

Use of Special Theorems to solve questions

- Jaha kuch samajh na aae waha inhe lagaye.

Conservation of Mechanical Energy (COME)

- In pure rolling, work done by friction is zero.
- $T.K.E_i + R.K.E_i + P.E_i = T.K.E_f + R.K.E_f + P.E_f$
- Use it in inclined/curved surface questions.

Work Energy Theorem (WET)

- In case of external torque or frictional torque, apply WET.
- $T.K.E_f + R.K.E_f - T.K.E_i - R.K.E_i = W.D_{\text{all forces}}$

PYQ PUNCH

Q17. A disc of radius 2m and mass 100 kg rolls on a horizontal floor. Its centre of mass has speed of 20 cm/s. How much work is needed to stop it? (NEET 2019)

Sol. $u = 0.2\,m/s \qquad k = r/\sqrt{2}$

Since Work Done by external force, apply WET

$T.K.E_f + R.K.E_f - T.K.E_i - R.K.E_i = W.D_{\text{all forces}}$

$0 + 0 - \frac{1}{2}mu^2 - \frac{1}{2}mk^2\frac{u^2}{r^2} = W.D$

$\Rightarrow -\frac{1}{2}\times 100\times(.2)^2\left(1+\frac{1}{2}\right) = W.D = -3J$

Q18. A solid cylinder of mass 2 kg and radius 4 cm is rotating about its axis at the rate of 3 rpm. The torque required to stop after 2π revolutions is (NEET 2019)

Sol. $\omega = \frac{2\pi}{60}\times 3 = \frac{\pi}{10}\,rad/s. \quad ; \quad r = 0.04\,m$

$I = \frac{mr^2}{2} = \frac{2\times 0.04^2}{2} = 0.0016 \quad ; \quad \theta = 2\pi\times 2\pi = 4\pi^2\,rad$

Since external torque is required, apply WET.

$T.K.E_f + R.K.E_f - T.K.E_i - R.K.E_i = W.D_{\text{all forces}}$

$0 + 0 - 0 - \frac{1}{2}I\omega^2 = -\tau\theta$

$\Rightarrow -\frac{1}{2}\times 0.0016\times\frac{\pi^2}{100} = -\tau\times 4\pi^2$

$\Rightarrow 2\times 10^{-6}\,Nm = \tau$

Q19. A small object of uniform density rolls up a curved surface with an initial velocity u. It reaches upto a maximum height of $3u^2/4g$ with respect to the initial position. The object is (NEET 2013)

Sol. Apply COME

$T.K.E_i + R.K.E_i + P.E_i = T.K.E_f + R.K.E_f + P.E_f$

$\frac{1}{2}mu^2 + \frac{1}{2}mk^2\frac{u^2}{r^2} + 0 = 0 + 0 + mgh$

$\Rightarrow u^2\left(1+\frac{k^2}{r^2}\right) = 2g\times\frac{3u^2}{4g} \Rightarrow 1+\frac{k^2}{r^2} = \frac{3}{2}$

$\Rightarrow k = r/\sqrt{2}$ Hence, a Disc.

12. Gravitation

Gravitational Force

- An attractive force due to mass.
- Weakest fundamental force
- Long range
- Conservotive force i.e. its work is path independent.
- Follows inverse square law i.e. $F \propto \frac{1}{r^2}$
- Doesn't depend upon the medium.

Newton's Law of Gravitation

$$F = \frac{Gm_1m_2}{r^2}$$

$$\vec{F}_{21} = \frac{Gm_1m_2}{|r^3|}\vec{r}_{12}$$

$$\vec{F}_{12} = \frac{Gm_1m_2}{|r^3|}\vec{r}_{21}$$

where $G = 6.67 \times 10^{-11}\ kg^{-1}m^3s^{-2}$ called as Universal Gravitational Constant

Validity of Gravitational Law

2 point bodies	2 spherical bodies	A spherical body and a point body
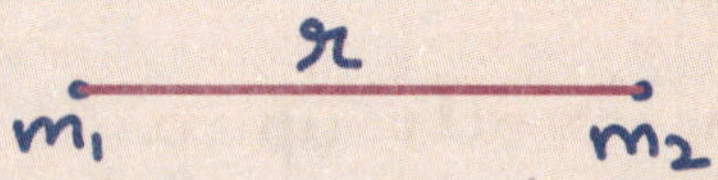		
$F = \frac{Gm_1m_2}{r^2}$	$F = \frac{Gm_1m_2}{r^2}$	$F = \frac{Gm_1m_2}{r^2}$

Superposition Theorem

- Force between two masses doesn't get affected by the presence of any third mass.
- Net force on a particle is vector addition of all the forces acting on a particle.

$$\vec{F}_{net} = \vec{F}_1 + \vec{F}_2 + \vec{F}_3 + \ldots$$

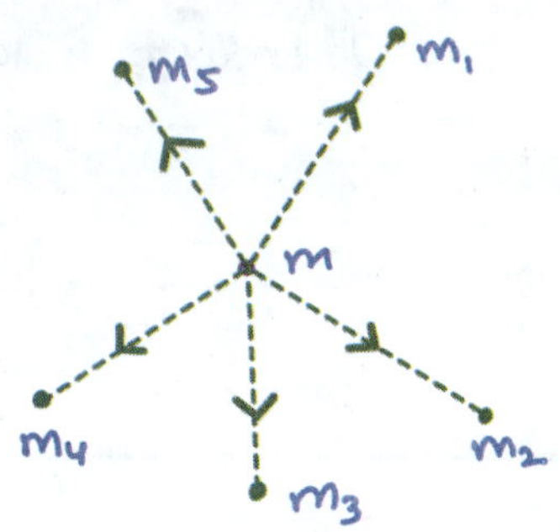

Net force on a particle

- **Particle placed at the centre of equilateral triangle**

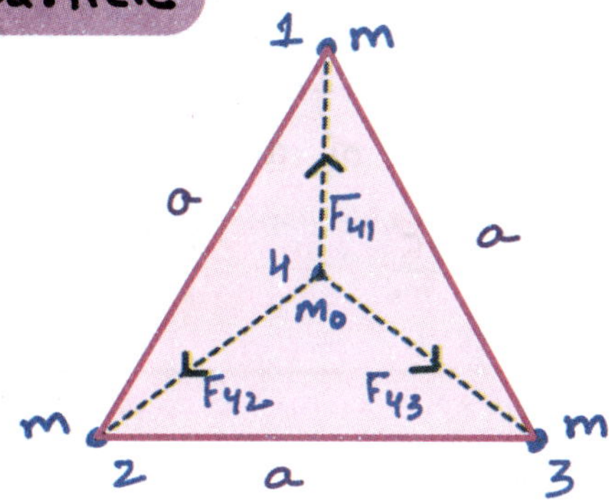

$|\vec{F_{41}}| = |\vec{F_{42}}| = |\vec{F_{43}}| = F$

$F_{net} = 0$

- **Particle placed at the centre of the square**

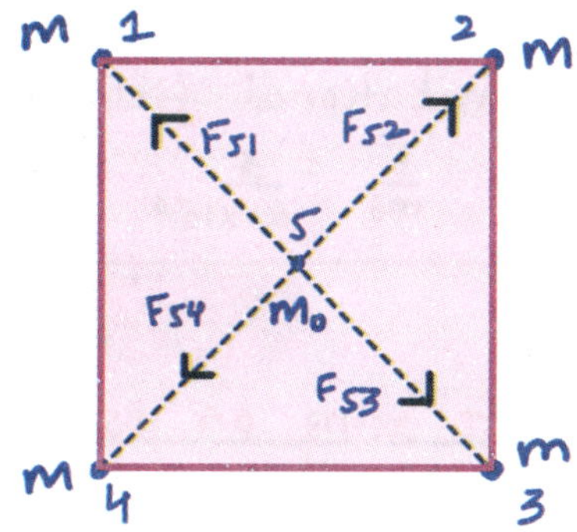

$|\vec{F_{51}}| = |\vec{F_{52}}| = |\vec{F_{53}}| = |\vec{F_{54}}| = F$

$F_{net} = 0$

- **Particle placed at the vertex of equilateral triangle**

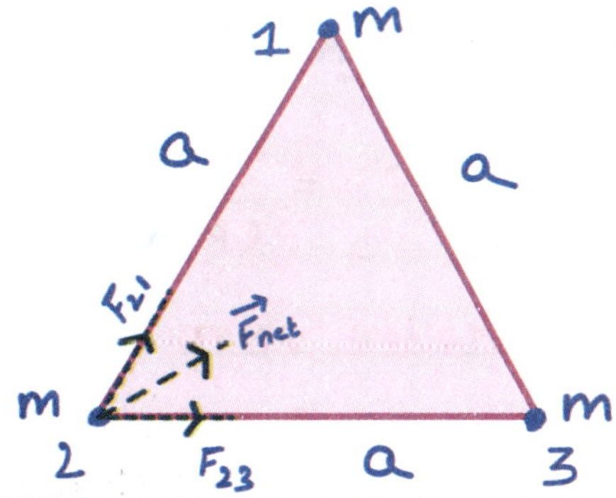

$|\vec{F_{21}}| = |\vec{F_{23}}| = F$

$$F_{net} = 2F\cos 30^\circ = \frac{\sqrt{3}\,Gm^2}{a^2}$$

NEET Accelerate

- For a regular polygon having equal masses placed at its vertices, net force is zero at the centre.
- If one mass is removed from the vertex of regular polygon, net force is then equal and opposite to the force at centre due to removed mass.

Gravitational Field

- It is a region around a mass in which its influence can be felt by other masses.

Gravitational Field Intensity ($\vec{E}$)

- It is the force experienced by a unit mass m_0 placed under the field of another mass m.

$\vec{E} = \frac{\vec{F}}{m_0}$; $|\vec{E}| = \frac{Gm}{r^2}$

PYQ PUNCH

Q1. A body of mass 60 g experiences a gravitational force of 3.0 N, when placed at a particular point. The magnitude of gravitational field intensity at that point is : (NEET 2022)

Sol. $E = \frac{F}{m_0} = \frac{3}{60 \times 10^{-3}} = 50$ N/kg

G. Field of Some Continuous Bodies

Due to ring on its axis

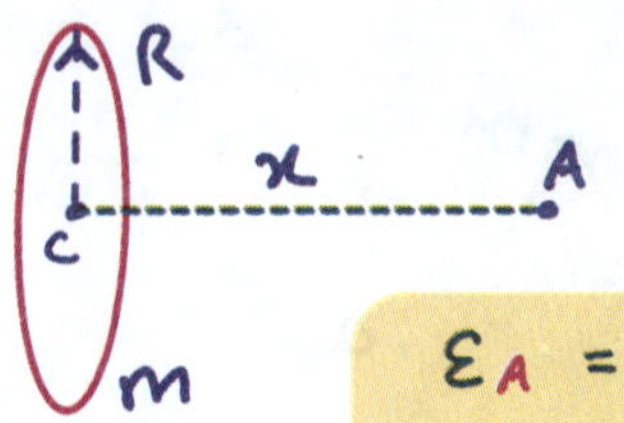

$$E_A = \frac{GMx}{(R^2+x^2)^{3/2}}$$

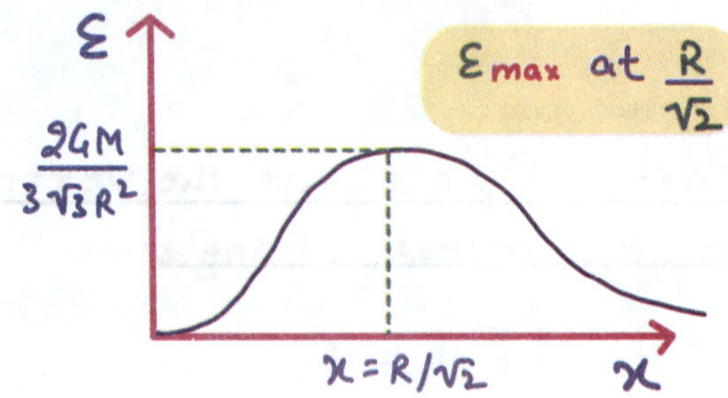

E_{max} at $\frac{R}{\sqrt{2}}$

Due to Hollow Sphere

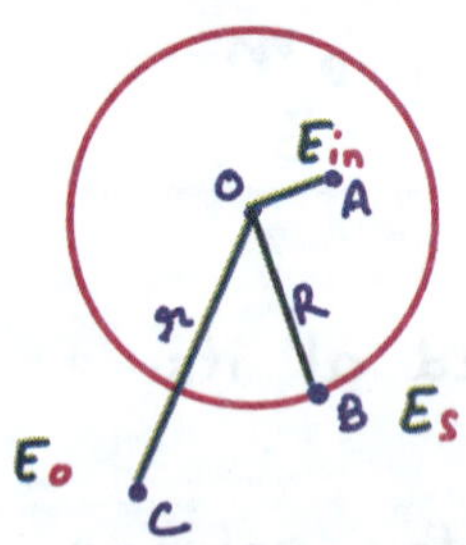

E_{out} $(E_o) = \frac{GM}{r^2}$

$E_{surface}$ $(E_s) = \frac{GM}{R^2}$

E_{inside} $(E_{in}) = 0$

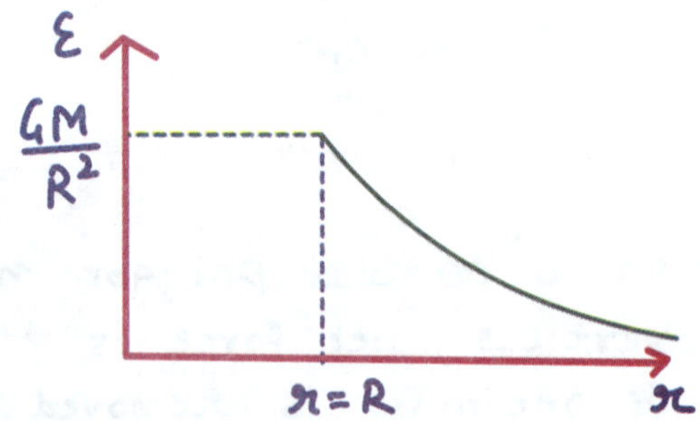

Due to Solid Sphere

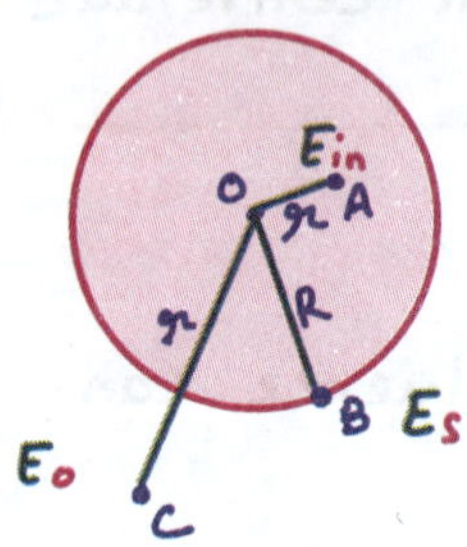

E_{out} $(E_o) = \frac{GM}{r^2}$

$E_{surface}$ $(E_s) = \frac{GM}{R^2}$

E_{inside} $(E_{in}) = \frac{GMr}{R^3}$

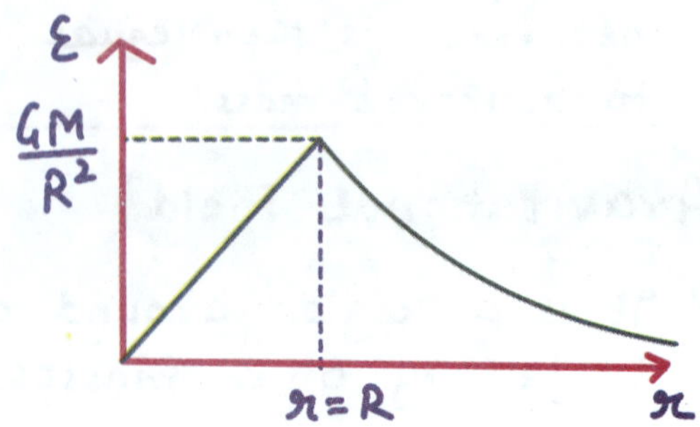

NEET Accelerate

- G. Force depends upon both the masses while G. Field is of individual mass.
- Indirectly G. Field measures the strength of mass to attract other masses.

Acceleration due to Gravity

- It is the acceleration of an object due to the G. Force of larger objects like planets, stars etc.
- In simple language, it is the Electric field intensity of large objects.
- It varies from place to place.

On surface

$$g = \frac{GM_e}{R_e^2} = \frac{4}{3}\pi R_e G \rho$$

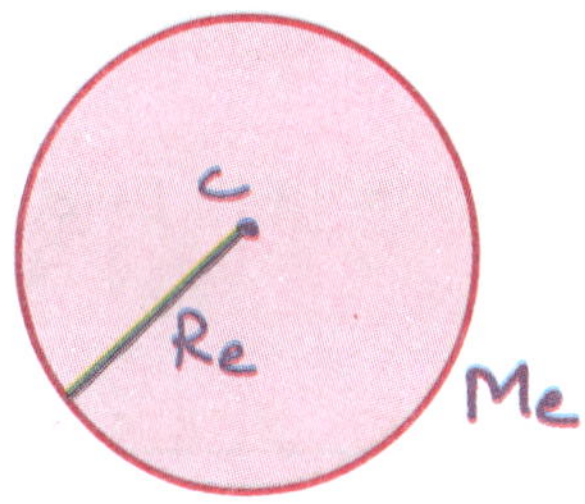

$M_e =$ constant: $g \propto \frac{1}{R_e^2}$

$\rho =$ constant: $g \propto R_e$

PYQ PUNCH

Q2. The mass of the planet is $\frac{1}{10}$ that of Earth and its diameter is half of the earth. The acceleration due to gravity on that planet is ? (NEET 2024)

Sol. $M_p = \frac{1}{10} M_e$; $R_p = \frac{1}{2} R_e$; $g = \frac{GM}{R^2}$

$$\Rightarrow \frac{g_p}{g_e} = \frac{M_p}{M_e} \times \left(\frac{R_e}{R_p}\right)^2 \Rightarrow g_p = 3.92 \text{ m/s}^2$$

Above Surface

- $g_h = \frac{g}{\left(1+\frac{h}{R_e}\right)^2}$; $W_h = \frac{W}{\left(1+\frac{h}{R_e}\right)^2}$

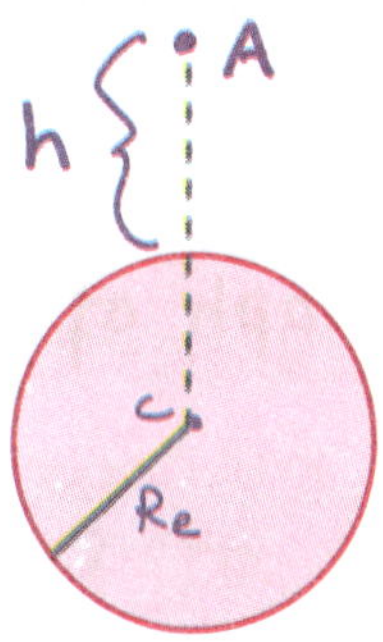

- For $h \lll R_e$

$g_h = g\left[1 - \frac{2h}{R_e}\right]$; $W_h = W\left[1 - \frac{2h}{R_e}\right]$

where W and W_h are the weight at surface of the Earth and at height h.

MCQ PUNCH

Q3. A body weighs 72 N on the surface of the Earth. What is the gravitational force on it, at a height equal to half the radius of the Earth ?

Sol. For h comparable to R_e,

$$W_h = \frac{W}{\left(1+\frac{h}{R_e}\right)^2} \Rightarrow W_h = \frac{72}{\left(1+\frac{R_e}{2R_e}\right)^2} = 32\text{ N}$$

Below Surface

$$g_d = g\left[1-\frac{d}{R_e}\right]$$

$$W_d = W\left[1-\frac{d}{R_e}\right]$$

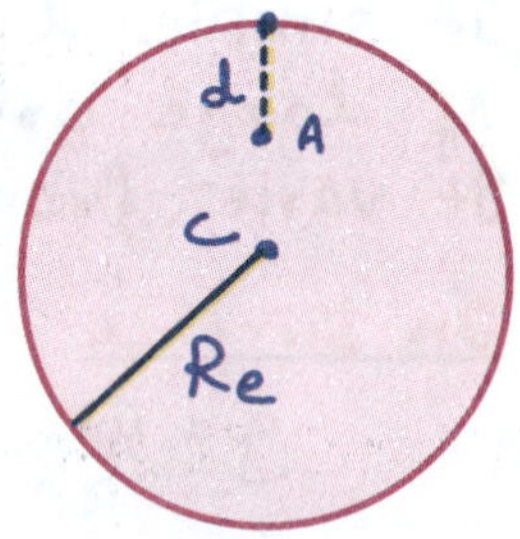

Due to Shape of the Earth

$R_E > R_P$

$\Rightarrow g_E < g_P$

$\Rightarrow W_E < W_P$

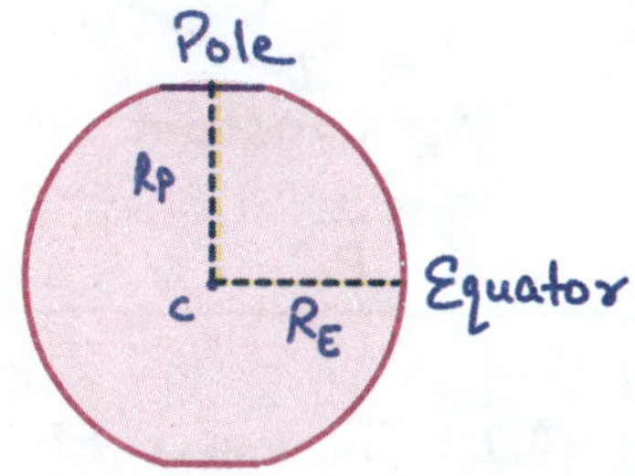

Due to Rotation of Earth

$$g_A = g - \omega^2 R\cos^2\theta$$

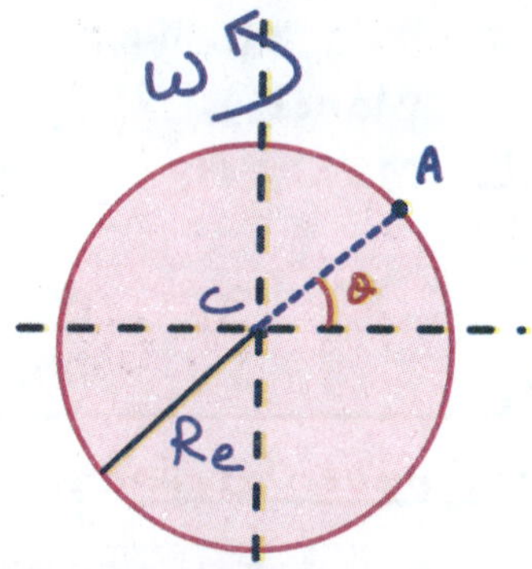

- $g \downarrow$ due to rotation
- $g_{eq} = g - \omega^2 R$
- $g_{pole} = g$
- For T= 84.6 min i.e. if Earth rotates 17 times its present rotational speed then objects becomes weightless.

Graph of variation of g with distance r

- r is measured from the centre of Earth till infinity.

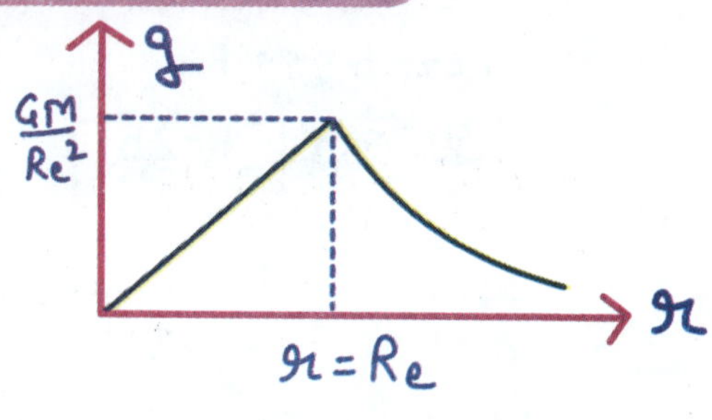

Change of G. Potential Energy (ΔU)

- It is the negative of Work done by gravitational force in changing the position.

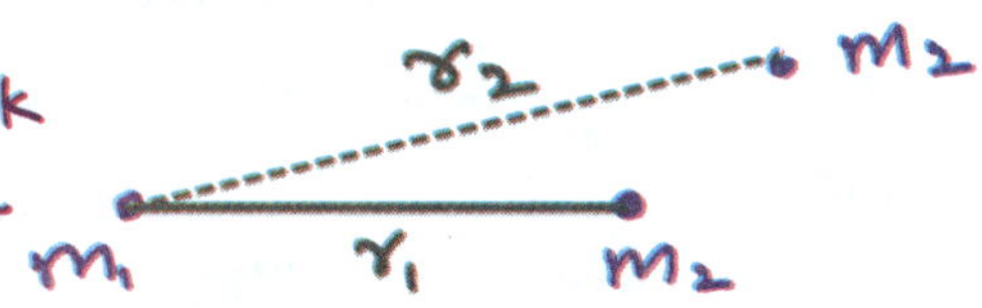

$$\Delta U = -W_g = -Gm_1m_2\left(\frac{1}{r_2} - \frac{1}{r_1}\right)$$

r_1 : Initial Separation
r_2 : Final Separation

G. Potential Energy (U)

- It is the negative of Work done by gravitational force while bringing a particle from infinity to a particular distance r.

$$U = -\frac{Gm_1m_2}{r}$$

(−) Indicates The force is attractive

Potential Energy of Earth - mass System

- PE at a height h from Earth's Surface

$$P.E = \cancel{mgh}\ -\frac{GMm}{R+h}$$

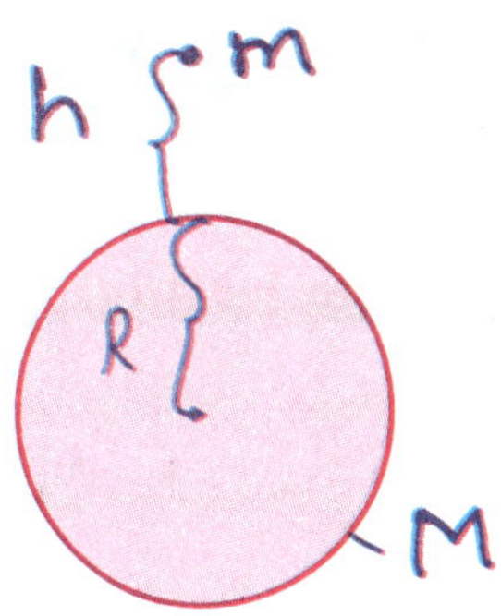

- For $h << R$

$\Delta U = mgh$ ← (Don't use this in this chapter)

- mgh is the change of PE rather than just P.E.

- Work Done to raise a mass by height h

$W.D = U_f - U_i$

PYQ PUNCH

Q4. The work done to raise a mass m from the surface of the earth to a heigh h, which is equal to the radius of the Earth is? (NEET 2019)

Sol. $W.D = U_f - U_i$

$$= -\frac{GMm}{R+R} - \left(-\frac{GMm}{R}\right)$$

$$= \frac{GMm}{2R} = \frac{mgR}{2}$$

Gravitational Potential (V)

- Just like G. Field, it also represents the strength of a mass but in scalar form.

$$V_P = -\frac{Gm}{r}$$

- Being a scalar quantity, it simply gets added.

$$V_P = -\frac{Gm_1}{r_1} - \frac{Gm_2}{r_2} - \frac{Gm_3}{r_3}$$

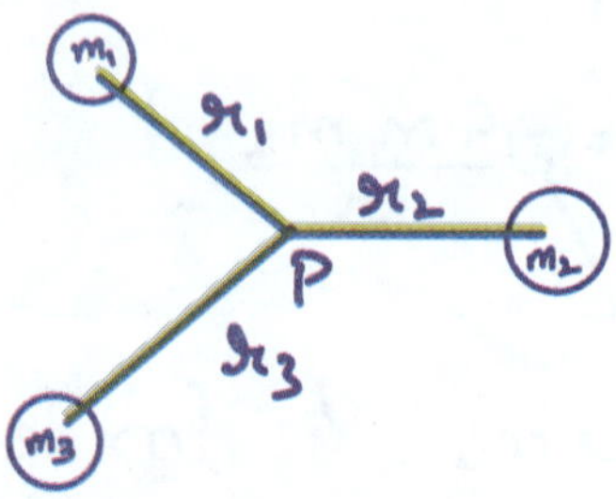

Potential of Some Continuous Bodies

- **Due to ring on its axis**

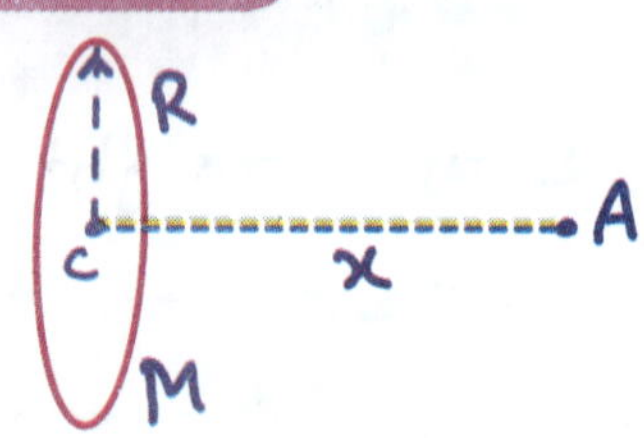

$$V_A = -\frac{GM}{(R^2+x^2)^{1/2}} \quad ; \quad V_{centre} = -\frac{GM}{R}$$

- **Due to hollow Sphere**

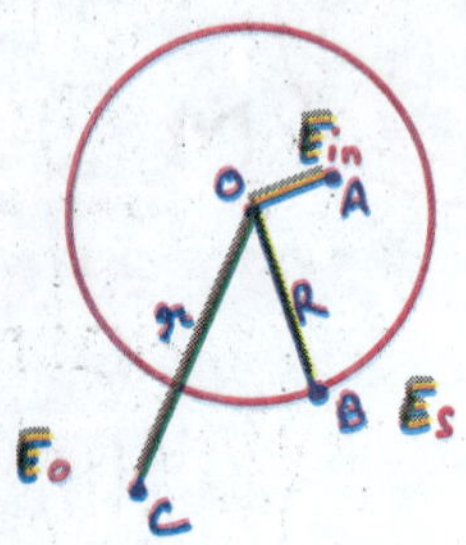

$$V_{out}\ (V_o) = -\frac{GM}{r}$$

$$V_{surface}\ (V_s) = -\frac{GM}{R}$$

$$V_{inside}\ (V_{in}) = -\frac{GM}{R}$$

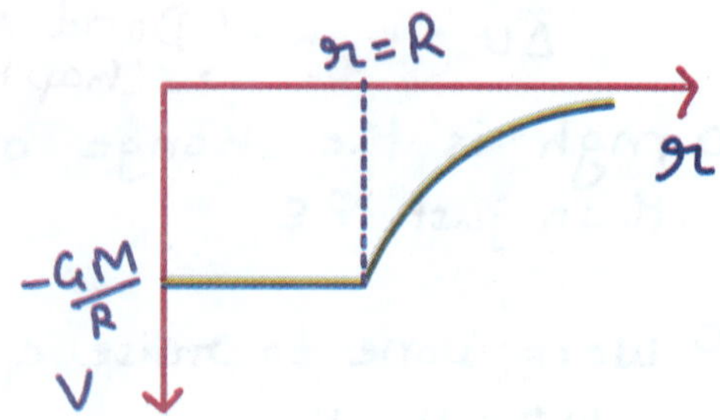

Due to Solid Sphere

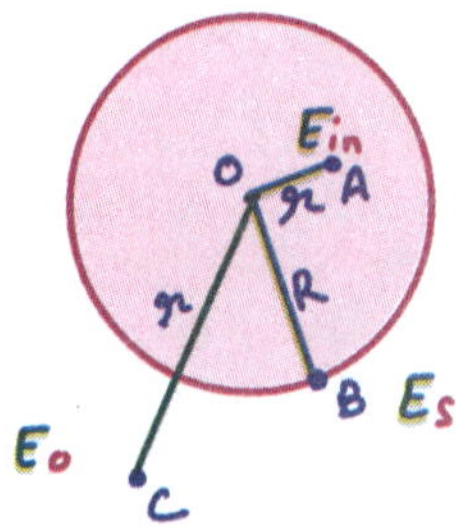

$$V_{out}\ (V_o) = -\frac{GM}{r}$$

$$V_{surface}\ (V_s) = -\frac{GM}{R}$$

$$V_{inside}\ (V_{in}) = -\frac{GM}{2R^3}\left(3R^2 - r^2\right)$$

$$V_{centre}\ (V_c) = -\frac{3GM}{2R}$$

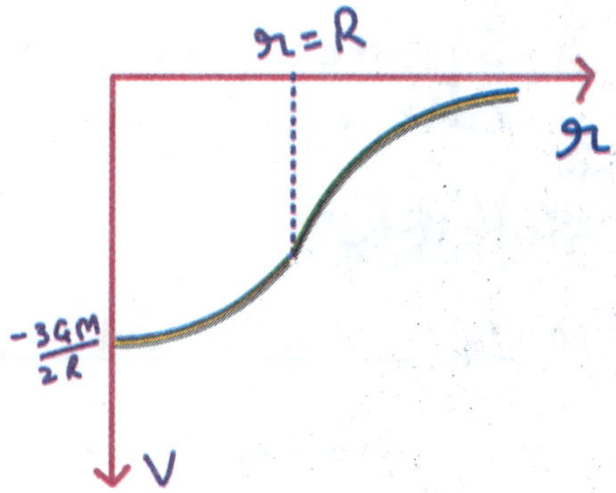

Kepler's Laws

1. All planets revolve around the sun in an elliptical orbit with sun at one of its foci.

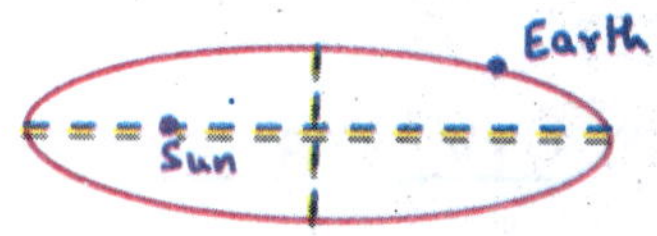

Conclusions

- Distance of the planet from the sun varies as its revolves.

2. Radius vector joining the Sun and the planet sweeps equal area in equal time.

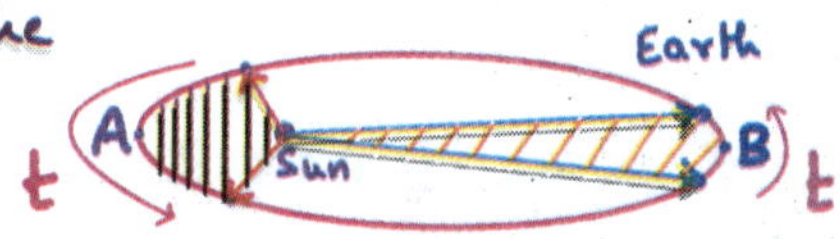

Conclusions

- Speed depends upon the distance. Lesser the distance more the speed. It is max at A and minimum at B.
- Rate of change of Area is constant.

$$\frac{dA}{dt} = \frac{L}{2m} = \text{constant}$$, where L is angular momentum.

PYQ PUNCH

Q5. The kinetic energies of a planet in an elliptical orbit about the sun, at positions A, B and C are k_A, k_B and k_C respectively. AC is the major axis and SB is perpendicular to AC at the position of the sun S as shown in the figure. Arrange energies in increasing order. (NEET 2018)

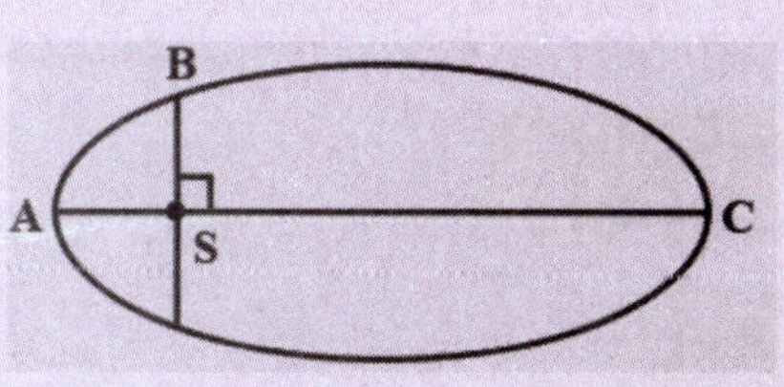

Sol. $V_o \propto \frac{1}{\text{Distance}}$

$V_A > V_B > V_C$

$k_A > k_B > k_C$

3. Square of the time period is directly proportional to cube of the semi-major axis.

Satellite

◎ Orbiting in an orbit of radius r.

Orbital Speed

$$V_o = \sqrt{\frac{GM}{r}}$$

Time Period

$$T = \frac{2\pi r^{3/2}}{\sqrt{GM}} \quad \text{or} \quad T^2 \propto r^3$$

◎ Orbiting near to Earth's Surface i.e. $r = R$

Orbital Speed

$$V_o = \sqrt{\frac{GM}{R}} = \sqrt{gR}$$

$$= \sqrt{\frac{4}{3}\pi G\rho}\, R$$

Time Period

$$T^2 = \frac{4\pi^2 R^3}{GM} = \frac{4\pi^2 R}{g}$$

$$= \frac{3\pi}{G\rho}$$

PYQ PUNCH

Q 6. A satellite is orbiting just above the surface of the Earth with period T. If d is the density of the earth and G is the universal constant of gravitation, the quantity $\frac{3\pi}{Gd}$ represents ? (NEET 2023)

Sol. $T^2 = \frac{3\pi}{Gd}$

Energy of Satellite

- $U = -\frac{GMm}{R+h}$
- $KE = \frac{GMm}{2(R+h)}$
- $TE = U + KE = -\frac{GMm}{2(R+h)}$
- $PE = 2\,TE = -2\,KE$

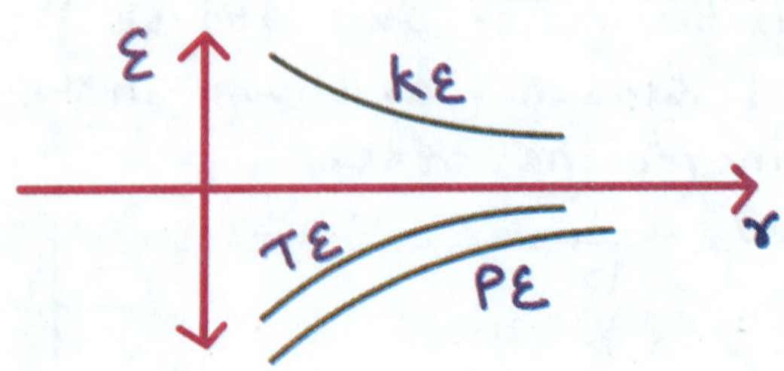

Energy required to launch a satellite

- $h = kR$
- $E_{min} = \frac{GMm}{2R}\left(\frac{1+2k}{1+k}\right)$

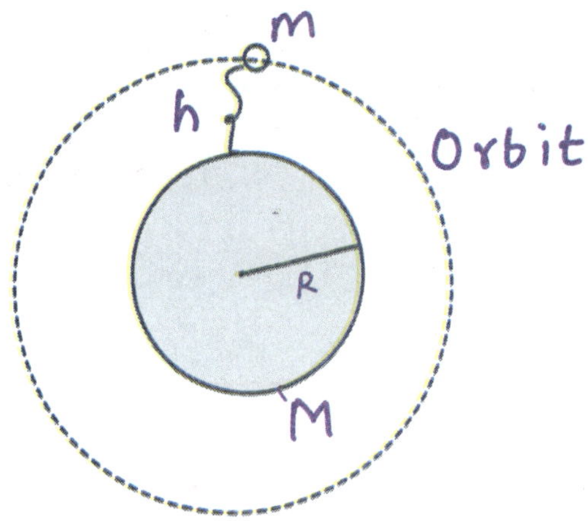

PYQ PUNCH

Q7. The minimum energy required to launch a satellite of mass m from the surface of earth of mass M and radius R in a circular orbit at an altitude of 2R from the surface of the earth is ? (NEET 2024)

Sol. $E_{min} = \frac{GMm}{2R}\left(\frac{1+2k}{1+k}\right)$

For $h = 2R$

$k = 2$

$E_{min} = \frac{5}{6}\frac{GMm}{R}$

Escape Velocity

- It is the minimum velocity of a particle to escape the G. Field of a planet.

◎ **From Earth's Surface**

$$V_e = \sqrt{\frac{2GM}{R}} = \sqrt{2gR} = \sqrt{\frac{8}{3}G\rho\pi R}$$

If ρ = Constant, $V_e \propto R$

M = constant, $V_e \propto \frac{1}{\sqrt{R}}$

- Orbiting at a height h above Earth's Surface

$$V_e = \sqrt{\frac{2GM}{R+h}} = \sqrt{2}\,V_o$$

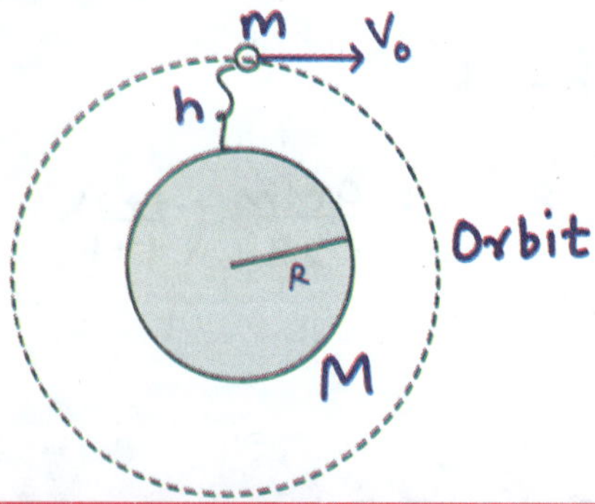

NEET Accelerate

- Escape velocity is independent of direction of throw.
- For earth, V_e = 11.2 km/hr

Conservation of Angular Momentum

- Planet experiences zero torque due to Sun Gravity.
- Thus angular momentum remains conserved.

$$L = mvr = \text{constant}$$

- 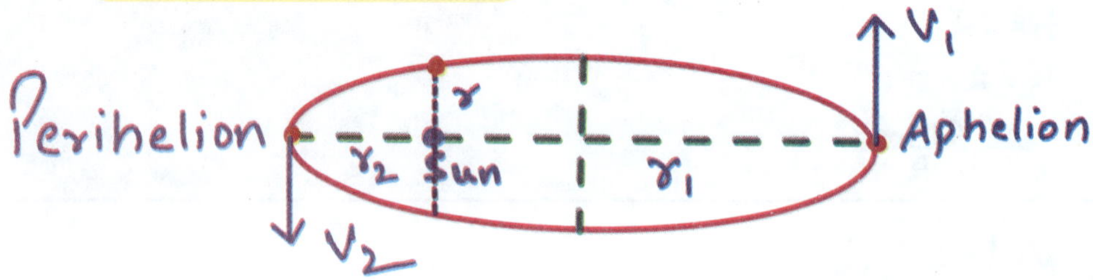

  - Perihelion is the closest distance.
  - Aphelion is the farthest distance.

$$m V_1 r_1 = m V_2 r_2$$

Maximum Height from Earth's Surface

- $V < V_e$

$$h_{max} = \frac{R}{\left(\frac{V_e^2}{V^2} - 1\right)}$$ where V is speed of throw.

◎ $V = kV_e$ $(k<1)$

$$h_{max} = \frac{Rk^2}{1-k^2}$$

PYQ PUNCH

Q8. A particle of mass m is projected with a velocity $V = kV_e$ $(k<1)$ from the surface of the Earth. The maximum height above the surface reached by the particle is :

Sol. $h_{max} = \frac{Rk^2}{1-k^2}$

(NEET 2021)

13. Elasticity

Elasticity

- When an external force is applied on a body, the body gets deformed.
- The property of a body to regain its original configuration (length, volume or shape) when the deforming forces are removed is called as Elasticity.
- It happens due to internal forces called as restoring force (f_R).
- Only at equilibrium, restoring force equals to external force.

Types of Bodies

- **Perfectly Elastic**
  - Bodies completely re-gain its natural shape after the removal of the deforming forces.

- **Perfectly Inelastic**
  - Bodies makes no effort to regain its original shape.

- **Partially Elastic or Plastic**
  - Bodies partially regain its original shape.

Stress (σ)

- It is the restoring force per unit area.

$$\sigma = \frac{f_R}{A}$$

- At equilibrium, $\sigma = \dfrac{F_{ext}}{A}$
- Unit is same as the pressure.

Types of Stress

Longitudinal or Normal Stress

- Restoring force acts along the axis of the rod.

Compressive Stress

Tensile Stress

$$\sigma = \frac{F_R}{A}$$

NEET Accelerate

- Restoring force is equal to external force only in equilibrium condition. Isliye stress nikalte samay external force pe viswas na kare.
- In the case of string, tension acts as restoring force.
- In all other cases, if restoring force is not given then you can safely consider external force for finding stress.
- Given below 2 cases are same, hence have same stress.

Case I

Case II

- Tension at any point in a string of mass m.

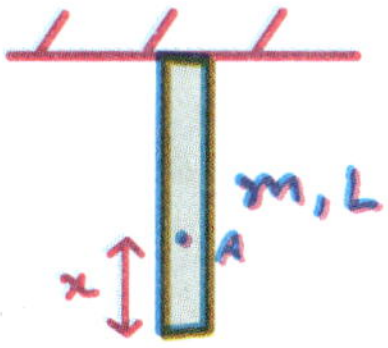

$$T_A = \frac{mgx}{L}$$

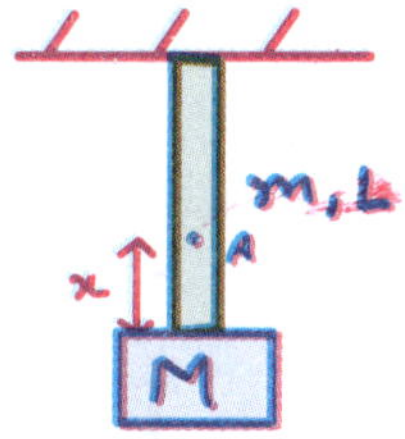

$$T_A = \left(M + \frac{mx}{L}\right)g$$

PYQ PUNCH

Q1. Let a wire be suspended from the ceiling (rigid support) and stretched by a weight W attached at its free end. The longitudinal stress at any point of cross-sectional area A of the wire is : (NEET 2023)

Sol. At equilibrium $F_R = F_{ext} = W$

$$\sigma = \frac{F_R}{A} = \frac{W}{A}$$

Shear Stress

- Restoring force acts tangentially.

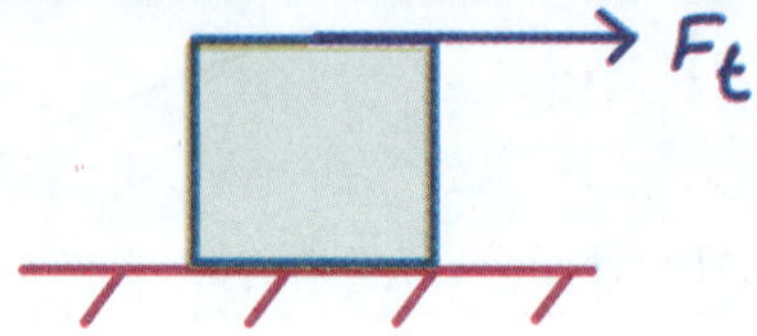

$$\sigma = \frac{F_t}{A}$$

Volumetric Stress

- Restoring force tries to re-gain original volume.

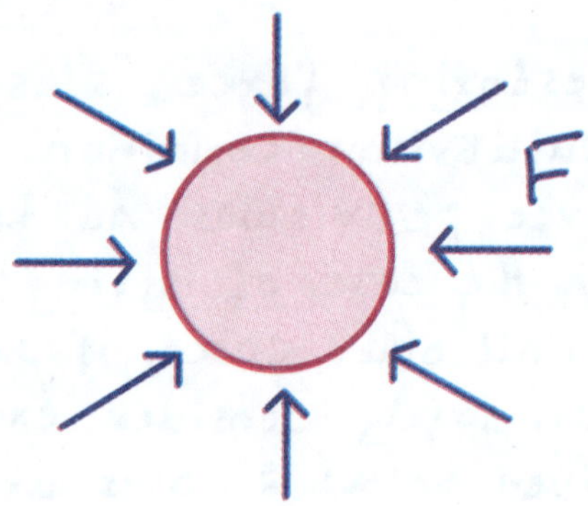

$$\sigma = \frac{F_R}{\text{Surface Area}}$$

Strain (ε)

- It is the ratio of change of shape to the original shape.
- Depending upon the type of stress, it is also of 3 types.

Types of Strain

Longitudinal Strain	Shear Strain	Volumetric Strain
$\frac{\Delta L}{L}$ 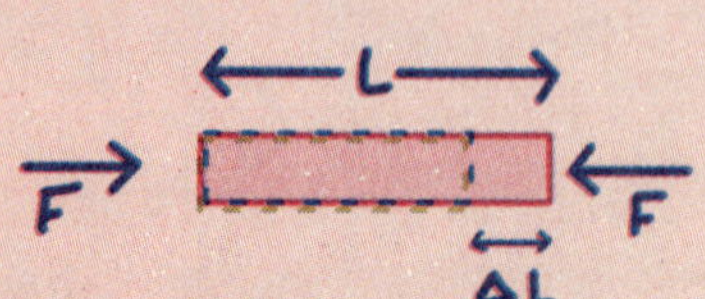	$\theta = \frac{x}{h}$ 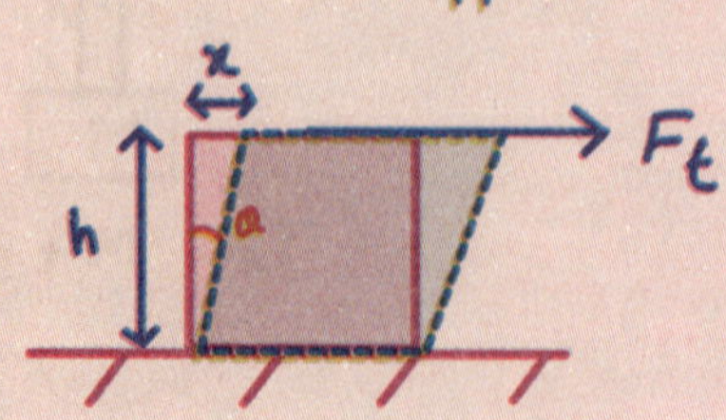	$\frac{\Delta V}{V}$ 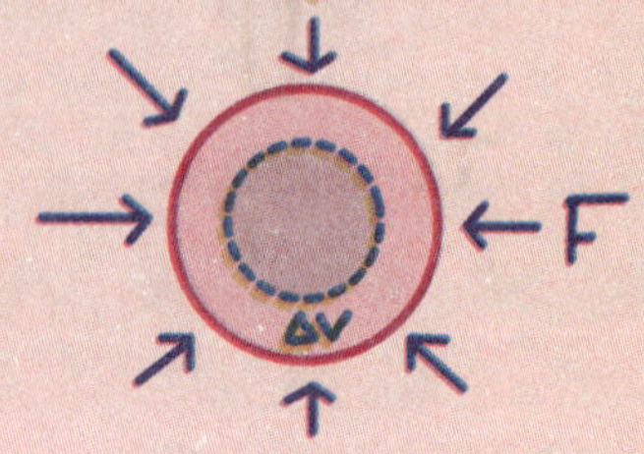

Hooke's Law

- For small strain,

  Stress ∝ Strain

  $\sigma \propto \varepsilon$

  $\sigma = E\varepsilon$

  $E = \dfrac{\sigma}{\varepsilon}$, where E is called as Modulus of Elasticity

Modulus of Elasticity

- It is the property of the material, which represents how difficult is to deform a body.
- More the value of E, more difficult to deform.
- Depending on the type of stress, it is also of 3 types.

Young's Modulus (Y)

$$Y = \frac{\text{Longitudinal Stress}}{\text{Longitudinal Strain}}$$

$$\Rightarrow Y = \frac{F_R/A}{\Delta L/L}$$

$$\Rightarrow Y = \frac{F_R L}{A\,\Delta L}$$

It is for Solids only

PYQ PUNCH

Q2. A wire of length L, area of cross-section A is hanging from a fixed support. The length of the wire changes to L_1 when mass M is suspended from its free end. The expression for Young's Modulus is (NEET 2020)

Sol. $\Delta L = L_1 - L$; $Y = \dfrac{MgL}{A(L_1 - L)}$

Shear Modulus (η)

$$\eta = \frac{\text{Shear Stress}}{\text{Shear Strain}}$$

$$\eta = \frac{F}{A\theta}$$

It is for Solids only

◎ **Bulk Modulus** (B)

It is mainly for fluids

- $B = \frac{\text{Volumetric Stress}}{\text{Volumetric Strain}}$

$$B = -V\left(\frac{\Delta P}{\Delta V}\right)$$

- On increasing the pressure, volume decreases, hence -ve sign is put to make the overall value +ve.

PYQ PUNCH

Q3. The bulk modulus of a spherical object is B. If it is subjected to uniform pressure p, the fractional decrease in radius is (NEET 2017)

Sol. From U & D chapter $\frac{\Delta V}{V} = \frac{3\Delta r}{r}$

Now $\frac{\Delta V}{V} = \frac{-\Delta P}{B} \Rightarrow \frac{3\Delta r}{r} = -\frac{P}{B}$

$\Rightarrow \frac{\Delta r}{r} = -\frac{P}{3B}$

Potential Energy Stored in a Wire

- When a rod is deformed using an external force, then part of work done by external force gets stored in the rod in the form of Elastic Potential Energy.

$$U = W.D = \frac{1}{2}Fx$$

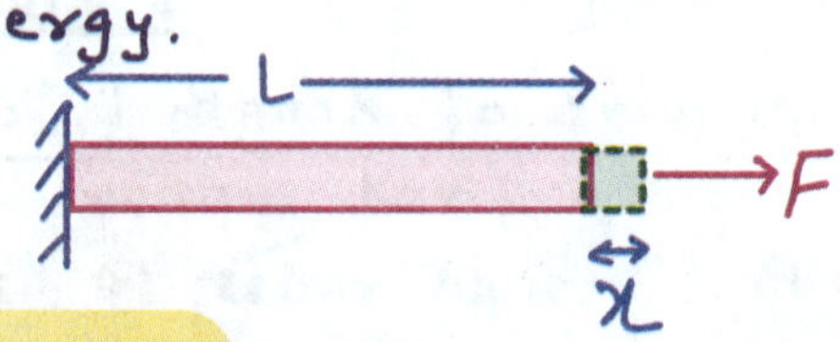

- Also, $U = \frac{1}{2} \times \text{Stress} \times \text{Strain} \times \text{Volume}$

$\frac{\sigma^2 A l}{2Y}$ ↙ ↘ $\frac{1}{2}\varepsilon^2 Y A l$

- Potential Energy per unit volume

$u = \frac{U}{V} = \frac{1}{2} \times \text{Stress} \times \text{Strain}$

$\frac{\sigma^2}{2Y}$ ↙ ↘ $\frac{1}{2}\varepsilon^2 Y$

PYQ PUNCH

Q4. When a block of mass M is suspended by a long wire of length L, the length of the wire becomes $(L+l)$. The elastic potential energy stored in the extended wire is : **(NEET 2019)**

Sol. $U = \frac{Fx}{2} = \frac{1}{2}Mgl$

Special cases of Elongation of Rod

◎ **Elongation in massless rod due to attached block**

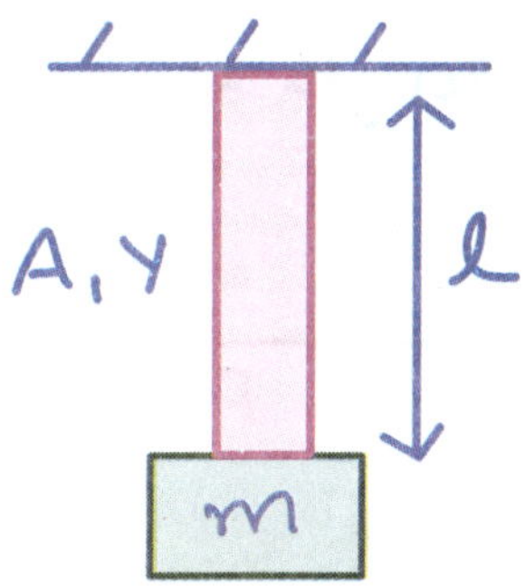

$$\Delta l = \frac{mgl}{AY}$$

◎ **Elongation due to Own Weight**

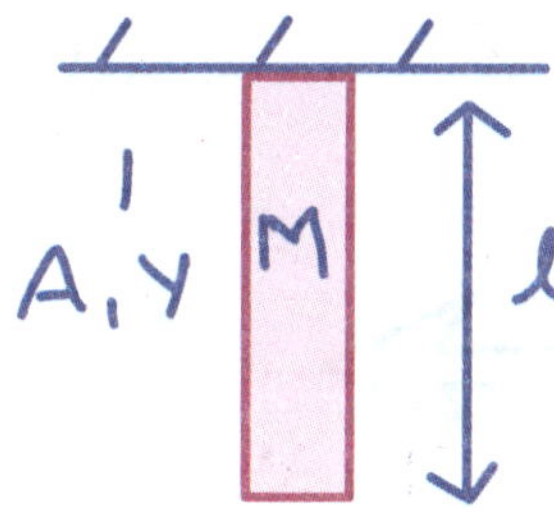

$$\Delta l = \left(\frac{M}{2}\right)\frac{gl}{AY}$$

◎ **Rod has mass M**

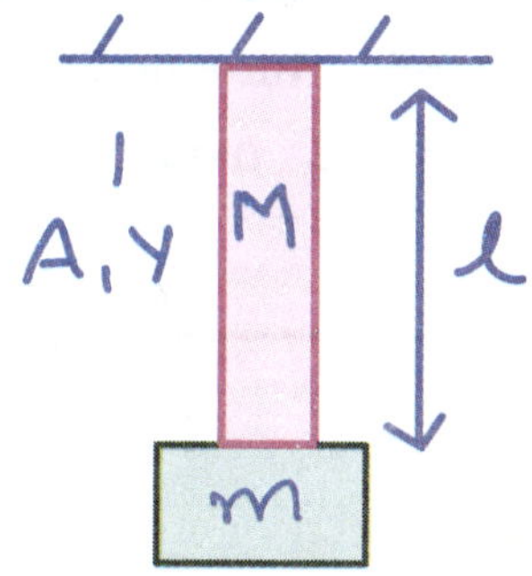

$$\Delta l = \left(m+\frac{M}{2}\right)\frac{gl}{AY}$$

◎ **Original length of wire from 2 forces**

- Length is l_1 for force T_1
- Length is l_2 for force T_2

$$l = \frac{T_1 l_2 - T_2 l_1}{T_1 - T_2}$$

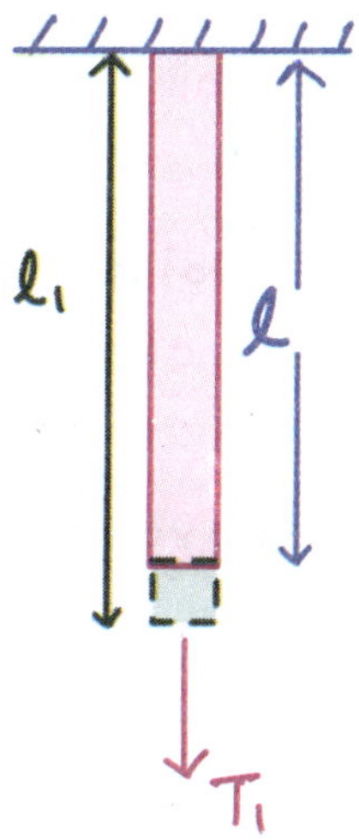

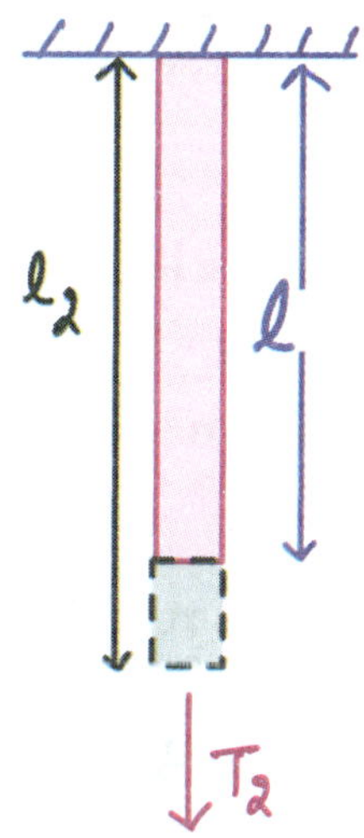

Parallel and Series Combination of Y

Parallel Combination

- 2 rods having same length L and Area A ⇒ Single rod of length L and area 2A

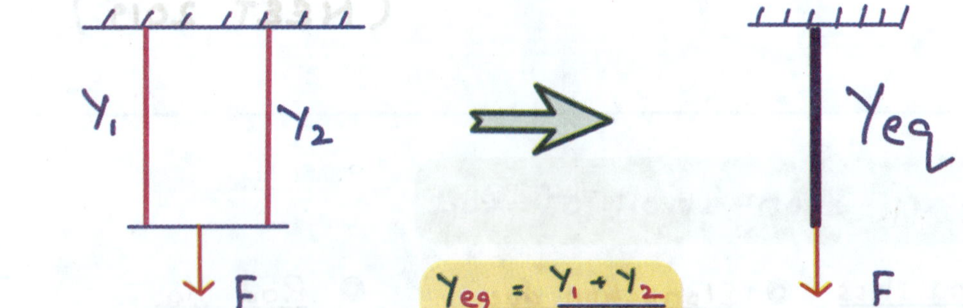

$$Y_{eq} = \frac{Y_1 + Y_2}{2}$$

Series Combination

- 2 rods having same length L and Area A ⇒ Single rod of length 2L and area A

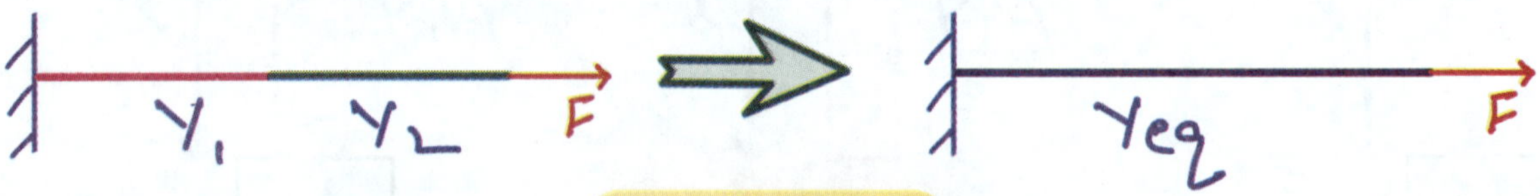

$$Y_{eq} = \frac{2Y_1Y_2}{Y_1 + Y_2}$$

Poisson's Ratio

- When a rod is elongated, its diameter decreases.

$$\nu = \frac{\text{Lateral Strain}}{\text{Longitudinal Strain}} = -\frac{\frac{\Delta D}{D}}{\frac{\Delta L}{L}}$$

- Theoretical value of poisson's ratio is −1 to 0.5
- For $\nu = 0.5$, there is no change of volume on compression though shape changes.

Few Important Relations

- $Y = 2\eta(1+\nu)$
- $Y = 3B(1-2\nu)$
- $Y = \frac{3B-2\eta}{6B-2\eta}$
- $Y = \frac{9\eta B}{3B+\eta}$

Stress - Strain Curve

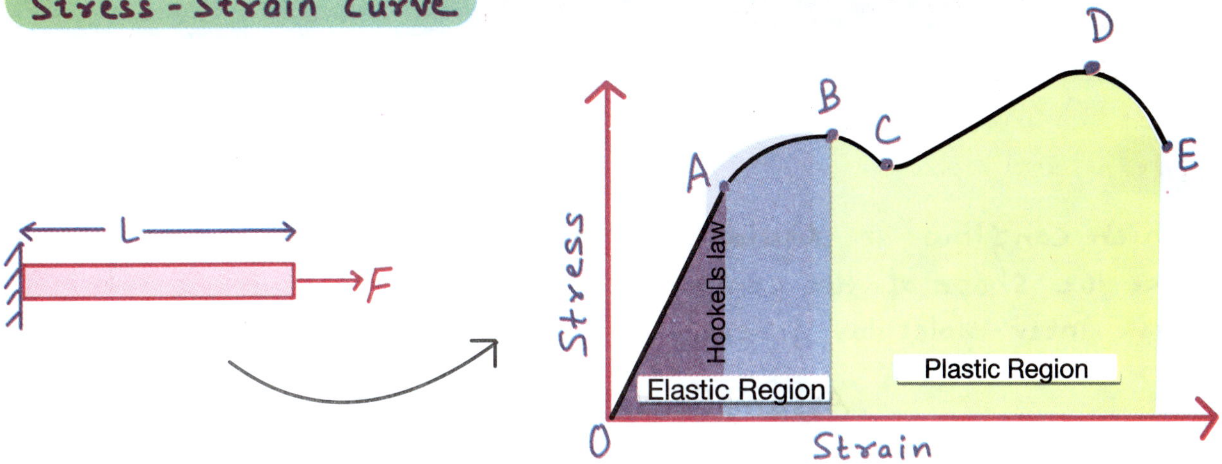

◎ Points

A → Proportional Limit
B → Elastic Limit
D → Breaking Stress
E → Fracture Point

◎ Region

OA → Hooke's Law Valid ($\sigma \propto \varepsilon$)
OB → Elastic Region
Complety regains its shape.
DE → Neck Region
BE → Plastic Region
Partially regains its shape.

NEET Accelerate

- Breaking stress is the property of material. It doesn't depend upon the area of the rod.
- Plastic region is large for ductile material.
- Plastic region is small for brittle material.
- Slope of Stress-Strain curve gives Young Modulus within the proportionality region.
- Steel is more elastic than rubber.

14. Mechanical Properties of Fluids

Fluids

- Which can flow i.e. liquids and gases.
- Take the shape of the container.
- Weak inter-molecular forces.

Assumptions

- Fluid is incompressible.
- Fluid is non-viscous.
- Fluid is irrotational.

Rotational

Irrotational

Pressure

- It is thrust per unit area.

$$P = \frac{\text{Thrust}}{\text{Area}} = \frac{F_\perp}{A}$$

- It is a scalar quantity.
- For a fluid, pressure is exerted in all direction and equal in magnitude.
- Units of Pressure are
  - Pascal
  - atm
  - Torr
  - mm of Hg
  - N/m^2
  - bar
  - PSI

Variation of Pressure in Static Fluids

- $P_2 = P_1 + \rho_f g h$

where ρ_f is the density of fluid.

Or $\Delta P = \rho g h$

- h is +ve downwards.
- h is −ve upwards.
- Pressure is same at same horizontal level.

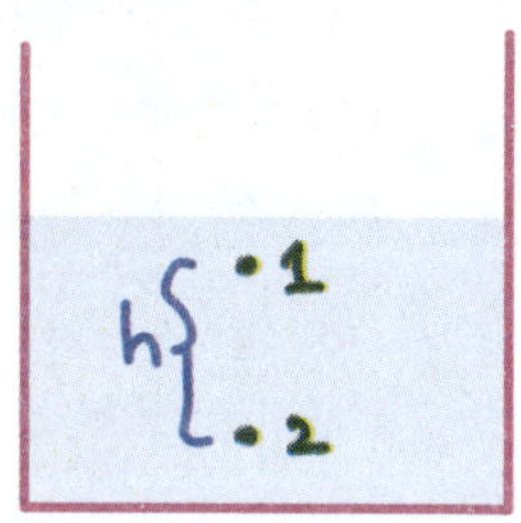

Atmospheric Pressure

- Pressure due to air particles.
- $P_0 = 1.013 \times 10^5 \, N/m^2 = 1 \, atm$
- Type of pressure
  - Absolute Pressure : Actual Pressure
  - Gauge Pressure : Pressure over atmospheric pressure

Gauge P = Absolute P − Atmospheric P

Barometer

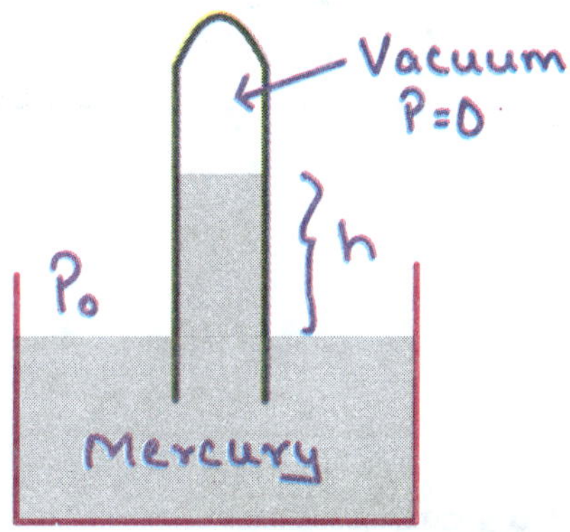

- A simple instrument to measure atmospheric pressure.
- $P_0 = \rho_m g h$

  where ρ_m is the density of mercury.
  h is the height of mercury rises.
- 760 mm of Hg = 1 atm
- Mercury is used because it is the heaviest liquid at room temperature. It also doesn't wet the walls.
- Length of any other liquid

$$h_l = \frac{\rho_m h}{\rho_l}$$

- Atmospheric Pressure in terms of other liquid.

$$P_0 = \rho_l g h_l$$

- For water $h_l = 10.3$ m at 1 atm.

PYQ PUNCH

Q1. A barometer is constructed using a liquid (density = 760 kg/m³). What would be the height of the liquid column, when a mercury barometer reads 76 cm ? Density of mercury = 13600 kg/m³).

(NEET 2020)

Sol. $h_l = \frac{\rho_m h}{\rho_l} = \frac{13600 \times 76}{760} = 13.6$ m

Compressibility of Water

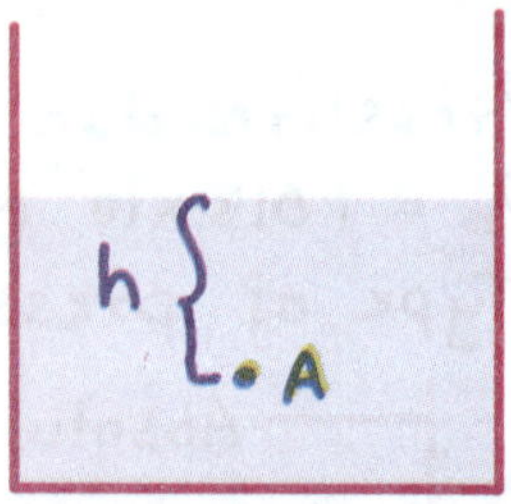

- Water get compressed due to pressure.
- Fraction compression of water

$$\frac{\Delta V}{V} = \rho g h k$$

where k is the compressibility of water.

MCQ PUNCH

Q2. The approximate depth of an ocean is 2700 m. The compressibility of water is $45.4 \times 10^{-11}\ Pa^{-1}$ and density of water is $10^3\ kg/m^3$. What fractional compression of water will be obtained at the bottom.

Sol. $\frac{\Delta V}{V} = \rho g h k$

$= 1000 \times 9.8 \times 2700 \times 45.4 \times 10^{-11}$

$= 1.2 \times 10^{-2}$

Pascal's Law

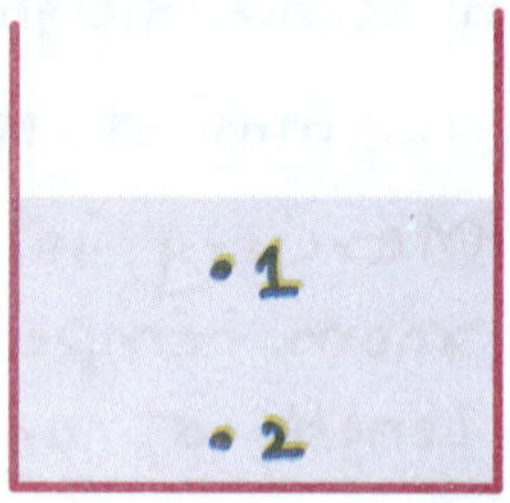

- It states that change of pressure at one point of fluid changes the pressure at all other points by same amount.

$$\Delta P_1 = \Delta P_2$$

Application of Pascal's Law

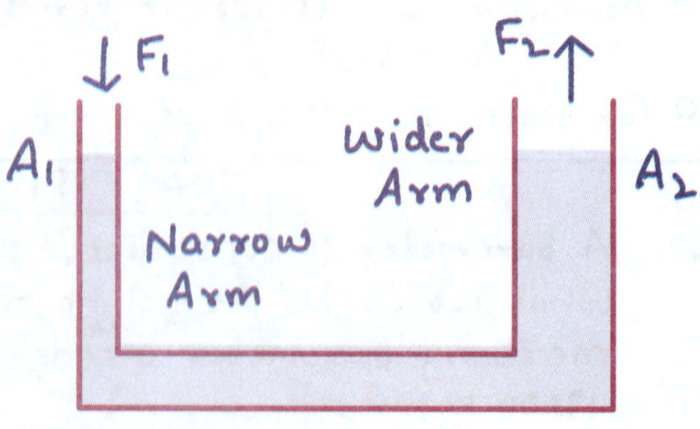

- **Hydraulic Lift**
- Used to Lift Heavy Objects
- Force F_1 at narrow arm produces Force F_2 at wider arm, such that

$$\frac{F_1}{A_1} = \frac{F_2}{A_2}$$

- If a mass M is placed at wider arm, then

$$F_2 = Mg$$

- If a mass m is put over narrower arm to provide force F_1, then

$$F_1 = mg$$

- It doesn't violate conservation of energy.

U-Tube

◎ Two Liquids

- Lighter fluid is always at higher height.
- At equilibrium

$$\rho_1 h_1 = \rho_2 h_2 \quad \& \quad h = h_2 - h_1$$

where h_1 & h_2 are height above common horizontal line of liquid 1 and liquid 2 respectively.

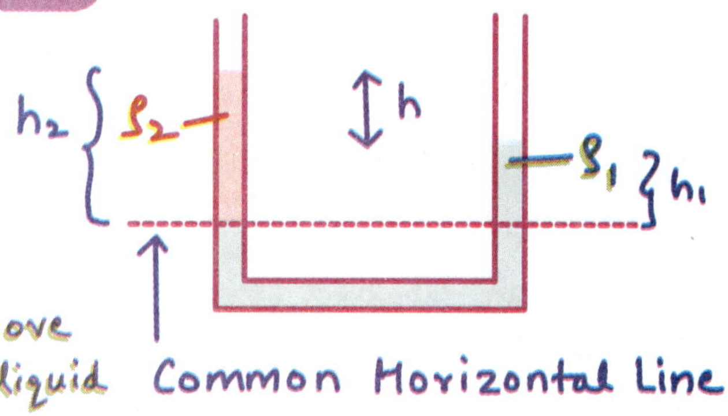

PYQ PUNCH

Q3. In a U-tube shown in a figure, water and oil are in the left side and right side of the tube, respectively. The heights from the bottom for water and oil columns are 15 cm and 20 cm, respectively. The density of the oil is (take $\rho_w = 1000\ kg/m^3$) (NEET 2019)

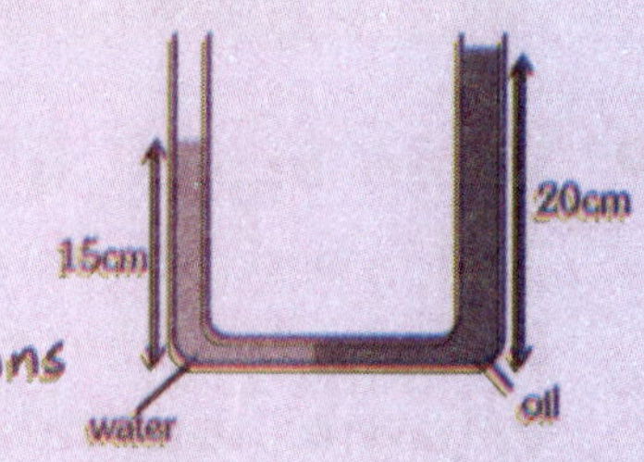

Sol. $\rho_1 = 1000\ kg/m^3$; $h_1 = 15\ cm$

$\rho_2 = ?$; $h_2 = 20\ cm$

$\rho_1 h_1 = \rho_2 h_2$

$\Rightarrow \rho_2 = 750\ kg/m^3$

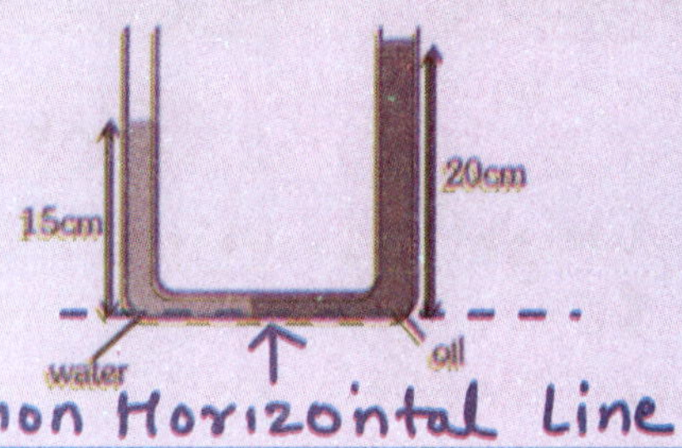

◎ Three Liquids

- At equilibrium

Left Side Balanced by Right Side

$$\rho_2 h_2 = \rho_1 h_1 + \rho_3 h_3$$

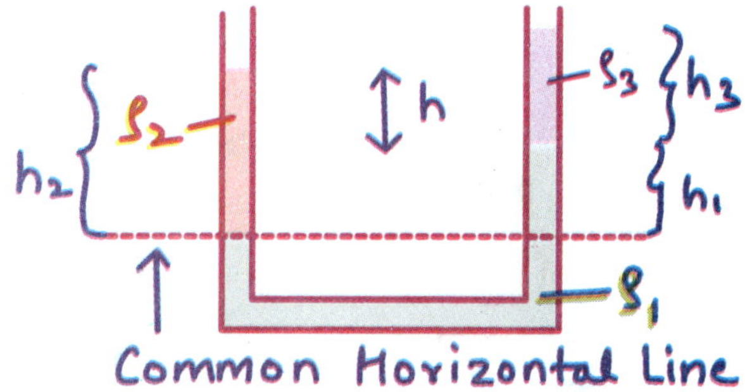

Relative Density or Specific Gravity

- It is the density of body with respect to water.
- Example, relative density of mercury $= \dfrac{\text{Density of Mercury}}{\text{Density of Water}}$

$$= \frac{13600}{1000} = 13.6$$

- It is a dimensionless quantity.

Archimedes' Principle

- When a body is fully or partially submerged in a fluid, it exerts an upward force, which is equal to weight of the fluid displaced.
- Buoyant Force or Upthrust

$$F_b = \rho_f g V_{sub}$$

where ρ_f is the density of fluid
V_{sub} is the volume submerged in the fluid.

- If an object is submerged in more than 1 liquid, then each liquid exerts buoyant force proportional to the volume submerged in it.

$$F_b = \rho_1 g V_1 + \rho_2 g V_2 + \ldots$$

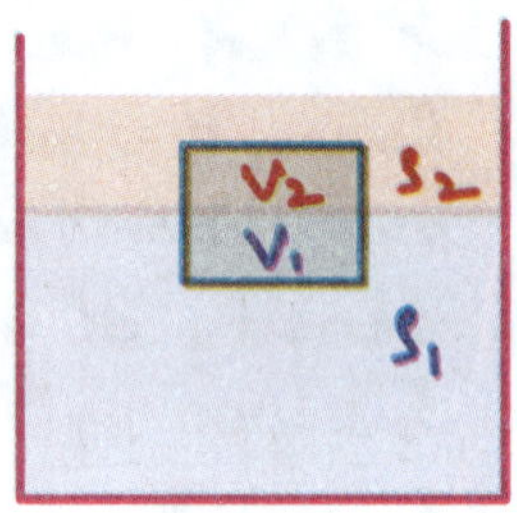

Sinking

- $F_b <$ Weight of Object
- $\rho_f < \rho_b$
- Specific Gravity > 1

Submerge and Float

- $F_b =$ Weight of Object
- $\rho_f = \rho_b$
- Specific Gravity $= 1$
- Object remains at the same place where it is placed.

Floating

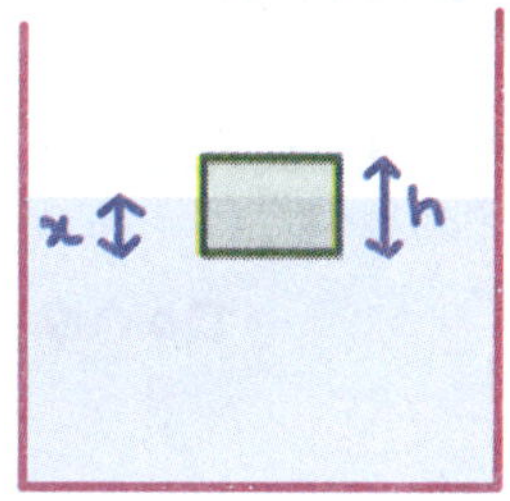

- $\rho_f > \rho_b$
- Specific Gravity < 1
- $\rho_f g V_{sub} = mg$
- Fractional Volume Submerged $\frac{V_{sub}}{V_{Total}} = \frac{\rho_b}{\rho_f}$
- Fractional Volume UnSubmerged $\frac{V_{out}}{V_{Total}} = 1 - \frac{\rho_b}{\rho_f}$
- Depth inside water $x = \frac{\rho_b h}{\rho_f}$

PYQ PUNCH

Q4. Two non-mixing liquids of densities ρ and $n\rho$ $(n>1)$ are put in a container. The height of each liquid is h. A Solid cylinder of length L and density d is put in this container. The cylinder floats with its axis vertical and length pL $(p<1)$ in the denser liquid. The density d is equal to (NEET 2016)

Sol. Let A be the cross-sectional area

For submerge and float

F_b = Weight of Object

$\rho_1 g V_1 + \rho_2 g V_2 = mg$

$n\rho A pL + \rho A(L - pL) = dAL$

$\Rightarrow d = (1 + (n-1)p)\rho$

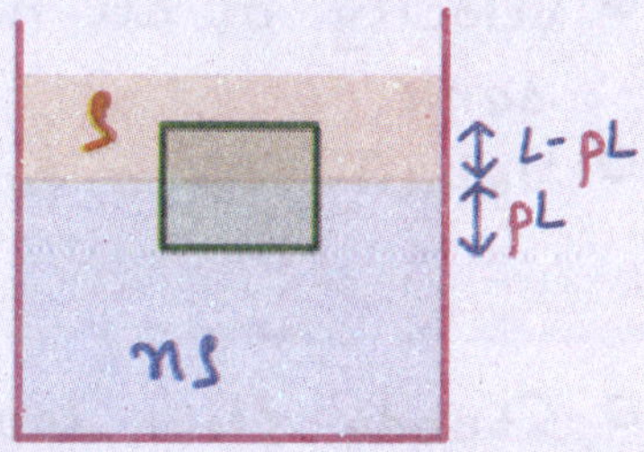

Weight of body in water

- Weight of an object decreases in water due to Buoyancy.
- For sinking

  $N = mg - F_b$

  $W_a = W_T - F_b$

  where W_a is apparent weight & W_T is the true weight
- Relative density of fluid using weight $\rho_r = \frac{W_T}{W_T - W_a}$
- For submerge and float $N = W_a = 0$
- For float $N = W_a = 0$

Variation of Pressure in Dynamic Fluid

- **Horizontal Acceleration**

$$\tan\theta = \frac{a}{g}$$

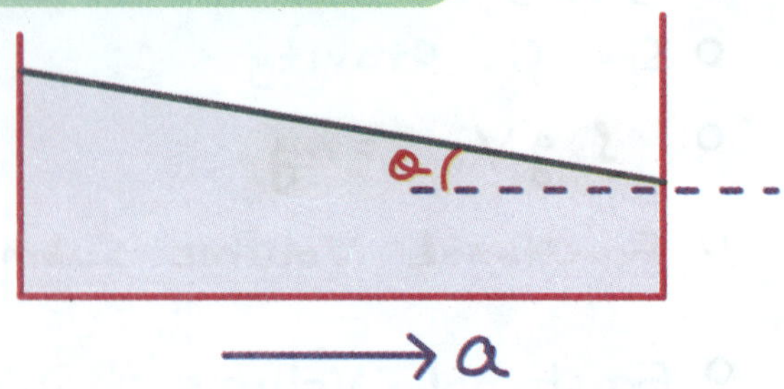

- **Vertical Acceleration**

- $P_2 - P_1 = \rho_f (g+a)h$ ($g+a$ = g_{eff})

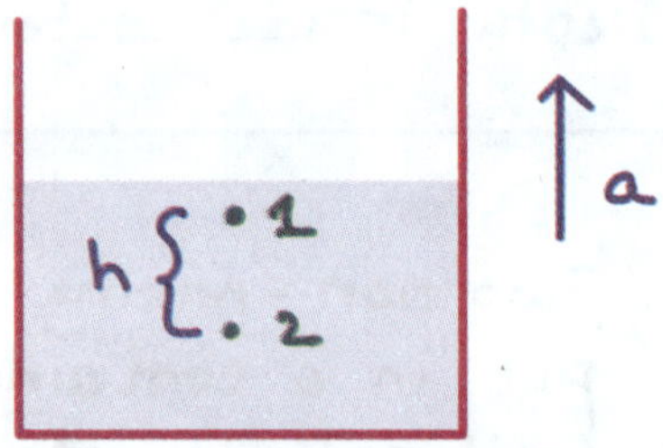

- During free fall, $a = -g$
  $P_2 = P_1$
  i.e. pressure becomes uniform

Steady Flow

- A flow that doesn't change with time.
- Velocity of all the particles passing through a point is same.
- Velocity of a particle can be different at different locations.

Streamline Flow

- Steady flow leads to formation of line. This line is called as Streamline.
- Two streamlines can never intersect each other otherwise there would be two direction of flow at the intersecting point, which is not possible.

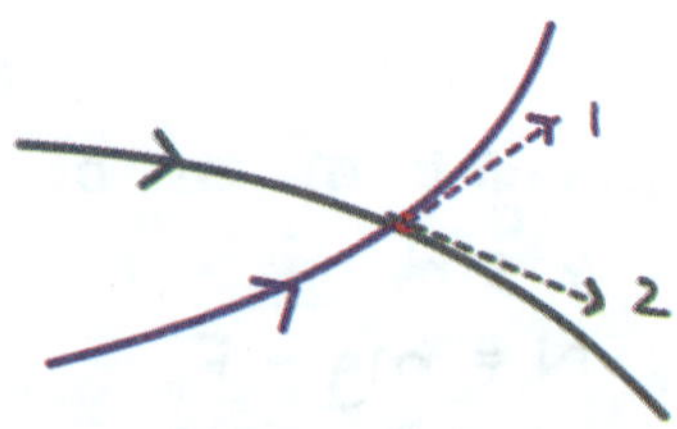

Laminar Flow

- Several streamlines form lamina.
- These lamina flows over each other forming Laminar Flow.
- Two lamina never intersect each other.

Equation of Continuity

- In a steady state
  Rate of mass entering = Rate of mass exiting
- $A_1 v_1 = A_2 v_2$

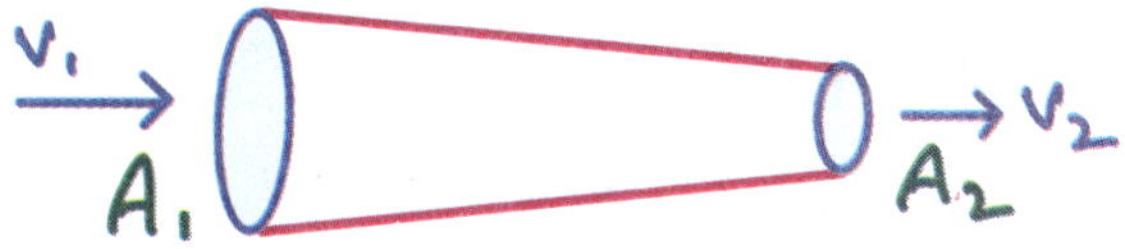

- In a pipe of uniform cross-section, speed is uniform irrespective of the orientation of pipe i.e. horizontal, vertical or inclined.

MCQ PUNCH

Q5. The cylindrical tube of a spray pump has radius R, one end of which has n fines holes, each of radius r. If the speed of the liquid in the tube is v, the speed of the ejection of the liquid through the holes is :

Sol. $A_1 v_1 = A_2 v_2$

$\pi R^2 v = n \pi r^2 v_2$

$\Rightarrow v_2 = \dfrac{vR^2}{nr^2}$

Bernoulli's Principle

- Based on conservation of energy.
- Fluid should
  - Incompressible
  - Non-viscous
  - Irrotational

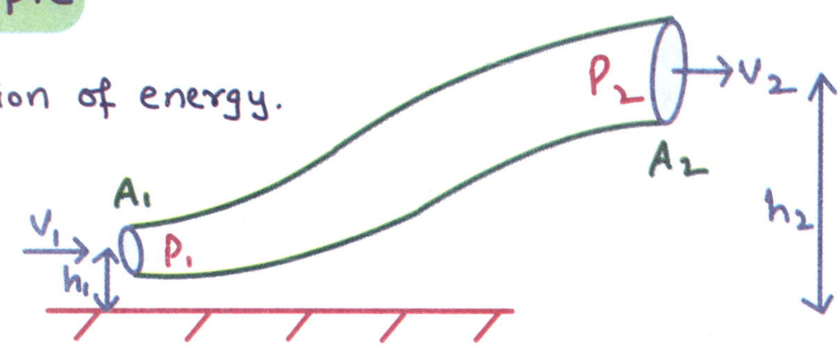

- $P + \frac{1}{2}\rho v^2 + \rho g h = \text{constant}$
- $\frac{P}{\rho g} + \frac{v^2}{2g} + h = \text{constant}$
  ($\frac{P}{\rho g}$: Pressure Head; $\frac{v^2}{2g}$: Kinetic Head; h: Potential Head)
- On a streamline, sum of 3 heads is constant.

Applications of Bernoulli's

Flying of Roof

- Due to pressure difference
- Outside pressure is less due to high speed.

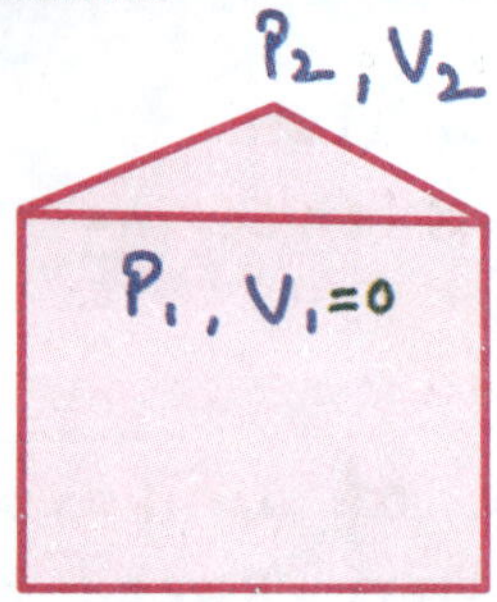

$$F = (P_1 - P_2) \times A$$

$$F = \frac{1}{2}\rho V_2^2 A$$

MCQ PUNCH

Q6. A wind with speed 40 m/s blows parallel to the roof of a house. The area of the roof is 250 m². Assuming that the pressure inside the house is atmospheric pressure, the force exerted by the wind on the roof and the direction of the force will be ($\rho_{air} = 1.2\ kg/m^3$)

Sol. $F = \frac{1}{2}\rho V_2^2 A$

$= \frac{1}{2} \times 1.2 \times 40^2 \times 250 = 2.4 \times 10^5\ N$ upward.

Flying of Aeroplane

- Due to pressure difference on wing.
- Lower side is rough, hence less speed and more pressure
- Upper side is smooth, hence more speed and less pressure.

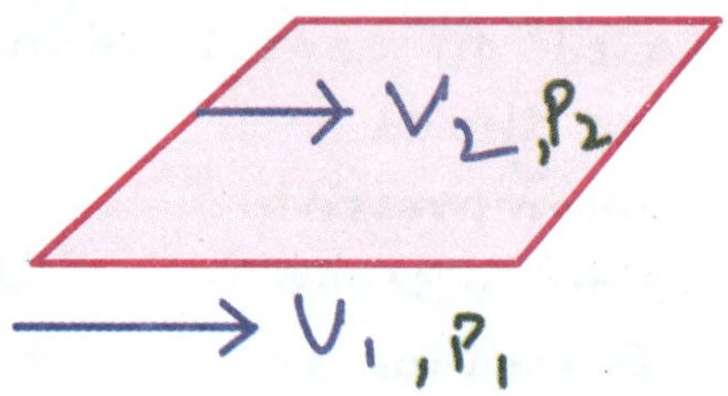

$$F = (P_1 - P_2) \times A$$

$$F = \frac{1}{2}\rho (v_2^2 - v_1^2) \times A$$

Velocity of Efflux

- $$V = \sqrt{\frac{2g(h_1 - h_2)}{\left[1 - \left(\frac{a}{A}\right)^2\right]}}$$

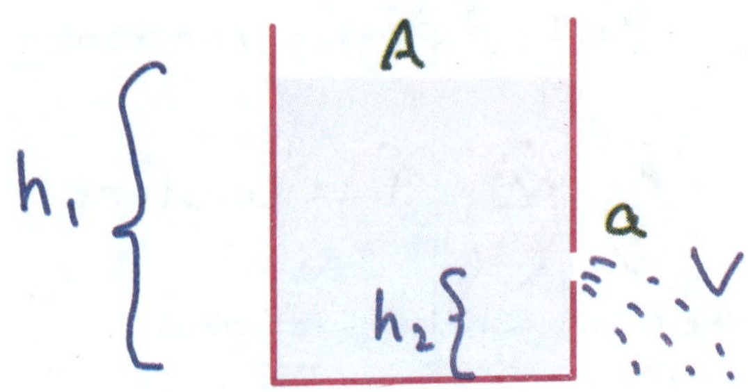

- If $A >> a$,

$$v = \sqrt{2g(h_1 - h_2)}$$ ← Torricelli's Law

- Doesn't depends upon density of fluid.
- Speed reduces as water level decreases.
- Rate of Volume flow

$$\dot{Q} = a\sqrt{2g(h_1 - h_2)}$$

- Time to empty from H_1 to H_2

$$T = \frac{A}{a}\sqrt{\frac{2}{g}}\left(\sqrt{H_1} - \sqrt{H_2}\right)$$

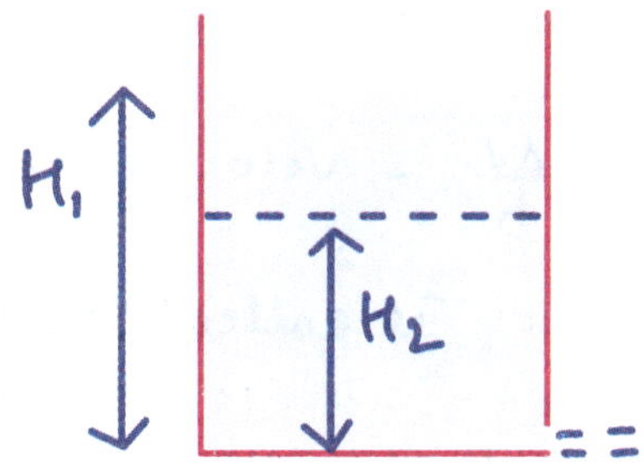

- Ratio of time to empty from H to $H/2$ and $H/2$ to 0 is

$$\frac{t_1}{t_2} = \sqrt{2} - 1$$

PYQ PUNCH

Q7. A small hole of cross-section 2 mm² is present near the bottom of a fully filled open tank of height 2m. Take $g = 10\ m/s^2$, the rate of flow of water through the open hole would be nearly (NEET 2019)

Sol. $h_1 = 2$; $h_2 = 0$

$$\dot{Q} = a\sqrt{2g(h_1 - h_2)} = 2\times10^{-6}\sqrt{2\times10\times2} = 12.6\times10^{-6}\ m/s$$

- **Venturimeter**
- Measure flow of liquid in a tube.

$$V = \sqrt{\frac{2g(h_1 - h_2)}{\left[\left(\frac{A}{a}\right)^2 - 1\right]}}$$

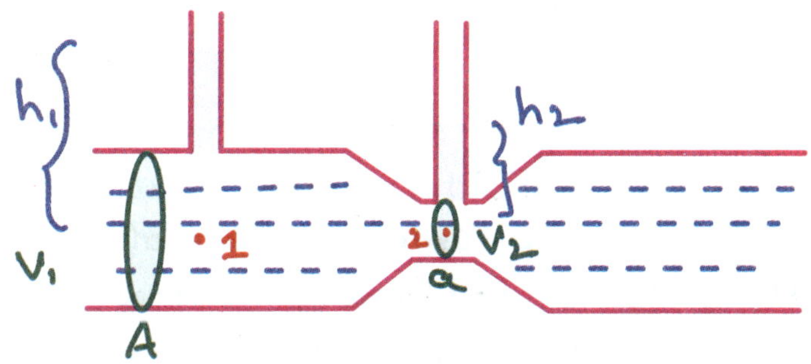

- $h_1 > h_2$

Viscosity

- Frictional force between layers in which atleast one is fluid layer to oppose the relative motion between them.

Viscous Force on Boat

- Viscous Force

$$f = \eta A \frac{\Delta V}{h}$$

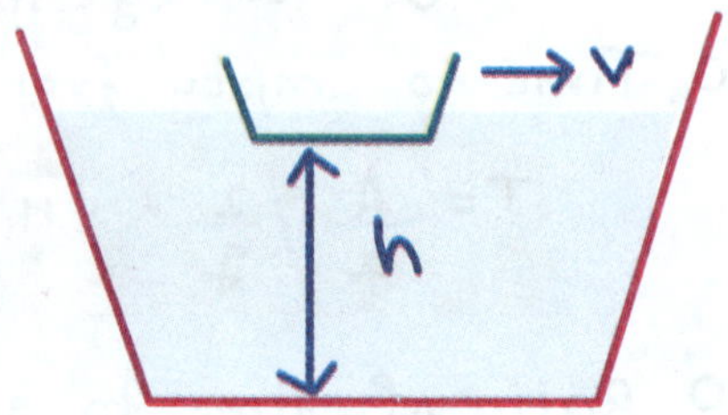

where $\frac{\Delta V}{h}$ is Velocity gradient

η is called coeff of viscosity

- CGS unit of η is Poise.
- SI unit is decaPoise.

Stoke's Law

- Valid only for spherical bodies of radius r.
- Viscous force experienced by a sphere in fluid.

$f = 6\pi\eta r v$ where v is the speed of sphere in fluid.

- **Terminal Velocity** (V_t)
- Net force on body becomes Zero.
- $V_t = \frac{2r^2}{9\eta}(\rho_b - \rho_f)$
- $f = 6\pi\eta r V_t$
- $V_t \propto r^2$ for a same material

NEET Accelerate

- Work done by viscous force till ball achieves terminal velocity is less than work done by it after achieving terminal velocity for the the same amount of distance covered.
- If $\rho_b > \rho_f$ body moves downward and viscous force acts upward.
- If $\rho_b < \rho_f$ body moves upward and viscous force acts downward.

PYQ PUNCH

Q8. The velocity of a small ball of mass M and density d when dropped in a container filled with glycerine becomes constant after some time. If the density of glycerine is d/2, then the viscous force acting on the ball will be : (NEET 2021)

Sol. $V_t = \frac{2r^2}{9\eta}(\rho_b - \rho_f) = \frac{2r^2}{9\eta}\left(d - \frac{d}{2}\right) = \frac{r^2 d}{9\eta}$

$f = 6\pi\eta r v_t = 6\pi\eta \times r \times \frac{r^2 d}{9\eta} = \frac{2}{3}\pi r^3 d = \frac{Mg}{2}$

Graph

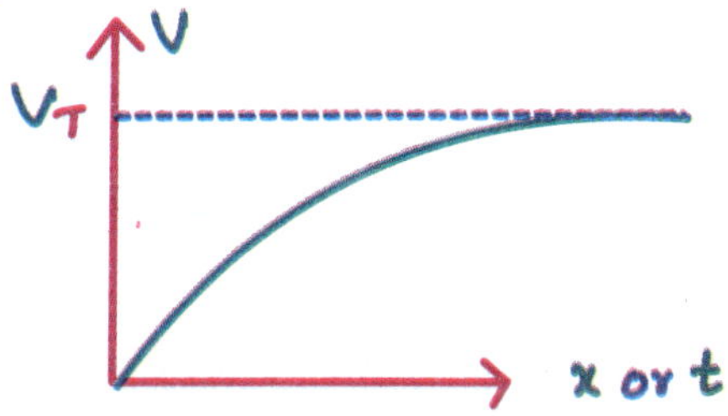

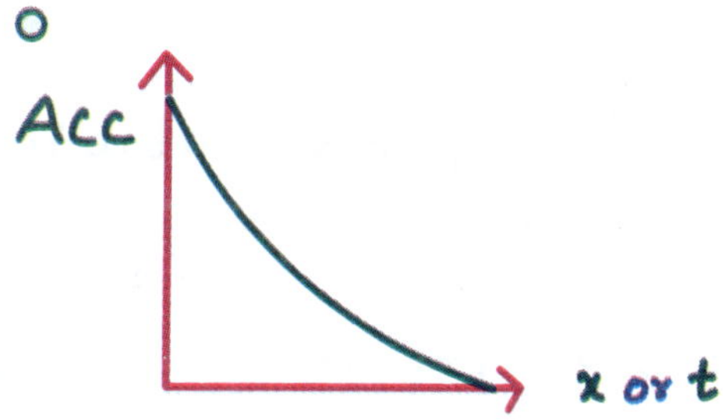

Coalesce of Drops

- When n identical drops each of radius r combine to form a bigger drop of radius R, then

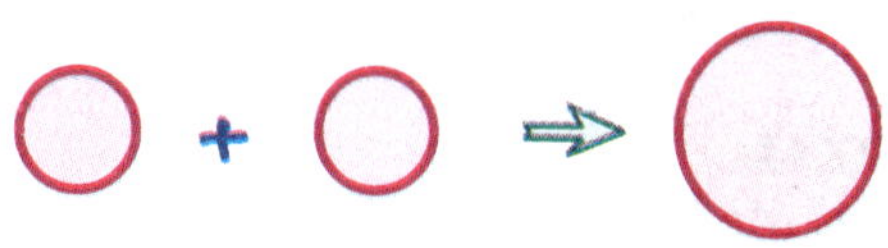

$$R = n^{1/3} r$$

- If V_t is the terminal velocity of smaller drop, then terminal velocity of bigger drop

$$V_t' = n^{2/3} V_t$$

Rate of Heat production

- During motion at constant speed in the fluid, heat get produced due to viscous force.
- Rate of Heat produced is

$$\dot{H} = 6\pi\eta r v_t^2$$

$$\dot{H} \propto r^5$$

PYQ PUNCH

Q9. A small sphere of radius r falls from rest in a viscous liquid. As a result, heat is produced due to viscous force. The rate of production of heat when the sphere attains its terminal velocity, is proportional to (NEET 2018)

Sol. $\dot{H} \propto r^5$

Surface Tension (S)

- Free surface of a liquid is a surface separating two mediums.
- It tends to expose its minimum surface to the surrounding for stability.
- Free surface behaves as it is under tension somewhat like a stretched elastic membrane.
- This property of a liquid is known as Surface Tension.
- Air bubble in water, and water drop have only one free surface.
- Soap bubble and a rectangular film have two free surfaces.
- $S = \dfrac{\text{Force}}{\text{Perimeter}}$
- Unit is N/m.
- Force required to raise an object over liquid surface.

  $F = mg + \text{Force due to Surface tension}$

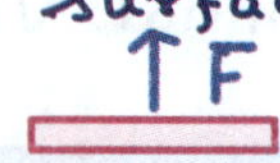

- Excess force required to raise an object.

  $F_{excess} = \text{Force due to Surface tension}$

	Rod	Disc	Ring
Surface Tension	$\frac{F}{2L}$	$\frac{F}{2\pi r}$	$\frac{F}{2\pi r + 2\pi R}$
Excess Force (F_{excess})	$S \times 2L$	$S \times 2\pi r$	$S \times (2\pi r + 2\pi R)$

PYQ PUNCH

Q10. A thin flat circular disc of radius 4.5 cm is placed gently over the surface of water. If surface tension of water is $0.07\ Nm^{-1}$, then the excess force required to take it away from the surface is: (NEET 2024)

Sol. $r = 4.5\ cm = 0.045\ m$

For a disc

$F_{excess} = S \times 2\pi r$

$= 0.07 \times 2\pi \times 0.045$

$= 19.8\ mN$

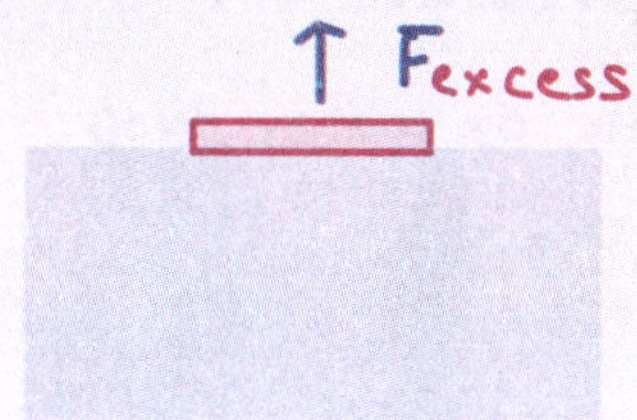

Surface Energy (ε)

- Free surface is stretched. It stores some energy known as surface energy.

$$E = S \times \text{Free Surface Area}$$

- Energy required to change the free surface area.

$$\Delta E = S \times \Delta A$$

- Small drops of radius r coalesce to form bigger drop of radius R. Surface area decreases, stability increases and energy get released.
  - $R = n^{1/3} r$
  - $\varepsilon_{released} = 3VS\left(\frac{1}{r} - \frac{1}{R}\right)$ where V is the volume of larger drop.
- To break a bigger drop into n small drops, energy is needed to supply.
  - $R = n^{1/3} r$
  - $\varepsilon_{absorbed} = 3VS\left(\frac{1}{R} - \frac{1}{r}\right)$
- Energy required to increase the width of rectangular film by x.

$$\Delta E = S \times 2 \times l x$$

Excess Pressure

- Pressure inside the bubble is more than outside pressure due to surface tension.
- $P_{excess}(\Delta P) = P_{inside}(P_1) - P_{outside}(P_2)$
- Excess pressure for

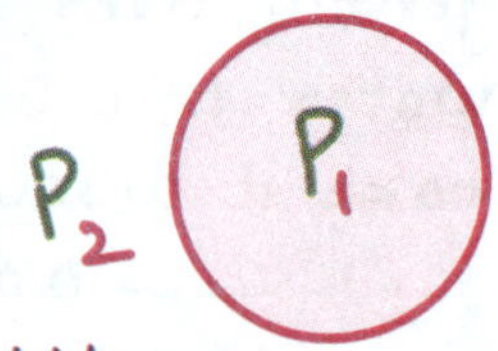

▹ Air bubble or water drop

$$\Delta P = \frac{2S}{R}$$

▹ Soap bubble

$$\Delta P = \frac{4S}{R}$$

- On increasing the radius, pressure inside decreases.

PYQ PUNCH

Q11. A soap bubble, having radius of 1 mm, is blown from a detergent solution having a surface tension of 2.5×10^{-2} N/m. The pressure inside the bubble equals at a point Z_0 below the free surface of water in a container. Taking $g = 10 \, m/s^2$, $\rho_{water} = 10^3 \, kg/m^3$, the value of Z_0 is (NEET 2019)

Sol. Pressure difference at depth Z_0

$\Delta P = \rho_w g Z_0$ ---------- eqn 1

Pressure difference in a soap bubble

$\Delta P = \frac{4S}{R}$ --------- eqn 2

Equating eqn 1 & eqn 2

$$\rho_w g Z_0 = \frac{4S}{R}$$

$$\Rightarrow 1000 \times 10 \times Z_0 = \frac{4 \times 2.5 \times 10^{-2}}{10^{-3}}$$

$$\Rightarrow Z_0 = 1 \text{ cm}$$

Radius of Interference

- Two drops of radius r_1 and r_2 interacts.
- $r_1 > r_2$

$\Rightarrow P_1 < P_2$

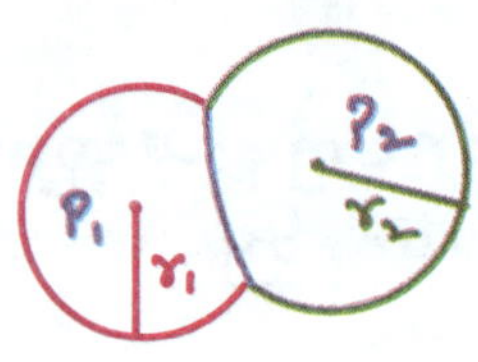

- $$\frac{1}{r} = \frac{1}{r_1} - \frac{1}{r_2}$$

Angle of Contact

- When a capillary is inserted in a liquid, the liquid level increases or decreases due to Adhesive or Cohesive force.
- Force between different types of molecules is adhesive force.
- Force between same types of molecules is Cohesive force.

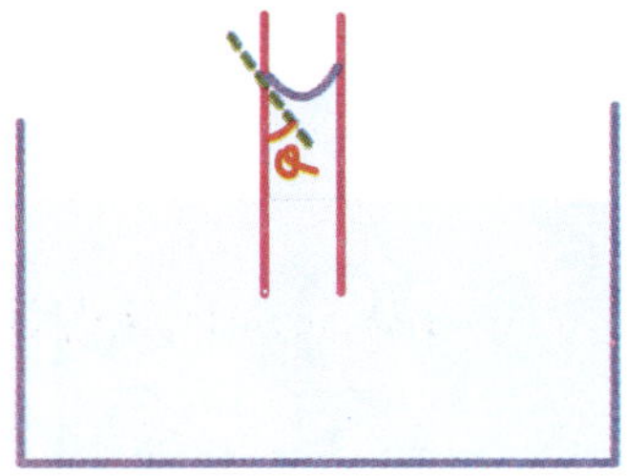

Adhesive Force
(Concave Meniscus)

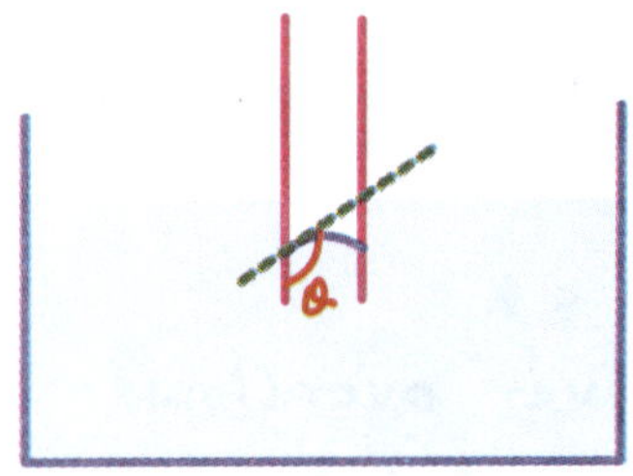

Cohesive Force
(Convex Meniscus)

- The angle between free surface and the solid surface is called as angle of contact θ.
- During adhesive force $\theta < 90°$ and cohesive force $\theta > 90°$.

Wetability

- For $\theta < 90°$, a liquid wets the surface.

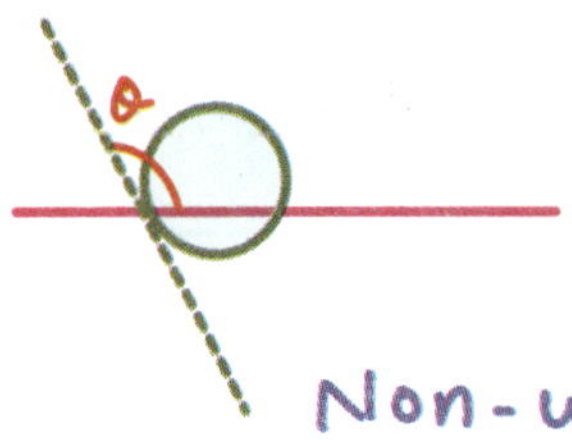

Non-wet

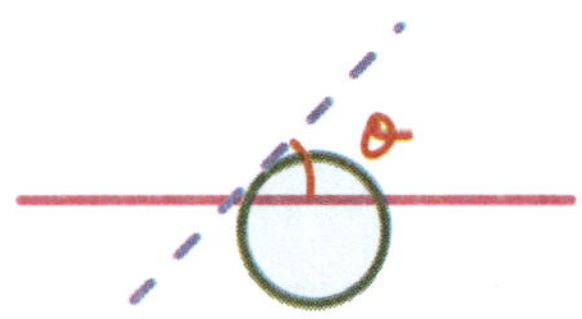

Wet

- Angle of contact between
  - Pure water and pure glass is 0°
  - Pure mercury and pure glass is 135°.

Capillary Tube

- The phenomenon of rising / falling water in a capillary tube is called as Capillarity.
- The weight of the liquid is balanced by adhesive or cohesive force.

- $h = \frac{2S\cos\theta}{\rho r g}$
- Pressure in the Capillary decreases with height.
- Mass of liquid rises ∝ radius of the tube

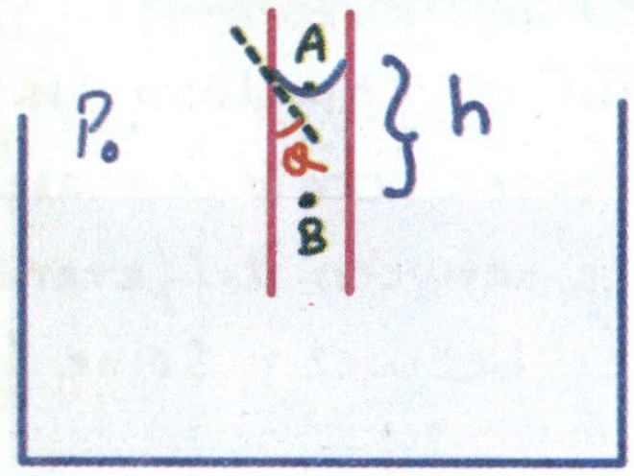

Tube of Insufficient Length

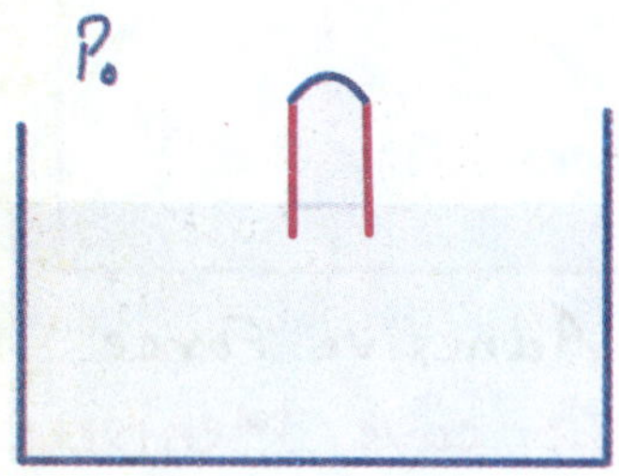

- For $h_{tube} < h$, Liquid never overflows.
- If it does, it would violate conservation of energy.
- Angle of contact changes as per the requirement.

Hole in the tube

- If a hole is made in the capillary tube, the liquid won't come out of it.
- If it does, it would violate conservation of energy.

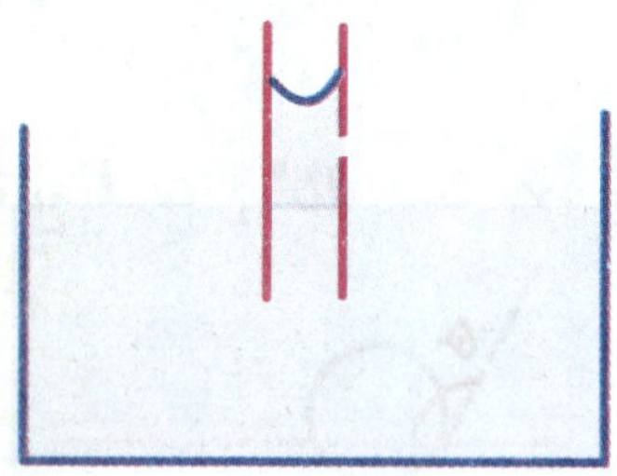

PYQ PUNCH

Q12. A capillary tube of radius r is immersed in water and water rises into a height h. The mass of the water in the capillary tube is 5 gm. Another capillary tube of radius 2r is immersed in water. The mass of the water that will rise in this tube is : (NEET 2020)

Sol. Mass ∝ r

$$\Rightarrow m_2 = \frac{m_1 r_2}{r_1}$$

$$= \frac{5 \times 2r}{r} = 10\,gm$$

15. Thermal Properties of Matter

Temperature

- Degree of hotness or coldness.
- Absolute unit is kelvin. It can never be negative.
- $K = 273.15 + °C$
- $F = 32 + \frac{9}{5} °C$

Conversion of Unit

Unit	Freezing Pt.	Boiling Pt.	Any Temp
X	T_{xf}	T_{xB}	T_x
Y	T_{yf}	T_{yB}	T_y

$$\left(\frac{T_x - T_{xf}}{T_{xB} - T_{xf}}\right)_x = \left(\frac{T_y - T_{yf}}{T_{yB} - T_{yf}}\right)_y$$

Bhramastra Formula for Temp Topic

MCQ PUNCH

Q1. On a new scale of temperature (which is linear) and called the W scale, the freezing and boiling points of water are 39°W and 239°W, respectively. What will be the temperature on the new scale, corresponding to a temperature of 39°C on the celsius scale?

Sol. For Celsius scale

$T_f = 0°C$ & $T_b = 100°C$

$$\left(\frac{T_x - T_{xf}}{T_{xB} - T_{xf}}\right)_x = \left(\frac{T_y - T_{yf}}{T_{yB} - T_{yf}}\right)_y$$

$$\Rightarrow \left(\frac{T_w - 39}{239 - 39}\right) = \left(\frac{39 - 0}{100 - 0}\right)$$

$$\Rightarrow T_w = 117°W$$

Thermometric Properties

- Property of a substance which varies linearly with temperature.
- Thermometers are designed on this property.

Types of Thermometer

- **Mercury Thermometer**
- Principle

Length of Column ∝ Temperature

$$\frac{L-L_0}{L_{100}-L_0} = \frac{T-T_0}{T_{100}-T_0}$$

$T_0 \rightarrow 0°C$, L_0 : Column length at 0°C
$T_{100} \rightarrow 100°C$ L_{100} : Column length at 100°C
L : Column length at T°C.

- **Constant Volume Gas Thermometer**
- At constant volume

Pressure of the Gas ∝ Temperature

- **Constant Pressure Gas Thermometer**
- At constant pressure

Volume of the gas ∝ Temperature

- **Platinum Resistance Thermometer**

Resistance of wire ∝ Temperature

Faulty Thermometer

- A faulty thermometer can be used to take correct reading using the following method.

	Freezing Pt.	Boiling Pt.	Any Temp
Faulty Reading	x	y	z
Correct Reading	0°C	100°C	T

$$\frac{Z-x}{y-x} = \frac{T-0°C}{100°C-0°C}$$

NEET Accelerate

- Change of temperature by 1°C changes temp in kelvin by 1 k.
  Fahrenhiet by 1.8°F
- At −40°C, temperature in Celsius and Fahrenhiet are same.
- Mercury is used over water in thermometer because
  a. Low coefficient of thermal expansion.
  b. Doesn't stick to the glass.
  c. Low melting point and high boiling point.
  d. No anomalous behaviour in density like water.

Thermal Equilibrium

- Two or more bodies are said to be in thermal equilibrium with each other if there is no flow of heat from one body to another when they are brought in contact.

Zeroth Law of Thermodynamics

- If two bodies A and B are in thermal equilibrium, and B and C are in thermal equilibrium, then A and C are also in thermal equilibrium.

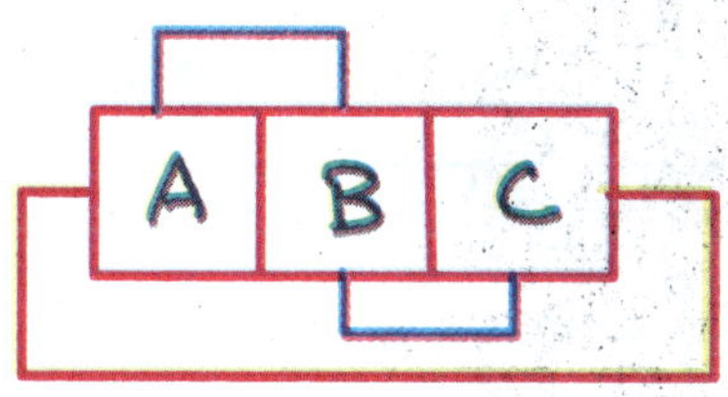

Thermal Expansion

- On heating, size of the body always increases.
- It may be treated as photographic enlargement
- For example, on increasing the temperature both r_1 and r_2 increases.

Types of Expansion

◎ Linear Expansion

- Increase in length on heating.

$\Delta L = L_0 \alpha \Delta T$ $L_f = L_0[1+\alpha \Delta T]$

α : Coefficient of Linear Expansion
ΔT : Change of Temperature.

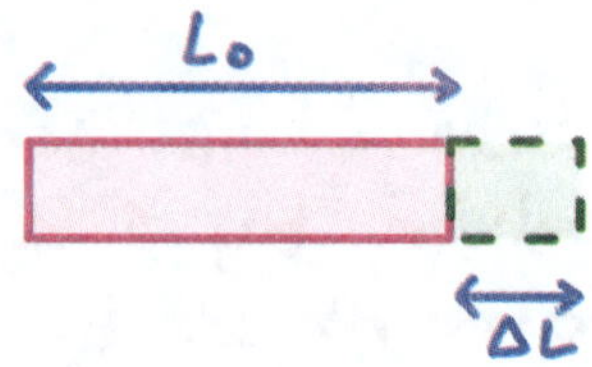

◎ Area Expansion

- Increase in area on heating.

$\Delta A = A_0 \beta \Delta T$ $A_f = A_0[1+\beta \Delta T]$

β : Coefficient of Area Expansion

◎ Volume Expansion

- Increase in volume on heating

$\Delta V = V_0 \gamma \Delta Q$ $V_f = V_0[1+\gamma \Delta Q]$

γ : Coefficient of Volume Expansion

Comparision of Expansion of two rods

- If difference of length $(l_2 - l_1)$ is independent of change of temperature then

$l_1 \alpha_1 = l_2 \alpha_2$

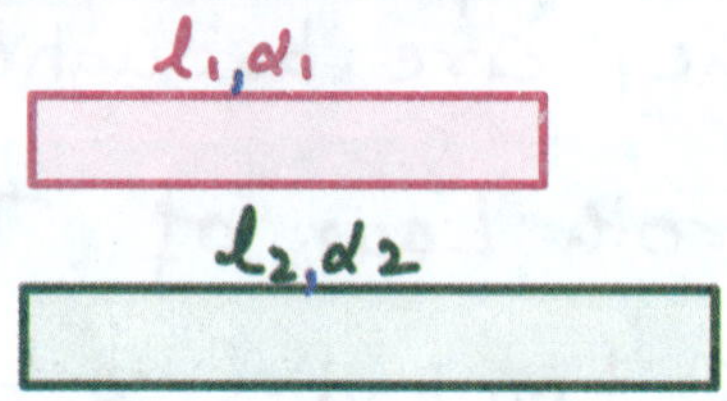

PYQ PUNCH

Q2. A copper rod of 88 cm and an aluminium rod of unknown length have their increase in length independent of increase in temperature. The length of aluminium rod is (NEET 2019)

Sol. $L_c - L_{al}$ = Constant

$L_{0_c} \alpha_c \Delta T = L_{0_{al}} \alpha_{al} \Delta T$

$\Rightarrow 88 \times 1.7 \times 10^{-5} = L_{0_{al}} \times 2.2 \times 10^{-5}$

$68 \text{ cm} = L_{0_{al}}$

Variation of Density with Temperature

- Density decreases with increase in temperature.

$\Delta \rho = -\rho_0 \gamma \Delta \theta$ $\rho_f = \rho_0 [1 - \gamma \Delta \theta]$

- It is mainly used for liquids.

PYQ PUNCH

Q3. The value of coefficient of volume expansion of glycerin is $5 \times 10^{-4}\ K^{-1}$. The fractional change in the density of glycerin for a rise of 40°C in its temperature is. (NEET 2015)

Sol. $\Delta \rho = -\rho_0 \gamma \Delta T$

$\Rightarrow \frac{\Delta \rho}{\rho_0} = -\gamma \Delta T = -5 \times 10^{-4} \times 40$

$= -0.02$

Relationship between α, β and γ

Isotropic material
- $\beta = 2\alpha$
- $\gamma = 3\alpha$
- $\alpha : \beta : \gamma = 1:2:3$

Anisotropic material
- $\beta = \alpha_1 + \alpha_2$
- $\gamma = \alpha_1 + \alpha_2 + \alpha_3$
- $\gamma = \beta + \alpha_3$

Relative Expansion

Liquid in a Beaker
- $\gamma_r = \gamma_e - \gamma_c$

Thermal Stress

- If a material is allowed to expand naturally on heating then there is no thermal stress in the material.
- Thermal stress in case of any external interference

$$\text{Thermal Stress} = \alpha Y \Delta T$$

$$\text{Thermal Strain} = \alpha \Delta T$$

PYQ PUNCH

Q4. A metallic bar of Young's modulus 0.5×10^{11} N/m and coefficient of linear thermal expansion 10^{-5} °C^{-1}, length 1m and area of cross-section 10^{-3} m^2 is heated from 0°C to 100°C without expansion or bending. The compressive force developed in it is (NEET 2024)

Sol. Thermal stress $= \alpha Y \Delta T$

$= 10^{-5} \times 0.5 \times 10^{11} \times 100$

$= 5 \times 10^{7}$ N/m^2

Compressive Force = Stress × Area

$= 5 \times 10^{7} \times 10^{-3}$

$= 5 \times 10^{4}$ N

Heat (Q)

- Thermal Energy in transit.
- Units are Joule, Calorie etc
- 1 Calorie is the amount of heat needed to increase the temperature of 1 gm of water from 14.5°C to 15.5°C at a pressure of 1 atm.
- 1 cal = 4.186 J ≃ 4.2 J

Calorimetry

- It is the process of measuring heat released or absorbed during a specific process.

Calorimeter

- Measure the heat required to raise the temperature of material by 1°C.
- It works on the principle that total heat given by hot objects is equal to the total heat received by cold objects.

Heat Capacities

Specific Heat Capacity

- It is the amount of heat required to raise the temperature of 1 kg mass by 1°C.

$$s = \frac{Q}{m\Delta T} \quad \text{or} \quad Q = ms\Delta T$$

- s_{water} = 4186 J/kgK ≈ 4200 J/kgK
  = 1 Cal/gK
- s_{ice} = 0.5 cal/gK

Heat Capacity

- Heat required to raise the temperature of m kg substance by 1°C.

$$C = ms$$

Latent Heat

- It is the amount of heat required to change the state of 1kg of substance.

$$L = \frac{Q}{m} \quad \text{or} \quad Q = mL$$

- During heating, temperature remains constant.
- Latent heat of fusion is used during conversion from solid to liq or vice-versa.
- Latent heat of vaporization is used during conversion from liq to gas or vice versa.
- L_{fusion} = 80 cal/g] For H_2O.
- L_{vap} = 540 cal/g]

NEET Accelerate

- Heat Capacities are specific to the materials.
- Practically it increases with temperature but for numerical purpose it is taken as constant.
- The unit of ΔT can be in °C or kelvin. They need not to be changed even if heat capacities are given in other unit.

Heating of Liquid using electricity

- Heater connected with V Volt supplying I current produces Q amount of heat in time t

$$Q = VIt$$

- This heat heats up liquid and changes its temperature by ΔT in time

$$t_s = \frac{ms\Delta T}{VI}$$

- To change the phase, time required is

$$t_l = \frac{mL}{VI}$$

MCQ PUNCH

Q5. An electric kettle takes 4A current at 220V. How much time will it take to boil 1 kg of water from temperature 20°C? (The temperature of boiling water is 100°C)

Sol. $S_w = 4200$ J/kgK

$$t_s = \frac{ms\Delta T}{VI} = \frac{1 \times 4200 \times (100-20)}{220 \times 4} = 382 \text{ sec}$$

Phase-Change Diagram of H_2O

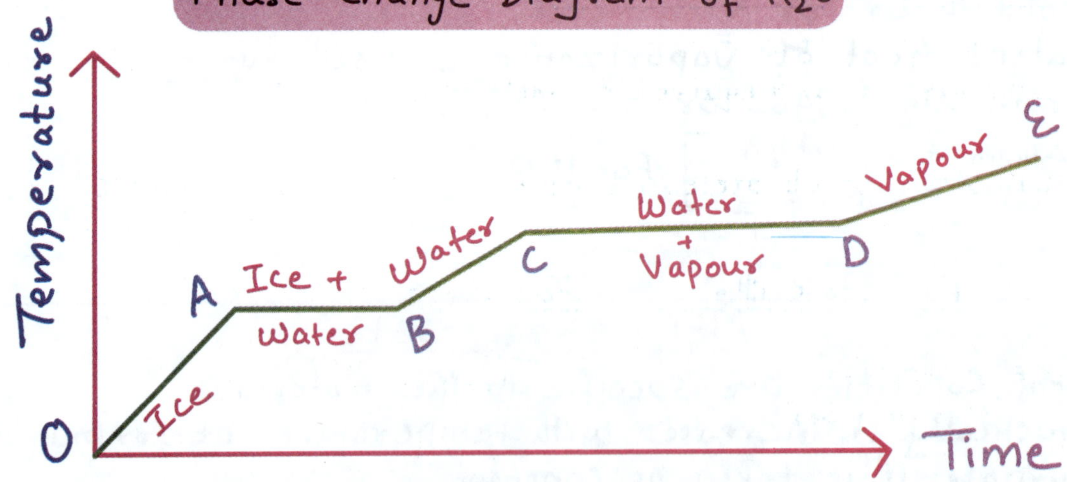

- OA : Heat increases the temperature of Ice.
- AB : Ice converts into water at 0°C.

- BC : Heat increases the temperature of Water.
- CD : Water converts into vapour at 100°C.
- DE : Heat increases the temperature of vapour.
- Slope represents the change of temperature per second.
- Slope OA > Slope BC > Slope DE

Specific Heat	Latent Heat
• OA • BC • DE	• AB • CD

Mixture

Fluids in Same phase

- Mixing two or more fluids leads to final temperature

$$T_{mix} = \frac{m_1s_1T_1 + m_2s_2T_2 + m_3s_3T_3 + \ldots}{m_1s_1 + m_2s_2 + m_3s_3 + \ldots}$$

Mixture of Ice & Water

- Steps to follow ÷
  - Calculate heat required to melt the ice.

$$Q_a = m_i s_i T_i + m_i L_f$$

  - Calculate heat released to bring the water at 0°C.

$$Q_r = m_w s_w T_w$$

For $Q_a < Q_r$:

$$T_{mix} = \frac{Q_r - Q_a}{(m_i + m_w) s_w}$$

Leftover Water : $m_i + m_w$

For $Q_a > Q_r$:

$$T_{mix} \le 0°C$$

Most of the time, it is 0°C.

Leftover ice = $\frac{Q_r - Q_a}{L_f} + 2m_i$

Mixture of Water & Steam at 100°C

- Steps to follow ÷
  - Calculate heat required to boil the water

$$Q_a = m_w s_w (100 - T_w)$$

  - Calculate heat released to convert the steam into water

$$Q_r = m_s L_v$$

For $Q_a > Q_r$

$$T_{mix} = \frac{m_s L_v + s_w(m_w T_w + m_s \times 100)}{(m_s + m_w) s_w}$$

Leftover Water = $m_w + m_s$

For $Q_a < Q_r$

$$T_{mix} = 100°C$$

Leftover water = $m_w + Q_a/L_v$

Leftover steam = $m_s - Q_a/L_v$

PYQ PUNCH

Q6. Steam at 100°C is passed into 20 gm of water at 10°C. When water acquires of 80°C, the mass of water present will be (Take specific heat of water = 1 cal/g-°C and Latent heat of steam = 540 g/cal) **(NEET 2014)**

Sol. $$T_{mix} = \frac{m_s L_v + s_w(m_w T_w + m_s \times 100)}{(m_s + m_w) s_w}$$

$$80 = \frac{m_s \times 540 + 1(20 \times 10 + m_s \times 100)}{(m_s + 20) \times 1}$$

$$\Rightarrow m_s = 2.5 \text{ gm}$$

Leftover water = $m_s + m_w$ = 22.5 gm

Mixture of Ice at 0°C and steam at 100°C

- Steps to follow :-
  - Calculate heat required to boil the ice

$$Q_a = m_i L_f + m_i s_w \times 100$$

  - Calculate heat released to convert the steam into water

$$Q_r = m_s L_v$$

For $Q_a > Q_r$

$$T_{mix} = \frac{m_s(s_w + L_v) - m_i L_f}{(m_i + m_s) s_w}$$

For $Q_a < Q_r$

$$T_{mix} = 100°C$$

MCQ PUNCH

Q7. If 1gm of steam is mixed with 1gm of ice, then the resultant temperature of the mixture is :

Sol. $Q_a = m_i L_f + m_i s_w \times 100$

$= 1 \times 80 + 1 \times 1 \times 100 = 180 \text{ cal}$

$Q_r = m_s L_v$

$= 1 \times 540 = 540 \text{ cal}$

Since $Q_r > Q_a$, $T_{mix} = 100°C$

Water Equivalent

- When heat is provided to water in a container, a part of heat is absorbed by the container.
- For simplification of calculation, container can be replaced by an imaginary water container.
- The mass of imaginary water container is called as water equivalent such that it absorbs the same amount of heat as absorbed by the original container.

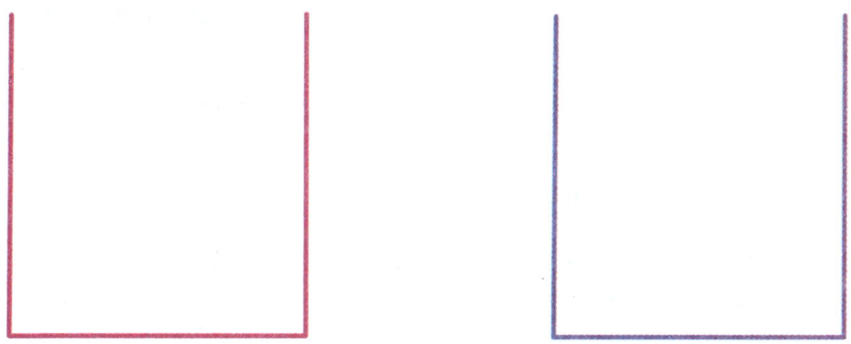

Copper Container	Water Container
Mass $= m_c$	Mass $= m_w$
Specific heat $= s_c$	Specific heat $= s_w$

Water Equivalent, $m_w = \dfrac{m_c s_c}{s_w}$

Conversion of Kinetic Energy into Heat

- During collision of matter with a surface, all its kinetic energy get converted into heat.
- Part of this heat raises the temperature of the fluid.
- Raise of Temp, $\Delta T = \frac{\text{Fraction of K.E converted into Heat}}{ms}$

$$\Delta T = \frac{\eta \times K.E}{ms}$$

where η is fraction

- Part of this heat may also changes the state of matter.

$$mL = \eta \times K.E.$$

- For example
  - ▷ Colliding of water tanker.
  - ▷ Falling of water.

PYQ PUNCH

Q8. A piece of ice falls from a height h so that it melts completely. Only one-quarter of the heat produced is absorbed by the ice and all energy of ice gets converted into heat during its fall. The value of h is (Latent heat of ice is 3.4×10^5 J/kg and g = 10 N/kg) (NEET 2016)

Sol. $\eta = 0.25$ $K.E_f = P.E_i = mgh$

Here, complete ice is getting converted in water

$$mL = \eta \times mgh$$

$$3.4 \times 10^5 = 0.25 \times 10 \times h$$

$$\Rightarrow h = 1.36 \times 10^5 \text{ m}$$

Heat Transfer

- Heat can be transferred from one place to another by three different methods.
  - Conduction – By oscillation of particles
  - Convection – By movement of particles
  - Radiation – By Electro-magnetic waves

Conduction

- It usually takes place in solids.
- Heat flows from hot end to cold end.

Law of Thermal Conductivity

- At steady state, rate of flow of heat is

$$\dot{Q} = \frac{Q}{t} = \frac{kA(T_1 - T_2)}{L}$$

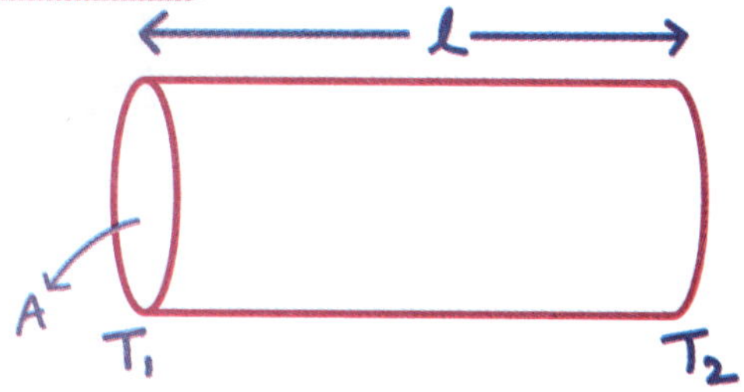

where k = Coefficient of Thermal Conductivity.

- More the value of k, more easily heat flows.
- $k_{conductor} > k_{insulators}$
- $k_{solids} > k_{liquids} > k_{gases}$

Temperature Variation

- At steady state, heat keeps up flowing in the rod but temperature of each point becomes constant.
- Temperature at any distance x from the hot end is given as

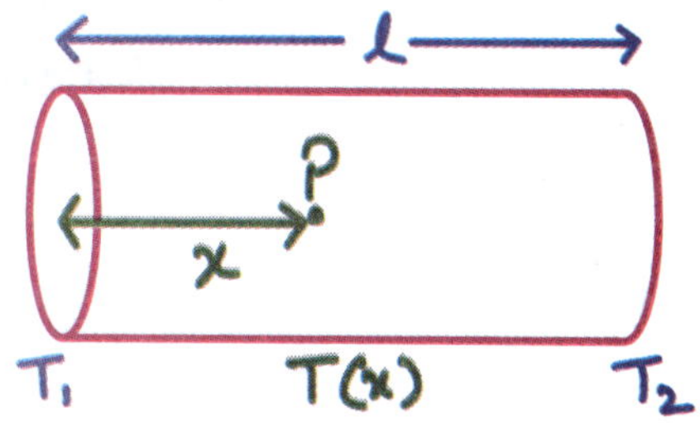

$$T(x) = T_1 - \frac{x}{L}(T_1 - T_2)$$

- It varies linearly.
- This temperature variation is independent of the material of rod and its cross-section.

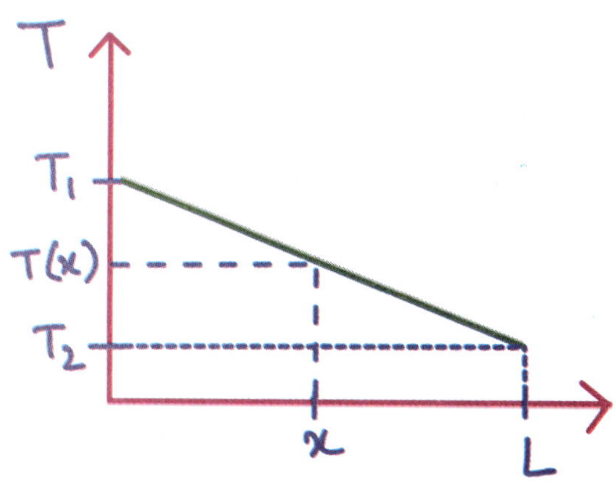

Heat Current

- $\dot{Q} = \frac{\Delta T}{R_T}$ where, $R_T = \frac{L}{kA}$

and called as Thermal Resistance

- For a same rod, R_T is constant.

$$\frac{\dot{Q}_1}{\Delta T_1} = \frac{\dot{Q}_2}{\Delta T_2}$$

MCQ PUNCH

Q9. The two ends of a metal rod are maintained at temperatures 100°C and 110°C. The rate of heat flow in the rod is found to be 4 J/s. If the ends are maintained at temperatures 200°C and 210°C, the rate of flow of heat will be

Sol. $\Delta T_1 = 110 - 100 = 10°C$

$\Delta T_2 = 210 - 200 = 10°C$

For $\Delta T_1 = \Delta T_2$

$\dot{Q}_1 = \dot{Q}_2 = 4 J/s$

Combination of Conductors

Series

- Heat flow is same through the rods.

$$\dot{Q}_1 = \dot{Q}_2 = \dot{Q}$$

- Thermal resistance get added up.

$$R_{eq} = R_1 + R_2 + \ldots$$

$$\frac{L_1 + L_2}{k_{eq} A_{eq}} = \frac{L_1}{k_1 A_1} + \frac{L_2}{k_2 A_2} + \ldots$$

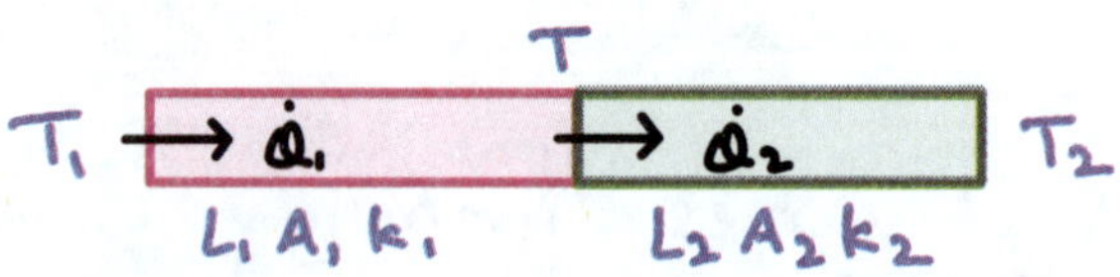

- Junction temperature T

$$\frac{k_1 A_1 (T_1 - T)}{L_1} = \frac{k_2 A_2 (T - T_2)}{L_2}$$

- Heat flow, $\dot{Q} = \frac{T_1 - T_2}{R_{eq}}$

- For equal cross-sectional area A

$$k_{eq} = \frac{L_1 + L_2}{\frac{L_1}{k_1} + \frac{L_2}{k_2}}$$

MCQ PUNCH

Q10. Consider a compound slab consisting of two different materials having equal thickness and thermal conductivities k and 2k, respectively. The equivalent thermal conductivity of the slab is :

Sol. $l_1 = l_2 = l$ and $A_1 = A_2 = A$

$$k_{eq} = \frac{L_1 + L_2}{\frac{L_1}{k_1} + \frac{L_2}{k_2}} = \frac{2}{\frac{1}{k} + \frac{1}{2k}} = \frac{4k}{3}$$

- **Parallel**
- Temperature is same at the ends.
- Reciprocal of Thermal Resistance get added up.

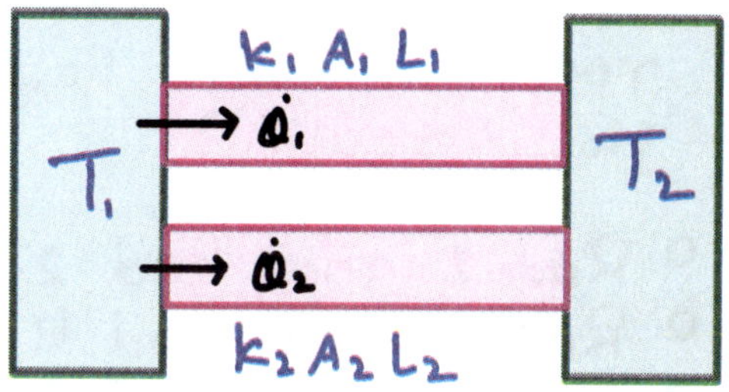

$$\frac{1}{R_{eq}} = \frac{1}{R_1} + \frac{1}{R_2} + \cdots$$

$$\frac{k_{eq}(A_1 + A_2)}{l_{eq}} = \frac{k_1 A_1}{l_1} + \frac{k_2 A_2}{l_2} + \cdots$$

- Total Heat flow, $\dot{Q} = \dot{Q}_1 + \dot{Q}_2$

$$= \frac{k_{eq}(A_1 + A_2)(T_1 - T_2)}{L_{eq}}$$

- For equal length rods

$$k_{eq} = \frac{k_1 A_1 + k_2 A_2}{A_1 + A_2}$$

PYQ PUNCH

Q11. Two rods A and B of different materials are welded together as shown in figure. Their thermal conductivities are k_1 and k_2. The thermal conductivity of the composite rod will be:

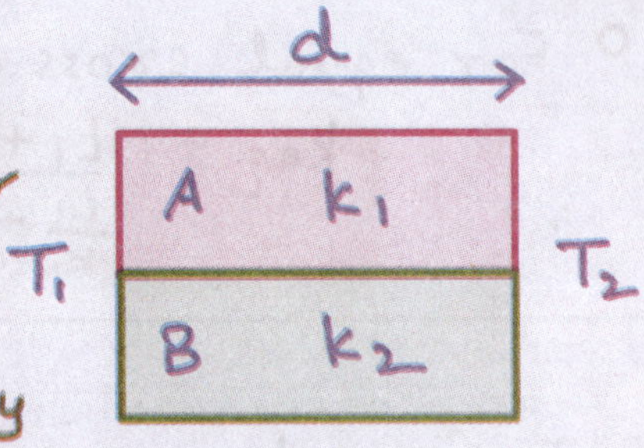

(NEET 2017)

Sol. $A_1 = A_2 = A$ and $l_1 = l_2 = d$

$$k_{eq} = \frac{k_1 A_1 + k_2 A_2}{A_1 + A_2}$$

$$= \frac{k_1 + k_2}{2}$$

Wheatstone Bridge

- For

$$\frac{k_1}{k_2} = \frac{k_3}{k_4}$$

Temperature at the ends of rod 5 is same. So, no heat flow through it.

- Rod 1 and Rod 2 are in series.
- Rod 3 and Rod 4 are in series.
- Then the combination is in parallel.

Ice formation in Lake

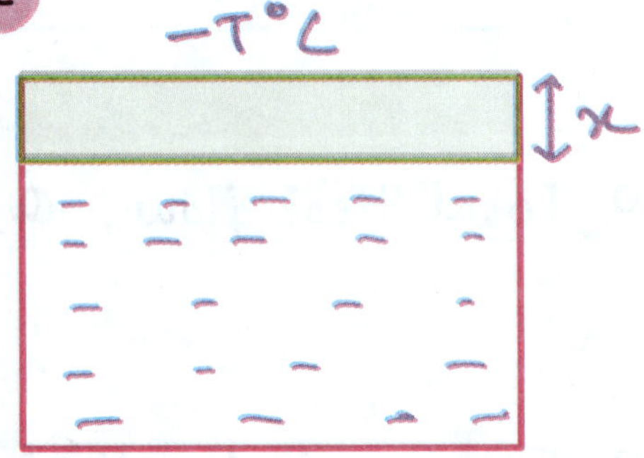

- Ice get formed in the lake in winter.
- The thickness with time

$$t = \frac{\rho L x^2}{2kT}$$

- Rate of formation of ice

$$\frac{dx}{dt} = \frac{kT}{\rho L x}$$

ρ : Density of water
L : Latent Heat of Water
k : Thermal Conductivity of ice

PYQ PUNCH

Q12. A deep rectangular pond of surface area A, containing water (density ρ, specific heat capacity s), is located in a region where the outside air temperature is a steady value at the $-26°C$. The thickness of the frozen ice layer in this pond, at a certain instant is x. Taking the thermal conductivity of ice as k, and its specific latent heat of fusion L, the rate of increase of the thickness of ice layer, at this instant would be given by (NEET 2019)

Sol. $\frac{dx}{dt} = \frac{kT}{\rho L x} = \frac{26k}{\rho L x}$

Convection

- Molecules carry heat from one place to another.
- Happens in fluid.
- Rate of heat transfer

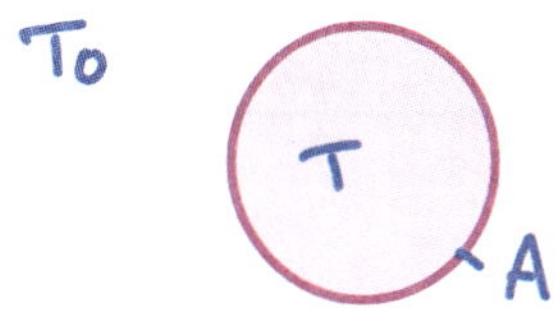

$$\dot{Q} = hA(T - T_0)$$

where h is Convection Heat Transfer Co-efficient

- h depends upon medium and speed of fluid.
- Natural convection is due to gravity.

Radiation

- It doesn't need any medium.
- All bodies radiates thermal radiation at all temperatures.
- The amount of thermal radiation radiated per unit time depends on the nature of emitting surface, its area and temperature.
- Besides emitting, a body also absorbs part of the thermal radiation falls on it.

Emissive Power

- It is the energy radiated per unit time per unit area of the surface.

$$E_{body} = \frac{\dot{Q}}{A}$$

Falling of Radiation on a body

Absorptive Power

- It is the ratio of energy absorbed by the body to the total energy falls on it.

$$a = \frac{\text{Energy Absorbed}}{\text{Energy Incident}}$$

Reflective Power

- It is the ratio of energy reflected by the body to the total energy falls on it.

$$r = \frac{\text{Energy Reflected}}{\text{Energy Incident}}$$

Transmittive Power

- It is the ratio of energy transmitted by the body to the total energy falls on it.

$$t = \frac{\text{Energy Transmitted}}{\text{Energy Incident}}$$

$$a + r + t = 1$$

art = काला 1 Number hai

16. Kinetic Theory Of Gases

Ideal Gas

- Gas which obeys gas low

$$PV = nRT$$

P: Pressure of the Gas
V: Volume of ~~container~~ Free Space
n: no. of moles
R: Universal Gas constant = 8.31 J/mol K
T: Absolute Temperature

- Other forms of Ideal Gas Equation

▷ $PV = \frac{mRT}{M_0}$ M_0: Molecular Weight
m: Total mass

▷ $P = \frac{\rho RT}{M_0}$ ρ: Mass Density

▷ $PV = \frac{N m_0 RT}{M_0}$ N: Total Particles
m_0: mass of one particle

- Real gases approach the ideal gas behaviour at low pressure and high temperature.

PYQ PUNCH

Q1. An ideal gas equation can be written as $P = \frac{\rho RT}{M_0}$, where ρ and M_0 respectively are:

Sol. Mass Density and molecular mass (NEET 2020)

Kinetic Theory of Gases (KTG)

- It is a theoretical model that explains all the properties of gas like pressure, temperature, speed, etc., that are related to the microscopic phenomenon.
- It helps in developing a correlation between the macroscopic properties and the microscopic phenomenon.

Assumptions of KTG

- For a gas, all particles are identical and for mono-atomic gas we consider them as spherical.
- No interaction between particles and with wall except during collision
  - Potential Energy = 0
  - Internal Energy = Kinetic Energy
- Collisions are elastic in nature.
  - No loss of energy.
- Actual volume of particles is negligible as compared to the volume of Container.
- Particles obey Newton's Laws of Motion.
- Effect of gravity is neglected.
  - Density is uniform.
- Number density $\left(\frac{N}{V}\right)$ should be less.
- Molecules should be moving randomly in all directions.
- When a gas is left for sufficient time, it comes to a steady state.

Pressure of the Gas

$$P = \frac{1}{3} \rho V_{rms}^2$$

Root Mean Square Speed

$$V_{rms} = \sqrt{\frac{3P}{\rho}} = \sqrt{\frac{3PV}{m}} = \sqrt{\frac{3RT}{M_0}} = \sqrt{\frac{3k_bT}{m_0}}$$

- Change of V_{rms} on change of P → Can't say
- As T ↑, V_{rms} ↑ $V_{rms} \propto \sqrt{T}$

NEET Accelerate

- If a quantity increases to n times then $x' = nx$
- If a quantity increase by n times then $x' = (n+1)x$
- If $V_{rms} > V_{escape}$ (11.2 km/hr), molecules escapes the atmosphere.
- On moon, $V_{rms} > V_{escape}$, hence there is no atmosphere on moon.

PYQ PUNCH

Q2. The temperature of a gas is -50°C. To what temp. the gas should be heated, so that the rms speed is increased by 3 times? (NEET 2022)

Sol. $T_1 = 273 - 50 = 223K$

Increased by 3 times $\Rightarrow V'_{rms} = 4V_{rms}$

$$\frac{V'_{rms}}{V_{rms}} = \sqrt{\frac{T'}{T}}$$

$$\Rightarrow \frac{4V_{rms}}{V_{rms}} = \sqrt{\frac{T'}{223}}$$

$\Rightarrow T' = 3568K$ or $3295°C$

Maxwell's Distribution Curve

- Area of the curve represents total number of particles.
- $V_{MP} = \sqrt{\frac{2RT}{M_0}} = \sqrt{\frac{2k_bT}{m_0}}$
- $V_{rms} = \sqrt{\frac{3RT}{M_0}} = \sqrt{\frac{3k_bT}{m_0}}$
- $V_{avg} = \sqrt{\frac{8RT}{\pi M_0}} = \sqrt{\frac{8k_bT}{\pi m_0}}$
- $V_{avg} > V_{rms} > V_{MP}$

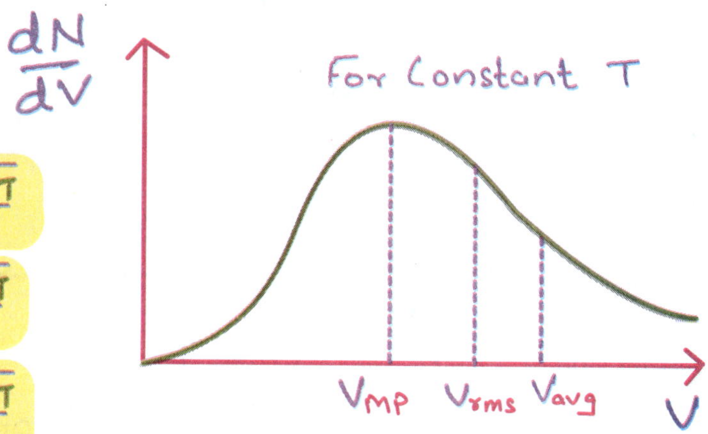

Boltzmann's Constant

$$k_b = \frac{R}{N_A} = 1.38 \times 10^{-23}\ J/K$$

Degree of freedom (f)

- It is the number of independent ways through which an atom or a molecule can attain energy while considering the atom as a point mass.

Type	Translatory	Rotational	Total
Monoatomic	3	0	3
Diatomic	3	2	5
Linear Triatomic	3	2	5
Triatomic	3	3	6
Polyatomic	3	3	6

- At higher temperature, there is vibrational mode also. Each Vibrational mode has 2 DOF. (1 K.E + 1 P.E)
- CO_2 is a linear triatomic, hence has 5 DOF.

Law of Equi-partition of Energy

- Internal Energy associated with each degree of freedom per molecule $\frac{1}{2}k_bT$
- Energy of n moles in f degree of freedom

$$U = \frac{nfk_bNT}{2} = \frac{nfRT}{2}$$

- Change of U on change of P → Can't comment
- As T ↑, U ↑

$$U \propto T$$

- Change of Internal Energy on changing of Temp.

$$\Delta U = \frac{nfR\Delta T}{2} \leftarrow \frac{\text{Nafrat (नफरत)}}{2}$$

- Translatory $K.E = \frac{3}{2}nRT$ $(f=3)$

- KE is independent of the mass of the molecule.
- If 2 or more gases are mixed in a container, total internal energy is the addition of individual internal energy.

$$U = U_1 + U_2$$
$$= \frac{n_1f_1RT}{2} + \frac{n_2f_2RT}{2}$$

PYQ PUNCH

Q3. A gas mixture consists of 2 moles of O_2 and 4 moles of Ar at temperature T. Neglecting all vibrational modes, the total internal energy of the system is : (NEET 2027)

Sol. For $O_2 \rightarrow f = 5$; $Ar \rightarrow f = 3$

$$U = U_1 + U_2$$

$$= \frac{n_1 f_1 RT}{2} + \frac{n_2 f_2 RT}{2}$$

$$= \frac{2 \times 5 \times RT}{2} + \frac{4 \times 3 \times RT}{2} = 11RT$$

Special Laws

◎ **Gay-Lusaac Law**
- Volume Constant

$$P \propto T$$

◎ **Charles's Law**
- Pressure Constant

$$V \propto T$$

◎ **Boyle's Law**
- Temp. Constont

$$PV = c$$

◎ **Avogadro's Law**
- At the same temperature and pressure, equal volume of all gases contain equal number of molecules.

Critical Temperature

- It is the temperature above which no amount of pressure can convert a gas into liquid.

Mean Free Path (λ)

- Average distance covered by an atom between two successive collision.

$$\lambda = \frac{1}{\sqrt{2}\pi n d^2} \quad ; \quad \lambda = \frac{RT}{\sqrt{2}\pi N_A P}$$

n : No. of molecules per unit volume

d : diameter of molecule.

17. Thermodynamics

System and Surrounding

- Anything under consideration is called system.
- Everything except system in universe is surrounding.
- Types of system :
  - Open System : Exchange of heat & mass.
  - Closed System : Exchange of heat only.
  - Isolated System : No exchange of heat and mass.

Thermodynamic Parameters

- They are the variables which describes the state of matter. Ex: pressure, volume, temperature, entholphy, entropy.

1st Law of Thermodynamics

- Net change in internal energy of a system is equal to net heat supplied to the system minus the net work done by the system.

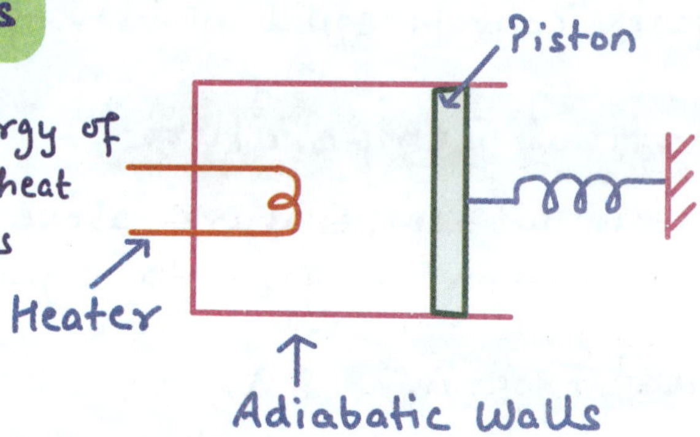

$$\Delta U = \Delta Q - \Delta W_{sys}$$

State Fn. (ΔU), Path Fn. (ΔQ), Path Fn. (ΔW_{sys})

- It is based on Conservation of Energy.
- State functions are path independent i.e. depends only on the initial and final state of the gas.
- Path functions are path dependent i.e. depends upon the nature of process followed.

Sign Convention

- Heat supplied to the system is taken as positive and

heat rejected by the system is taken as negative.

- Work done by the system is taken as positive and work done on the system is taken as negative.

Work Done by a Gas

- $W = \int_{V_1}^{V_2} P dV$
- Always positive on expansion.
- Always negative on compression.
- For constant volume, work done is Zero.

Conversion of Water into Steam

- M amount of water of volume V_1 at 100°C and pressure P_0 is converted into steam of volume V_2.
- For the specific heat of vaporisation L, the change in internal energy is

$$\Delta U = \Delta Q - \Delta W_{sys}$$

$$\Delta U = ML - P(V_2 - V_1)$$

PYQ PUNCH

Q1. 1 g of water of volume 1 cm^3 at 100°C is converted into steam of same temperature under normal atmospheric pressure ($\simeq 1 \times 10^5$ Pa). The volume of steam formed equals 1671 cm^3. If the specific latent heat of vaporisation of water is 2256 J/g, the change in internal energy is : (NEET 2019)

Sol. $M = 1g$

$V_1 = 1 cm^3 = 10^{-6} m^3$; $V_2 = 1671 cm^3 = 1671 \times 10^{-6} m^3$

$P = 1 \times 10^5$ Pa

$$\Delta U = ML - P(V_2 - V_1)$$
$$= 1 \times 2256 - 10^5 (1671 - 1) 10^{-6}$$
$$= 2256 - 167$$
$$= 2089 \text{ J}$$

Area under PV Curve

- Represents work done by the gas.
- If cycle is clock-wise, then work done is positive.

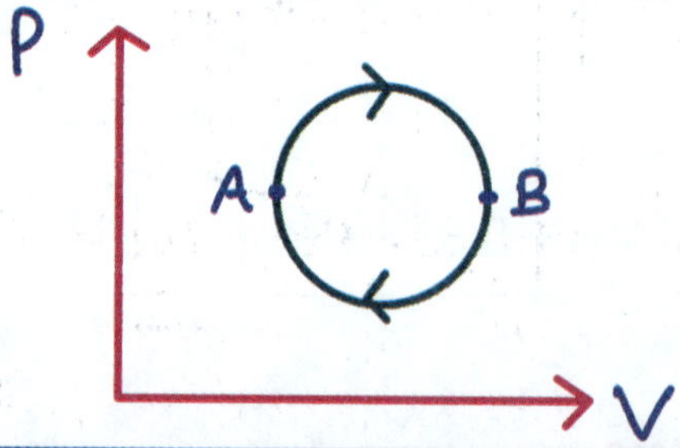

- If cycle is anti-clockwise, then work done is negative.

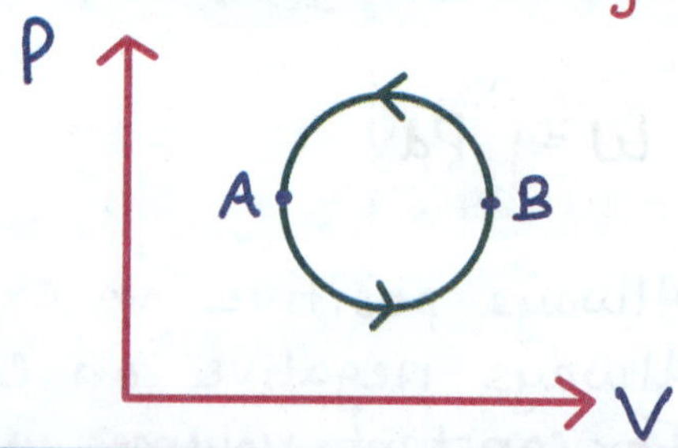

PYQ PUNCH

Q2. A thermodynamics system is taken through the cycle abcda. The work done by the gas along the path bc is: (NEET 2024)

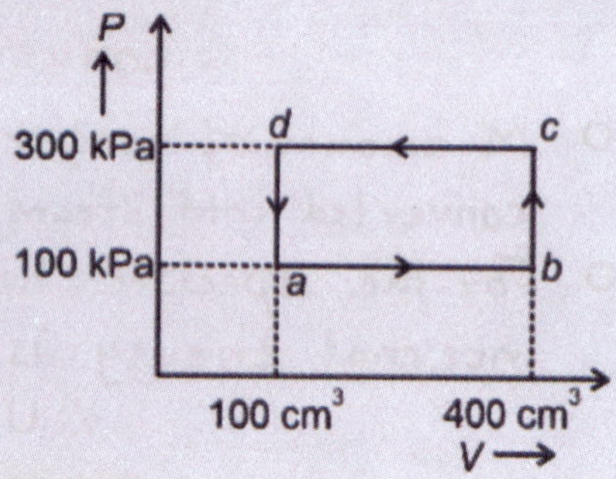

Sol. bc path is constant volume path, hence work done is zero.

Standard Processes

Isobaric Process

- Pressure is constant.
- $V \propto T$
- Work done by the gas

$\Delta W = nR\Delta T$ and

$\Delta W = P(V_2 - V_1)$

- Change in Internal Energy

$\Delta U = \frac{nfR\Delta T}{2}$

- Heat given to the system

$\Delta Q = \left(\frac{f}{2} + 1\right) nR\Delta T$

$\Delta Q = \left(\frac{f}{2} + 1\right) P\Delta V$

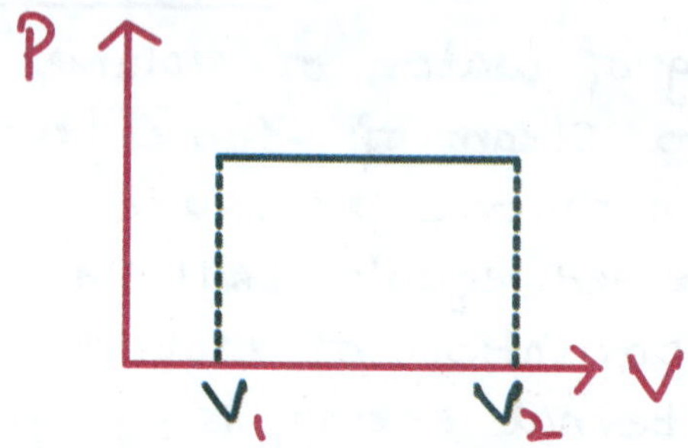

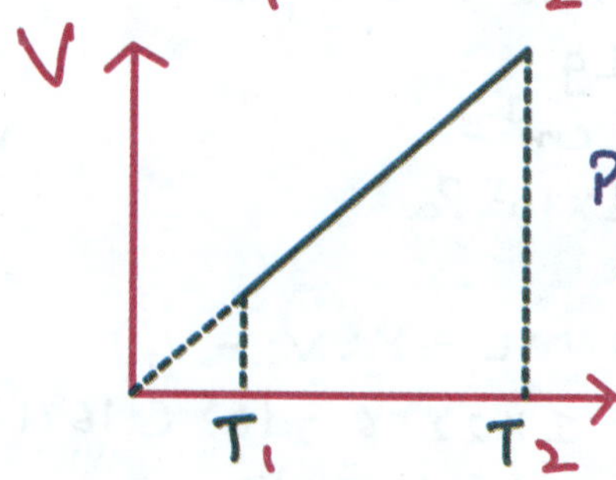

Passes thr. origin.

- $\frac{\Delta W}{\Delta Q} = \frac{2}{f+2}$

PYQ PUNCH

Q3. The volume V of a monoatomic gas varies with its temparature T, as shown in the graph. The ratio of work done by the gas, to the heat absorbed by it, when it undergoes a change from state A to state B is: (NEET 2018)

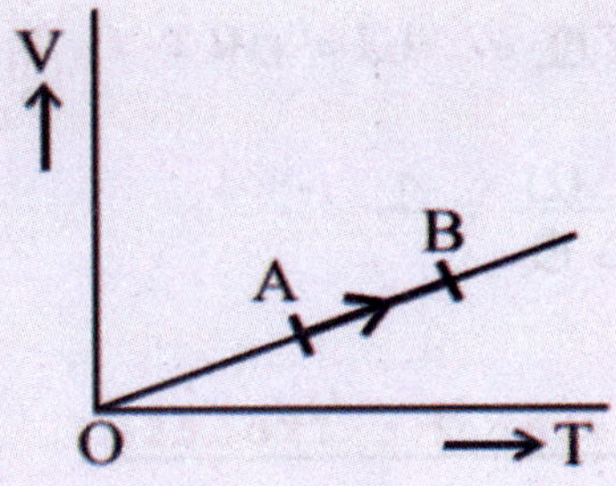

Sol. Since V-T curve passes through origin hence, it is the isobaric process.

$\Rightarrow \frac{\Delta W}{\Delta Q} = \frac{2}{f+2}$

For monoatomic gas, $f = 3$

$\Rightarrow \frac{\Delta W}{\Delta Q} = \frac{2}{5}$

Isochoric Process

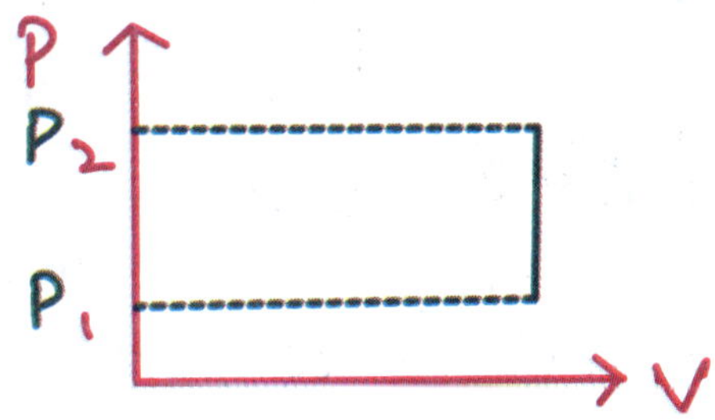

- Volume is constant.
- $P \propto T$
- Work done by the gas
  $\Delta W = 0$
- Change in Internal Energy
  $\Delta U = \frac{nfR\Delta T}{2}$
- Heat given to the system
  $\Delta Q = \frac{nfR\Delta T}{2}$

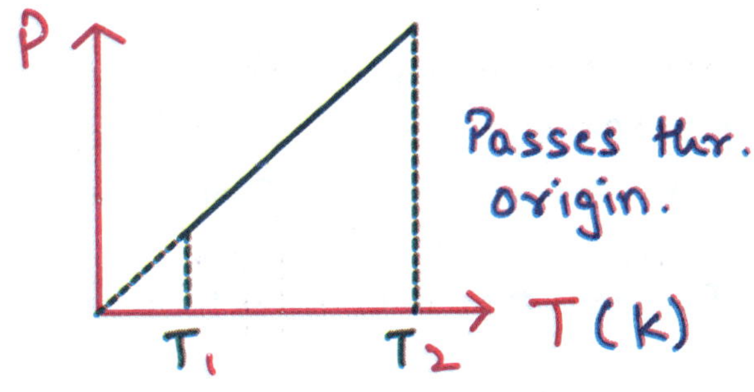

Isothermal Process

- Temperature is constant.
- $PV = C$
- Work done by the gas
  $\Delta W = nRT \ln \frac{V_2}{V_1}$; $\Delta W = nRT \ln \frac{P_1}{P_2}$

- Heat given to the system

$$\Delta Q = \Delta W = nRT \ln \frac{V_2}{V_1}$$

$$\Delta Q = \Delta W = nRT \ln \frac{P_1}{P_2}$$

- $\frac{\Delta W}{\Delta Q} = 1$

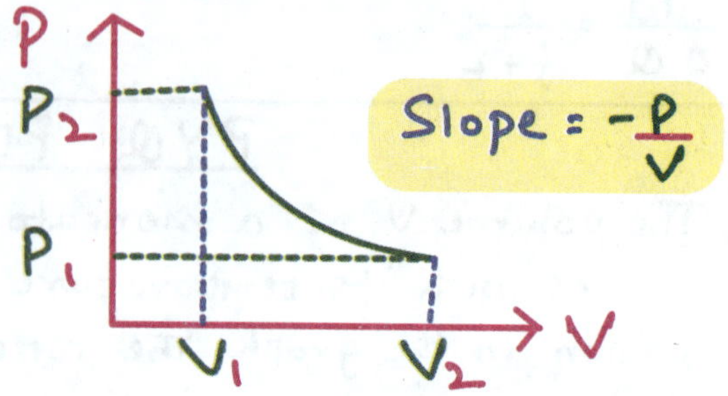

Adiabatic Process

- No exchange of heat.
- $\Delta Q = 0$
- $\Delta W = \frac{fnR}{2}(T_1 - T_2)$
- $\Delta W = \frac{f}{2}(P_1V_1 - P_2V_2)$
- $\Delta U = -\Delta W$

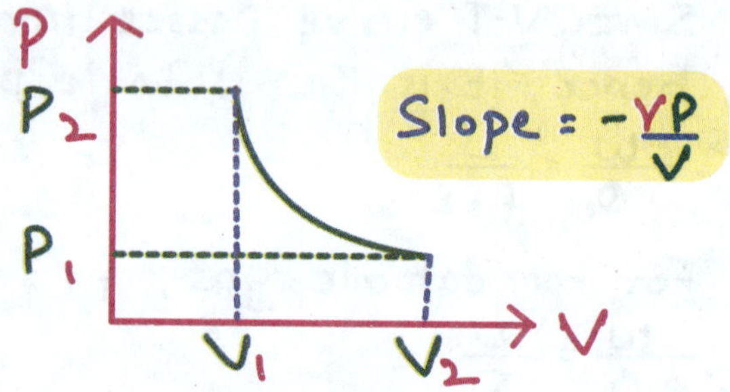

NEET Accelerate

- For Isobaric Process, a part of heat given to the gas changes its internal energy and other part performs work.
- For Isochoric Process, complete heat changes the internal energy.
- For same change of internal energy, more heat is required in Isobaric process as compared to Isochoric Process.
- Slope of P-T graph of adiabatic process is more steeper as compared to Isothermal Process.

Molar Heat Capacities of Gases (C)

- It is the amount of heat required to raise the temperature of 1 mole of gas by 1°C.

$$\Delta Q = nC\Delta T$$

- It depends upon the process followed.

C for Different Processes

Adiabatic	Isochoric	Isobaric	Isothermal
$C_a = 0$	$C_V = \frac{fR}{2}$	$C_P = \left(1+\frac{f}{2}\right)R$	$C_T \to \infty$
Constant	Variable	Variable	

- Mayer's Relation
  $$C_P - C_V = R$$
- Ratio of Specific Heats
  $$\gamma = \frac{C_P}{C_V} = 1 + \frac{2}{f}$$

Gas	C_V	C_P	γ
Monoatomic	$\frac{3}{2}R$	$\frac{5}{2}R$	$\frac{5}{3}$
Diatomic or Linear Triatomic	$\frac{5}{2}R$	$\frac{7}{2}R$	$\frac{7}{5}$
Non-Linear Triatomic	$3R$	$4R$	$\frac{4}{3}$

Adiabatic Equation

- $PV^{\gamma} = C$
- $TV^{\gamma-1} = C$
- $PT^{\frac{\gamma}{1-\gamma}} = C$

MCQ PUNCH

Q4. A mass of diatomic gas ($\gamma = 1.4$) at a pressure of 2 atm is compressed adiabatically so that its temperature rises from 27°C to 927°C. The pressure of the gas in the final state :

Sol. $P_1 = 2$ atm ; $T_1 = 27°C = 300K$; $T_2 = 927°C = 1200K$

For adiabatic compression

$$PT^{\frac{\gamma}{1-\gamma}} = C$$

$$\Rightarrow P_1T_1^{\frac{\gamma}{1-\gamma}} = P_2T_2^{\frac{\gamma}{1-\gamma}}$$

$$\Rightarrow 2\left(\frac{300}{1200}\right)^{\frac{1.4}{1-1.4}} = P_2$$

$$\Rightarrow P_2 = 256 \text{ atm}$$

Polytropic Process

- All processes including the 4 standard processes can be represented by polytropic process.

- Its equation is

$$PV^a = C$$

- Work done by the gas

$$\Delta W = \frac{P_1V_1 - P_2V_2}{a-1}$$

$$\Delta W = \frac{nR(T_1 - T_2)}{a-1}$$

a	Process
0	Isobaric
1	Isothermal
γ	Adiabatic
∞	Ischoric

- Molar Heat Capacity

$$C = C_V + \frac{R}{1-a}$$

PYQ PUNCH

Q5. One mole of ideal monoatomic gas undergoes a process described by the equation $PV^3 = C$. The heat capacity of the gas during this process is: (NEET 2016)

Sol. Comparing given equation with polytropic equation $PV^a = C$

$\Rightarrow a = 3$

For monoatomic, $C_V = \frac{3R}{2}$

Heat Capacity, $C = C_V + \frac{R}{1-a}$

$\Rightarrow C = \frac{3R}{2} + \frac{R}{1-3}$

$\Rightarrow C = R$

Graph Related Theory

◉ Isothermal Curves

- $T_2 > T_1$

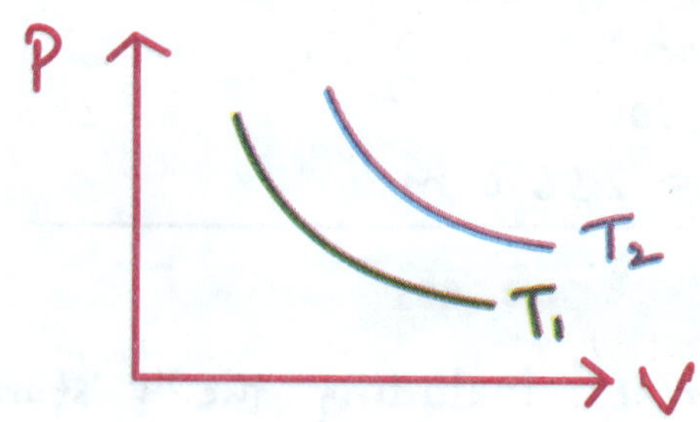

Work Done Graph

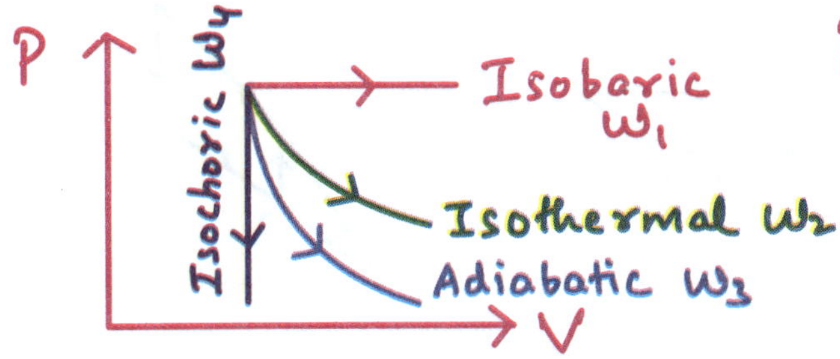

Expansion

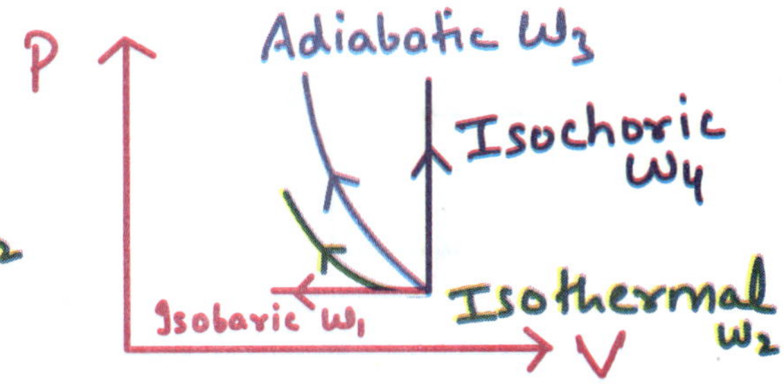

Compression

Expansion:

- Work Done is +ve
- $W_1 > W_2 > W_3$
- $W_4 = 0$

Compression:

- Work Done is −ve
- $W_3 > W_2 > W_1$
- $W_4 = 0$

Adiabatic Curves

- More the γ, steeper the slope.

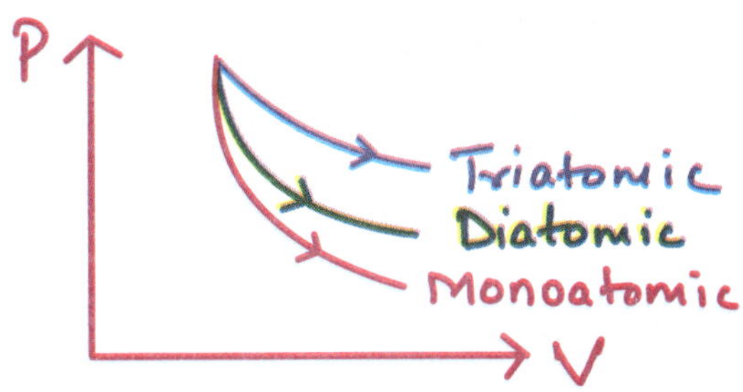

Table for 4 Standard Processes

Process	Equation	WD	ΔU	ΔQ
Isobaric $P = C$	$\frac{V}{T} = C$	$P(V_2 - V_1)$ $nR\Delta T$	$\frac{nfR\Delta T}{2}$	$\left(\frac{f}{2} + 1\right) nR\Delta T$
Isochoric $V = C$	$\frac{P}{T} = C$	0	$\frac{nfR\Delta T}{2}$	$\frac{nfR\Delta T}{2}$
Isothermal $T = C$	$PV = C$	$nRT \ln(V_2/V_1)$ $nRT \ln(P_1/P_2)$	0	$nRT \ln(V_2/V_1)$ $nRT \ln(P_1/P_2)$
Adiabatic $\Delta Q = 0$	$PV^{\gamma} = C$ $TV^{\gamma-1} = C$ $PT^{\frac{\gamma}{1-\gamma}} = C$	$\frac{fnR}{2}(T_1 - T_2)$ $\frac{f}{2}(P_1V_1 - P_2V_2)$	$-\frac{fnR}{2}(T_1 - T_2)$ $-\frac{f}{2}(P_1V_1 - P_2V_2)$	0

Graph Conversion

1. 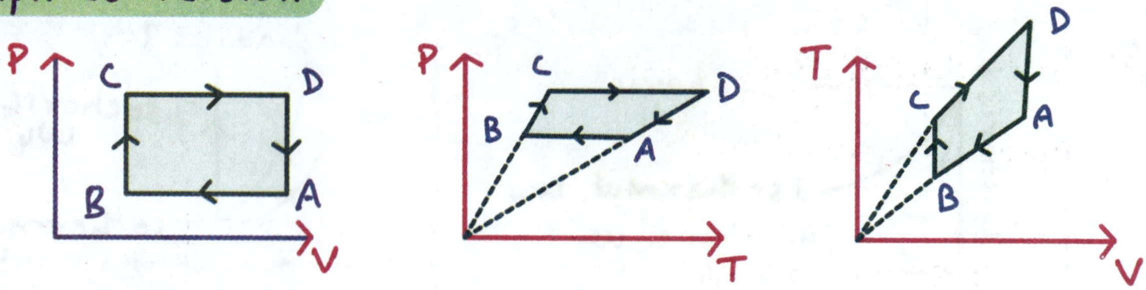

- AB → Isobaric V↓, T↓
- BC → Isochoric P↑, T↑
- CD → Isobaric V↑, T↑
- DA → Isochoric P↓, T↓

2. 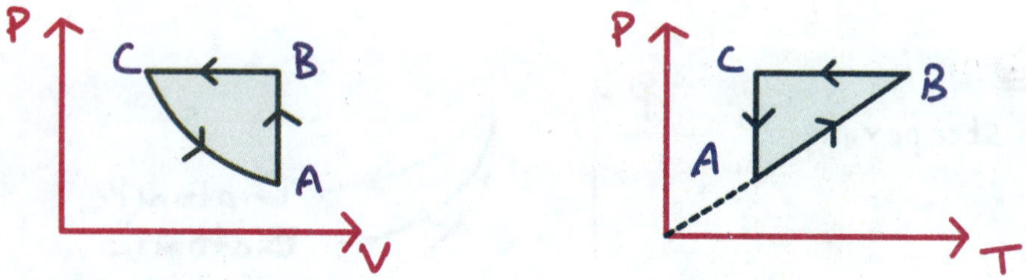

- AB → Isochoric P↑, T↑
- BC → Isobaric V↓, T↓
- CD → Isothermal P↓ V↑

3. 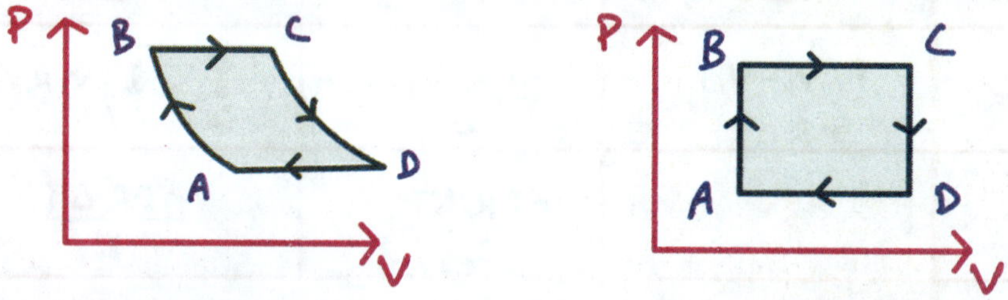

- AB → Isothermal P↑, V↓
- BC → Isobaric T↑, V↑
- CD → Isothermal P↓, V↑
- DA → Isobaric T↓, V↓

18. Oscillations

Periodic Motion

- Repeats itself after a regular interval of time.
- Example - Revolution of Earth

Oscillatory Motion

- To and fro motion about a mean point.
- Example - Swing

Simple Harmonic Motion (SHM)

- It is the special case of oscillatory motion in which
  - a particle oscillates in a straight line.
  - the acceleration of the particle is always directed towards a fixed point on the line. This point is called as equilibrium point or mean point or center of oscillation.
  - Net force at mean point is zero.
  - Magnitude of acceleration is proportional to the displacement of the particle from this point.

$$\vec{a} \propto -\vec{x}$$

or

$$a = -kx$$

Where x is the displacement from mean position.

- If the position of mean point from origin is X_0 and X is is the position of particle, then

$$\vec{a} \propto -(\vec{X} - \vec{X_0})$$

or

$$\vec{a} \propto -\vec{x}$$

Where x is the displacement from mean position.

- Example - Spring - mass system

Differential Equation of SHM

- $$\frac{d^2x}{dt^2} + \omega^2 x = 0$$

- Time period of SHM

$$T = \frac{2\pi}{\omega}$$

Equation of SHM

- **For displacement from mean position**
- $x = A \sin(\omega t + \phi)$
- $v = A\omega \cos(\omega t + \phi)$
- $a = -A\omega^2 \sin(\omega t + \phi)$

where A : Amplitude of SHM
ω : Angular frequency
ϕ : Initial phase
$\omega t + \phi$: Phase at any time t.

- **For position from origin**
- $X = X_0 + A \sin(\omega t + \phi)$
- Take $X - X_0 = x$ $\Rightarrow$ $x = A \sin(\omega t + \phi)$
- $v = A\omega \cos(\omega t + \phi)$
- $a = -A\omega^2 \sin(\omega t + \phi)$

PYQ PUNCH

Q1. If $x = 5 \sin\left(\pi t + \frac{\pi}{3}\right) m$ represents the motion of a particle executing SHM, the amplitude and time period of motion are: (NEET 2024)

Sol. Comparing $x = 5 \sin\left(\pi t + \frac{\pi}{3}\right)$

with $x = A \sin(\omega t + \phi)$

$\Rightarrow A = 5 m$

$\omega = \pi$

$\Rightarrow T = \frac{2\pi}{\omega} = \frac{2\pi}{\pi} = 2 sec$

Circular Representation of SHM

- Particle rotating in a circle of radius A with constant angular speed ω.
- Initial phase or angle is ϕ.
- Rotates by ωt in time t.
- Final phase or angle is $\omega t + \phi$.
- Projection length on x-axis at any time t

$x = A \sin(\omega t + \phi)$
↑
Projection undergoes SHM

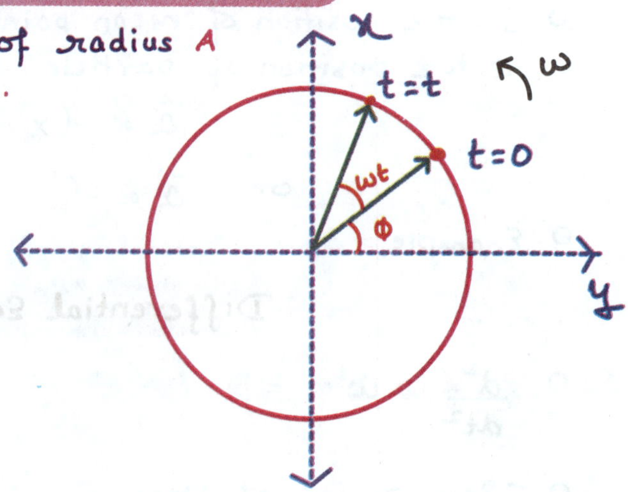

- Phase represents the position of the particle at any time t.

Phase - Position Relation

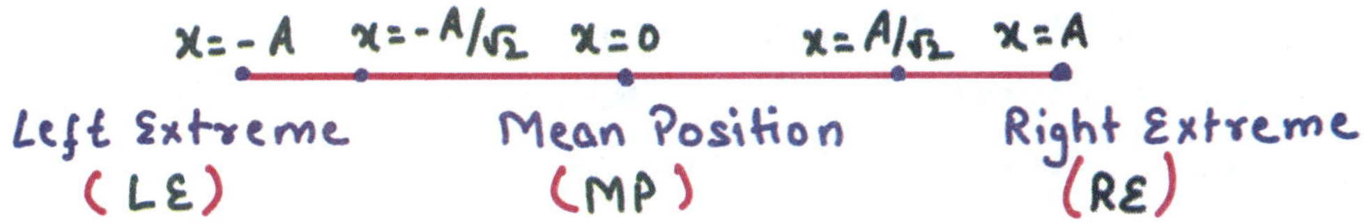

Phase	Disp.	Position	Direction	Diagram
0°	0	At MP	Towards RE	
30°	$A/2$	Btw MP & RE	Towards RE	
45°	$A/\sqrt{2}$	Btw MP & RE	Towards RE	
90°	A	At RE	Stationary	
135°	$A/\sqrt{2}$	Btw MP & RE	Towards MP	
150°	$A/2$	Btw MP & RE	Towards MP	
180°	0	At MP	Towards LE	
210°	$-A/2$	Btw MP & LE	Towards LE	
225°	$-A/\sqrt{2}$	Btw MP & LE	Towards LE	
270°	$-A$	At LE	Stationary	
315°	$-A/\sqrt{2}$	Btw MP & LE	Towards MP	
330°	$-A/2$	Btw MP & LE	Towards MP	
360°	0	At MP	Towards RE	

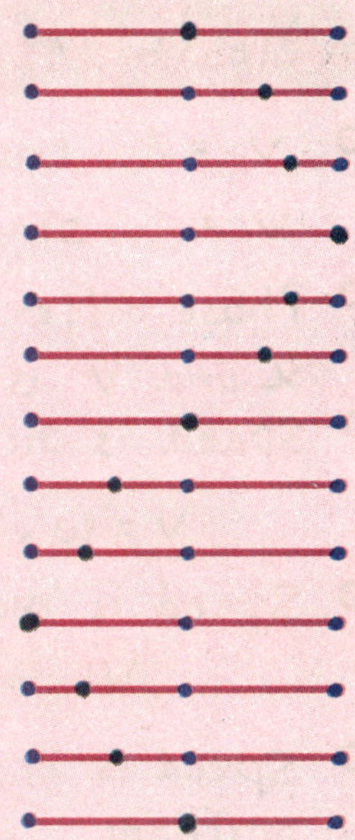

Time of Motion

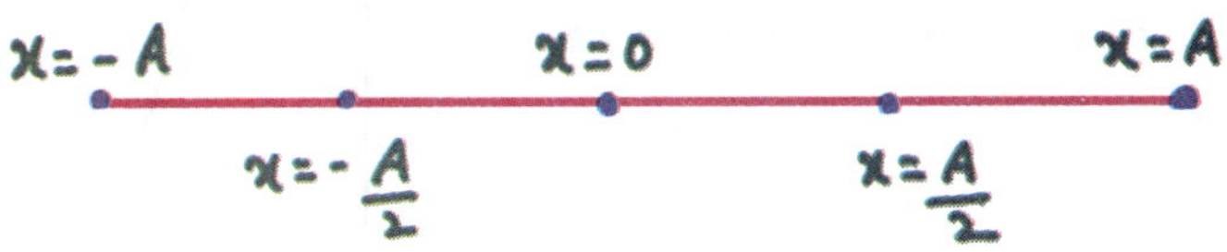

From	To	Time
0	$\pm A/2$	$T/12$
$A/2$	A	$T/6$
0	$\pm A$	$T/4$
$-A/2$	$-A$	$T/6$
$A/2$	$-A/2$	$T/6$
A	$-A$	$T/2$

- T is the Time of One oscillation.
- Incoming Time = Outgoing Time
- From 0 to $A/2$, time is $T/12$ while from $A/2$ to A, time is $T/6$. For same distance, time taken can be different.

NEET Accelerate

- All SHM are oscillatory motion but vice-versa not true.
- All are periodic motion but vice-versa not true.
- Total displacement in 1 Oscillation is Zero.
- Total distance covered in 1 Oscillation is 4A.
- Mean position doesn't depends upon the initial position of the particle.
- Calculations for initial position is adjusted by initial phase.

Velocity of SHM

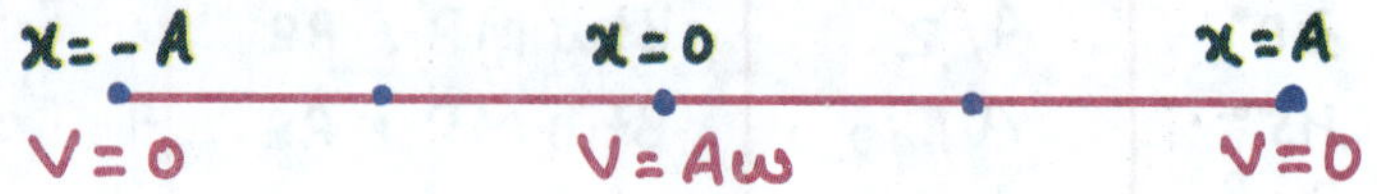

- $v = A\omega \cos(\omega t + \phi)$
  $v = A\omega \sin(\omega t + \phi + 90°)$
- Phase difference between x and v is 90°.

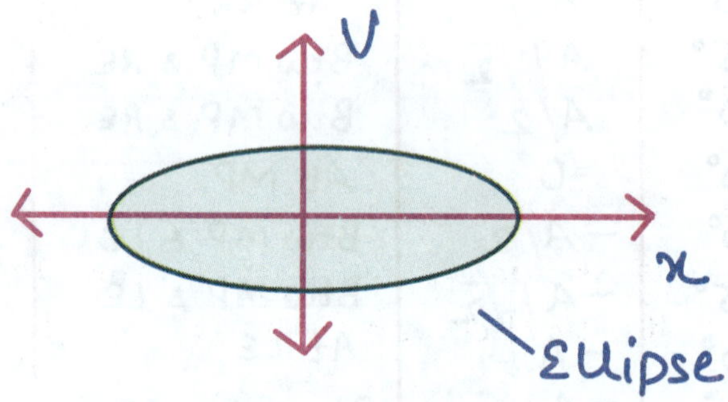

- Speed is related to x as
  $$v = \omega\sqrt{A^2 - x^2}$$
- Speed is maximum at MP.
  $$V_{max} = A\omega$$
- Speed is zero at extreme positions.

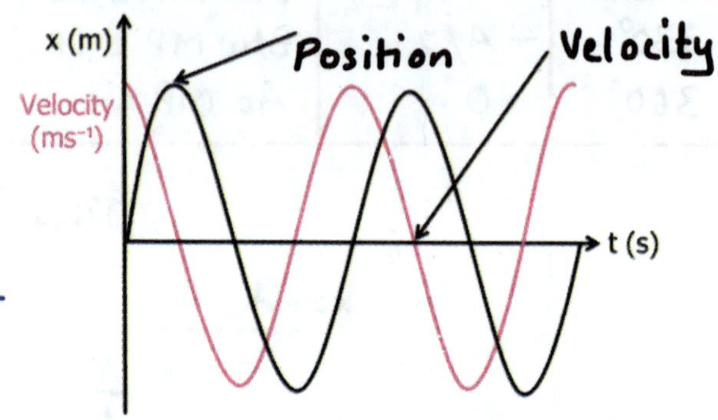

- Average speed in one complete oscillation is $\frac{2A\omega}{\pi}$.
- Average velocity in one complete oscillation is 0.

Acceleration of SHM

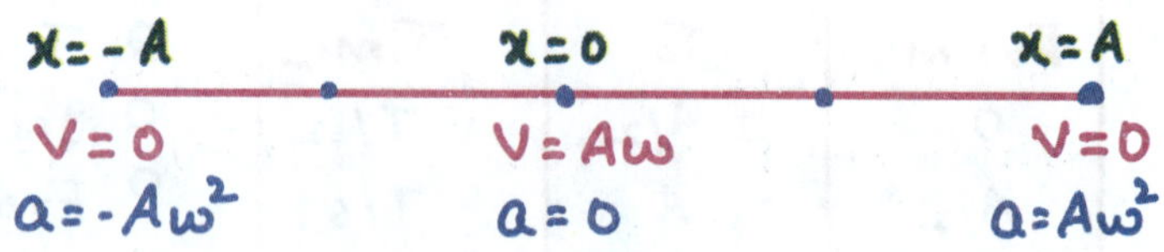

- $a = -A\omega^2 \sin(\omega t + \phi)$
  $a = A\omega^2 \sin(\omega t + \phi + 180°)$
- Phase difference between x and a is 180°.
- Phase difference between v and a is 90°.

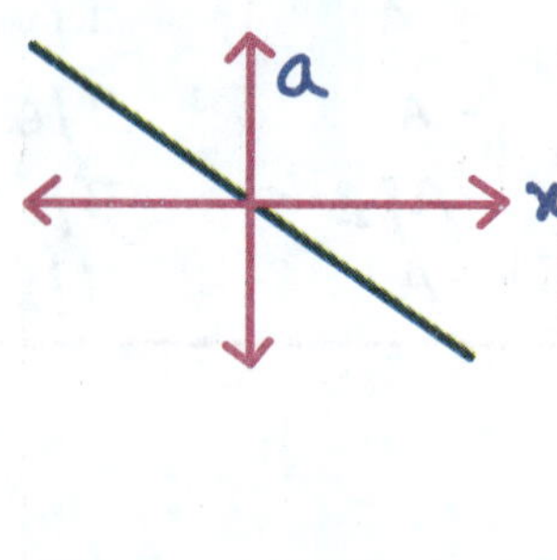

- Acceleration at any position x is given as $a = -\omega^2 x$

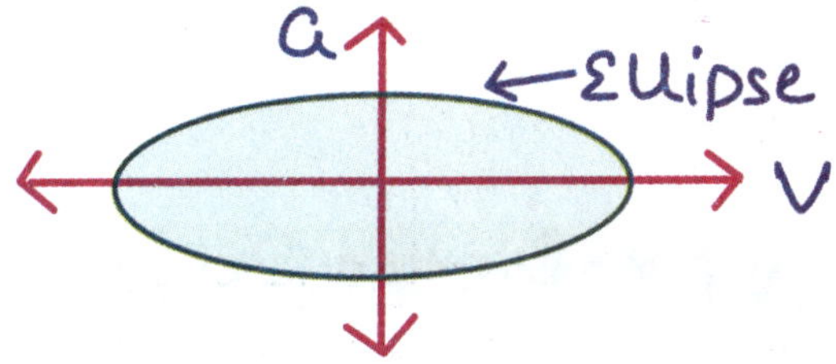

- Acceleration is related to v as $a = \omega\sqrt{A^2\omega^2 - v^2}$
- Acceleration is maximum at extreme positions. $a = -A\omega^2$
- Acceleration is zero at MP.

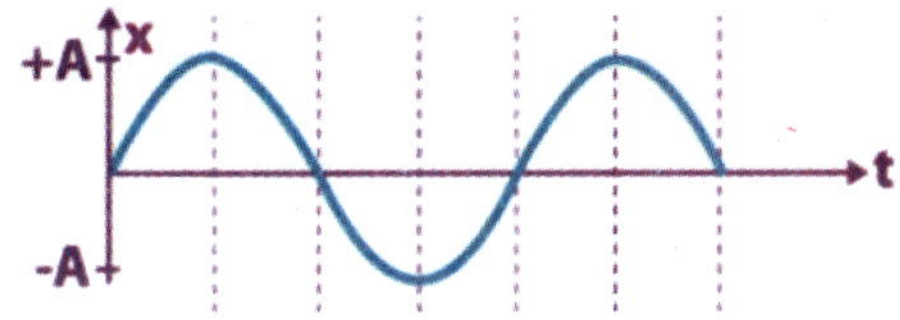

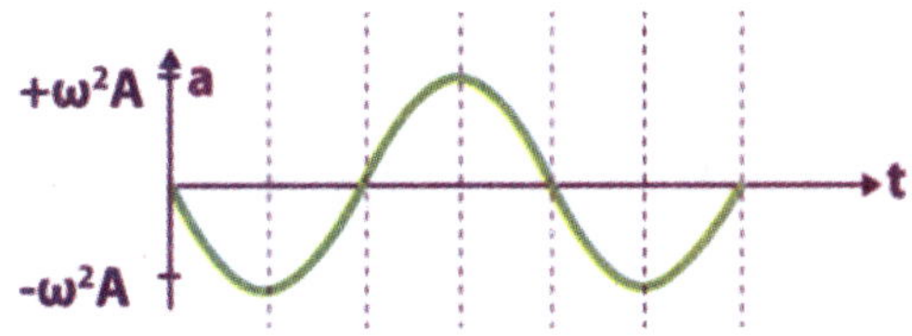

PYQ PUNCH

Q2. The x-t graph of a particle performing SHM is shown in the figure. The acceleration of the particle at t=2s is (NEET 2023)

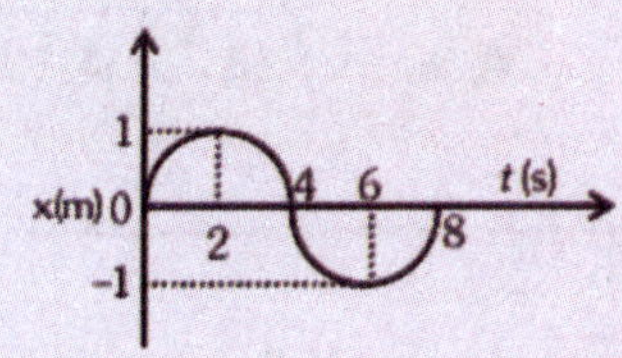

Sol. Time Period = 8 sec

$$\omega = \frac{2\pi}{T} = \frac{2\pi}{8} = \frac{\pi}{4}$$

At t = 2s, x = 1m

So, acceleration at any instant

$$a = -\omega^2 x$$

$$= -\left(\frac{\pi}{4}\right)^2 \times 1 = -\frac{\pi^2}{16}\ m/s^2$$

Special Cases

- Time period of particle executing SHM for which velocities at displacements x_1 and x_2 are v_1 and v_2 respectively is

$$T = 2\pi\sqrt{\frac{x_2^2 - x_1^2}{v_1^2 - v_2^2}}$$

- Maximum speed equals to maximum acceleration

$\omega = 1$ rad/s

$T = 2\pi$ sec

- TP in terms of maximum speed v and max acceleration a

$$TP = \frac{2\pi v}{a}$$

Super-Position Principle

In same axis

- Two or more SHM are superimposed on a particle.
- Displacement due to 1st SHM

$$x_1 = A_1 \sin(\omega t + \phi_1)$$

- Displacement due to 2nd SHM

$$x_2 = A_2 \sin(\omega t + \phi_2)$$

- By superposition principle

$$x = x_1 + x_2$$

- Amplitude

$$A = \sqrt{A_1^2 + A_2^2 + 2A_1A_2\cos(\phi_2 - \phi_1)}$$

PYQ PUNCH

Q3. The displacement of a particle executing SHM is given by

$$y = A_0 + A\sin\omega t + B\cos\omega t$$

Then the amplitude of its oscillation is given by (NEET 2019)

Sol. $y = A_0 + A\sin\omega t + B\cos\omega t$

Rewrite it as

$y - A_0 = A\sin\omega t + B\cos\omega t$

$\Rightarrow Y = A\sin\omega t + B\cos\omega t$

$y_1 = A\sin\omega t$; $y_2 = B\sin(\omega t + 90°)$

$\Rightarrow$ Thus, this is SHM of 2 super-imposed motion having

$A_1 = A$; $A_2 = B$; $\phi_1 = 0°$; $\phi_2 = 90°$

$$Amp = \sqrt{A_1^2 + A_2^2 + 2A_1A_2\cos(\phi_2 - \phi_1)}$$

$$Amp = \sqrt{A^2 + B^2 + 2AB\cos(90° - 0°)}$$

$$Amp = \sqrt{A^2 + B^2}$$

◎ In perpendicular axis

- Two or more SHM are imposed on a particle.
- Displacement due to 1st SHM

  $x = A_1 \sin(\omega t + \phi_1)$
- Displacement due to 2nd SHM

  $y = A_2 \sin(\omega t + \phi_2)$
- By super-position principle

  Net Displacement $= \vec{x} + \vec{y}$

- If two SHMs with some amplitude and time period, when acting together in perpendicular directions with a phase difference $(\phi_2 - \phi_2)$ of

a. $0° \rightarrow$ Straight inclined line motion at 45° with x-axis

b. $\pi/2 \rightarrow$ Circular motion

Spring - Mass System

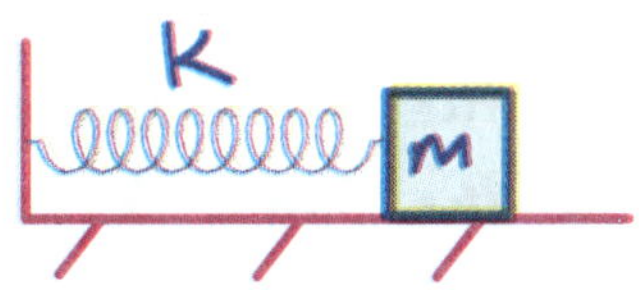

- Time Period (TP)

  $$T = 2\pi\sqrt{\frac{m}{k}}$$

  $k = m\omega^2$ & $k = F/x$

- TP is independent of the orientation of the system.
- Also independent of the amplitude of the mass.
- It doesn't stop at mean position. Infact speed is maximum at mean position.

PYQ PUNCH

Q4. A spring is stretched by 5cm by a force 10 N. The time period of the oscillations when a mass of 2 kg is suspended by it is: (NEET 2021)

Sol. $F = 10\,N$; $x = 5cm = 0.05m$; $m = 2\,kg$

$k = F/x = 10/0.05 = 200\,N/m$

$$T = 2\pi\sqrt{\frac{m}{k}} = 2\pi\sqrt{\frac{2}{200}} = 0.628s$$

Combination of Spring

Series

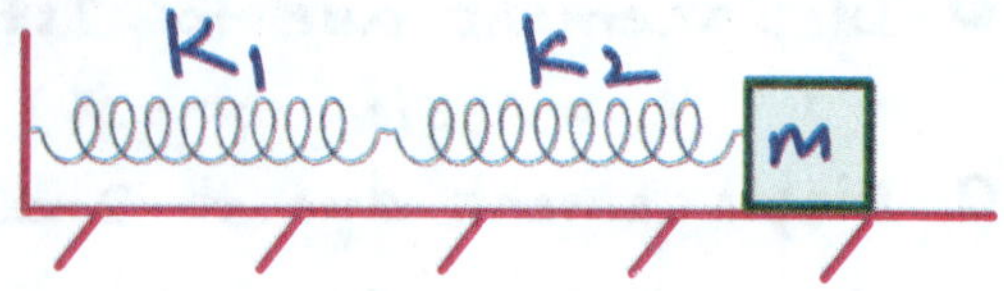

- $T = 2\pi\sqrt{\dfrac{m}{k_{eq}}}$ where $\dfrac{1}{k_{eq}} = \dfrac{1}{k_1} + \dfrac{1}{k_2}$
- $T_{eq}^2 = T_1^2 + T_2^2$

where T_1 is the Time Period with spring k_1
T_2 is the Time Period with spring k_2

Parallel

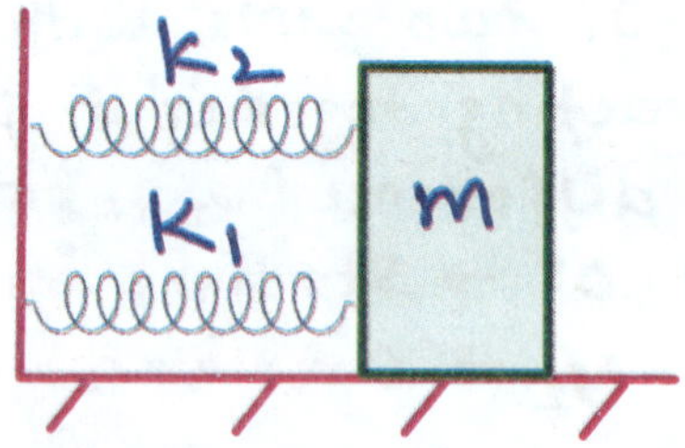

- $T = 2\pi\sqrt{\dfrac{m}{k_{eq}}}$ where $k_{eq} = k_1 + k_2$
- $\dfrac{1}{T_{eq}^2} = \dfrac{1}{T_1^2} + \dfrac{1}{T_2^2}$

where T_1 is the Time Period with spring k_1
T_2 is the Time Period with spring k_2

Reduced Mass Concept

- $T = 2\pi\sqrt{\dfrac{m_1 m_2}{(m_1 + m_2)k}}$

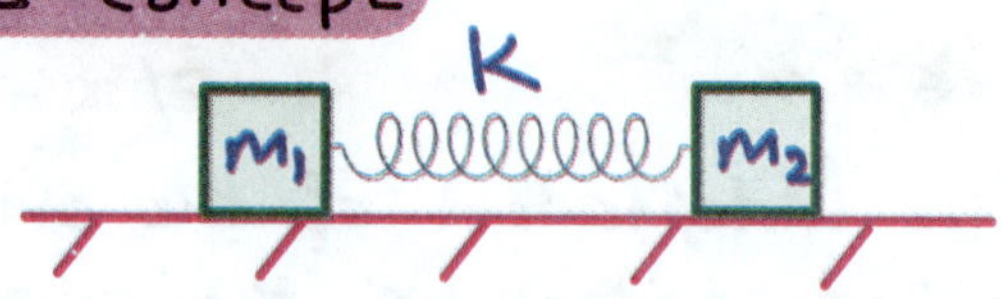

Simple Pendulum

$$T = 2\pi\sqrt{\frac{l}{g_{eff}}}$$

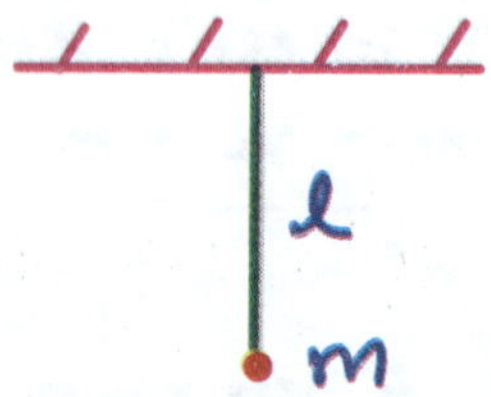

- TP is independent of the mass of the bob.
- l is the length from the point of rotation to the centre of the bob.

Special Cases of Simple Pendulum

In an accelerating train

- $T = 2\pi\sqrt{\dfrac{l}{\sqrt{g^2 + a^2}}}$ where a is the acceleration of train.
- Time Period decreases.

Lift Acc Up

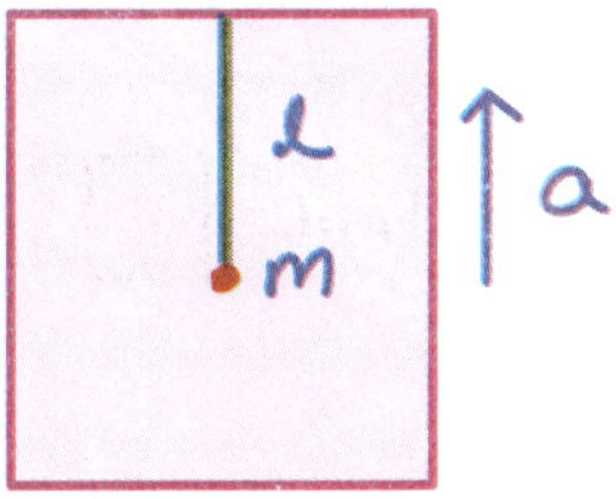

$$T = 2\pi\sqrt{\frac{l}{g+a}}$$

Lift Acc Down

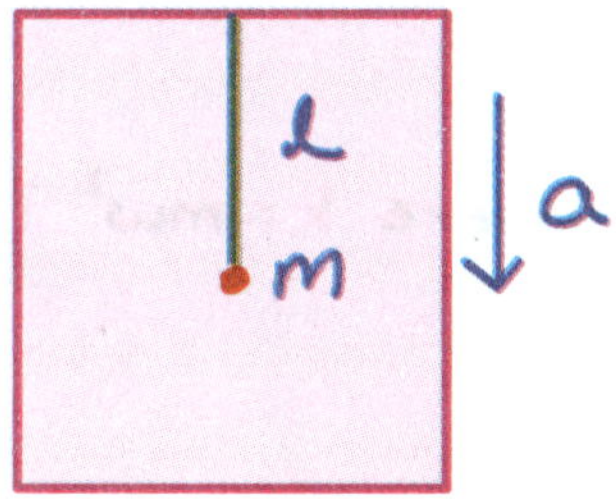

$$T = 2\pi\sqrt{\frac{l}{g-a}}$$

Free Fall

- $T \rightarrow \infty$

Time Period in non-viscous fluid

$$T = 2\pi\sqrt{\frac{l}{g}\left(\frac{\rho_b}{\rho_b - \rho_f}\right)}$$

where ρ_b and ρ_f are the densities of body and the fluid respectively.

Two Pendulums

- Minimum number of oscillations for longer pendulums to be in phase starting from their mean position

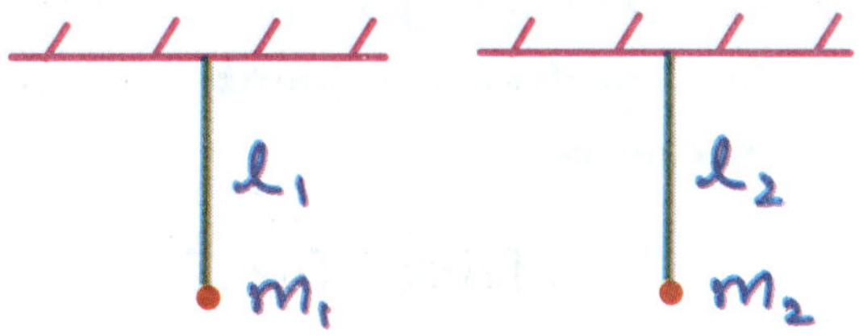

$l_1 > l_2$

$$n_l = \frac{\sqrt{l_2}}{\sqrt{l_1} - \sqrt{l_2}}$$

$$n_s = n_l + 1$$

PYQ PUNCH

Q5. Two pendulums of length 121 cm and 100 cm start vibrating in phase. At some instant, the two are at their mean position in the same phase. The minimum number of vibrations of the shorter pendulum after which the two are again in phase at the mean position is : (NEET 2022)

Sol. $n_l = \frac{\sqrt{l_2}}{\sqrt{l_1} - \sqrt{l_2}} = \frac{\sqrt{100}}{\sqrt{121} - \sqrt{100}} = 10$

For shorter pendulum, $n_s = n_l + 1 = 11$

Energies in SHM

- Kinetic Energy

$KE = \frac{1}{2}k(A^2 - x^2)$ where $k = m\omega^2$ is a Force Constant.

- Potential Energy

$PE = \frac{1}{2}kx^2$

Conservation of Energy

- Total Energy = Kinetic Energy + Potential Energy
  $= \frac{1}{2}kA^2$
  = Constant

- Total energy remains conserved.
- It only changes its form.
  - At extreme points, KE is 0
  - At equilibrium point, KE is maximum.

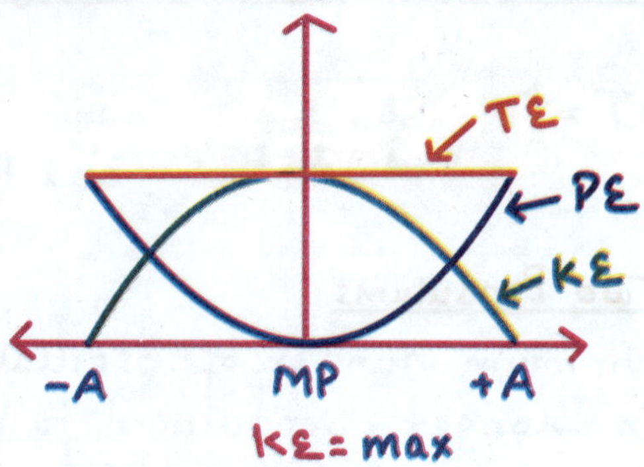

Tricks for Relationship between Energies

- Displacement of particle for

PE = nKE

- $A\sqrt{\frac{n}{n+1}}$
- For n = 1

$x = \frac{A}{\sqrt{2}}$

KE = nPE

- $\frac{A}{\sqrt{n+1}}$
- For n = 1

$x = \frac{A}{\sqrt{2}}$

TE = nPE

- $\frac{A}{\sqrt{n}}$
- For n = 1

$x = A$

i.e. Extreme Position

TE = nKE

- $A\sqrt{\frac{n-1}{n}}$
- For n = 1

$x = 0$,

i.e. Mean Position

Frequency

- Number of times a physical quantity repeats.

$$f \propto \frac{1}{TP}$$

Physical Quantity	Time Period	Frequency
Position	T	f
Velocity	T	f
Speed	T/2	2f
Acceleration	T	f
KE	T/2	2f
PE	T/2	2f
TE	∞	0

PYQ PUNCH

Q6. A body is executing simple harmonic motion with frequency n, the frequency of its potential energy is: (NEET 2021)

Sol. Frequency of PE is 2n.

19. Waves

Wave

- It is a disturbance through which energy gets transferred from one point to another.

Types of Wave

- **On the basis of Medium**

Mechanical Wave
- Needs medium to propagate.
- Sound wave, String wave etc.

Non-Mechanical Wave
- Doesn't need medium to propagate.
- EMW

- **On the basis of Displacement of particle**

Transverse Wave
- Particles oscillate perpendicular to the direction of wave motion.
- Uses shear elasticity of medium.
- In solids only.
- EMW, string wave, waves on water surface. (due to surface tension)

Longitudinal Wave
- Particles oscillate parallel to the direction of wave motion.
- Uses volume elasticity of the medium.
- Both in solids and fluids
- Sound wave, waves inside water.

◎ On the basis of Energy Propagation

Progressive Wave
- Energy keeps on moving in a particular direction.

Stationary Wave
- Energy gets confined in segments.

Equation of Transverse Wave

- Every particle of wave performs individual SHM according to an equation

▷ $y = A\sin(kx - \omega t)$

Ek +ve and ek –ve, then ⟶ Travelling in +ve x-direction

▷ $y = A\sin 2\pi\left(\frac{x}{\lambda} - \frac{t}{T}\right)$

▷ $y = A\sin(kx + \omega t)$

Dono +ve ya dono –ve, then ⟶ Travelling in –ve x-direction

▷ $y = A\sin 2\pi\left(\frac{x}{\lambda} + \frac{t}{T}\right)$

where y is the displacement of particle at a distance x and time t.

A is the amplitude of oscillation of each particle.

PYQ PUNCH

Q1. A wave travelling in the positive x-direction having displacement along y-direction as 1m, wavelength 2π m and frequency of $1/\pi$ Hz is represented by (NEET 2013)

Sol. $A = 1\text{m}$; $\lambda = 2\pi$ m ; $f = 1/\pi$ Hz

Now

$T = \frac{1}{f} = \pi$ sec

So, equation becomes

$$y = A\sin 2\pi\left(\frac{x}{\lambda} - \frac{t}{T}\right) = 1\sin 2\pi\left(\frac{x}{2\pi} - \frac{t}{\pi}\right) = \sin(x - 2t)$$

- Velocity of wave $V = \frac{\omega}{k} = \frac{\lambda}{T} = \lambda f$

Particle Velocity

- $V_p = A\omega \cos(kx - \omega t)$
- $(V_p)_{max} = A\omega$
- In terms of wave velocity

$$(V_p)_{max} = AkV$$

String Wave

- **Velocity in string**
- Velocity $v = \sqrt{\frac{T}{\mu}}$

where T is the tension in the string

μ is the mass per unit length.

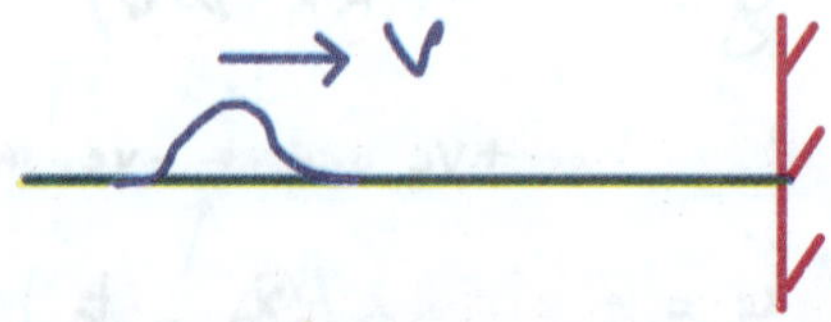

PYQ PUNCH

Q2. If the initial tension on a stretched string is doubled, then the ratio of the initial and final speeds of a transverse wave along the string is : (NEET 2022)

Sol. $v \propto \sqrt{T}$

$$\Rightarrow \frac{V_1}{V_2} = \sqrt{\frac{T_1}{T_2}} = \sqrt{\frac{1}{2}}$$

- **Velocity in vertical mass string**
- Tension is different at different point.
- Speed at a distance x

$$v = \sqrt{gx}$$

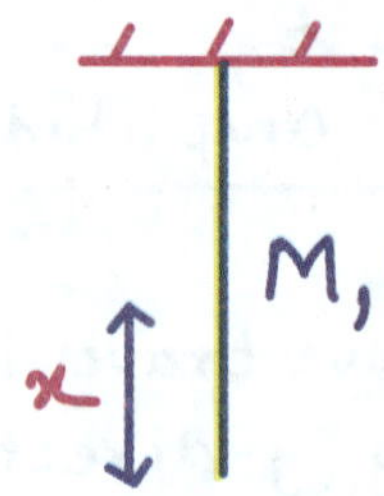

- Time to reach at top

$$T = 2\sqrt{\frac{L}{g}}$$

- **Ratio of transverse wave at bottom to top**

$$\frac{\lambda_1}{\lambda_2} = \sqrt{\frac{m}{M+m}}$$

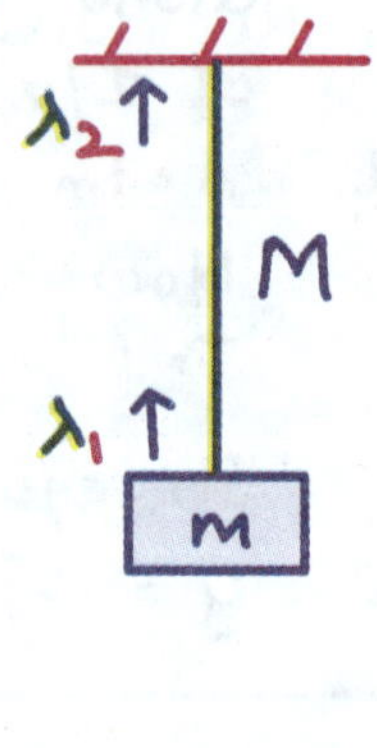

Intensity of Wave

- $I = \frac{1}{2}\rho v A^2 \omega^2$ where ρ is the density of string
- $I \propto A^2$

Reflection of Wave

Thinner to Thicker

	Original	Reflected	Transmitted
Frequency	f	f	f
Speed	v	Same	↓
Wavelength	λ	Same	↓
Phase Diff.	0°	π	0°
Amp. Dir	+ve	−ve	+ve
Amp. Mag	A	↓	↓

Thicker to Thinner

	Original	Reflected	Transmitted
Frequency	f	f	f
Speed	v	Same	↑
Wavelength	λ	Same	↑
Phase Diff.	0°	0°	0°
Amp. Dir	+ve	+ve	+ve
Amp. Mag	A	↓	↓

Free End

- No transmitted wave
- Amplitude at free end becomes 2A.
- Reflected wave phase change 0°

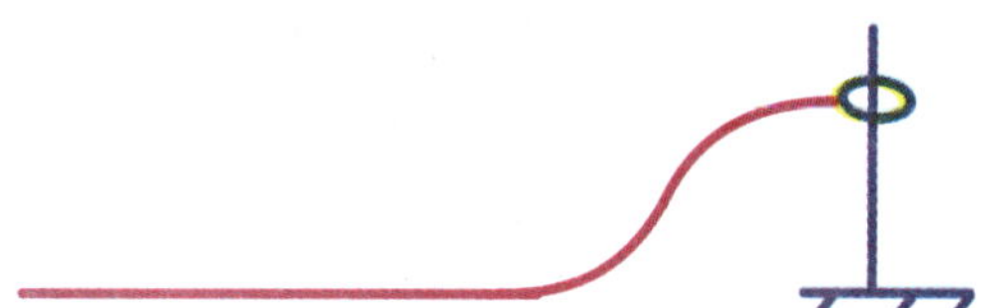

Fixed End

- No transmitted wave
- Amplitude at free end becomes 0.
- Reflected wave phase change π.

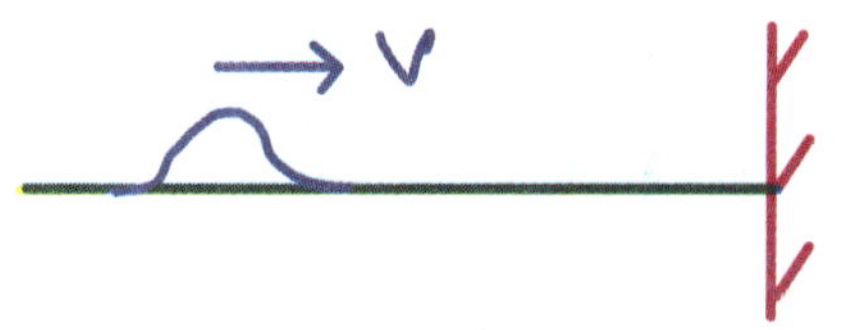

Sound Wave

Speed of Sound

- $v_{solid} > v_{liq} > v_{gas}$
- $v_{solid} = \sqrt{\frac{Y}{\rho}}$ where Y is the Young's Modulus
- $v_{fluid} = \sqrt{\frac{B}{\rho}}$ where B is the Bulk Modulus

Newton's Formula
- Process is Isothermal
  $\Rightarrow B = P$
- $v_{fluid} = \sqrt{\frac{P}{\rho}}$

Laplace's Correction
- Process is Adiabatic
  $\Rightarrow B = \gamma P$
- $v_{fluid} = \sqrt{\frac{\gamma P}{\rho}}$

- $v_{moist\ air} > v_{dry\ air}$
- $v_{rms} > v_{sound\ in\ gas}$

Wavelength of Sound

- Wavelength changes as it travels from one medium to another.
- Frequency remains the same.

$$\frac{v_1}{\lambda_1} = \frac{v_2}{\lambda_2}$$

MCQ PUNCH

Q3. Sound wave travel at 350 m/s through a warm air and at 3500 m/s through brass. The wavelength of a 700 Hz acoustic wave as it enters from warm air:

Sol. $\lambda_2 = \frac{v_2}{v_1} \times \lambda_1 = \frac{3500}{350} \lambda_1$

$\Rightarrow \lambda_2 = 10\lambda_1$

Intensity of Wave

Point source

$I \propto \frac{A^2}{r^2}$

Linear Source

$I \propto \frac{A^2}{r}$

Planar Source

$I \propto \frac{A^2}{r^0}$

Reflection of Wave

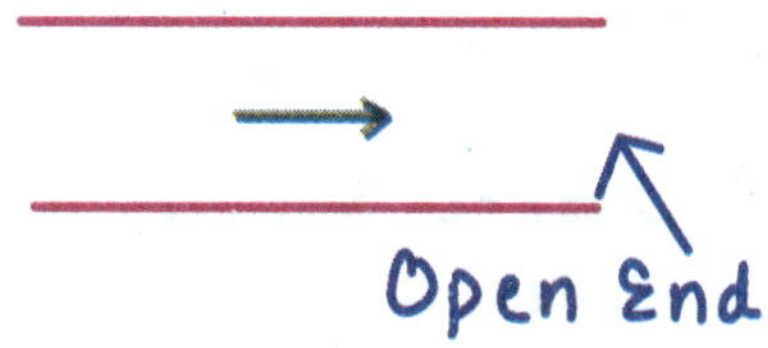

- **Open End**
- Reflected wave phase change π
- Compression reflects as rarefaction
- Rarefaction reflects as compression.

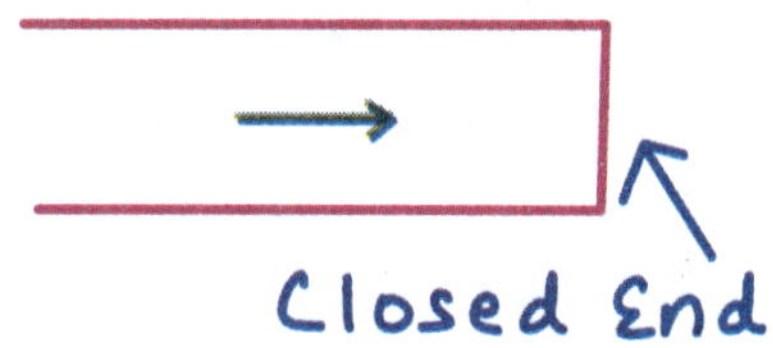

- **Closed End**
- Reflected wave phase change 0°
- Compression reflects as compression.
- Rarefaction reflects as rarefaction

Loudness of Sound Wave

- Unit is Decibel (dB)
- $L = 10 \log_{10}\left(\frac{I}{I_0}\right)$ where $I_0 = 10^{-12}$ Watt/m^2

Interference and Principle of Superposition

- Displacement of particle during interference of two waves is given by Principle of Superposition as

$$\vec{y} = \vec{y}_1 + \vec{y}_2$$

where y_1 and y_2 are the displacement of waves 1 & 2 respectively.

- Amplitude during interference is given as

$$A = \sqrt{A_1^2 + A_2^2 + 2A_1A_2\cos\phi}$$

where A_1 and A_2 are the amplitudes of waves 1 & 2 respectively.
ϕ is the phase difference of 2 waves at the point of interference.

Stationary Wave

- Interference of two waves having same speed, frequency, wavelength, amplitude but opposite speed.

- **Nodes**
  - Points of Zero displacement.
  - Position $x = \frac{n\lambda}{2}$ where, $n = 0, 1, 2, \ldots$
  - Distance between 2 consecutive nodes is $\lambda/2$.

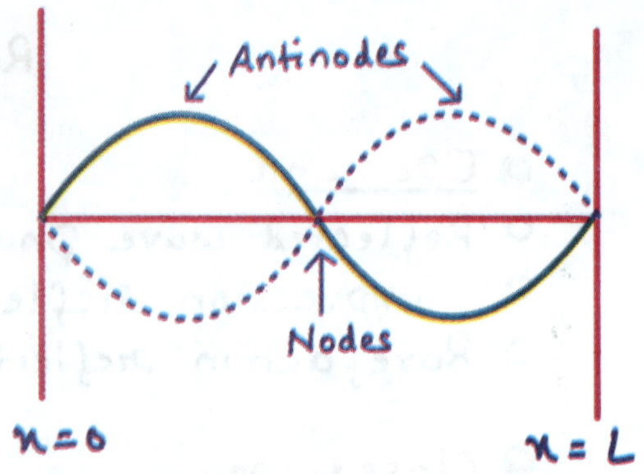

- **Anti-nodes**
  - Points of Maximum Displacement i.e. $2A$
  - Position $x = (2n-1)\frac{\lambda}{4}$ where, $n = 1, 2, \ldots$
  - Distance between 2 consecutive anti-nodes is $\lambda/2$.
- Amplitude of each point is different.
- All the particles in a same segment vibrate in phase.
- Phase difference of two consecutive segment is π.

Standard Terms for Standing Wave

◎ **Natural Frequency** (f)

- These are all the posible frequencies in which an instrument can vibrate.

◎ **Fundamental Frequency** (f_0)

- It is the minimum frequency with which an instrument can vibrate.

◎ **Overtone**

- All the natural frequencies other than fundamental frequency are called as overtone.
- 1st overtone is 2nd natural frequency.
- 2nd overtone is 3rd natural frequency.
- And so on.

◎ **Harmonics**

- They are the multiple of fundamental frequency.
- 1st Harmonic $= 1 \times f_0$

- 2nd Harmonic $= 2 \times f_0$
- And so on.

Equations of Stationary Wave

- $Y = 2A \sin(kx) \cos(\omega t)$
- $Y = 2A \cos(kx) \sin(\omega t)$
- $Y = 2A \sin(kx) \sin(\omega t)$
- $Y = 2A \cos(kx) \cos(\omega t)$

Formation of Stationary Wave in Sonometer Wire

- Natural frequencies

  $f = \frac{nv}{2L}$ where, $n = 1, 2, \ldots$

- No. of Antinodes $= n$
- No. of Nodes $= n+1$
- Fundament frequency

  $f_0 = \frac{v}{2L}$

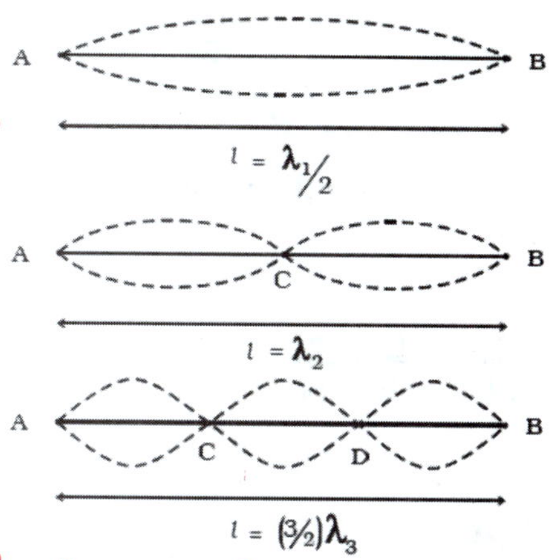

Fundamental or 1st Harmonic $n=1$

1st overtone or 2nd Harmonic $n=2$

2nd overtone or 3rd Harmonic $n=3$

- Fundamental frequency in terms of two nearby frequencies f_1 and f_2 is

  $f_0 = f_2 - f_1$

- Permissible wavelengths in the string, $\lambda = \frac{2L}{n}$ where, $n = 1, 2, \ldots$

PYQ PUNCH

Q4. The length of the string of a musical instrument is 90 cm and has a fundamental frequency of 120 Hz. Where should it be pressed to produce fundamental frequency of 180 Hz? (NEET 2020)

Sol. $f_0 = \frac{v}{2L}$

$\Rightarrow 120 \times 2 \times .9 = v \Rightarrow v = 216 \text{ m/s}$

For fundamental frequency of 180 Hz

$L = \frac{v}{2f_0} = \frac{216}{2 \times 180} = 60 \text{ cm}$

Sonometer Wire

- Bridges divide the string into segments.
- Weight produces the same tension in each segment.
- On plucking, each segment vibrates with same frequency but with different harmonic as per the length of the segment.

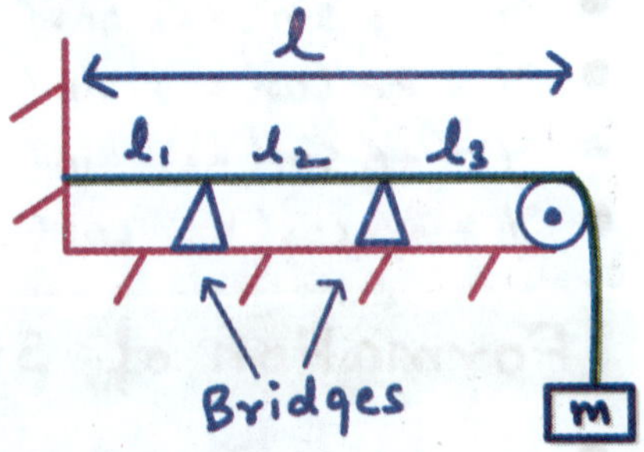

- $$\frac{n_1}{l_1} = \frac{n_2}{l_2} = \frac{n_3}{l_3}$$

where n_1, n_2 and n_3 are the harmonics of each part.

- If N_1, N_2 and N_3 are the fundamental frequencies of each part respectively, then fundamental frequency of complete string is given by

$$\frac{1}{N} = \frac{1}{N_1} + \frac{1}{N_2} + \frac{1}{N_3}$$

Open Organ Pipe

- Natural frequencies

$$f = \frac{nV}{2L}$$ where, $n = 1, 2, \ldots$

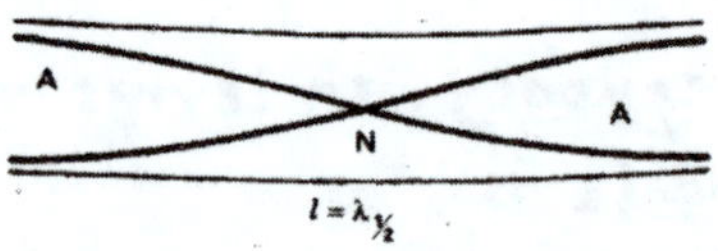

Fundamental or 1st Harmonic $n = 1$

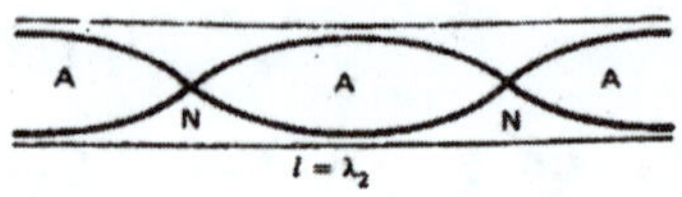

1st overtone or 2nd Harmonic $n = 2$

- No. of Antinodes $= n + 1$
- No. of Nodes $= n$
- Fundamental frequency

$$f_0 = \frac{V}{2L}$$

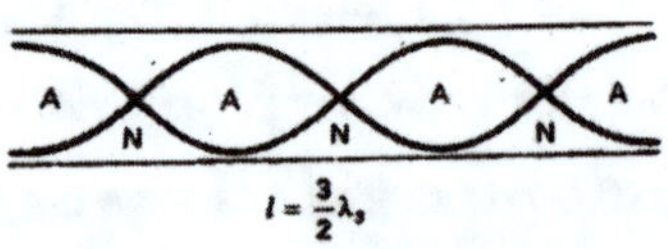

2nd overtone or 3rd Harmonic $n = 3$

- Fundamental frequency in terms of two nearby frequencies f_1 and f_2 is

$$f_0 = f_2 - f_1$$

- Permissible wavelengths in the pipe, $\lambda = \frac{2L}{n}$ where, $n = 1, 2, \ldots$

- Variation of frequency with temperature, $f \propto \sqrt{T}$

Closed Organ Pipe

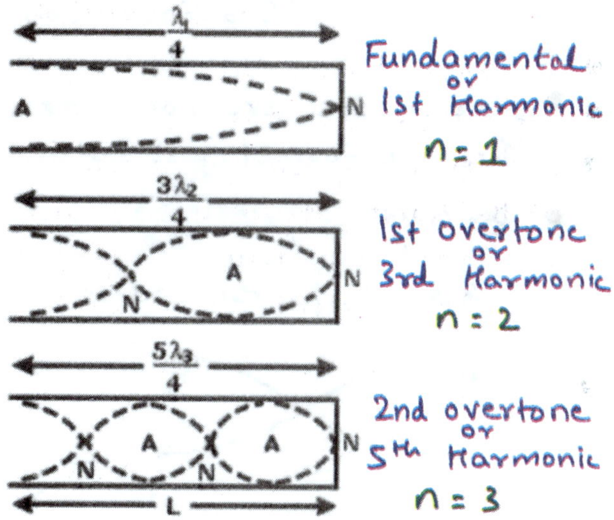

- Natural frequencies

$$f = \frac{(2n-1)V}{4L}$$ where, $n = 1, 2, \ldots$

- No. of Antinodes = n
- No. of Nodes = n
- Fundamental frequency

$$f_0 = \frac{V}{4L}$$

- Fundamental frequency in terms of two nearby frequencies f_1 and f_2 is

$$f_0 = \frac{f_2 - f_1}{2}$$

- Permissible wavelengths in the pipe, $\lambda = \frac{4L}{(2n-1)}$ where, $n = 1, 2, \ldots$
- Even harmonics are missing.
- Variation of frequency with temperature, $f \propto \sqrt{T}$

PYQ PUNCH

Q5. The ratio of frequencies of fundamental harmonics produced by an open pipe to that of closed pipe having the same length is : (NEET 2023)

Sol. For open pipe and for closed pipe

$$(f_0)_{open} = \frac{V}{2L} \quad ; \quad (f_0)_{closed} = \frac{V}{4L}$$

$$\frac{(f_0)_{open}}{(f_0)_{closed}} = \frac{2}{1}$$

Q6. The two nearest harmonics of a tube closed at one end and open at other end are 220 Hz and 260 Hz. What is the fundamental frequency of the system? (NEET 2017)

Sol. $f_0 = \frac{f_2 - f_1}{2} = \frac{260 - 220}{2} = 20 \text{ Hz}$

End Correction in Organ Pipes

- Anti-nodes are not formed exactly at the open end. Infact they are formed just outside of it.
- $e = 0.6r$

  where r is the radius of the tube

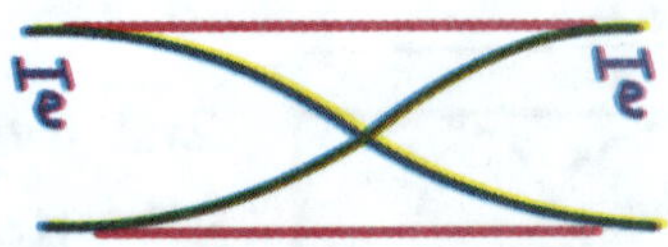

$$f = \frac{nV}{2(L+2e)}$$

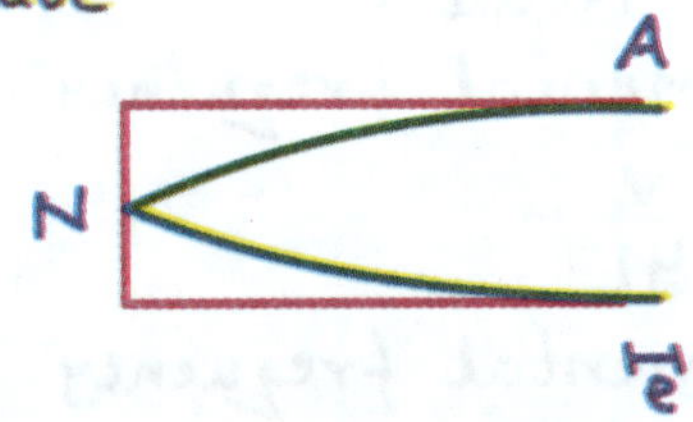

$$f = \frac{(2n-1)V}{4(L+e)}$$

Resonance Tube

- Use to measure the Speed of Sound.
  - $V = 2f(\ell_2 - \ell_1)$
  - End correction

    $$e = \frac{\ell_2 - 3\ell_1}{2}$$

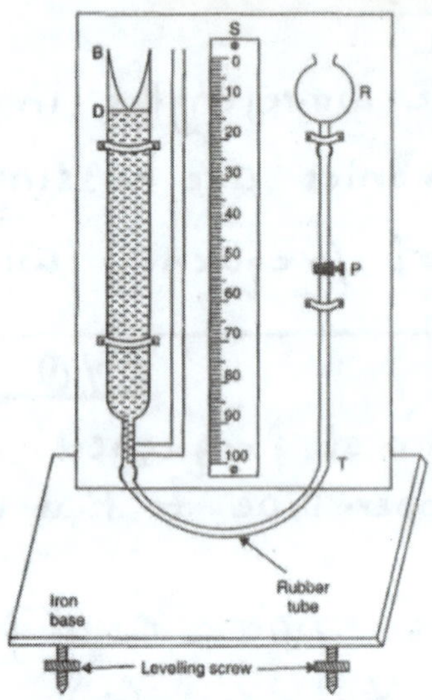

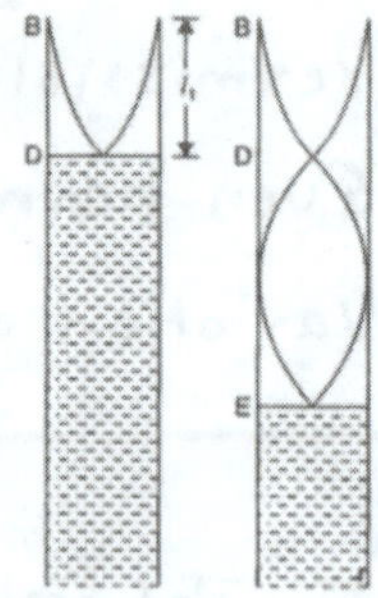

(b)

PYQ PUNCH

Q7. A tuning fork with frequency 800 Hz produces resonance in a resonance Column tube with upper end open and lower end closed by water surface. Successive resonance are observed at length 9.75 cm, 31.25 cm and 52.75 cm. The speed of sound in air is: (NEET 2019)

Sol. $V = 2f(\ell_2 - \ell_1)$

$= 2 \times 800(31.25 - 9.75) \times 10^{-2}$

$= 1600 \times 10^{-2} \times 21.50$

$= 344$ m/s

Beats

- When two waves of same amplitude but of slightly different frequencies interfere, the phenomenon of beats occurs.
- Occasionally the sound of high intensity is heard.
- Beat frequency

$$f_b = |f_1 - f_2|$$

- Frequency of tuning fork decreases on waxing.
- Frequency of string increases on increasing the tension.

PYQ PUNCH

Q8. In a guitar, two strings A and B made of same material are slightly out of tune and produce beats of frequency 6 Hz. When tension in B is slightly decreased, the beat frequency increases to 7 Hz. If the frequency of A is 530 Hz, the original frequency of B will be ? (NEET 2020)

Sol. $f_A = 530$ Hz

On decreasing tension, frequency decreases but f_b increases.

$\Rightarrow f_B < f_A$

Now using

$$f_b = |f_1 - f_2|$$

$$6 = f_A - f_B$$

$$f_B = 524 \text{ Hz}$$

- If 3 sound waves of equal amplitudes have frequencies $(n-1)$, n and $(n+1)$ are super-imposed, then the no. of beats per second is 2.

20. Electric Charges and Fields

Charge

- Particles in an atom that attract or repel each other.
- Just like mass, they are also the fundamental attribute of matter.

Properties of Charge

- Min Charge is 1.6×10^{-19} C.
- Positive - Positive repel
- Positive - Negative attract
- Positive - Neutral attract.
- Net charge is conservative.
- Additive in nature.
- Quantized

$Q = ne$ where n is integer.

- Moves due to potential difference.
- Invariant i.e. doesn't depend upon speed.
- Scalar

Electrostatic Force

- An attractive or a repulsive force due to charges.
- Long range
- Conservotive force i.e. its work is path independent.
- Follow inverse square law i.e. $F \propto \frac{1}{r^2}$
- Depends upon the medium.

Coulomb's Law

- $F = \frac{k q_1 q_2}{r^2}$
- $\vec{F}_{21} = \frac{k q_1 q_2}{|r^3|} \vec{r}_{21}$ where $k = \frac{1}{4\pi\varepsilon_0} = 9 \times 10^9$ Nm^2C^{-2}
- $\vec{F}_{12} = \frac{k q_1 q_2}{|r^3|} \vec{r}_{12}$ is permittivity of free space.
- Depends upon the permittivity of the medium.

Permittivity

- It is a measure of ability of medium to resist the formation of Electric Field in it.
- For vacuum, it is $8.854 \times 10^{-12}\ C^2 N^{-1} m^{-2}$

Validity of Coulomb's Law

2 point bodies	2 spherical bodies	A spherical body and a point body
 $F = \frac{kq_1q_2}{r^2}$	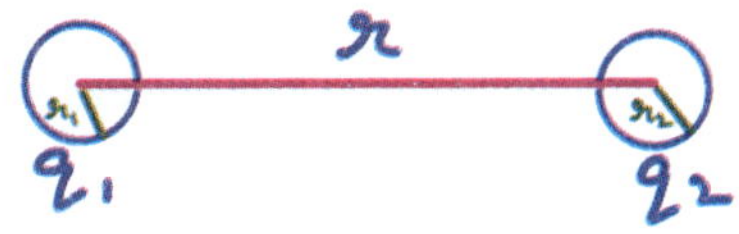 $F = \frac{kq_1q_2}{r^2}$	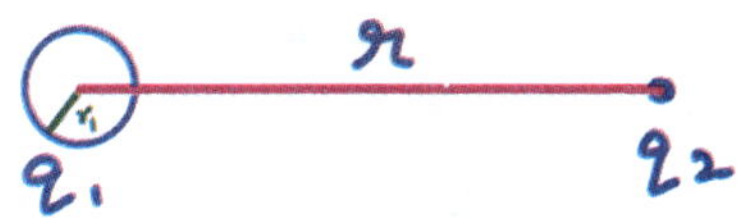 $F = \frac{kq_1q_2}{r^2}$

PYQ PUNCH

Q1. The acceleration of an electron due to the mutual attraction between the electron and a proton when they are 1.6 Å apart is, ($m_e = 9 \times 10^{-31}$ kg, $e = 1.6 \times 10^{-19}$ C). (NEET 2020)

Sol. $r = 1.6\ \text{Å} = 1.6 \times 10^{-10}$ m

$$F = \frac{kq_1q_2}{r^2}$$

$$= \frac{9 \times 10^{9} \times 1.6 \times 10^{-19} \times 1.6 \times 10^{-19}}{(1.6 \times 10^{-10})^2}$$

$$= 9 \times 10^{-9}\ N$$

Now

$$a = \frac{F}{m} = \frac{9 \times 10^{-9}}{9 \times 10^{-31}} = 10^{22}\ m/s^2$$

Superposition Theorem

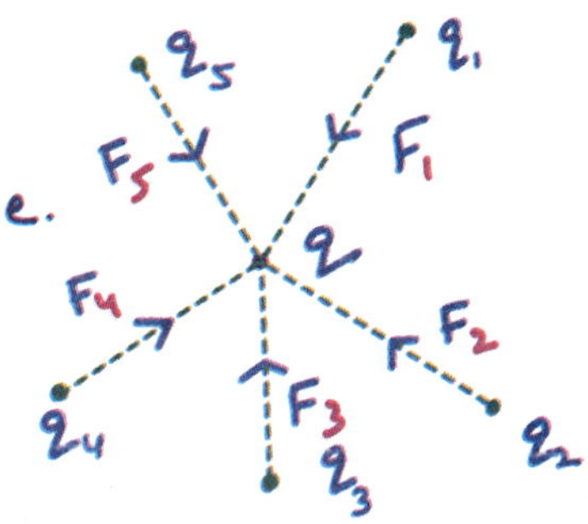

- Force between two charges doesn't get affected by the presence of any third charge.
- Net force on a particle is vector addition of all the forces acting on a particle.

$$\vec{F}_{net} = \vec{F_1} + \vec{F_2} + \vec{F_3} + \ldots$$

Shortcuts to Solve Coulomb's Law Questions

Change of Medium

$$F_w = \frac{F_a}{k}$$

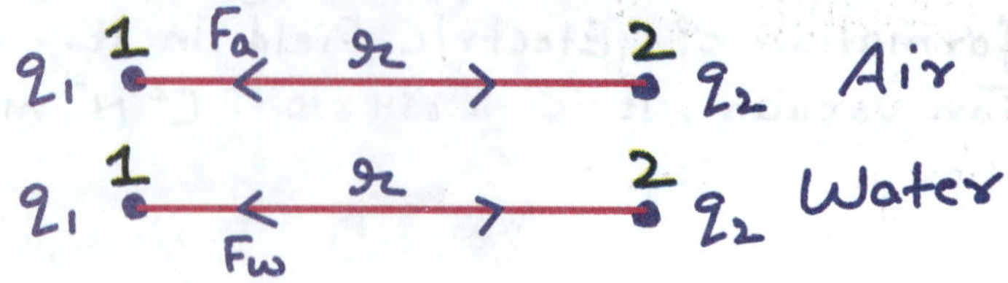

where k is the dielectric constant of water.

Transfer of Charge

$$F_1 = \frac{kq_1q_2}{r^2}$$

Now q charge is transferred

$$F_2 = \frac{k(q_1+q)(q_2-q)}{r^2}$$

$$F_2 = \frac{(q_1+q)(q_2-q)}{q_1q_2} F_1$$

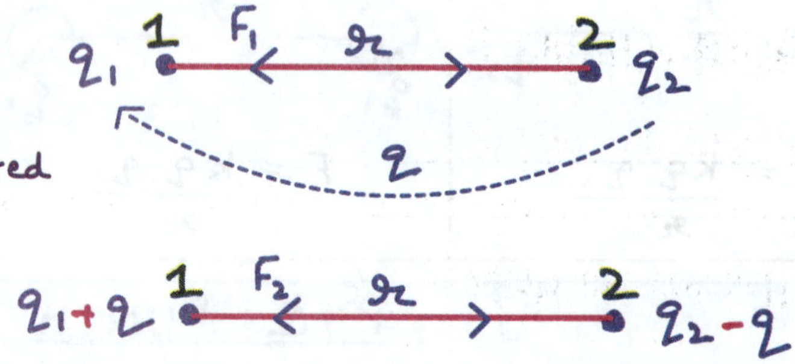

Charge on Pendulum

- $\tan\theta = \dfrac{kq^2}{mgr^2}$
- $T = \sqrt{(mg)^2 + \left(\dfrac{kq^2}{r^2}\right)^2}$

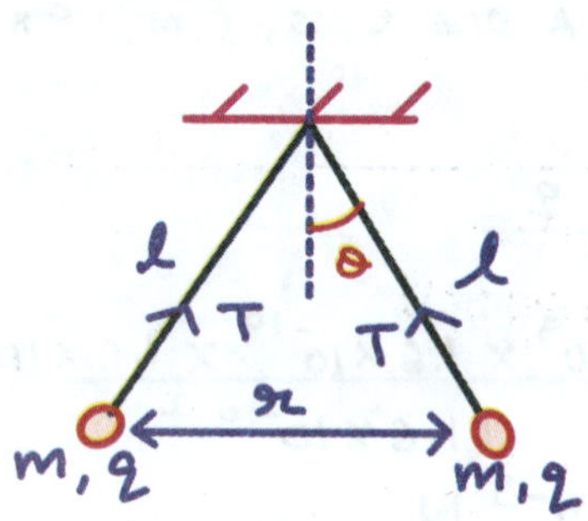

3 masses system in equilibrium

- Charge q is placed in the middle of system.
- For the system to be in equilibrium

$$q = -\frac{Q}{4}$$

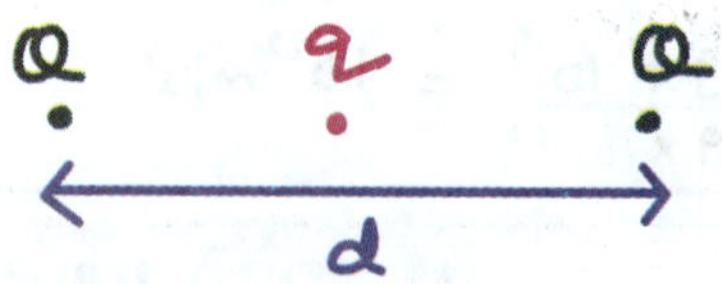

Placement of charge for zero net force

- Placing a +ve q charge for zero net force on it.

- If both (Q_1 and Q_2) are of same nature, then put q charge in region II.
- If charges are of opposite nature and $Q_1 > Q_2$, then put q Charge in region III.
- If charges are of opposite nature and $Q_1 < Q_2$, then put q Charge in region I.

Breaking of Q charge for maximum force between them.

- Q charge breaks into q_1 and q_2 and placed r distance apart.
- For maximum force between them
  - $q_1 = q_2 = \frac{Q}{2}$

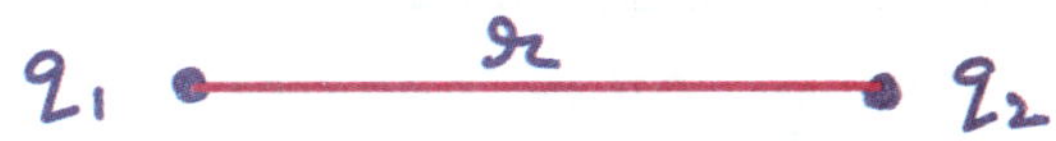

Charges placed at the centre of equilateral triangle

$|\vec{F}_{41}| = |\vec{F}_{41}| = |\vec{F}_{41}| = F$

$F_{net} = 0$

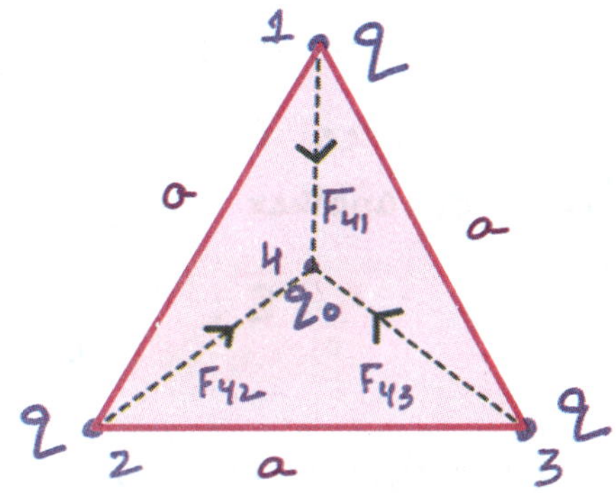

Charges placed at the centre of the square

$|\vec{F}_{51}| = |\vec{F}_{52}| = |\vec{F}_{53}| = |\vec{F}_{54}| = F$

$F_{net} = 0$

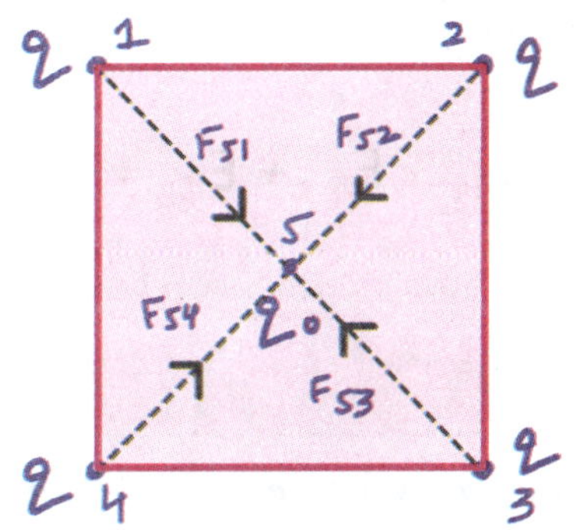

Charges placed at the vertex of equilateral triangle

$|\vec{F}_{21}| = |\vec{F}_{23}| = F$

$F_{net} = 2F\cos 30°$

$= \frac{\sqrt{3}kq^2}{a^2}$

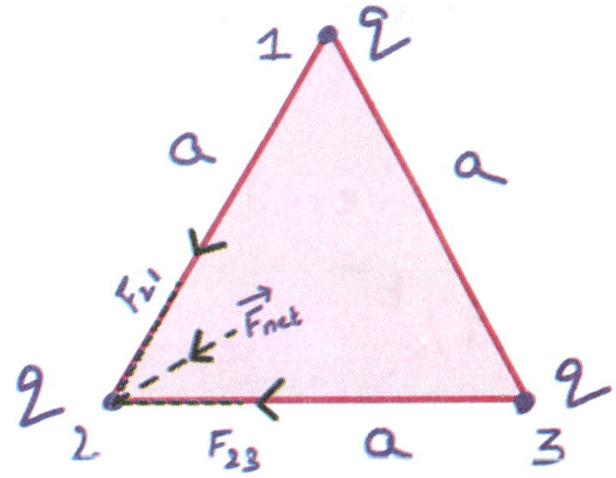

NEET Accelerate

- For a regular polygon having equal charges placed at its vertexes, net force is zero at the centre.
- If one charge is removed from the vertex of regular polygon, net force is then equal and opposite to the force at centre due to removed charge.

Electric Field

- It is a region around a charge in which its influence can be felt by other charges

Electric Field Intensity ($\vec{E}$)

- It is the force experienced by a unit charge q_0 placed under the field of another charge q.

$$\vec{E} = \frac{\vec{F}}{q_0} \quad ; \quad |\vec{E}| = \frac{kq}{r^2}$$

- Just like force, it also follows principle of super-position.

$$\vec{E}_A = \vec{E}_{q_1} + \vec{E}_{q_2} + \vec{E}_{q_3} + ---.$$

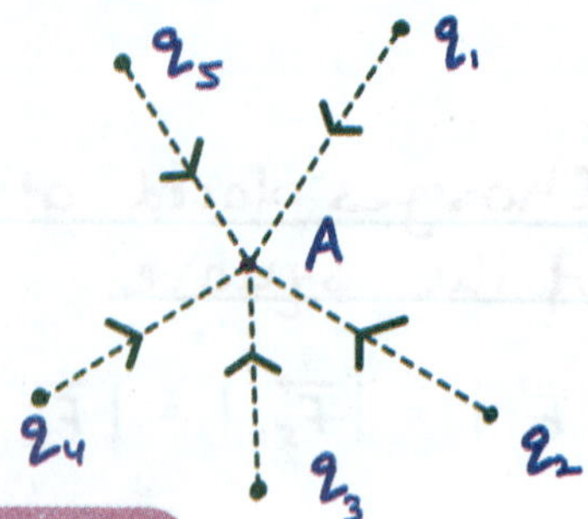

Movement of charge in Electric Field

- q charge placed in external uniform electric field E.
- $F = qE$

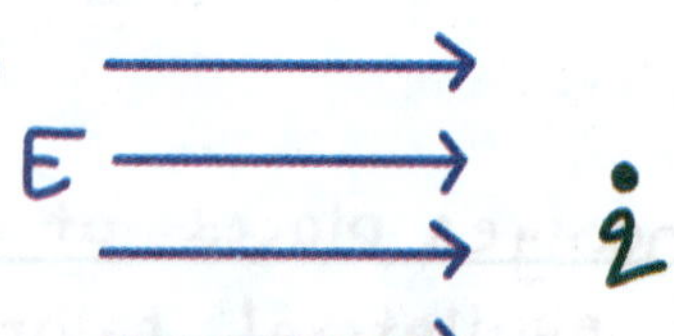

- Distance covered in time t

$$y = \frac{1}{2}\left(\frac{qE}{m}\right)t^2$$

- Speed after time t

$$v = \frac{qEt}{m}$$

○ Kinetic Energy after time t

$$KE = \frac{1}{2}\frac{q^2E^2t^2}{m}$$

MCQ PUNCH

Q2. A particle of mass m and charge q is placed at rest in a uniform electric field E and then released. The kinetic energy attained by the particle after moving a distance y is

Sol. $y = \frac{1}{2}\left(\frac{qE}{m}\right)t^2$ ---- eq. 1

$KE = \frac{1}{2}\frac{q^2E^2t^2}{m}$ ---- eq. 2

From equations 1 and 2 $KE = qEy$

E. Field of Some Continuous Bodies

◎ Due to ring on its axis

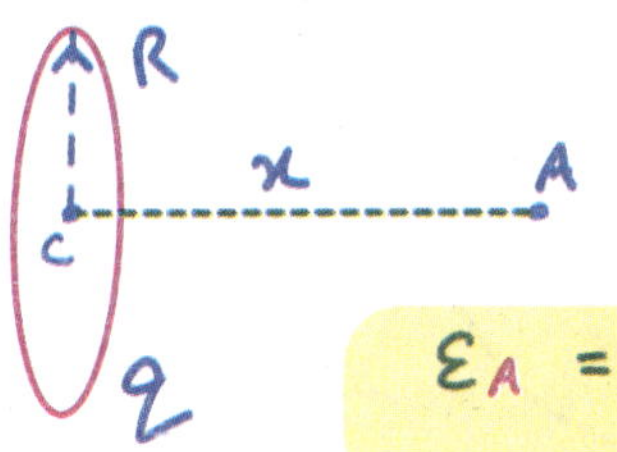

$$E_A = \frac{kqx}{(R^2+x^2)^{3/2}}$$

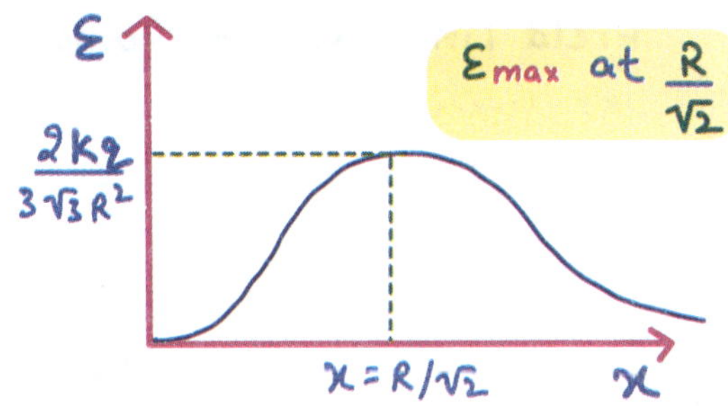

E_{max} at $\frac{R}{\sqrt{2}}$

◎ Due to Hollow Sphere

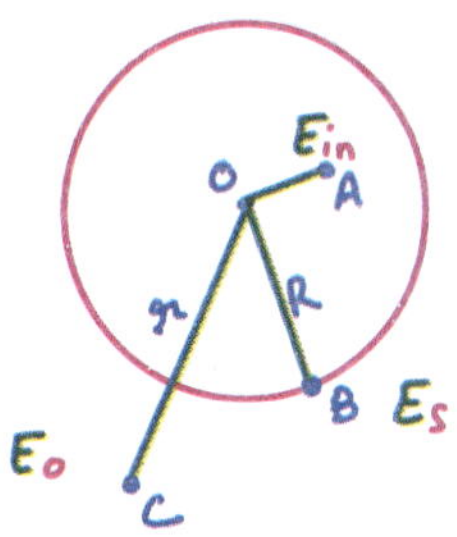

$E_{out}\ (E_o) = \frac{kq}{r^2}$

$E_{surface}\ (E_s) = \frac{kq}{R^2}$

$E_{inside}\ (E_{in}) = 0$

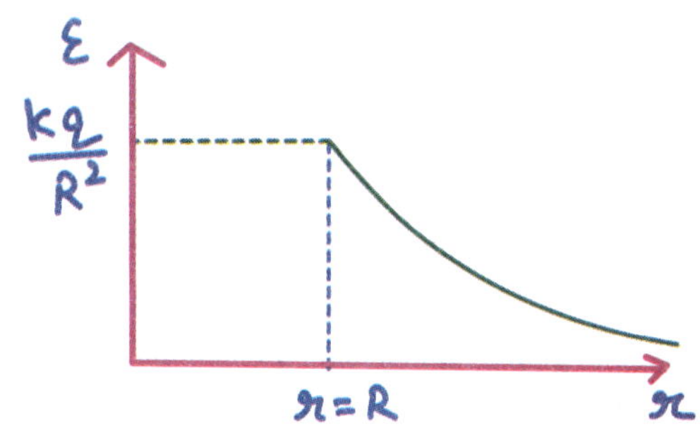

◎ Due to Solid Insulating Sphere

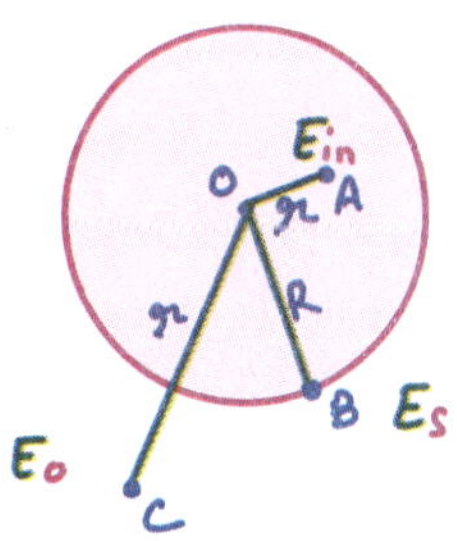

$E_{out}\ (E_o) = \frac{kq}{r^2}$

$E_{surface}\ (E_s) = \frac{kq}{R^2}$

$E_{inside}\ (E_{in}) = \frac{kqr}{R^3}$

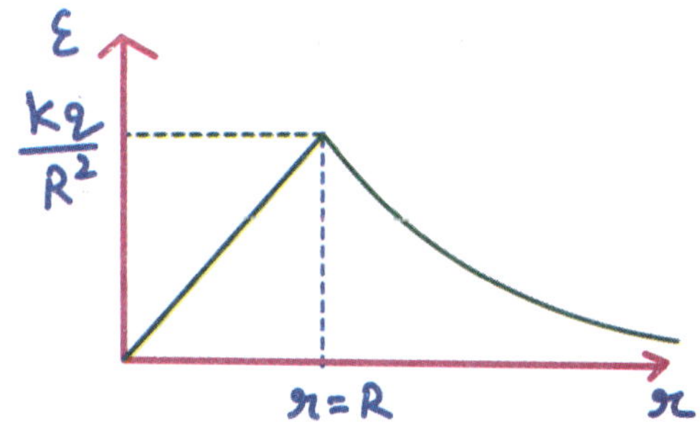

Due to Solid conducting Sphere

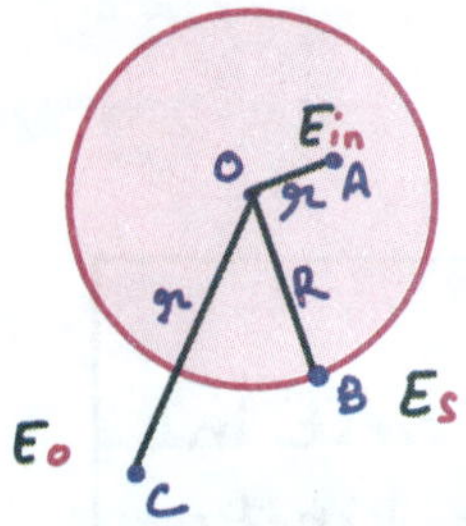

$$E_{out}\ (E_o) = \frac{kq}{r^2}$$

$$E_{surface}\ (E_s) = \frac{kq}{R^2}$$

$$E_{inside}\ (E_{in}) = 0$$

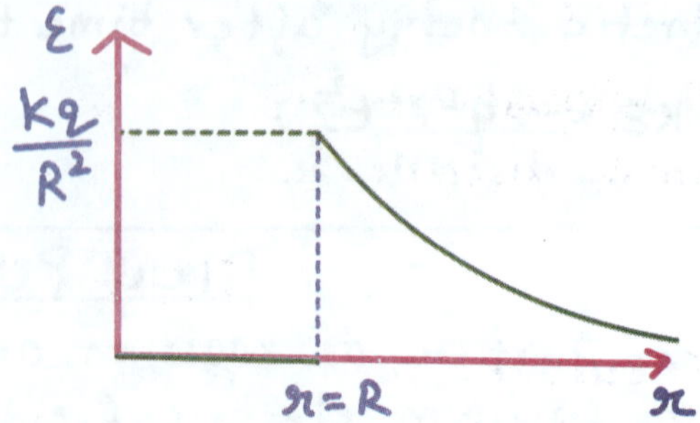

Electric Field Lines

- These are imaginary lines tangent to which gives the direction of net electric field at that point due to configuration of charges.

Properties

- Originates from +ve charge and terminates at −ve charge.
- Two field lines never intersect each other.

Field Lines due to some configuration of charges

Positive Charge

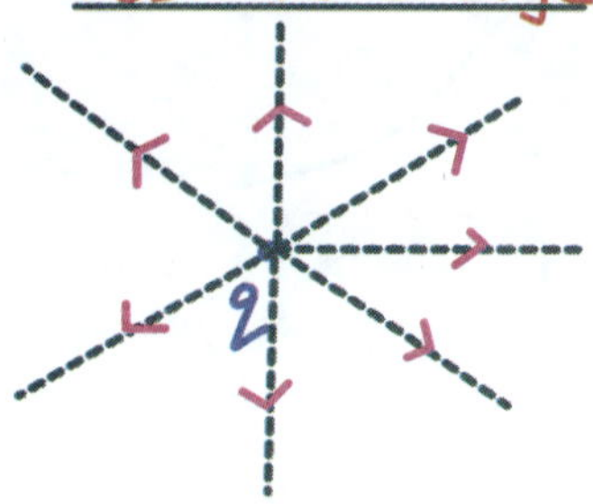

Negative Charge

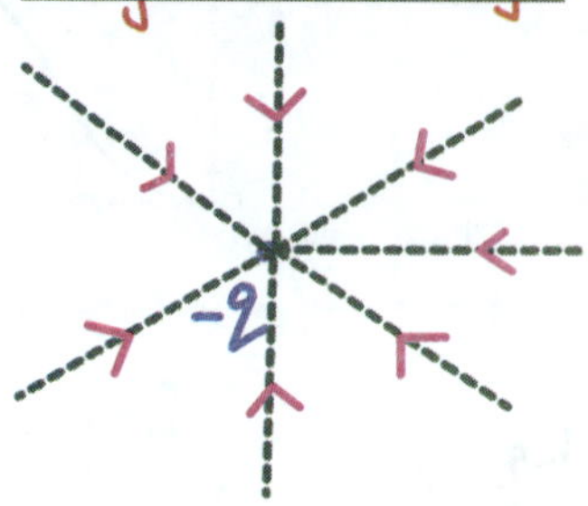

Negative - Negative

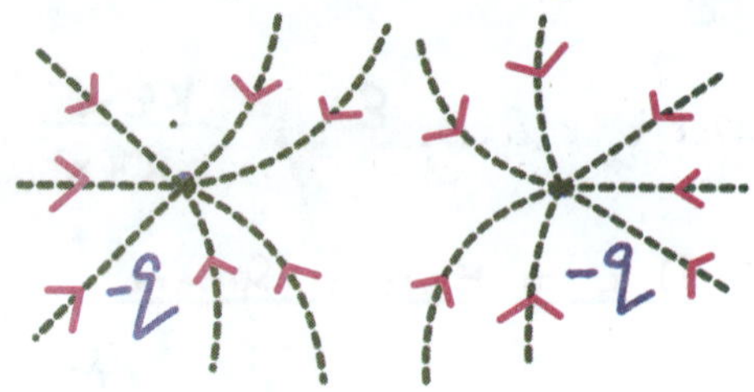

Positive - Negative

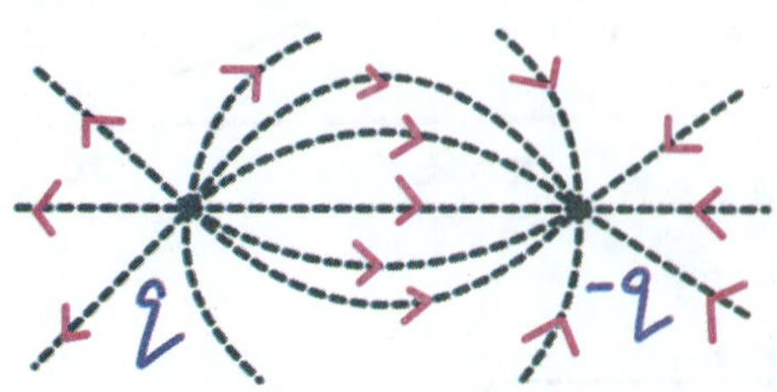

Positive - Positive

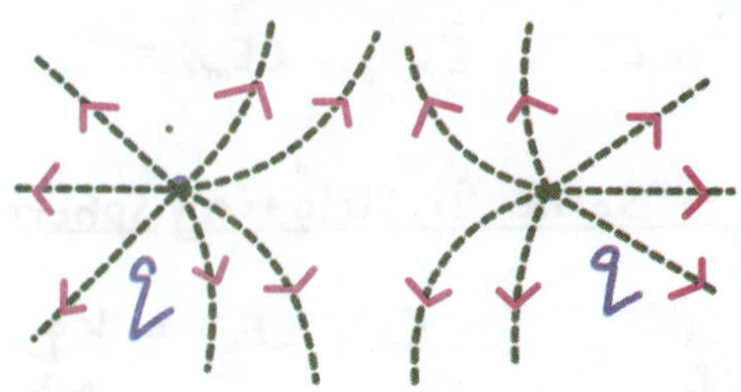

Electric Dipole

- Two equal and opposite charges placed at a small distance 2a.

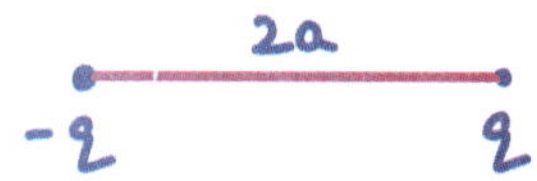

Electric Dipole Moment (p)

- Measures the strength of electric dipole.
- $\vec{p}$ = (Magnitude of charge) × (Distance between them)

$$\vec{p} = q \times 2\vec{a}$$

- Direction is from -ve to +ve charge.
- Unit is Cm.

E. Field due to Dipole

Position	Diagram	EF at pt. P	x >> a
Axial	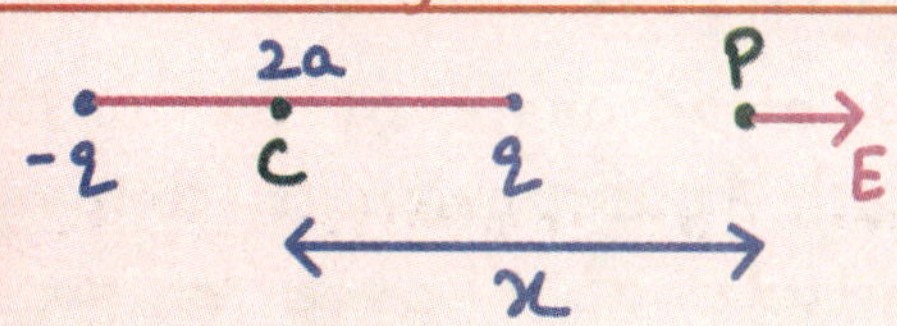	$\frac{2k\vec{p}x}{(a^2-x^2)^2}$	$\frac{2k\vec{p}}{x^3}$
Equitorial	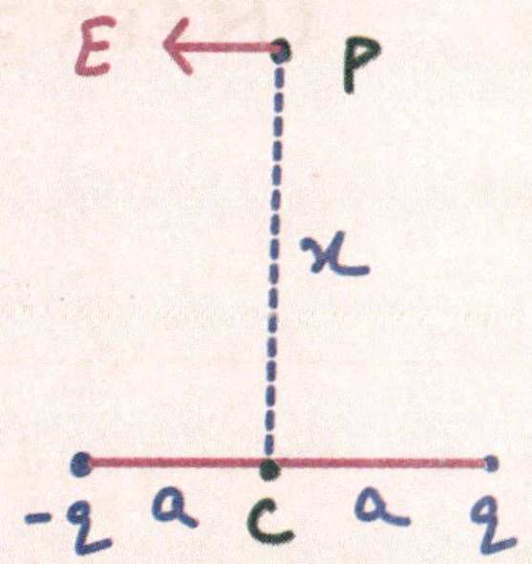	$\frac{-k\vec{p}x}{(a^2-x^2)^2}$	$\frac{-k\vec{p}}{x^3}$
At any point	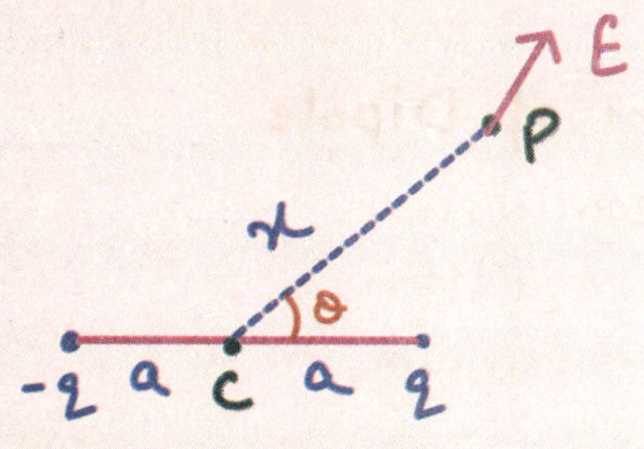		$\frac{k\vec{p}}{x^3}\sqrt{3\cos^2\theta+1}$

- $\frac{E_{axial}}{E_{equi}} = \frac{1}{2}$
- E_{axial} is along the direction of dipole moment if pt. P is on the side of positive charge.

- E_{axial} is opp. to the direction of dipole moment if pt P is on the side of negative charge.
- E_{equi} is opposite to the direction of dipole moment.
- For $\theta = \tan^{-1}\sqrt{2}$, Electric field is perpendicular to dipole moment.
- $E \propto \frac{1}{x^3}$

Torque on Dipole

- A dipole placed in external uniform electric field $\vec{E}$.
- It experiences a torque

$$\vec{\tau} = \vec{p} \times \vec{E}$$

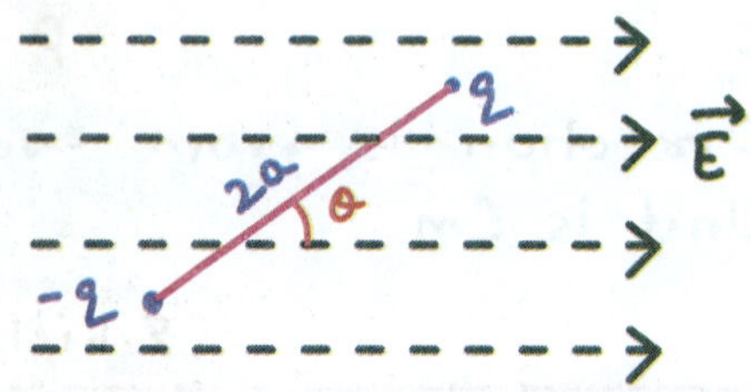

PYQ PUNCH

Q3. An electric dipole is placed at an angle of 30° with an electric field of intensity 2×10^5 N C^{-1}. It experiences a torque equal to 4 Nm. Calculate the magnitude of charge on the dipole, if the dipole length is 2cm. **(NEET 2023 & 2016)**

Sol. $\vec{\tau} = \vec{p} \times \vec{E}$

$4 = q \times 2 \times 10^{-2} \times 2 \times 10^5 \times \sin 30°$

$q = 2 \times 10^{-3}$ C

- If a dipole is placed in non-uniform electric field, it will do both
  - Rotational Motion
  - Translatory Motion

Equilibrium of Dipole

- For $\theta = 0°$, $\tau = 0$ and stable equilibrium.
- For $\theta = 180°$, $\tau = 0$ and unstable equilibrium.
- For $\theta = 90°$ or $270°$, torque is maximum.

Work Done in Rotating a Dipole

- Work Done in rotating the dipole from θ_1 to θ_2

$$W = pE(\cos\theta_1 - \cos\theta_2)$$

Potential Energy of Dipole

- Change of Potential Energy

$$\Delta PE = pE(\cos\theta_1 - \cos\theta_2)$$

- Potential Energy

  $\theta_1 = 90^\circ$ and $\theta_2 = \theta$

$$PE = -pE\cos\theta$$

- Potential Energy reduces in self process.

PYQ PUNCH

Q4. A dipole is placed in an electric field as shown. In which direction will it move?

a. Towards the left as its potential energy will ↑

b. Towards the right as its potential energy will ↓

c. Towards the left as its potential energy will ↓

d. Towards the right as its potential energy will ↑

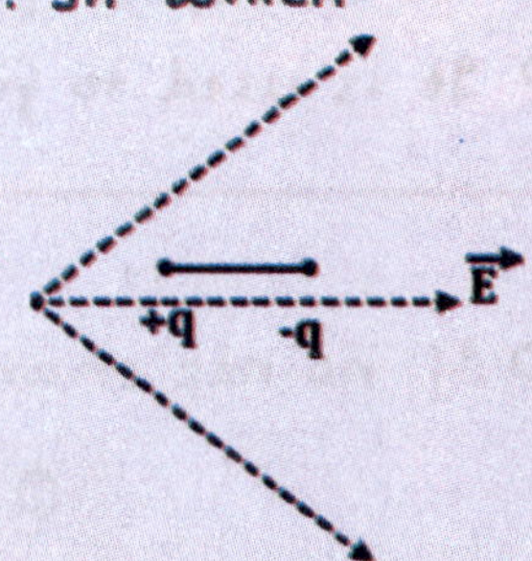

(NEET 2020)

Sol. This is the electric field due to a point positive charge, hence non-uniform. Dipole will move towards right due to repulsion of +ve - +ve charge.
Since, it is a self occuring process, potential energy will decrease.
Option b.

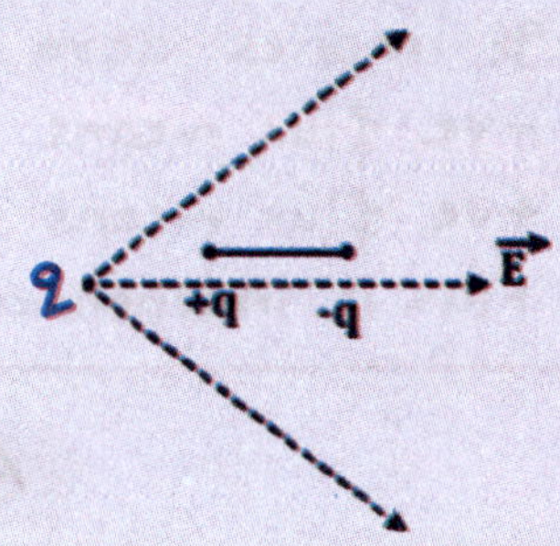

Electric Flux

- It is the number of field lines passing through an area.

$$\phi = \vec{E}\cdot\vec{A} = EA\cos\theta$$

where θ is the angle between the Electric field and area.
- It is a scalar quantity.
- Unit is Nm^2C^{-1}

- Lines coming into the surface, ϕ_{in} = −ve
- Lines going out of the surface, ϕ_{out} = +ve

Gauss's Law

- It states that flux through a closed surface is equal to q_{inside} multiplied by $\frac{1}{\varepsilon_0}$.

$$\phi = \oint \vec{E}.d\vec{A} = \frac{q_{inside}}{\varepsilon_0}$$

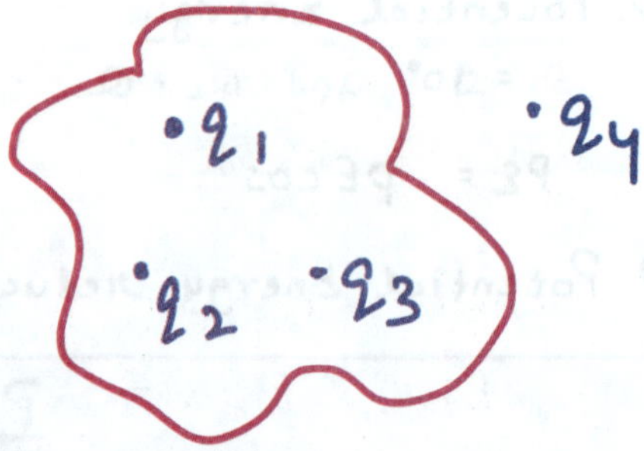

- ϕ is due to internal charges only.
  For example q_1, q_2 and q_3.
- E is due to all charges.
  For example q_1, q_2, q_3 and q_4.
- It is used to find out Electric field in case of symmetry.

NEET Accelerate

- If no net charge inside, then ϕ is zero.

$$\phi = \oint \vec{E}.d\vec{A} = 0$$

- Zero flux through the surface doesn't imply no charge inside. It implies zero net charge.
- −ve flux means net charge is −ve inside.
- +ve flux means net charge is +ve inside.
- Flux is independent of the position of charge & size of surface.

Applications of Gauss's Law

- **Infinite thin charged wire**

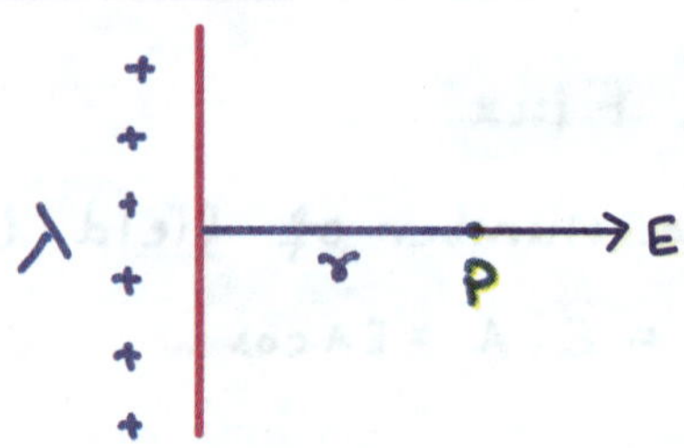

- λ is the uniform linear charge density.
- Electric Field at point P

$$E_P = \frac{2k\lambda}{r}$$

- $E \propto \frac{1}{r}$

PYQ PUNCH

Q5. Two parallel infinite line charges with linear charge densities $+\lambda$ C/m and $-\lambda$ C/m are placed at a distance of $2R$ in free space. What is the electric field between the two line charges? (NEET 2019)

Sol. $\vec{E}_\lambda = \frac{2k\lambda}{R}\hat{i}$

$\vec{E}_{-\lambda} = \frac{2k\lambda}{R}\hat{i}$

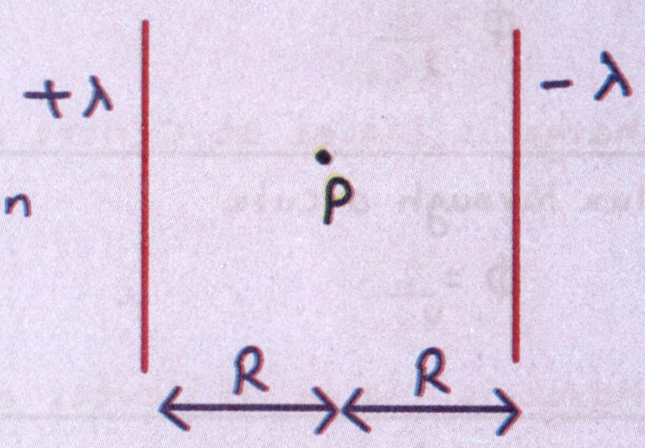

By principle of super-position

$$\vec{E}_{net} = \vec{E}_\lambda + \vec{E}_{-\lambda}$$
$$= \frac{2k\lambda}{R}\hat{i} + \frac{2k\lambda}{R}\hat{i}$$
$$= \frac{4k\lambda}{R}\hat{i}$$

◎ **Infinite thin Insulating Charged Plate**

- σ is the uniform surface charge density.
- Electric Field at point P

$$E_P = \frac{\sigma}{2\varepsilon_0}$$

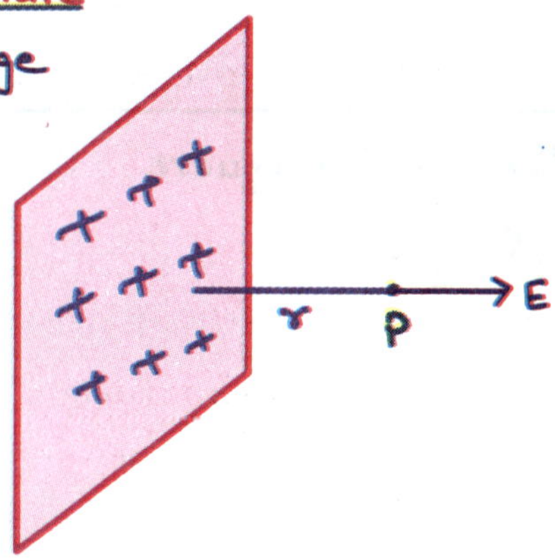

- Electric Field is independent of the distance.

Special Cases of Gauss's Law

◎ **If charge q is placed inside a cube**

- Flux through a cube

$$\phi = \frac{q}{\varepsilon_0}$$

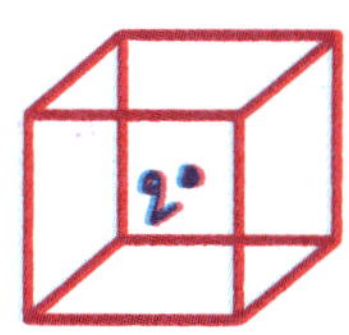

- Flux through one face

$$\phi = \frac{q}{6\varepsilon_0}$$

- **If charge q is placed outside a cube**
  - Flux through a cube

$$\phi = 0$$

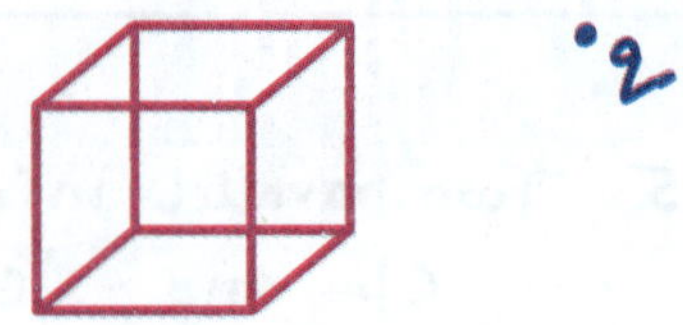

- **Charge is placed at one face of the cube**
  - Flux through a cube

$$\phi = \frac{q}{2\varepsilon_0}$$

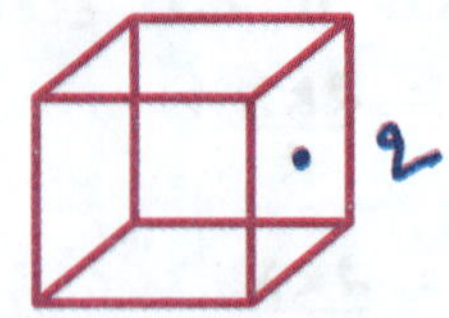

- **Charge is placed at centre of the edge**
  - Flux through a cube

$$\phi = \frac{q}{4\varepsilon_0}$$

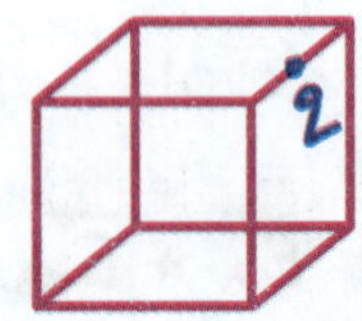

- **Charge is placed at vertex of the cube**
  - Flux through a cube

$$\phi = \frac{q}{8\varepsilon_0}$$

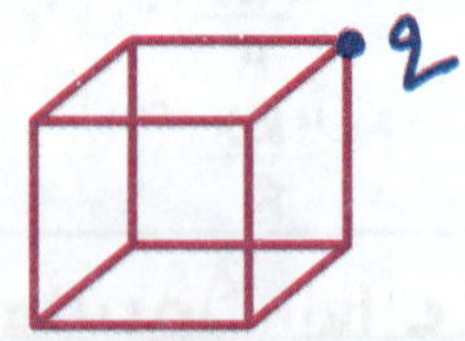

- **Charge is placed at a distance $a/2$ from the square of side a**
  - Flux through the square

$$\phi = \frac{q}{6\varepsilon_0}$$

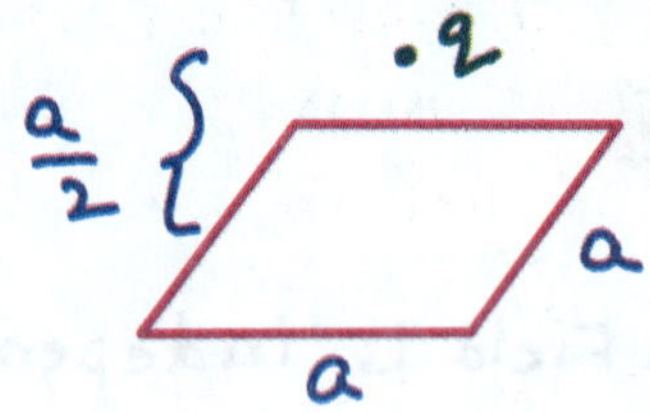

21. Electrostatics Potential and Capacitance

Change of E. Potential Energy (ΔU)

- It is the negative of work done by electrostatics force in changing the position of charge.

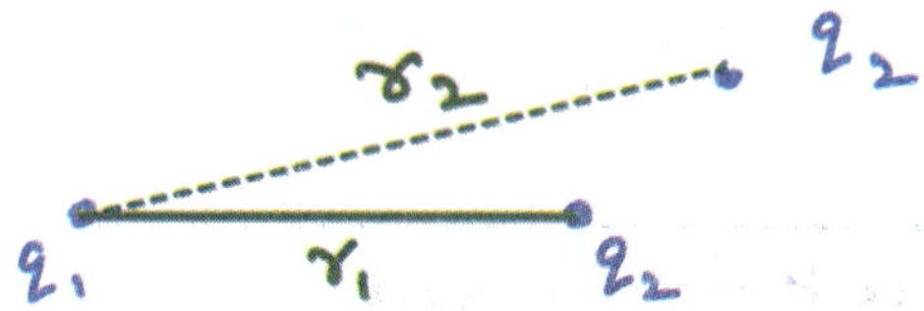

$$\Delta U = -W_e = kq_1q_2\left(\frac{1}{r_2} - \frac{1}{r_1}\right)$$

r_1 : Initial Separation
r_2 : Final Separation

- It is always of a system i.e. 2 charges.
- For no change of kinetic Energy

$$W_{ext} = \Delta U$$

MCQ PUNCH

Q1. Charges $+q$ and $-q$ are placed at points A and B, respectively which are at a distance $2L$ apart. C is the mid-point between A and B. The work done in moving a charge $+Q$ along the semi-circle CRD is :

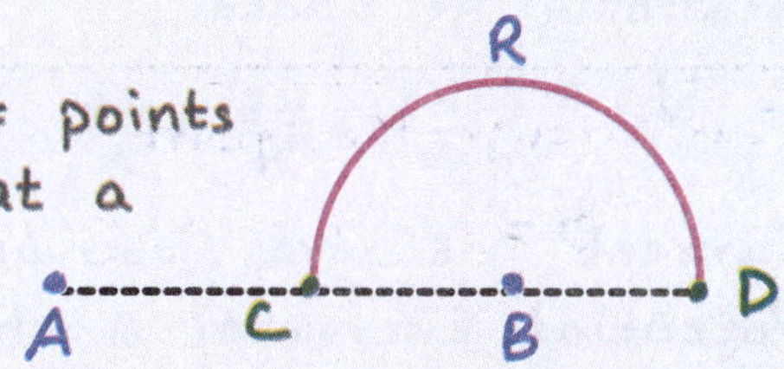

Sol. $W_{ext} = \Delta U$

$$\Delta U = kq_1q_2\left(\frac{1}{r_2} - \frac{1}{r_1}\right)$$

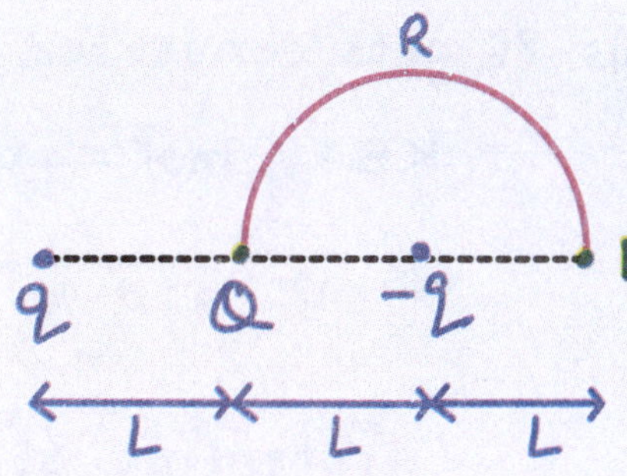

For q and Q

$$\Delta U_1 = kqQ\left(\frac{1}{3L} - \frac{1}{L}\right) = -\frac{2kqQ}{3L}$$

For $-q$ and Q

$$\Delta U_2 = -kqQ\left(\frac{1}{L} - \frac{1}{L}\right) = 0$$

$$\Delta U = \Delta U_1 + \Delta U_2 = -\frac{2kqQ}{3L}$$

$$W_{ext} = \Delta U = -\frac{2kqQ}{3L}$$

E. Potential Energy (U)

- It is the negative of work done by electrostatics force while bringing a particle from infinity to a particular distance r.

$$U = \frac{kq_1q_2}{r}$$

Electric Potential (V)

- Just like G. Field, it also represents the strength of a charge but in scalar form.

$$V_P = \frac{kq}{r}$$

- Being a scalar quantity, it simply get added.

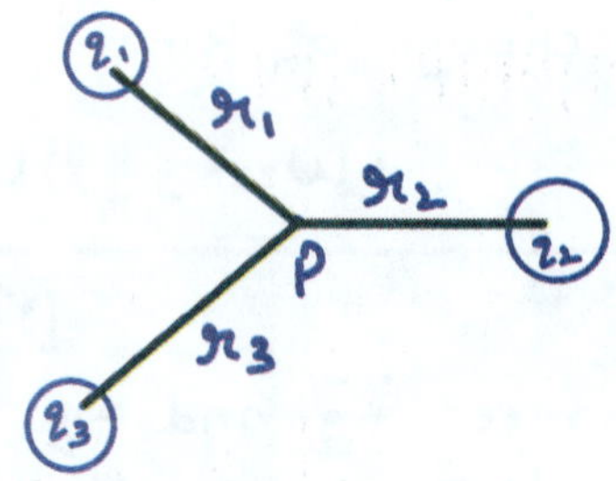

$$V_P = \frac{kq_1}{r_1} + \frac{kq_2}{r_2} + \frac{kq_3}{r_3}$$

- Current in a wire flows because of potential difference.
- Potential Energy of a charge q when accelerated by a potential difference of V volts is

$$PE = qV$$

- This PE gets converted into kinetic energy

$$KE = \frac{1}{2}mv^2 = qV$$

$$\Rightarrow v = \sqrt{\frac{2qV}{m}}$$

Potential of Some Continuous Bodies

- Due to ring on its axis

$$V_A = \frac{kq}{(R^2+x^2)^{1/2}} \quad ; \quad V_{center} = \frac{kq}{R}$$

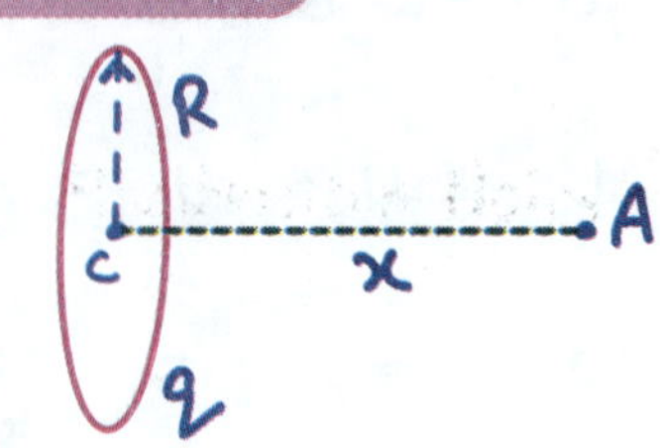

Due to hollow Sphere

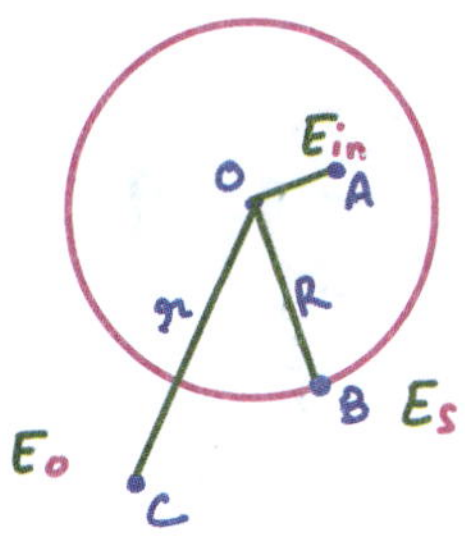

$V_{out}\ (V_o) = \frac{kq}{r}$

$V_{surface}\ (V_s) = \frac{kq}{R}$

$V_{inside}\ (V_{in}) = \frac{kq}{R}$

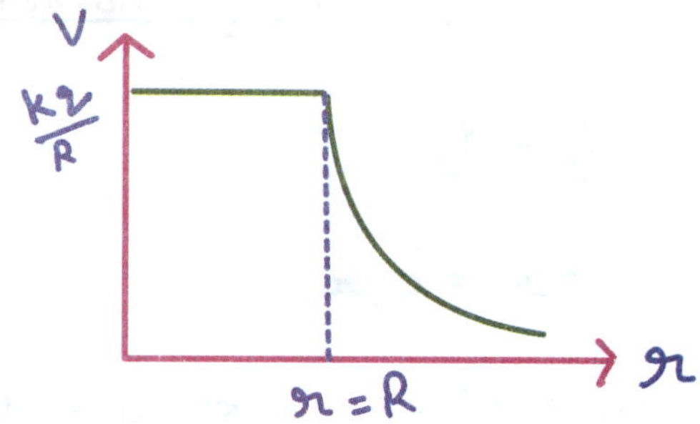

PYQ PUNCH

Q2. A thin spherical shell is charged by some source. The potential difference between the two points C and P (in V) shown in the figure is :
(Take $\frac{1}{4\pi\varepsilon_0} = 9\times10^9$ SI units)

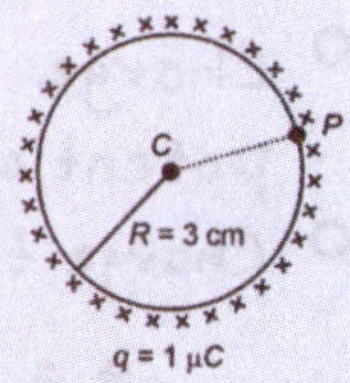

(NEET 2024)

Sol. For thin shell

$V_C = \frac{kq}{R}$; $V_P = \frac{kq}{R}$

$\Rightarrow V_P - V_C = 0$

Due to Solid Sphere

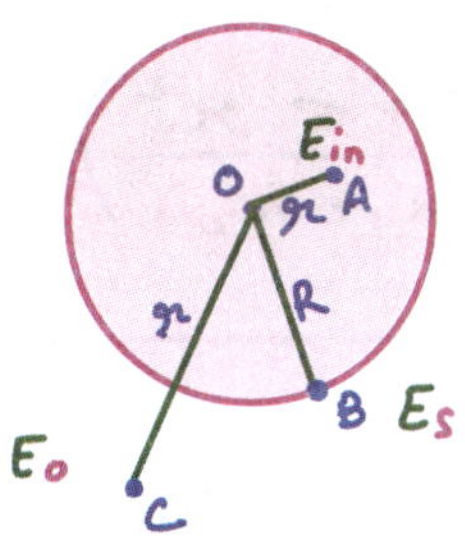

$V_{out}\ (V_o) = \frac{kq}{r}$

$V_{surface}\ (V_s) = \frac{kq}{R}$

$V_{inside}\ (V_{in}) = \frac{kq}{2R^3}(3R^2 - r^2)$

$V_{center}\ (V_c) = \frac{3kq}{2R}$

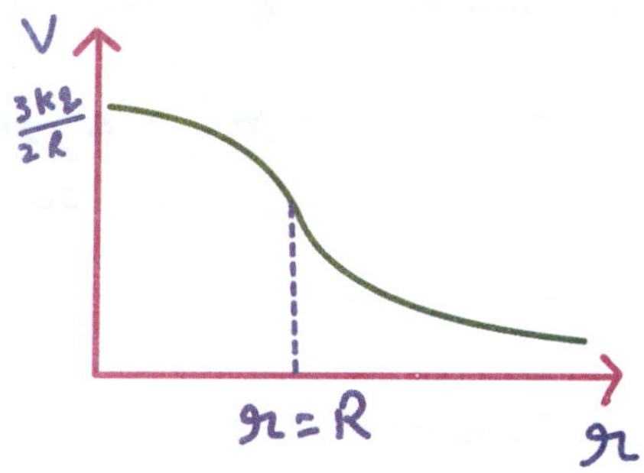

Shortcut Formulae related to Spheres

Coalescing of Charged Drops

- n identical drops of radius r at potential V_s coalesce to form a bigger drop of radius R, then
  - Charge on smaller drop $Q_s = \frac{rV}{k}$
  - $R = n^{1/3} r$
  - Potential of bigger drop $V_b = n^{2/3} V_s$
  - Charge on bigger drop $Q_b = nQ_s$

Two differently charged hollow sphere at same potential

- $\dfrac{q_1}{r_1} = \dfrac{q_2}{r_2}$
- $\sigma_1 r_1 = \sigma_2 r_2$

where σ_1 and σ_2 are the surface charge densities.

Two charged spheres are connected by a wire

- Charge flow between them till potential becomes same
- Charge transfers from B to A is

$$q = \frac{q_2 r_1 - q_1 r_2}{r_1 + r_2}$$

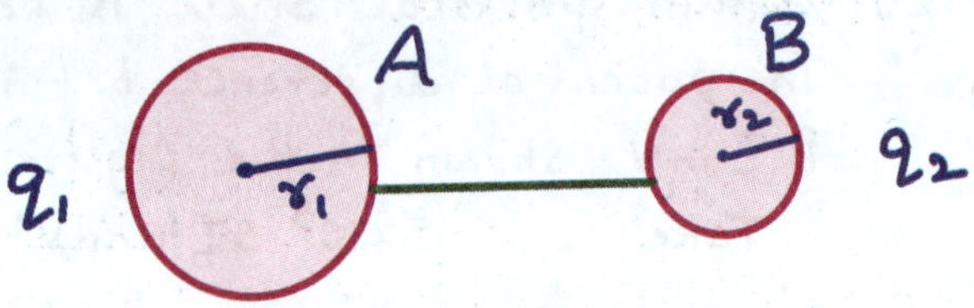

- New Charge on A is
$$q_1' = r_1\left(\frac{q_1 + q_2}{r_1 + r_2}\right)$$
- New Charge on B is
$$q_1' = r_2\left(\frac{q_1 + q_2}{r_1 + r_2}\right)$$
- New charge density on A is
$$\sigma_1' = \left(\frac{\sigma_1 r_1^2 + \sigma_2 r_2^2}{r_1(r_1 + r_2)}\right)$$
- New charge density on B is
$$\sigma_2' = \left(\frac{\sigma_1 r_1^2 + \sigma_2 r_2^2}{r_2(r_1 + r_2)}\right)$$

PYQ PUNCH

Q3. Two metal spheres, one of radius R and other of radius 2R, respectively have the same surface charge density σ. They are brought in contact and separated. What will be the new surface charge densities on them? (NEET 2019)

Sol. Given $\sigma_1 = \sigma_2 = \sigma$; $R_1 = R$; $R_2 = 2R$

$$\sigma_1' = \left(\frac{\sigma_1 r_1^2 + \sigma_2 r_2^2}{r_1(r_1 + r_2)}\right) \qquad \sigma_2' = \left(\frac{\sigma_1 r_1^2 + \sigma_2 r_2^2}{r_2(r_1 + r_2)}\right)$$

$$\sigma_1' = \left(\frac{\sigma R^2 + \sigma(2R)^2}{R(R + 2R)}\right) \qquad \sigma_2' = \left(\frac{\sigma R^2 + \sigma(2R)^2}{2R(R + 2R)}\right)$$

$$= \frac{5\sigma}{3} \qquad = \frac{5\sigma}{6}$$

Relationship between Electric Field and Potential

- $dV = -\vec{E}\cdot d\vec{r}$
  - Electric Field is from higher to lower potential.
  - Potential decreases in the direction of Electric Field.
  - If E is zero, then potential is constant.
  - Potential is constant in a surface perpendicular to Electric field.
- $V_2 - V_1 = -\int_{x_1}^{x_2} E_x dx - \int_{y_1}^{y_2} E_y dy - \int_{z_1}^{z_2} E_z dz$
- $E_x = -\left(\frac{\partial V}{\partial x}\right)_{y\,\&\,z = \text{constant}}$ Partial Differentiation of V w.r.t x taking y & z as constant.
- $E_y = -\left(\frac{\partial V}{\partial y}\right)_{x\,\&\,z = \text{constant}}$ Partial Differentiation of V w.r.t y taking x & z as constant.
- $E_z = -\left(\frac{\partial V}{\partial z}\right)_{x\,\&\,y = \text{constant}}$ Partial Differentiation of V w.r.t z taking x & y as constant.
- $\vec{E} = E_x\hat{i} + E_y\hat{j} + E_z\hat{k}$
- $\vec{E} = -\left(\frac{\partial V}{\partial x}\right)\hat{i} - \left(\frac{\partial V}{\partial y}\right)\hat{j} - \left(\frac{\partial V}{\partial z}\right)\hat{k}$

MCQ PUNCH

Q4. If potential (in volts) in a region is expressed as

$$V(x, y, z) = 6xy - y + 2yz,$$

the electric field (in N/C) at point (1, 1, 0) is:

Sol. $V(x, y, z) = 6xy - y + 2yz$

$E_x = -\left(\frac{\partial V}{\partial x}\right) = -6y$ $\quad E_y = -\left(\frac{\partial V}{\partial y}\right) = -6x + 1 - 2z$ $\quad E_z = -\left(\frac{\partial V}{\partial z}\right) = -2y$

Now $\vec{E} = -\left(\frac{\partial V}{\partial x}\right)\hat{i} - \left(\frac{\partial V}{\partial y}\right)\hat{j} - \left(\frac{\partial V}{\partial z}\right)\hat{k}$

$= (-6y)\hat{i} + (-6x + 1 - 2z)\hat{j} + (-2y)\hat{k}$

At (1, 1, 0)

$\vec{E} = -6\hat{i} - 5\hat{j} - 2\hat{k}$

Equi-potential Surface

- A surface whose potential is equal at every point.

Properties of Equi-potential Surface

- Work done in moving a charge on it is Zero.
- They are always perpendicular to Electric Field.
- Two equipotential surfaces can never intersect each other.

NEET Accelerate

- Two hollow spheres having same charge, then the potential of lesser radius sphere would be more.
- A positive charge can move from higher equi-potential surface to lower equi-potential surface i.e. B to A.

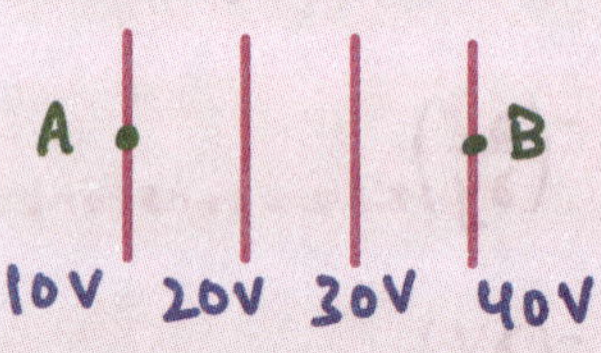

- More the spacing between the equi-potential surfaces, lesser the electric field.
  $E_B < E_A$

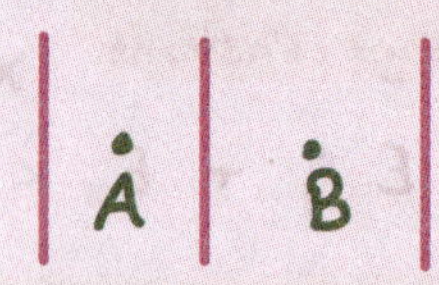

Shapes of Equi-potential Surface

- Point Charge - Spherical (Fig. a)
- Infinite Line charge - Cylindrical
- Infinite charged plate - Plate
- Equi-potential surface of an electric dipole. (Fig. b)
- Equi-potential surface of two positive charges. (Fig. c)

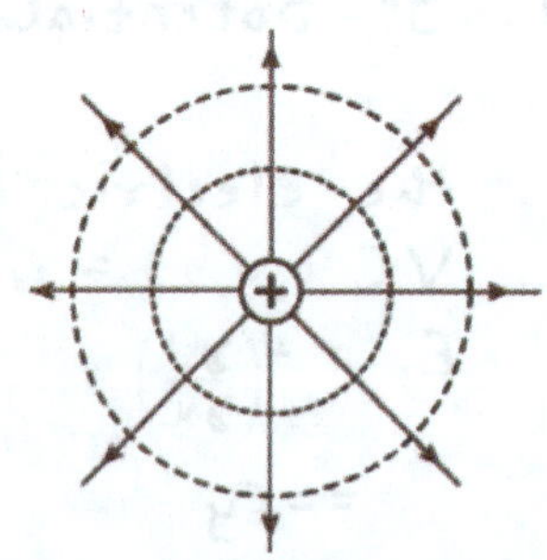

Fig. a

Fig. c

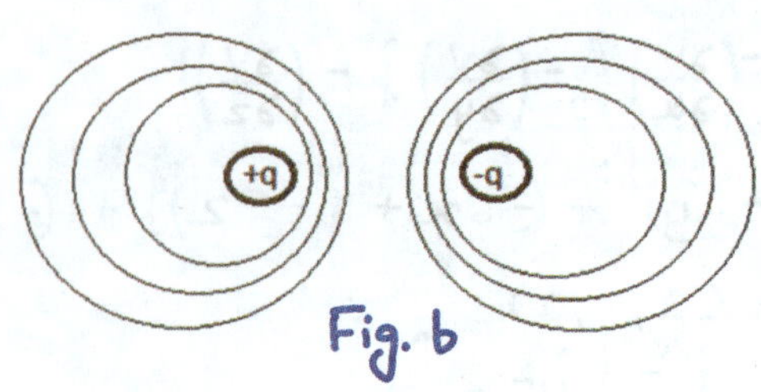

Fig. b

- At large distance from ring or any charge distribution – Spherical

Potential of Electric Dipole

◎ **Axial Line**

$$V_P = \frac{kp}{(x^2-a^2)}$$

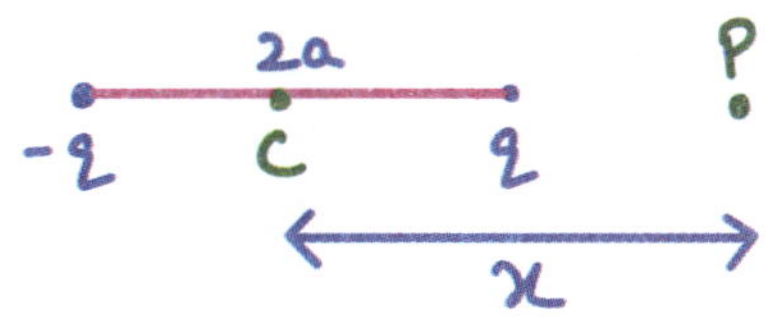

If $x >> a$

$$V_P = \frac{kp}{x^2}$$

◎ **Equitorial Line**

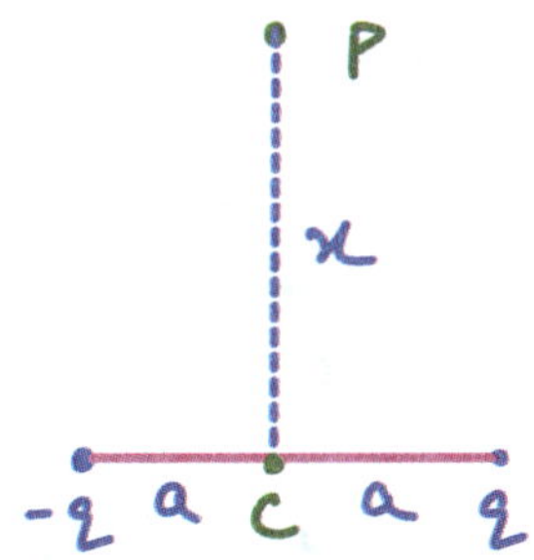

$$V_P = 0$$

◎ **At any point**

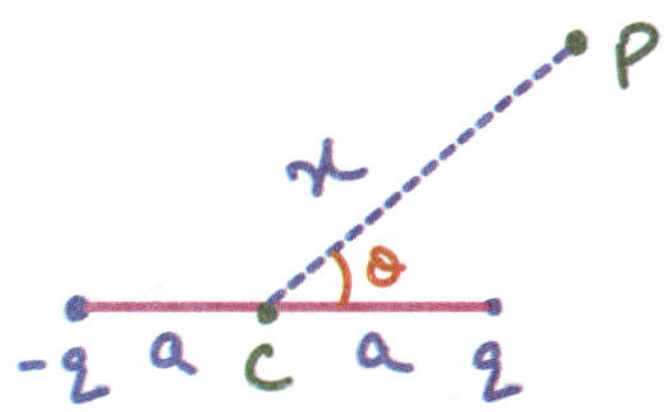

For $x >> a$

$$V_P = \frac{kp\cos\theta}{x^2}$$

PYQ PUNCH

Q5. An electric dipole is placed as shown in the figure. The electric potential (in 10^2 V) at point P due to the dipole is :

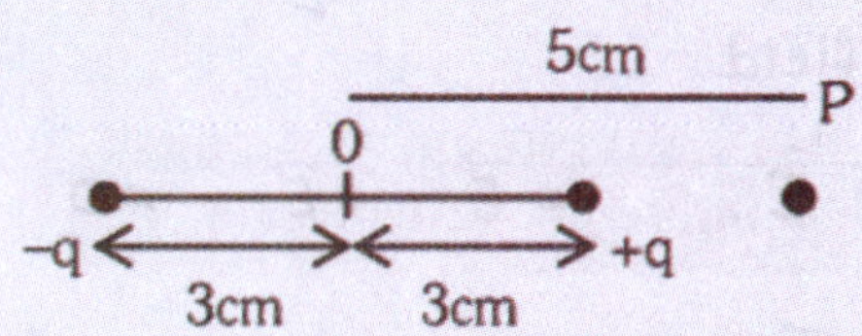

(NEET 2023)

Sol. $V_P = \frac{kp}{(x^2-a^2)}$

$$= \frac{k \times q \times 6 \times 10^{-2}}{(5^2-3^2) \times 10^{-4}}$$

$$= \frac{3}{8} \times 10^2 kq \quad \text{or} \quad \text{Ans is } \frac{3}{8}kq$$

Electrostatics of Conductor

- Charge given to a conductor always resides on its surface.
- If a charge q is placed in a cavity of conductor, then charge on conductor re-distributes such that

Initial State | Charge q placed in cavity | Re-distribution

  - $q_{inner} = -q_{cavity}$
  - $q_{outer} = q_{conductor} + q_{cavity}$

- Potential of Conductor is constant.
- Electric field lines are always perpendicular to the surface of conductor.

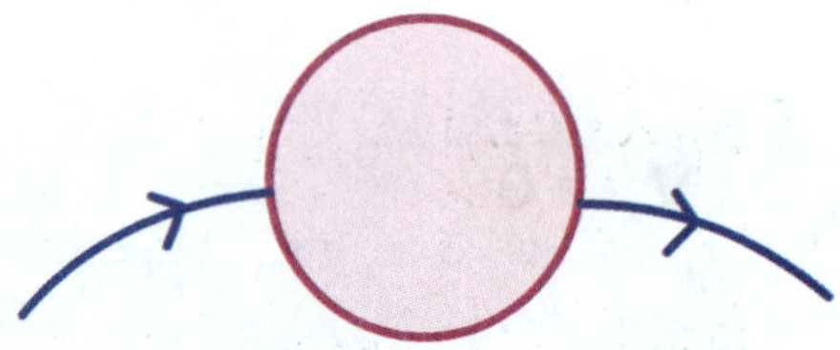

- Electric field due to a conductor near its surface is

$$E = \frac{\sigma}{\varepsilon_0}$$

Electro-static Shielding

- If a conductor is placed in an external field, charge of conductors re-distribute to induce an equal and opposite electric field.

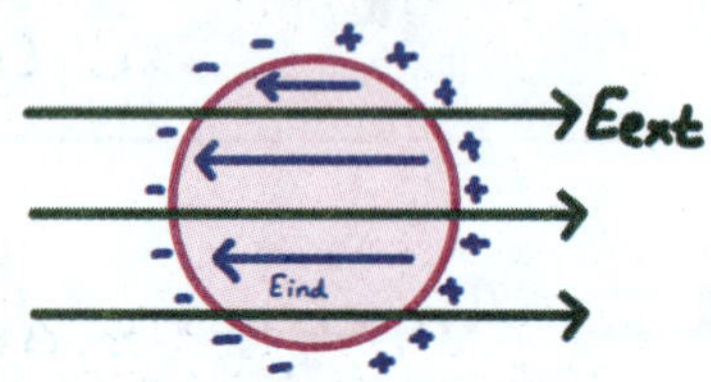

- $\vec{E}_{inside} = \vec{E}_{ext} + \vec{E}_{ind} = 0$
- This net zero electric field inside the conductor is called as electro-static shielding.

NEET Accelerate

- For all calculation purposes, treat conducting sphere as hollow sphere.
- Electric field inside the conductor is always zero.
- Conductor is an equi-potential surface.

Earthing of a Conductor

- Due to its vast size, earth's potential is almost zero.
- Whenever a conductor is connected with earth, its potential also becomes zero.
- It is not necessary that charge on the conductor also becomes zero.
- Earth can accept or donate electrons as per requirement.
- Lightning conductor is earthed to protect the homes from lightning. They have sharp vertex to increase charge density.

$$\text{Charge Density} \propto \frac{1}{\text{Radius}}$$

Capacitors

- It is a device used to store energy in the form of electric field (charge).
- It consists of two metallic bodies separated by an insulating medium.

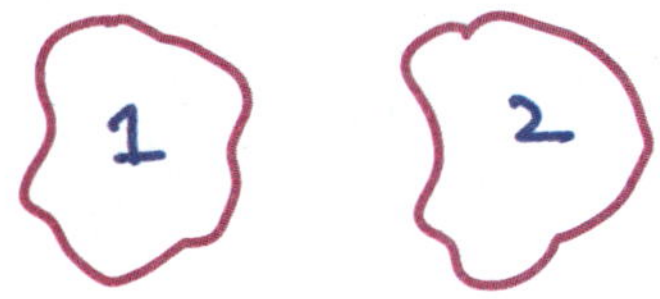

- Charge stored

$$Q = CV$$

where C is the Capacitance of the Capacitor.

Capacitance

- Measure the ability of a conductor to store charge.
- SI unit is Farad (F).
- It is a very big unit. Most general used limit is nF or pF.
- Dimensional Formula $[M^{-1} L^{-2} T^{4} A^{2}]$
- Depends upon the
  - Size of the conductor
  - Shape of the conductor
  - Medium between the conductor.

Parallel Plate Capacitor

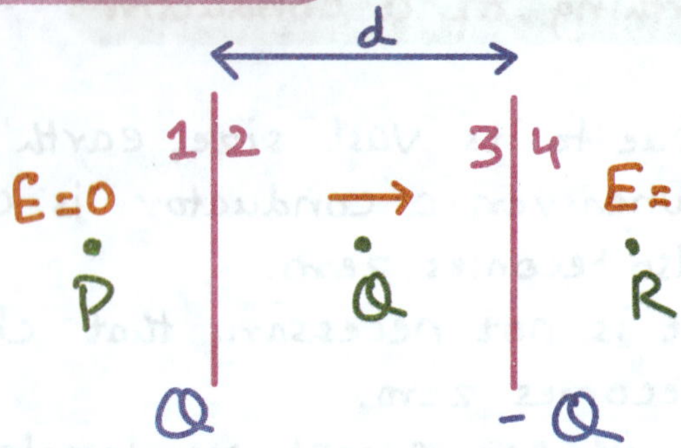

- $E_Q = \frac{\sigma}{\varepsilon_0}$ (Uniform Inside)
- $V = Ed$
- $E_P = E_R = 0$
- $C = \frac{A\varepsilon_0}{d}$
- Charge resides only on inner surfaces i.e. 2 and 3.
- Electro-static force between the plates

$$F = \frac{Q^2}{2A\varepsilon_0} = \frac{\sigma^2 A}{2\varepsilon_0}$$

Spherical Capacitor

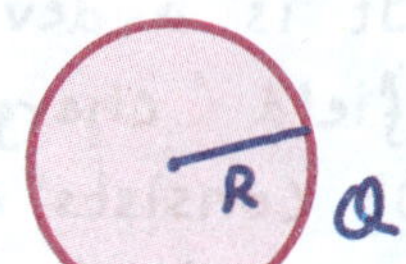

- Q charge on the surface of sphere.
- Other conductor at infinity.
- Capacitance

$$C = 4\pi\varepsilon_0 R$$

Energy stored in Capacitor

- $U = \frac{1}{2}CV^2 = \frac{1}{2}\frac{Q^2}{C} = \frac{1}{2}QV$
- Energy density $u = \frac{\sigma^2}{2\varepsilon_0} = \frac{Q^2}{2CAd}$

PYQ PUNCH

Q6. A parallel plate capacitor has a uniform electric field E in the space between the plates. If the distance between the plates is d and the area of each plate is A, the energy stored in the capacitor is : (NEET 2021, AIPMT 2011)

Sol. $C = \frac{A\varepsilon_0}{d}$; $V = Ed$

$$U = \frac{1}{2}CV^2 = \frac{1}{2} \times \frac{A\varepsilon_0}{d} \times E^2 d^2 = \frac{1}{2}A\varepsilon_0 d E^2$$

Charging of a Capacitor

- Work Done by battery $= CV^2$
- Energy stored $= \frac{1}{2}CV^2$
- Energy lost in the form of Heat or EMW

$$E_{lost} = \frac{1}{2}CV^2$$

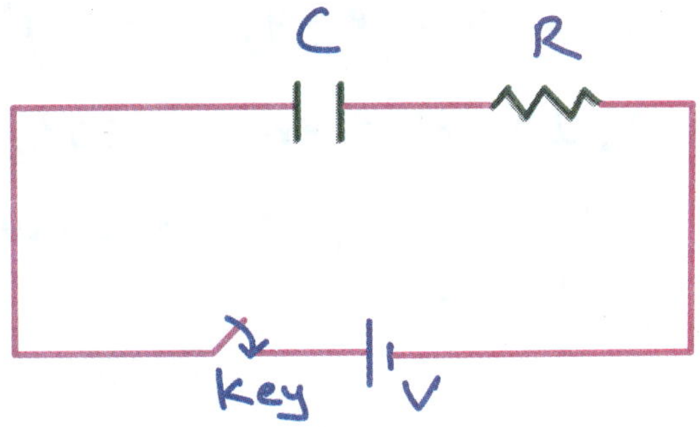

Connection of a Charged Capacitor with uncharged Capacitor

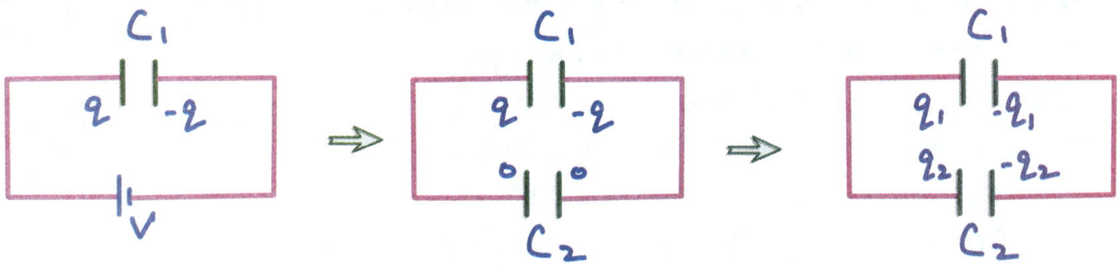

- C_1 was initially charged to q by battery V.
- It is then disconnected and connected to an uncharged capacitor.
- $q = C_1 V$
- $q_2 = \frac{qC_2}{C_1+C_2}$; $q_1 = \frac{qC_1}{C_1+C_2}$; $\frac{q_1}{q_2} = \frac{C_1}{C_2}$
- Initial Energy, $U_i = \frac{1}{2}\frac{q^2}{C_1}$
- Final Energy, $U_f = \frac{1}{2}\frac{q^2}{(C_1+C_2)}$
- Loss of Energy, $\Delta U = \frac{q^2 C_2}{2C_1(C_1+C_2)}$
- % loss of energy $= \frac{C_2}{(C_1+C_2)} \times 100$
- If $C_1 = C_2 = C$
  - $q_1 = q_2 = \frac{q}{2}$
  - Initial Energy, $U_i = \frac{1}{2}\frac{q^2}{C}$

- Final Energy, $U_f = \frac{1}{4}\frac{q^2}{C}$
- Loss of Energy, $\Delta U = \frac{1}{4}\frac{q^2}{C}$
- % loss of energy = 50%
- Total energy of the resulting system decreases by a factor of 2.

PYQ PUNCH

Q7. A capacitor of capacitance C = 900 pF is charged fully by 100 V battery B as shown in figure (a). Then, it is disconnected from the battery and connected to another uncharged capacitor of capacitance C = 900 pF as shown in figure (b). The electrostatic energy stored by the system (b) is:

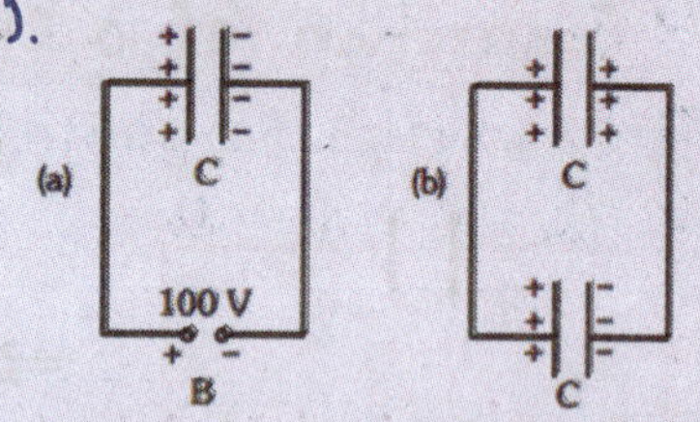

(NEET 2021)

Sol. $C_1 = 900$ pF ; $C_2 = 900$ pF ; $V = 100$ V

$q = C_1V$

$= 900\times10^{-12}\times100 = 9\times10^{-8}$ C

Now $U_f = \frac{1}{4}\frac{q^2}{C} = \frac{1}{4}\times\frac{(9\times10^{-8})^2}{900\times10^{-12}} = 2.25\times10^{-6}$ J

Changing of Capacitance

Battery is attached

	Plate Gaps Increased	Plate Gaps Decreased
Capacitance	↓	↑
Potential	Same	Same
Charge	↓	↑
Energy stored	↓	↑

Battery is unattached

	Plate Gaps Increased	Plate Gaps Decreased
Capacitance	↓	↑
Potential	↑	↓
Charge	Same	Same
Energy stored	↑	↓

Combinations of Capacitors

Series

- $\frac{1}{C_{eq}} = \frac{1}{C_1} + \frac{1}{C_2} + \frac{1}{C_3} + ---.$
- Q remains same
- $V = V_1 + V_2 + V_3 + ---.$

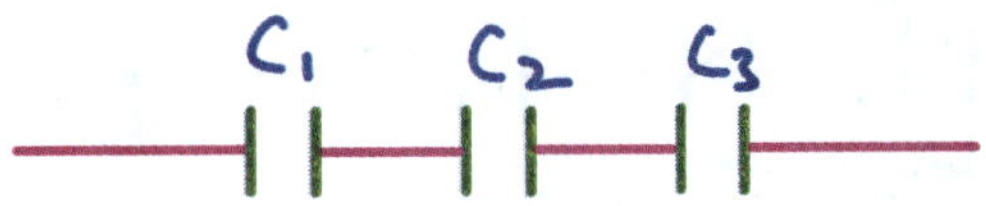

Parallel

- $C_{eq} = C_1 + C_2 + C_3 + ---.$
- V remains same
- $Q = Q_1 + Q_2 + Q_3 + ---.$

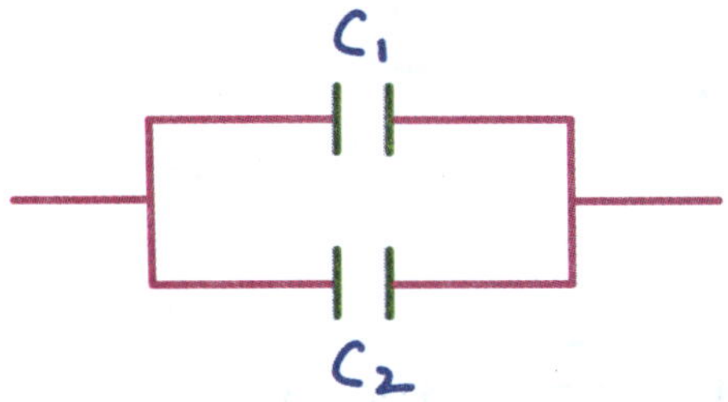

PYQ PUNCH

Q8. The equivalent capacitance of the system shown in the following circuit is :

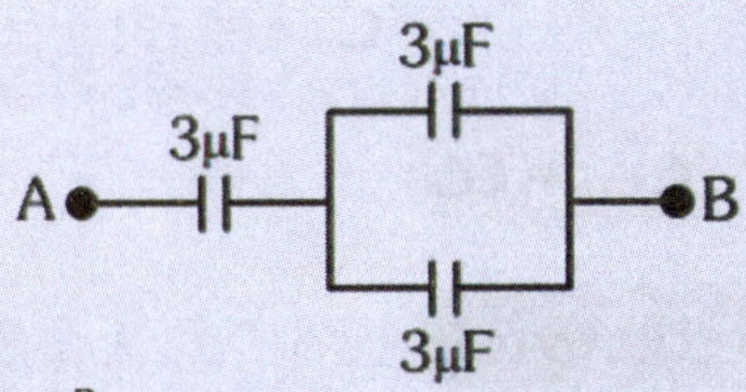

(NEET 2024)

Sol. 2 & 3 are in parallel and then in series with 1.

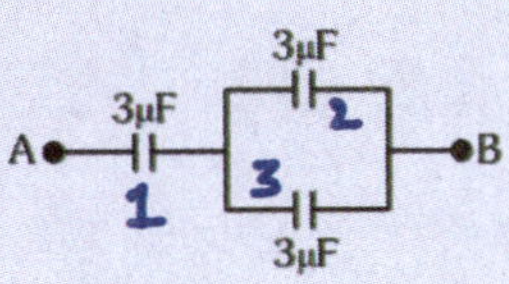

C_{eq} of 2 and 3 is 6 μF

C'_{eq} of 1 and C_{eq} is 2 μF.

Wheatstone Bridge

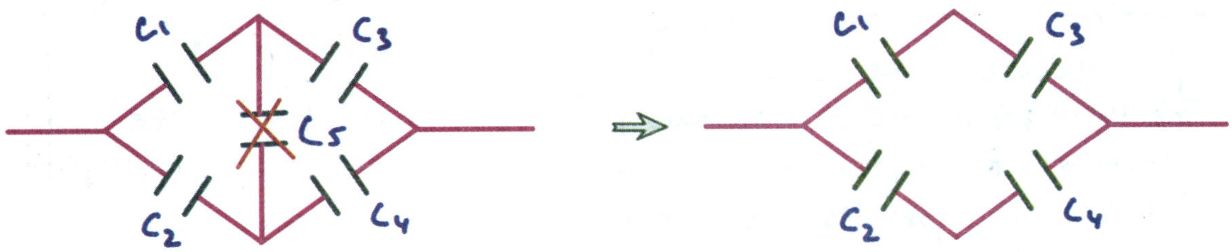

- If $\frac{C_1}{C_2} = \frac{C_3}{C_4}$, then C_5 can be removed.

⇒ C_1 and C_3 are in series
C_2 and C_4 are in series
Then their resultant are in parallel.

Applications of Wheatstone Bridge

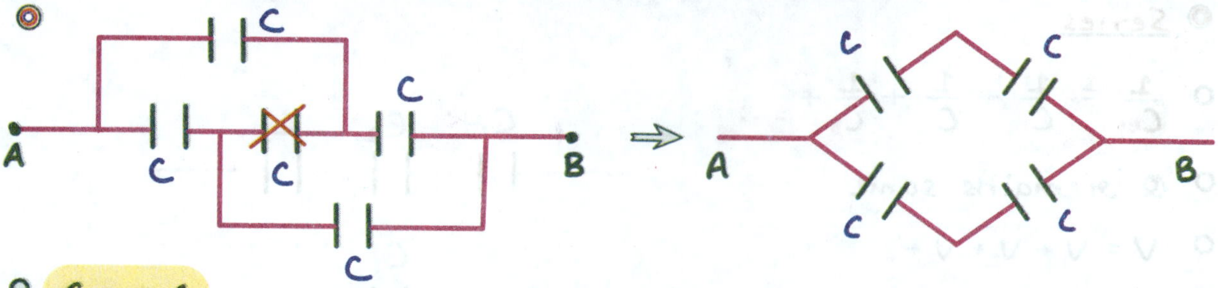

- $C_{eq} = C$

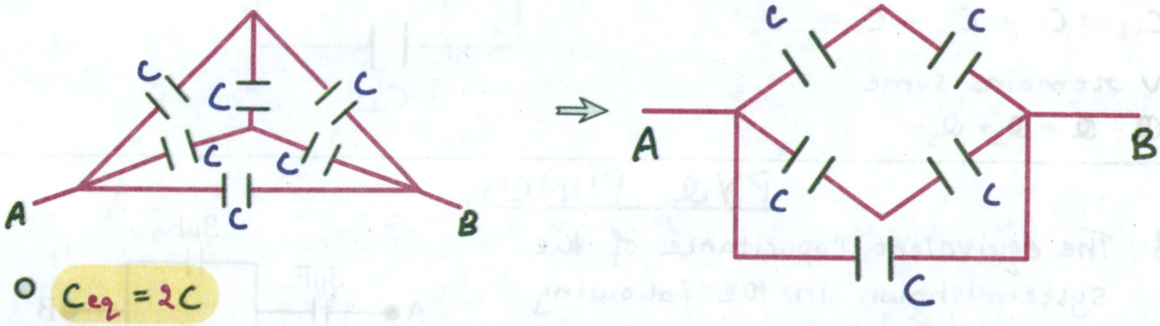

- $C_{eq} = 2C$

Dielectrics

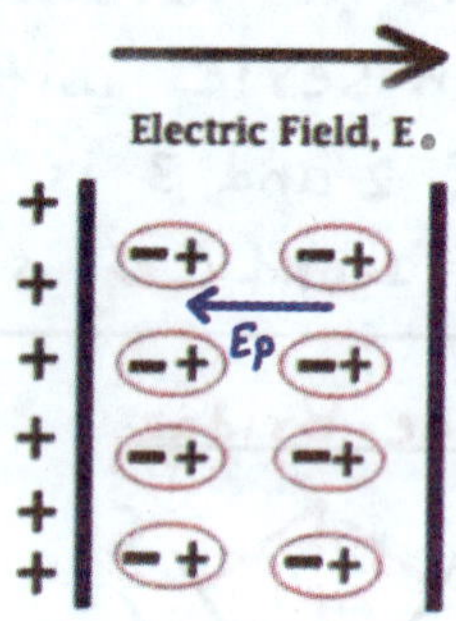

- It is an insulator.
- Can be non-polar i.e. zero dipole.
- Can be polar i.e. non-zero dipole.
- When placed in external electric field, polarization of molecules take place.
- The field produced due to the polarization of the material minimize the effect of external field.
- Unlike conductors, the net field doesn't become zero.
- $E_m = E_0 - E_p \neq 0$

Dielectric Constant (k)

- Ratio of External Electric Field to medium electric field.

$$K = \frac{E_0}{E_m}$$

- $k \geq 1$

- $K_{vacuum} = 1$ (Perfect Insulator)
- $K_{air} \simeq 1$
- $K_{conductor} \to \infty$

Relative Permeability

- Ratio of permittivity of medium to vacuum.

$$\varepsilon_r = \frac{\varepsilon_m}{\varepsilon_0} = k \text{ (Dielectric Constant)}$$

Breakdown of Dielectric

- It is the minimum external field which breaks an insulator into a conductor.

Dielectric in Capacitor

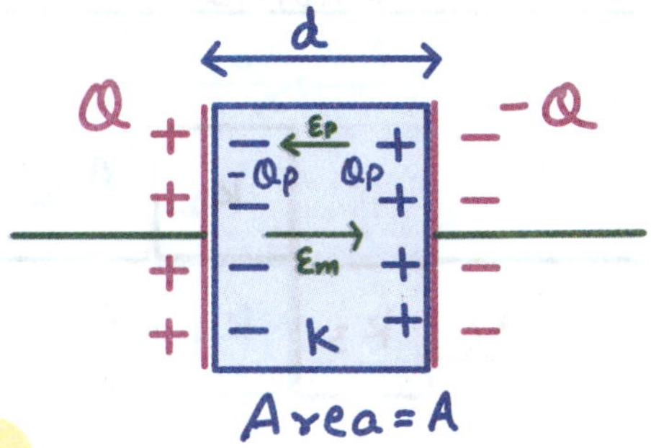

- $E_m = \frac{E_0}{k} = E_0 - E_p$
- Electric field decreases by k times.
- Polarised charge on dielectric

$$Q_p = Q\left(1 - \frac{1}{k}\right)$$

- New Capacitance $C' = \frac{kA\varepsilon_0}{d} = kC$
- Capacitance increased by k times.
- Series Combination of Dielectrics

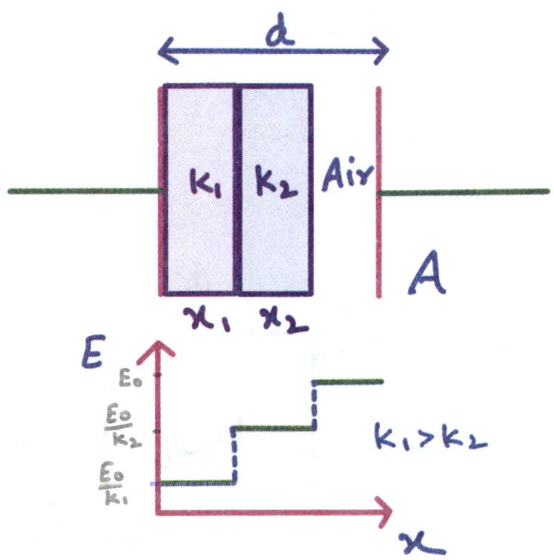

⇒

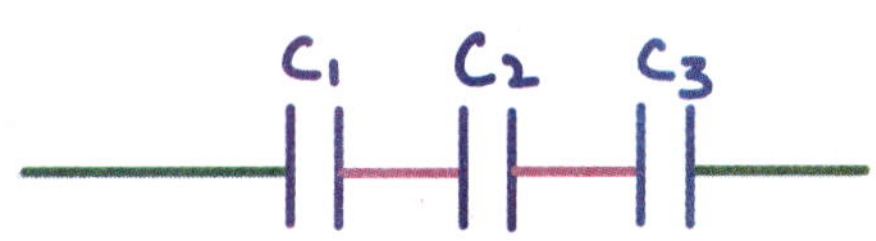

$$C_1 = \frac{k_1 A\varepsilon_0}{x_1} \; ; \; C_2 = \frac{k_2 A\varepsilon_0}{x_2} \; ; \; C_3 = \frac{A\varepsilon_0}{d - x_1 - x_2}$$

$$\frac{1}{C_{eq}} = \frac{1}{C_1} + \frac{1}{C_2} + \frac{1}{C_3}$$

Parallel Combination of Dielectric

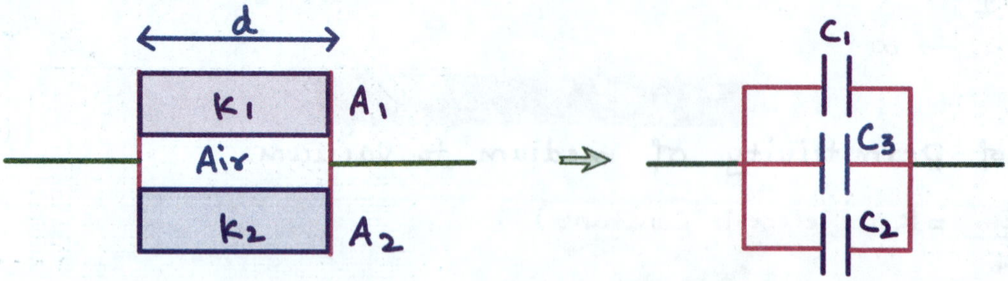

$$C_1 = \frac{K_1 A_1 \varepsilon_0}{d} \; ; \; C_2 = \frac{K_2 A_2 \varepsilon_0}{d} \; ; \; C_3 = \frac{(A - A_1 - A_2)\varepsilon_0}{d}$$

$$C_{eq} = C_1 + C_2 + C_3$$

Mixed Combination of Dielectrics

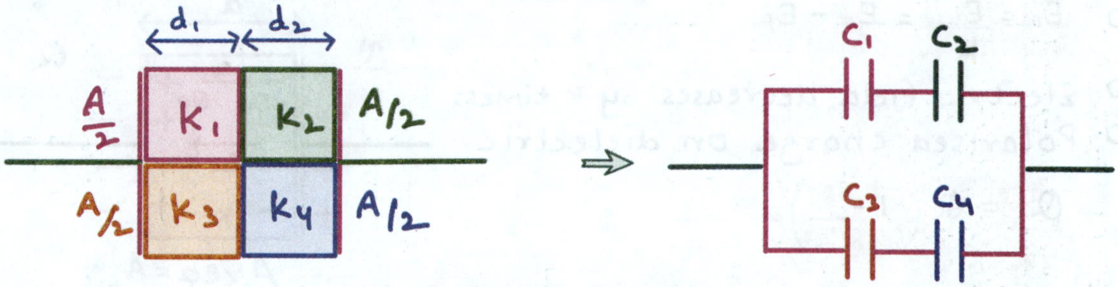

$$C_1 = \frac{K_1 A \varepsilon_0}{2d_1} \; ; \; C_2 = \frac{K_2 A \varepsilon_0}{2d_2} \; ; \; C_3 = \frac{K_3 A \varepsilon_0}{2d_1} \; ; \; C_4 = \frac{K_4 A \varepsilon_0}{2d_2}$$

- K_1 and K_3 parallel mein ~~hai~~ Nahi hai.
- K_2 and K_4 parallel mein ~~hai~~ Nahi hai.
- K_1 and K_2 series mein hai.
- K_3 and K_4 series mein hai.

K equivalent

- $\frac{K_{eq} A \varepsilon_0}{d} = C_{eq}$

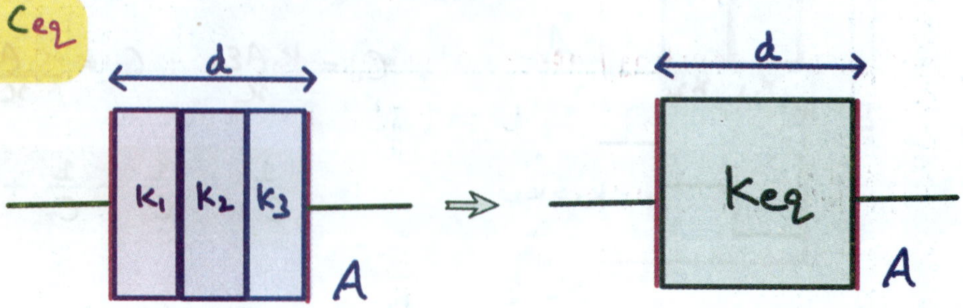

PYQ PUNCH

Q9. A parallel plate capacitor of area A, plate separation d and Capacitance C is filled with four dielectric materials having dielectric constant k_1, k_2, k_3 and k_4 as shown in the figure. If a single dielectric material is to be used to have the same capacitance C in this capacitor, then its dielectric constant k is given by: (NEET 2021)

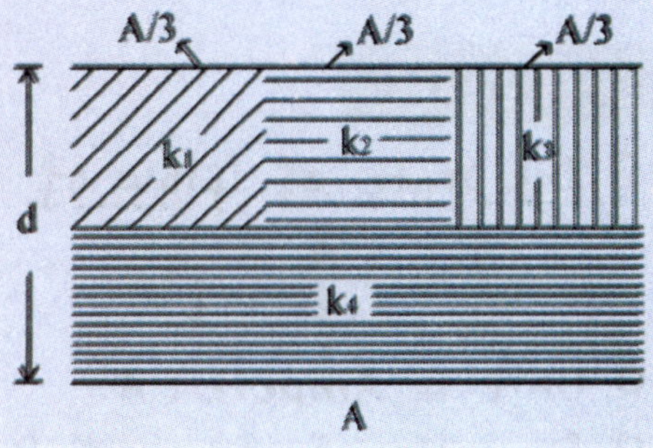

Sol.

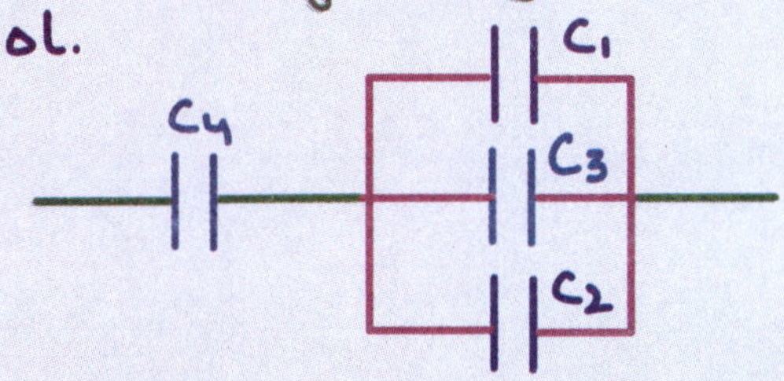

$$C_1 = \frac{2k_1 A\varepsilon_0}{3d} \; ; \quad C_2 = \frac{2k_2 A\varepsilon_0}{3d_2} \; ;$$

$$C_3 = \frac{2k_3 A\varepsilon_0}{3d_1} \; ; \quad C_4 = \frac{2k_4 A\varepsilon_0}{d}$$

$$C'_{eq} = C_1 + C_2 + C_3 = \frac{2A\varepsilon_0}{3d}(k_1 + k_2 + k_3)$$

$$\frac{1}{C_{eq}} = \frac{1}{C_4} + \frac{1}{C'_{eq}} = \frac{d}{2k_4 A\varepsilon_0} + \frac{3d}{2A\varepsilon_0(k_1+k_2+k_3)} = \frac{d}{2A\varepsilon_0}\left(\frac{1}{k_4} + \frac{3}{(k_1+k_2+k_3)}\right)$$

Now

$$\frac{k_{eq} A\varepsilon_0}{d} = C_{eq} \quad \text{or}$$

$$\frac{d}{k_{eq} A\varepsilon_0} = \frac{1}{C_{eq}} = \frac{d}{2A\varepsilon_0}\left(\frac{1}{k_4} + \frac{3}{(k_1+k_2+k_3)}\right)$$

$$\frac{2}{k_{eq}} = \frac{1}{k_4} + \frac{3}{(k_1+k_2+k_3)}$$

Self Energy

◎ Hollow Conducting / non-conducting or solid conducting sphere

$$U = \frac{kQ^2}{2R}$$

◎ Solid non-conducting sphere

$$U = \frac{3kQ^2}{5R}$$

22. Current Electricity

Current

- The rate of flow of charge through a cross-sectional area.

  ▹ $I_{avg} = \frac{Q}{t} = \frac{ne}{t}$ ▹ $I_{ins} = \frac{dq}{dt}$

- Unit is Ampere (A).
- Direction is towards the flow of positive charge.
- Scalar because doesn't obey triangle law of vector addition.

Current Density

- Current per unit area.

  $$j = \frac{I}{A}$$

- A vector quantity
- Unit is A/m^2.

Drift velocity

- It is the average velocity of all the electrons at a particular instant of time, which is independent of time, though electrons are accelerating in the presence of electric field.
- $\vec{V}_d = -\frac{e\vec{E}\tau}{m}$ where τ is the mean relaxation time.
- It is due to electric field.
- Extremely low in magnitude. A fraction of mm/s.
- In terms of Current

  $$I = neAV_d$$

Mobility

- $\mu = \frac{V_d}{E} = \frac{e\tau}{m}$
- Unit is $m^2V^{-1}s^{-1}$
- Property of a charge carrier.
- Doesn't depend upon V_d & E.

PYQ PUNCH

Q1. A charged particle having drift velocity of 7.5×10^{-4} m/s in an electric field of 3×10^{-10} V/m, has a mobility of ? (NEET 2020)

Sol. $\mu = \frac{V_d}{E}$

$= \frac{7.5 \times 10^{-4}}{3 \times 10^{-10}} = 2.5 \times 10^{6}\ m^2 V^{-1} s^{-1}$

Ohm's Law

- $\vec{J} = \sigma \vec{E}$ where $\sigma = \frac{ne^2\tau}{m}$ is conductivity.
- $V = RI$ where R is the resistance of the conductor.

Resistance

- It is the hindrance to the flow of current.
- For ohmic conductors, it doesn't depend upon the voltage applied and current passing through the conductor.
- $R = \frac{\rho L}{A}$ where $\rho = \frac{1}{\sigma}$ is the resistivity of the material.
- Slope of V-I curve gives Resistance.
  - For AB, resistance is positive.
  - For BC, resistance is negative.
  - For CD, resistance is positive.

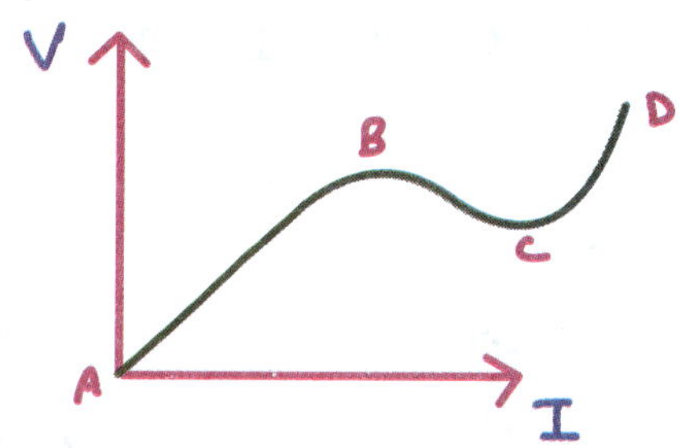

Resistivity or Specific Resistance

- Resistivity is the property of material.
- Depends upon the temperature only.
- Doesn't depend upon the shape and size of the material.
- Use to compare the conductivity of different materials.

Variation of Resistance

- On stretching
- On stretching a conductor, its length ↑ and area ↓.

- For $L' = nL$

$$R' = n^2 R$$

- For twice the length, take $n = 2$
- For thrice the length, take $n = 3$
- For $x\%$ increase in length, take $n = 1 + \frac{x}{100}$

MCQ PUNCH

Q2. A wire of certain material is stretched slowly by 10 percent. Its new resistance and specific resistance become :

Sol. $n = 1 + \frac{x}{100} = 1 + \frac{10}{100} = 1.1$

$$R' = n^2 R = (1.1)^2 R = 1.21 R$$

So, Resistance becomes 1.21 times while Specific resistance remains same.

On Temperature

- On increasing temperature, both resistance and resistivity of a conductor increases.
- $\rho_T = \rho_0 (1 + \alpha T)$ where ρ_0 is the resistivity at 0°c, ρ_T is the resistivity at T°c, α is the coefficient of resistivity.
- 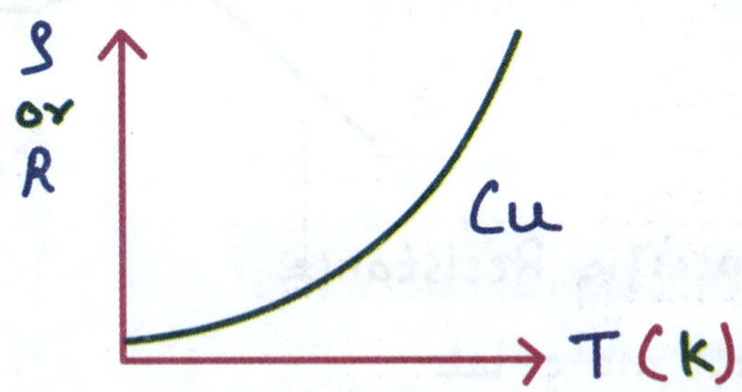

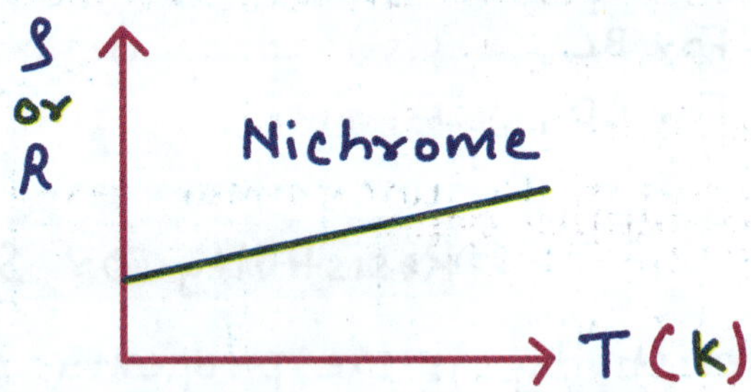

- $R_T = R_0 (1 + \alpha T)$ where R_0 is the resistance at 0°c, R_T is the resistance at T°c
- $\frac{R_{T_2}}{R_{T_1}} = \frac{R_0 (1 + \alpha T_2)}{R_0 (1 + \alpha T_1)}$ where R_0 is the resistance at 0°c, R_{T_1} is the resistance at T_1°c, R_{T_2} is the resistance at T_2°c

PYQ PUNCH

Q3. The resistance of platinum wire at 0°C is 2 Ω and 6.8 Ω at 80°C. The temperature coefficient of resistance of the wire is. (NEET 2023)

Sol. $R_T = R_0(1+\alpha T)$

$6.8 = 2(1+\alpha\, 80)$

$\Rightarrow \alpha = 0.03\ °C^{-1}$

On melting and re-drawing

- Volume remains the same.
- For $L' = nL$

$$R' = n^2 R$$

- For twice the length, take $n = 2$
- For thrice the length, take $n = 3$
- For $x\%$ increase in length, take $n = 1 + \frac{x}{100}$

Combination of Resistors

Series

- Method to identify series combination
  - Only 1 terminal should be common.
  - No diversion at the common terminal.
  - Replace the equivalent resistance between the uncommon terminals.

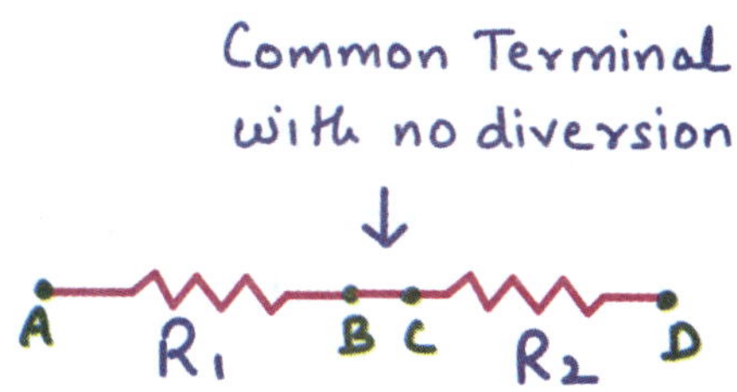

- Current is same.
- $V = V_1 + V_2$
- $R_{eq} = R_1 + R_2 + R_3 + ---$
- If n resistors of same value are attached in series, then

$$R_{eq} = nR$$

Parallel

- Method to identify parallel combination
  - Both the terminals should be common.
  - Diversion doesn't matter.
  - Replace the equivalent resistance between the common terminals.

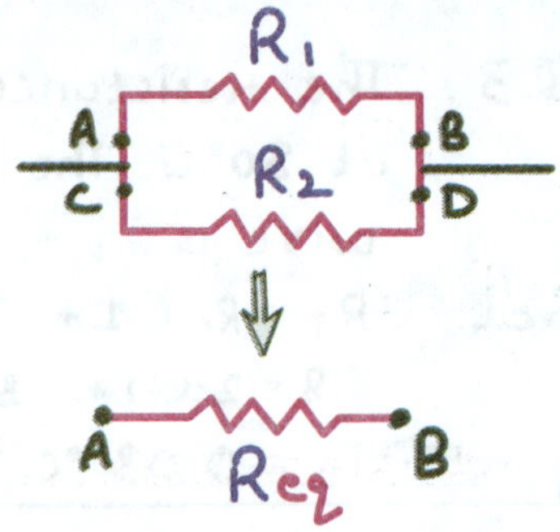

- Voltage is same.
- $I = I_1 + I_2$
- $\frac{1}{R_{eq}} = \frac{1}{R_1} + \frac{1}{R_2} + \frac{1}{R_3} + \ldots$
- If n resistors of same value of attached in parallel, then

$R_{eq} = \frac{R}{n}$

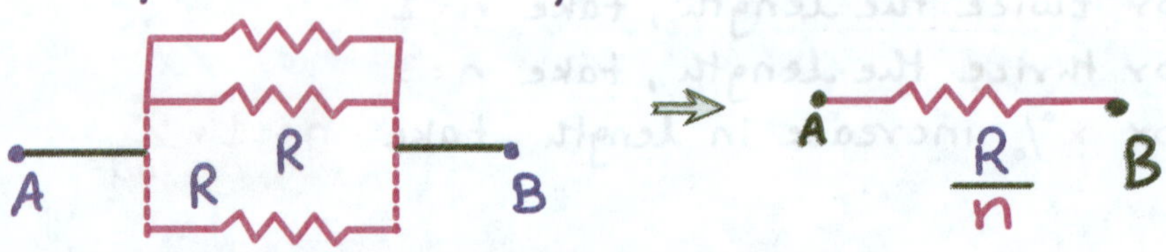

PYQ PUNCH

Q4. A wire of length l and resistance $100\,\Omega$ is divided into 10 equal parts. The first 5 parts are connected in series while the next 5 parts are connected in parallel. The two combinations are again connected in series. The resistance of this final combination is (NEET 2024)

Sol. As $R \propto l$

$\Rightarrow R = \frac{R_{total}}{n} = \frac{100}{10} = 10\,\Omega$

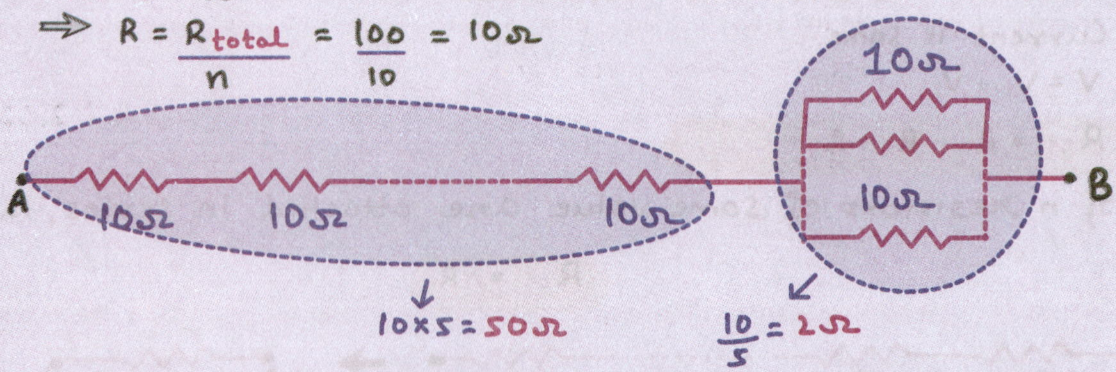

Now the two combinations are in series

$R_{eq} = 50 + 2 = 52\,\Omega$

Special cases of Combination of Resistors

n resistors first in series then in parallel

- $R_s = nR$; $R_p = \frac{R}{n}$
- $\frac{R_s}{R_p} = n^2$

Resistance of Circular Wire

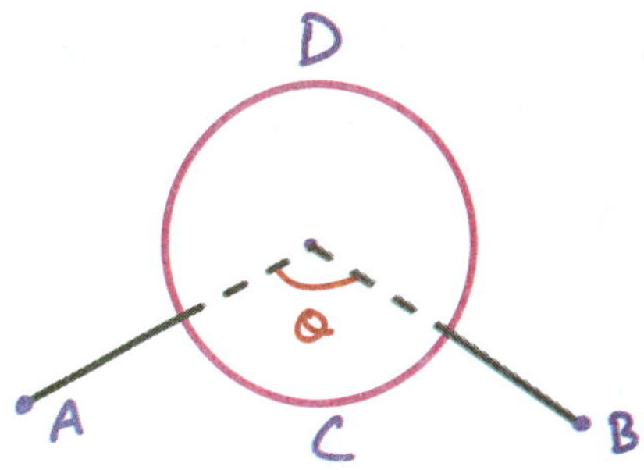

- R is the resistance of circular wire.
- ACB and ADB are in parallel
- $R_{eq} = \frac{R\,\theta(360° - \theta)}{360° \times 360°}$
- For terminals at two diametrically opposite points $\theta = 180°$

  $R_{eq} = R/4$

Resistance of a triangular wire

- R is the resistance of triangular wire.
- Equivalent Resistance

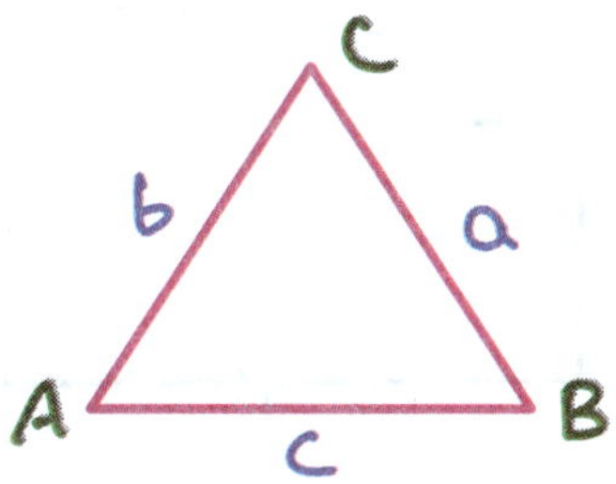

Points	R_{eq}
AB	$\frac{c(a+b)R}{(a+b+c)^2}$
BC	$\frac{a(b+c)R}{(a+b+c)^2}$
AC	$\frac{b(a+c)R}{(a+b+c)^2}$

PYQ PUNCH

Q5. A 12 cm wire is given a shape of a right angled triangle ABC having sides 3 cm, 4 cm and 5 cm. The resistance between the two ends (AB, BC, CA) of the respective sides are measured one by one by a multimeter. The resistances will be the ratio **(NEET 2013)**

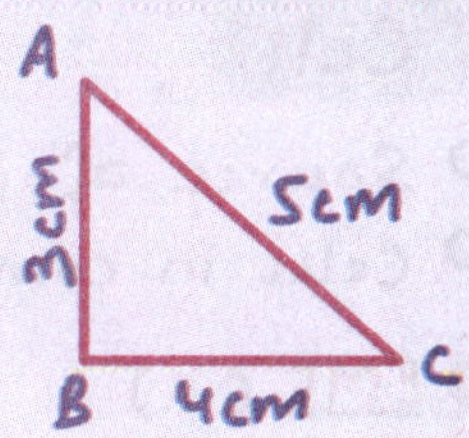

Sol. $a = 4\text{cm}$; $b = 5\text{cm}$; $c = 3\text{cm}$

$R_{AB} = \frac{c(a+b)R}{(a+b+c)^2} = \frac{3(4+5)}{(3+4+5)} \times 12 = 27\,\Omega$

Similarly

$R_{BC} = 32\,\Omega$

$R_{CA} = 35\,\Omega$

Ratio is 27 : 32 : 35

Equivalent Resistivity and Conductivity

Series

- Two wires of resistivities ρ_1 and ρ_2, conductivities σ_1 and σ_2, lengths l_1 and l_2 and same area A.
- $\rho_{eq} = \dfrac{\rho_1 l_1 + \rho_2 l_2}{l_1 + l_2}$
- $l_1 = l_2$

  $\rho_{eq} = \dfrac{\rho_1 + \rho_2}{2}$

  $\sigma_{eq} = \dfrac{2\sigma_1\sigma_2}{\sigma_1 + \sigma_2}$

Parallel

- Two wires of resistivities ρ_1 and ρ_2, conductivities σ_1 and σ_2, areas A_1 and A_2 and same length L.
- $\rho_{eq} = \dfrac{\rho_1\rho_2 (A_1 + A_2)}{\rho_1 A_1 + \rho_2 A_2}$
- $A_1 = A_2$

  $\rho_{eq} = \dfrac{2\rho_1\rho_2}{\rho_1 + \rho_2}$

  $\sigma_{eq} = \dfrac{\sigma_1 + \sigma_2}{2}$

Current through non-uniform cross-sectional area

Quantity	Change
Current	No
Current Density	Yes
Electric Field	Yes
Resistance	Yes
Drift Velocity	Yes

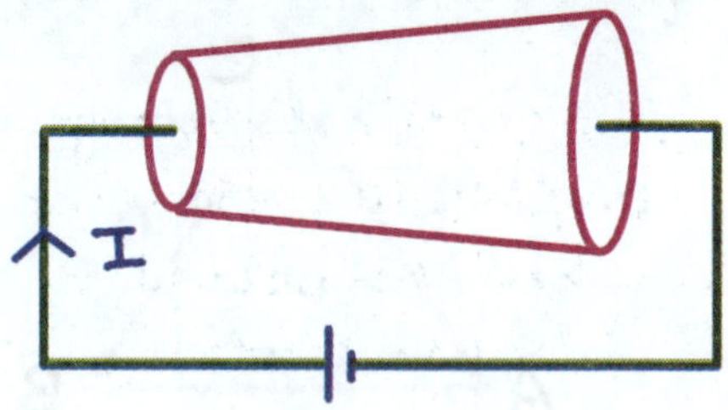

Cell

- Source of Constant Current.
- Cells in combination is called Battery.

EMF (E)

- WD in moving a unit positive charge from negative terminal to positive terminal when circuit is opened.
- Yeh battery ki dikhane wali aukaat hai.

Internal Resistance (r)

- Resistance offered by the cell to the flow of current.
- Depends upon
  - Concentration of electrolyte.
  - Distance between the terminals.
  - Temperature

◎ **Terminal Voltage** (V)

- WD in moving a unit positive charge from negative terminal to positive terminal when circuit is closed.
- Yeh battery ki asli aukaat hai.

Relationship between E, V and r

◎ **While Discharging**

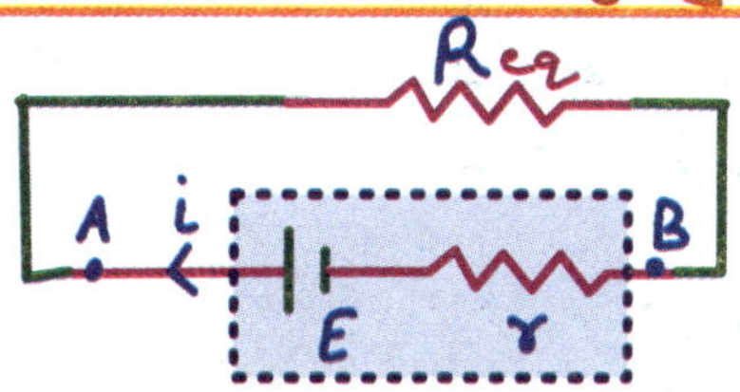

- $V = \mathcal{E} - ir$
- $i = \dfrac{\mathcal{E}}{r + R_{eq}}$
- $V = \dfrac{\mathcal{E} R_{eq}}{r + R_{eq}}$

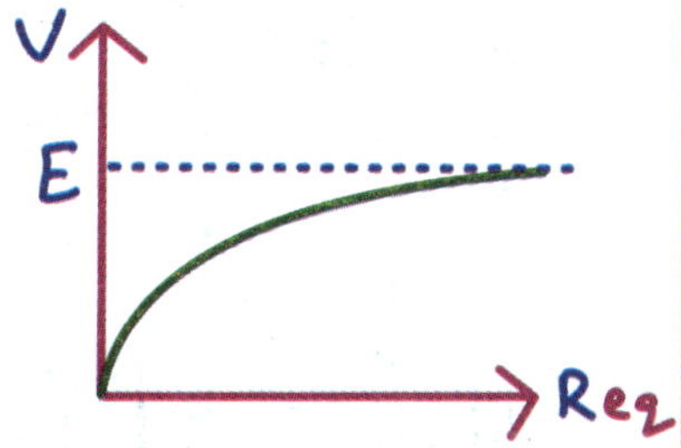

◎ **While Charging**

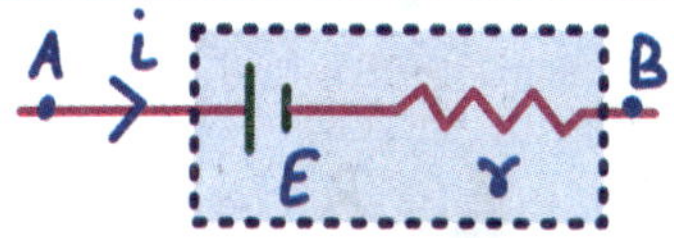

- $V = \mathcal{E} + ir$
- $V > E$

PYQ PUNCH

Q6. The terminal voltage of the battery, whose emf is 10V and internal resistance 1Ω when connected through an external resistance of 4Ω as shown in the fig is :

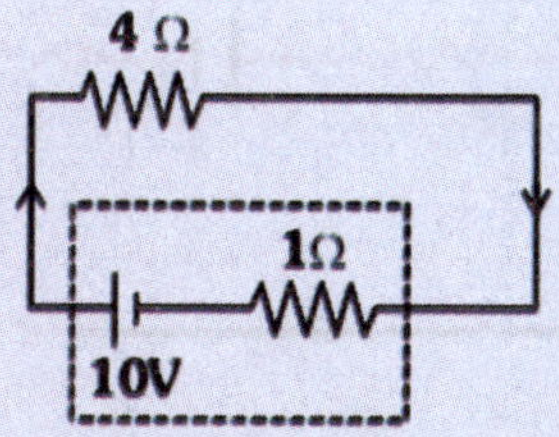

(NEET 2024)

Sol. $E = 10V$; $r = 1\Omega$; $R_{eq} = 4\Omega$

$$V = \frac{\mathcal{E} R_{eq}}{r + R_{eq}} = \frac{10 \times 4}{1 + 4} = 8V$$

Cells in Combination

◎ **Series**

- n identical cells
- $E_{eq} = nE$
- $r_{eq} = nr$
- Both EMF & r ↑
- $I = \dfrac{E_{eq}}{nr + R}$

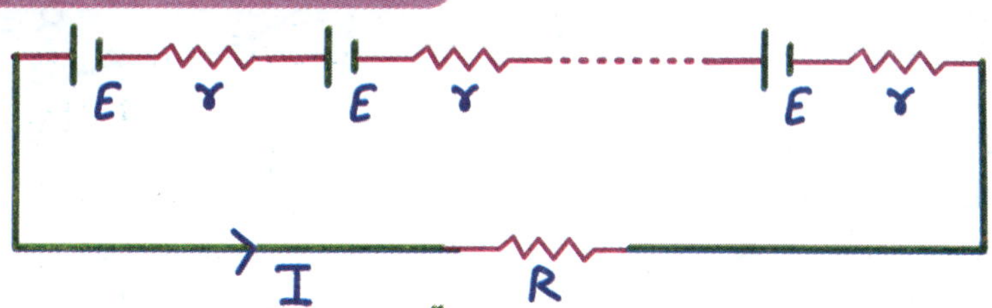

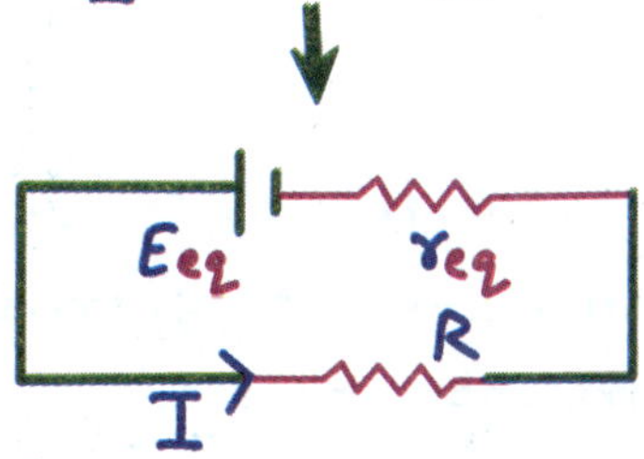

Parallel

- m identical rows
- $E_{eq} = E$
- $r_{eq} = \frac{r}{m}$
- EMF remain same
- Resistance ↓
- $I = \frac{E}{\frac{r}{m} + R}$

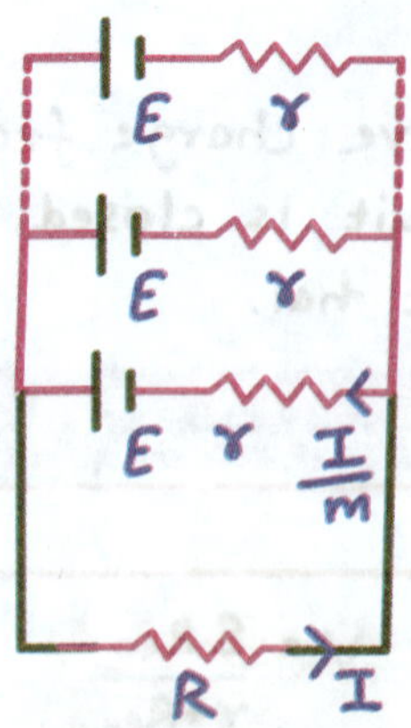

⇒

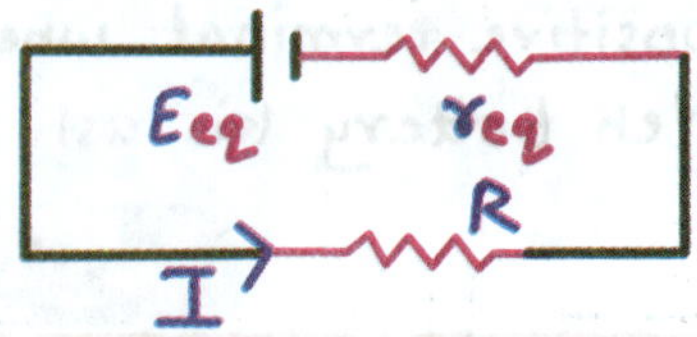

Mixed Grouping

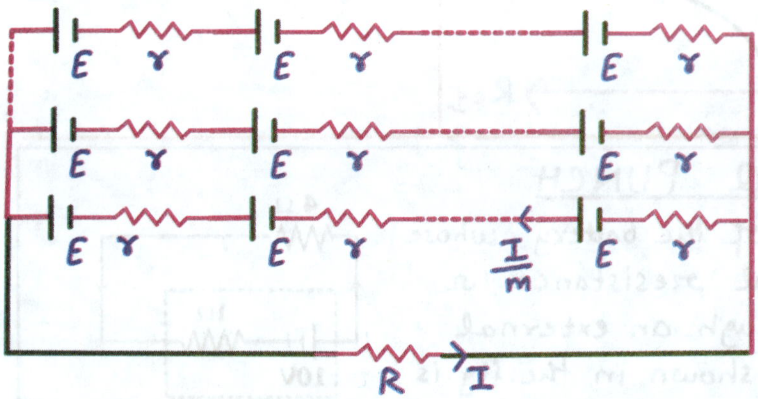

⇒

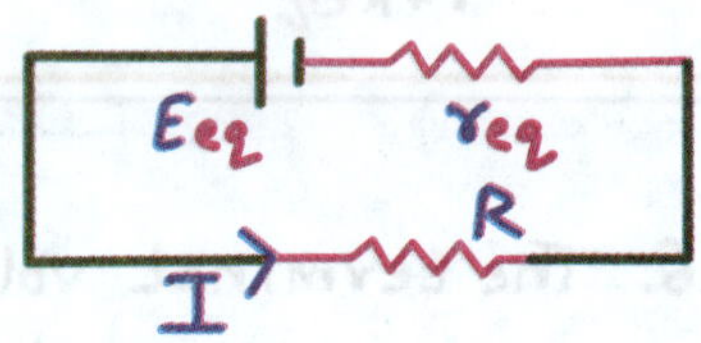

- m identical rows having n identical cells in each row.
- $E_{eq} = nE$
- $r_{eq} = \frac{nr}{m}$
- EMF ↑
- Resistance ↑ or ↓
- $I = \frac{nE}{\frac{nr}{m} + R}$

For maximum current
$R = \frac{nr}{m}$

NEET Accelerate

- While charging of cell, the graph between V and I has
  - ▹ Slope representing -ve of internal resistance.
  - ▹ Intercept represents EMF.

Unidentical Cells in Parallel

Same Polarity attached

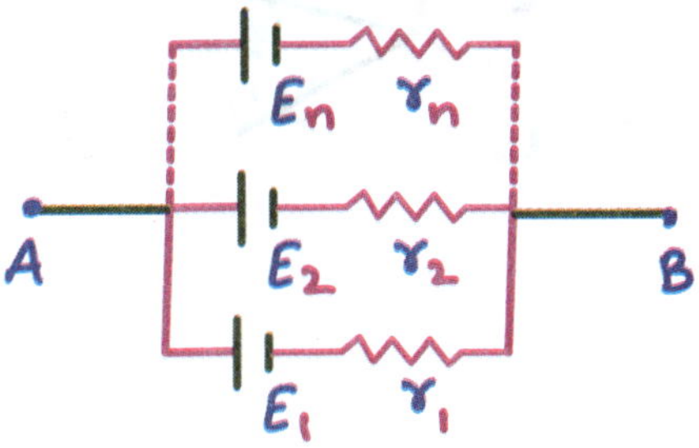

⇒

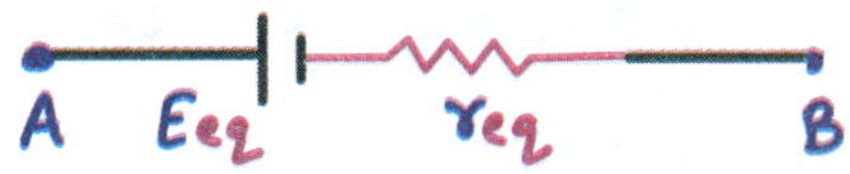

▷ $E_{eq} = \left(\frac{E_1}{r_1} + \frac{E_2}{r_2} + \cdots + \frac{E_n}{r_n}\right) r_{eq}$

▷ $\frac{1}{r_{eq}} = \frac{1}{r_1} + \frac{1}{r_2} + \cdots + \frac{1}{r_n}$

Random Polarity Attached

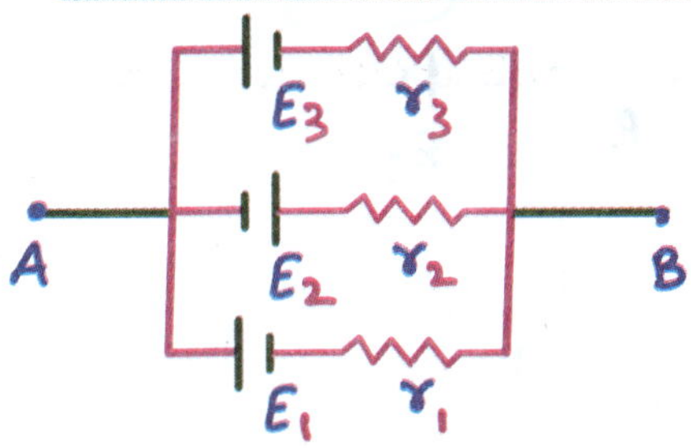

⇒

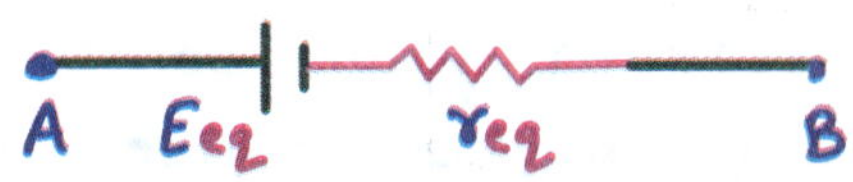

▷ $E_{eq} = \left(\frac{E_1}{r_1} + \frac{-E_2}{r_2} + \frac{E_3}{r_3}\right) r_{eq}$

Becomes Negative

▷ $\frac{1}{r_{eq}} = \frac{1}{r_1} + \frac{1}{r_2} + \frac{1}{r_3}$

No effect on resistance

MCQ PUNCH

Q7. Two batteries, one of emf 18V and internal resistance 2Ω and other of emf 12V and internal resistance 1Ω, are connected as shown. The voltmeter V will record a reading of :

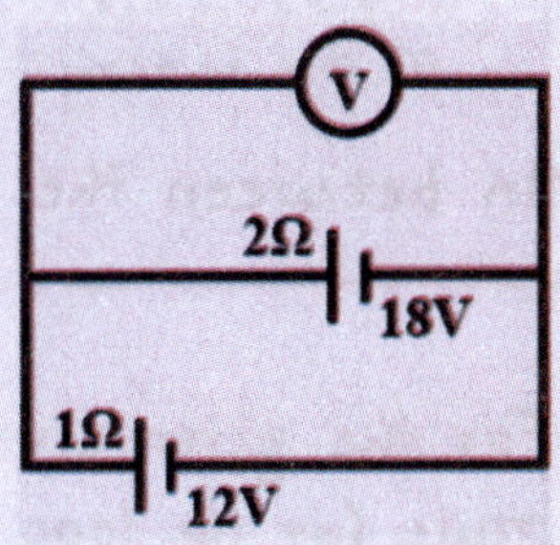

Sol. $E_1 = 12V$; $r_1 = 1\Omega$; $E_2 = 18V$; $r_2 = 2\Omega$

$$\frac{1}{r_{eq}} = \frac{1}{r_1} + \frac{1}{r_2} = \frac{1}{1} + \frac{1}{2} = \frac{3}{2}$$

$$V = E_{eq} = \left(\frac{E_1}{r_1} + \frac{E_2}{r_2}\right) r_{eq} = \left(\frac{12}{1} + \frac{18}{2}\right) \times \frac{2}{3} = 14V$$

Kirchoff's Law

1st Law or Junction Rule

- Based on Conservation of Charge.
- Incoming current = Outgoing Current

$$i_1 + i_2 + i_3 = i_4 + i_5$$

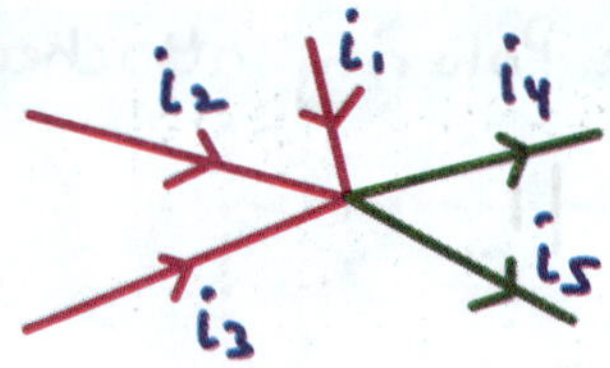

2nd Law or KVL

- Based on Conservation of Energy.
- Algebric sum of potential drop in a closed loop is zero.
- Steps to apply KVL.
  - Take a point on a loop. (Let say A)
  - Assume the current in the loop in any direction. (Let say I anti-clockwise)
  - Choose the direction of loop (Let say anti-clockwise)
  - Now starting from point A and moving anti-clockwise, use

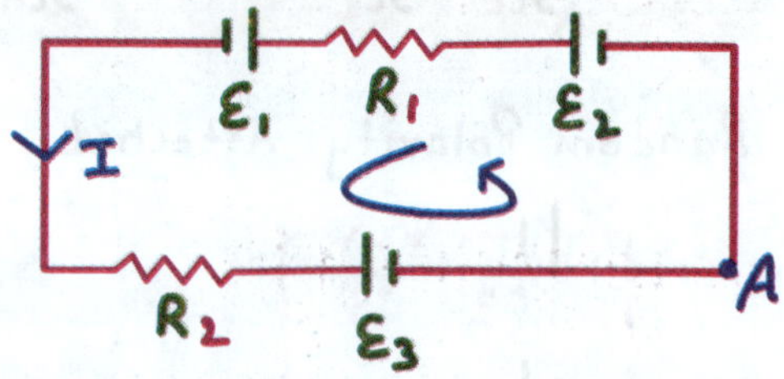

+ve sign as we reach on +ve terminal of the battery

$$V_A - (-E_3) - (+IR_1) - (+E_1) - (+IR_2) - (+E_3) = V_A$$

Potential at pt A

−ve sign as we reach on −ve terminal of the battery

+ve as dir. of current & loop is same

  - In between the terms, there comes negative sign.

PYQ PUNCH

Q8. For the given circuit, the kirchoff's loop rule for the loop BCDEB is given by the equation.

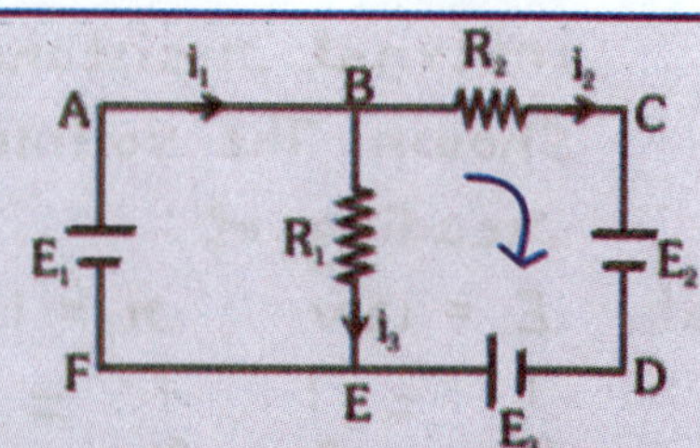

(NEET 2020)

Sol. Let us take the loop clock-wise and starts from point B.

$$V_B - (i_2 r_2) - (E_2) - (-E_3) - (-i_3 r_1) = V_B$$

$$\Rightarrow -i_2 r_2 - E_2 + E_3 + i_3 r_1 = 0$$

- KVL can also be applied in a part of loop.

  Moving from A to B

  $V_A - (-E_1) - (iR_1) - (+E_2) = V_B$

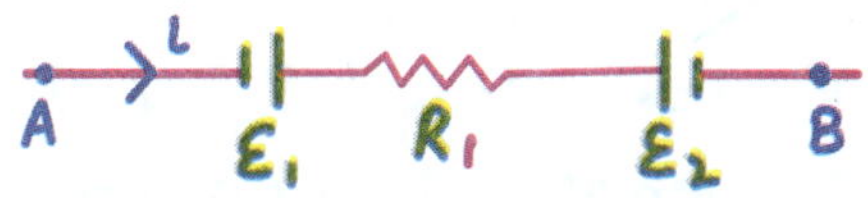

PYQ PUNCH

Q.9. The potential difference $(V_A - V_B)$ between the points A and B in the given figure is :

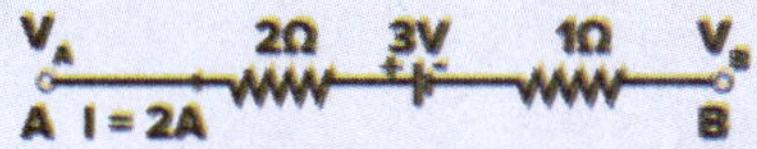

(NEET 2016)

Sol. Moving from A to B

$V_A - (2\times2) - (3) - (1\times2) = V_B$

$\Rightarrow V_A - V_B = 9V$

Joule's Heating Effect

- When current i passes through a resistor R, heat get produced in it

- $H = i^2Rt$
- $H = \frac{V^2}{R}t$
- $H = Vit$ (use to find total heat)

In series

- $H \propto R$
- $H_1 = i^2R_1t$
- $H_2 = i^2R_2t$
- $\frac{H_1}{H_2} = \frac{R_1}{R_2}$

In Parallel

- $H \propto \frac{1}{R}$
- $H_1 = \frac{V^2t}{R_1}$
- $H_2 = \frac{V^2t}{R_2}$
- $\frac{H_1}{H_2} = \frac{R_2}{R_1}$

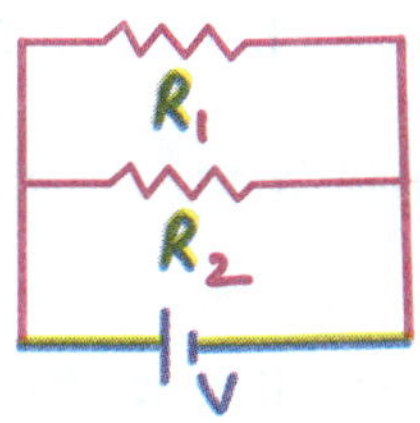

Power

- Rate of production of heat.
- Unit is Watt (W)
- 1 HP = 746 W

- $H = i^2R$
- $H = \frac{V^2}{R}$
- $H = Vi$ (use to find total power)

Power Rating of Bulb

- Power rating (P_R , V_R)
- It means, bulb consumes P_R power at V_R voltage.
- Resistance of the bulb

$$R = \frac{V_R^2}{P_R}$$

- If power consumption at V_R Volt is P_R and at V Volt is P , then

$$P = \left(\frac{V}{V_R}\right)^2 P_R$$

Series

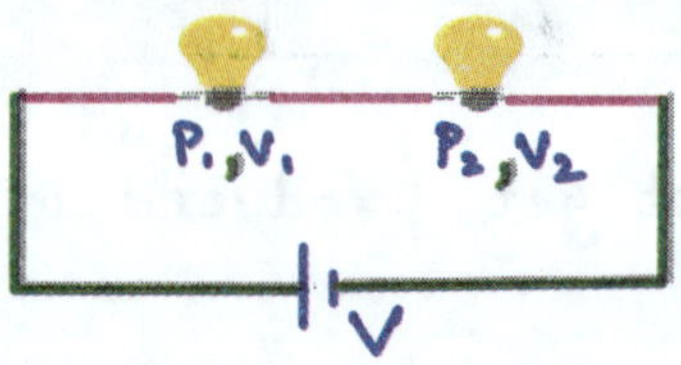

- $$\frac{1}{P} = \frac{1}{P_1} + \frac{1}{P_2}$$

- One with lesser power glows more.

Parallel

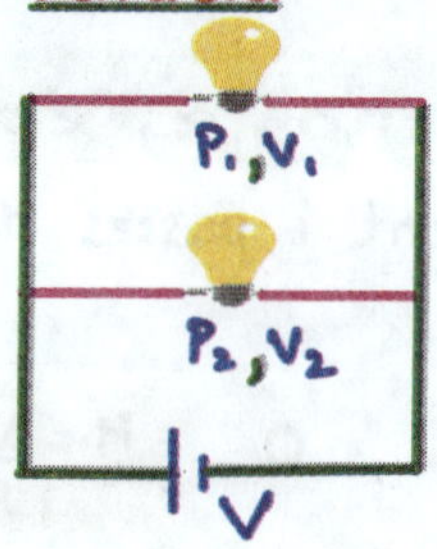

$$P = P_1 + P_2$$

- One with more power glows more.

Galvanometer

- Used to detect small amount of current.
- Shows no deflection when current is zero.

Wheatstone Bridge

- It is a network of four resistances on four arms of the quadrilateral, a key and a battery on one of its diagnols and a galvanometer on other diagnol.

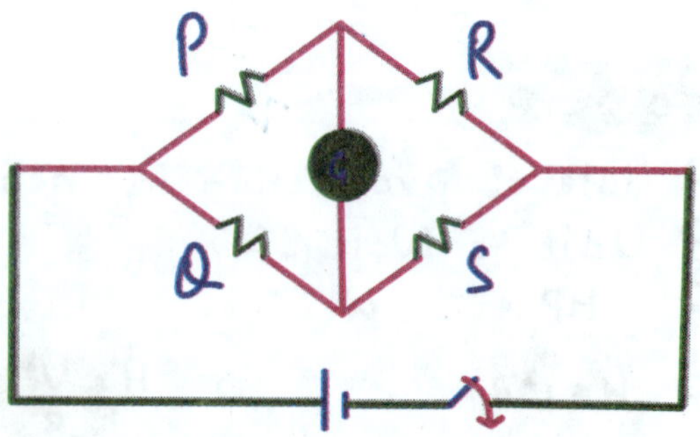

Balanced Wheatstone Bridge

- No current in the Galvanometer.
- $\frac{P}{Q} = \frac{R}{S}$

Application

- **Meter Bridge**
- Use to find unknown resistor.
- S is known resistance
- R is unknown resistance
- C is balanced point.

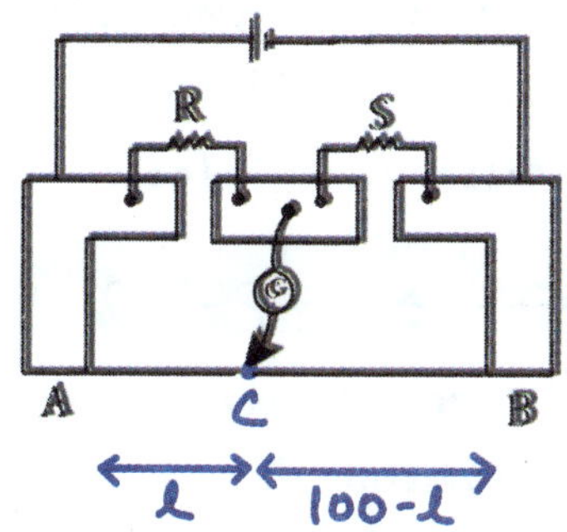

$$\frac{R}{S} = \frac{l}{100-l}$$

Wheatstone Bridge in Combination of Resistors

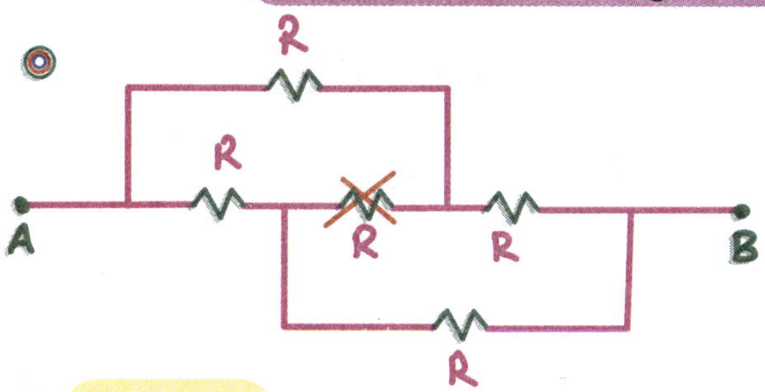

⇒

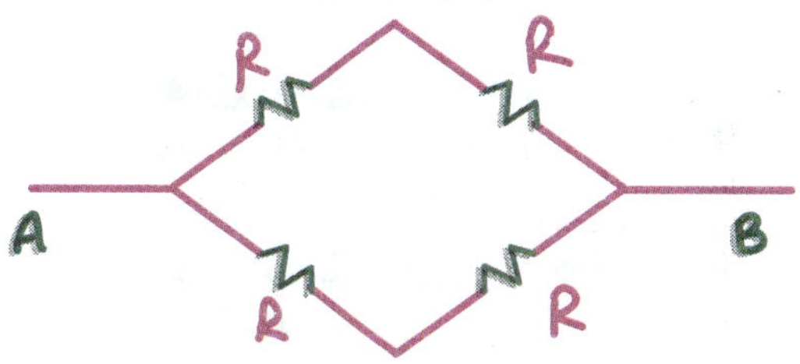

- $R_{eq} = R$

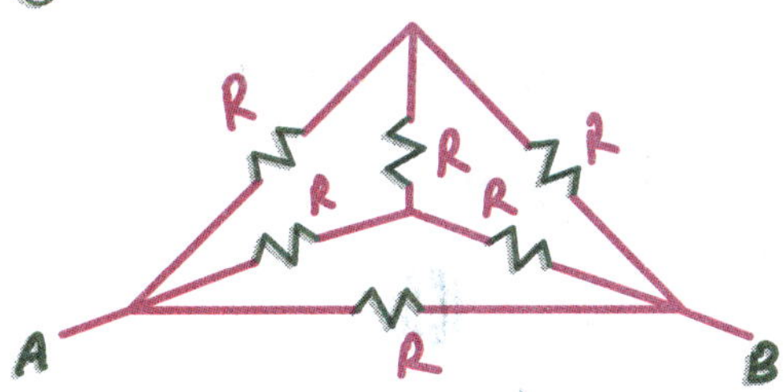

⇒

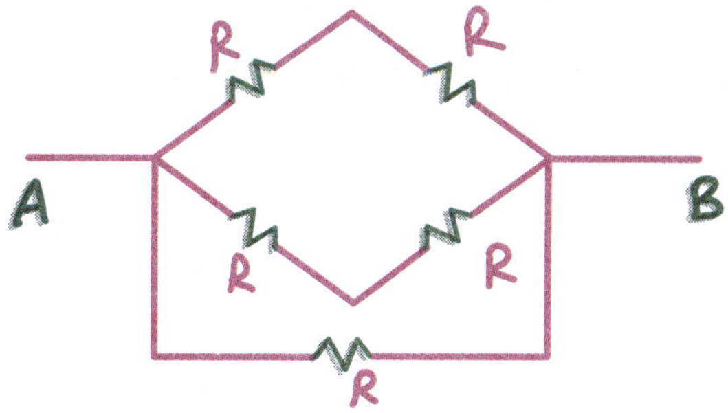

- $R_{eq} = 2R$

23. Moving Charges and Magnetism

Magnetic Field (MF)

- The space around a magnet or a current carrying conductor in which its magnetic influence can be experienced.
- SI unit is Tesla (T)
- 1 Gauss = 10^{-4} Tesla

Oersted's Experiment

- It demonstrated that the current carrying wire produces magnetic field around it.

Biot - Savart's Law

- It gives the magnetic field due to a small current carrying element dl.

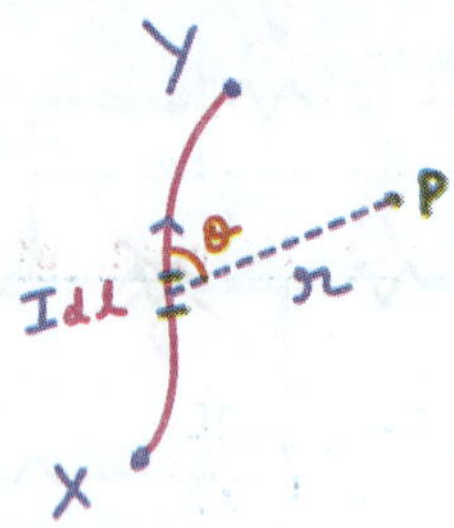

- $dB = \frac{\mu_0}{4\pi} \cdot \frac{I\,dl \sin\theta}{r^2}$ Scalar Form
- $d\vec{B} = \frac{\mu_0}{4\pi} \cdot \frac{I\,d\vec{l} \times \hat{r}}{|\vec{r}|^2}$ Vector Form

where $\frac{\mu_0}{4\pi} = 10^{-7}\ Tm^{-1}A^{-1}$

μ_0 is the permeability of free space

r is the distance of point P from current carrying element.

- Direction is given by Right Hand Thumb Rule. Place your thumb along the element Idl. Curl the fingers to the point P. Fingers will give the direction of magnetic field.

Permeability

- It is the measure of ability of the medium to allow the formation of magnetic field in it.
- $\frac{1}{\mu_0 \varepsilon_0} = c^2$ where c is the speed of light in vacuum.

Applications of Biot-Savart's Law

MF at the centre of a circular current carrying coil

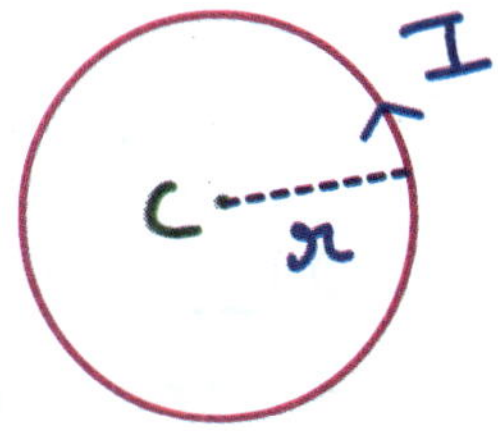

- $B_C = \frac{\mu_0 I}{2r}$
- Curl the fingers in the direction of current, thumb will give the direction of magnetic field.
- For N turns of coil

$$B_C = \frac{\mu_0 N I}{2r}$$

PYQ PUNCH

Q1. A tightly wound 100 turns coil of radius 10 cm carries a current of 7A. The magnitude of the magnetic field at the centre of the coil is (Take $\mu_0 = 4\pi \times 10^{-7}$ SI units) (NEET 2024)

Sol. $N = 100$; $r = 10\text{cm} = 0.1\text{m}$; $I = 7\text{A}$

$$B_C = \frac{\mu_0 N I}{2r}$$

$$= \frac{4\pi \times 10^{-7} \times 100 \times 7}{2 \times 0.1} = 4.4\text{mT}$$

MF at the centre of a semi-circular coil

$$B_C = \frac{\mu_0 I}{4r}$$

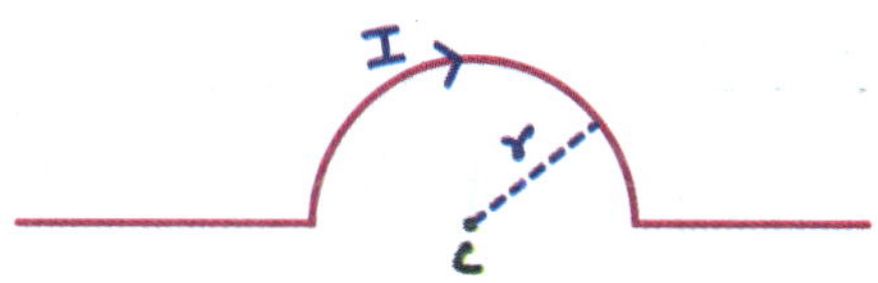

MF at the centre of an arc of circular conductor

$$B_C = \frac{\mu_0}{4\pi} \cdot \frac{I\theta}{r}$$

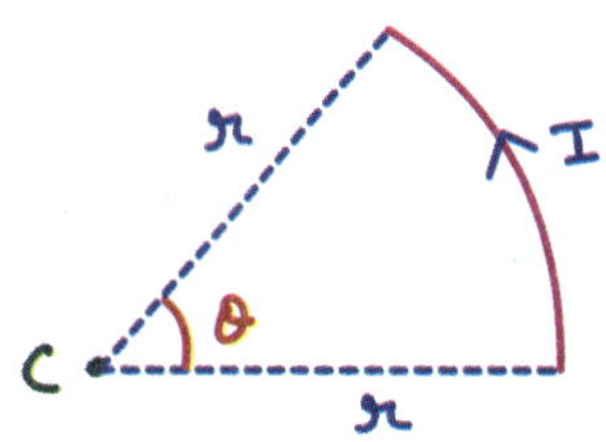

MF due to looping of wire

- r of loop is constant

$$B_n = nB_1$$

- Same wire rebound i.e. $L = 2\pi r$ = constant

$$B_n = n^2 B_1$$

MF at the centre of a circular loop in a circuit

- Loop ADBEA has a resistance r.
- Current entering through point A and leaves at point B.
- The net magnetic field at point C due to 2 segments AEB and ADB is

$$B_C = 0$$

- It doesn't depends upon the angle θ.

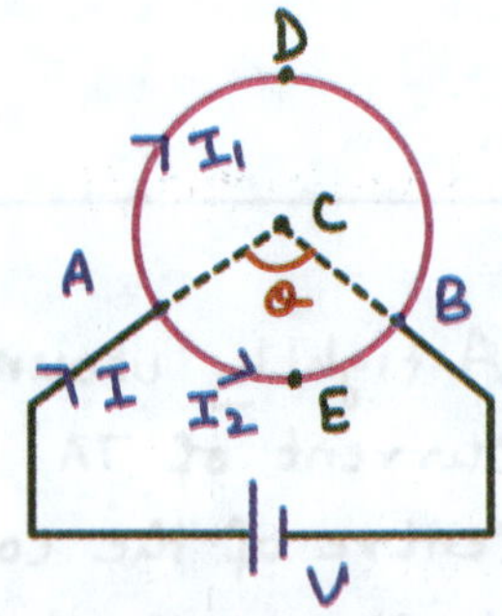

NEET Accelerate

- Magnetic field due to an electron rotating in a circular orbit of radius r making n rotations per second is

$$B_C = \frac{\mu_0 n e}{2r}$$

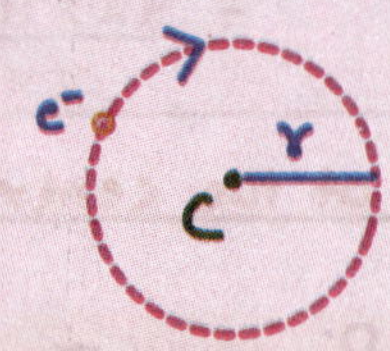

- Magnetic field at the centre of a uniformly charged ring rotating with frequency f is

$$B_C = \frac{\mu_0 q f}{2r}$$

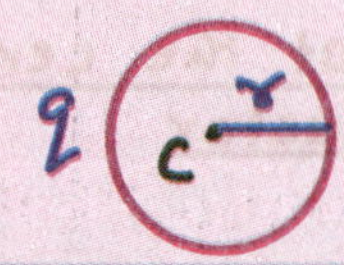

MF due to a straight wire

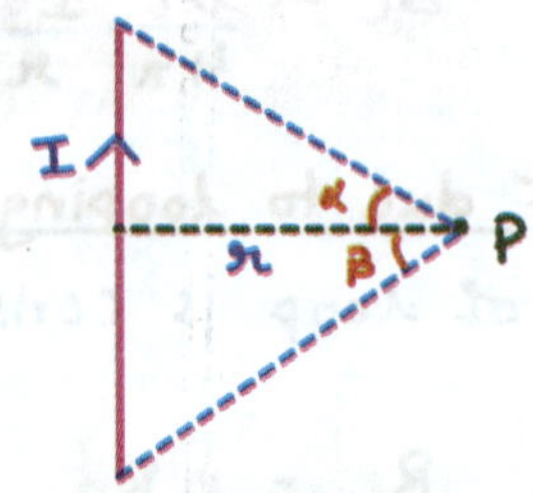

- $$B_P = \frac{\mu_0 I}{4\pi r}(\sin\alpha + \sin\beta)$$
- For semi-infinite wire

$$B_P = \frac{\mu_0 I}{4\pi r}$$

PYQ PUNCH

Q2. A very long conducting wire is bent in a semi-circular shape from A to B as shown in figure. The magnetic field at a point P for a steady current configuration is given by: (NEET 2023)

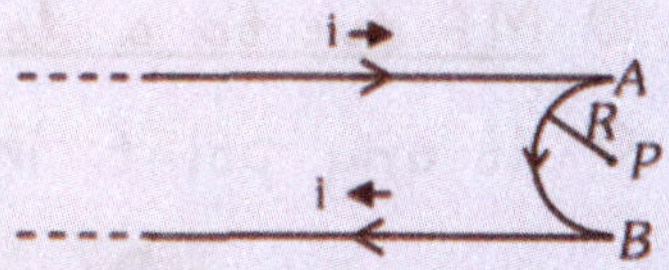

Sol. Wires 1 and 3 are semi-infinite wires.

$$\vec{B}_1 = \frac{\mu_0 I}{4\pi r}(-\hat{k})$$

$$\vec{B}_3 = \frac{\mu_0 I}{4\pi r}(-\hat{k})$$

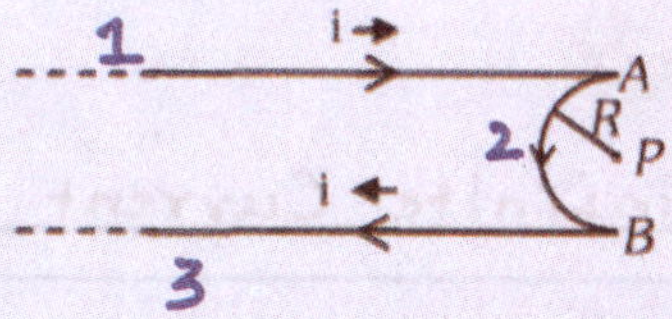

$$\vec{B}_2 = \frac{\mu_0 I}{4r}(\hat{k})$$

$$\vec{B}_{net} = \vec{B}_1 + \vec{B}_2 + \vec{B}_3$$

$$= \frac{\mu_0 I}{4r}\left(1 - \frac{2}{\pi}\right)(\hat{k})$$

MF at any point on the axis of circular loop

$$B_P = \frac{\mu_0 I r^2}{2(r^2+x^2)^{3/2}}$$

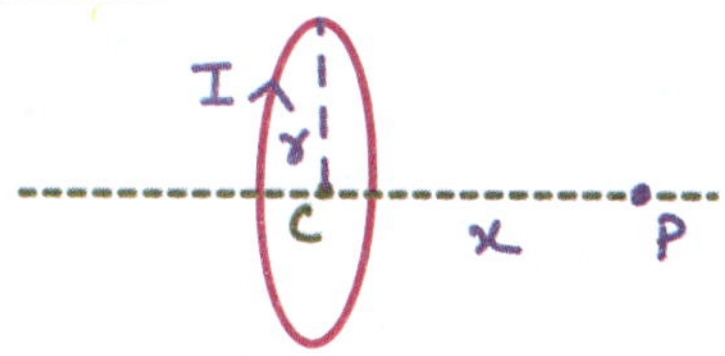

Ampere's Circuital Law

- The line integral of magnetic field B around any closed path in vacuum is equal to μ_0 times of the total current I threading through the closed loop.

$$\oint \vec{B}\cdot d\vec{l} = \mu_0 I$$

Applications of Ampere's Circuital Law

MF due to a infinite straight wire

$$B_P = \frac{\mu_0 I}{2\pi r}$$

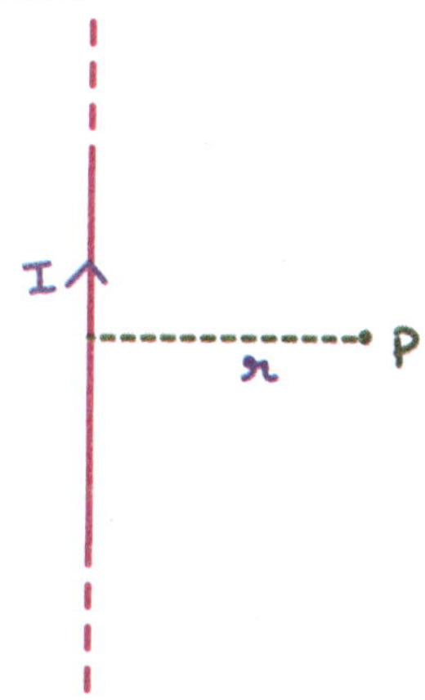

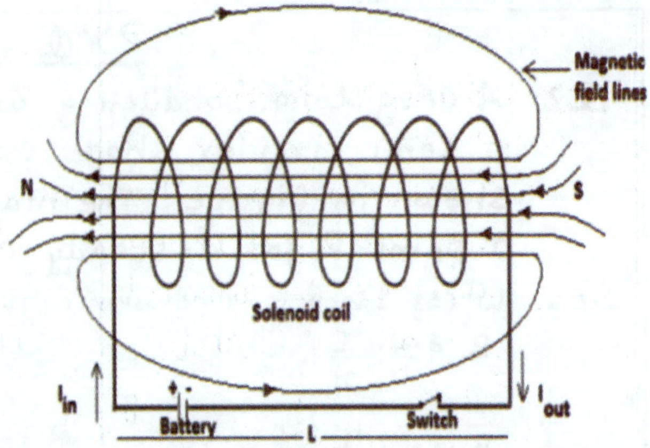

MF due to a long solenoid

- At any point inside the solenoid

$$B_i = \mu_0 n I$$

Where n is number of turns per unit length.

- At any point outside

$$B_o = 0$$

MF due to a infinite Current Carrying

	Solid Cylinder	Hollow Cylinder
Current	Uniformly Distributed	Only on Surface
Inside	$B_P = \frac{\mu_0 I a}{2\pi R^2}$	$B_P = 0$
Surface	$B_S = \frac{\mu_0 I}{2\pi R}$	$B_S = \frac{\mu_0 I}{2\pi R}$
Outside	$B_Q = \frac{\mu_0 I}{2\pi b}$	$B_Q = \frac{\mu_0 I}{2\pi b}$
Graph	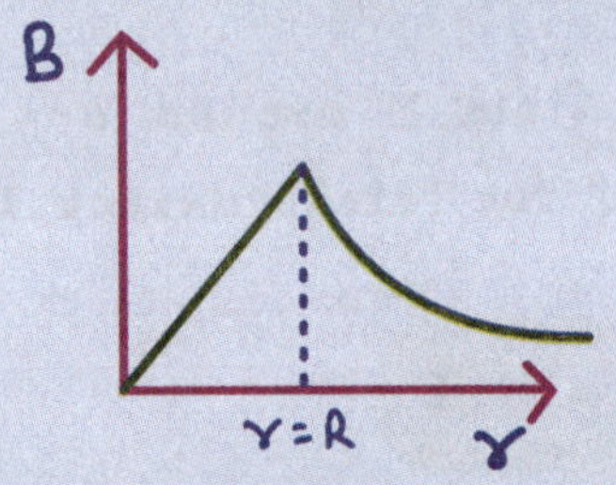	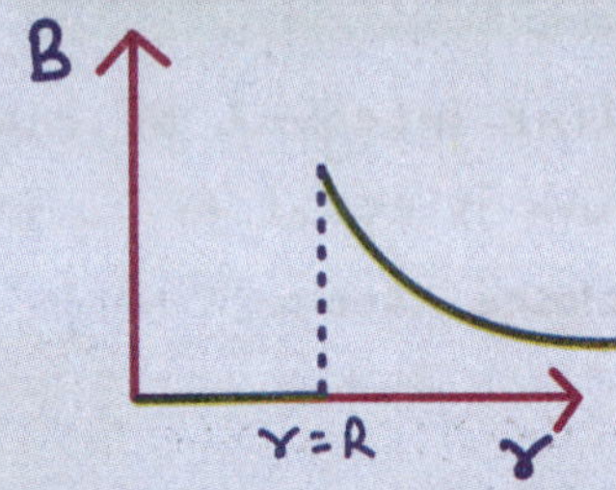
Diagram	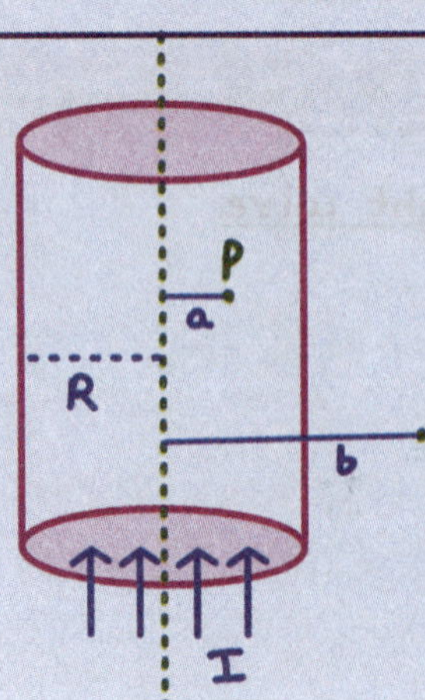	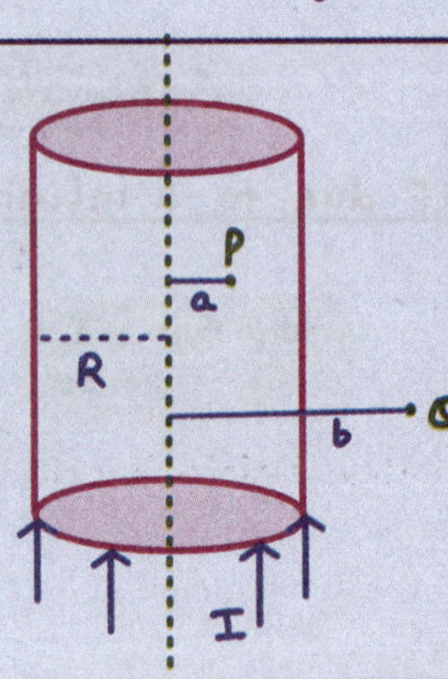

PYQ PUNCH

Q3. A long straight wire of radius a carries a steady current I. The current is uniformly distributed over its cross-section. The ratio of the magnetic fields B and B' at radial distances a/2 and 2a respectively, from the axis of the wire is (NEET 2016)

Sol. $R = a$; $a = a/2$; $b = 2a$

$B_P = \frac{\mu_0 I a}{2\pi R^2}$; $B_Q = \frac{\mu_0 I}{2\pi b}$

$B = \frac{\mu_0 I}{2\pi a^2} \times \frac{a}{2}$; $B' = \frac{\mu_0 I}{2\pi \times 2a}$

$\Rightarrow \frac{B}{B'} = 1$

Magnetic Force

- It acts only on moving charge
- $\vec{F} = q(\vec{V} \times \vec{B}) = qVB\sin\theta \, \hat{n}$
- θ is the angle between V and B.
- Work Done by magnetic force on a charge particle is always 0.

Motion of a Charged Particle in Uniform MF

- **θ is 0° or 180°**
- Force is 0.
- Motion is a straight line.

- **θ is 90°**
- Motion is circular.
- Magnetic Force acts as a centripetal force.
- Time Period $T = \frac{2\pi m}{qB}$
- Time Period is independent of speed.
- Radius of Circle $r = \frac{mv}{qB} = \frac{p}{qB}$
- For same momentum $r \propto \frac{1}{q}$

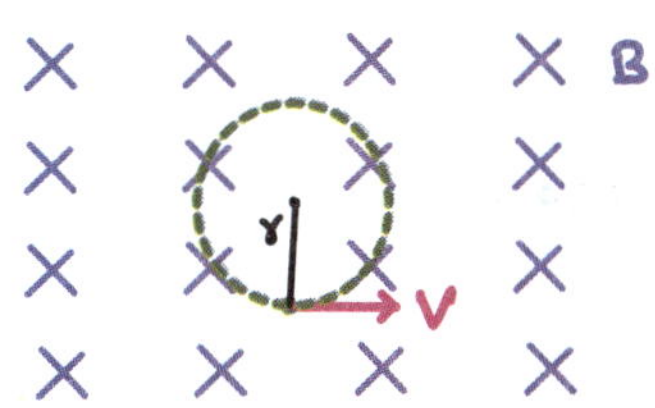

- Cyclotron frequency $f = \frac{qB}{2\pi m}$
- Kinetic Energy $KE = \frac{q^2B^2r^2}{2m}$
- KE is constant as Work Done by force is zero.

PYQ PUNCH

Q4. Ionised hydrogen atoms and α-particles with same momenta enters perpendicular to a constant magnetic field, B. The ratio of their radii of their paths $r_H : r_\alpha$ will be (NEET 2019)

Sol. $q_H = e$; $q_\alpha = 2e$

For same momentum

$r \propto \frac{1}{q}$

$$\Rightarrow \frac{r_H}{r_\alpha} = \frac{q_\alpha}{q_H} = 2$$

- $\theta \neq 90°$
- Path is helical.
- Time Period $T = \frac{2\pi m}{qB}$
- Radius of Circle $r = \frac{mv\sin\theta}{qB}$
- Pitch $P = \frac{2\pi m v\cos\theta}{qB}$

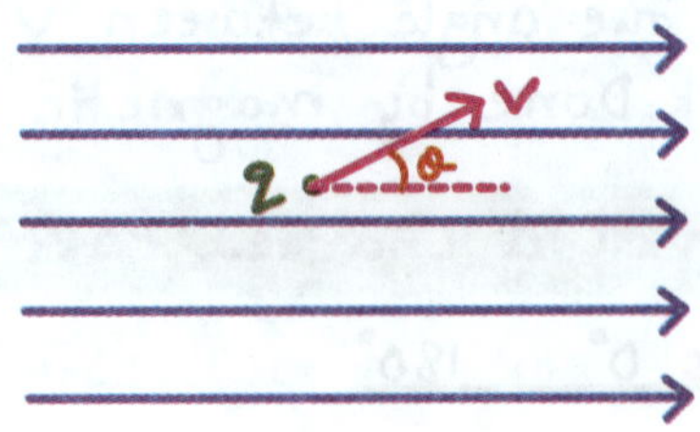

Lorentz Force

- For a charge moving in magnetic field and the electric field, it experiences a net force called as Lorentz Force.
- $\vec{F_L} = q\vec{E} + q(\vec{V} \times \vec{B})$
- For no deflection of charge

  Case I

  ▷ E and B are mutually perpendicular and perpendicular to the direction of velocity.

  ▷ $V = E/B$

Case II

- Both E and B along the direction of velocity.
- Speed increases or decreases.

Magnetic Force on Current Carrying Conductor

- Current carrying conductor of length l is placed in magnetic field B at an angle θ experiences

$$\vec{F} = I(\vec{l} \times \vec{B})$$

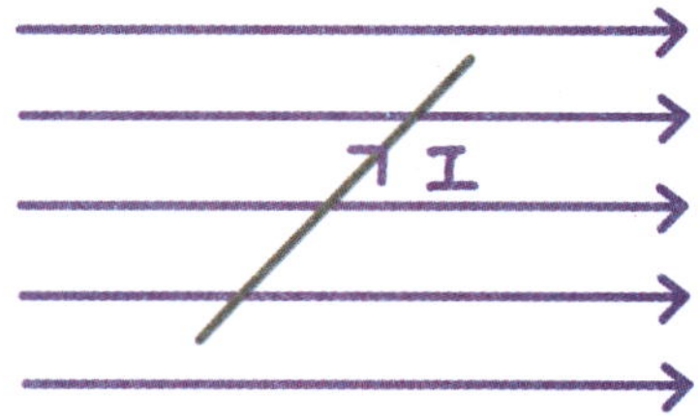

where $\vec{l}$ is along the direction of current

PYQ PUNCH

Q5. A wire carrying a current I along the positive X-axis has length L. It is kept in a magnetic field $\vec{B} = (2\hat{i} + 3\hat{j} - 4\hat{k})$ T. The magnitude of magnetic force acting on the wire is (NEET 2023)

Sol. $\vec{L} = L\hat{i}$; $\vec{B} = 2\hat{i} + 3\hat{j} - 4\hat{k}$

$$\vec{F} = I(\vec{l} \times \vec{B})$$
$$= IL(3\hat{k} + 4\hat{j})$$
$$|\vec{F}| = 5IL$$

- For random shape wire, take l_{eff}

$$\vec{F} = I(\vec{l}_{eff} \times \vec{B})$$

- l_{eff} is the shortest distance between the ends
- Force on closed loop is zero as l_{eff} is zero.

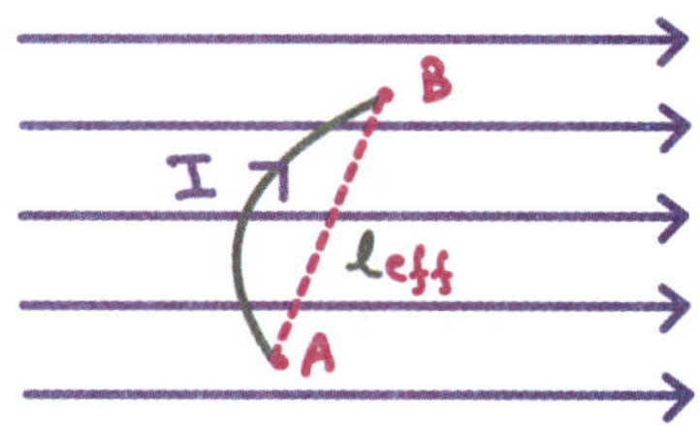

Applications

- **To determine the force on a segment**

- $\vec{F}_1 + \vec{F}_2 + \vec{F}_3 + \vec{F}_4 + \vec{F}_5 = 0$

- If F_1 is unknown then

$$\vec{F}_1 = -(\vec{F}_2 + \vec{F}_3 + \vec{F}_4 + \vec{F}_5)$$

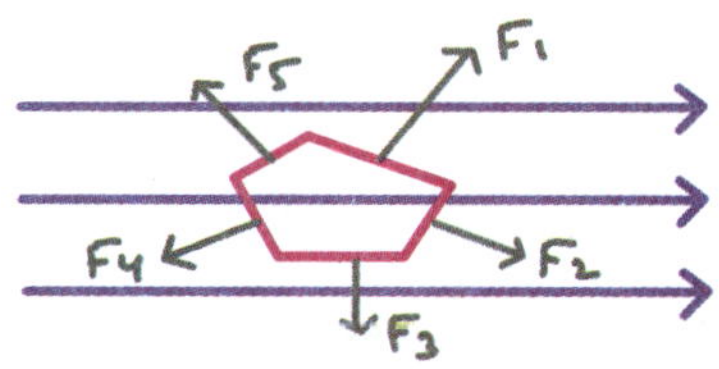

MCQ PUNCH

Q6. A circular coil ABCD carrying a current i is placed in a uniform magnetic field. If the magnetic force on the segment AB is $\vec{F}$, the force on the remaining segment BCDA is

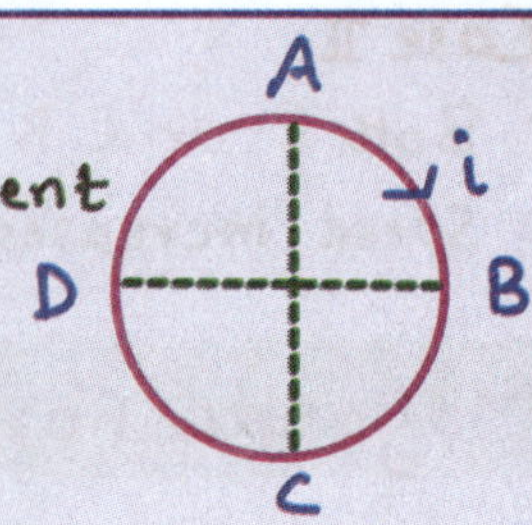

Sol. Force on the closed loop is zero

$$\vec{F_1} + \vec{F_2} = 0$$

$$\Rightarrow \vec{F_2} = -\vec{F_1} = -\vec{F}$$

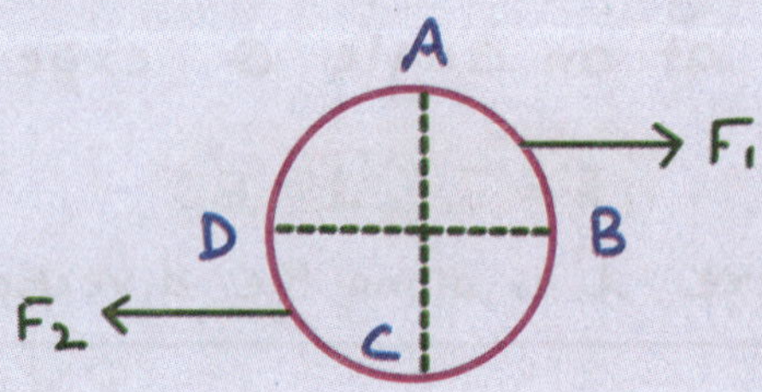

Q7. A current carrying closed loop in the form of a right angled isosceles Δ ABC is placed in a uniform magnetic field acting along AB. If the magnetic force on the arm BC is F, the force on the arm AC is

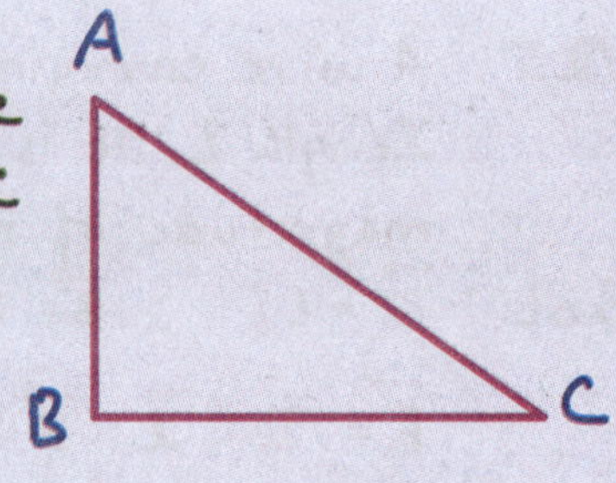

Sol. Since magnetic field is along AB, hence, force on this segment is 0.
Now

$$\vec{F_1} + \vec{F_2} + \vec{F_3} = 0$$

$$\Rightarrow \vec{F_2} = -\vec{F_1} = -\vec{F}$$

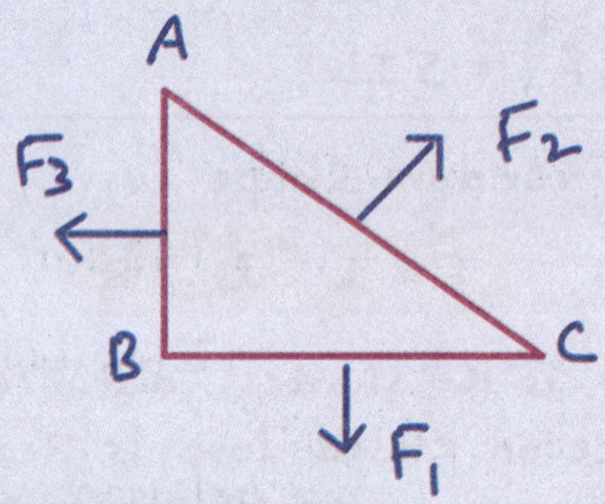

M. Force Between 2 Infinite Parallel Wires

- **Current in Same Direction**
  - $\frac{F_{12}}{l} = \frac{F_{21}}{l} = \frac{\mu_0 i_1 i_2}{2\pi d}$
  - They attract each other.
- **Current in Opposite Direction**
  - Force remains the same.
  - They repel each other.

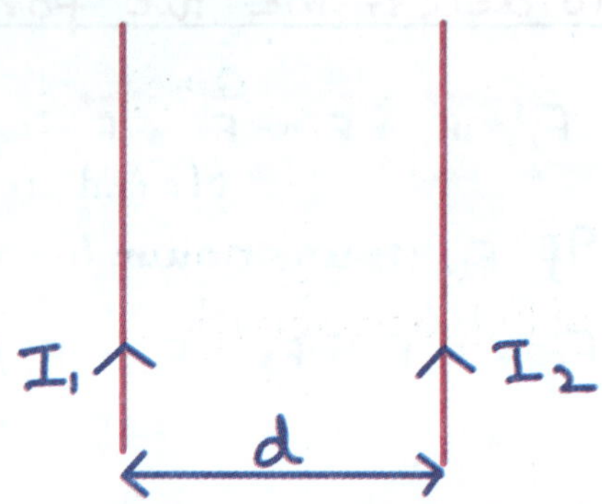

Application

- **M. Force on a square loop**
- Force on loop ABCD

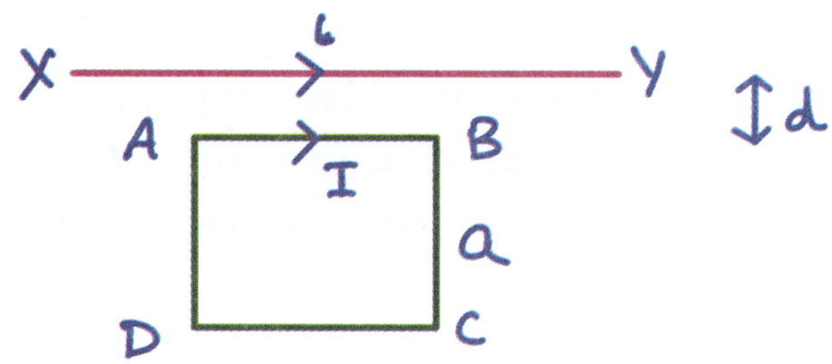

$$F = \frac{\mu_0 i I a^2}{2\pi d(a+d)}$$

- If $d \ll a$

$$F = \frac{\mu_0 i I a}{2\pi d}$$

- If current in AB is in same direction as XY, then square gets attracted.
- If current in AB is in opposite direction as XY, then square gets repelled.

Torque on Current Carrying Loop

- Coil ABCD is placed in uniform magnetic field.
- It has n turns carrying current I and has area A.
- Torque experienced by it

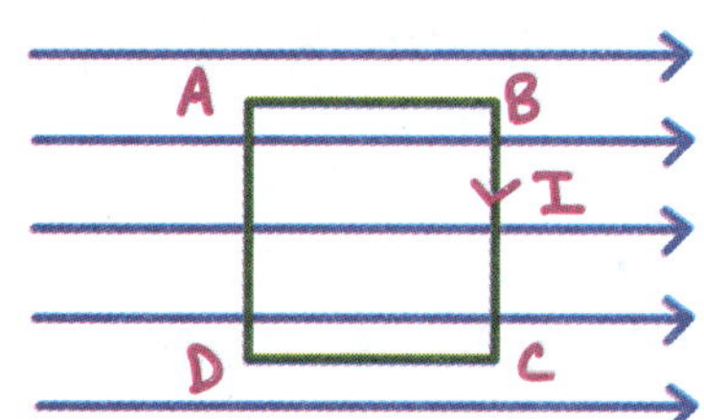

$$\vec{\tau} = \vec{M} \times \vec{B} = MB\sin\theta\,\hat{n}$$

where $M = nIA$ is called as magnetic dipole moment of coil.
M unit is Am^2.
θ is the angle between area vector and magnetic field.

- If α is the angle between the plane of the coil and magnetic field, then

$$\theta = 90° - \alpha$$

- If a loop is placed in non-uniform magnetic field, it will do both
  - Rotational Motion
  - Translatory Motion

MCQ PUNCH

Q8. A rectangular coil of length 0.12m and width 0.1m having 50 turns of wire is suspended vertically in a uniform magnetic field of strength 0.2 Wb/m^2. The coil carries a current of 2 A. If the plane of the coil is inclined at an angle of 30° with the direction of the field, the torque required to keep the coil in stable equilibrium will be:

Sol. $\alpha = 30°$

$\Rightarrow \quad \theta = 90° - 30° = 60°$

Now

$$\tau = MB\sin\theta = nIAB\sin 60°$$

$$= 50 \times 2 \times 0.12 \times 0.1 \times 0.2 \times \frac{\sqrt{3}}{2} = 0.2 \text{ Nm}$$

Equilibrium of Loop

- For $\theta = 0°$, $\tau = 0$ and stable equilibrium.
- For $\theta = 180°$, $\tau = 0$ and unstable equilibrium.
- For $\theta = 90°$ or $270°$, torque is maximum.

Work Done in Rotating a Loop

- Work Done is rotating the loop from θ_1 to θ_2

$$W = MB(\cos\theta_1 - \cos\theta_2)$$

Potential Energy of Loop

- Change of Potential Energy

$$\Delta PE = MB(\cos\theta_1 - \cos\theta_2)$$

- Potential Energy

$\theta_1 = 90°$ and $\theta_2 = \theta$

$$PE = -MB\cos\theta$$

- Potential Energy reduces in self process.

Circular Current Loop as a Magnetic Dipole

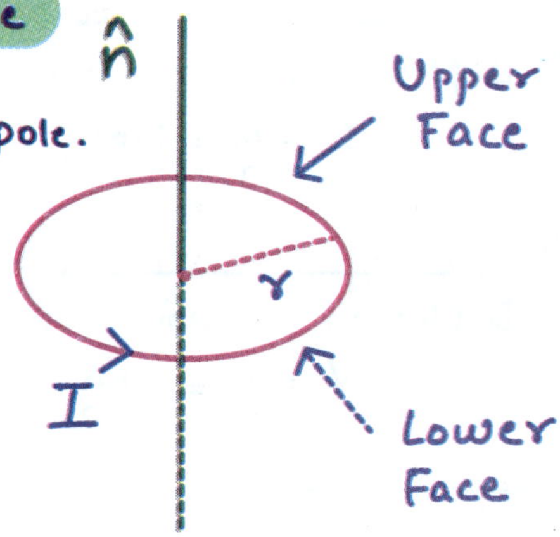

- Circular loop behaves as a magnetic dipole.
- $M = nIA$ where, n is no. of turns
- If we look at the upper face, current is anti-clockwise, so it has North Polarity.
- If we look at the lower face, current is clockwise, so it has South Polarity.
- Magnetic Field at the axial point

$$B_P = \frac{\mu_0 n I r^2}{2(r^2+x^2)^{3/2}}$$

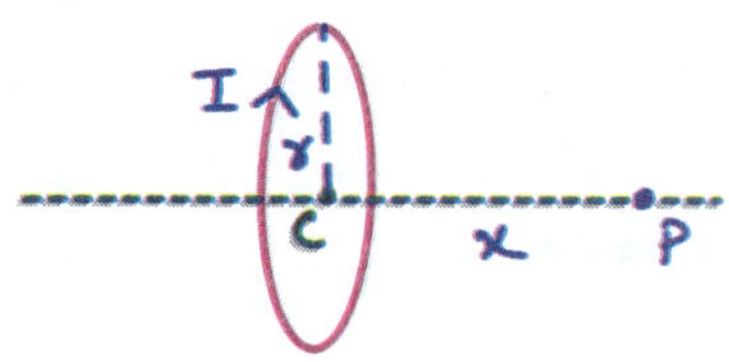

- If $x >> r$

$$B_P = \frac{\mu_0 n I r^2}{2x^3} = \frac{\mu_0 M}{2\pi x^3}$$

Moving Coil Galvanometer

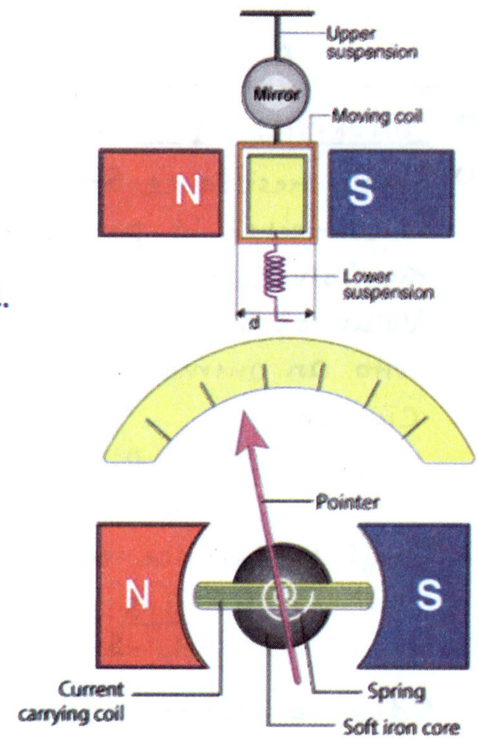

- **Working Principle**
- Current carrying loop experiences torque when placed in a uniform magnetic field.
- Magnetic Fields are radial to the coil.
- Deflection $\theta = GI$

  where $G = \frac{NBA}{k}$ is the Galvanometer Constant.

  k is the torsional spring constant.
- More the current, more the deflection.

$$\theta \propto I$$

Current Sensitivity

- Deflection per unit current.

$$I_s = \frac{\theta}{I} = \frac{NBA}{k}$$

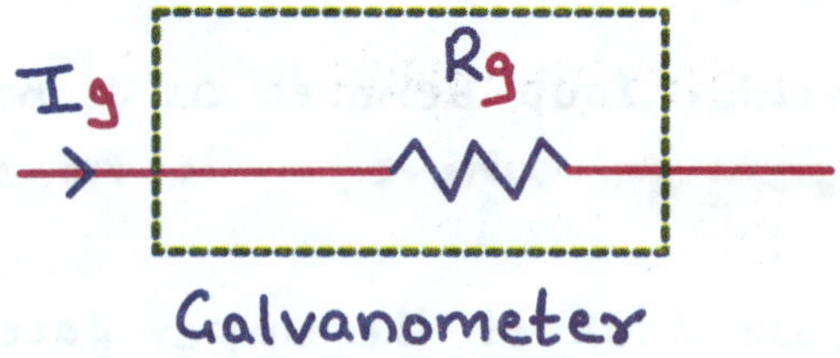

Voltage Sensitivity

- Deflection per unit voltage.

$$V_s = \frac{\theta}{V} = \frac{NBA}{kR}$$

PYQ PUNCH

Q9. Current sensitivity of a moving coil galavanometer is 5 div/mA and its voltage sensitivity (angular deflection per unit voltage applied) is 20 div/V. The resistance of the galvanometer is (NEET 2018)

Sol. $I_s = \frac{NBA}{k} = 5 \text{ div/mA} = 5 \times 10^3 \text{ div/A}$ --- (1)

$V_s = \frac{NBA}{kR} = 20 \text{ div/V}$ ---- (2)

Divide equation 1 by 2

$R = 250\,\Omega$

Conversion of Galvanometer into Ammeter.

- Small resistance Shunt (S) is connected in parallel to the Galvanometer.
- Value of S for converting into an ammeter of maximum current I

$$S = \frac{I_g R_g}{I - I_g}$$

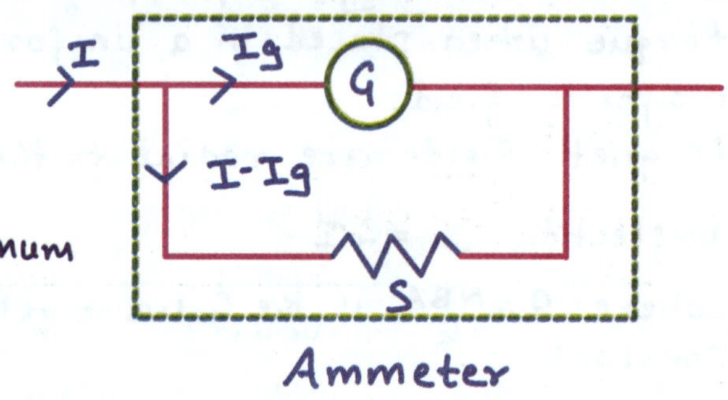

- Total resistance of Ammeter

$$R = \frac{R_g S}{R_g + S}$$

- Ideal ammeter has $R = 0$
- Ammeter is connected in series to the circuit.

Conversion of Galvanometer into Voltmeter.

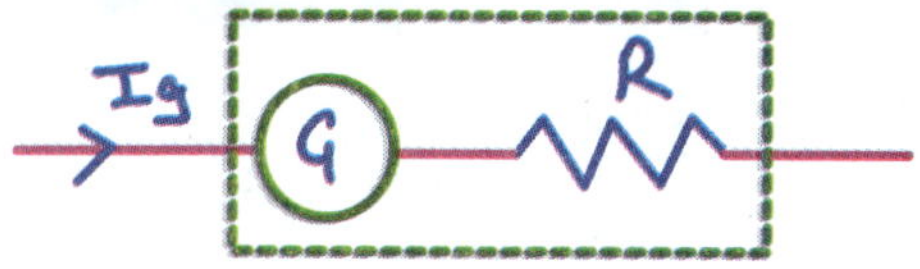

Voltmeter

- Large resistance (R) is connected in series to the Galvanometer.
- Value of R for converting into an Voltmeter of maximum voltage V

$$R = \frac{V}{I_g} - R_g$$

- Total resistance of Voltmeter
  $R' = R_g + R$
- Ideal voltmeter has $R \to \infty$
- Voltmeter is connected in parallel to the circuit.

NEET cases of Ammeter and Voltmeter

Resistance in series of Ammeter for no change of current

- Conversion of Galvanometer into Ammeter reduces its resistance, which in turn increases the current in the circuit.
- To keep the main current in the circuit unchanged, the resistance to be put in series with the ammeter is

$$S' = \frac{R_g^2}{(S+R_g)}$$

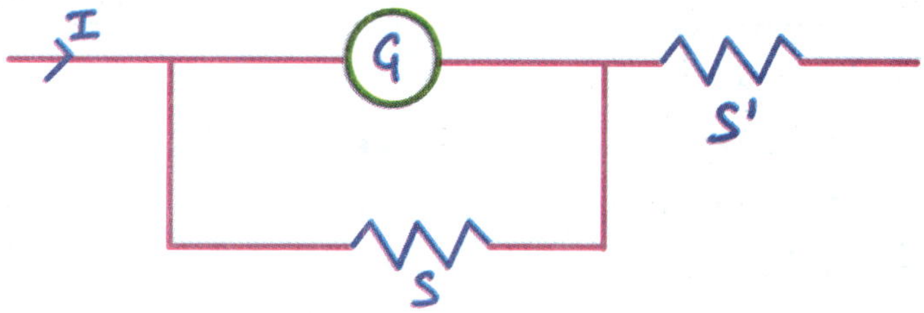

Conversion of Voltmeter into Ammeter

- Resistance of Voltmeter $R' = R_g + R$
- R' becomes equivalent resistance of new Galvanometer.
- $I_g = V/R'$
- Shunt Resistance $S = \frac{I_g R'}{I - I_g}$
- If $I_g << I$, then Shunt Resistance $S = \frac{I_g R'}{I}$

24. Magnetism and matter

Magnet

- A magnet is a material or an object that produces a magnetic field.

Properties of Magnet

- A freely suspended bar magnet points in the North-South direction.
- The tip which points to the geographic north is called the north pole of the magnet.
- The tip which points to the geographic South is called the South pole of the magnet.
- We can't isolate north or south pole of a magnet. In short magnetic mono-pole doesn't exist.
- Magnets are made up of iron, nickel and their alloys.

Pole strength (m)

- Magnet strong hai ya weak usko judge karne ke kaam aati hai.
- It is replica of charge.
- It is a scalar quantity.
- Unit is Ampere-metre (A-m).

Force between two poles

- $F = \frac{\mu_0 m_1 m_2}{4\pi r^2}$

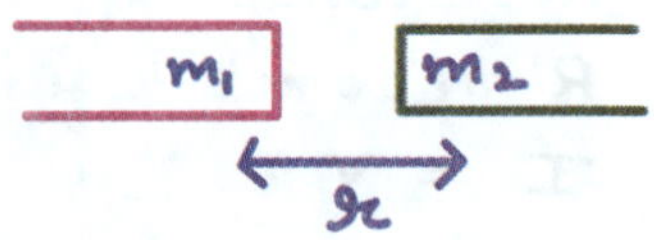

- Repulsion in case of same type of poles.
- Attraction in case of opposite type of poles.
- In case of charge

$$F = \frac{K q_1 q_2}{r^2}$$

$\Rightarrow$ $K \rightarrow \frac{\mu_0}{4\pi}$

Magnetic Field

- It is a region around a magnetic pole in which other magnetic pole could experience force due to it.

Magnetic Field Strength (B)

- It is the force experienced by a unit north pole placed at a distance r under the field of another pole m.
- $\vec{B} = \frac{\mu_0 m}{4\pi r^2}$
- Unit is Tesla ($NA^{-1}m^{-1}$)
- Force experienced by a magnetic pole placed in an external magnetic field $\vec{B}$ is

$$\vec{F} = m\vec{B}$$

Magnetic Dipole

- An arrangement of two equal and opposite magnetic poles separated by a small distance. e.g. A bar magnet.

Magnetic Dipole Moment (M)

- It measures the strength of magnets.
- M of a bar magnet

$$\vec{M} = m \times 2\vec{l}$$

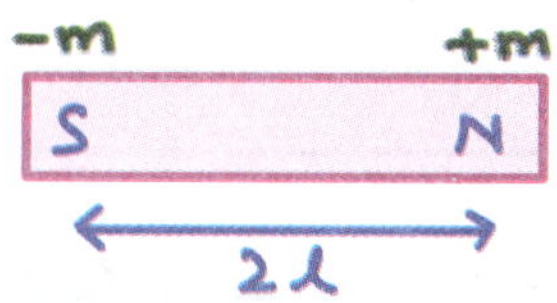

- A vector quantity
- Direction is from South pole to north pole.
- Unit is $A\text{-}m^2$.

Equivalent Magnet Dipole Moment of a Bar Magnet

- Cutting along longitudinal axis
- Pole strength becomes half.
- $m' = m/2$
- $M' = M/2$

◉ **Cutting perpendicular to longitudinal axis**

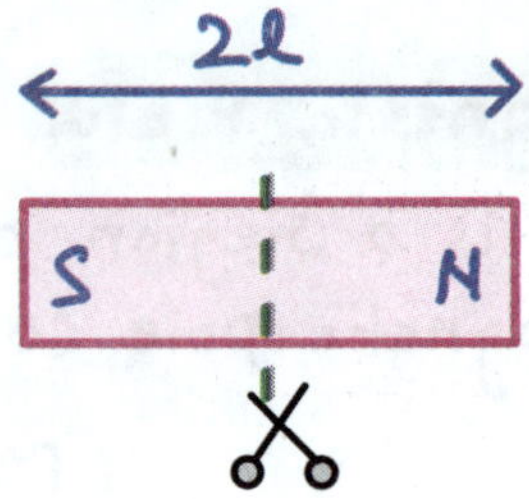

- Pole strength remains same.
- $l' = 2l/2$
- $M' = M/2$

◉ **Bending in the form of arc**

- L becomes L_{eff}
- $L_{eff} = 2r\sin\theta/2$
- $M' = \dfrac{M\sin\theta/2}{\theta/2}$

PYQ PUNCH

Q1. A bar magnet of length l and magnetic dipole moment M is bent in the form of an arc as shown in the figure. The new magnetic moment will be:

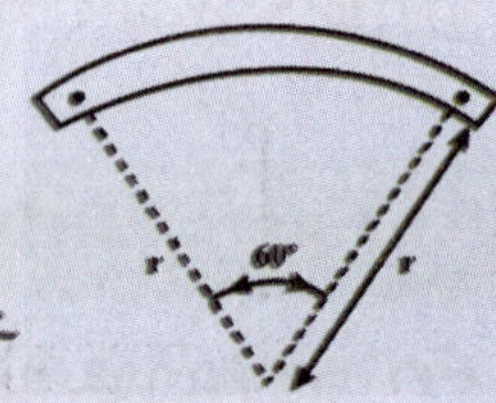

(NEET 2013)

Sol. $\theta = 60^\circ = \pi/3$

$$M' = \frac{M\sin\theta/2}{\theta/2}$$

$$= \frac{M \times \sin\pi/6}{\pi/6} = \frac{3M}{\pi}$$

◉ **Bending in the form of sides**

- $L_{eff} = 2l\sin\theta/2$
- $M' = M\sin\theta/2$

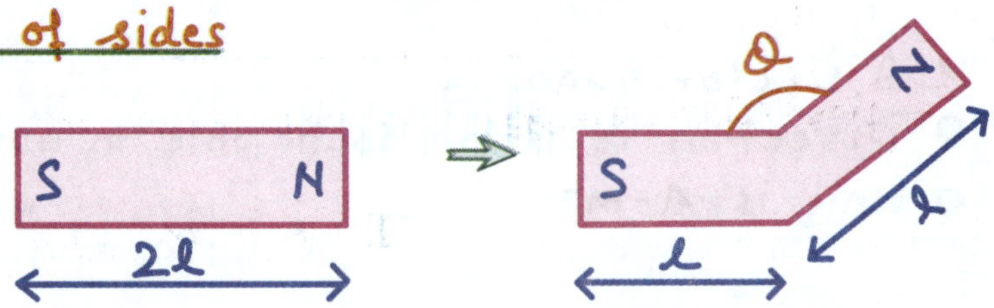

◉ **2 Magnets**

$M' = 2M$

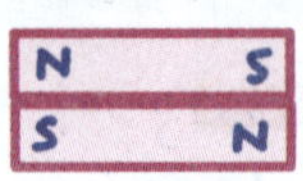

$M' = 0$

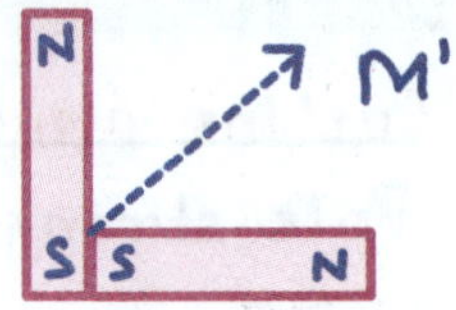

$M' = \sqrt{2}M$

- 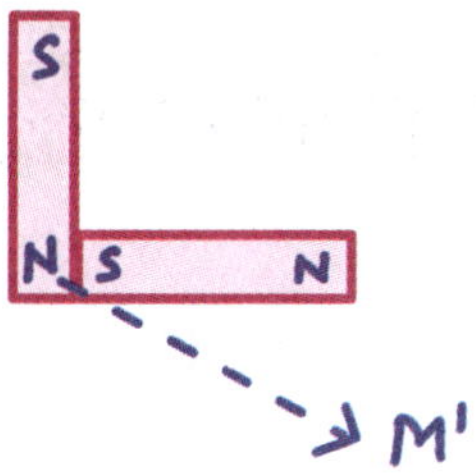

$M' = \sqrt{2}M$

- 

  - $M' = 2M\cos\theta/2$
  - More the angle, lesser the magnetic dipole moment.

MCQ PUNCH

Q2. Following figures show the arrangement of bar magnets in different configurations. Each magnet has magnetic dipole moment M. Which configuration has highest net magnetic dipole moment?

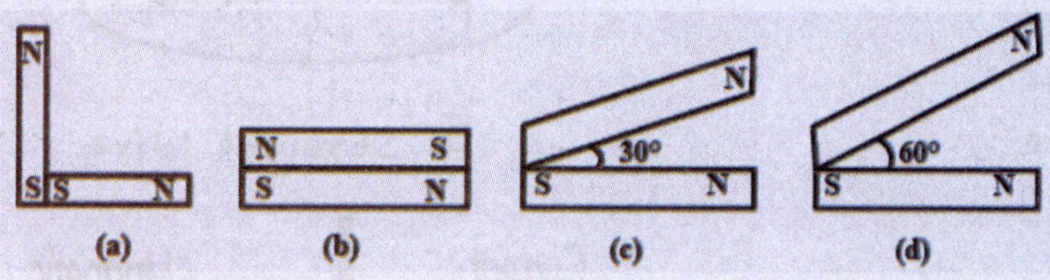

Sol.
a. $\theta = 90°$
b. $\theta = 180°$
c. $\theta = 30°$
d. $\theta = 60°$

Lesser the angle, more the magnetic dipole moment.
So, option c.

Relationship between a magnet and a current carrying loop

$$I \times \vec{A} = m \times 2\vec{l}$$

Magnetic Field Lines (MFL)

- These are imaginary lines tangent to which gives the direction of net magnet field at that point.

Properties

- They form continuous closed loops.
- Non-conservative field.

- Don't intersect each other.
- Outside the magnet, they runs from North to South Pole.
- Inside the magnet, they appear to run from South to North Pole.
- Larger the density of the lines, Stronger will be the magnetic field.

MFL of few Magnets

- Bar Magnet

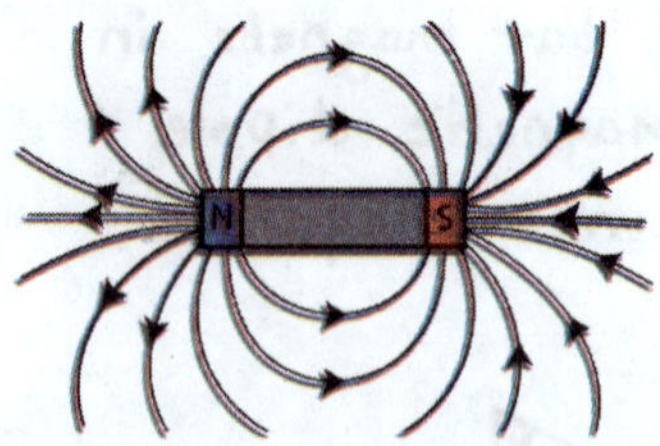

- Solenoid

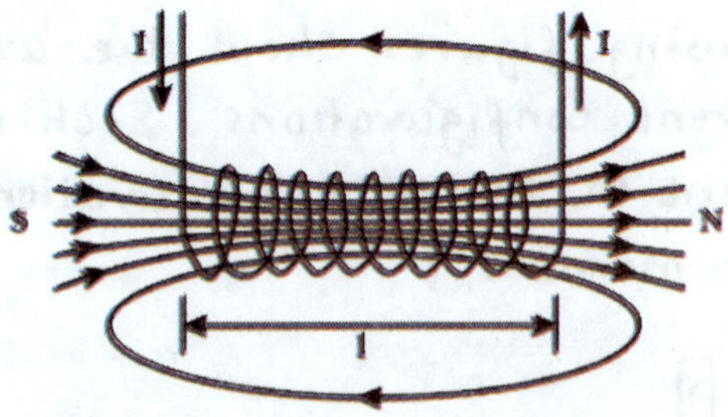

- Circular Wire

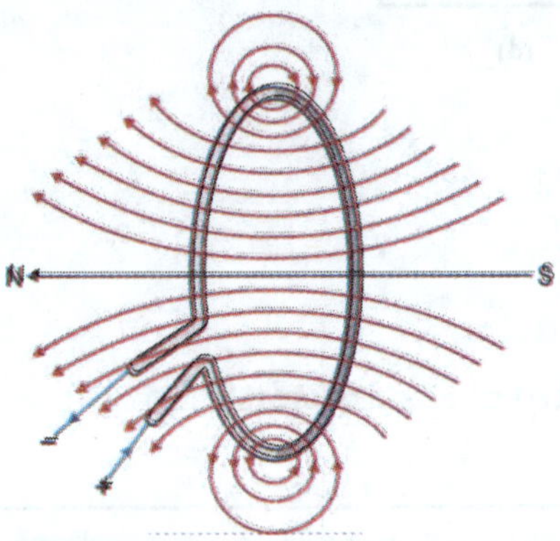

- Straight Wire

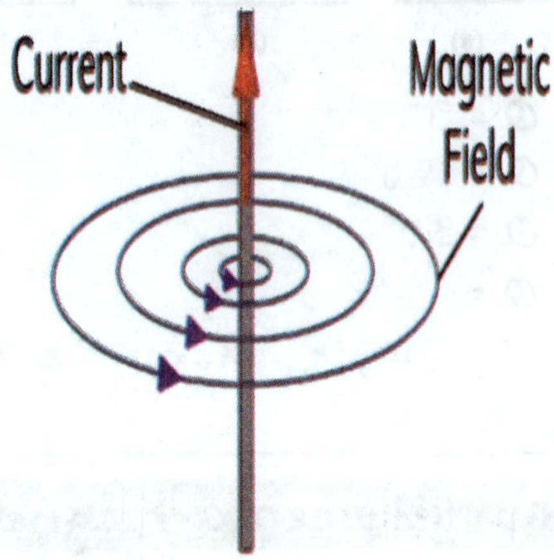

NEET Accelerate

- Magnetic moment of a charged particle moving in a circle of radius R with uniform speed v is

$$m = \frac{qvR}{2}$$

- Magnet moment of an equilateral triangle of side a carrying current I & have n turns is

$$m = nIa^2 \frac{\sqrt{3}}{4}$$

Magnetic Field Strength at a point due to bar magnet

On axial line (end-on-position)

- $\vec{B}_P = \frac{\mu_0}{4\pi} \cdot \frac{2\vec{M}r}{(r^2-l^2)^2}$

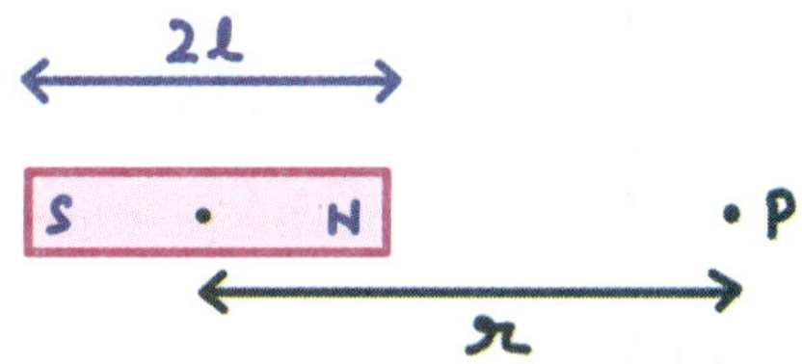

- For a short bar magnet

  $r >> l$

  $\vec{B}_P = \frac{\mu_0}{4\pi} \cdot \frac{2\vec{M}}{r^3}$

On equitorial line (broadside-on-position)

- $\vec{B}_P = -\frac{\mu_0}{4\pi} \cdot \frac{\vec{M}}{(r^2+l^2)^{3/2}}$

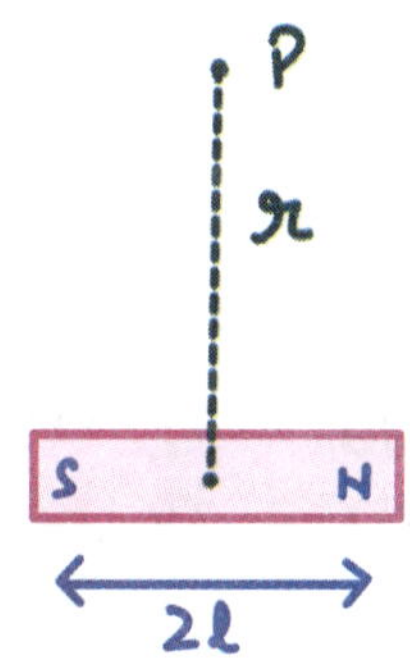

- For a short bar magnet

  $r >> l$

  $\vec{B}_P = -\frac{\mu_0}{4\pi} \cdot \frac{\vec{M}}{r^3}$

Force and Torque on Bar Magnet

- Bar magnet experiences zero force.

- Torque experienced by it

  $\vec{\tau} = \vec{M} \times \vec{B} = MB\sin\theta \, \hat{n}$

where θ is the angle between M and B.

- For $\theta = 0°$, $\tau = 0$ and stable equilibrium.
- For $\theta = 180°$, $\tau = 0$ and unstable equilibrium.
- For $\theta = 90°$ or $270°$, torque is maximum.
- If a bar is placed in non-uniform magnetic field, it will do both
  - Rotational Motion
  - Translatory Motion

Work Done in Rotating a bar magnet

- Work Done in rotating the bar magnet from θ_1 to θ_2

$$W = MB(\cos\theta_1 - \cos\theta_2)$$

Potential Energy of bar magnet

- Change of Potential Energy

$$\Delta PE = MB(\cos\theta_1 - \cos\theta_2)$$

- Potential Energy

  $\theta_1 = 90°$ and $\theta_2 = \theta$

$$PE = -MB\cos\theta$$

- Potential Energy reduces in self process.

PYQ PUNCH

Q3. A bar magnet is hung by a thin cotton thread in a uniform horizontal magnetic field and is in equilibrium state. The energy required to rotate it by 60° is W. Now the torque required to keep the magnet in this new position is: (NEET 2016)

Sol. $\theta_1 = 0°$; $\theta_2 = 60°$

$\Delta PE = MB(\cos\theta_1 - \cos\theta_2)$

$W = \frac{MB}{2}$

$\tau = MB\sin\theta$

Here θ is θ_2

$\tau = 2W\sin 60° = \sqrt{3}W$

Oscillation of Freely Suspended Magnet

- Bar magnet performs SHM.
- Time Period

$$T = 2\pi\sqrt{\frac{I}{MB}}$$

where I is the moment of inertia of the magnet
B is external magnetic field.
M is magnetic dipole moment.

Force between two Short Magnetic Dipoles

- $F = \frac{\mu_0}{4\pi} \cdot \frac{6\vec{M_1}\vec{M_2}}{r^4}$

  where M_1 and M_2 are magnetic dipole moments of two different magnets.
- $F \propto \frac{1}{r^4}$

Bar Magnet as an Equivalent Solenoid

- Magnetic Field due to both bar magnet and solenoid at axial point is same.
- Further both have same Magnetic Field Lines representation.
- Hence, bar magnet is equivalent to that of bar magnet.

The Electrostatic Analogy

Electrostatics	Magnetism
$1/\varepsilon_0$	μ_0
Charge q	Pole strength m
Electric Dipole Moment $\vec{p} = q2\vec{a}$	Magnetic Dipole Moment $\vec{M} = m2\vec{a}$
$\frac{q_1 q_2}{4\pi\varepsilon_0 r^2}$	$\frac{\mu_0 m_1 m_2}{4\pi r^2}$
$\vec{F} = q\vec{E}$	$\vec{F} = m\vec{B}$

Gauss's Law in Magnetism

- The net magnetic flux through any closed surface is always zero.
- This is because magnet mono-poles doesn't exist.
- $\phi_B = \oint \vec{B} \cdot d\vec{s} = 0$

Magnetic Susceptibity (χ)

- It is the measure of how easily a material gets magnitized.
- It has no unit.
- It is a scalar quantity.

Relative Permeability

- $\mu_r = \frac{\mu_m}{\mu_0}$
- $\mu_r = 1 + \chi$
- $\mu_m = \mu_0(1+\chi)$

PYQ PUNCH

Q4. An iron rod of susceptibility 599 is subjected to a magnetising field of 1200 Am^{-1}. The permeability of the material of the rod is : (Take $\mu_0 = 4\pi \times 10^{-7}\ TmA^{-1}$) (NEET 2020)

Sol. $\chi = 599$

$\mu_m = \mu_0(1+\chi)$

$= 4\pi \times 10^{-7}(1+599)$

$= 2.4\pi \times 10^{-4}\ TmA^{-1}$

Classification of Magnetic Substance

- On the basis of mutual interactions or their behaviours, the magnetic materials placed in a uniform magnetic field are classified into three parts.

Paramagnetic Materials

- $M_{atom} \neq 0$
- $M_{material} = 0$ in absence of external M.F.
- $M_{material} \neq 0$ in presence of external M.F.
- According to Curie Law

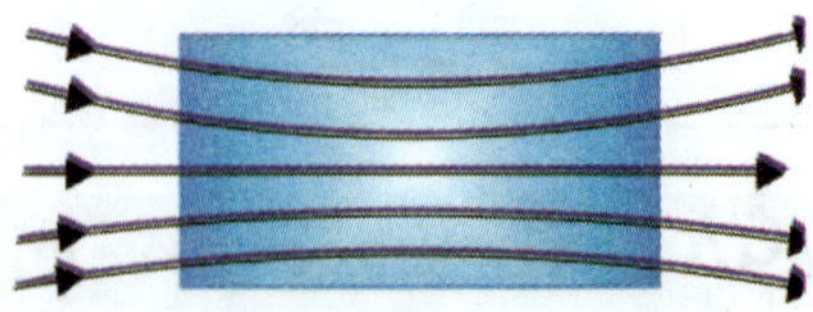

$\chi \propto \frac{1}{T}$

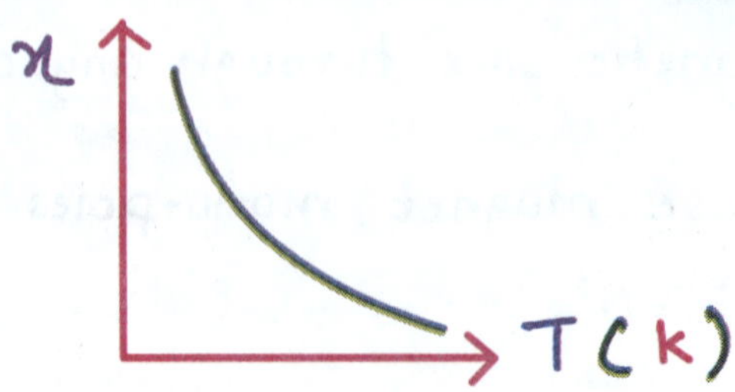

Diamagnetic Materials

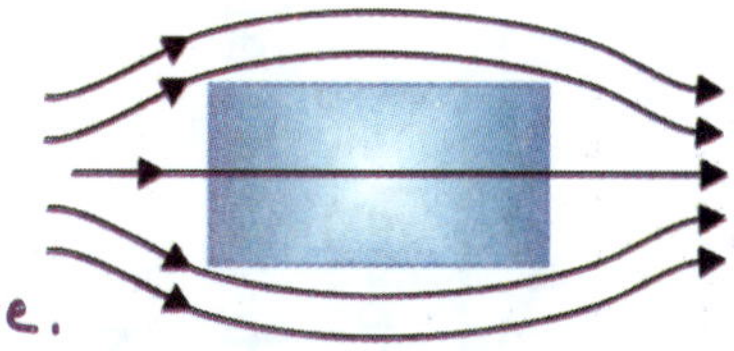

- $M_{atom} = 0$
- $M_{material} = 0$ in absence of external M.F.
- $M_{material} \neq 0$ in presence of external M.F.
- Susceptibility is independent of temperature.
- Every material exhibits Dia-magnetism behaviour.

Ferro-magnetic Material

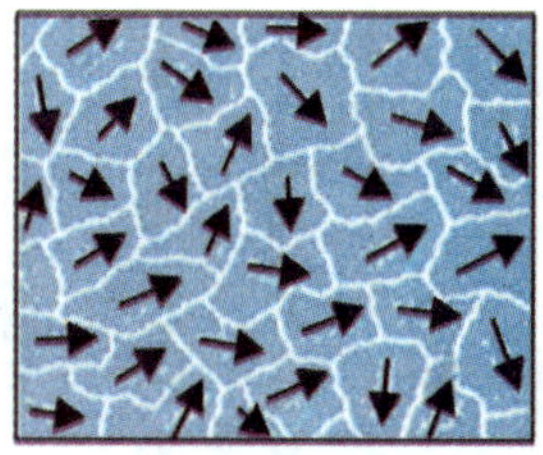

(a)

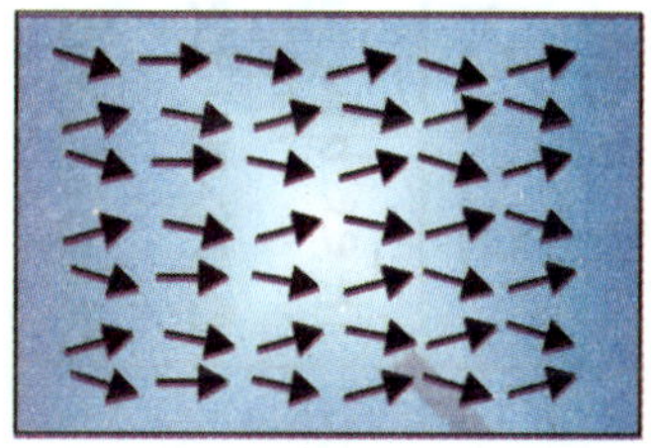

- $M_{domain} \neq 0$
- $M_{material} = 0$ in absence of external M.F.
- $M_{material} \neq 0$ in presence of external M.F.
- Domains are macroscopic volume having magnetic moment in a particular direction.
- Curie Temperature is the temperature above which ferro converts into para.
- Curie Weiss Law

$$\chi \propto \frac{1}{T - T_c}$$

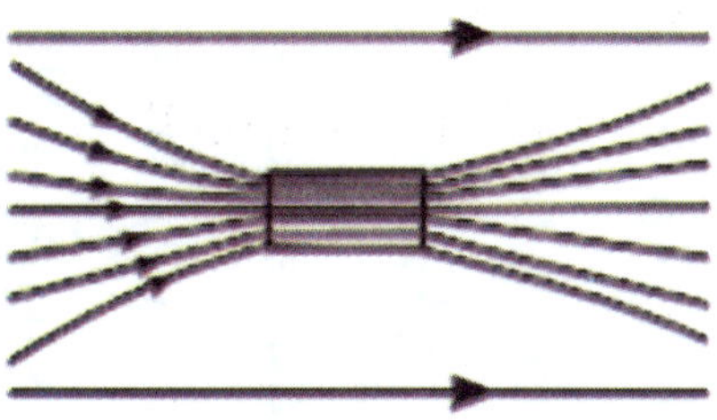

Ferromagnetic

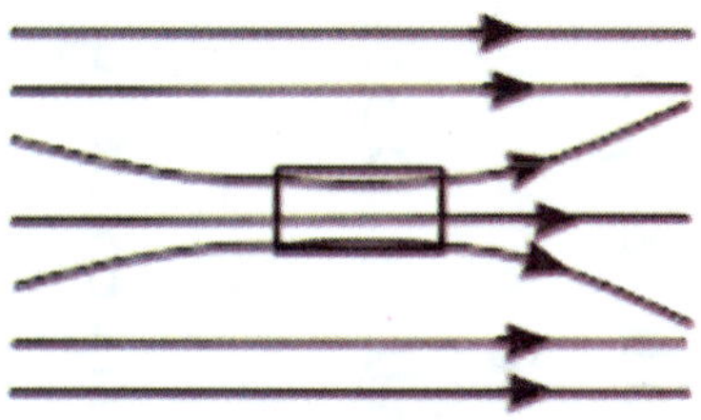

Paramagnetic

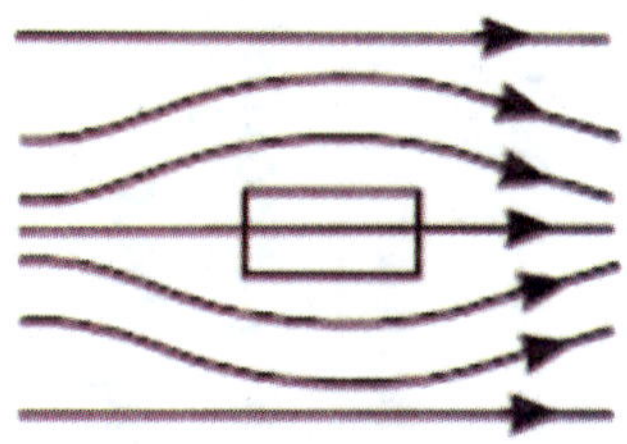

Diamagnetic

NEET Accelerate

- The work done in the magnetism is not by magnetic field. Infact, it comes indirectly from other sources mainly from battery or current.
- For protecting a sensitive equipment from the external magnetic field, it should be placed inside a ferro-magnetic materials like iron can.

Properties of Magnetic Materials

Property	Paramagnetic Substance	Diamagnetic Substance	Ferromagnetic Substance
When placed in uniform MF	Feebly magnitized along M.F.	Feebly magnitized opposite to MF or repelled by magnets	Strongly magnitized along MF
χ	Small & positive $0 < \chi$	Small & Negative $-1 < \chi < 0$	Very large $\chi >> 1$
μ_r	Small & positive $1 < \mu_r$	Positive & less than 1 $0 < \mu_r < 1$	Very large $\mu_r >> 1$
Effect of Temperature	Inversely $\chi \propto \frac{1}{T}$	Independent of Temperature	Inversely $\chi_m \propto \frac{1}{T-T_c}$
In a non-uniform MF	Tends to move from weaker to stronger magnetic field.	Tends to move from stronger to weaker magnetic field.	Tends to move quickly from weaker to stronger MF.
Examples	Ph, H_2O, NaCl, Bi, Cu, Si, Sb	Na, Ca, O_2, $CuCl_2$, Al	Ni, Co, Fe, Fe_2O_3, Gd

25. Electromagnetic Induction

Magnetic Flux

- It is the total magnetic lines passing through a given area.
- $\phi_B = \int \vec{B}.\vec{ds}$

  where B is the magnetic field and
  ds is the area of element
- For constant B,

  $\phi_B = \vec{B}.\vec{A} = BA\cos\theta$
- If magnetic field is parallel to the plane of loop, then flux through the loop is zero.
- SI unit is Weber (Wb).
- It is a scalar quantity.
- Dimensional Formula is $[ML^2T^{-2}A^{-1}]$.

PYQ PUNCH

Q1. A square loop of side 1m and resistance 1 Ω placed in a magnetic field of 0.5 T. If the plane of the loop is perpendicular to the direction of magnetic field, the magnetic flux through the loop is (NEET 2022)

Sol. $\theta = 0°$

$A = 1^2 = 1m^2$

$B = 0.5T$

$\phi_B = BA\cos\theta$

$= 0.5 \times 1 \times \cos 0°$

$= 0.5$ Wb

Faraday's law

- Whenever the magnetic flux linked with the closed loop changes, an emf gets induced in the circuit which lasts so long as change in flux continues. The phenomenon is called as Electro-Magnetic Induction (EMI).

- The magnitude of induced emf is directly proportional to the rate of change of flux linked with the closed loop.

$$e = N\left|\frac{d\phi}{dt}\right|$$

where N = number of turns in loop.

- If R is the resistance of the loop, then the induced current is

$$i = \frac{e}{R} = \frac{N}{R}\left|\frac{d\phi}{dt}\right|$$

- Average Induced EMF

$$e_{avg} = N\left|\frac{\Delta\phi}{\Delta t}\right|$$

- Average Induced Current

$$i_{avg} = \frac{N}{R}\left|\frac{\Delta\phi}{\Delta t}\right|$$

PYQ PUNCH

Q2. The magnetic flux linked with a coil (in Wb) is given by the equation $\phi = 5t^2 + 3t + 16$. The magnitude of induced emf in the coil at the fourth second will be: (NEET 2020)

Sol. $e = \left|\frac{d\phi}{dt}\right|$

$e = \frac{d}{dt}(5t^2 + 3t + 16) = 10t + 3$

$e_{t=4} = 10 \times 4 + 3 = 43\ V$

Lenz's law

- In simple words, induced emf induces current in such a direction, which opposses the bar magnet to induce EMF.

$$e = -N\frac{d\phi}{dt}$$

where $-ve$ sign is the consequence of Conservation of Energy

- If North pole moves towards a loop, then loop should try to stop it. It can be done by creating North Pole. Thus, current is anti-clockwise.

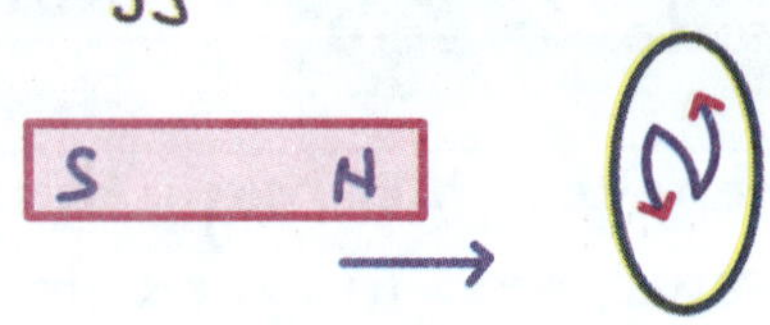

Anti-clockwise

- If North pole moves away from a loop, then loop Should try to stop it. It can be done by creating South Pole. Thus, current is clockwise.

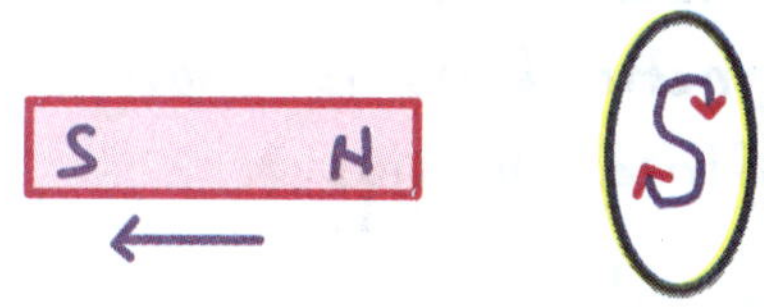

Clockwise

Note: Jo paas aaega wo banega and jo dur jaega uska opposite banega

PYQ PUNCH

Q3. In the diagram, a strong bar magnet is moving towards solenoid-2 from solenoid-1. The direction of induced current in solenoid-1 and that in solenoid-2, respectively, are through the directions.

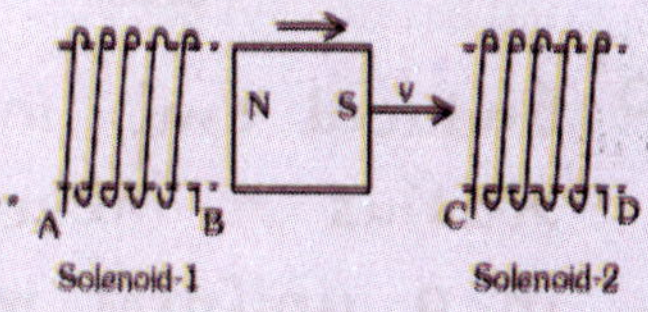

a. AB and DC b. BA and CD
c. AB and CD d. BA and DC

(NEET 2024)

Sol. As south moving towards Solenoid-2, thus South will form.
⇒ Clockwise direction. Hence, DC.
As north moving away from Solenoid-1, thus south will form.
⇒ Clockwise direction. Hence, AB.
Option a.

Ways to change the flux

◎ Change of Magnetic Field

- $e = -NA\left(\frac{dB}{dt}\right)$

Similarity with North Pole

Magnetic Field	Similarity	Current
↑	North Pole Approaching	Anti-clockwise
↓	North Pole Receding	Clock-wise

- Induced emf in a loop of radius R where magnetic field is change at a rate $\frac{dB}{dt}$ in a confined radius r.

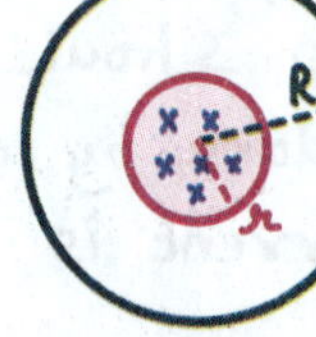

$$e = -\frac{dB}{dt}\pi r^2$$

Change of Area

- $e = -NB\left(\frac{dA}{dt}\right)$
- Induced emf in a Circular coil of radius r increasing at a rate of $\frac{dr}{dt}$ in a uniform magnetic field B is

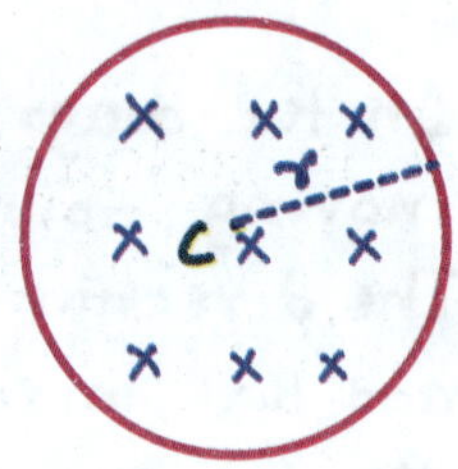

$$e = -2NB \times \pi r \frac{dr}{dt}$$

Change of Angle between B and A

- This can be achieved by rotating the coil around any axis.
- If Coil is rotated by constant angular speed ω, then
  - $\phi = NBA\cos\omega t$
  - $e = -NB\omega A\sin\omega t$
  - $i = -\frac{NB\omega A\sin\omega t}{R}$

Initial Angle
$\theta_i = 0°$
$\theta = \omega t$

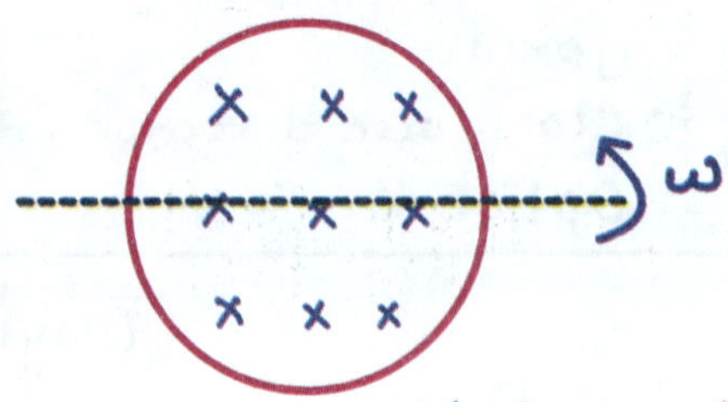

- Average emf induced over a time interval Δt when angle changes from θ_1 to θ_2.

$$e = -\frac{NBA(\cos\theta_2 - \cos\theta_1)}{\Delta t}$$

- If f is the frequency of rotation of coil then frequency of change of direction of
  - flux is $2f$
  - induced emf is $2f$
  - induced current is $2f$

PYQ PUNCH

Q4. A coil of 800 turns effective area $0.05\,m^2$ is kept perpendicular to a magnetic field 5×10^{-5} T. When the plane of the coil is rotated by $90°$ around any of its co-planar axis in 0.1 s, the emf induced in the coil will be : (NEET 2019)

Sol. $\theta_1 = 0°$; $N = 800$; $A = 0.05\,m^2$; $B = 5\times10^{-5}$ T

$\theta_2 = 90°$

Now

$$e = -\frac{NBA(\cos\theta_2 - \cos\theta_1)}{\Delta t}$$

$$= -\frac{800\times5\times10^{-5}\times0.05\,(\cos 90° - \cos 0°)}{0.1}$$

$$= 0.02\text{ V}$$

Charge flow through the loop

- If flux changes by $\Delta\phi$ in time Δt through a loop of resistance R, then the total charge passes through a cross-section of loop is

$$q = \frac{\Delta\phi}{R}$$

- It depends upon the total change of flux and resistance.

Motional EMF

Due to Translatory Motion

- Rod moving with constant speed v.
- EMF induced is

$$e = \vec{l}\cdot(\vec{v}\times\vec{B})$$

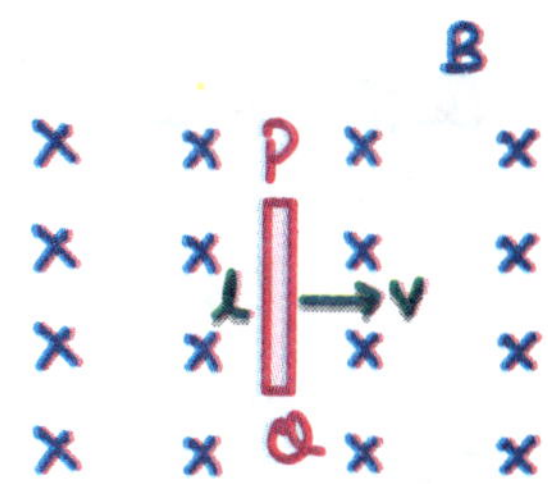

- Rod behaves like a battery of Voltage e.
- Battery Terminals

B	V	P	Q
⊗	Right	+ve	−ve
⊗	Left	−ve	+ve
⊙	Right	−ve	+ve
⊙	Left	+ve	−ve

- Electric field in the rod is

$$E = \vec{V} \times \vec{B}$$

- For conductor moving perpendicular to magnetic field

$$e = Blv$$

$$E = vB$$

Due to Rotation Motion

- Hinged at one end.
  - Rod is rotated with constant ω anti-clockwise about point O.

$$e = \frac{B\omega l^2}{2}$$

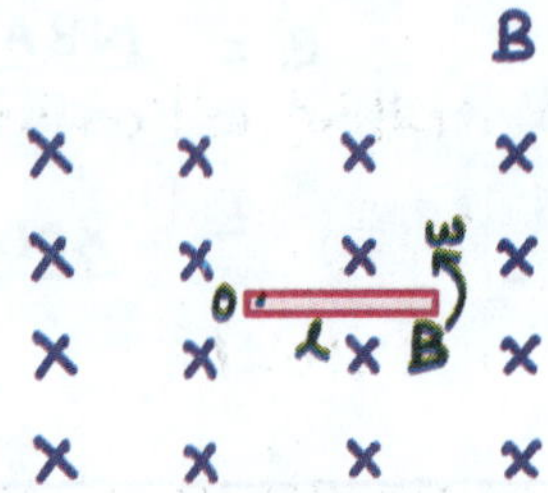

  - Time Period

$$T = \frac{2\pi}{\omega}$$

  - Battery Terminals

B	ω	O	B
⊗	Anti-clockwise	+ve	−ve
⊗	Clockwise	−ve	+ve
⊙	Anti-clockwise	−ve	+ve
⊙	Clockwise	+ve	−ve

PYQ PUNCH

Q5. A wheel with 20 metallic spokes each 1m long is rotated with a speed of 120 rpm in a plane perpendicular to a magnetic field of 0.4G. The induced emf between the axle and rim of the wheel will be ($1G = 10^{-4}$ T) (NEET 2020)

Sol. $l = 1m$; $\omega = 120$ rpm $= 4\pi$ rad/s ; $B = 0.4G = 4 \times 10^{-5}$ T

Now

$$e = \frac{B\omega l^2}{2} = \frac{4\times10^{-5} \times 4\pi \times 1^2}{2}$$

$$= 2.51 \times 10^{-4} \text{ V}$$

- Hinged at centre

$$e = 0$$

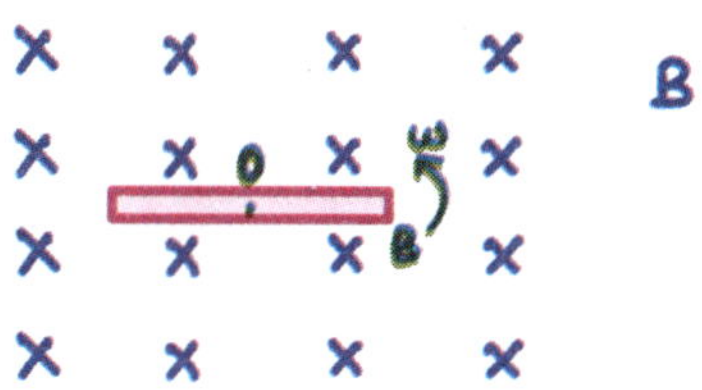

- Hinged unequally

$$e = \frac{B\omega(l_1^2 - l_2^2)}{2}$$

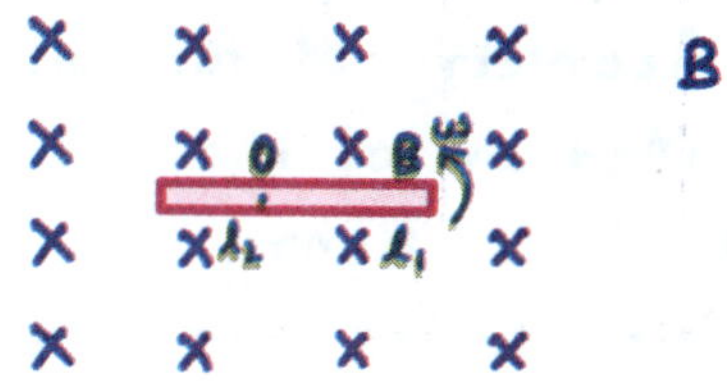

- Rotation of arbitrary shape object
  - $l_{eff} = OB$
  - $$e = \frac{B\omega l_{eff}^2}{2}$$

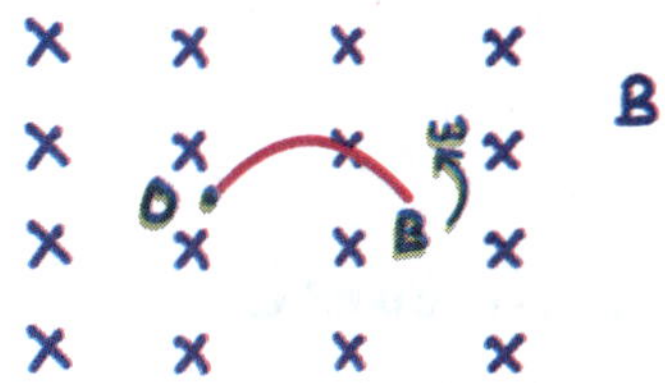

Eddy Current

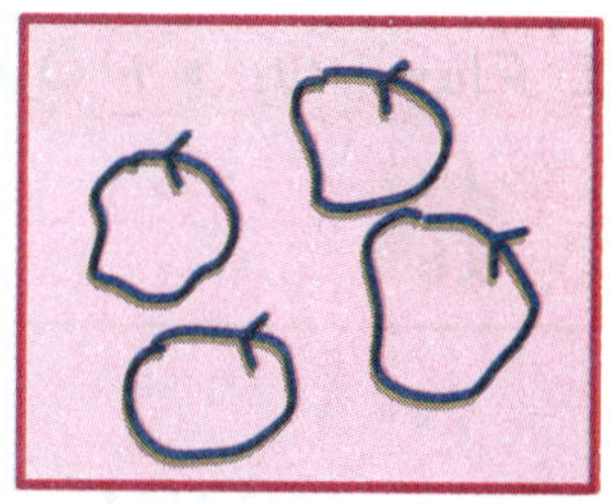

- In a solid conductor, when flux changes, it leads to the formation of random current loops called as Eddy Current.
- It is mainly produced due to time-varying current.
- It causes generation of heat.
- It is used in
  - Electro-magnetic damping
  - Magnetic braking in train
  - Induction furnace.
  - Wireless charging

Induction

- Flux linkage of a closely wound coil is directly proportional to the current.

$$\phi_B \propto I$$

$$\phi_B = LI$$

where, L is called as Inductance of the Coil.

- It is the property of the electrical conductor by virtue of which it opposses the change of magnetic flux in the coil by inducing an emf in the coil.
- It depends upon the
  - Geometry of the coil
  - Medium of the coil
- Unit is Henry.
- Other units are Vs/A , Tm^2/A , ohm-s
- EMF induced in terms of Inductor

$$e = -L\frac{dI}{dt}$$

Self-Inductance

- It is the property of the electrical conductor by virtue of which it opposses the change of magnetic flux in the coil due to the change of current in itself by inducing an emf in the coil.
- Total Flux $\phi_t = N\phi = LI$
- $e = -L\frac{dI}{dt}$

PYQ PUNCH

Q6. A long solenoid has 1000 turns. When a current of 4A flows through it, the magnetic flux linked with each turn of the solenoid is 4×10^{-3} Wb. The self-inductance of the solenoid is: (NEET 2016)

Sol. $N\phi = LI$

$\Rightarrow L = \frac{N\phi}{I} = \frac{1000 \times 4 \times 10^{-3}}{4} = 1H$

Self Inductance of a Long Solenoid

- A long solenoid is the one whose length is very large as compared to its radius.
- $L = \frac{\mu_0 N^2 \pi r^2}{l}$

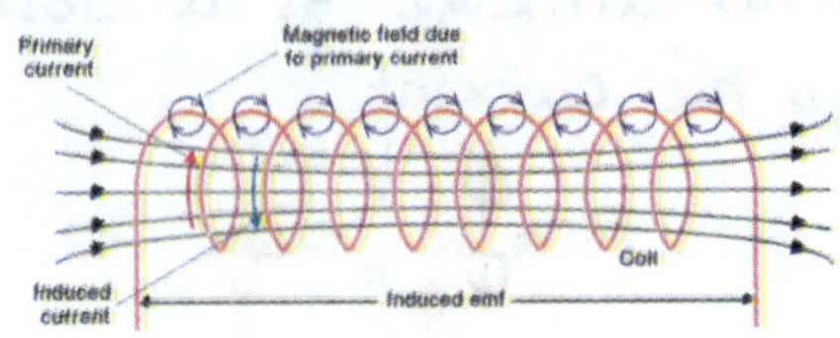

Inductor

- It is a solenoid of negligible resistance and considerable self inductance.
- It is used to store energy in the form of Magnetic Field.
- Energy stored is

$$E = \frac{1}{2} L I^2$$

- Potential drop across inductor is equal to back emf (induced emf)

$$V = e = L\frac{dI}{dt}$$

PYQ PUNCH

Q7. The magnetic energy stored in an inductor of inductance 4 μH carrying a current of 2A is (NEET 2023)

Sol. $L = 4\,\mu H = 4 \times 10^{-6} H$; $I = 2A$

$$E = \frac{1}{2} L I^2 = \frac{1}{2} \times 4 \times 10^{-6} \times 2^2$$

$$= 8\,\mu J$$

Mutual Inductance

- It is the property of the electrical conductor by virtue of which it opposes the change of magnetic flux in the coil due to the change of current in other coil by inducing an emf in the coil.
- Total Flux $= N_2 \Phi_{21} = M_{21} I_1$
- $e_{21} = -M_{21} \frac{dI_1}{dt}$

Reciprocity Theorem

- $M_{12} = M_{21} = M$

Coupling Factor

- Mutual Inductance of two inductors L_1 and L_2 when flux of one coil gets completely linked with other.

$$M = \sqrt{L_1 L_2}$$

MCQ PUNCH

Q8. Two coils of self inductance 2mH and 8mH are placed so close together that the effective flux in one coil is completely linked with the other. The mutual inductance between these coils is :

Sol. $L_1 = 2mH$; $L_2 = 8 mH$

Now

$$M = \sqrt{L_1 L_2}$$
$$= \sqrt{2 \times 8}$$
$$= 4 mH$$

Charge Flown

- Change of Current in 1 coil causes flow of current in other coil.
- Total charge passes through coil 2 due to change of current in 1

$$q_{21} = \frac{M}{R_2}(i_i - i_f)_1$$ where R_2 is the resistance of the coil 2.

- Total charge passes through coil 1 due to change of current in 2

$$q_{12} = \frac{M}{R_1}(i_i - i_f)_2$$ where R_1 is the resistance of the coil 1.

Mutual Inductance of 2 Circular Coils

- For $r_1 << r_2$,

$$M_{12} = M_{21} = M = \frac{\mu_0 \pi r_1^2}{2 r_2}$$

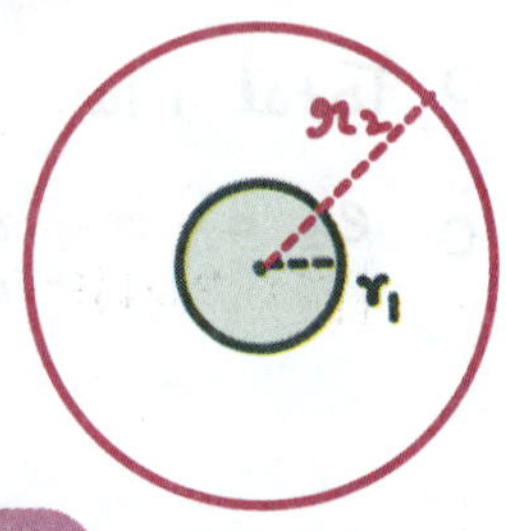

- Total charge

Mutual Inductance of 2 Solenoids

- S_1 has n_1 turns per unit length.
- S_2 has n_2 turns per unit length.

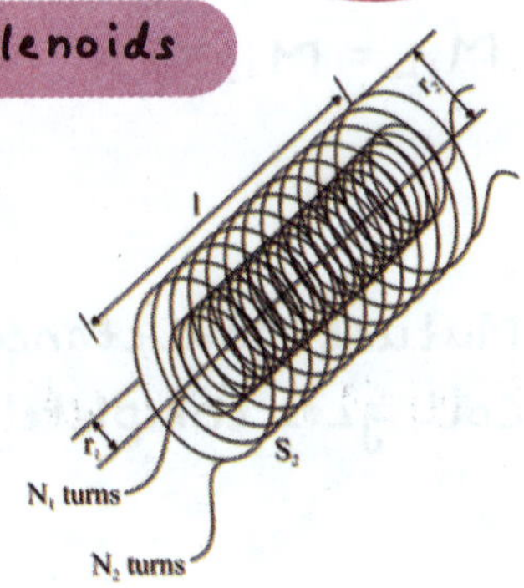

$$M_{12} = M_{21} = M = \mu_0 \pi n_1 n_2 r_1^2 l$$

Mutual Inductance of a Solenoid and a Coil

- Coil of radius r_2 and number of turns N_2 is placed coaxially with a solenoid of radius r_1 and n_1 number of turns per unit length.
- For $r_2 < r_1$

  $M = \mu_0 N_1 n_2 \pi r_2^2$
- For $r_2 > r_1$

  $M = \mu_0 N_1 n_2 \pi r_1^2$

PYQ PUNCH

Q9. A long solenoid of diameter 0.1m has 2×10^4 turns per metre. At the centre of the solenoid, a coil of 100 turns and radius 0.01 m is placed with its axis coinciding with the solenoid axis. The current in the solenoid reduces at a constant rate of 0 A from 4A in 0.05s. If the resistance of the coil is $10\pi^2\,\Omega$, the total charge flowing through the coil during this time is: (NEET 2017)

Sol. $n_1 = 2\times10^4$; $d_1 = 0.1m$; $r_1 = 0.05m$

$N_2 = 100$; $r_2 = 0.01m$

$i_i = 4A$; $i_f = 0A$; $t = 0.05s$; $R_2 = 10\pi^2\,\Omega$

Now

$M = \mu_0 N_1 n_2 \pi r_2^2 = \mu_0 \times 100 \times 2\times10^4 \times \pi \times 0.01^2 = 8\pi^2\times10^{-5} H$

Charge passes

$q_{21} = \frac{M}{R_2}(i_i - i_f)_1 = \frac{8\pi^2\times10^{-5}}{10\pi^2}(4-0) = 32\,\mu C$

Conversion of i-t graph to e-t

- $e = -L\frac{di}{dt}$
- Slope of i-t graph gives $-\frac{e}{L}$
-

i-t		e-t
▹ Inclined Straight Line above x-axis	⇒	Straight horizontal line below x-axis.
▹ Inclined Straight Line below x-axis	⇒	Straight horizontal line above x-axis.
▹ Straight Horizontal Line	⇒	Straight horizontal line on x-axis.

26. Alternating Current

AC Generator

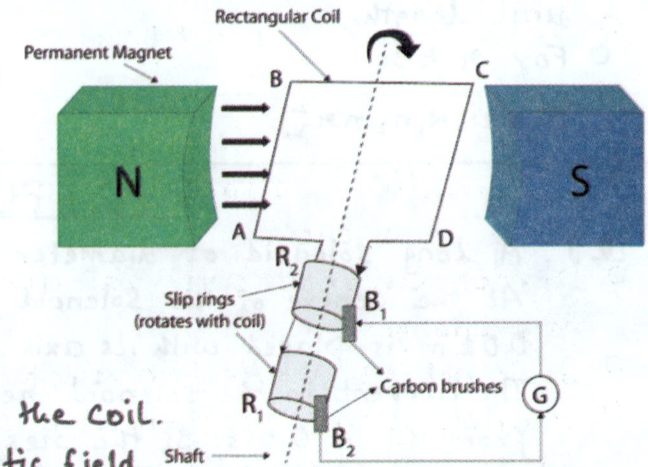

- Converts Mechanical Energy of turbine into electrical energy.
- Works on the Principle of Electro-magnetic Induction.
- Magnetic Flux

  $\phi = NBA\cos\omega t$

  where N = number of turns in the coil.
  B = strength of magnetic field.
  A = area of each turn of the coil.
  ω = angular velocity of rotation of the coil.

- Peak flux

  $\phi_0 = NBA$

- Induced emf

  $e = NBA\omega\sin\omega t = V$

- Peak induced emf

  $e_0 = NBA\omega = V_0$

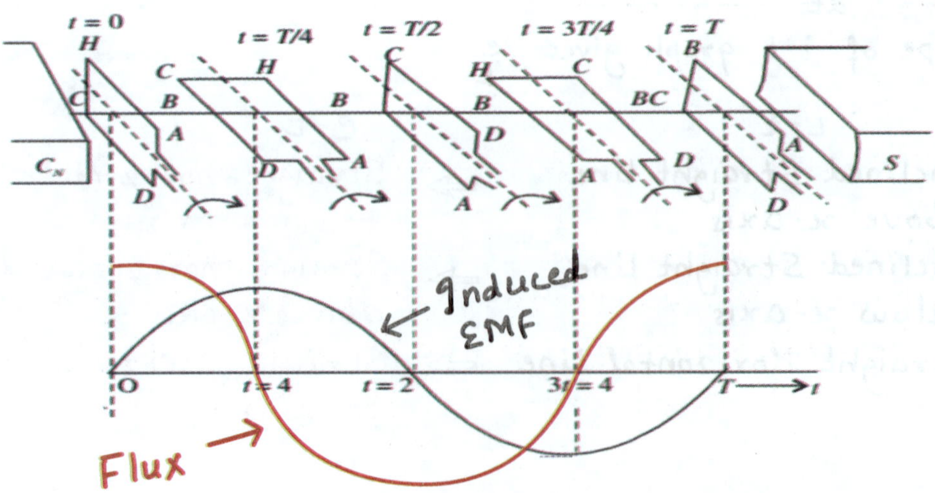

- Flux leads voltage and current by 90°.
- Induced Current is

$$i = \frac{NBA\omega \sin \omega t}{R}$$ where R is the resistance of the coil.

- Peak current $i_0 = \frac{NBA\omega}{R}$

NEET Accelerate

- Alternating voltage and current changes its direction twice in a cycle.
- Direct current are uni-directional, however, magnitude may changes.
- It is not necessary for AC to be sinusoidal.
- Multiple strands of thin wire are used for AC transmission because of skin effect.
- DC can be transmitted through thick or multiple strands of thin wire.

Average or Mean Value of AC

Over a half cycle

- It is defined as the value of AC which would send same amount of charge through a circuit in half-cycle that is sent by steady current in the same time.
- $i_{av} = \frac{2i_0}{\pi} = 63.7\% \; i_0$

Over a complete cycle

- $i_{av} = 0$

Effective Current or RMS Current

- It is defined as the value of AC over a complete cycle which would generate same amount of heat in a given resistor that is generated by steady current in the same resistor in the same time during a complete cycle.

For sinusoidal AC

1. $i = i_0 \sin \omega t$

- $I_{rms} = \frac{I_0}{\sqrt{2}} = 0.707 I_0 = 70.7\%$ of I_0
- Similarly,

$V_{rms} = \frac{V_0}{\sqrt{2}} = 0.707 V_0 = 70.7\%$ of V_0

2. $i = a + i_0 \sin \omega t$ or $V = a + V_0 \sin \omega t$

- $I_{rms} = \sqrt{a^2 + \frac{i_0^2}{2}}$
- Similarly, $V_{rms} = \sqrt{a^2 + \frac{V_0^2}{2}}$

For Square-wave AC

1. $I_{rms} = I_0$

$V_{rms} = V_0$

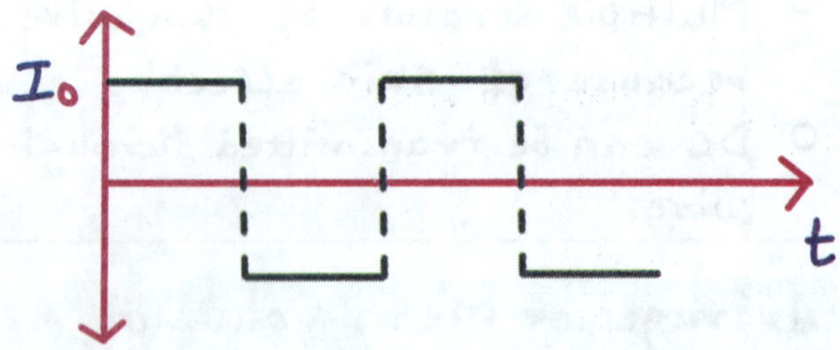

2. $I_{rms} = \frac{I_0}{\sqrt{2}}$

$V_{rms} = \frac{V_0}{\sqrt{2}}$

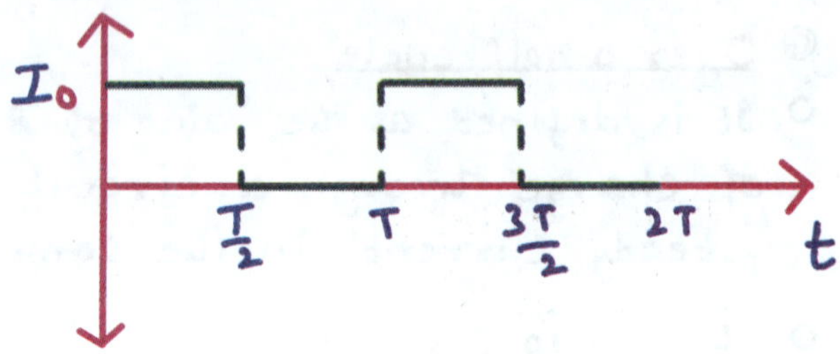

For triangular-wave AC

1. $I_{rms} = \frac{I_0}{\sqrt{3}}$

$V_{rms} = \frac{V_0}{\sqrt{3}}$

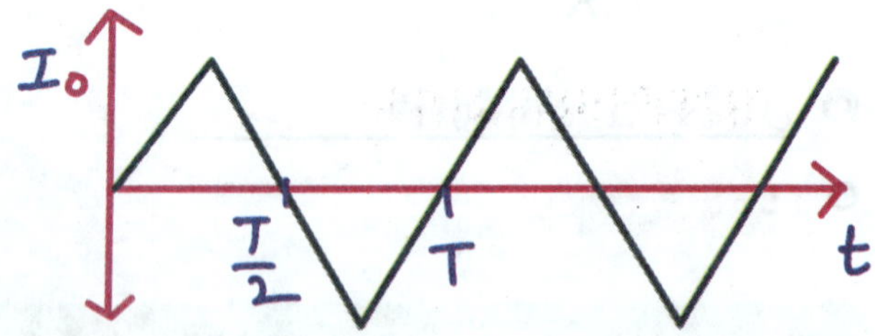

2. $I_{rms} = \frac{I_0}{\sqrt{3}}$

$V_{rms} = \frac{V_0}{\sqrt{3}}$

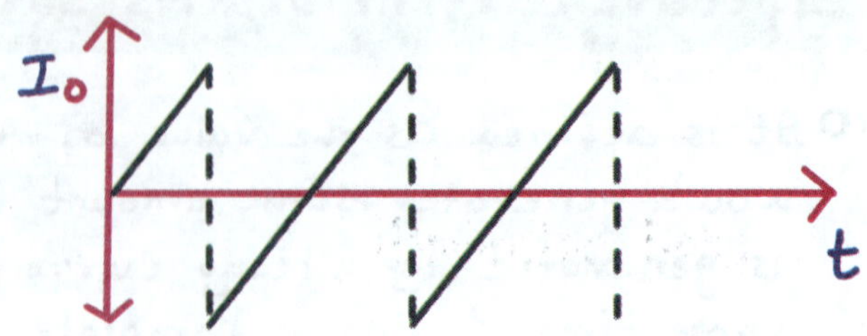

3. $I_{rms} = \frac{I_0}{\sqrt{6}}$

$V_{rms} = \frac{V_0}{\sqrt{6}}$

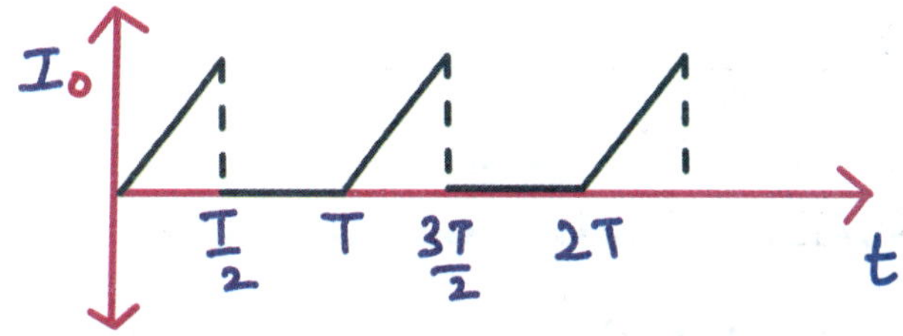

NEET Accelerate

- In the question, if only voltage is given instead of instantaneous voltage, then it is rms voltage.
- In the question, if only voltage or current is asked, then it means rms voltage or rms current.

R-Circuit

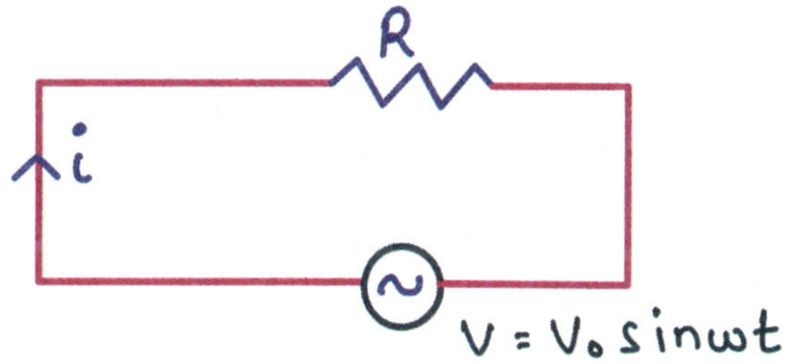

- $i = i_0 \sin\omega t$
- $i_0 = \frac{V_0}{R}$
- $i_{rms} = \frac{V_{rms}}{R}$
- Current and voltage are in phase.
- Average Power Consumption is

$$P_{avg} = \frac{i_0 V_0}{\sqrt{2}} = i_{rms} V_{rms}$$

- 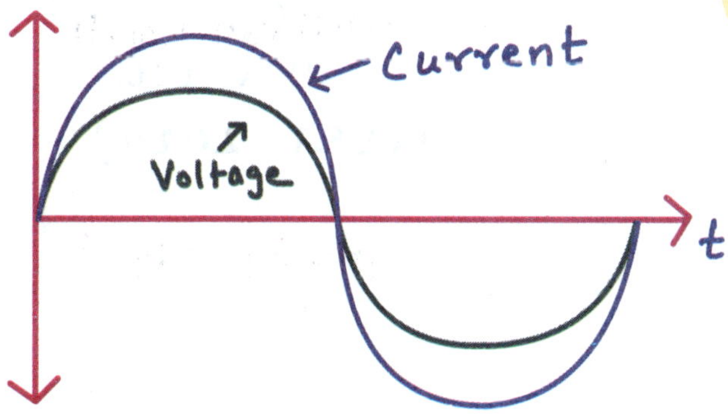

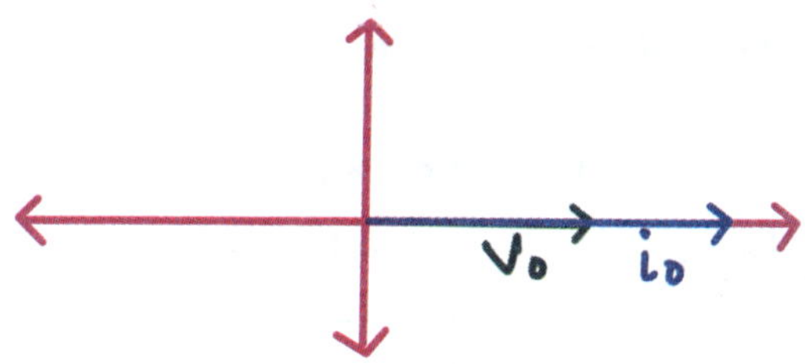

Phasor Diagram

C-Circuit

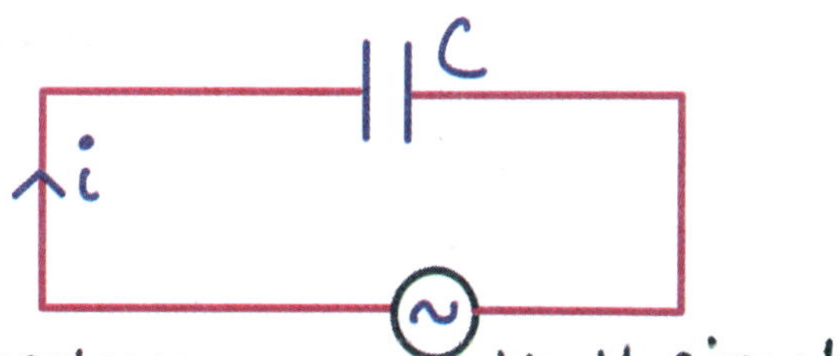

- $i = i_0 \sin(\omega t + 90°)$
- $i_0 = \frac{V_0}{X_C}$

where $X_C = \frac{1}{\omega C}$ is Capacitive Reactance

- $i_{rms} = \frac{V_{rms}}{X_C}$
- X_C unit is ohm.
- Average Power Consumption is $P_{avg} = 0$
- Capacitor provides potential drop without consuming any power
- Current leads voltage by 90°.
(Remember ICE - Current Capacitor EMF)
- 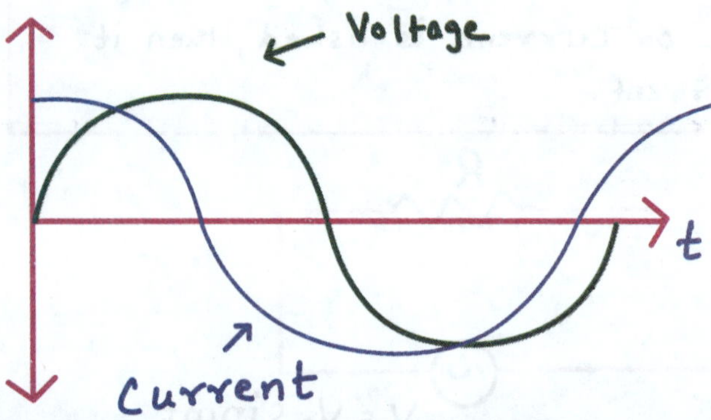

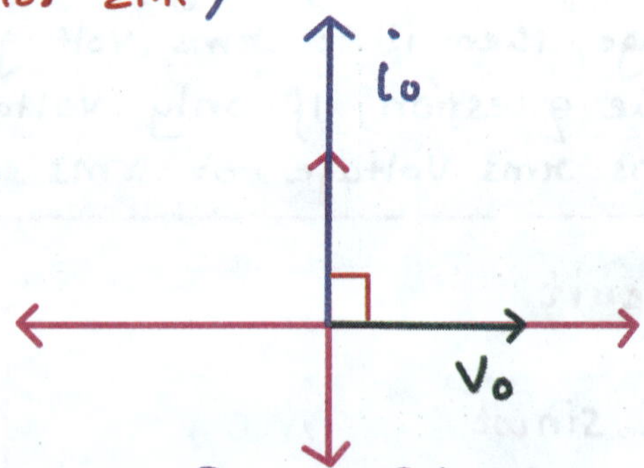

Phasor Diagram

PYQ PUNCH

Q1. A 10 μF capacitor is connected to a 210 V, 50 Hz source as shown in figure. The peak current in the circuit is nearly ($\pi = 3.14$).

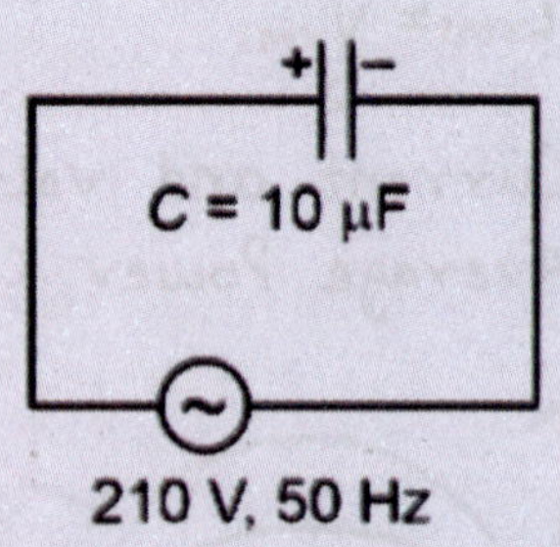

(NEET 2024)

Sol. $V_{rms} = 210\text{ V}$; $f = 50\text{ Hz}$; $C = 10\ \mu F$

$\omega = 2\pi f = 100\pi$ rad/s

$X_C = \frac{1}{\omega C} = \frac{1}{100\pi \times 10 \times 10^{-6}} = \frac{10^3}{\pi}$

$i_{rms} = \frac{V_{rms}}{X_C} = \frac{210 \times \pi}{10^3}$

$i_0 = \sqrt{2} \times i_{rms} = \frac{\sqrt{2} \times 210 \times 3.14}{10^3} = 0.93\text{ A}$

Variation of X_C

- Variation of X_C with ω
- If Capacitor is filled with dielectric, C increases and X_C decreases. Thus current increases in C-R circuit.

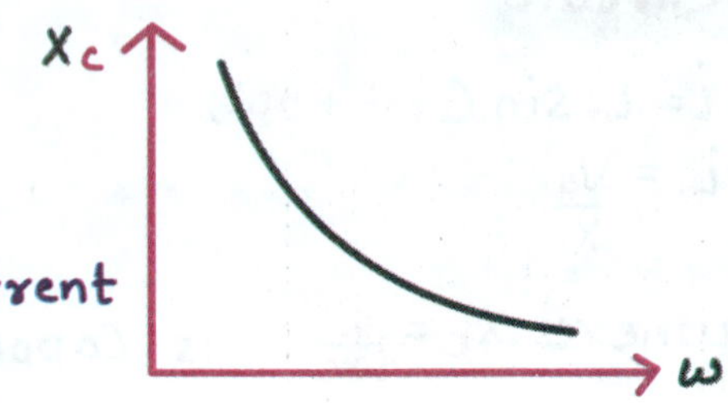

L-Circuit

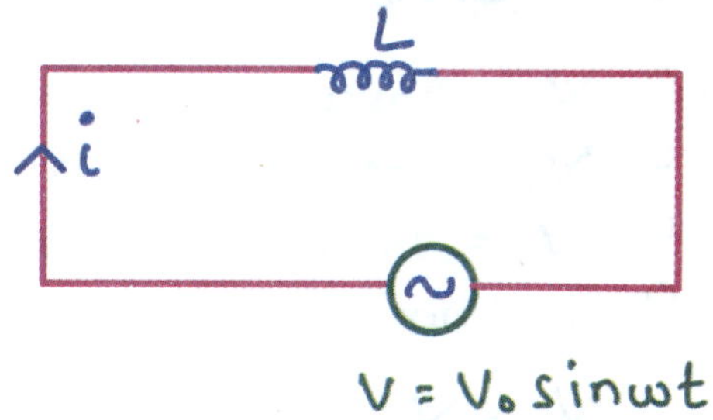

- $i = i_o \sin(\omega t - 90°)$
- $i_o = \dfrac{V_o}{X_L}$

where $X_L = \omega L$ is Inductive Reactance

- $i_{rms} = \dfrac{V_{rms}}{X_C}$
- X_L unit is ohm.
- Average Power Consumption is $P_{avg} = 0$
- Inductor provides potential drop without consuming any power.
- Current lags voltage by 90°.
  (Remember ELI - EMF Inductor Current)
- 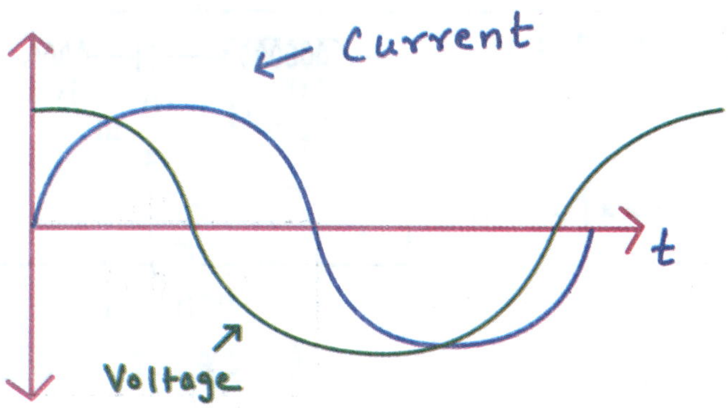

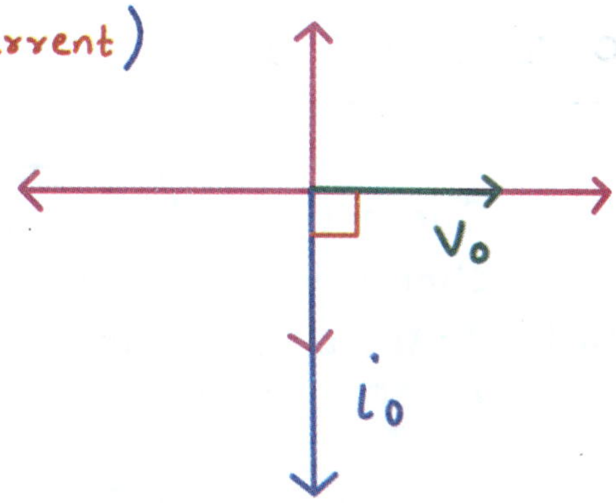

Phasor Diagram

Variation of X_L

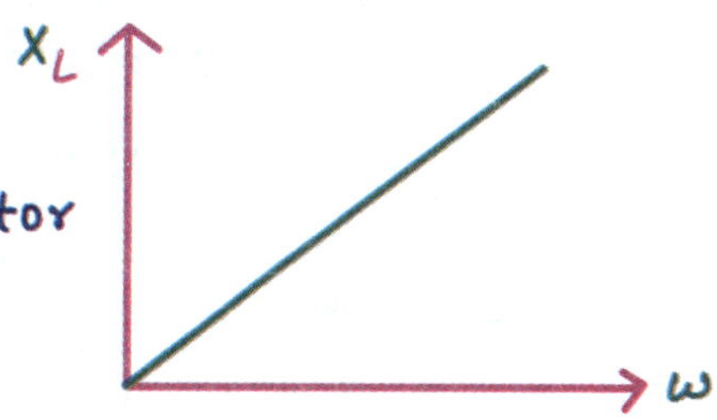

- Variation of X_L with ω
- If a metallic rod is inserted in an inductor L increases and X_L also increases. Thus Current decreases in L-R circuit.

NEET Accelerate

- As soon as the key is closed, for DC
  - Inductor acts as Open wire
  - Capacitor acts just like a simple wire.
- At steady state, for DC
  - Capacitor acts as Open wire
  - Inductor acts just like a simple wire.

LCR-Circuit

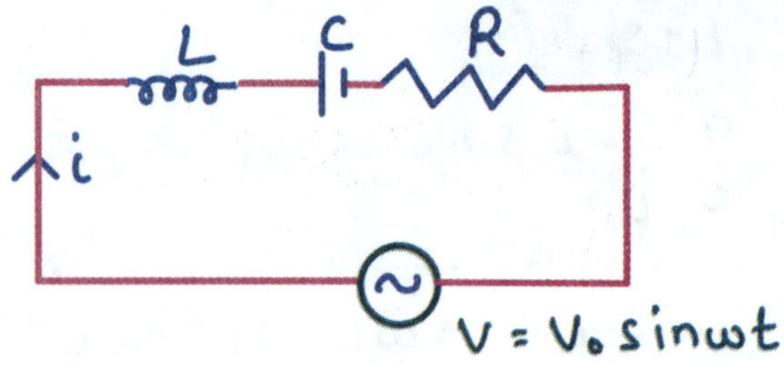

- V_L = Instantaneous Voltage of L
- V_C = Instantaneous Voltage of C
- V_R = Instantaneous Voltage of R
- By Ohm's Law

$$V_0 = V_L + V_C + V_R$$

- $i = i_0 \sin(\omega t + \phi)$
- $i_0 = \frac{V_0}{Z}$ where Z is the impedence of the circuit.
- $Z = \sqrt{R^2 + (X_C - X_L)^2}$
- Z unit is ohm.

PYQ PUNCH

Q2. The net impedence of circuit as shown in figure will be :

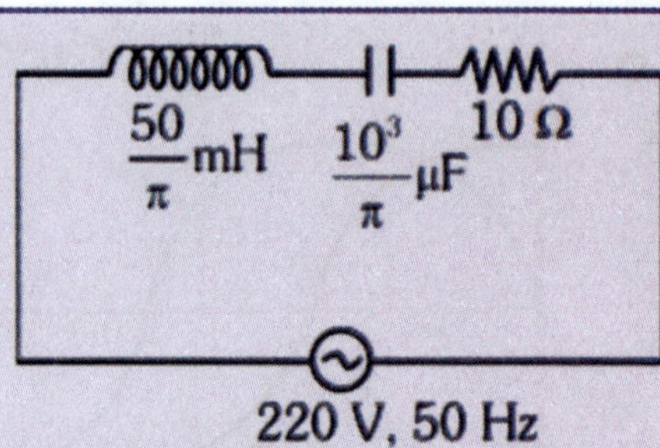

(NEET 2023)

Sol. $f = 50\text{ Hz}$; $R = 10\,\Omega$; $\omega = 2\pi f = 100\pi$

$L = \frac{50}{\pi}\text{ mH} = \frac{50}{\pi} \times 10^{-3}\text{ H}$

$C = \frac{10^3}{\pi}\,\mu F = \frac{10^3}{\pi} \times 10^{-6}\text{ F} = \frac{10^{-3}}{\pi}\text{ F}$

$X_C = \frac{1}{\omega C} = \frac{\pi}{100\pi \times 10^{-3}} = 10\,\Omega$

$X_L = \omega L = 100\pi \times \frac{50}{\pi} \times 10^{-3} = 5\,\Omega$

$Z = \sqrt{R^2 + (X_C - X_L)^2}$
$= \sqrt{10^2 + (10-5)^2}$
$= 5\sqrt{5}\,\Omega$

- $(V_L)_{max}$ = Maximum Voltage of L
- $(V_C)_{max}$ = Maximum Voltage of C
- $(V_R)_{max}$ = Maximum Voltage of R

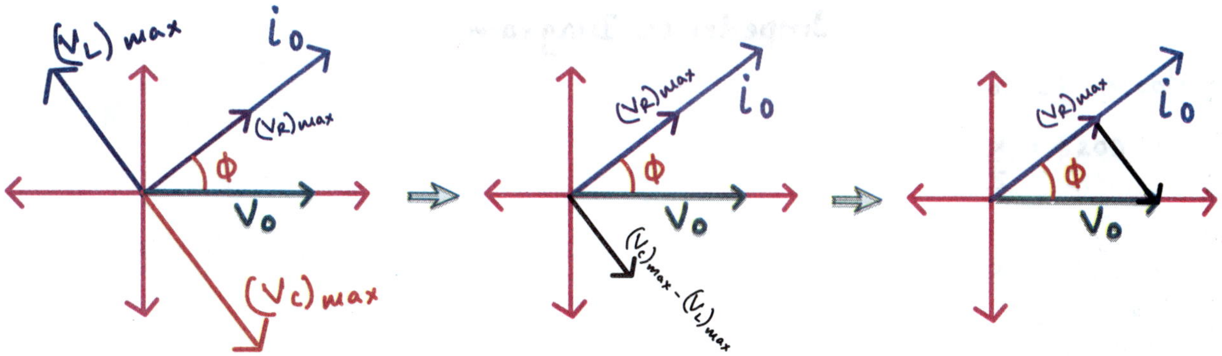

- $V_0 = \sqrt{(V_R)^2_{max} + ((V_C)_{max} - (V_L)_{max})^2}$
- $\tan\phi = \dfrac{X_C - X_L}{R}$ where ϕ is the phase by which current leads source voltage.
- $V_{rms} = \sqrt{(V_R)^2_{rms} + ((V_C)_{rms} - (V_L)_{rms})^2}$
- $i_{rms} = \dfrac{V_{rms}}{Z}$

PYQ PUNCH

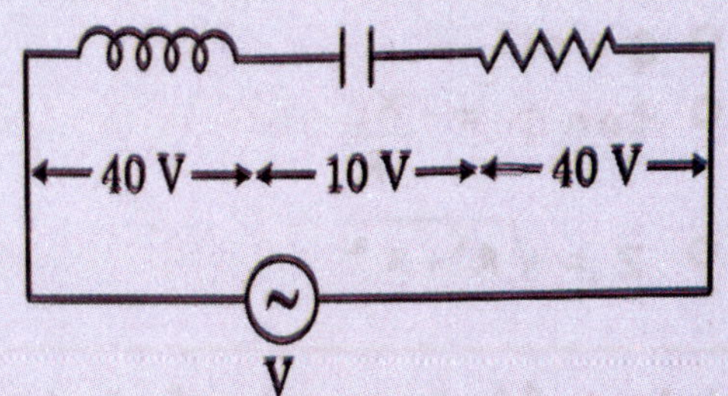

Q3. An inductor of inductance L, a capacitor of Capacitance C and a resistor of resistance R are connected in series to an AC source of potential difference V volts as shown in figure. Potential difference across L, C and R is 40 V, 10 V and 40 V respectively. The amplitude of current flowing through L-C-R series circuit is $10\sqrt{2}$ A. The impedence of the circuit is : (NEET 2021)

Sol. $(V_L)_{rms} = 40V$; $(V_C)_{rms} = 10V$; $(V_R)_{rms} = 40V$; $i_0 = 10\sqrt{2}$ A

$$V_{rms} = \sqrt{(V_R)^2_{rms} + ((V_C)_{rms} - (V_L)_{rms})^2}$$
$$= \sqrt{40^2 + (40-10)^2} = 50V$$
$$i_{rms} = \frac{i_0}{\sqrt{2}} = \frac{10\sqrt{2}}{\sqrt{2}} = 10A$$
$$Z = \frac{V_{rms}}{i_{rms}} = \frac{50}{10} = 5\Omega$$

Impedence Diagram

- Power factor

$$\cos\phi = \frac{R}{Z}$$

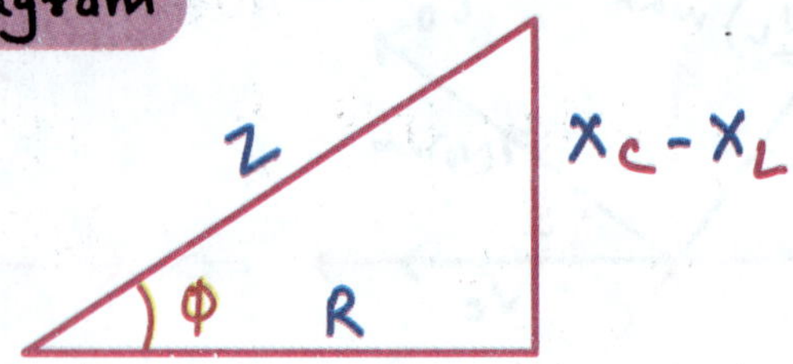

- For $X_C = X_L$, $Z = R$
  $\cos\phi = 1$

- If $\phi > 0°$
  - $X_C > X_L$
  - Capacitive Circuit
- If $\phi < 0°$
  - $X_C < X_L$
  - Inductive Circuit
- If $\phi = 0°$
  - $X_C = X_L$
  - Resistive Circuit

Other Circuits

L-R Circuit	C-R Circuit
○ If $X_C = 0$, L-C-R becomes L-R circuit. ○ $\phi < 0°$ ○ $\tan\phi = -\frac{X_L}{R}$ ○ $Z = \sqrt{R^2 + X_L^2}$	○ If $X_L = 0$, L-C-R becomes C-R circuit. ○ $\phi > 0°$ ○ $\tan\phi = \frac{X_C}{R}$ ○ $Z = \sqrt{R^2 + X_C^2}$

Note: If removal of L from L-C-R makes $\phi = \phi_0$ and removal of C from LCR also makes $\phi = \phi_0$, then $X_C = X_L$

PYQ PUNCH

Q4. A series L-C-R circuit is connected to an AC Voltage Source. When L is removed from the circuit, the phase difference between the Current and the voltage is $\pi/3$. If instead C is removed from the circuit, the phase difference is again $\pi/3$ between the current and the voltage. The power factor of the circuit is : (NEET 2020)

Sol. Without Inductor, $\phi = \pi/3$
Without Capacitor, $\phi = \pi/3$

$\Rightarrow X_C = X_L$

$\Rightarrow \cos\phi = 1$

Average Power Consumption

- $P_{avg} = i_{rms} V_{rms} \cos\phi$
  $= i_{rms} V_{rms} \times \frac{R}{Z}$
  $= i_{rms}^2 R$
  $= \left(\frac{V_{rms}}{Z}\right)^2 \times R$
- $P_{avg} = \frac{i_0 V_0 \cos\phi}{2}$
  $= \frac{i_0 V_0 R}{2Z}$
- Power is only consumed by Resistance.
- For same value of R,
  - P_{avg} of R-Circuit > P_{avg} of L-R Circuit
  - P_{avg} of R-Circuit > P_{avg} of C-R Circuit
  - P_{avg} of R-Circuit > P_{avg} of L-C-R Circuit ($X_C \neq X_L$)
  - P_{avg} of R-Circuit = P_{avg} of L-C-R Circuit ($X_C = X_L$)
- For purely inductive or capacitive circuit,
  - $\phi = 90°$
  - $P_{avg} = 0$
  - Current is flowing in the circuit but doesn't consume any power, hence, called as Wattless Current.

PYQ PUNCH

Q5. An inductor 20 mH, a capacitor 100 μF and a resistor 50 Ω are connected in series across a source of emf, $V = 10 \sin 314t$. The power loss in the circuit is : (NEET 2018)

Sol. $V = 10 \sin 314t$; $\omega = 314$ rad/s

$\Rightarrow V_0 = 10$

As, $V_{rms} = \frac{V_0}{\sqrt{2}} = \frac{10}{\sqrt{2}}$ V

Now

$L = 20\text{ mH} = 20 \times 10^{-3}$ H ; $C = 100\ \mu F = 100 \times 10^{-6}$ F $= 10^{-4}$ F

$X_L = \omega L = 314 \times 20 \times 10^{-3}\ \Omega$; $X_C = \frac{1}{\omega C} = \frac{1}{314 \times 10^{-4}}\ \Omega$

$Z = \sqrt{R^2 + (X_C - X_L)^2}$
$= 56\ \Omega$

$$P_{avg} = \left(\frac{V_{rms}}{Z}\right)^2 \times R = \left(\frac{10}{\sqrt{2} \times 56}\right)^2 \times 50 = 0.79\text{ W}$$

Resonance

- At resonance $X_C = X_L$
- $\omega_0 = \frac{1}{\sqrt{LC}}$; $f_0 = \frac{1}{2\pi\sqrt{LC}}$
- $Z = R$ is minimum
- $\phi = 0°$
- Power factor = $\cos\phi = 1$
- $P_{avg} = i_{rms} V_{rms} = \frac{i_0 V_0}{2}$
- Current is maximum.

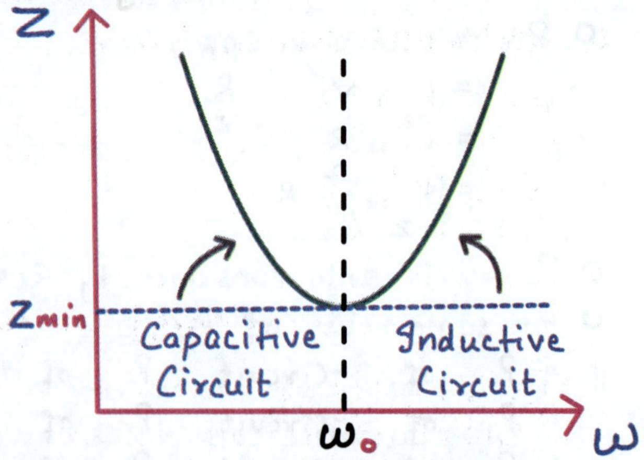

PYQ PUNCH

Q6. In a series L-C-R circuit, the inductor L is 10 mH, capacitance C is 1 μF and resistance R is 100 Ω. The frequency at which resonance occurs is: (NEET 2023)

Sol. $L = 10\ mH = 10^{-2}\ H$; $C = 1\ \mu F = 10^{-6}\ F$

$$\omega_0 = \frac{1}{\sqrt{LC}} = \frac{1}{\sqrt{10^{-2} \times 10^{-6}}} = 10^4\ rad/s$$

$$f_0 = \frac{\omega_0}{2\pi} = \frac{10^4}{2\pi} = 1.59\ kHz$$

- If V_{rms} is same across L, C and R, then $X_C = X_L = R$ i.e. circuit is in Resonance. Removing of

Capacitor leads to
- $\phi' = -45°$
- $i'_{rms} = i_{rms}/\sqrt{2}$
- $(V'_R)_{rms} = (V_R)_{rms}/\sqrt{2}$
- $(V'_L)_{rms} = (V_L)_{rms}/\sqrt{2}$

Inductor leads to
- $\phi' = 45°$
- $i'_{rms} = i_{rms}/\sqrt{2}$
- $(V'_R)_{rms} = (V_R)_{rms}/\sqrt{2}$
- $(V'_C)_{rms} = (V_C)_{rms}/\sqrt{2}$

Transformer

- Converts high voltage AC into low voltage DC and vice-versa.
- Works on the Principle of Mutual Induction.
- Primary winding has N_p turns.

- Secondary winding has N_s turns.
- For an ideal transformer

$$P_{input} = P_{output}$$

- $$\frac{V_p}{V_s} = \frac{N_p}{N_s} = \frac{I_s}{I_p}$$

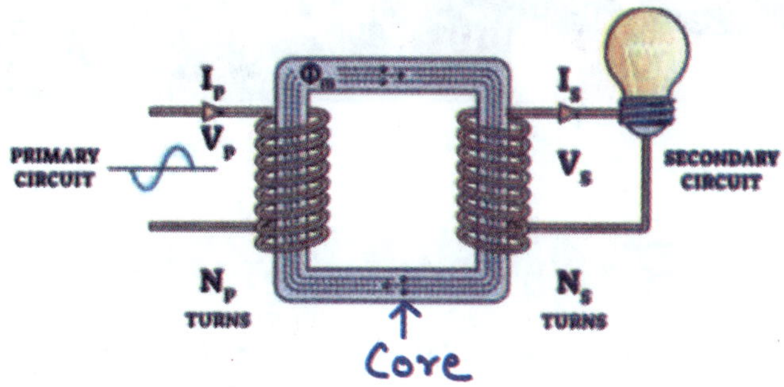

Energy Losses in Transformer

- In a practical transformer, energy losses due to
  - Eddy Current Loss - Reduces by laminating the core of transformer.
  - Flux Leakage - Reduces by using single-limb transformer.
  - Copper Loss - Reduces by using less resistance wire.
  - Hysteris Loss - Reduces by using soft iron core.
  - Humming Loss
- $P_{output} = \eta\%$ of P_{input}
  where η is the efficiency of transformer.

Types of Transformer

◉ Step-up Transformer ($N_s > N_p$)

- Increases the output voltage.
- Used to transmit electricity over long distances as losses in the form of heat get minimised.

◉ Step-down Transformer ($N_s < N_p$)

- Decreases the output voltage.
- Used in power consumption area.

PYQ PUNCH

Q7. In an ideal transformer, the turns ratio is $\frac{N_p}{N_s} = \frac{1}{2}$. The ratio $V_s : V_p$ is equal to: (NEET 2024)

Sol. $\frac{V_p}{V_s} = \frac{N_p}{N_s} = \frac{1}{2}$

$\Rightarrow \frac{V_s}{V_p} = \frac{2}{1}$

27. Electromagnetic Waves

Displacement Current

- It is the current inside the Capacitor during charging.
- Produced due to changing of electric flux (ϕ_E) inside the Capacitor.

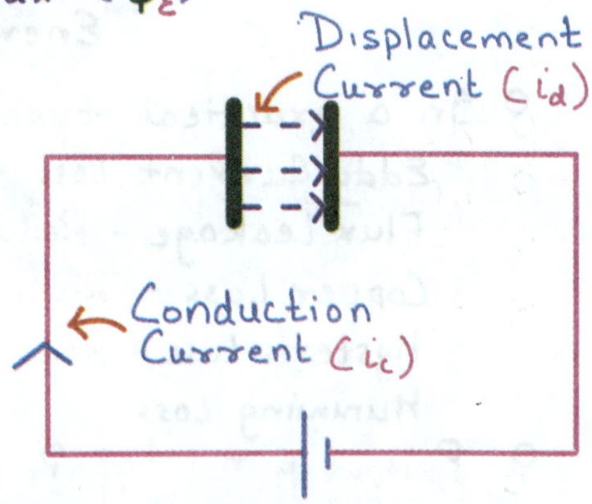

- $i_d = \varepsilon_0 \frac{d\phi_E}{dt} = \varepsilon_0 A \frac{dE}{dt}$
- $i_d = C.\frac{dV}{dt} = \frac{\varepsilon_0 A}{d}\frac{dV}{dt}$
- $i_c = i_d$
- Doesn't exist during steady state.

PYQ PUNCH

Q1. A capacitor of capacitance C, is connected across an AC Source of voltage V, given by $V = V_0 \sin\omega t$. The displacement current between the plates of the capacitor, would then be given by (NEET 2021)

Sol. $V = V_0 \sin\omega t$

In a Capacitor, current is

$i_c = V_0 \omega C \cos\omega t$

As $i_d = i_c = V_0 \omega C \cos\omega t$

Maxwell's Equations

- These four equations define the properties of EMW.

1. Gauss Law of Electrostat

$$\phi_E = \oint \vec{E}.\vec{ds} = \frac{q_{in}}{\varepsilon_0}$$

2. Gauss Law of Magnetism

$$\phi_B = \oint \vec{B}.\vec{ds} = 0$$

3. Faraday's Law

$$e = \oint \vec{E} \cdot d\vec{l} = \frac{-d\phi_B}{dt}$$

4. Ampere's - Maxwell Law

$$\oint \vec{B} \cdot d\vec{l} = \mu_0 (i_c + i_d) = \mu_0 \left(i_c + \varepsilon_0 \frac{d\phi_E}{dt}\right)$$

Sources of EMW

- Accelerating charge
- LC Oscillation
- Transition of electrons from higher orbit to lower orbit.
- Radioactivity

Characteristics of EMW

- It is a time varying electric and magnetic field.
- It doesn't require a medium to propagate.
- Electric field, magnetic field and direction of propagation all are mutually perpendicular.

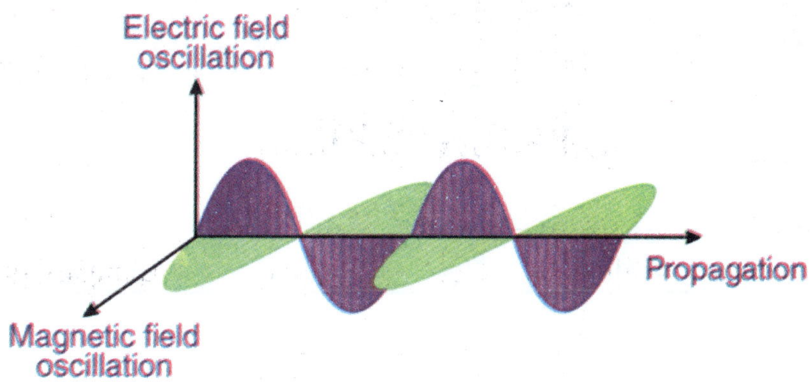

- Electric field and magnetic field are always in phase.
- It is transverse in nature i.e. it can be polarized.
- It carries both momentum and energy.

Nature of EMW

- Variation of Electric Field with time

$$E_x = E_0 \sin(\omega t - kz)$$

- Variation of Magnetic Field with time

$$B_y = B_0 \sin(\omega t - kz)$$

- Speed of light in vacuum

$$c = \frac{1}{\sqrt{\mu_0 \varepsilon_0}} = 3 \times 10^8 \text{ m/s}$$

- Speed of light in medium

$$v = \frac{1}{\sqrt{\mu_m \varepsilon_m}} = \frac{c}{\sqrt{\mu_r \varepsilon_r}}$$

where μ is the magnetic permeability
ε is the electric permittivity

- Angular frequency $\omega = \frac{2\pi}{T}$
- Angular wave number $k = \frac{2\pi}{\lambda} = \frac{\omega}{v}$
- Direction of propagation of EMW $\hat{E} \times \hat{B}$
- $E_0 = B_0 v$ or $E = Bv$

PYQ PUNCH

Q2. In a plane EMW travelling in free space, the electric field component oscillates sinusoidally at a frequency of 2×10^{10} Hz and amplitude 48 V/m. Then the amplitude of oscillating magnetic field is ? (Speed of light in free space = 3×10^8 m/s) (NEET 2023)

Sol. $B_0 = \frac{E_0}{v} = \frac{48}{3 \times 10^8} = 1.6 \times 10^{-7}$ T

- If medium is changed
  - Wavelength changes
  - Speed changes
  - Frequency remains the same.

Energy Density

Electrostatic Energy Density (u_E)

- $u_E = \frac{1}{2}\varepsilon_0 E^2$
- $(u_E)_{avg} = \frac{1}{4}\varepsilon_0 E^2$

Magnetic Energy Density (u_B)

- $u_B = \frac{B^2}{2\mu_0}$
- $(u_B)_{avg} = \frac{B_0^2}{4\mu_0}$

EM Wave Energy Density (u)

- $u = u_E + u_B = \varepsilon_0 E^2 = \frac{B^2}{\mu_0}$
- Both electric energy density and magnetic energy density contributes equally to totally energy density of EM Wave.
- $u_{avg} = \frac{\varepsilon_0 E^2}{2} = \frac{B^2}{2\mu_0}$

Intensity of EM Wave

- $I_{avg} = \frac{1}{2}\varepsilon_0 E_0^2 c = \frac{1}{2}\frac{B_0^2 c}{\mu_0}$

Force and Radiation Pressure

	Completely Reflecting Surface	Completely Absorbing Surface
Change of Momentum	$\frac{2E}{c}$	$\frac{E}{c}$
Force	$\frac{2E}{ct}$	$\frac{E}{ct}$
Pressure	$\frac{2E}{cAt}$ or $\frac{2I}{c}$	$\frac{E}{cAt}$ or $\frac{I}{c}$

I = Intensity ; E = Energy ; c = Speed ; t = Time

Energy Flux

- It is the power falling per unit area. In other words, it is Intensity.
- Energy due to flux on a given area in given time

U = Energy Flux × Area × Time

PYQ PUNCH

Q3. Light with an average flux of $20 W/cm^2$ falls on a non-reflecting surface at normal incidence having surface area $20 cm^2$. The energy received by the surface during time span of 1 min is : (NEET 2020)

Sol. U = Energy Flux × Area × Time

= 20 × 20 × 60

= 24 kJ

Electromagnetic Spectrum

- It is the orderly arrangement of EMW on the basis of their wavelength or frequency.

Radiation	Frequency Range (Hz)	Wavelength Range
γ-Rays	10^{20} - 10^{24}	< 10^{-3} nm
X-Rays	10^{17} - 10^{20}	10^{-3} nm - 1 nm
UV-Rays	10^{15} - 10^{17}	1 nm - 400 nm
Light	10^{14} - 10^{15}	400 nm - 700 nm
Infra-red	10^{13} - 10^{14}	700 nm - 1 mm
Microwave	10^{11} - 10^{13}	1 mm - 0.1 m
Radiowave	< 10^{11}	> 0.1 m

- Energy and frequency decreases from γ-rays to Radiowave.
- Wavelength increases from γ-rays to Radiowave.
- γ-rays to UV-rays are harmful rays.

Important Features of EMW

- Microwaves are called as Short wavelength Radio Waves.
- In microwaves, resonance of rotational water molecules causes heating effect.
- Infra-red waves are also called as Heat waves.
- Snakes can detect infrared.
- UV rays induces melanin, which causes tanning of skin.
- UV rays can be absorbed by ordinary glass.

Different Types of EMW

	Radio	Micro	IR	Light	UV	X-Ray	γ-Ray
Production	Acceleration of electrons in wires	Klystron, Magnetron, Gunn Diode	Hot Bodies and Molecules through vibration of atoms and molecules.	Jumping of electrons from higher orbit to lower orbit	Jumping of inner shell e⁻ from higher orbit to lower orbit, Very hot bodies	X-Ray tube, Inner Shell electron.	Radioactive decay of the nucleus
Detection	Receiver's Antenna	Point Contact Diode	Bolometer, IR Photographic plate, Thermopiles	Human Eye, Photographic Films, Photocells	Diodes, Photographic films.	Gieger Counter, Ionisation Chamber, Photographic Plates	Same as X-Ray
Uses	FM (88-108 MHz) AM (530-1710 kHz) TV (54-890 MHz) Cellular Phones (UHF)	Radar Navigation, Measuring Speed of Balls, Microwave Oven	Remotes, Hi-Fi Systems, Physical Theraphy, Green House Effect, In Satellite for military purpose & to observe the growth of Crops	To see objects	UV Lamps, LASIK,	Diagnostic Tools, Radio-therapy	Radio-therapy

28. Ray Optics

Object

- The point of intersection of Incident Rays.
- Types of Object

Real Object

- Incident rays actually meet.

Virtual Object

- Incident rays appear to meet.

Image

- The point of intersection of Reflected / Refracted Rays.
- Types of Object

Real Image

- Reflected rays actually meet.

Virtual Image

- Reflected rays appears to meet.

Reflection

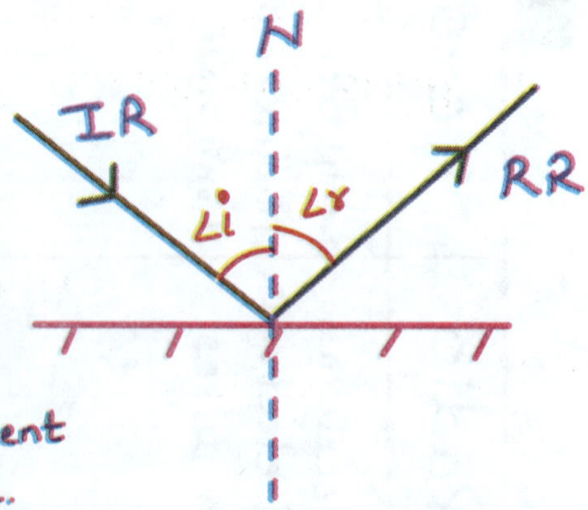

- Bouncing back of light in the same medium.
- $\angle i = \angle r$
- If Image medium appears to same as object medium, then real image.
- If Image medium appears to different as object medium, then virtual image.

Image formation by Plane Mirror

- Real Object → Virtual Image
- Virtual Object → Real Image
- Same distance of object and image from the mirror.
- Laterally inverted image
- Magnification is 1.

Deviation from Plane Mirror

It is the angle formed between the undeflected incident ray and the reflected ray.

By a Mirror

- $\delta = 180 - 2i$

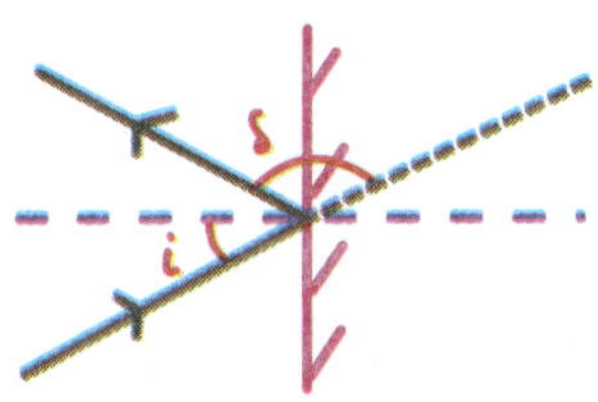

- If mirror is rotated by θ, new angle of deviation $\delta' = \delta - 2\theta$

By two inclined Mirror

- $\delta = 360 - 2\theta$

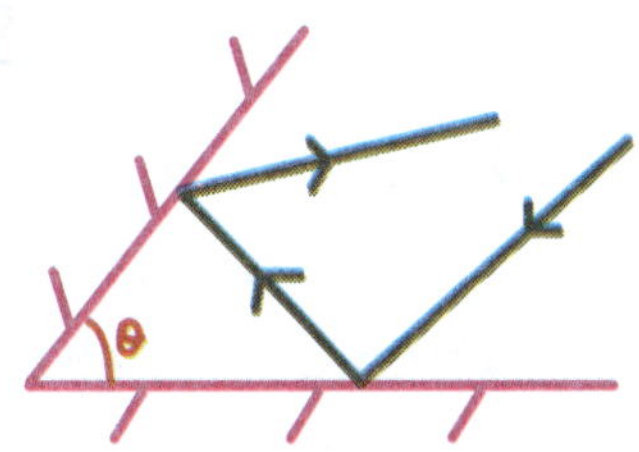

- For $\delta = 180°$, $\theta = 90°$

Height of Mirror

To see full height of Self

- $H_{mirror} = H_{person}/2$
- It is independent of the distance of person from the mirror.

Velocity of Image

Object moving towards mirror with speed u

- $\vec{V}_{IG} = -\vec{V}_{OG}$
- $\vec{V}_{IO} = -2\vec{V}_{OG}$

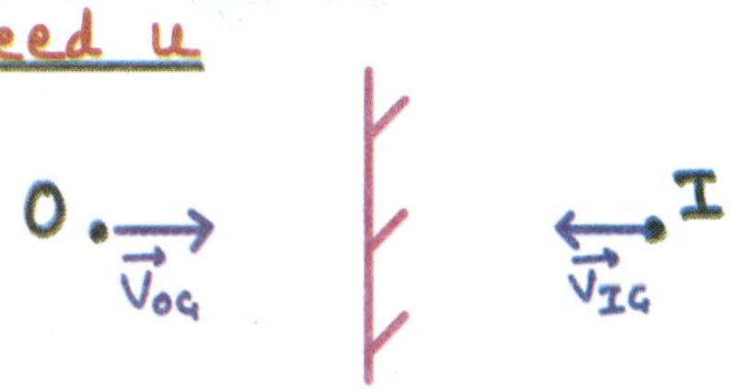

◉ Object moving away from the mirror with speed u

- $\vec{V}_{IG} = -\vec{V}_{OG}$
- $\vec{V}_{IO} = -2\vec{V}_{OG}$

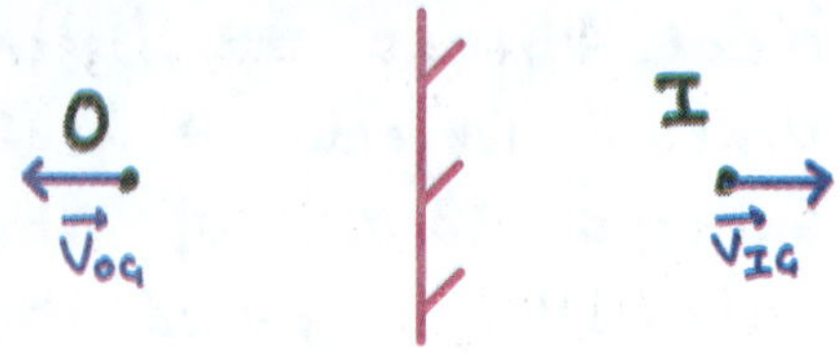

Spherical Mirror

Concave Mirror	Convex Mirror
• Converging • Focal length –ve. • u is –ve for (RO) • v is –ve for (RI) • v is +ve for (VI)	• Diverging • Focal length +ve. • u is –ve for (RO) • v is +ve for (VI)

Sign Convention

- All the horizontal distances are measured from Pole.
- Distances measured along the incident ray are taken as +ve.
- All the vertical heights are measured from Principal Axis.
- Heights measured above the Principal Axis are taken as +ve.

Equations for Mirror

1. $\frac{1}{v} + \frac{1}{u} = \frac{2}{R}$
2. $f = \frac{R}{2}$ Focal Length
3. $\frac{1}{v} + \frac{1}{u} = \frac{1}{f}$ Mirror Equation
4. $m = -\frac{v}{u}$ Lateral Magnification

m	+ve	–ve
>1	V & E Mag.	R & I Mag.
<1	V & E Small	R & I Small
=1	V & E Same Size	R & I Same Size

Image Formation By Convex Mirror

Object	Image	Nature	Size
• At infinity	At F	V & E	Highly Diminished
• At any point	Btw P & F	V & E	Diminished

- Convex mirror always forms EVS (Erect, Virtual, Small).

Image Formation By Concave Mirror

Object	Image	Nature	Size
At infinity	At F	R & I	Highly Diminished
Btw ∞ & C	Btw C & F	R & I	Diminished
At C	At C	R & I	Same Size
Btw C & F	Btw ∞ & C	R & I	Enlarged
At F	At infinity	R & I	Highly Enlarged
Btw F & P	Behind Mirror	V & E	Enlarged

- For concave mirror, as object comes close to the mirror, image goes away from the mirror and size increases.

PYQ PUNCH

Q1. An object is placed on the principal axis of a concave mirror at a distance of 1.5f (f is the focal length). The image will be at : (NEET 2020)

Sol. $u = -1.5f$; $f = -f$

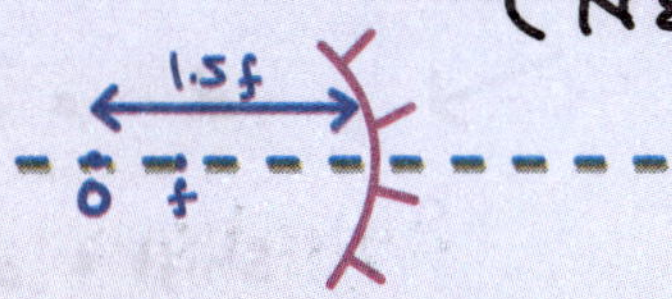

For mirror

$$\frac{1}{v} + \frac{1}{u} = \frac{1}{f}$$

$$\Rightarrow \frac{1}{v} - \frac{1}{1.5f} = -\frac{1}{f}$$

$$\Rightarrow v = -3f$$

Refraction

- Bending of ray when it travels from one medium to another.
- By Snell's law,

$$\frac{\sin\angle i}{\sin\angle r} = \frac{\mu_2}{\mu_1}$$

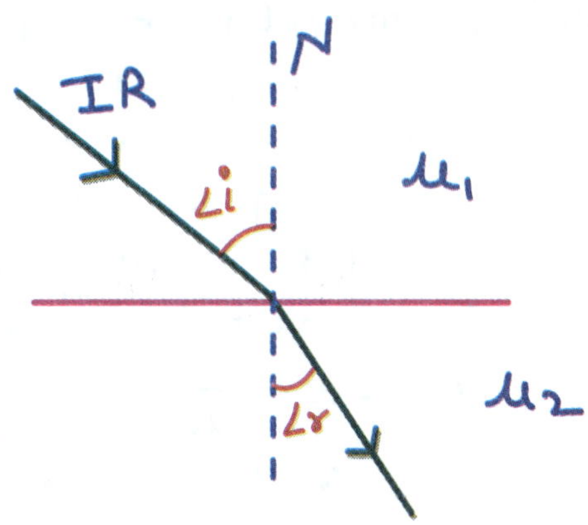

μ_1 is always the medium of Incident Ray.

Angle between Reflected and Refracted Ray

- During refraction, reflection also takes place.
- For $\tan i = \frac{\mu_2}{\mu_1}$
  - $\alpha = 90^\circ$
  - Reflected and Refracted are perpendicular to each other.

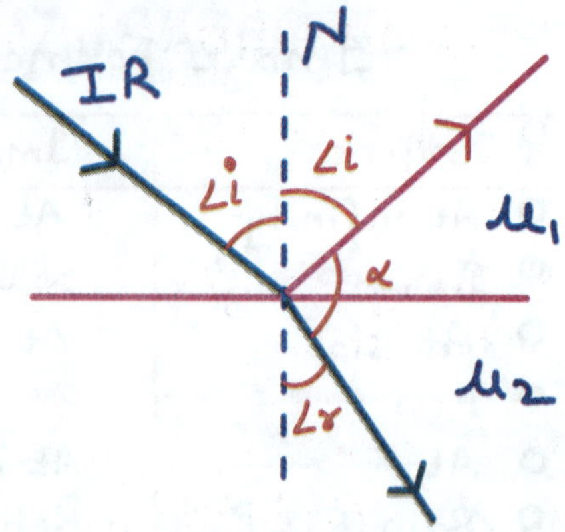

Real and Apparent Depth

Object in Denser Medium

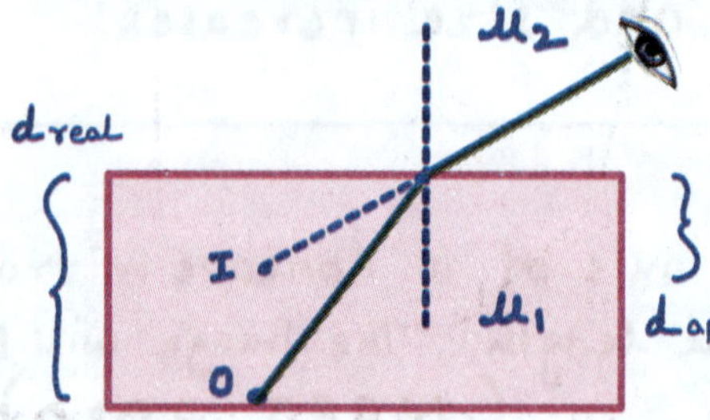

Object in rarer medium

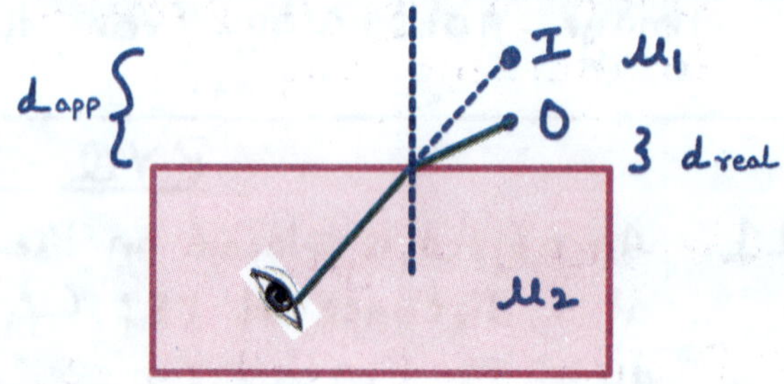

- $d_{app} = d_{real} \frac{\mu_2}{\mu_1}$
- $\text{Shift} = \left| d_{real}\left(1 - \frac{\mu_2}{\mu_1}\right) \right|$

- Object kahi bhi rakha ho, formula same rahega. Bas yaad rakhna ki μ_1 object ka medium hota hai.

PYQ PUNCH

Q3. An air bubble in a glass slab with refractive index 1.5 (near normal incidence) is 5cm deep when viewed from one surface and 3 cm deep when viewed from the opposite face. The thickness (in cm) of the slab is: (NEET 2016)

Sol. $\mu_1 = 1.5$; $\mu_2 = 1$

For apparent depth 5cm ;

$d_{real} = d_{app} \frac{\mu_1}{\mu_2}$

$= 5 \times 1.5 = 7.5 \text{ cm}$

For apparent depth 3 cm

$d_{real} = d_{app} \frac{\mu_1}{\mu_2}$

$= 3 \times 1.5 = 4.5 \text{ cm}$

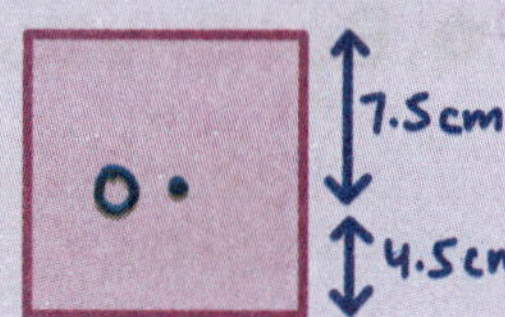

The thickness is $7.5 + 4.5 = 12 \text{ cm}$

Rectangular Slab

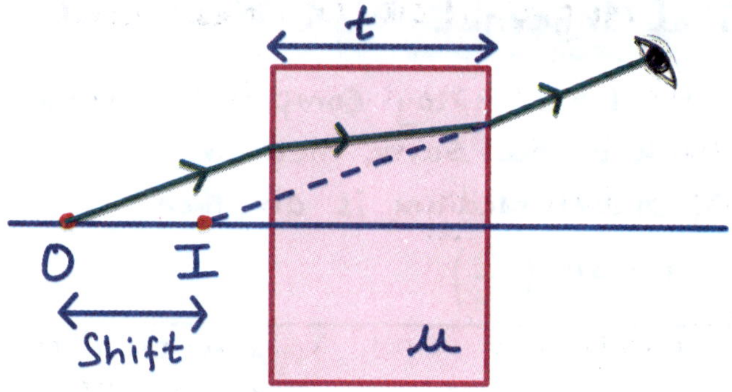

Longitudinal Shift

- $\text{Shift} = t\left(1 - \frac{1}{\mu}\right)$
- Image shifts towards the slab.

Lateral Shift

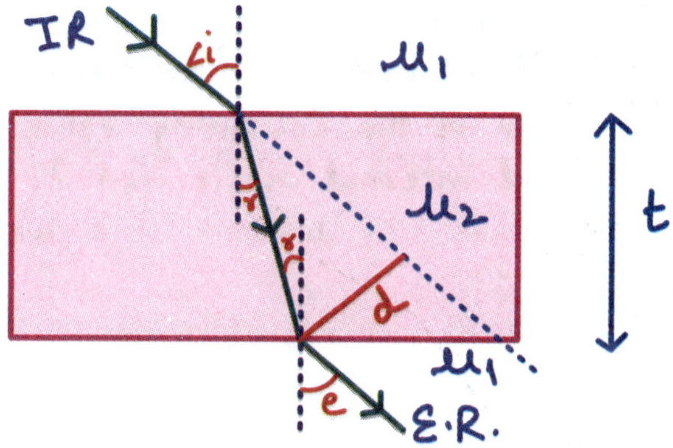

- $d = t \sec r \sin(i - r)$
- $\angle i = \angle e$
- Emergent ray is parallel to incident ray.

Critical Angle

- During the travelling of light ray from denser to rarer medium, the angle of incidence for which $\angle r = 90°$ is called as Critical Angle.
- $\sin i_c = \frac{\mu_2}{\mu_1}$
- If rarer medium is air, then $\sin i_c = \frac{1}{\mu}$ where μ is the refractive index of denser medium

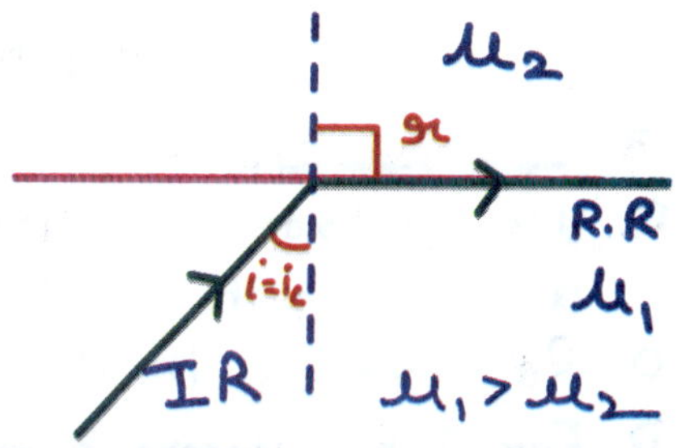

PYQ PUNCH

Q4. Light travels a distance x in time t_1 in air and $10x$ in time t_2 in another denser medium. What is the critical angle for this medium? (NEET 2023)

Sol. For air ; For Denser medium

$c = x/t_1$; $v = 10x/t_2$

Now $\mu = \frac{c}{v} = \frac{t_2}{10t_1}$

Critical angle

$\sin i_c = \frac{1}{\mu} = \frac{10t_1}{t_2} \Rightarrow i_c = \sin^{-1}\left(\frac{10t_1}{t_2}\right)$

Total Internal Reflection (TIR)

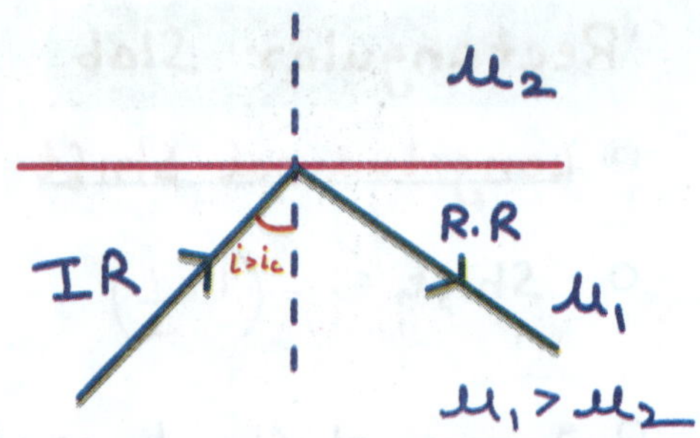

- For $i > i_c$, ray completely returns back to the same medium.
- If rarer medium is air, then

$$i > \sin^{-1}\left(\frac{1}{\mu}\right)$$

MCQ PUNCH

Q5. A ray of light travelling in a transparent medium of refractive index μ, falls on a surface separating the medium from air at an angle of incidence of 45°. For which of the following value of μ the ray can undergo total internal reflection?

a. $\mu = 1.33$ b. $\mu = 1.4$ c. $\mu = 1.5$ d. $\mu = 1.25$

Sol. $i = 45°$

For TIR $i > \sin^{-1}\left(\frac{1}{\mu}\right)$

$\Rightarrow \sin i > \frac{1}{\mu} \Rightarrow \mu > \frac{1}{\sin 45°} \Rightarrow \mu > \sqrt{2} \Rightarrow \mu > 1.414$

Hence, option c

Applications of TIR

Optical Fibre

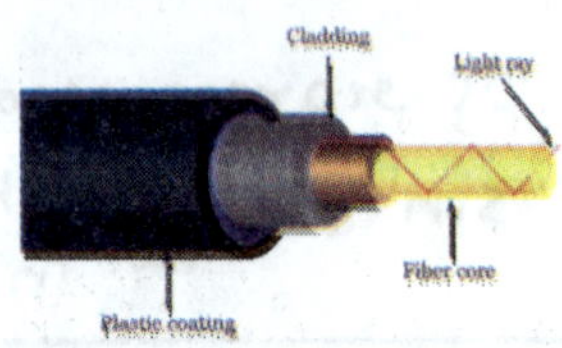

- Use to transmit signals over a large distance without loosing much strength.
- Ray travels in the core.
- For TIR, $\mu_{core} > \mu_{cladding}$
- Angle at which, the ray enters in the core

$$\sin \angle i \leq \sqrt{\mu_{core} - \mu_{cladding}}$$

Radius of Visibility

- $R = \dfrac{d}{\sqrt{{}^1\mu_2^2 - 1}}$

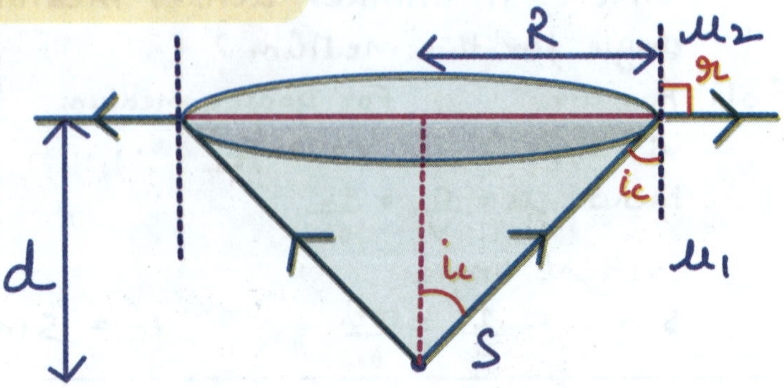

Refraction at Spherical Surface

- $\frac{\mu_2}{v} - \frac{\mu_1}{u} = \frac{\mu_2 - \mu_1}{R}$
- $m = \frac{\mu_1 v}{\mu_2 u}$

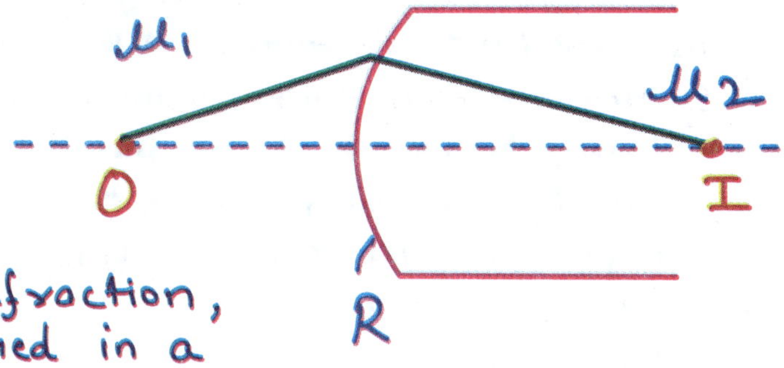

- In case of single refraction, image is always formed in a medium other than object medium.
- If image appears to be formed in the same medium as object, then it is a virtual image.
- These formulae are valid for real and apparent depth when R is taken as infinity.

Prism

- $\angle A \rightarrow$ Angle of Prism or Refracting Angle
- $\angle A = r_1 + r_2$
- $\delta = i + e - A$
- For 2 different i, δ is same.

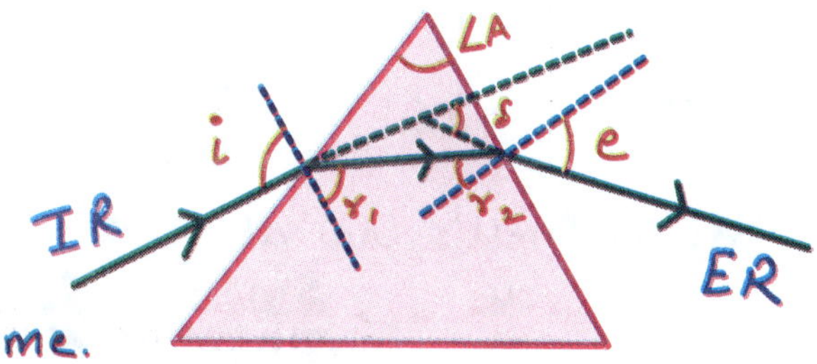

Minimum Deviation

- $r_1 = r_2 = r$ or $A = r/2$
- $i = e$
- $\delta_{min} = 2i - 2r$
- $$\mu = \frac{\sin\left(\frac{\delta_m + A}{2}\right)}{\sin\left(\frac{A}{2}\right)}$$
- For small angles

$\delta_{min} = (\mu - 1) A$

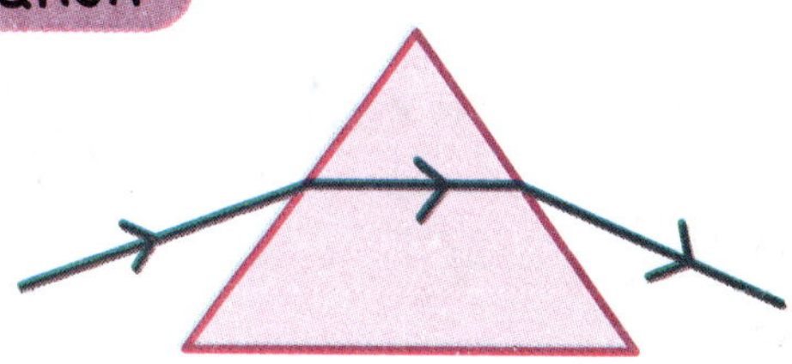

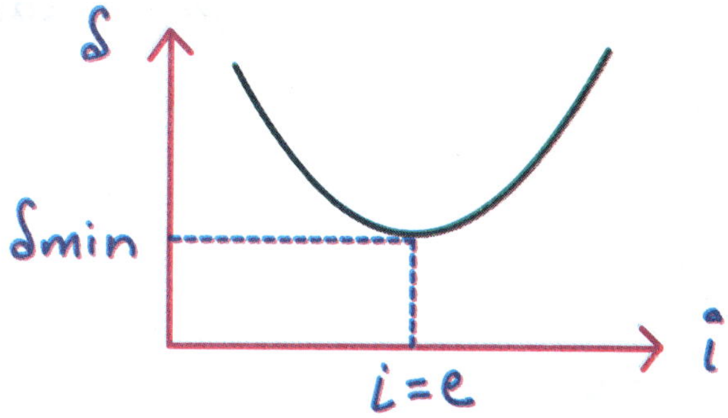

PYQ PUNCH

Q6. A light ray enters through a right angled prism at point P with the angle of incidence 30° as shown in the figure. It travels through the prism parallel to its base BC and emerges along the face AC. The refractive index of the prism is

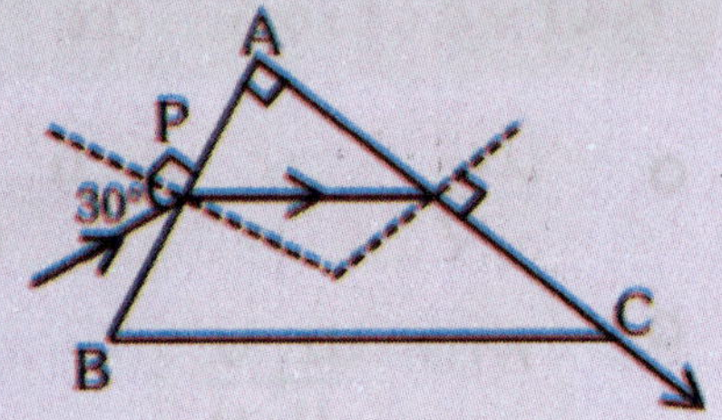

(NEET 2024)

Sol. $\angle A = 90°$; $\mu_{air} = 1$; $\mu_{prism} = \mu$

For prism

$\angle A = r_1 + r_2$

$r_2 = \angle A - r_1$

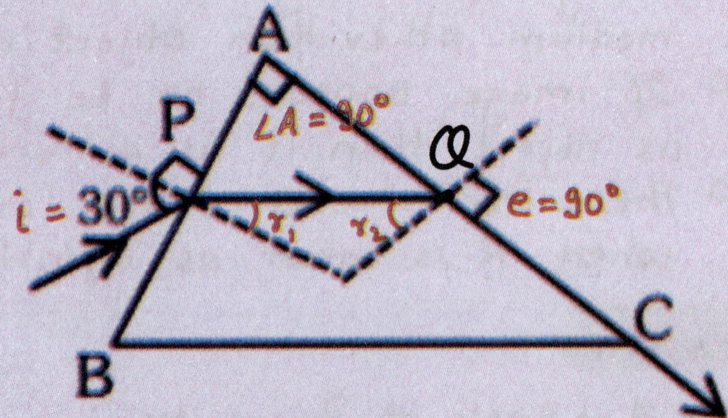

Apply Snell's Law at pt. P

$$\frac{\sin\angle i}{\sin\angle r} = \frac{\mu_2}{\mu_1}$$

$$\Rightarrow \frac{\sin 30°}{\sin\angle r_1} = \frac{\mu}{1}$$

$$\Rightarrow \sin\angle r_1 = 1/2\mu \text{ ------- } (1)$$

Apply Snell's Law at pt. Q

$$\frac{\sin\angle i}{\sin\angle r} = \frac{\mu_2}{\mu_1} \Rightarrow \frac{\sin\angle r_2}{\sin 90°} = \frac{1}{\mu} \Rightarrow \frac{\sin(\angle A - r_1)}{\sin 90°} = \frac{1}{\mu} \Rightarrow \cos\angle r_1 = \frac{1}{\mu} \text{ ------- } (2)$$

Square and add equations (1) and (2)

$$\sin^2\angle r_1 + \cos^2\angle r_1 = \left(\frac{1}{2\mu}\right)^2 + \left(\frac{1}{\mu}\right)^2$$

$$\Rightarrow \mu = \frac{\sqrt{5}}{2}$$

Special Cases of Prism

◎ **Emergent Ray normal to the Surface**

- $e = 0°$
- $r_2 = 0°$
- $A = r_1$
- $\delta = i - A$
- $\mu = \frac{\sin i}{\sin A}$

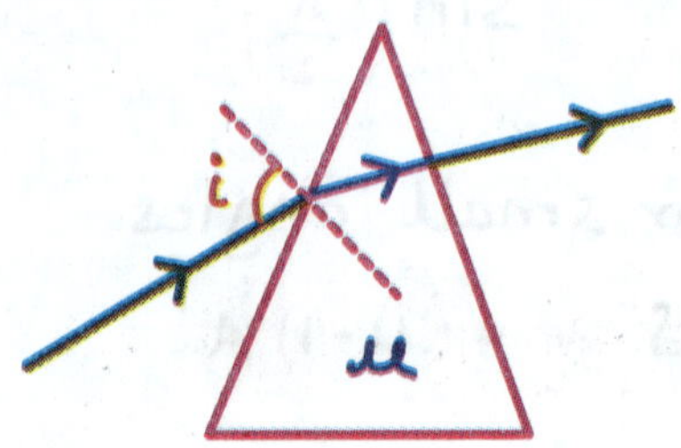

PYQ PUNCH

Q7. A ray of light is incident at an angle of incidence i, on one face of a prism of angle A (assumed to be small) and emerges normally from the opposite face. If the refractive index of the prism is μ, the angle of incidence i, is nearly equal to : (AIPMT 1989, 2012) (NEET 2020)

Sol. $\mu = \frac{\sin i}{\sin A}$

For small angles, $\sin i \approx i$ and $\sin A \approx A$

$\Rightarrow \mu = \frac{i}{A}$

$\Rightarrow i = \mu A$

◎ Refracted ray traces its path back

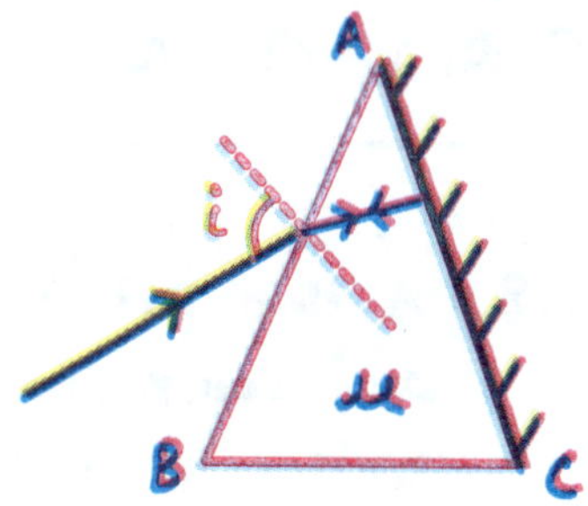

- Face AC is silvered.
- Refracted ray traces its path back after striking the surface AC.
- $A = r_1$
- $\delta = i - A$
- $\mu = \frac{\sin i}{\sin A}$

Dispersion

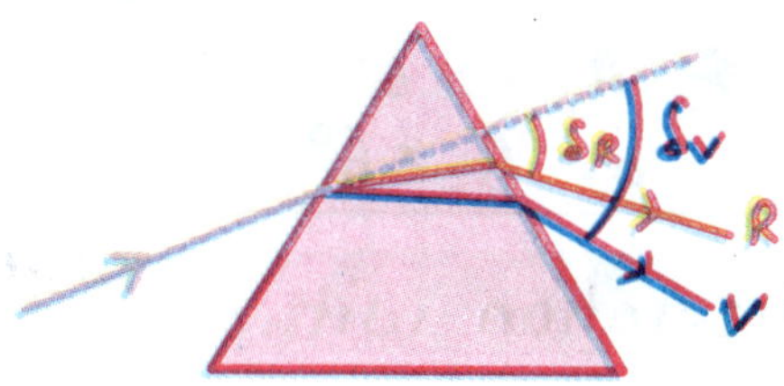

- Splitting of white light into seven constituents.
- It is due to different color has different speed (refractive index) in glass.
- $\mu \propto \frac{1}{\lambda^2}$
- Angular Dispersion

  $\theta = \delta_V - \delta_R = (\mu_V - \mu_R)A$
- Mean Deviation

  $\delta_{mean} = \frac{\delta_V + \delta_R}{2} = \delta_y$

- $\delta_{mean} = A\left(\frac{\mu_R + \mu_V}{2} - 1\right)$
- $\delta_{mean} = (\mu_{mean} - 1)$
- $\delta_{mean} = (\mu_{yellow} - 1)$

- Dispersive Power

$$\omega = \frac{\theta}{\delta_y} = \frac{\mu_V - \mu_R}{\mu_y - 1}$$

Dispersion without Deviation

- Emergent ray parallel to Incident ray.
- $\delta_{y_1} + \delta_{y_2} = 0$
- $A_1(\mu_1 - 1) + A_2(\mu_2 - 1) = 0$
- $\theta_{net} = \theta_1 + \theta_2$

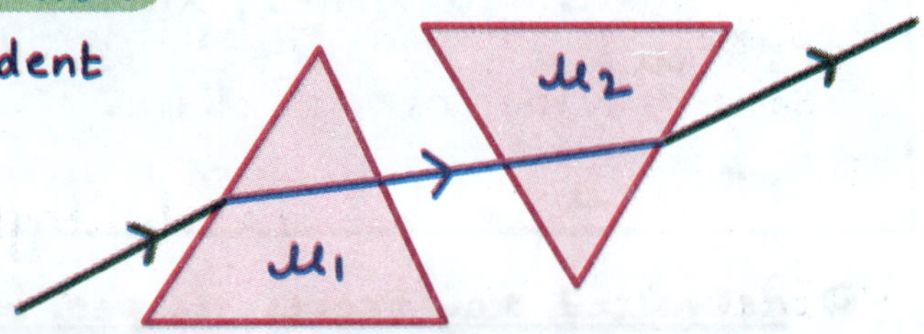

PYQ PUNCH

Q8. A thin prism having refracting angle 10° is made of glass of refractive index 1.42. The prism is combined with another thin prism of glass of refractive index 1.7. This combination produces dispersion without deviation. The refracting angle of second prism should be : (NEET 2017)

Sol. $A_1 = 10°$; $\mu_1 = 1.42$; $\mu_2 = 1.7$

$A_1(\mu_1 - 1) + A_2(\mu_2 - 1) = 0$

$\Rightarrow 10°(1.42 - 1) + A_2(1.7 - 1) = 0$

$\Rightarrow A_2 = -6°$

or $A_2 = 6°$ (Inverted)

Deviation without Dispersion

- White light enters, white ligit exists.
- $\theta_1 + \theta_2 = 0$
- $(\delta_{V_1} - \delta_{R_1}) + (\delta_{V_2} - \delta_{R_2}) = 0$
- Total Deviation

  $\delta_y = \delta_{y_1} + \delta_{y_2}$

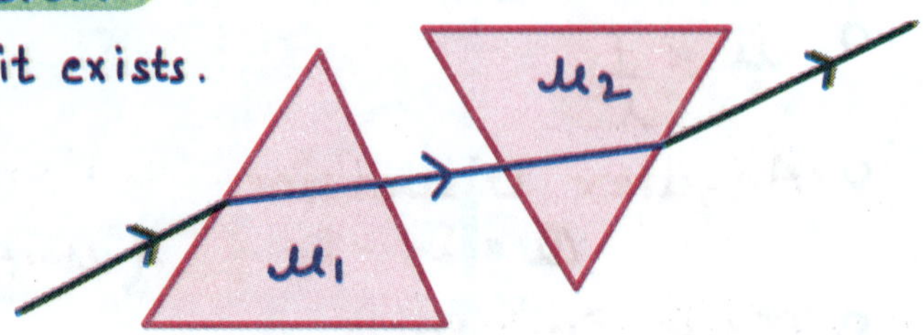

Lens

- It has 2 refracting surfaces out of which atleast one is curved.
- Types

Double Convex | Plano Convex | Concavo Convex | Double Concave | Plano Concave | Convexo Concave

- Since lens has 2 refracting surface, hence formed image in the same medium as of object.

Focal length of Lens

- Both $f_1 = f_2$
- It doesn't depend upon orientation.
- Depends upon the
  - shape of the lens
  - medium of lens
  - medium in which lens is placed

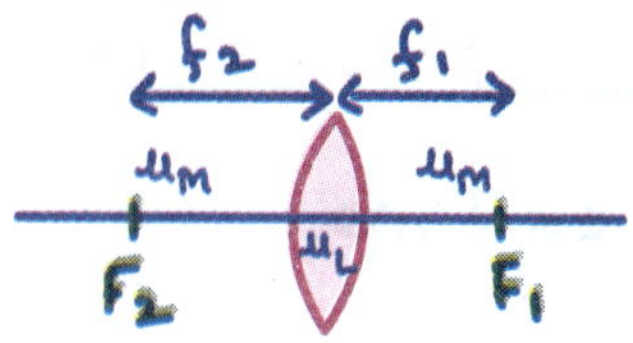

$$\frac{1}{f} = \left(\frac{\mu_L}{\mu_M} - 1\right)\left(\frac{1}{R_1} - \frac{1}{R_2}\right)$$

- For equi-convex & equi-concave lens

$$f = \frac{R}{2\left(\frac{\mu_L}{\mu_M} - 1\right)}$$

- For plano-convex & plano-concave lens

$$f = \frac{R}{\left(\frac{\mu_L}{\mu_M} - 1\right)}$$

  - For same radius of curvatures and refractive index of lenses

$$f_{concave} = -f_{convex}$$

- If a lens is dipped in water

$$f_w = 4 f_{air}$$

- If a lens is placed in a medium denser than its own medium,
  - Convergent lens become divergent i.e. Convex becomes Concave.

- Divergent lens become Convergent i.e. Concave becomes Convex.

PYQ PUNCH

Q9. A double convex len has focal length 25 cm. The radius of curvature of one of the surfaces is doubled of the other. Find the radii, if the refractive index of the material of the lens is 1.5. (NEET 2019)

Sol. $R_1 = R$; $R_2 = -2R$; $\mu_L = 1.5$; $\mu_m = 1$

Now

$$\frac{1}{f} = \left(\frac{\mu_L}{\mu_M} - 1\right)\left(\frac{1}{R_1} - \frac{1}{R_2}\right) \Rightarrow \frac{1}{25} = \left(\frac{1.5}{1} - 1\right)\left(\frac{1}{R} - \frac{1}{-2R}\right)$$

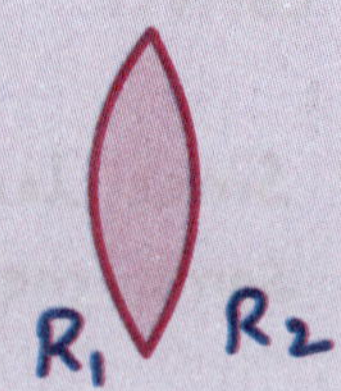

$\Rightarrow R = 18.75$ cm

Hence

$R_1 = R = 18.75$ cm ; $R_2 = 2R = 37.5$ cm

Ray Diagram

Ray is Parallel to Principal Axis

- Convex Lens

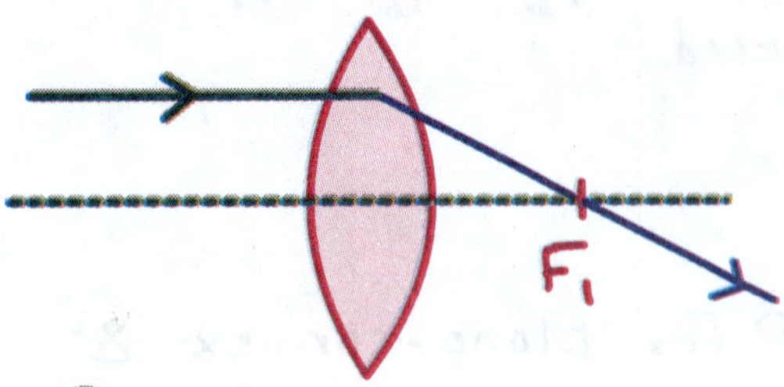

- Passes through focus.

- Concave Lens

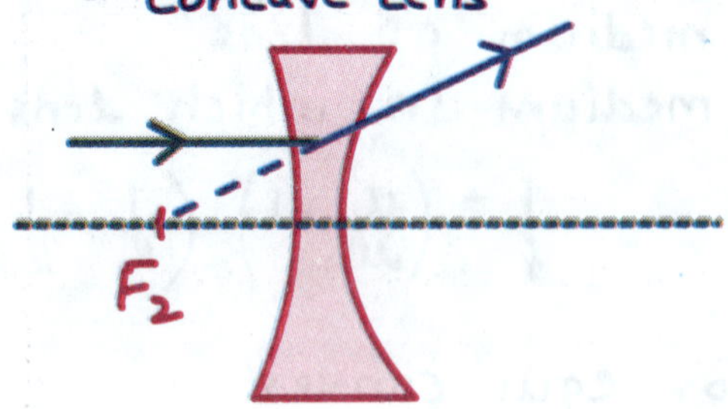

- ~~Passes~~ Appears to pass through focus.

Ray passes through Optical Centre

- Convex Lens

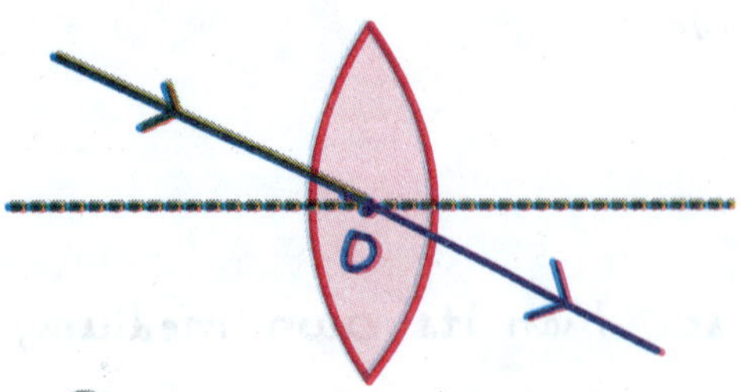

- Passes undeviated

- Concave Lens

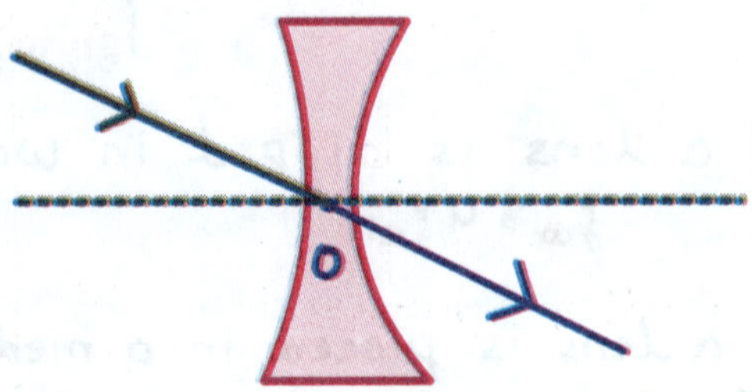

- Passes undeviated

Ray passes through Focus

- Convex Lens

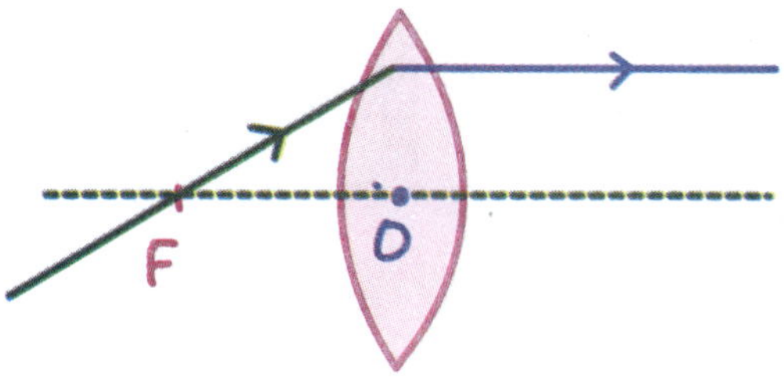

- Concave Lens

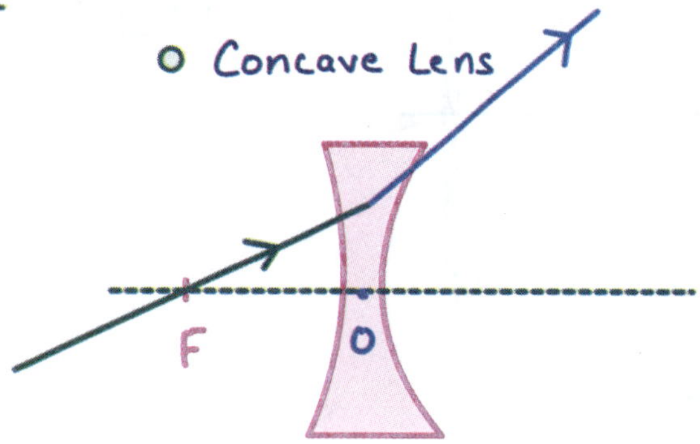

  - Parallel to Principal Axis.

Lens Formulae

- $\frac{1}{v} - \frac{1}{u} = \left(\frac{\mu_L}{\mu_M} - 1\right)\left(\frac{1}{R_1} - \frac{1}{R_2}\right)$ Lens Maker Formula
- $\frac{1}{v} - \frac{1}{u} = \frac{1}{f}$
- $m = \frac{v}{u}$ Lateral Magnification

Power of a Lens

- Ability to bend the ray of light.
- $P_{lens} = \frac{1}{f}$
- Types of Power

Positive Power
- Bends the rays towards the principal axis.
- Convergent Lens

Negative Power
- Bends the rays away from the principal axis.
- Diverging Lens

Cutting of Lens

- **Longitudinally**

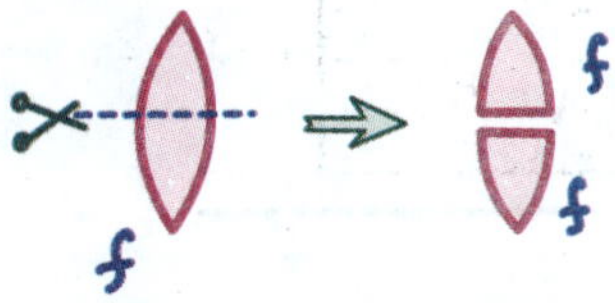

- No change in f.
- No change in P.
- Complete image get formed by each part but of less intensity.

- **Laterally**

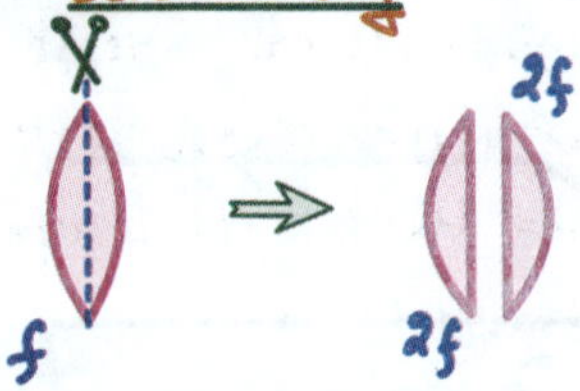

- Focal length increases.
- Power increases
- Complete image get formed by each part and of same intensity.

PYQ PUNCH

Q10. An equi-convex lens has power P it is cut into two symmetrical halves by a plane containing the principal axis. The power of one part will be: (NEET 2019)

Sol. Since cut longitudinally.
Power remains the same

$P' = P$

Combination of Lens

- Image get formed in the same medium as of object.

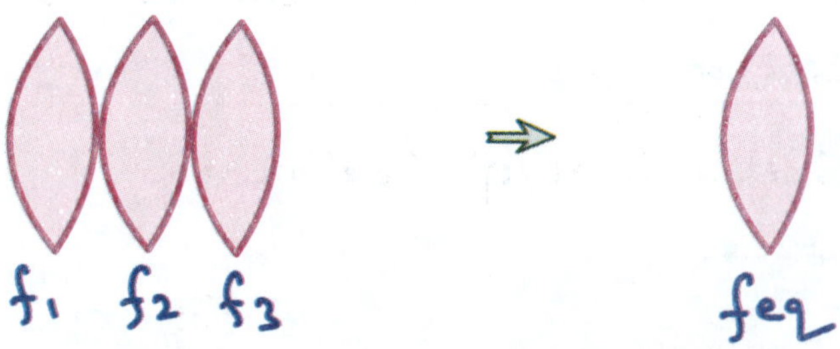

$$\frac{1}{f_{eq}} = \frac{1}{f_1} + \frac{1}{f_2} + \frac{1}{f_3} + \text{--------}$$

- Focal length of each lens is taken in the medium of object.
- Equivalent Power

$$P_{eq} = P_1 + P_2 + P_3 + \text{--------}$$

PYQ PUNCH

Q11. In the figure shown here, what is the equivalent focal length of the combination of lenses (Assume that all layers are thin)

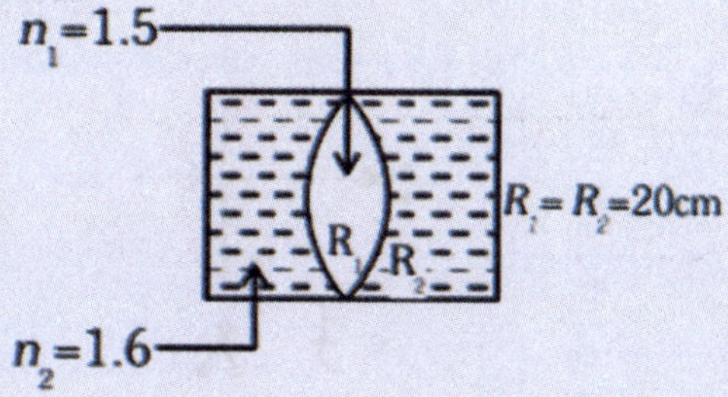

(NEET 2023)

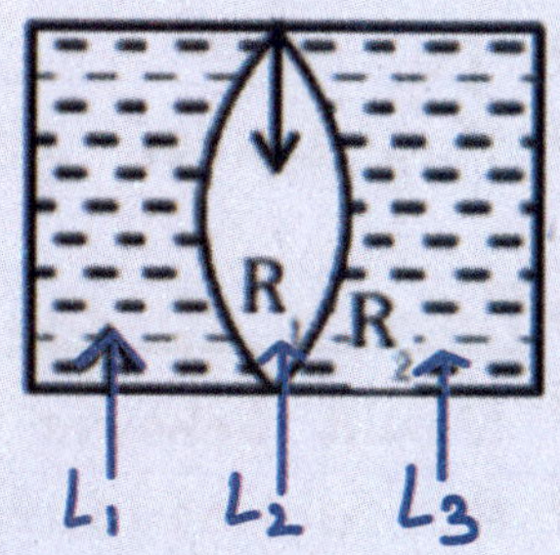

Sol. L_1 and L_3 are the same lenses.

$\mu_L = 1.6$; $\mu_m = 1$

$$\frac{1}{f} = \left(\frac{\mu_L}{\mu_M} - 1\right)\left(\frac{1}{R_1} - \frac{1}{R_2}\right)$$

$$\Rightarrow \frac{1}{f} = \left(\frac{1.6}{1} - 1\right)\left(\frac{1}{\infty} - \frac{1}{20}\right)$$

$$\Rightarrow f_1 = \frac{-20}{0.6} = f_3$$

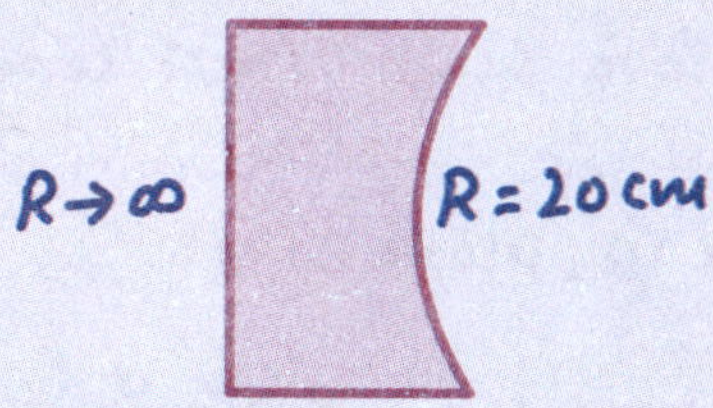

Lens 2 is a equi-convex lens

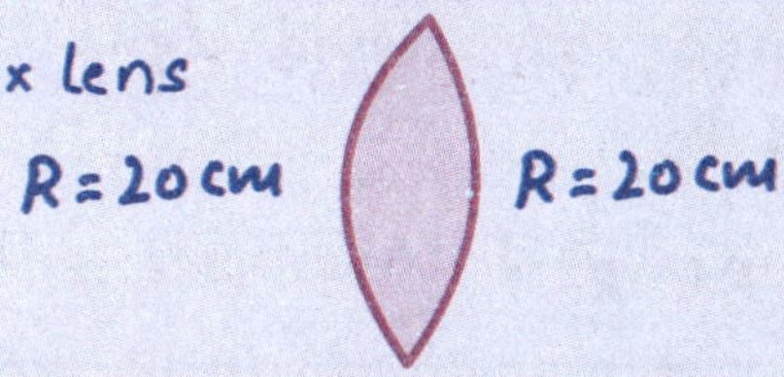

$$f = \frac{R}{2\left(\frac{\mu_L}{\mu_M} - 1\right)}$$

$$\Rightarrow f = \frac{20}{2\left(\frac{1.5}{1} - 1\right)} = 20 \text{ cm}$$

Now $\frac{1}{f_{eq}} = \frac{1}{f_1} + \frac{1}{f_2} + \frac{1}{f_3}$ $\Rightarrow \frac{1}{f_{eq}} = -\frac{0.6}{20} + \frac{1}{20} - \frac{0.6}{20}$

$$\Rightarrow f_{eq} = -100 \text{ cm}$$

Special Cases of Combination

◎ 2 pieces of lens

▹ Laterally

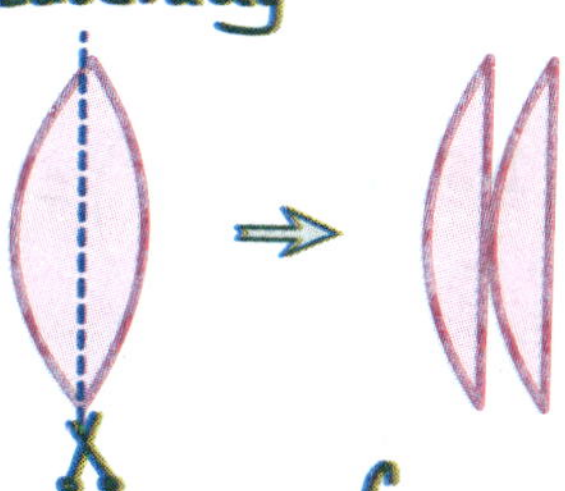

f $\quad$ $f_{eq} = f$

▹ Longitudinally

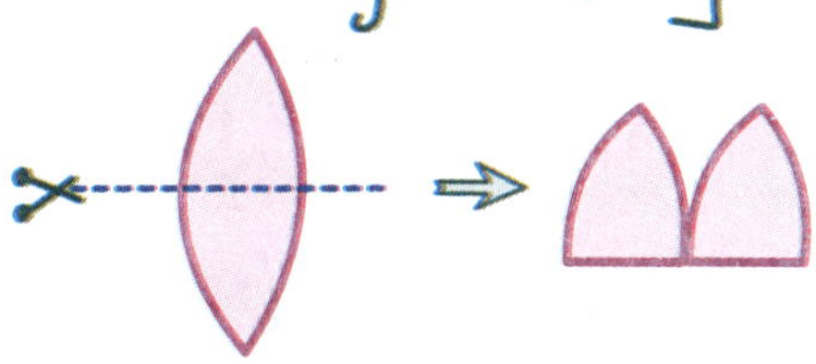

f $\quad$ $f_{eq} = \frac{f}{2}$

4 pieces of lens

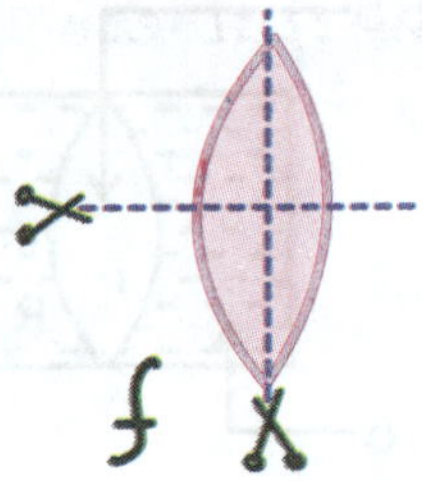

$\Rightarrow$

$$f_{eq} = \frac{f}{2}$$

Concave and Convex lenses of Equal Focal Length

- Both the lenses have same focal length f.
- $f_{eq} \rightarrow \infty$
- They behave like a plane sheet.

Pouring of Liquid between 2 lenses in contact

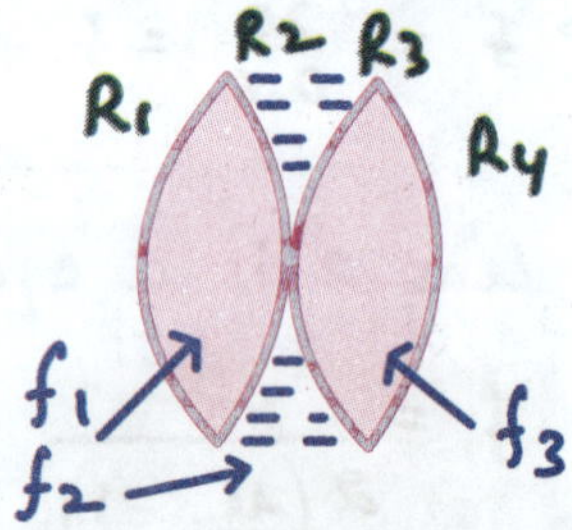

- Liquid behaves like a lens
- Refracting surfaces of liquid lens would be R_2 and R_3

$$\frac{1}{f_2} = \left(\frac{\mu_L}{\mu_M} - 1\right)\left(\frac{1}{R_2} - \frac{1}{R_3}\right)$$

PYQ PUNCH

Q12. Two similar thin equi-convex lenses, of focal length f each, are kept coaxially in contact with each other such that the focal length of the combination is F_1. When the space between the two lenses is filled with glycerine (which has the same refractive index $\mu = 1.5$ as that of glass), then the equivalent focal length is F_2. The ratio $F_1 : F_2$ will be **(NEET 2019)**

Sol. Focal length of each lens f.

$$\frac{1}{f} = \left(\frac{\mu_L}{\mu_M} - 1\right)\left(\frac{1}{R_1} - \frac{1}{R_2}\right) \Rightarrow \frac{1}{f} = \left(\frac{1.5}{1} - 1\right)\left(\frac{1}{R} + \frac{1}{R}\right)$$

Without Glycerine $\frac{1}{f_{eq}} = \frac{1}{f_1} + \frac{1}{f_2} \Rightarrow \frac{1}{F_1} = \frac{1}{f} + \frac{1}{f} \Rightarrow F_1 = \frac{f}{2}$ ---- ①

With glycerine $\frac{1}{f_2} = \left(\frac{\mu_L}{\mu_M} - 1\right)\left(\frac{1}{R_2} - \frac{1}{R_3}\right) \Rightarrow \frac{1}{f_2} = \left(\frac{1.5}{1} - 1\right)\left(\frac{-1}{R} - \frac{1}{R}\right) = \frac{-1}{f}$

$$\frac{1}{f_{eq}} = \frac{1}{f_1} + \frac{1}{f_2} + \frac{1}{f_3} \Rightarrow \frac{1}{F_2} = \frac{1}{f} - \frac{1}{f} + \frac{1}{f} = \frac{1}{f} \text{ ---- ②}$$

Using ① & ② $\Rightarrow \frac{1}{F_2} = \frac{1}{2F_1} \Rightarrow \frac{F_1}{F_2} = \frac{1}{2}$

Combination of lens with a distance between them

- Ray comes parallel to the principal axis and exists parallel to the principal axis from the combination of lens.

Both equi-convex lenses

- $d = f_1 + f_2$

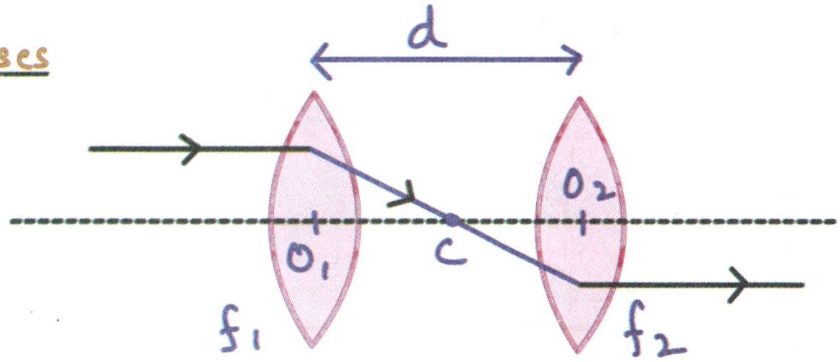

One Concave and one Convex

- $d = f_1 - f_2$

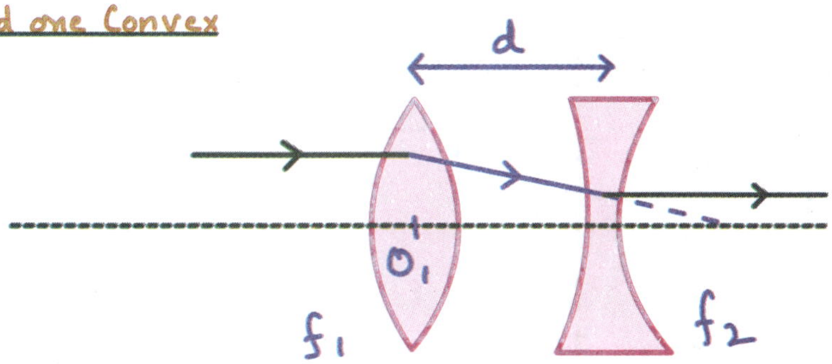

NEET Accelerate

- Radius of Curvature of the curved surface can be measured using Spherometer.
- If a lens is dipped in a liquid which has same refractive index as of lens, then it acts just as a plane sheet i.e. focal length becomes infinity.
- For a same lens, ray of different colors have different focal length. More the refractive index of the color in the glass, lesser the focal length.

  $f_V < f_I < f_B < f_G < f_Y < f_O < f_R$
- An achromatic combination of lenses is formed by joining 1 convex lens and 1 concave lens.
- Covering a part of lens only effects the intensity of image. Image height, size and location of image remains the same.

	Mirror	Spherical Surface	Lens
	$\frac{1}{v}+\frac{1}{u}=\frac{2}{R}$	$\frac{\mu_2}{v}-\frac{\mu_1}{u}=\frac{\mu_2-\mu_1}{R}$	$\frac{1}{v}-\frac{1}{u}=\left(\frac{\mu_2}{\mu_1}-1\right)\left(\frac{1}{R_1}-\frac{1}{R_2}\right)$
Focal Length	$\frac{1}{f}=\frac{2}{R}$	$\frac{\mu_2}{f}=\frac{\mu_2-\mu_1}{R}$	$\frac{1}{f}=\left(\frac{\mu_2}{\mu_1}-1\right)\left(\frac{1}{R_1}-\frac{1}{R_2}\right)$
	$\frac{1}{v}+\frac{1}{u}=\frac{1}{f}$	$\frac{\mu_2}{v}-\frac{\mu_1}{u}=\frac{\mu_2}{f}$	$\frac{1}{v}-\frac{1}{u}=\frac{1}{f}$
Lateral Magnification	$m=-\frac{v}{u}$	$m=\frac{\mu_1 v}{\mu_2 u}$	$m=\frac{v}{u}$
Image Medium	Same as Object	Different from Object	Same as Object
Image Speed	$\frac{dv}{dt}=-\frac{v^2}{u^2}\frac{du}{dt}$	$\frac{dv}{dt}=\frac{\mu_1 v^2}{\mu_2 u^2}\frac{du}{dt}$	$\frac{dv}{dt}=\frac{v^2}{u^2}\frac{du}{dt}$

Displacement Method

- It is used to find the focal length of convex lens.
- Object and screen are fixed while lens is moved.

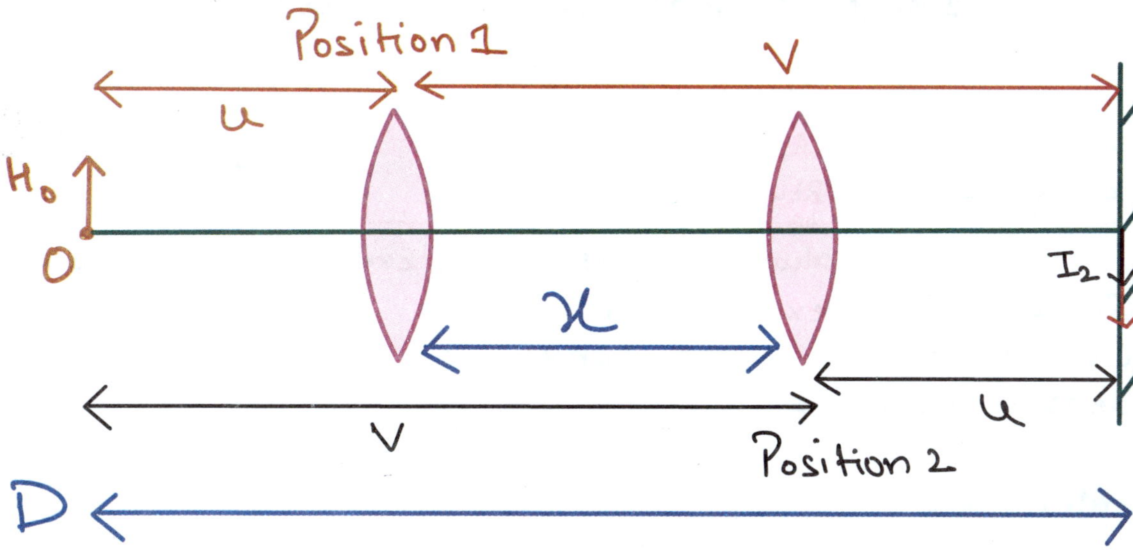

- While moving lens, u becomes v & v becomes u.
- $f = \frac{D^2 - x^2}{4D}$
- $H_o = \sqrt{I_1 I_2}$
- Area of Image I_1 be A_1. Area of Image I_2 be A_2. Then, area of object

$$A_o = \sqrt{A_1 A_2}$$

Image Formation by Convex Lens

Object	Image	Nature	Size
At infinity	At F	R & I	Highly Diminished
Btw ∞ & 2F	Btw 2F & F	R & I	Diminished
At 2F	At 2F	R & I	Same Size
Btw 2F & F	Btw ∞ & 2F	R & I	Enlarged
At F	At infinity	R & I	Highly Enlarged
Btw F & O	Behind Mirror	V & E	Enlarged

- Same as Concave Mirror.
- Convex lens becomes diverging if placed in a denser medium.
- An air bubble in water behaves like a diverging lens.

Image Formation By Concave Lens

Object	Image	Nature	Size
At infinity	At F	V & E	Highly Diminished
At any point	Btw O & F	V & E	Diminished

- Concave Lens always forms EVS (Erect, Virtual, Small).
- Same as Convex Mirror.
- Concave lens becomes converging, if placed in a denser medium.

Human Eye

- Near point of human eye is 25cm (D). Eyes are strained.
- D is also called as Distance of Distinct Vision.
- Far point of human eye is Infinity. Eyes are relaxed.
- Myopia
  - Near Sightedness
  - Person not able to see far away objects clearly.
  - Concave lens is used.
- Hypermetropia
  - Far Sightedness
  - Person not able to see near by objects clearly.
  - Convex lens is used.

Optical Instrument

- Any device which helps our eyes to see object.
- Normal Adjustment
  - Instrument forms image at infinity (far point) from eye.
- Nearby Adjustment
  - Instrument forms image at D (near point) of eye.

Simple Microscope

- It consists of a simple convex lens.
- Used for magnification upto 9 times.
- **Nearby Adjustment**
  - Object is placed just inside the focus.
  - Image is virtual, erect and magnified.
  - Magnification

$$m = \left(1 + \frac{D}{f}\right)$$

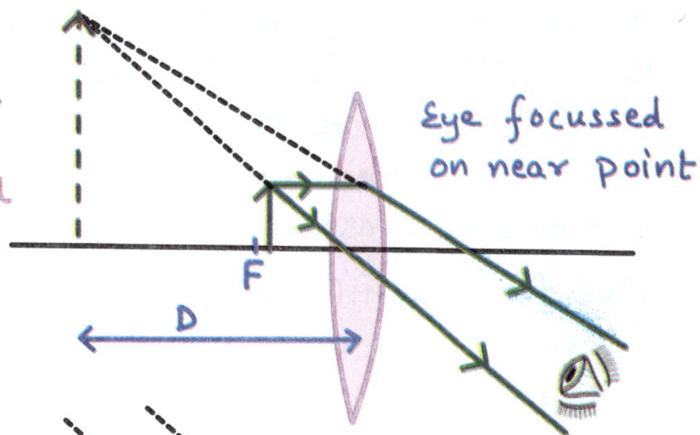

- **Normal Adjustment**
  - Object is placed at focus.
  - Image is virtual, erect and magnified.
  - Angular Magnification

$$m = \frac{D}{f}$$

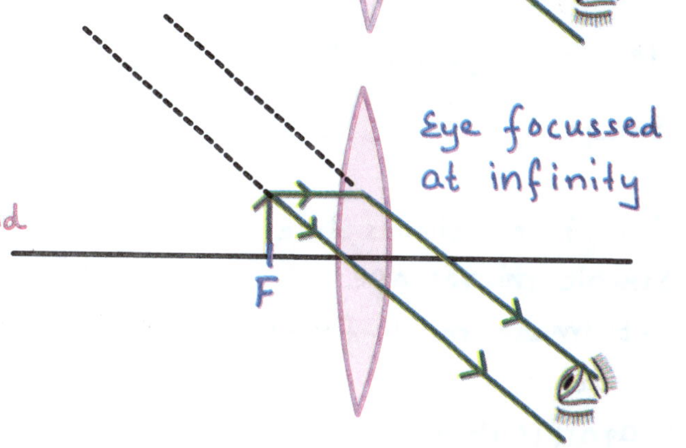

MCQ PUNCH

Q13. A microscope is focussed on a mark on a piece of paper and then a slab of glass of thickness 3cm and refractive index 1.5 is placed over the mark. How should the microscope be moved to get the mark in focus again?

Sol. Due to rectangular slab, there is a shift of object.

Shift $= t\left(1 - \frac{1}{\mu}\right) = 3\left(1 - \frac{1}{1.5}\right) = 1\text{cm}$

The shift is upward, hence the microscope is to be moved upward 1 cm.

Compound Microscope

- It has 2 lenses.
  - One near to eye is called as eye-piece (f_e)

- One near the object is called as objective lens (f_o)

- $f_o < f_e$
- Object is placed just outside the F_o.
- The distance L i.e. the distance between the second focal point of the objective and the first focal point of the eye-piece is called the tube length of the compound microscope.
- Distance between two lenses can be adjusted using a screw.
- L remains constant for a microscope.
- Use for magnification upto 100 times. Beyond that electron microscope is used, which works on the theory of wave optics.

- **Nearby Adjustment**
  - Image is virtual, erect and magnified.
  - Eye-piece behaves like a simple microscope.
  - 1st image must form inside Fe.
  - Magnification

$$m = -\frac{L}{f_o}\left(1 + \frac{D}{f_e}\right)$$

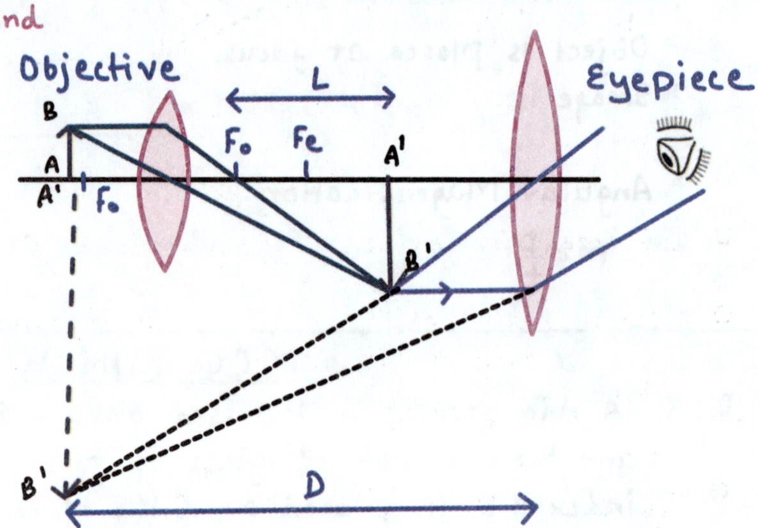

- **Normal Adjustment**
  - Image is virtual, erect and magnified.
  - Eye-piece behaves like a simple microscope.
  - 1st image must form at Fe.
  - Angular Magnification

$$m = -\frac{L}{f_o}\left(\frac{D}{f_e}\right)$$

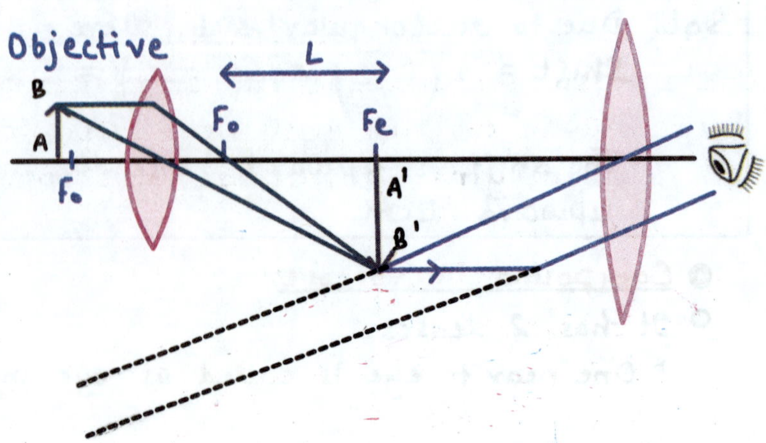

Astronomical Telescope

- Used to see far-away objects.
- It is just like a compound microscope. Infact reversing a compound microscope leads to telescope.
- $f_o > f_e$
- Objective lens is made bigger so that more amount of light could enter. This helps in resolution.

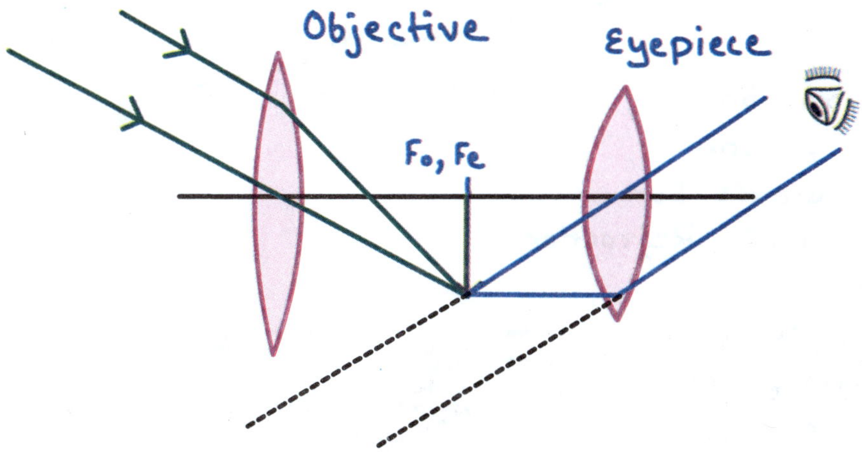

- 1st image is formed at focal plane as object is at infinity.
- **Nearby Adjustment**

  $m = f_o\left(\frac{1}{f_e} + \frac{1}{D}\right)$

- **Normal Adjustment**

  $m = \frac{-f_o}{f_e}$

- **Tube Length** $L = |f_o| + |f_e|$

PYQ PUNCH

Q14. A small telescope has an objective of focal length 140 cm and an eye piece of focal length 5 cm. The magnifying power of telescope for viewing a distant object is (NEET 2024)

Sol. $f_o = 140\,cm$; $f_e = 5\,cm$

$m = \frac{-f_o}{f_e} = \frac{-140}{5} = -28$

$\Rightarrow m = 28$ inverted

Galileo Telescope

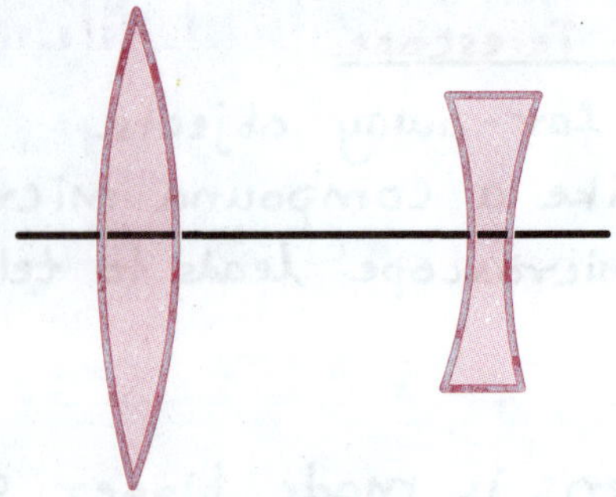

- **Tube Length**

  $L = |f_o| - |f_e|$

- Rest everything same.

Rainbow

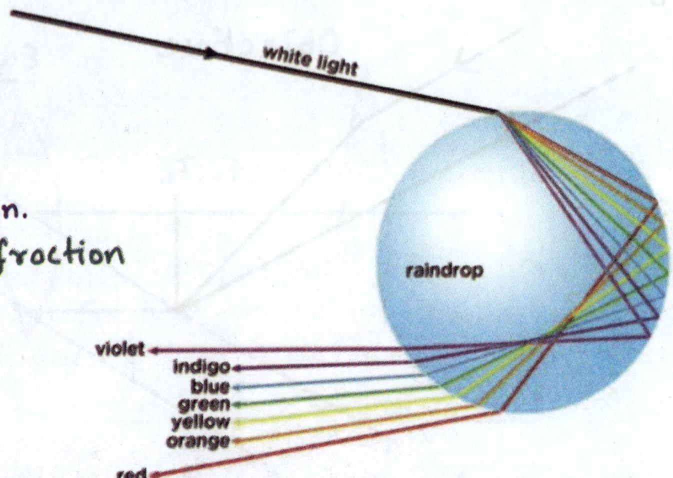

Primary Rainbow

- To see the rainbow, back of the person should be towards Sun.
- Refraction - TIR - Refraction takes place.
- In primary rainbow, violet is above and red is below.
- Secondary rainbow is formed above the primary rainbow.
- In secondary rainbow, red is above and violet is below.

29. Wave Optics

Dual Nature

- Newton - Light made up of particles
  Explain Rectilinear propagation, Reflection, Refraction.
- Huygen - Light is a disturbance.
  Explains Rectilinear Propagation, Interference, Diffraction, Reflection, Refraction.

Wavefront

- Light being a wave, its phase changes as it travels.
- Wavefront is a surface formed by joining the points of same phase.
- Each point on the wavefront acts as a secondary source emitting secondary waves in all directions.
- Direction of propagation of wave is always perpendicular to the wavefront.

Types of Wavefront

Spherical

- Formed by point source.

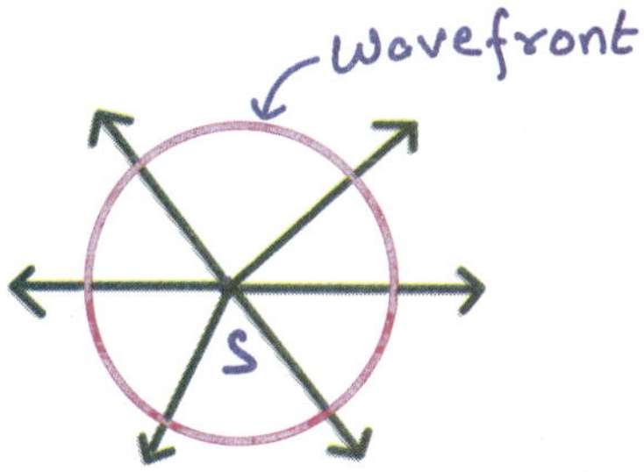

Cylindrical

- Formed by wire source.

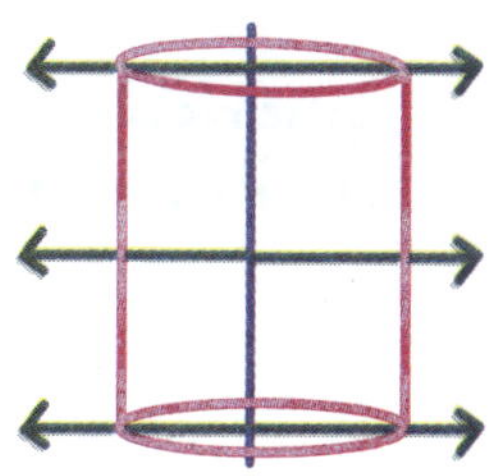

Plane

- Formed by plane source or by point source at infinite distance.

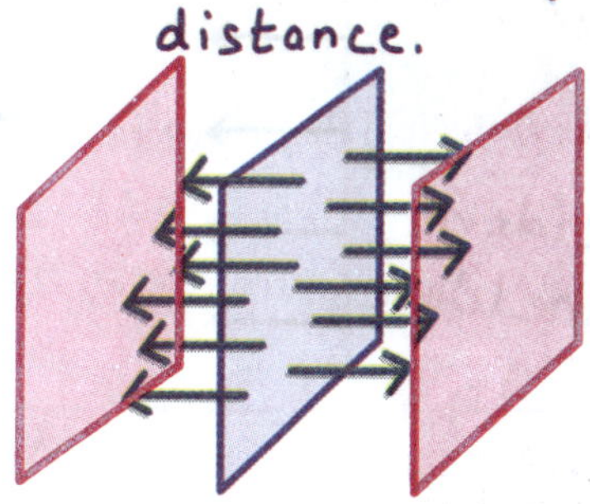

Huygens' Principle

- It is essentially a geometrical construction method which gives the shape of wavefront at a later time τ if we know the shape of wavefront at current time.

- Steps to draw wavefront at time τ.
  - Consider points of initial wavefront as a secondary sources of light.
  - Draw an arc of radius vτ from each secondary sources.
  - Draw the common tangent of all these arcs. This is the required wavefront.

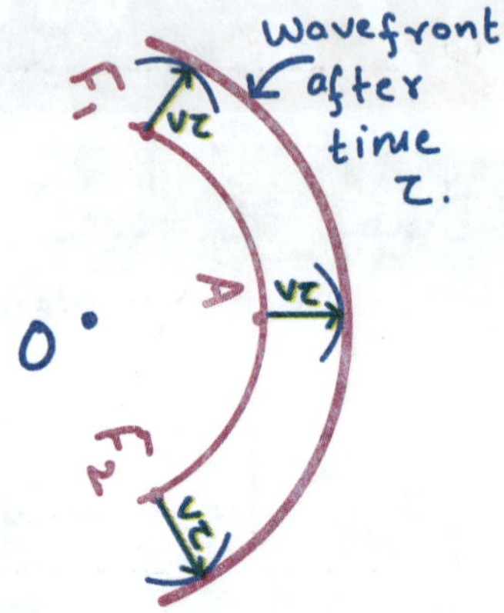

Reflection/ Refraction of Plane Wave

- **Prism**

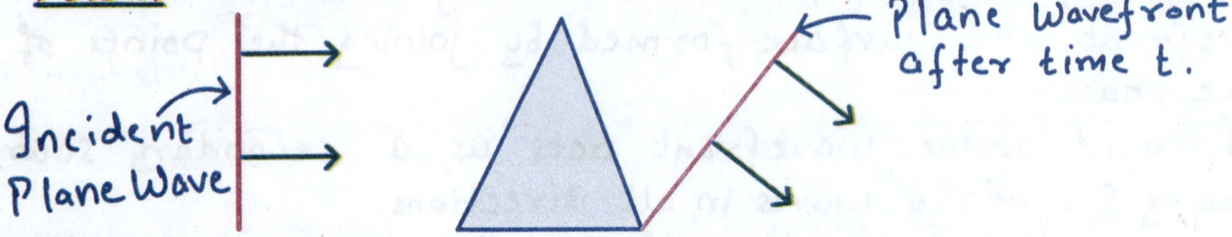

- **Convex Lens**

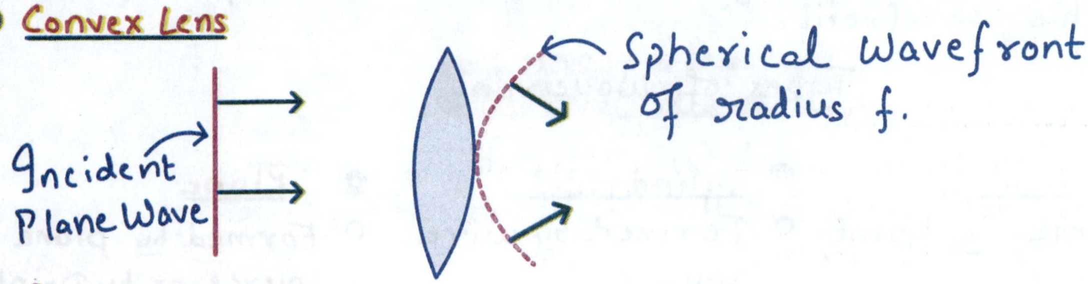

- **Concave Mirror**

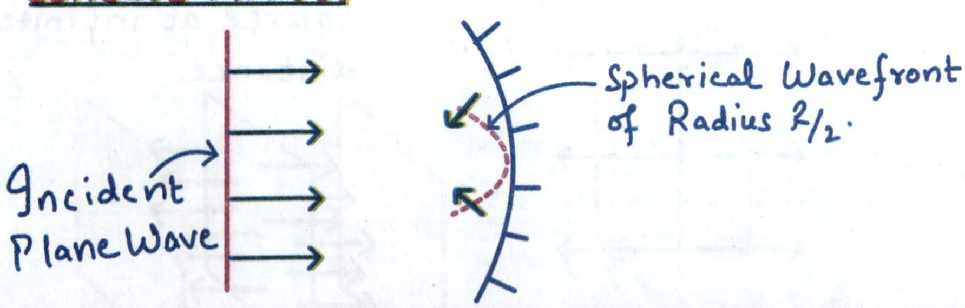

NEET Accelerate

- Easy way to draw wavefront is to replace wave by particle travelling on a straight path with speed v_1 in air and $v_2 < v_1$ in medium. Join their location after τ time to get the shape of new wavefront.

Reflection by Plane Mirror

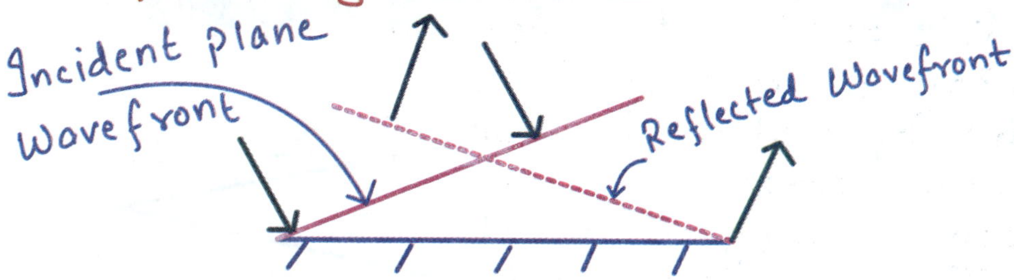

Refraction by Plane Surface

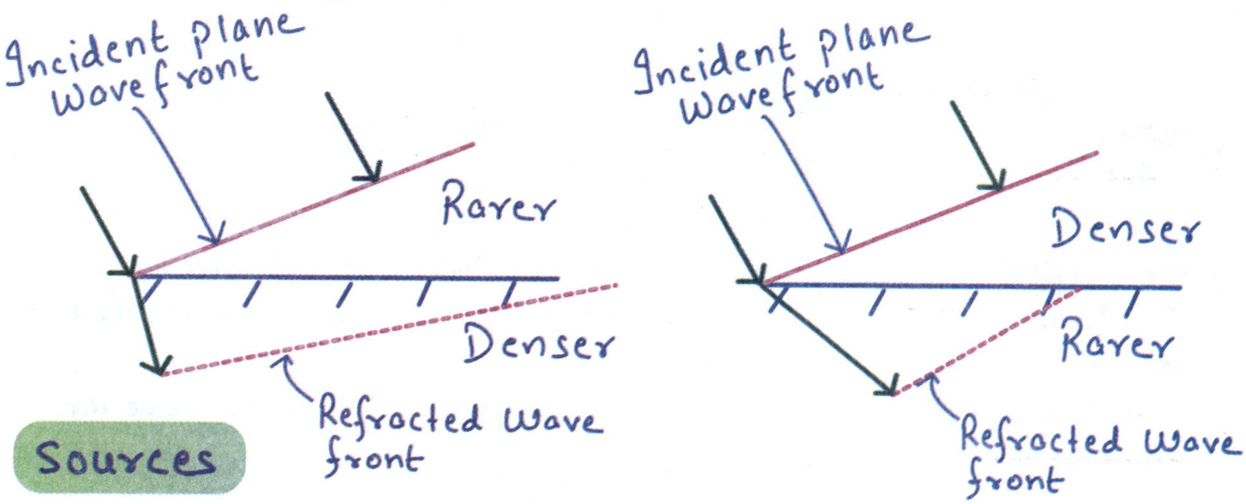

Sources

Coherent Sources

- Sources have same wavelength.
- Phase difference at the point of interference doesn't change with time.
- It is impossible to have 2 coherent sources of light.
- LASER lights are the nearest example of coherent sources.
- Only coherent sources can form dark and bright fringe pattern on the screen.

Incoherent Sources

- Phase difference at a point of interference changes continuously.
- They don't form dark and bright fringe pattern.
- Average intensity at the point of interference is the algebric sum of Intenties of two waves.

Relationship between Phase Diff. and Path Diff.

- Path difference at pt. P

$$\Delta x = x - y$$

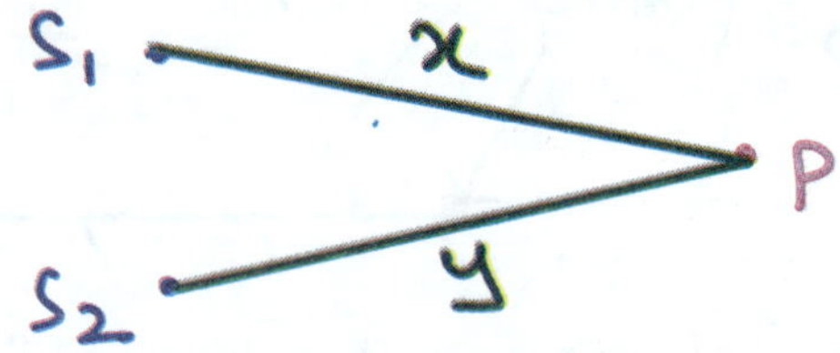

- $$\Delta\phi = \frac{2\pi}{\lambda}.\Delta x$$

$\Delta\phi$ is the phase difference at the pt. of interference.

Interference & Principle of Super-position

- It is the phenemonen when two waves meet.
- Principle of super-position states that the net electric field at the point of interference is the vector addition of electric field of 2 waves at that point.
- Amplitude of Electric Field at the point of interference is given by

$$A_{net} = \sqrt{A_1^2 + A_2^2 + 2A_1A_2\cos\Delta\phi}$$

where A_1 is the max Electric Field of Wave 1
A_2 is the max Electric Field of Wave 2

Types of Interference

Constructive Interference

- Amplitude is max

$A_{max} = A_1 + A_2$ for $\Delta\phi = 2n\pi$, $\Delta x = n\lambda$ where $n = 0, \pm1, \pm2, \pm3, \ldots$

Destructive Interference

- Amplitude is minimum

$A_{min} = |A_1 - A_2|$ for $\Delta\phi = (2n+1)\pi$, $\Delta x = \left(n+\frac{1}{2}\right)\lambda$ where $n = 0, \pm1, \pm2, \pm3, \ldots$

Intensity

- For a spherical wave, $I \propto A^2$

Net Intensity at Interference

- In terms of phase difference

$$I_{net} = I_1 + I_2 + 2\sqrt{I_1 I_2}\cos\Delta\phi$$

where I_1 & I_2 are the intensities of wave 1 and 2 respectively.

- In terms of path difference

$$I_{net} = I_1 + I_2 + 2\sqrt{I_1 I_2}\cos\frac{2\pi}{\lambda}\Delta x$$

- Most of the time $I_1 = I_2 = I_0$

$$I_{net} = 4I_0\cos^2\frac{\Delta\phi}{2}$$

- **Constructive Interference**
  - $I_{max} = (\sqrt{I_1} + \sqrt{I_2})^2$
  - If $I_1 = I_2 = I_0$
    - $I_{max} = 4I_0$

- **Destructive Interference**
  - $I_{min} = (\sqrt{I_1} - \sqrt{I_2})^2$
  - If $I_1 = I_2 = I_0$
    - $I_{min} = 0$

- **Incoherent sources**
  - $I_{net} = I_1 + I_2$
  - If $I_1 = I_2 = I_0$
    - $I_{net} = 2I_0$

Young's Double Slit Experiment

- For $d << D$

$$\Delta x = d\tan\theta = \frac{yd}{D}$$

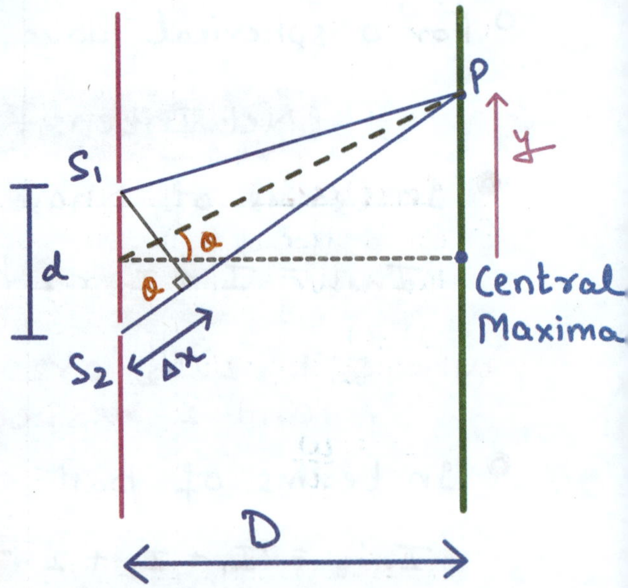

For Constructive Interference

- $y = \frac{n\lambda D}{d}$, where $n = 0, 1, 2, 3, ..$

n	Name	Distance	$\Delta\phi$	Δx
0	Central Maxima	$y_0 = 0$	0	0
1	Ist Maxima	$y_1 = \frac{\lambda D}{d}$	2π	λ
2	2nd Maxima	$y_2 = \frac{2\lambda D}{d}$	4π	2λ
3	3rd Maxima	$y_3 = \frac{3\lambda D}{d}$	6π	3λ

- Intensity is Maximum

For Destructive Interference

- $y = \left(n+\frac{1}{2}\right)\frac{\lambda D}{d}$, where $n = 0, 1, 2, 3, ..$

n	Name	Distance	$\Delta\phi$	Δx
0	Ist Minima	$y_1 = \frac{\lambda D}{2d}$	π	$\frac{\lambda}{2}$
1	2nd Minima	$y_2 = \frac{3\lambda D}{2d}$	3π	$\frac{3\lambda}{2}$
2	3rd Minima	$y_3 = \frac{5\lambda D}{2d}$	5π	$\frac{5\lambda}{2}$
3	4th Minima	$y_4 = \frac{7\lambda D}{2d}$	7π	$\frac{7\lambda}{2}$

- Intensity is minimum

Fringe width (β)

- It is the distance between 2 consecutive bright or dark fringes. $\beta = \frac{\lambda D}{d}$
- d should be comparable to λ so that β is sufficiently large to observe the pattern.

Angular Fringe width

- $\theta = \frac{\omega}{D} = \frac{\lambda}{d}$
- Angular separtion of the fringes ↑ with ↑ of wavelength.

Complete set up in Fluid

- On immersing the set up in fluid of refractive index μ, the wavelength changes to

  $\lambda' = \frac{\lambda}{\mu}$

- $\omega' = \frac{\omega}{\mu}$

Intensity pattern

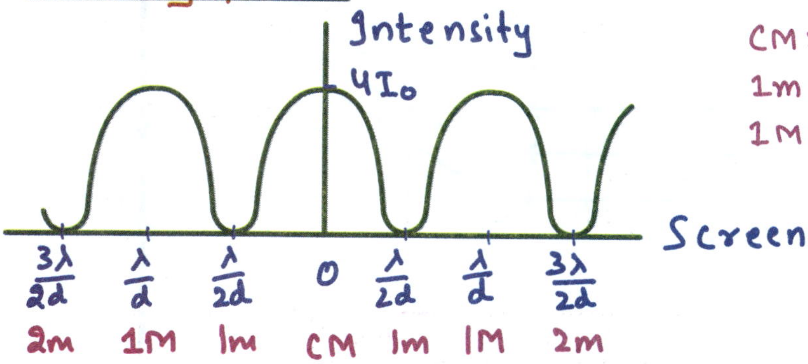

CM: Central Maxima
1m: Ist minima
1M: Ist Maxima

PYQ PUNCH

Q1. In a Young's double slit experiment, if there is no initial phase-difference between the light from the two slits, a point on the screen corresponding to the fifth minimum has path difference. (NEET 2020)

Sol. For minimum

$\Delta x = \left(n + \frac{1}{2}\right)\lambda \quad n = 0, \pm 1, \pm 2, \pm 3, \ldots$

For 5th minimum, $n = 4$

$\Rightarrow \Delta x = \left(4 + \frac{1}{2}\right)\lambda$

$= \frac{9\lambda}{2}$

NEET Accelerate

- Number of fringes in the same region of the screen for two different wavelengths are related as

$$\lambda_1 n_1 = \lambda_2 n_2$$

- If a mono-chromatic light is replaced by a white light, then there will be a central bright white fringe surrounded by a few coloured fringes.
- Intensity of light is directly proportional to width of the slit.

Single Slit

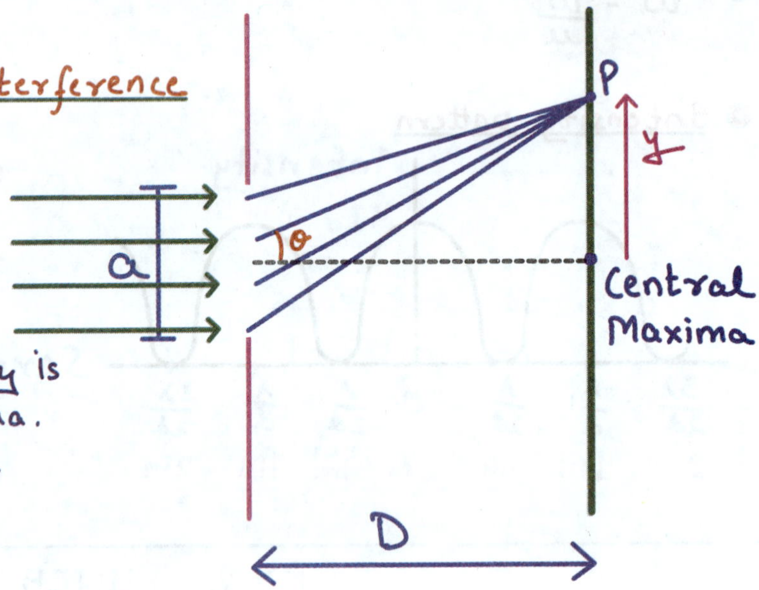

- **For constructive Interference**
- $\theta = \left(n+\frac{1}{2}\right)\frac{\lambda}{a}$

  where $n = 0, 1, 2, \ldots$
- Intensity varies at each maxima
- Most of the intensity is within central maxima.
- Angular width of the central maxima

$$\theta = \frac{2\lambda}{a}$$

- **For Destructive Interference**
- $\theta = \frac{n\lambda}{a}$ where $n = 1, 2, \ldots$

- **Intensity pattern**

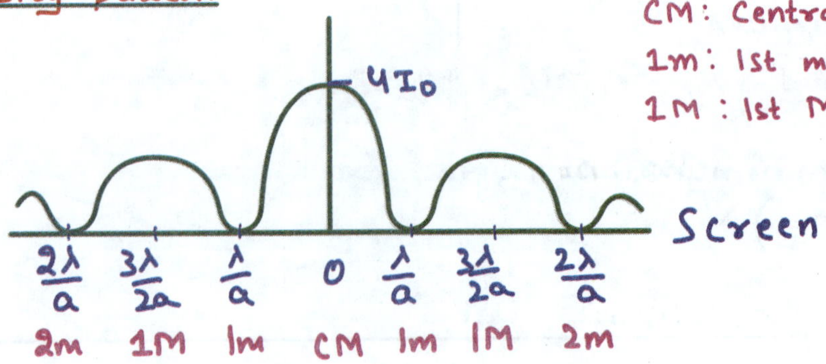

CM : Central Maxima
1m : 1st minima
1M : 1st Maxima

Polarization

- It is the property of transverse wave specifies the geometrical orientation of the oscillation.

Classification of waves on the basis of Polarization

Polarised Wave	Unpolarized Wave
Particles oscillate perpendicular to the propagation of wave in a fixed direction.	Direction of displacement of the particle changes randomly with time though it will always be perpendicular to the direction of propagation of wave.

Polarization of Light Wave

- Light wave is transverse in nature i.e. the electric field associated with a propagating light wave is always at right angle to the direction of propagation of the wave.
- Light emitted from an ordinary sources (like sodium lamp) is unpolarized.
- An unpolarized light can be polarized using Polaroids Sheets.

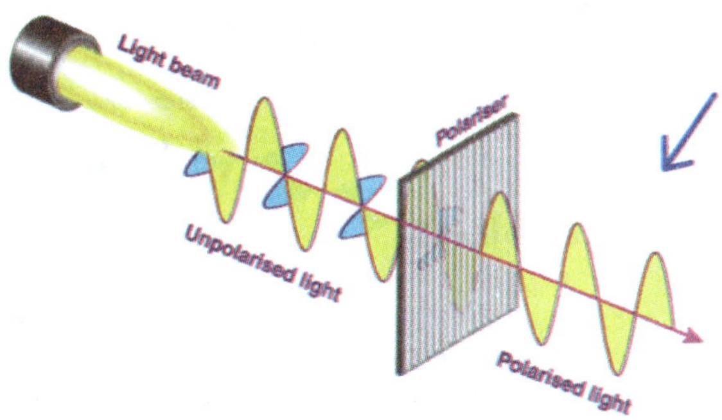

Oscillation along Pass-axis

- When an unpolarized light passes through a polaroid sheet, intensity becomes half.
- Pass-axis of the polaroid sheet is the one in which Electric field oscillates once it get polarized.

Law of Malus

- When a polarized light passes through a polaroid sheet, its intensity changes as per the law

$$I = I_0 \cos^2\theta$$

where θ is the angle between the Electric Field & Polarizer pass-axis.

A Polaroid sheet is rotated between crossed Polaroids

- An unpolarized light is passed through a system of 3 polaroid sheets placed such that their pass-through axis are inclined to each other.
- P_1 and P_3 are crossed polaroids i.e. their pass axes are at right angle.

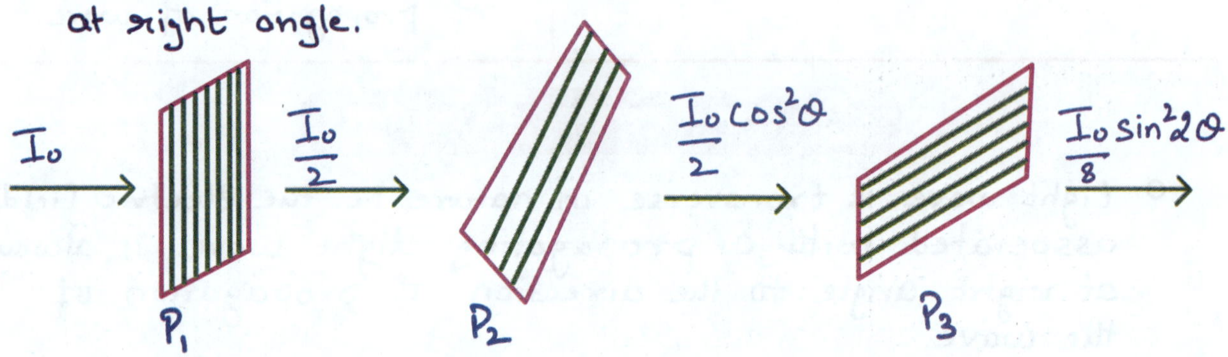

- Angle between P_1 and P_2 is θ.
- $I_f = \frac{I_0}{8}\sin^2 2\theta$

Brewster's Angle

- Unpolarized ray is incident on a reflecting surface.
- The reflected beam is completely polarised.
- The refracted beam is perpendicular to the reflected beam.
- The angle of incidence is Brewster's angle.
- $\tan i = \frac{\mu_2}{\mu_1}$

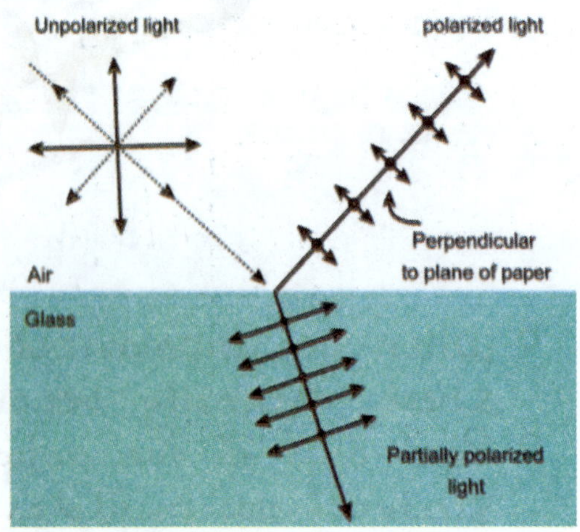

30. Dual Nature of Matter & Radiation

Some phenomenons of light can only be understood by wave nature and some by particle nature. Hence, light has dual nature.

Photon Theory of Light

- When light of sufficient low wavelength falls on a surface, e^-(s) are ejected. This phenomenon is called the Photoelectric Effect (PE Effect) and can be understood in terms of the particle nature of light.
- The particles of light are called photons.

Properties of Photon

- Photon is electrically neutral.
- It's rest mass is zero.
- Photons travel with the speed of 3×10^8 m/s.
- Photon doesn't get deviated in electro-magnetic field but gets deviated in gravitational field.
- Photons carry momentum.

$$p = \frac{h}{\lambda}$$

- Photons carry energy

$$E = \frac{hc}{\lambda} = h\nu = pc \simeq \frac{1240 \text{ eVnm}}{\lambda (\text{nm})}$$

where λ is wavelength
ν is frequency
h is Planck's Constant
$h = 6.626 \times 10^{-34}$ J/s

Irony of Light

Photon describes the particle nature of light but its momentum and energy are being described by wave nature of light.

- During collision of a photon and an electron the total energy and the total momentum remain conserved.

The photon may get absorbed or a new photon may get emitted. Thus the number of photons may not be conserved.

- Number of photons ∝ Intensity of Light
- Total energy of light = n × Energy of a photon.

$$TE = n \times \frac{hc}{\lambda}$$

- Power of Light Source = $\dot{n}$ × Energy of a photon.

$$P = \dot{n} \times \frac{hc}{\lambda}$$ where $\dot{n}$ is number of photons emitting per second.

PYQ PUNCH

Q1. The correct statements about photon among the following are

A. The energy of a photon is $E = h\nu$.

B. The velocity of a photon is c.

C. The momentum of a photon $p = \frac{h\nu}{c}$

D. In a photon-electron collision, both total energy and total momentum are conserved.

E. Photon possesses positive charge. (NEET 2024)

Sol. Options A, B, C and D are properties of photon.

Photoelectric Effect

- Photons lead to emission of electrons from the metal. The electrons are called as photo-electrons.
- It is the instantaneous process.
- A single photon can emit maximum of 1 electron.
- Energy of the photon must be greater than work function ϕ of the material.
- Maximum kinetic Energy of emitted photon

$$KE_{max} = \frac{hc}{\lambda} - \phi$$ ← Einstein Photoelectric Equation

- **Threshold Wavelength** (λ_0)
  - Maximum wavelength of photon for PE effect

$$\lambda_0 = \frac{hc}{\phi}$$

- **Threshold Frequency** (ν_0)
  - Minimum frequency of photon for PE effect.

$$\nu_0 = \frac{c}{\lambda_0} = \frac{\phi}{h}$$

PYQ PUNCH

Q2. The work function of Caesium, Potassium and Sodium are 2.14eV, 2.3eV and 2.75 eV respectively. If incident electromagnetic radiation has an incident energy of 2.2eV, which of these photosensitive surfaces may emit photoelectrons?

(NEET 2023)

Sol. $\phi_{caesium} < \frac{hc}{\lambda}$

Hence, only in this case P.E effect takes place.

Stopping Potential (V_0)

- It is the minimum negative potential of the discharge tube to stop the photoelectrons
- $eV_0 = KE_{max}$

or

$$V_0 = \frac{hc}{e}\left(\frac{1}{\lambda}\right) - \frac{\phi}{e}$$

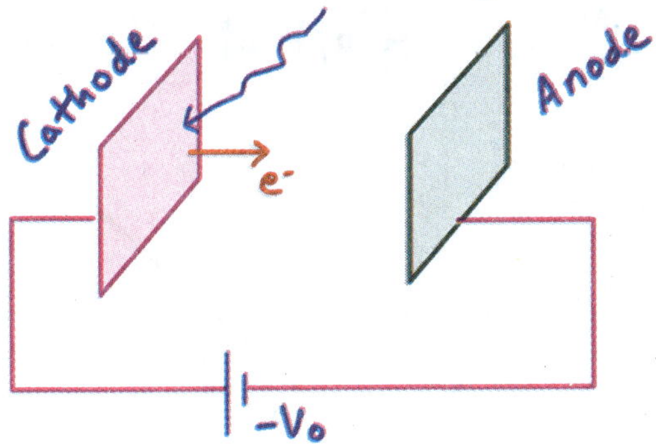

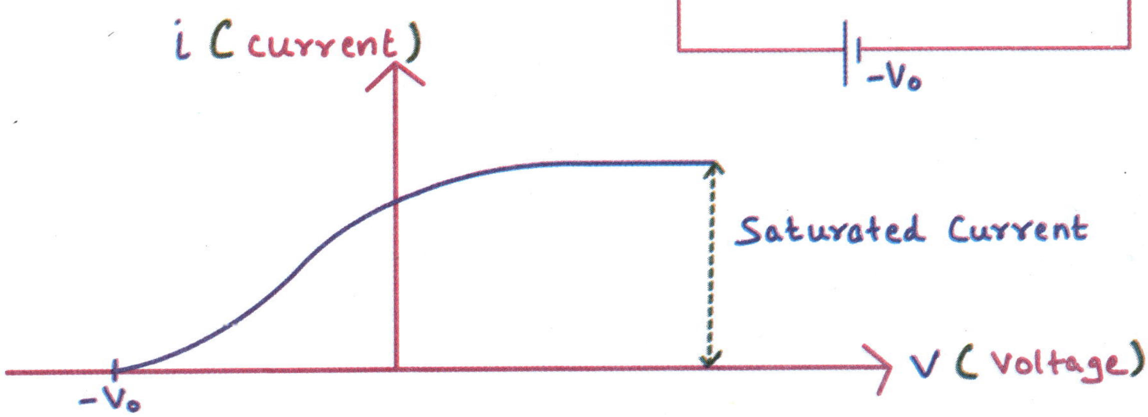

NEET Accelerate

- KE of photon during threshold is zero.
- Practically KE of photonelectrons varies from 0 to KE_{max}.
- Two photons having combined energy greater than work function can't cause PE effect.

Factors on which V_0 depends upon

Frequency of Light (ν)

$V_0 \uparrow$ as $\nu \uparrow$

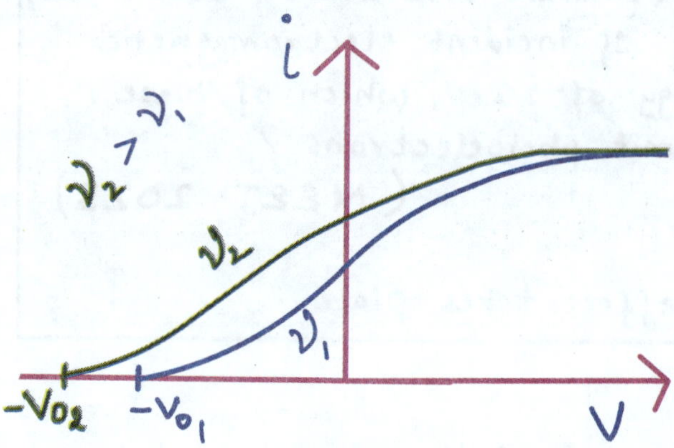

Intensity of Light (I)

V_0 is independent of Intensity

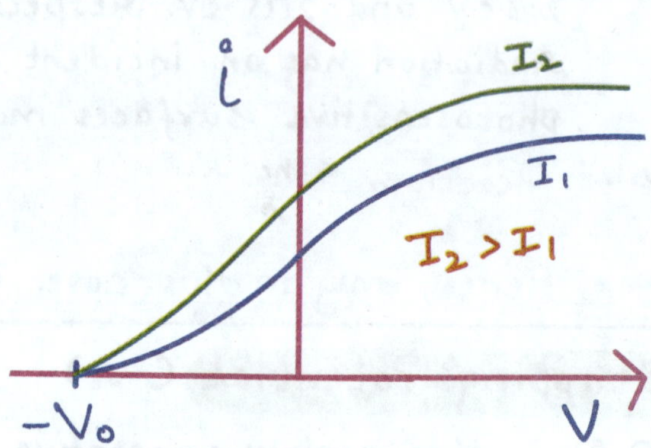

Graph of Stopping Potential vs Frequency

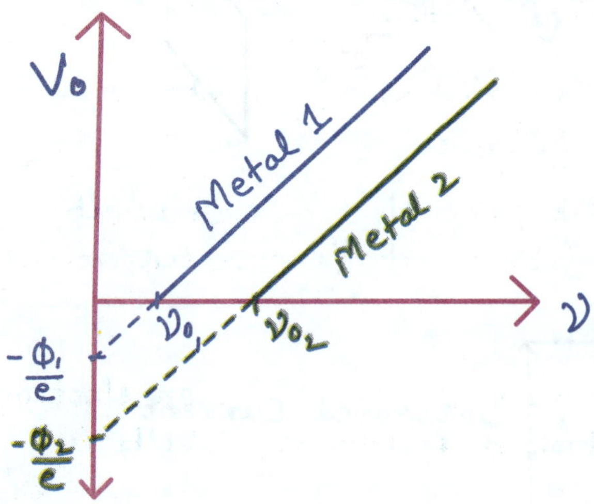

Slope $= \frac{h}{e}$

↑

- Independent of Material
- X-intercept gives threshold frequency.
- Y-intercept gives work function.

NEET Accelerate

- On increasing the distance between source and plate, both the intensity and photo-current decreases.

$$i \propto I \propto \frac{1}{r^2}$$

- More the Intensity, more the photons, more the photo-electrons, more the current.

$$i \propto \text{photo-electrons} \propto \text{photons} \propto \text{Intensity}$$

- More the frequency, more the energy, more the kinetic energy, more the Stopping potential.

$$V_0 \propto KE_{max} \propto E \propto \nu$$

- If ν is doubled, KE becomes more than double.

Wave Nature Failure to explain PE Effect

- Instantaneous Process.
- Threshold wavelength and frequency.

Wavelength of X-Ray produced

- X-Rays are produced by bombarding high energy electrons on metal.
- Minimum wavelength of produced X-Rays

$$\lambda_{min} = \frac{hc}{KE}$$ where KE is the maximum KE of bombarded electron.

$$\lambda_{min} = \frac{hc}{eV}$$ where V is the potential through which the electron was accelerated.

PYQ PUNCH

Q3. The minimum wavelength of X-rays produced by an electron accelerated through a potential difference of V volts is proportional to (NEET 2023)

Sol. $\lambda_{min} = \frac{hc}{eV} \Rightarrow \lambda_{min} \propto \frac{1}{V}$

Matter Wave

- According to de-Broglie, nature loves symmetry. If light has dual nature, then matter also possesses dual nature.
- Matter being particle, behaves like wave during travelling.

de-Broglie Wavelength of Matter

$$\lambda_d = \frac{h}{p}$$

where

λ_d : de-Broglie wavelength

p : momentum of particle

NEET 2015 & 2022

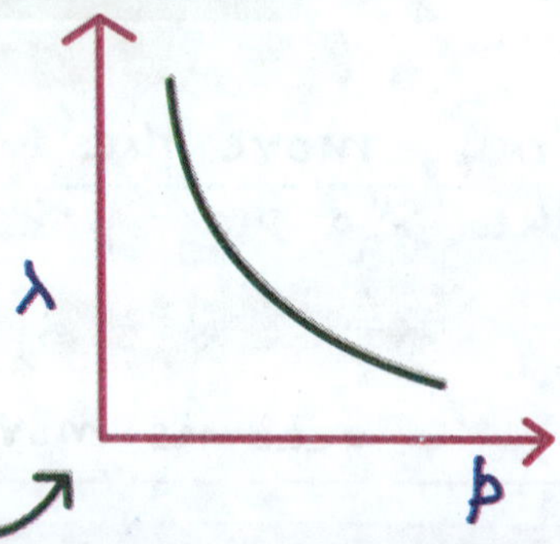

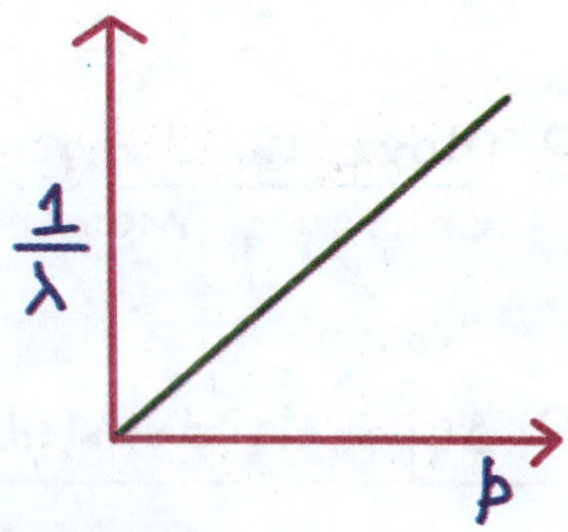

Various Forms of de-Broglie Wavelength

◉ Fundamental Particles accelerated through Potential V

$$\lambda_d = \frac{12.27}{\sqrt{V}}\ \text{Å}$$

Electron

$$\lambda_d = \frac{0.286}{\sqrt{V}}\ \text{Å}$$

Proton

$$\lambda_d = \frac{0.101}{\sqrt{V}}\ \text{Å}$$

α - Particle

PYQ PUNCH

Q4. An electron is accelerated from rest through a potential difference of V Volts. If the de-Broglie wavelength of the electron is 1.227×10^{-2} nm, the potential difference is: (NEET 2020)

Sol. $\lambda_d = \frac{12.27}{\sqrt{V}}$ Å

$$\Rightarrow V = \left(\frac{1.227}{\lambda_d}\right)^2 = \left(\frac{1.227}{1.227 \times 10^{-2}\ \text{nm}}\right)^2$$

$$\Rightarrow V = 10^4\ \text{V}$$

Particle at Speed v

$$\lambda_d = \frac{h}{mv}$$

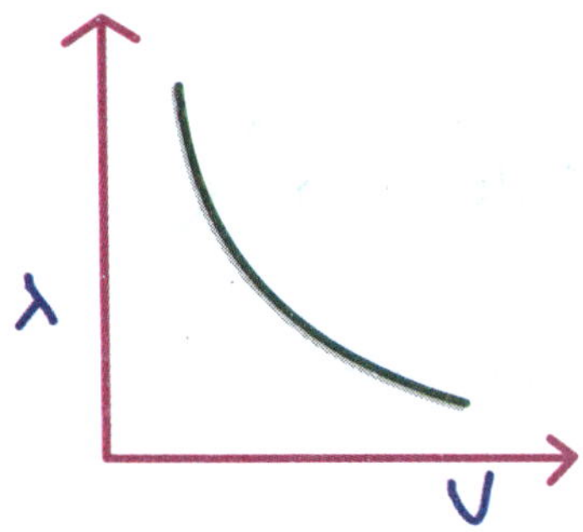

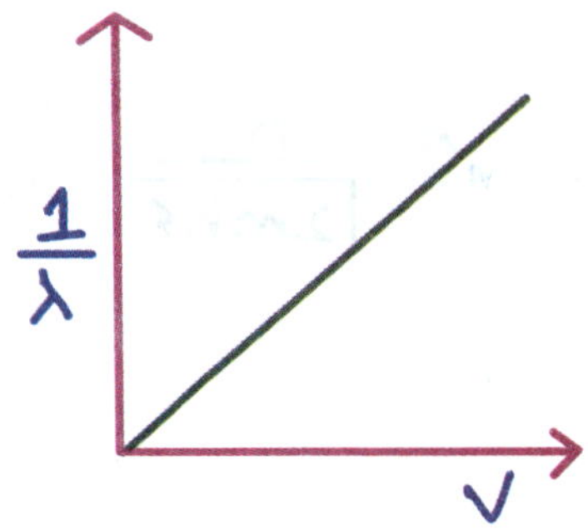

Charge particle accelerated through potential V

$$\lambda_d = \frac{h}{\sqrt{2mqV}}$$

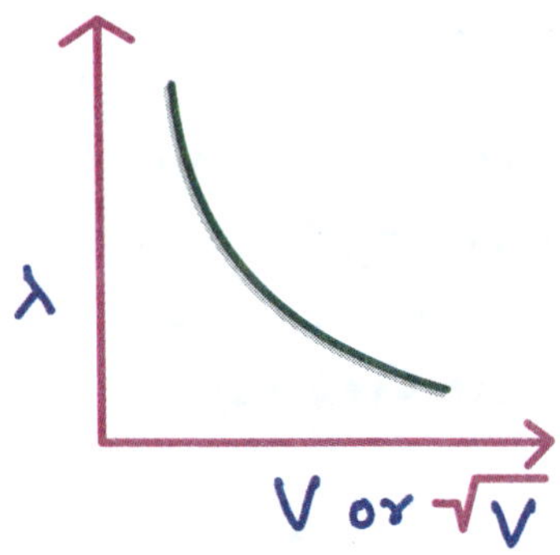

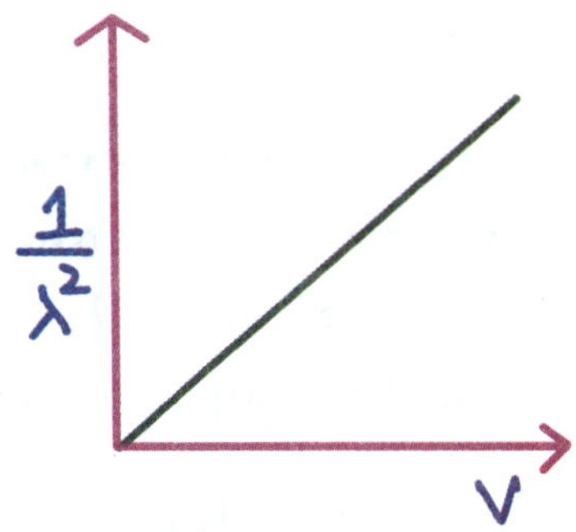

Gas molecules at Temperature T

$$\lambda_d = \frac{h}{\sqrt{3mk_BT}}$$

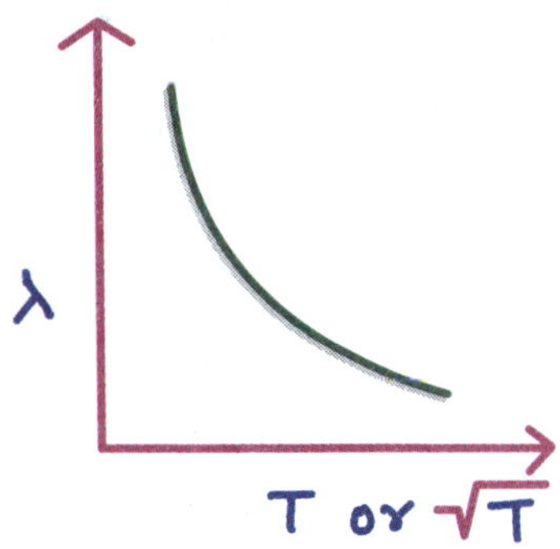

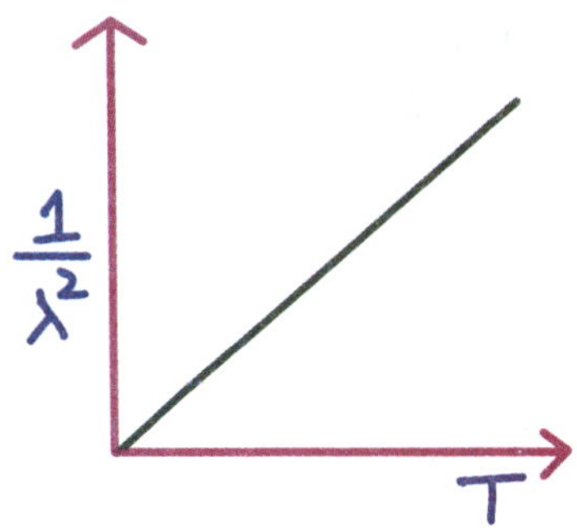

PYQ PUNCH

Q5. The de-Broglie wavelength of neutron in thermal equilibrium with heavy water at a Temperature T (Kelvin) and mass m is :

Sol. $\lambda_d = \frac{h}{\sqrt{3mk_bT}}$

(NEET 2017)

Particle with KE

$$\lambda = \frac{h}{\sqrt{2mK.E}}$$

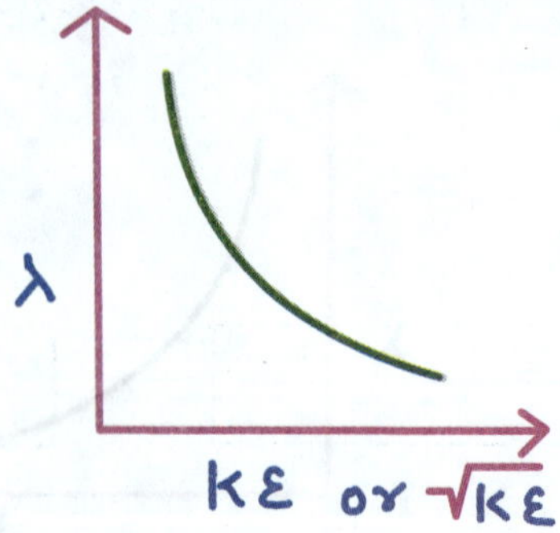

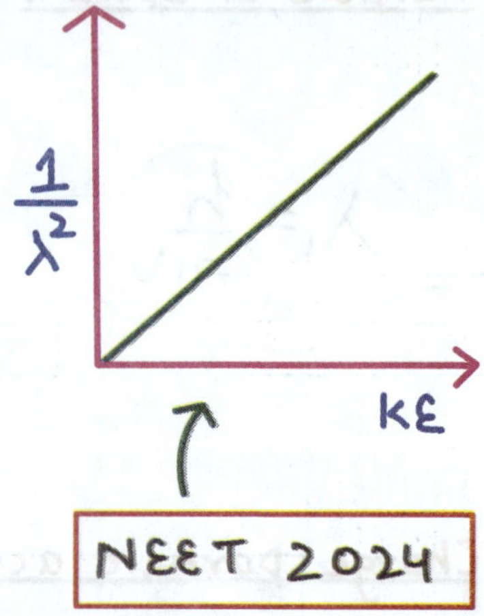

NEET Accelerate

- Most of the graphs of de-Broglie concept are either straight line or a rectangular hyperbola.
- The wavelength λ_e of an electron and λ_p of a photon of same energy E are related as

$$\lambda_e^2 = \frac{h\lambda_p}{2mc} \quad \text{or} \quad \lambda_e^2 \propto \lambda_p$$

- More the mass of the matter lesser the de-Broglie wavelength at same speed

$$\lambda_{electron} > \lambda_{proton} > \lambda_{neutron} > \lambda_{\alpha\text{-particle}}$$

31. Atoms

Discovery

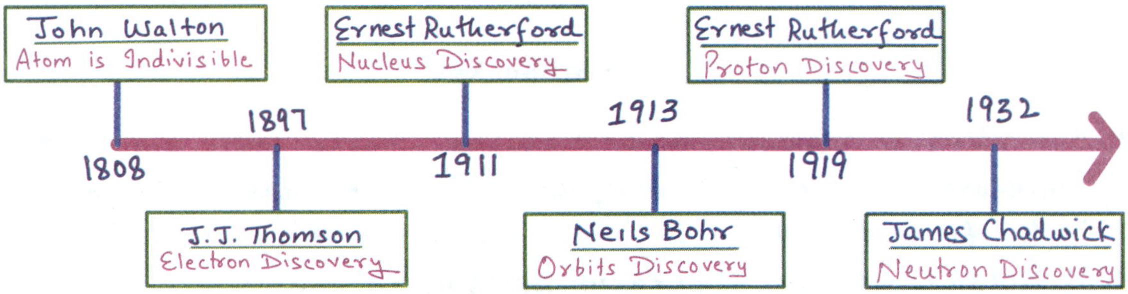

α- particle scattering experiment

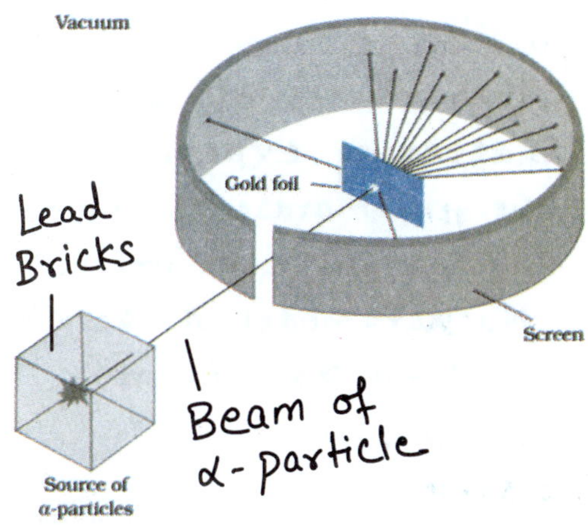

- $^{214}_{83}Bi$: Source of α-particle.
- Lead Bricks : Absorbs unrequired α-particles.
- Screen : Coated with ZnS (a fluorescent material)
- Thin Gold foil : 100nm thickness.

Observations and Conclusion

- Observation 1 Most of the α-particles passes the gold foil undeviated.
- Conclusion Most of the atom is empty.

- Observation 2 Only about 0.14% α-particles get scattered by more than 1°.
- Conclusion Small deflection due to positive particle of atom.

- Observation 3 About 1 in 8000 α-particles get deflected by more than 90°.
- Conclusion Positive charge of the atom is concentrated in a very small volume. This region was named nucleus by Rutherford.

◎ Observation 4 Electrons reside in the empty space of the atom.

○ Conclusion For stability of the electrons within the atom, they must revolve around the nucleus with the help of electrostatic force.

$$\frac{kZe^2}{r^2} = \frac{mv^2}{r}$$

Drawbacks

- According to Maxwell, an accelerated charge must emit EMW. Therefore, electrons revolving around the nucleus must emit energy in the form of EMW and finally get falls in the nucleus.
- It doesn't explain Hydrogen Spectrum.

NEET Accelerate

- Other names of α-particle Scattering experiment are
  - Geiger - Mardsen Experiment.
  - Rutherford Experiment.
  - Nuclear model of the atom.
  - Gold foil Experiment.

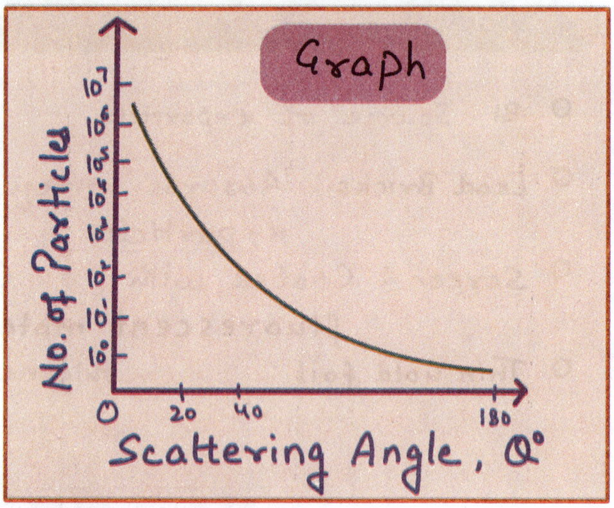

Distance of Closest Approach (d)

- Rutherford predicted that α-particles returns back without striking the gold nucleus.
- The least distance between them is called distance of closest approach

$$d = \frac{2kZe^2}{K.E.}$$

where KE is the initial energy of α-particle.

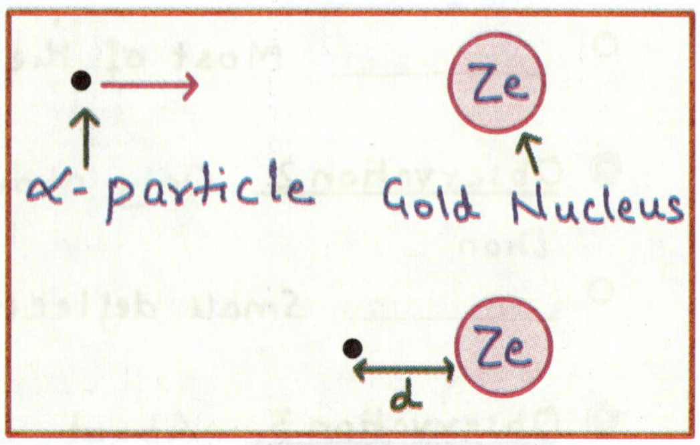

PYQ PUNCH

Q1. When an α-particle of mass m moving with velocity v bombards on a heavy nucleus of charge Ze, its distance of closest approach from the nucleus depends on m as: (NEET 2016)

Sol. $d = \frac{2kZe^2}{K.E.} = \frac{2kZe^2}{\frac{1}{2}mv^2}$

$\Rightarrow d \propto \frac{1}{m}$

Impact Parameter (b)

- Angle of Deflection (θ) of α-particle depends upon the impact parameter.
- $$b = \frac{kZe^2 \cot\left(\frac{\theta}{2}\right)}{K.E.}$$

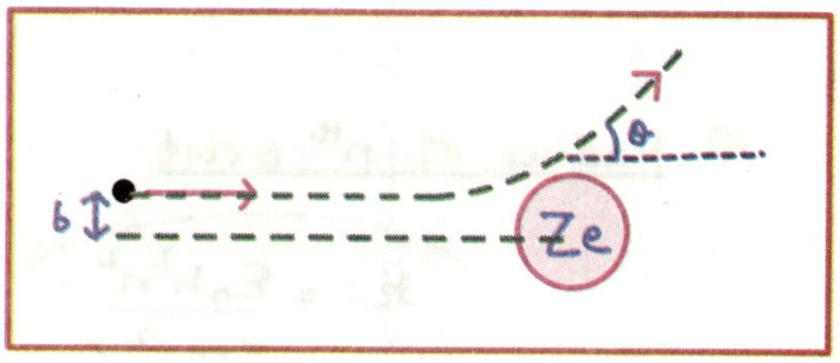

Bohr's Atomic Model

Bohr Studied Rutherford model and found that neither Rutherford nor Maxwell were wrong. To justify Rutherford model, he presented few postulates called as Bohr's postulates which are valid for Hydrogen or Hydrogen like ions.

Bohr's Postulates

- Electrons revolve around the nucleus in such orbits where they don't emit EMWs. These orbits are called as Stationary Orbits.
- The angular momentum of electrons in such orbits is integral multiple of $\frac{h}{2\pi}$.

$$L = mvr = \frac{nh}{2\pi} \quad \text{where } n = 1, 2, 3, ----$$

- Electrons can jump between the orbits. Stability of electron decreases as they jump from lower orbit to higher orbit.
- On gaining the energy, electrons jump from lower to higher orbit.
- To attain stability, they jump from higher to lower orbit. During the process, energy get released in the form of photon.

Bohr Quantization Formulae

◎ **Speed of electron in n^{th} orbit**

$$V_n = \frac{e^2 Z}{2\varepsilon_0 h n}$$

$$V_n = V_0 \frac{Z}{n} \qquad V_n \propto \frac{Z}{n}$$

where $V_0 = 2.18 \times 10^6$ m/s

◎ **Radius of nth orbit**

$$r_n = \frac{\varepsilon_0 h^2 n^2}{\pi m e^2 Z}$$

→ For Hydrogen Inner Most Orbit

$n = 1$ & $Z = 1$

$\Rightarrow r_1 = r_0$

Called as Bohr Orbit.

$$r_n = r_0 \frac{n^2}{Z} \qquad r_n \propto \frac{n^2}{Z}$$

where $r_0 = 0.53$ Å

PYQ PUNCH

Q2. The radius of inner most orbit of hydrogen atom is 5.3×10^{-11} m. What is the radius of third allowed orbit of hydrogen atom? (NEET 2023)

Sol. For Hydrogen atom, inner-most orbit

$r_1 = r_0 = 5.3 \times 10^{-11}$ m

Radius of third orbit

$n = 3$; $Z = 1$

$r_n = r_0 \frac{n^2}{Z}$

$\Rightarrow r_n = \frac{5.3 \times 10^{-11} \times 3^2}{1}$

$= 47.7 \times 10^{-11}$ m

◎ **Time Period of electron in n^{th} orbit**

$$T = \frac{2\pi r}{v} \propto \frac{n^3}{Z^2}$$

◎ **Energy of electron in n^{th} orbit**

$$\frac{mZ^2e^4}{8\epsilon_0^2h^2n^2} \quad \frac{-mZ^2e^4}{4\epsilon_0^2h^2n^2} \quad \frac{-mZ^2e^4}{8\epsilon_0^2h^2n^2}$$

K.E P.E T.E

- Negative total energy represents that electron is bounded to nucleus
- $TE = E_n = -\frac{13.6Z^2}{n^2}eV$
- $E_n \propto \frac{Z^2}{n^2}$
- $PE = 2TE = -2KE$

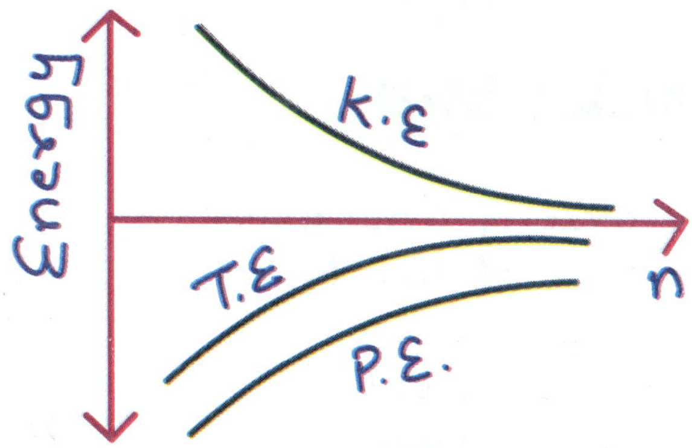

PYQ PUNCH

Q3. Let T_1 and T_2 be the energy of an electron in the first and second excited states of hydrogen atom respectively. According to the Bohr's model of an atom, the ratio $T_1 : T_2$ is (NEET 2022)

Sol. $E_n = -\frac{13.6Z^2}{n^2}eV$

$$\frac{T_1}{T_2} = \left(\frac{n_2}{n_1}\right)^2$$

$$= \left(\frac{2}{1}\right)^2$$

$$= \frac{4}{1}$$

Energy Level Diagram

Hydrogen Atom

$n \to \infty$	0 eV
$n=4$	-0.85 eV
$n=3$	-1.51 eV
$n=2$	-3.4 eV
$n=1$	-13.6 eV

Hydrogen Like Ions

$n \to \infty$	0 eV
$n=4$	$-0.85\,Z^2$ eV
$n=3$	$-1.51\,Z^2$ eV
$n=2$	$-3.4\,Z^2$ eV
$n=1$	$-13.6\,Z^2$ eV

Atomic Spectra

- Orderly arrangement of wavelength emitted by gas on heating.
- It is of two types

Continuous

- All the wavelengths in a given range are present.
- Emitted on heating the gas at normal or high pressure.

Discrete

- Only few particular wavelengths in a given range are present.
- Emitted on heating the gas at low pressure.

Bohr's Explanation of Hydrogen Spectrum

- On heating, electron gains energy and jumps to the excited state. It returns back by emitting a photon of particular wavelength.
- For an electron making jump from n_H to n_L orbit

$$\lambda = \frac{hc}{E_h - E_L}$$

$$\frac{1}{\lambda} = RZ^2\left(\frac{1}{n_L^2} - \frac{1}{n_H^2}\right)$$

where R is the Rydberg Constant

$R = 1.1 \times 10^7/m$

Number of Spectral Lines

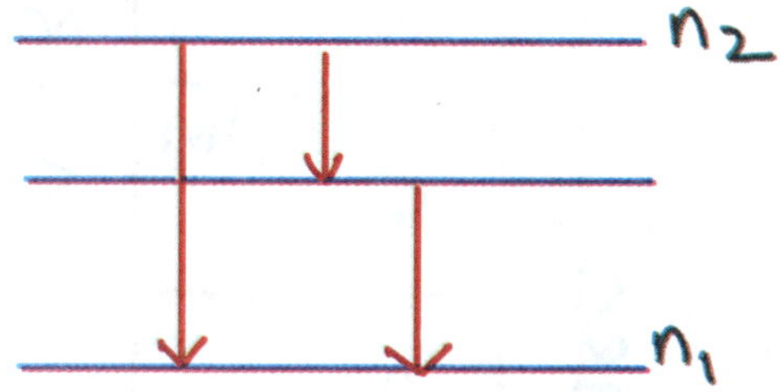

- Number of Spectral Lines

$$N = \frac{(n_2 - n_1)(n_2 - n_1 + 1)}{2}$$

PYQ PUNCH

Q4. Hydrogen atom in ground state is excited by a monochromatic radiation of $\lambda = 975\,Å$. Number of spectral lines in the resulting spectrum emitted will be : (NEET 2014)

Sol. $\frac{1}{\lambda} = RZ^2\left(\frac{1}{n_1^2} - \frac{1}{n_2^2}\right)$

Putting $\lambda = 975\,Å$ and $n_1 = 1$, we get $n_2 = 4$.

Number of Spectral Lines

$$N = \frac{(n_2 - n_1)(n_2 - n_1 + 1)}{2} = 6$$

Bohr's Quantum Condition from de-Broglie

- $2\pi r = n\lambda = \frac{nh}{mv}$
- Number of waves in n^{th} orbit is n.
  - 1st orbit has 1 wave.

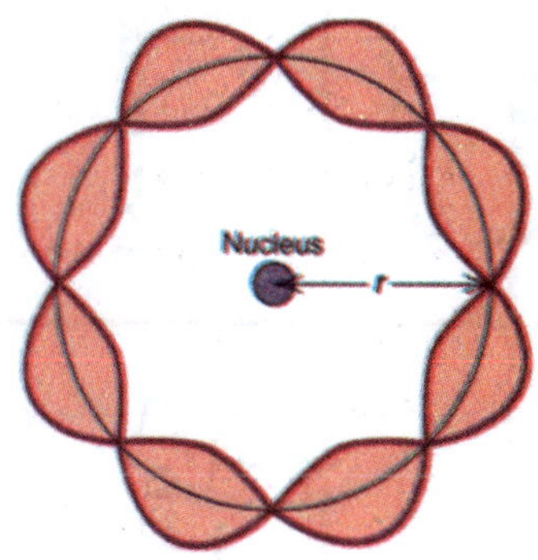

Recoiling of an atom

- When photon is emitted during transition of electron, atom get recoiled.
- Momentum of the re-coil atom
- Momentum of the system remains conserved.
- Momentum of atom = Momentum of photon

$$p = \frac{h}{\lambda} = RZ^2h\left(\frac{1}{n_L^2} - \frac{1}{n_H^2}\right)$$

Spectral Series

	Wavelength	Final Orbit	Hydrogen Region	Hydrogen λ_{min}	Hydrogen λ_{max}
Lyman	$\frac{1}{\lambda} = RZ^2\left[\frac{1}{1^2} - \frac{1}{n^2}\right]$ $n = 2, 3, ---$	Ground State	Ultraviolet	$n \to \infty$ $\frac{1}{R}$	$n = 2$ $\frac{4}{3R}$
Balmer	$\frac{1}{\lambda} = RZ^2\left[\frac{1}{2^2} - \frac{1}{n^2}\right]$ $n = 3, 4, ---$	1st Excited State	Visible	$n \to \infty$ $\frac{4}{R}$	$n = 3$ $\frac{36}{5R}$
Paschen	$\frac{1}{\lambda} = RZ^2\left[\frac{1}{3^2} - \frac{1}{n^2}\right]$ $n = 4, 5, ---$	2nd Excited State	Infrared	$n \to \infty$ $\frac{9}{R}$	$n = 4$ $\frac{144}{7R}$
Brackett	$\frac{1}{\lambda} = RZ^2\left[\frac{1}{4^2} - \frac{1}{n^2}\right]$ $n = 5, 6, ---$	3rd Excited State	Infrared	$n \to \infty$ $\frac{16}{R}$	$n = 5$ $\frac{400}{9R}$
P. Fund	$\frac{1}{\lambda} = RZ^2\left[\frac{1}{5^2} - \frac{1}{n^2}\right]$ $n = 6, 7, ---$	4th Excited State	Infrared	$n \to \infty$ $\frac{25}{R}$	$n = 6$ $\frac{900}{11R}$

Energy of the re-coil atom

$$E = \frac{p^2}{2m} = \frac{h^2}{2m\lambda^2}$$ where m is the mass of re-coiled atom.

NEET Accelerate

- As electron jumps to higher orbit, potential energy and total energy increases while kinetic energy decreases.
- Difference of energy in Hydrogen orbit
  - $E_2 - E_1 = 10.2\ eV$
  - $E_3 - E_1 = 12.6\ eV$
  - $E_3 - E_2 = 1.9\ eV$
- If electron is replaced by an hypothetical particle of mass m_o and charge e, then new Rydberg constant is

$$R' = \frac{R \times m_o}{m_e}$$

32. Nuclei

Atomic Mass Unit (u)

- It is a very small unit of mass.
- It is $\frac{1}{12}^{th}$ the mass of the carbon atom.

$$1u = 1.660539 \times 10^{-27} \text{ kg}$$

Composition of nucleus

Proton

- Mass of proton $m_p = 1.00727u$
- Number of proton in an atom is represented by Z.
- Z is called atomic number.
- Periodic table is arranged on the basis of Z.

Neutron

- Mass of neutron, $m_n = 1.00866u$.
- It is slightly heavier than proton.
- Number of neutrons in an atom is represented by N.
- A free neutron is unstable outside the nucleus.

Nucleons

- Protons and neutrons together are called as Nucleons.
- Number of nucleons in an atom is represented by A.
- $A = Z + N$ is called mass number.
- A nucleus is symbolically expressed as $_ZX^A$, where X is the chemical symbol of element.

Size of Nucleus

- $R = R_0 A^{1/3}$
- $R \propto A^{1/3}$

PYQ PUNCH

Q1. If radius of the $^{27}_{12}Al$ nucleus is taken to be R_{Al}, then the radius of $^{125}_{53}Te$ nucleus is nearly: (NEET 2015)

Sol. $R \propto A^{1/3}$

$$\Rightarrow \frac{R_{Te}}{R_{Al}} = \left(\frac{A_{Te}}{A_{Al}}\right)^{1/3}$$

$$\Rightarrow \frac{R_{Te}}{R_{Al}} = \left(\frac{125}{27}\right)^{1/3} = \frac{5}{3}$$

$$\Rightarrow R_{Te} = \frac{5}{3} R_{Al}$$

Density of Nucleus

- $\rho = 10^{17}$ kg/m^3 for all elements.

Rest Mass Energy

- According to Einstein, it is necessary to treat mass as the form of energy for the conservation of energy.
- Energy equivalent to mass is

$$E = mc^2$$

- Energy of 1u mass is 931.5 MeV.

Mass Defect (Δm)

- Combined mass of nucleus is slightly less than its constituents masses in free state. This difference of mass is called as Mass Defect (Δm).

$$\Delta m = \text{Free State mass} - \text{Nucleus mass}$$

$$\Delta m = (Z m_p + (A - Z) m_n - m_{nucleus})$$

Nuclear Binding Energy

- Binding Energy is the energy released when a nucleus is formed.
- It is also defined as the energy required to break a nucleus.

- It doesn't imply the stability of nucleus.
- A nucleus with more Binding Energy may be unstable.
- A nucleus with less Binding Energy may be Stable.

Nuclear Force

- It is a short range force.
- It is both attractive and repulsive force.

Distance
- $< .8$ fm → Repulsive
- $= .8$ fm → Zero
- $> .8$ fm → Attractive

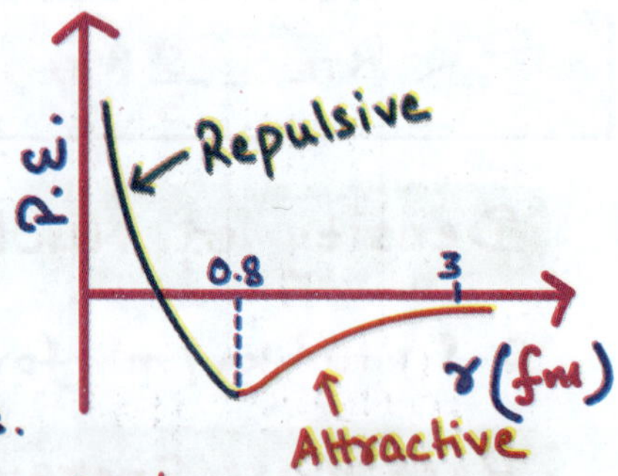

- It is a non-central force.
- It is non-conservative.
- Strongest among all fundamental forces.
- Acts between neutron-neutron, neutron-proton, and proton-proton only. Doesn't depend upon the charge of the particle.
- Depends upon the spin of nucleons.
- Parallel Spin → Strong Force
- Anti-parallel Spin → Weak Force
- It is a saturated force.

Binding Energy per Nucleon (ε_{bn})

- It judges the stability of the nucleus.
- It is defined as the energy required to separate a nucleon from the nucleus.

$$\varepsilon_{bn} = \frac{\varepsilon_b}{A}$$

Variation of ε_{bn} vs A

- As mass number increases, stability 1st increases, then decreases.
- ε_{bn} is practically constant for $30 < A < 170$.
- Iron has the most stable nucleus.

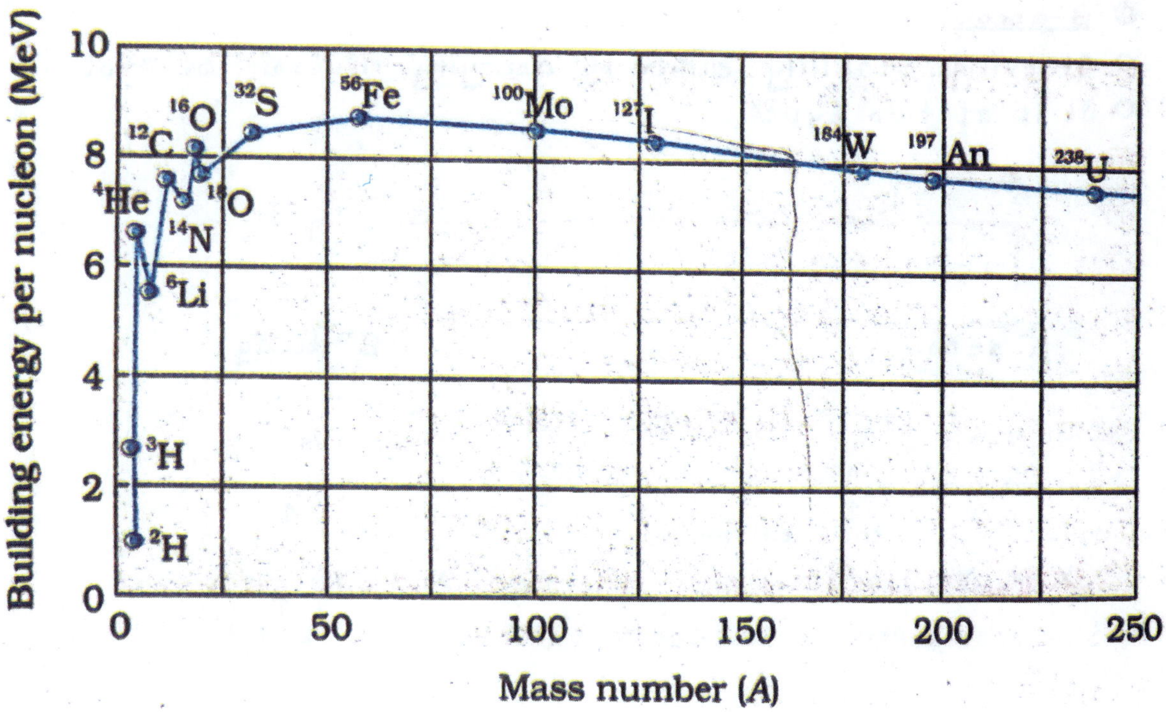

- Lighter nuclei fuse for stability and in doing so release energy. This process is called as Nuclear Fusion.
- Nuclei of higher mass number break for stability. In doing so, they release energy. This process is called as Nuclear Fission.
- Stability of nucleus ultimately depends upon the $\frac{N}{Z}$ ratio. Ideal range is 1 to 1.6.

Radioactivity

- The process of spontaneous disintegeration shown by unstable nuclei is called as natural radioactivity or radioactive decay.
- Decay process main aim is to alter the ratio of $\frac{N}{Z}$ to attain stability.

Types of Decay Processes

- **α-decay**
- The unstable nucleus emits an alpha-particle (Helium nucleus) reducing its Z and N by 2 each and A by 4.

$$_{Z}^{A}X \longrightarrow {}_{Z-2}^{A-4}Y + {}_{2}^{4}He \text{ (Helium nucleus)}$$

Parent Nuclei — Daughter Nuclei

β-decay

- It brings stability either by decaying neutron or proton.
- It is of two types

β^- decay

- Neutron decays
- $n \rightarrow p + e^- + \bar{\nu}$ (↑ Anti-neutrino)
- ${}^{A}_{Z}X \rightarrow {}^{A}_{Z+1}Y + e^- + \bar{\nu}$ (↑ e^-: β^- particle)
- Z increases by 1.
- A remains constant.

β^+ decay

- Proton decays
- $p \rightarrow n + e^+ + \nu$ ← neutrino
- ${}^{A}_{Z}X \rightarrow {}^{A}_{Z-1}Y + e^+ + \nu$ (↑ e^+: β^+ particle)
- Z decreases by 1.
- A remains constant.

PYQ PUNCH

Q2. $${}^{290}_{82}X \xrightarrow{\alpha} Y \xrightarrow{e^+} Z \xrightarrow{\beta^-} P \xrightarrow{e^-} Q$$

In the nuclear emission stated above, the mass number and the atomic number of the product Q respectively are: (NEET 2024)

Sol. $\alpha \rightarrow$ Alpha decay, Z ↓ by 2 and A ↓ by 4.

$e^+ \rightarrow \beta^+$ decay, Z ↓ by 1

$\beta^- \rightarrow \beta^-$ decay, Z ↑ by 1

$e^- \rightarrow \beta^-$ decay, Z ↑ by 1

So, ${}^{286}_{81}Q$

33. Semiconductor

Energy Band

- Valence electrons of one atom are shared by more that one atom causes splitting of energy level.
- The collection of these closely spaced energy levels are called energy bands.
- Types of energy bands
  - Valence Band (VB) : The highest fully filled energy band.
  - Conduction Band (CB) : The lowest partially filled or completely empty energy band. It lies just above the valence band.

Energy Band Gap (E_g)

- It is the energy gap between 2 consecutive energy gaps.
- Forbidden band gap is the energy gap between top of the valence band and bottom of the conduction band.

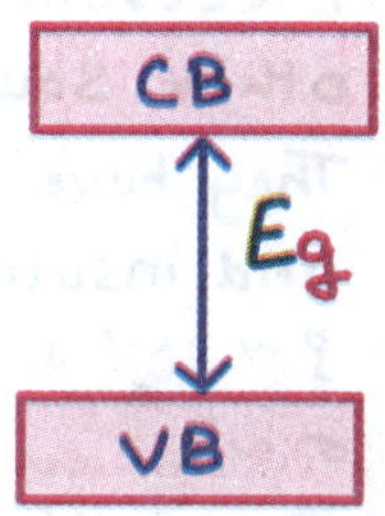

Solids

- **Conductors**
- CB and VB either overlap or very little gap between them.

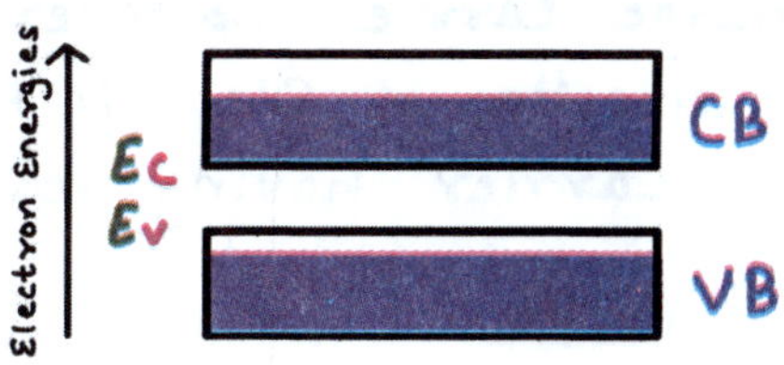

Very less E_g

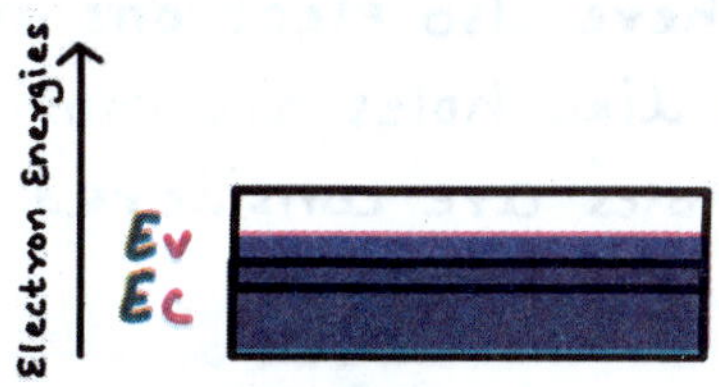

Over-lapping Bands

- Electrons easily jump to CB by acquiring a little more energy from any other source.
- Possesses very low resistivity or high conductivity.
- $\rho \sim 10^{-2}$ to 10^{-8} Ωm
- $\sigma \sim 10^{2}$ to 10^{8} Sm^{-1}

Insulators

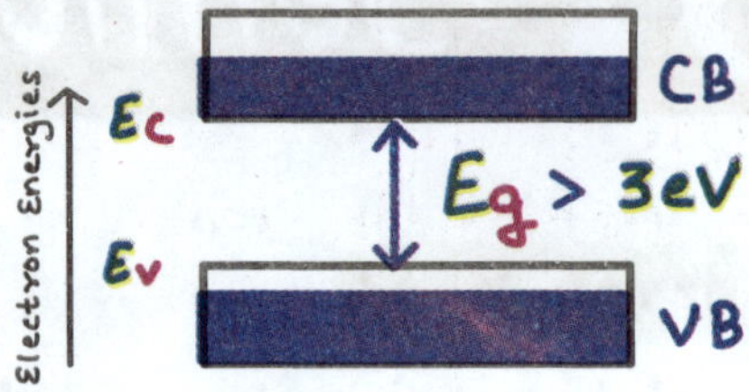

- VB is completely filled, CB is completely empty and energy gap between CB and VB is quite large that small energy from any other source cannot overcome it.
- They have high resistivity and low conductivity.
- $\rho \sim 10^{11}$ to 10^{19} Ωm
- $\sigma \sim 10^{-11}$ to 10^{-19} Sm^{-1}

Semi-Conductor (SC)

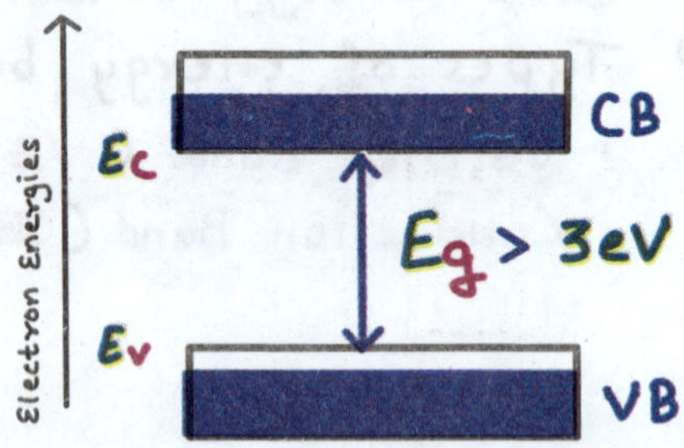

- Just like insulator, VB is completely filled and the CB is empty but the energy gap between them is comparetivaly small.
- Electrons from VB jump to CB from gaining energy from other source.
- They have resistivity or conductivity intermediate to conductors and insulators.
- $\rho \sim 10^{-5}$ to 10^{6} Ωm
- $\sigma \sim 10^{5}$ to 10^{-6} Sm^{-1}
- Flow of current can be controlled, hence, used widely in sensors.

Charge carrier in SC

- In VB, electrons act as charge carrier.
- In CB, here also electrons act as charge carrier, however, it looks like holes are moving in the direction of Electric Field. Hence, holes are considered as charge carrier having positive charge.

Types of Semi-conductor

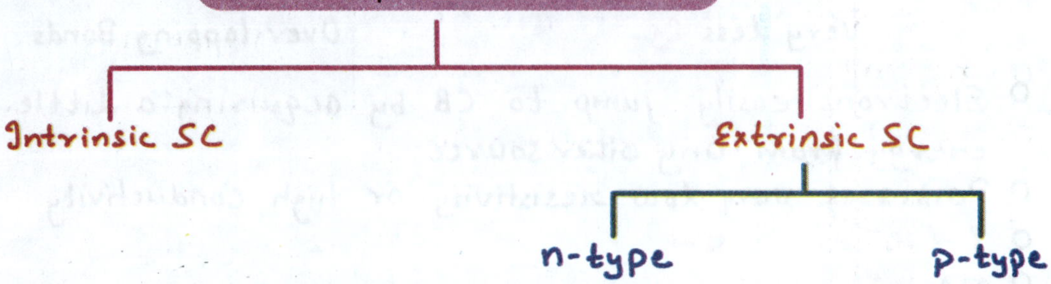

Intrinsic SC

- It is a pure semi-conductor.
- $n_e = n_h = n_i$ where n_e is the number density of electrons
  n_h is the number density of holes
  n_i is called intrinsic carrier concentration.
- Conductivity is very weak.

Extrinsic SC

- They are doped with impurities to increase conductivity.
- According to type of impurity, it is of two types :

n-type

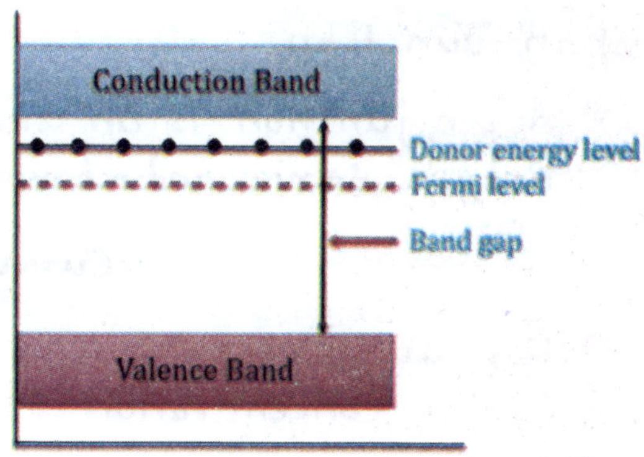

- Penta-valent impurity is doped.
- Impurity level is formed near the CB.
- Major charge carriers are e^-(s), hence called as n-type.
- Minor charge carriers are holes.
- $n_e > n_h$
- Dopant donates the electron, hence also called as Donar Impurity.

p-type

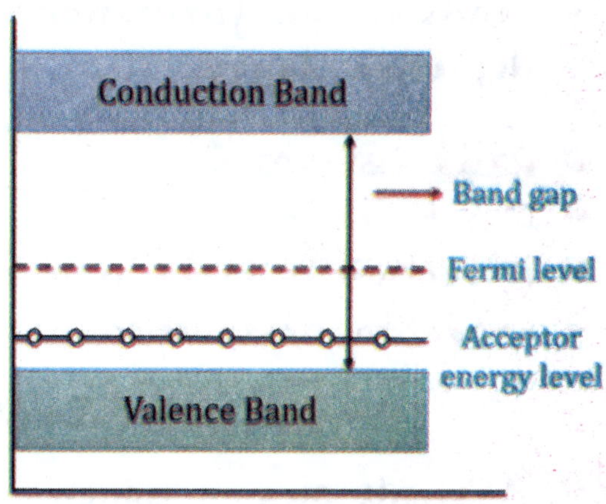

- Tri-valent impurity is doped.
- Impurity level is formed near the VB.
- Major charge carriers are holes, hence called as p-type.
- Minor charge carriers are e^-(s).
- $n_e < n_h$
- Dopant accepts the electron, hence also called as Donar Impurity.

NEET Accelerate

- At equilibrium $n_e n_h = n_i^2$
- Electrical Conductivity $\sigma = e(\mu_e n_e + \mu_h n_e)$
  where μ_e and μ_h are the mobilities of electron and holes resp.
- Doped sc is electrically neutral.
- For a same concentration of majority charge carrier in n-type and p-type, more current will be in n-type.
- In conductors, conductivity decreases with temperature.
- In sc and insulators, conductivity increases with temperature.

p-n Junction

- A p-n junction is an arrangement made by a close contact of n-type semi-conductor with p-type semi-conductor.

Current in p-n junction

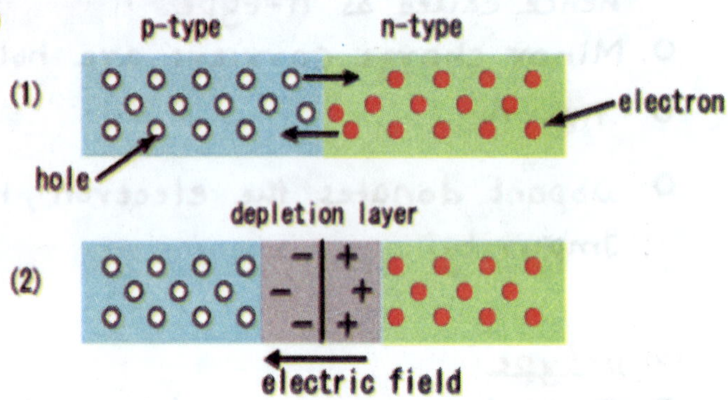

Diffusion Current ($i_{Diffusion}$)
- Due to concentration difference.
- Holes diffuse from p to n.
- Electrons diffuse from n to p.
- Current is from p to n.
- Leads to the formation of depletion layer.

Drift current (i_{Drift})
- Due to Electric Field.
- Direction is from n to p.
- Leads to destruction of depletion layer.

Depletion Layer

- A small region which is free from any free charge.
- Width of Depletion Region $\propto \dfrac{1}{\text{Concentration of doping}}$

- The potential difference developed across the depletion region is called the Potential Barrier.
- At steady state,
  $i_{Diffusion} = i_{Drift}$

⇒ Size of depletion layer becomes constant.

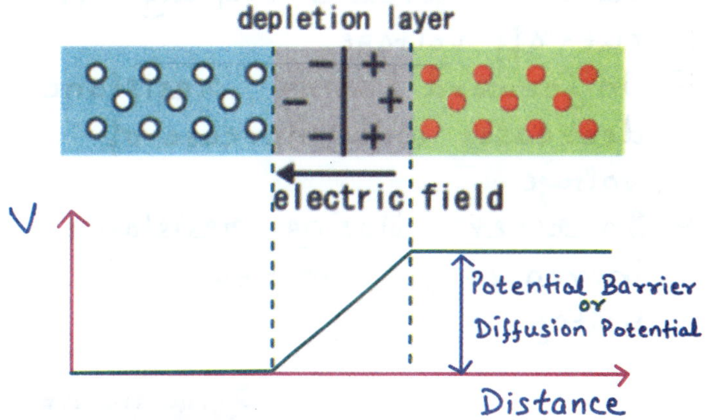

Biasing of p-n junction

- Applying the potential difference across the p-n junction.
- It is of two types

Forward Biasing

- Positive terminal is connected with p-side.
- Size of depletion layer decreases.
- Potential Barrier decreases.
- Current from p to n increases.
- At a particular voltage, size of depletion layer reduces to 0. This voltage is called as Cut-off Voltage or knee Voltage.
- Cut-off voltage for Si is 0.7V & Ge is 0.3V.

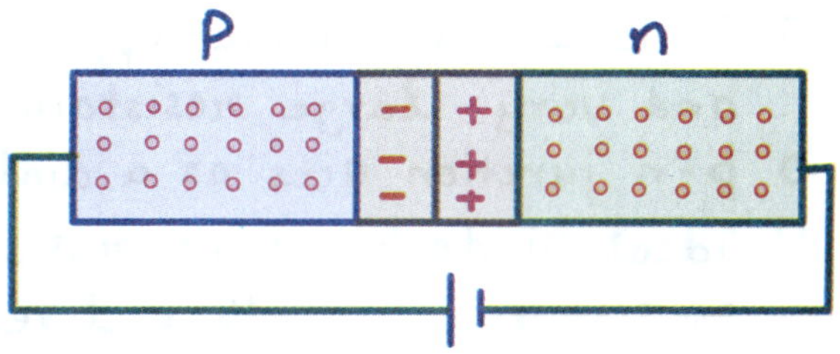

Reverse Biasing

- Positive terminal is connected with n-side.
- Size of depletion layer increases.
- Potential Barrier increases.
- Current from n to p increases marginally.

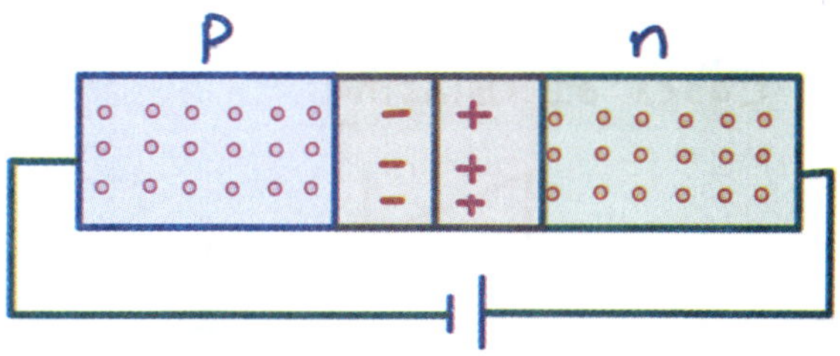

I-V Characteristics Curve

- Unlike conductors, current in semi-conductor varies non-linearly with the magnitude and direction of applied voltage.

- Current increases rapidly after cut-off voltage.
- In forward biasing, resistance decreases with increase of voltage.
- In reverse biasing, resistance increases with increase of Voltage.

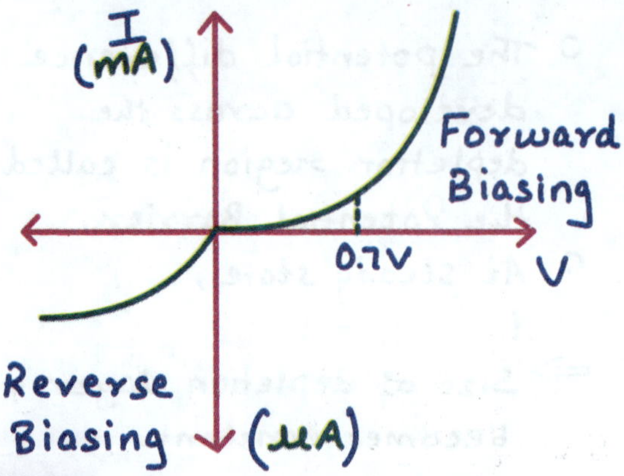

Dynamic Resistance

- As resistance varies with voltage, thus SC doesn't follow Ohm's Law.
- The resistance is called as Dynamic Resistance.

$$R_{AC} = \frac{\Delta V}{\Delta I}$$

Diode

- It is a device which offers negligible resistance in one-direction and very large resistance in reverse direction.
- p-n junction acts as a diode.
- Ideal Diode has zero resistance in one direction and infinite resistance in other direction.

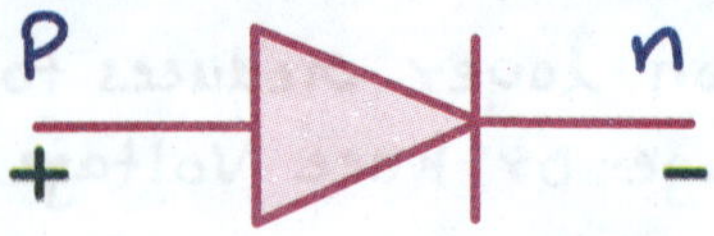

Forward Bias

- Current flow freely

Reverse Bias

- Current not allowed to flow.

- Cases of Biasing

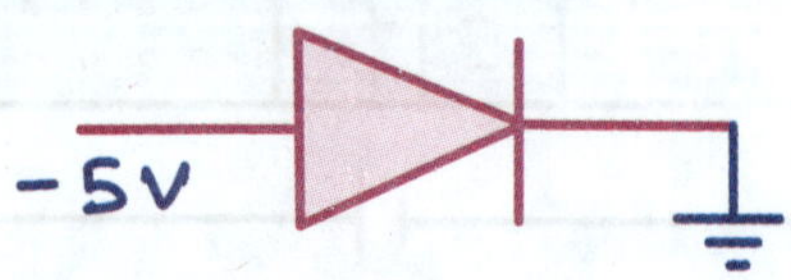

Reverse Biasing

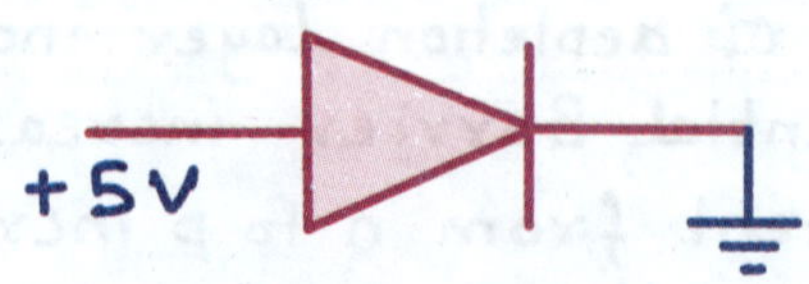

Forward Biasing

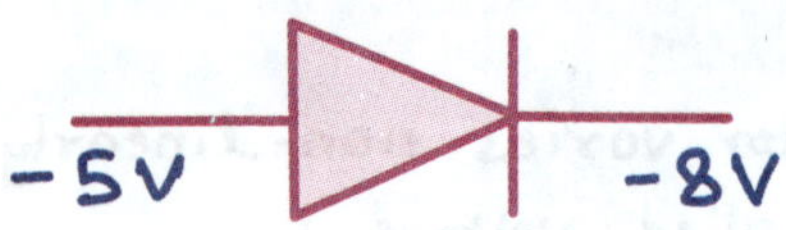

Forward Biasing

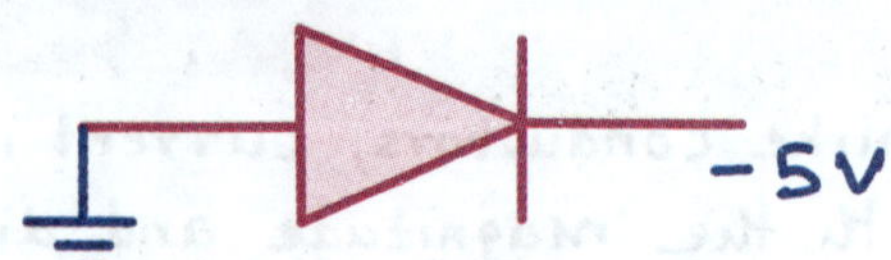

Forward Biasing

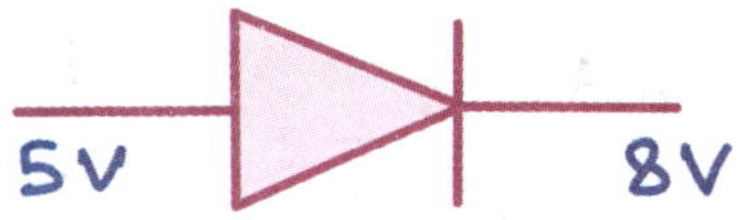

Reverse Biasing

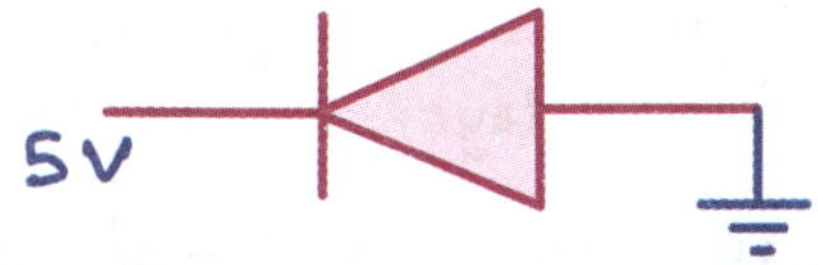

Reverse Biasing

PYQ PUNCH

Q1. Out of the following, which one is a forward biased diode ? (NEET 2020)

a. 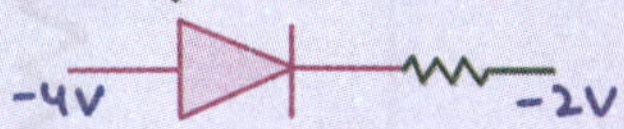

b. 

c. 

d. 

Sol. In option d, 0V > -3V

Q2. The given circuit has two ideal diodes connected as shown in the figure below. The current flowing through the resistance R_1 will be :

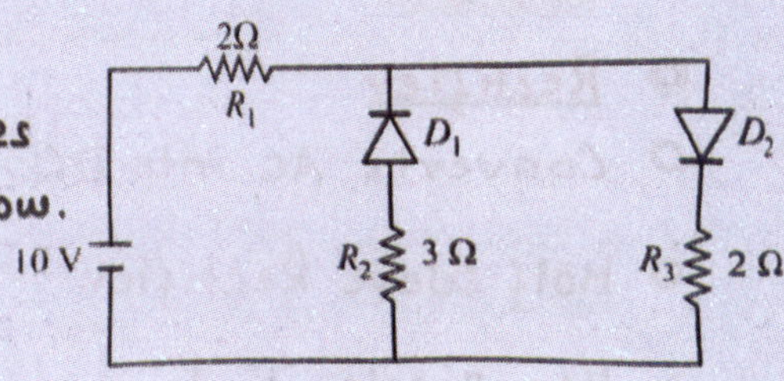

(NEET 2016)

Sol. Since D_1 is reversed biased, hence, no current flow through it.

D_2 is forward biased, hence offer no resistance.

$$i = \frac{V}{R_{eq}} = \frac{10}{2+2} = 2.5\text{ A}$$

Application of Diode

◉ **Zener Diode**

- In reverse biasing of p-n junction, over a certain voltage, electric field breaks the co-valent bond and increases the minority charge carriers. Such diode is called as Zener-Diode.
- The sudden increase of reverse current is called as zener breakdown.

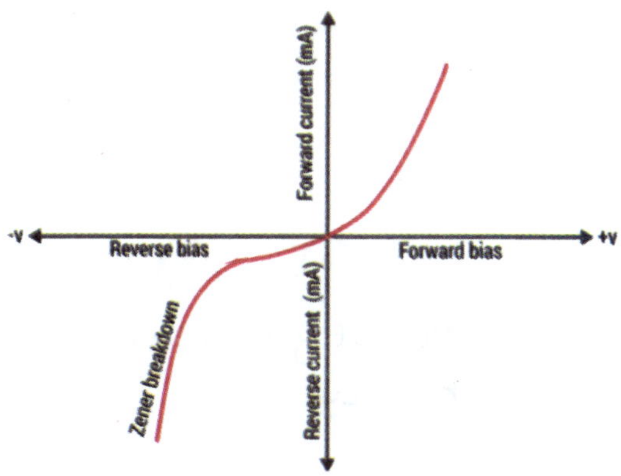

- It happens in highly doped sc. Depletion layer should be thin.

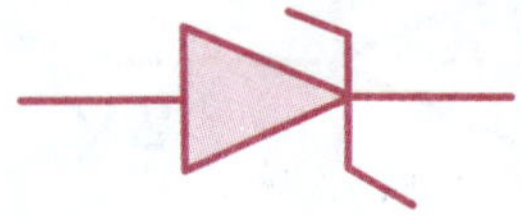

Zener Diode

- **It is used as a voltage regulator**
  - Put in parallel to a device in which we desire to regulate the voltage.
  - Let R_L be the resistance of load.
  - Voltage of Zener Diode is same as of the regulating voltage of load.

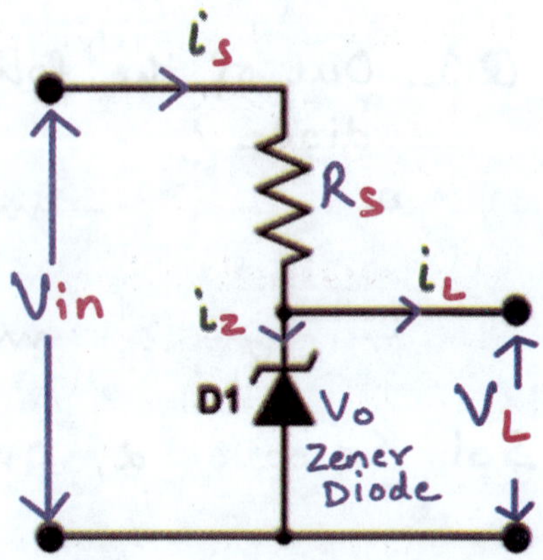

  - $i_L = \frac{V_L}{R_L}$
  - $V_s = V_{in} - V_L$
  - $i_s = \frac{V_s}{R_s}$
  - $i_z = i_s - i_L$

Rectifier

- Converts AC into DC.

- **Half Wave Rectifier**
  - Use single diode.

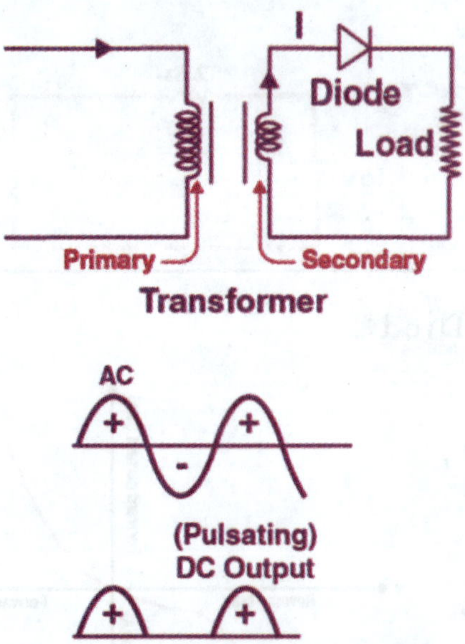

  - Output gives current only in half cycle.

- **Full-Wave Rectifier**
  - Center-tap transformer uses two diodes.

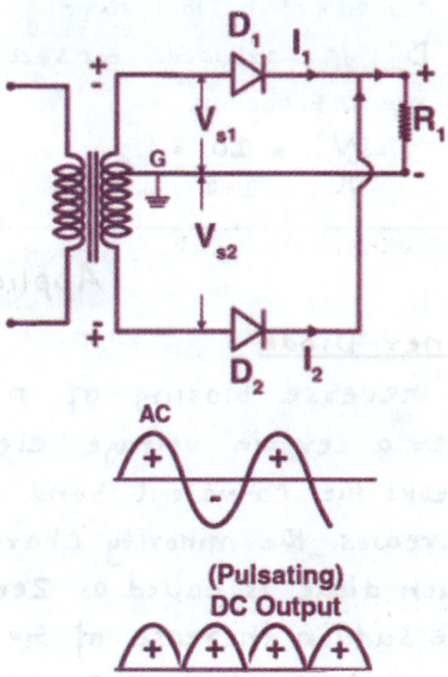

- If input frequency is f, then output frequency is also f.
- If input frequency is f, then output frequency is also 2f.

NEET Accelerate

- Pulsating DC from rectifier can be converted into constant DC through a process called as Filtering.
- Either a high value of Capacitor is put in parallel to the Load Resistance or a high value of Inductor is put in series to the Load Resistance for filtering.

Photodiode

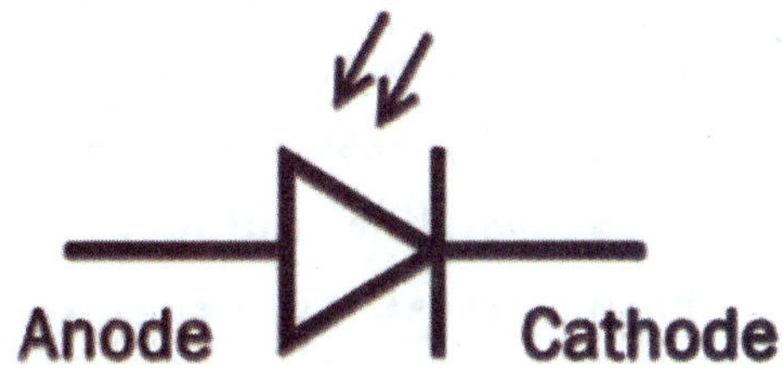

- Operated under reverse bias to
  - Increase the width of Depletion Layer.
  - For small current due to battery.
- Photo-current is controlled by light.
- Light energy must be greater than band gap. $h\nu > E_g$
- Develops a voltage called as photo-voltage.
- Photo-current is from n to p.
- Photo-current increases with intensity of light.

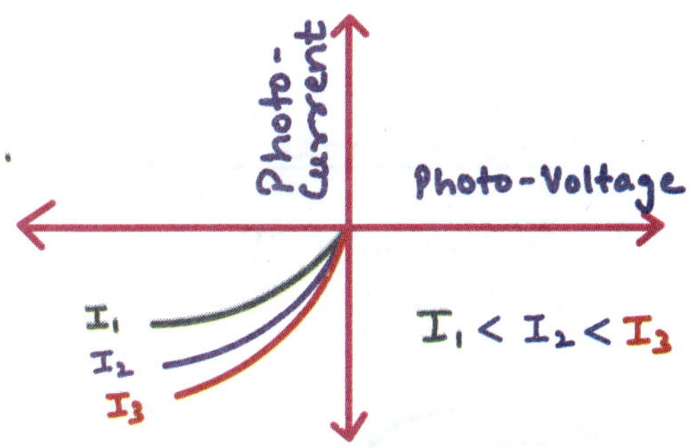

Solar Cell

- No biasing
- Photo-current is controlled by light.
- Light energy must be greater than band gap. $h\nu > E_g$
- Develops a voltage called as photo-voltage.
- Photo-current is from n to p.
- Photo-current increases with intensity of light.
- In absence of load, photo-voltage is called as Open-Circuit Voltage (V_{oc}).
- In presence of zero resistance load, current is maximum and called as Short-Circuit Current (i_{sc}).

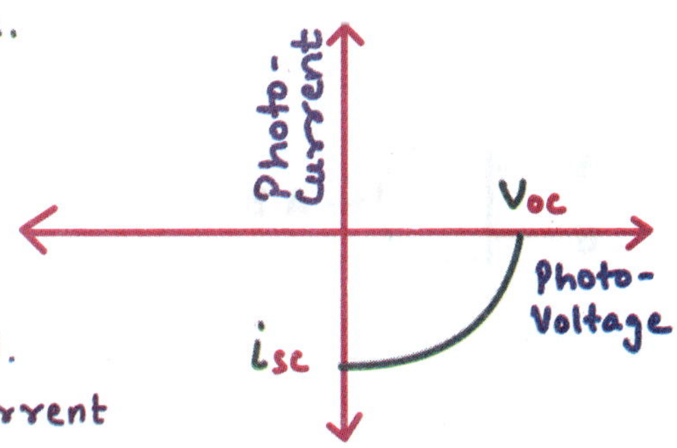

LED

- Operated under forward bias.
- Material used having band-gap lies between 1.8 to 3eV

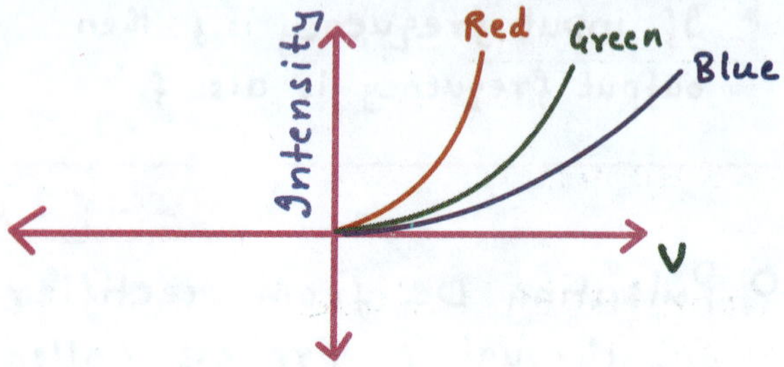

Logic Gates

- It is a digital circuit which is based on certain logical relationship between the input and the output voltages of the circuit.
- They are built using p-n juntion and transistors.
- The operation of a logic gate is indicated in a table, known as truth table. This table contains all possible combinations of input and the corresponding output.
- High Voltage is represented by 1.
- Low Voltage is represented by 0.

Types of Gates

Fundamental Gates

1. **OR Gate** (या)

- $Y = A + B$

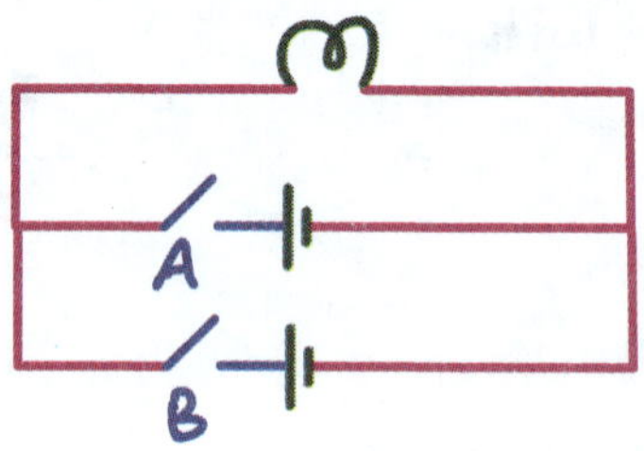

A	B	Y
0	0	0
0	1	1
1	0	1
1	1	1

2. **AND Gate** (और)

- $Y = A.B$

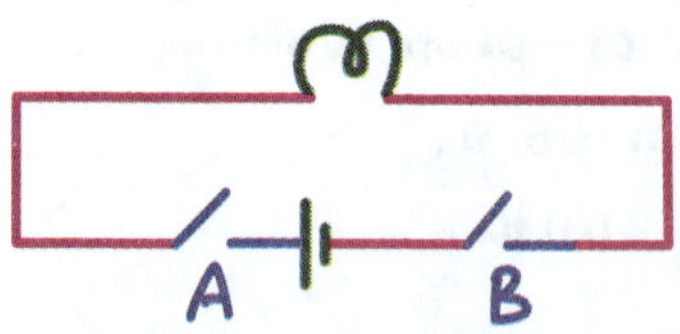

A	B	Y
0	0	0
0	1	0
1	0	0
1	1	1

3. **NOT-Gate**

- $Y = \overline{A}$

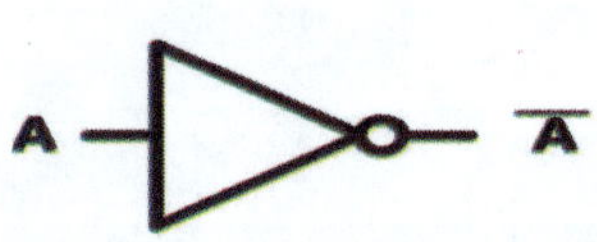

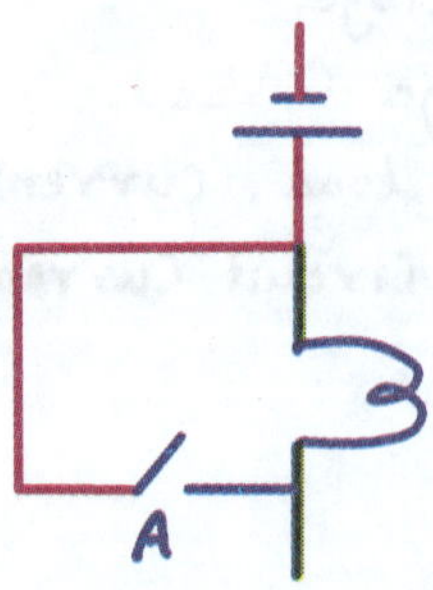

A	Y
0	1
1	0

Universal Gate

1. NAND Gate

- Opposite of AND Gate.
- $Y = \overline{A.B}$

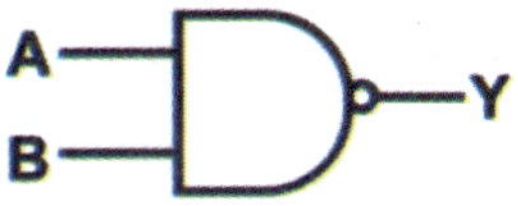

or

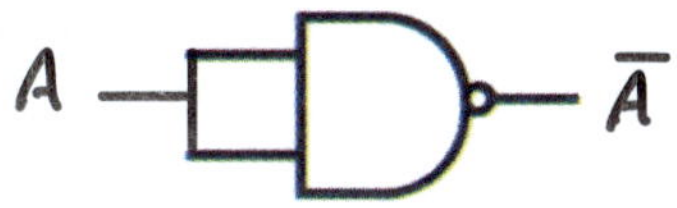

A	B	Y
0	0	1
0	1	1
1	0	1
1	1	0

2. NOR - Gate

- Opposite of OR Gate.
- $Y = \overline{A+B}$

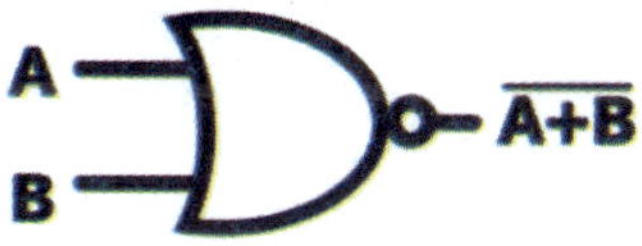

or

A	B	Y
0	0	1
0	1	0
1	0	0
1	1	0

Exclusive Gates

1. XNOR Gate

- $Y = AB + \bar{A}\bar{B}$

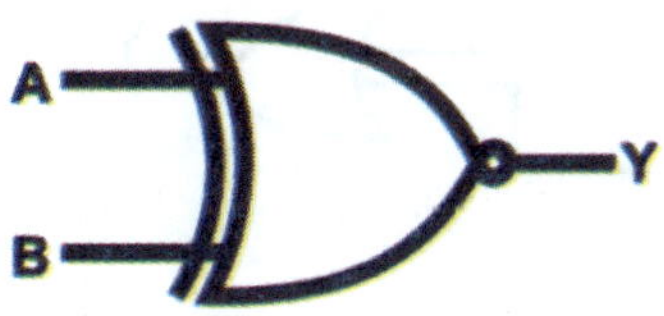

A	B	Y
0	0	1
0	1	0
1	0	0
1	1	1

2. XOR Gate

- $Y = \bar{A}B + A\bar{B}$

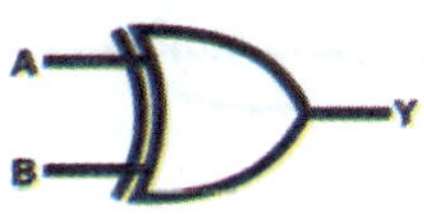

A	B	Y
0	0	0
0	1	1
1	0	1
1	1	0

Boolean Algebra

Commutative Law
- $A \cdot B = B \cdot A$
- $A + B = B + A$

Associative Law
- $(A \cdot B) \cdot C = A \cdot (B \cdot C)$
- $(A + B) + C = A + (B + C)$

Distributive Law
- $A \cdot (B + C) = A \cdot B + A \cdot C$
- $A + (B \cdot C) = (A + B) \cdot (A + C)$

Inversion Law
- $\bar{\bar{A}} = A$

AND Law
- $A \cdot 0 = 0$
- $A \cdot 1 = A$
- $A \cdot A = A$
- $A \cdot \bar{A} = 0$

OR Law
- $A + 0 = A$
- $A + 1 = 1$
- $A + A = A$
- $A + \bar{A} = 1$

De Morgan's Law

1st Law
- $(A \cdot B)' = A' + B'$

2nd Law
- $(A + B)' = A' \cdot B'$

PYQ PUNCH

Q3. The output Y of the given logic gate is similar to the output of an/a :

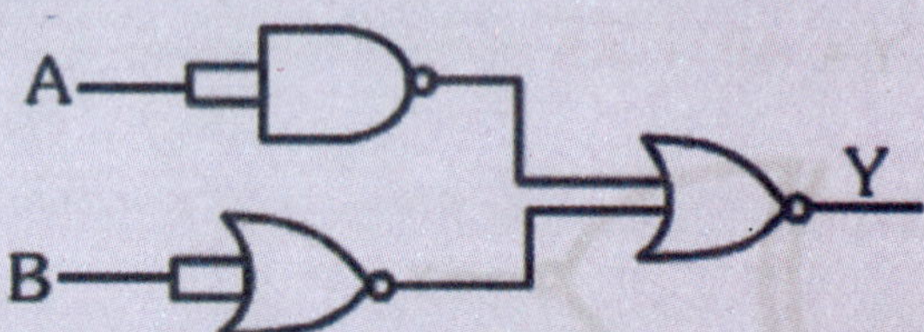

(NEET 2024)

Sol. For NAND Gate

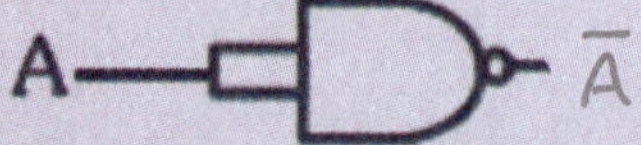

For Ist NOR Gate

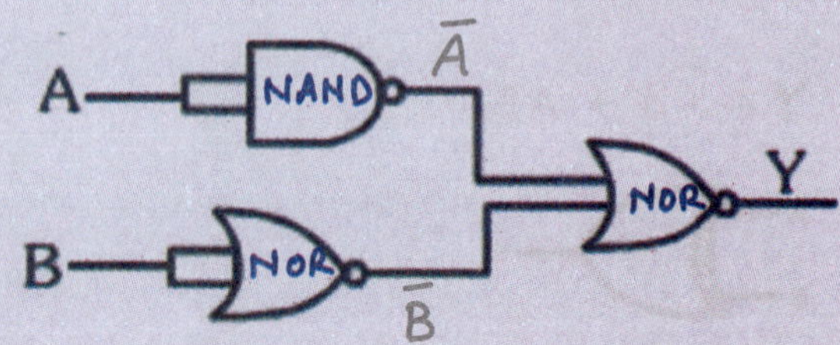

For the 2nd NOR Gate, Inputs are $\bar{A}$ and $\bar{A}$.

$Y = \overline{A + B} = \overline{\bar{A} + \bar{B}} = \bar{\bar{A}} \cdot \bar{\bar{B}} = A \cdot B$

AND GATE

Time Varying Voltage

MCQ PUNCH

Q.4. The figure shows a logic circuit with two inputs A and B and the output C. The voltage wave forms across A, B and C are given. The logic circuit is :

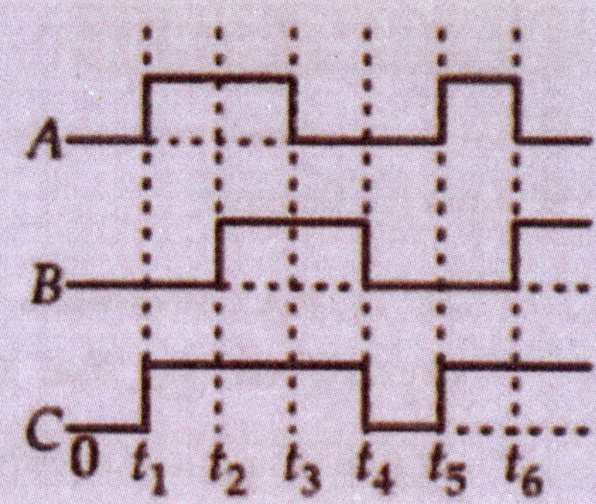

Sol. From the given waveforms, the following truth table can be made

Time	A	B	C
0 to t_1	0	0	0
t_1 to t_2	1	0	1
t_2 to t_3	1	1	1
t_3 to t_4	0	1	1
t_4 to t_5	0	0	0
t_5 to t_6	1	0	1
$> t_6$	0	1	1

This truth table obtained is of OR gate.
So, logic circuit gate is OR gate.

34. Experimental Skills

Vernier Calliper (VC)

- Use to measure very small thickness. (0.1mm)
- **Least Count**
  - It is the minimum thickness measured by the VC.
  - LC = 1 MSD - 1 VSD
  - If n VSD coincides with n-1 MSD, then

    $LC = \frac{1\ MSD}{n}$

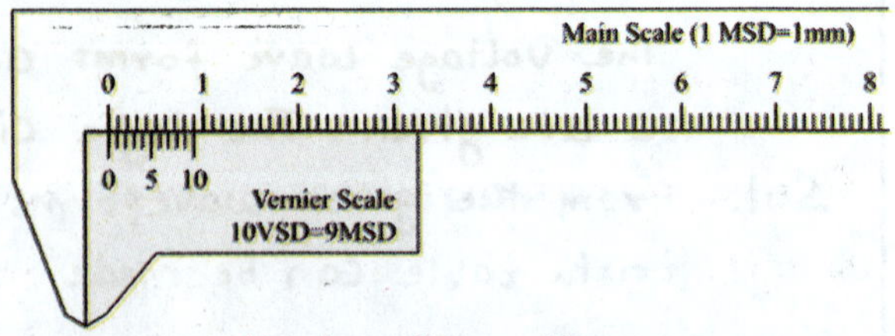

Vernier calipers with no zero error

- **Zero Error**
  - Error in the measurement, if zero of Main Scale and Vernier scale doesn't coincide.
  - Positive Error when zero of Vernier scale lies right of zero of main scale.
  - Negative Error when zero of Vernier scale lies left of zero of main scale.
  - ZE = MSR + VSR Coinciding × LC where, MSR is main scale reading. VSR is Vernier Scale reading

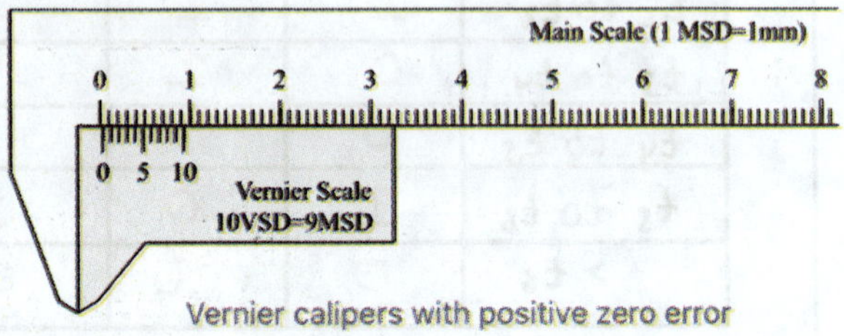

Vernier calipers with positive zero error

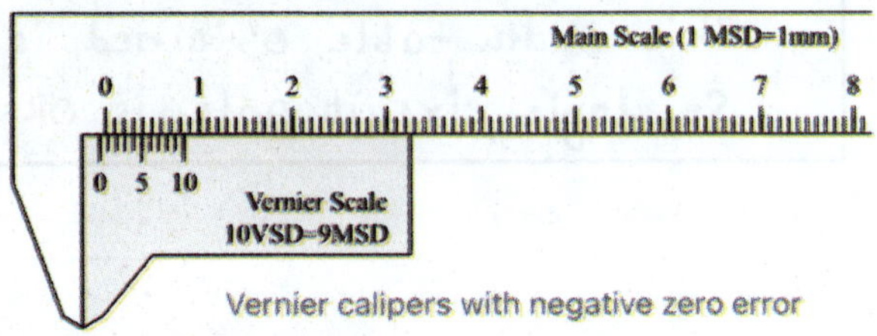

Vernier calipers with negative zero error

PYQ PUNCH

Q1. The main scale of a vernier calliper has n divisions/cm. n divisions of the vernier scale coincide with (n-1) divisions of main scale. The least count of the vernier callipers is: (NEET 2019)

Sol. MSD = n divisions/cm = $\frac{1}{n}$ cm

If n VSD coincides with n-1 MSD, then

$LC = \frac{1\ MSD}{n} = \frac{1 \times 1\ cm}{n \times n} = \frac{1\ cm}{n^2}$

- **Total Reading**
  - TR = MSR + VSR Coinciding × LC − ZE

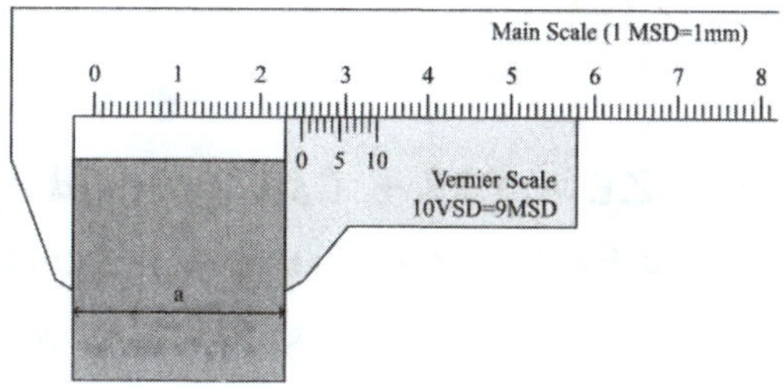

Measuring edge length of a cube

Screw Gauge

- Use to measure very-very small thickness. (0.01mm)
- **Pitch**
  - Linear distance covered in one complete rotation
  - $\text{Pitch} = \dfrac{\text{MSR}}{\text{no. of rotation}}$

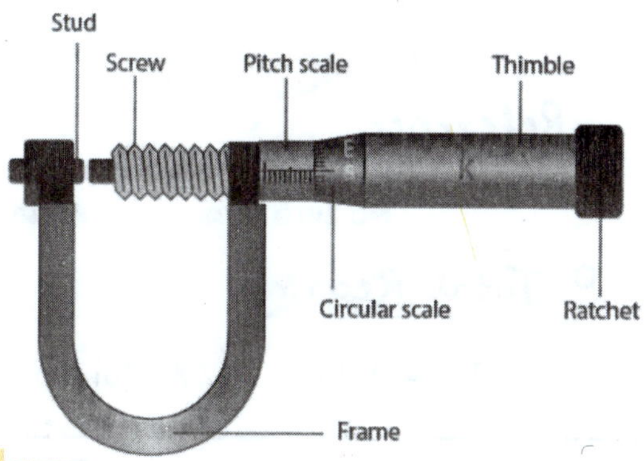

- **Least Count**
  - $LC = \dfrac{\text{Pitch}}{\text{Total no. of division on Circular Scale}}$

PYQ PUNCH

Q2. A screw gauge has least count of 0.01 mm and there are 50 divisions in its circular scale. The pitch of the screw gauge is: (NEET 2020)

Sol. $LC = \dfrac{\text{Pitch}}{\text{Total no. of division on Circular Scale}}$

→ Pitch = LC × Total no. of division on Circular Scale

= 0.01 mm × 50

= 0.5 mm

- **Zero Error**
  - Error in the measurement, if zero of circular scale and reference line doesn't coincide.
  - Positive Error when zero of circular scale lies below the reference line.

- Negative Error when zero of circular scale lies above the reference line.
- ZE = PSR + CSR Coinciding × LC

where PSR is pitch scale reading or main scale reading.
CSR is circular scale reading

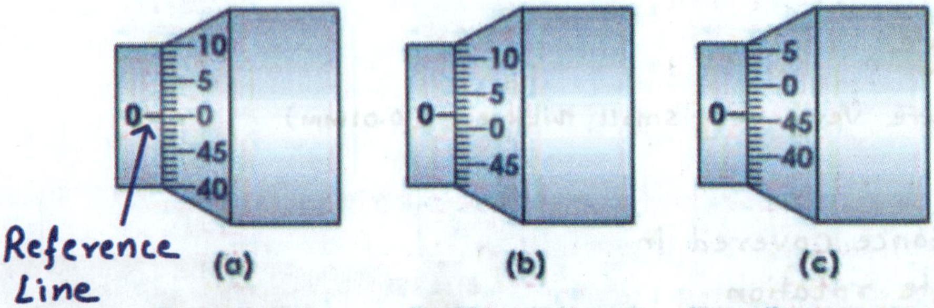

(a) No zero error (b) Positive zero error (c) Negative zero error

Total Reading

- TR = PSR + CSR Coinciding × LC − ZE

PYQ PUNCH

Q3. A screw gauge gives the following readings when used to measure the diameter of the wire.
Main Scale Reading : 0 mm
Circular Scale Reading : 52 divisions
Given that 1 mm on main scale corresponds to 100 divisions on the circular scale. The diameter of the wire from the above data is : (NEET 2021)

Sol. Pitch = 1mm ; No. of division on Circular Scale = 100

$$LC = \frac{\text{Pitch}}{\text{Total no. of division on Circular Scale}}$$

$$= \frac{1\text{ mm}}{100}$$

$$= 0.01\text{ mm}$$

Now,
PSR = 0mm ; CSR = 52 ; ZE = 0mm
TE = PSR + CSR Coinciding × LC − ZE
⇒ TE = 0 + 52 × 0.01 mm − 0
⇒ TE = .52 mm

Simple Pendulum

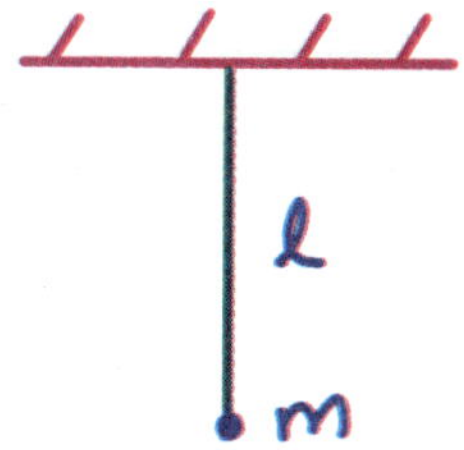

- Time Period of Simple Pendulum

$$T = 2\pi\sqrt{\frac{l}{g}}$$

- Error in Time Period

$$\frac{\Delta T}{T} = +\frac{1}{2}\frac{\Delta l}{l} + \frac{1}{2}\frac{\Delta g}{g}$$

- Energy lost in Simple Pendulum due to air friction. Amplitude decreases with time.

  a : amplitude of oscillation

  t : time

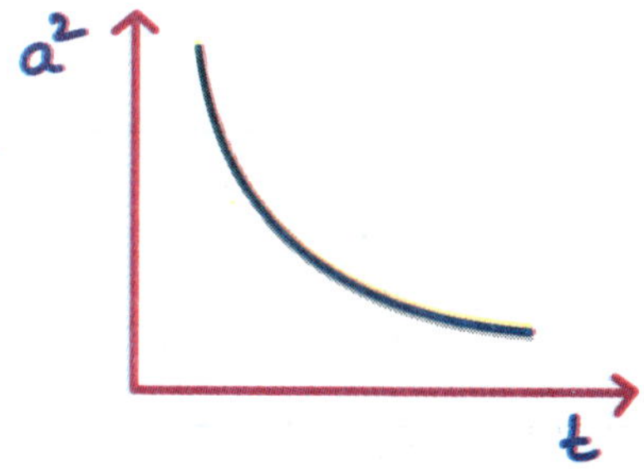

Meter Scale

- Use to calculate the mass of a given object.
- Works on the principle of moments.
- $F = 0$
- $\tau = 0$
- Unknown mass is equal to

$$m_1 = \frac{m_2 l_2}{l_1}$$

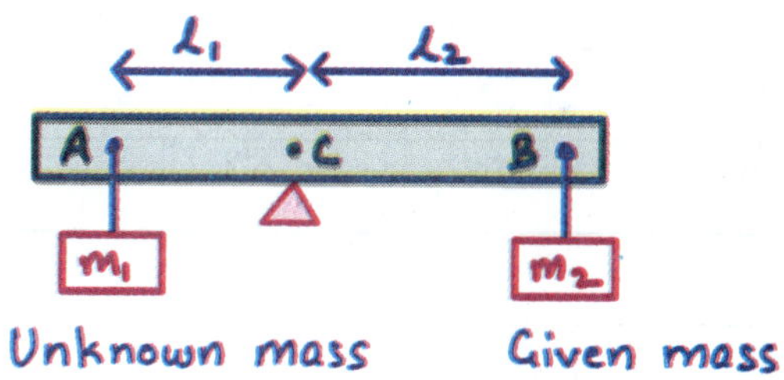

- For a scale of 1m length
  - $l_1 = 100 - l_2$
  - $m_1 = \dfrac{m_2 l_2}{100 - l_2}$

NOTES

NOTES

NOTES